D0882873

THE
BLACK
FIVES

THE
BLACK
FIVES

✶✶✶✶✶

THE EPIC
STORY OF
BASKETBALL'S
FORGOTTEN
ERA

✶✶✶✶✶

CLAUDE JOHNSON

ABRAMS PRESS, NEW YORK

Copyright © 2021 Claude Johnson

Jacket © 2021 Abrams

Published in 2021 by Abrams Press, an imprint of ABRAMS. All rights reserved. No portion
of this book may be reproduced, stored in a retrieval system, or transmitted in any form or by
any means, mechanical, electronic, photocopying, recording, or otherwise, without written
permission from the publisher.

Library of Congress Control Number: 2021933480

ISBN: 978-1-4197-4436-5
eISBN: 978-1-68335-908-1

Printed and bound in the United States
10 9 8 7 6 5 4 3 2 1

Abrams books are available at special discounts when purchased in quantity for premiums and
promotions as well as fundraising or educational use. Special editions can also be created to
specification. For details, contact specialsales@abramsbooks.com or the address below.

Abrams Press® is a registered trademark of Harry N. Abrams, Inc.

ABRAMS The Art of Books
195 Broadway, New York, NY 10007
abramsbooks.com

For
my Mama, who had a book in her
my Dad, who wanted to finish his book
my Siblings, who have always been there
my Sons, who inspire me to keep at it and keep at it
my 5 x 7s

CONTENTS

CHAPTER 1

AN UNMARKED GRAVE

ON A NARROW PATCH OF grass and dirt in Tier 4 of the Villa Palmeras section at the back of Rosedale Cemetery in Linden, New Jersey, there is a flat chunk of rocky cement with "47" scrawled on it, as if written by hand using a crooked stick while the concrete was still wet. This is Plot Number 47, an unmarked grave. It contains the remains of William Anthony "Will" Madden.[1] He died at age eighty-nine on Tuesday, February 20, 1973, in the Greenwich Village section of New York City, alone, with no family or friends.

Rosedale is an old burial ground that occupies ninety acres of flatland along the New Jersey Turnpike, about thirteen miles southwest of Manhattan. Developed in 1900, it is one of the longest-running businesses in Linden, a town best known for its dozens of gigantic, white, million-gallon petroleum storage tanks, familiar to drivers using Interstate 95 in that section. Hiding behind those vast containers is Rosedale. Though its vintage buildings and tree-lined paths hint at better days gone by, no one famous was ever buried there.

In the early 1970s, New York City ran out of graveyard space and, as a cost-saving move due to financial troubles, began sending its unclaimed dead to various cemeteries in New Jersey. These unaccountable goners were people with no next of kin and nobody else who had known them. Rosedale was one of those sites and the Villa Palmeras section there became filled with the untitled graves of those voiceless souls.

By law, investigation of their cases had to be assigned to the city's Office of the Public Administrator. That's what happened to Will, after whose death the PA's office searched his last known residence for personal belongings that might offer clues about next of kin or acquaintances. That came up empty.

No surviving spouse, children, grandchildren, siblings, cousins, or other relatives could be traced. No friends, acquaintances, or former coworkers stepped
forward. He had left behind no will and no instructions for what to do with
his body or his property. Its efforts having reached a dead end, the PA's office
issued a final statement: "Nothing was found among decedent's effects which
would assist your petitioner in who the distributees of decedent were or where
they might be located."[2]

According to the city's legal terminology, Will had died intestate, not
only without a will but also without anyone to speak on his behalf. Following
protocol, the handling of his affairs and burial arrangements were sent to the
Surrogate's Court, whose responsibilities included forwarding his mail, paying
his bills, settling his debts, and closing out his accounts. The court selected the
Gannon Funeral Home in Manhattan from New York City's list of approved
funerary service providers for such cases, which were usually low-budget.

Even though Gannon prepared Will's body, there was no funeral service.
No mourners gathered, no final farewells. The corpse was transported to
Rosedale, but the cemetery's chapel went unused, and instead of a casket, he
got a plain pine coffin.

Will was anonymous on the day of his interment, February 26, 1973. No
obituary was published in any newspaper. No headstone was placed, then or
later, which meant no epitaph would list his life's accomplishments. Just that
jagged edged "47" slab to mark the spot where he was put into the ground. Only
the gravediggers on duty were present at Will's burial. The nearby mound of
displaced soil was twice as high as usual because the hole was double depth.
To save money, graves for the city's intestate clients were dug deep enough for
two coffins, stacked one on top of the other.[3] The box containing Will's remains
went in first. Instead of resting six feet under, his coffin was placed twelve feet
down, like being stuck at the bottom of a bunk bed. Forever.

Any last words spoken at the burial were purely symbolic. "Even if we just
say, 'We consign the remains to the earth,' at least we give them a reasonably
dignified sendoff and show respect," said Wilson Beebe, executive director of
the New Jersey State Funeral Directors Association, in a 1995 interview about
the state's handling of all those unclaimed bodies.[4]

The pile of dirt next to the grave was moved back into the open hole, one
shovelful at a time. William Anthony Madden was the former "king of the
basket ball world and Beau Brummel of New York City," but as the pine box

containing his remains gradually became covered up, the pioneering African American sports history to which he had contributed was buried with him, and this case of an elderly man from Greenwich Village who had died alone was officially closed. But the soul of the dearly departed had far to go before it could rest in peace. That history was Will's story, and it had never been unburied or fully told. Until now.

CHAPTER 2

SURVIVAL

WILL MADDEN, THE FIRST RIGHTFUL king of Black basketball in America, ascended to that throne because he came from a family of survivors. This was established during the Civil War, on the evening of Tuesday, July 14, 1863, in New York City, as bloodthirsty mobs of enraged working-class Whites roamed Midtown Manhattan "armed with clubs, pitchforks, iron bars, swords, and many with guns and pistols," looking for any African Americans they could find.[1] Marching through the streets, those with weapons fired toward anyone in their way, even at New York City policemen. On the corner of Twenty-Ninth Street, "a crowd who had been engaged all day in hunting down and stoning to death every negro they could spy" lingered in plain view of the Twenty-First Precinct police station. It was undermanned because thousands of New York State Militia troops who would have served as backup had been sent to the Battle of Gettysburg.[2] Nothing was spared. The Colored Orphan Asylum at Forty-Fourth Street and Fifth Avenue, home to more than two hundred disadvantaged Black children, had been burned to the ground. Horses pulling streetcars had been shot to death and the cars smashed to pieces. The homes of prominent abolitionists were being looted and destroyed. Railroad tracks had been torn up and telegraph wires cut. Dozens of public buildings, including churches, were ransacked and torched. Even the house of the New York City mayor, George Opdyke, was raided and set on fire. It was mayhem.

Ever since President Abraham Lincoln had issued the Emancipation Proclamation in January 1863, the city's poorest Whites feared that freed slaves would migrate to Manhattan and steal their jobs. Then in March, Congress passed the Enrollment Act, which made all able-bodied adult males immediately eligible to be drafted into the Union Army. This reality sank in when the names of New York City draftees were published leading up to "Draft Week." Making matters worse was that under the Enrollment Act, any wealthy man could escape the draft by paying a $300 fee (the equivalent of more than $6,500 today).[3] He would be replaced by some poor fellow who simply couldn't afford to pay that. Over the weekend, what started out as heated protests escalated into angry demonstrations that gathered force and spiraled into raging mobs that, looking for scapegoats, became brutally violent toward African Americans. "Terror seized pedestrians and storekeepers," one witness observed, "the former hurried out of the way; the latter hastily closed and barred doors and windows."[4] Black people stayed indoors to remain safe. But mob instigators knew where they lived, not only from sight but also because the *New York City Directory* listed every "colored" resident with the abbreviation "(col'd)" next to the name.[5] The rioters specifically targeted neighborhoods where numerous mixed-race families lived.

York Street, a short lane just below Canal Street in what is Tribeca today, contained "two rows of small wooden and brick houses" that were "mostly occupied by negro whitewashers and ironers."[6] The surrounding neighborhood housed most of the "3,000 mulattoes in our city," according to a "careful perusal" of census returns by the *New York Daily Herald* in 1861. "It is in this ward that we find eighteen of the thirty-two intermarriages between Whites and blacks," the newspaper continued. "Six of these happy couples occupy a single house," it stated, and "in all these cases the wife is white." The *Herald* added, "Of the thirty-two white women whose husbands are black, eighteen were born in Ireland."[7] This apparently didn't sit well with Irishmen, at a time when a quarter of New York City's residents had ancestors from there.

In a tavern at the corner of York and West Broadway known to be frequented by lowlifes, "a crowd of Irish, about a hundred strong" began gathering to plot an attack on their innocent neighbors.[8] Just then, an unfortunate African American man named William Jones who lived a few blocks away was "returning from a bakery with a loaf of bread under his arm."[9] The brutal mob "instantly set upon and beat him and after nearly killing him, hung him to a lamp-post" near the pub at the end of the block. "A fire was made underneath him, and he was literally roasted as he hung, the mob reveling in their demoniac act."[10] The body of William Jones was intentionally left hanging. His murderers meant for their heinous deed to serve as a warning for the block.

Around midnight, the tavern mob began their premeditated York Street onslaught by hurling a barrage of bricks and stones through every window of each African American home on the block. Residents fled for their lives, many out of their back windows. Doors were torn away, and "amid the shrieks and groans of the unfortunate women and children the whole precinct was devoted to destruction."[11] Female rioters from the neighborhood brought pushcarts "to remove all the furniture which seemed of value" from certain pre-targeted apartments. "Several pianos were stolen, sofas, chairs and tables were appropriated." Their work was efficient.[12] "Of course the negroes offered no resistance," a witness testified. "The leaders said that if they kept quiet all would be right."[13]

Amid this violence and chaos, a thirty-one-year-old Black waiter named Anthony Harder; his wife, a twenty-seven-year-old Irish immigrant named Ellen Corbett; and their daughter, a five-year-old named Margaret Ann, nicknamed "Maggie," slipped away from their home at 3 York Street.[14] Someone went for help. A company of 250 police officers was mustered from its Mulberry Street headquarters and rushed up Broadway to York. When the officers arrived, the rioters ran.[15] But by then, every home on the block had been looted, leaving the buildings "a complete wreck."[16] The mob had "carried off the little all of these unfortunate creatures" and rendered "upwards of two hundred blacks thrown homeless upon the streets."[17]

This savagery, which became known as the New York City Draft Riots, was finally squashed on Friday, July 17, 1863, a week after it began. Reports claimed that 119 defenseless citizens lost their lives, most of them African Americans. Officials further estimated that the number of violent protesters "killed by the police and the military" citywide was "from four to five hundred."[18] Thousands of Black people were displaced, and according to reports there was more than $1 million of property damage, equivalent to more than $20 million today. Eventually, York Street and its "colored" residences were restored with financial help from the city, as well as through donations from merchants and sympathizers in the surrounding community. "Some four or five white women, wives of colored men applied for relief," a fundraising committee reported afterward. "In every instance they had been severely dealt with by the mob."[19] Some Black families who had escaped never returned, but Anthony Harder and Ellen Corbett came back to their York Street block. Their survival of this tragic event would prove pivotal because it changed the course of history. In the years that followed, their little girl, Maggie, would grow up in New York City, graduate from high school, and attend college. Eventually, she would get married and have three children, one of them a son, William Anthony Madden, who would rise to power, seize the throne, and reign over the land of basketball among Black Americans.

CHAPTER 3

SEEDS

THE ORIGINAL SEEDS FOR BLACK basketball were planted with a series of events, including the births of three men who would have a profound influence on the game, that took place during a one-year period beginning on November 4, 1882. That's the day the future "Father of Black Basketball" was born in the Newtown section of Basseterre, the capital city of the Caribbean island nation of St. Kitts. He was named Robert Isaac Lewis "Bob" Douglas, and his origins were humble. Newtown, where his parents lived, was a Black enclave, one of the oldest settled wards in the city, and the poorest. Effectively a slum, its inhabitants lived in one- and two-room wooden shacks and shanties along alleyways so tightly spaced that a horse and wagon could barely make it through. There was no running water or sewage system. Diseases like yellow fever, dengue, and malaria prevailed. Infant mortality was high. The section was located out of sight, behind and to the east of the church and courthouse buildings that faced lovely Pall Mall Square, the city's busy administrative, commercial, and social center. This square was where enslaved Africans had been sold at auction after disembarking from ships at one of the main piers in Basseterre Harbor a hundred yards away, from the mid-1700s until the abolition of slavery on St. Kitts in 1834. The people of Newtown got by, preparing locally produced foods such as sweet potatoes, eddoes, peas, yams, cassava, pumpkin, breadfruit tania, and dasheen. Peelings from these were reserved for the pigs, goats, and sheep some residents kept. Robert's father was a seventeen-year-old clerk named Robert Gould Douglas, and his mother, of undocumented age, was named Margaret Ann Permelia. (Coincidentally, she had the same first name as Will Anthony Madden's mother.) Local civil registrations and church records indicate that the baby's parents were never married, and no father was yet listed when Robert was baptized more than three months later.[1] Yet the youngster was cared for, educated, and raised to possess a sense of ambition that would soon take him far. In fact, the throne of the king of Black basketball would one day rightfully be his as well.

Less than two months after Robert Douglas's birth, there was an article in the January 1883 edition of a publication that rested with a stash of leading magazines on the tables in the reading rooms of practically every reputable American library. The reading room magazines that month included *Art Journal, Harper's Bazaar, Nineteenth Century, Scientific American, Youths' Companion*, and one, *North American Review*, that contained the article "Physical Education in Colleges." The highly esteemed *North American Review*, founded in Boston in 1815, was the oldest literary magazine in the country. This contribution was composed by a thirty-four-year-old White assistant professor of physical training at Harvard College named Dudley Allen Sargent. Sargent didn't imagine that he would one day become the "Grandfather of Basketball," as the man behind the man who was to invent the game itself. And what the assistant professor wrote about the need for physical education had never been considered. Sargent argued:

> But when it shall be generally known that the object of muscular exercise is not to develop muscle only, but to increase the functional capacity of the organs of respiration, circulation, and nutrition: not to gain in physical endurance merely, but to augment the working power of the brain: not to attain bodily health and beauty alone, but to break up morbid mental tendencies, to dispel the gloomy shadows of despondency, and to insure serenity of spirit; when men shall have learned that much of the ill-temper, malevolence, and uncharitableness which pervade society arises from the feeble health, and that the great mental and moral disturbances which sometimes threaten the stability of a government may be traded to physical causes, then will the training of the body rival in dignity and importance the training of the mind, for the interests of the mind and body will be recognized as inseparable.[2]

In other words, all students should receive physical training, not just those who wanted to become athletes. These concepts were seen as vitally important. Widespread industrialization and urbanization combined with waves of European immigration had fed America's booming economy with the labor it needed to thrive. But what at first had looked like progress became a crisis when unprepared cities became overcrowded and overrun by social problems. For example, Pittsburgh's population exploded from 8,000 to 46,000 between 1820 and 1850. Cincinnati went from 9,600 to 115,000 during the same period.[3] So many impoverished rural transplants or European newcomers were eking out their existences in overcrowded tenements and on unsanitary streets that morbid health, immorality, and criminality had become rampant. In their search for ideas on how to handle this ever-worsening issue, social reformers looked to England during its Industrial Revolution, when a massive population shift from rustic farming to urban industry had led to similar conditions. Efforts to improve that situation had led to the formation of the Young Men's Christian Association in London in 1844. Its organizers originally offered activities rooted in Bible study and prayer to keep young men from becoming spiritually lost.

By the early 1850s, this idea had spread to North America with the opening of YMCA branches in Montreal, Boston, and Springfield, Massachusetts. But they added a twist. The economy now included large numbers of office workers, and they, too, were succumbing to moral decay. Health specialists theorized that too much "brain work" could throw a man's physique out of harmony with his soul. This required realignment in the form of daily exercise to restore his "physical culture," his natural state of well-being. The linkage of exercise with spiritual growth became known as "muscular Christianity," a notion so powerful that by 1866 the YMCA had revised its mission statement to include it: "The improvement of the spiritual, mental, social and physical condition of young men."[4] That's when these concepts caught Dudley Allen Sargent's attention. Then still in high school, Sargent became so interested in gymnastics and their related apparatus that nearby Bowdoin College invited him to run its gymnasium. Two years later, he enrolled at the college as a student. But to Sargent, physical culture and muscular Christianity weren't just ideas, they constituted a movement. And during the following decade, he would emerge as its leader.

After graduating from Bowdoin, Sargent obtained a medical degree from Yale University in 1878 and a year later became the first associate professor of physical training at Harvard. He simultaneously ran the college's main fitness facility, the Hemenway Gymnasium, and opened his own school in Cambridge in 1881, called Sargent's Normal School of Physical Training. During this time, three systems of exercise were widely accepted as the norm. The first was the gymnastics-based "German system," which emphasized exercising in groups. Next was the "Swedish system," based on the needs of the individual, with body development through certain well-defined exercises. Finally, the "Delsarte system," named after the French singer and orator François Alexandre Nicolas Chéri Delsarte, was "not so much a system of physical exercise" as it was a training of the whole individual through "careful analysis of the facts of human nature and experience."[5]

But to Sargent, the typical gymnasium was inadequate. His original gym "occupied the second floor of a carriage shed next to a blacksmith shop across the street from a livery stable." Many of the exercise devices available were "never used twice by the same person," Sargent wryly observed in his 1883 article. The seventy-five-pound sandbag for heavy punching "was covered with heavy canvas that caused skinned knuckles." Tumbling mats, which weighed four hundred pounds, were filled with corn husks that "soon became matted and lumpy and caused sprained ankles." The gym's parallel bars were "broad at the base and narrow at the top, leading to insecure grip." And the "rough rungs" of the horizontal ladders used for climbing exercises caused blisters.[6]

In response, Sargent masterminded and taught a groundbreaking approach to exercise at his Normal School of Physical Training. It used sound physiological principles, custom-built gym apparatus he designed like the chest pulley weight system, and unique ways of measuring results. These were so compelling that as the school's students graduated, his ideas went forth "into college gymnasiums and athletic clubs of the whole country" and became known as the "Sargent system." Of all these approaches, many professionals considered his to be "the most efficient" by combining principles and truths of each. "The strength-giving qualities of the German, the beauty of the French calisthenics, the poise and mechanical precision of the Swedish system, it is sought to unite in the Sargent's method."[7] That set up what became known as the "Battle of the Systems" within the physical education field, and when "Physical Education in Colleges" was published, this clash was at its peak. But something much more important would soon be at stake: It was how these principles could be applied in Black communities to help counteract the effects of systematic oppression under White supremacy.

About four months after Sargent's article was published, on May 9, 1883, in the small town of Athens, Ohio, a twenty-five-year-old African American steamboat captain named Cumberland Willis "CW" Posey and a statuesque twenty-one-year-old Black schoolteacher named Angeline "Anna" Stevens applied for their marriage license, stated their wedding vows, and were solemnized in matrimony.[8] They soon had a child named Cumberland Willis Posey, Jr., nicknamed "Cum," who would ultimately become the second rightful king of Black basketball.

CW had been born into slavery in 1858 near the village of Port Tobacco, Maryland, the oldest of three children. After enslaved persons in Maryland were declared free in 1864, a few months before Congress approved the Thirteenth Amendment to the U.S. Constitution, abolishing slavery, his father, a farmer named Alexander Posey, Jr., became a minister serving the African Methodist Episcopal Church. CW's mother, Elizabeth Willis Posey, died a year later. By 1869, the thirty-five-year-old widowed clergyman took his family and moved to Marietta, Ohio, a commerce center on the banks of the Ohio River, across from Williamstown, West Virginia.[9]

After settling there, CW became captivated by the region's river life, which was dominated by its steam-powered paddle wheelers. These marvelously designed and engineered vessels, which carried passengers and towed barges, were romanticized in newspapers with breathless daily details. By the time CW was thirteen years old, he had found work as a deck sweeper aboard a paddle wheel passenger ferry connecting Belpre, Ohio, a small town about twelve miles downriver from Marietta, and Parkersburg, West Virginia, an important junction for the Baltimore & Ohio Railroad. Making that three-quarter-mile crossing about eighty times a day gave the young deckhand continual, repetitive, accelerated learning about the boat's machinery, engineering, navigation, and construction.[10] A certain kind of a man took to the river. Operating these craft while handling their business was risky, requiring grit and determination at every turn. The water levels of the Ohio River were ever-changing and highly unpredictable. On some days, a section of river was deep enough to navigate, which meant that a heavy barge load could be delivered and its haulers paid. On other days, however, when the water level there was too low, steamboats towing barges could not pass, which would bring all river commerce to a stop. Yet there was a steady rhythm to a riverman's doings, and CW became a keen student, developing an amazing knack for business and entrepreneurship. Cum would inherit these essential traits and apply them fearlessly in the world of sports.

CW learned as well about boilers, the defining feature of any steamboat, while working aboard the fifty-six-ton stern-wheeler *Sallie J. Cooper* as a fireman, responsible for feeding and stoking the burning coal that kept a steamer's engines going.[11] A boiler that wasn't carefully tended could become over-pressurized and spontaneously explode. That's what happened aboard the 1,700-ton steamboat *Sultana,* whose boilers blew up catastrophically on the Mississippi River north of Memphis in April 1865. More than 1,700 passengers were killed, which exceeded the number of lives that would be lost from the sinking of the *Titanic* and still ranks as the worst maritime disaster in U.S. history.

There were so many such tragedies on American waterways throughout the 1800s that by 1877, when CW was nineteen years old, the U.S. government had begun requiring the operators of steam-powered river vessels to be certified. Obtaining that much-sought-after credential was rare for anyone, and especially for Black applicants. Though authorities at first rejected the young riverman's multiple applications, citing race, CW's expertise eventually prevailed, and he became what was believed to be the first federally licensed African American steamboat engineer in the country.

This was a life-changing qualification for CW. From then on, he would be known as Captain Posey. More importantly, it landed him a coveted post as chief engineer of steam navigation for a White boat builder, coal merchant, and captain named William Seward Brenneman "SB" Hays. Based in Pittsburgh, Captain Hays was a descendant of an early settler of a nearby town called Homestead who had owned hundreds of acres of farmland in the area that contained parts of what today are Mifflin Township, Munhall, Whitaker, and Baldwin.[12] He lived on the family estate, known as Harden Station, which was located alongside the Monongahela River.[13] Captain Hays was also one of the Ohio River Valley's most prominent rivermen. The vessels he had built were well-known for their durability and performance, like the *Little Bill*, a 122-foot-long, 110-ton steam-powered tug built in 1880 that would tow six million bushels of coal into Pittsburgh during a single year, or the ninety-one-ton double-smokestack rear paddle wheeler *Abe Hays*, named after his father, Abraham Hays, which was legendary in river circles because it sank numerous times in freak collisions, only to be resurrected and pressed back into service shortly after each accident.[14] Captain Posey's association with Hays would soon alter the entire Posey family trajectory. For the next several years, the young steamboat engineer plied the Ohio River between Cincinnati and Pittsburgh while Hays, who was twenty years older, mentored him regarding the unseen aspects of the river trade, like how to team up with investors, acquire real estate, obtain facilities, hire men, procure materials, construct vessels, and secure hauling contracts.

Soon, Captain Posey began to consider building and piloting ships of his own. That's when he met Anna Stevens, a uniquely gifted woman with her own set of exceptional qualities. The oldest of eleven children, she was born in 1862 in Athens Township, Ohio, a rural area near the village of Athens.[15] Hers was the only non-White family in the vicinity, which was populated by farmers and skilled laborers. Anna's father, a stonecutter named Aquilla Stevens, had served in the Union Army as a private in the Ohio Volunteer Infantry.[16] Anna attended Athens High School, becoming its first African American graduate in 1879. An intelligent and visionary student, she was asked to deliver a commencement address, which a local newspaper praised. In her remarks, entitled "The Visible and Invisible," Anna said, "As potent as is the influence upon life's experience of the visible it is of importance, secondary to the moulding and directing of the invisible influences by which we are constantly surrounded in life."[17] Coming from a solitary person of color, her powerful words reminded people that their own unseen deeds, whether good or bad, were more influential on her than they may have known. After obtaining a teacher's certificate from the local Board of School Examiners, Anna became a schoolteacher in Athens in 1880.[18] At a countywide average salary of $22 per month, she demonstrated "rare tact and efficiency" and was in "wide demand," the *Athens Messenger* reported in 1882.[19] Cum would inherit these attributes as well, becoming not only popular, but also brilliant at working methodically behind the scenes to get his way.

In 1884, a year after Captain Posey and Anna were married, they relocated out of the Belpre area one hundred miles up the Ohio River to the outskirts of Pittsburgh, a progressive city smoldering with red-hot social and business opportunities. The move would set up Cum's future success.

On May 24, 1883, three weeks after the Poseys' wedding, the East River Bridge connecting Manhattan and Brooklyn, known today as the Brooklyn Bridge, opened for traffic and pedestrians in the presence of President Chester A. Arthur, his entire cabinet, and thousands of spectators.[20] Its completion was considered one of the most significant technical accomplishments mankind had ever achieved, a triumph of will over nature, a feat that captured the world's imagination. That's because the bridge was built over the dangerous East River, whose powerful currents reversed direction with every changing tide. In terms of setting up its massive underwater foundations and spans, this project presented a safety challenge so profound that it required a never-before-seen level of ingenuity in design, engineering, and construction that was a quarter century in the making. When it was finished, the East River Bridge was the tallest structure on the continent, a symbol of America's might and determination. Suddenly, the previously inconceivable seemed doable. A world of possibilities was opening up, and people couldn't contain their awe, giddy about the vastness of human potential that was brilliantly on display.

But not in "Little Africa." That was a poor section of Greenwich Village where most of New York City's Black residents lived, many the descendants of formerly enslaved people. Neglected and overcrowded, this area stretched along lower Sixth Avenue four blocks east to South Fifth Avenue (later renamed West Broadway), from West Fourth Street down to Bleecker Street. The term "Little Africa" was once used euphemistically outside of the South to describe any "negro district." These sections were often subject to severe restrictions or located in an undesirable part of a city or town.[21] So, even though the large and magnificently landscaped green space known as Washington Square Park was just one block to the north of Little Africa, its residents were not allowed to use it for recreation, and children were strictly forbidden.

This is the neighborhood where William Anthony Madden was born, in a cramped four-story wooden tenement at 99½ West Third Street on Friday, August 24, 1883, three months to the day after the East River Bridge's grand opening.[22] The site of that building is now occupied by Vanderbilt Hall of New York University's School of Law. At one end of that block is Sullivan Street. At the other end is the corner of Sixth Avenue where the outdoor basketball court known as the West Fourth Street Cage can be found today. William made a grand entrance into the world, amid drama and flair. On the morning of his birth, a dangerous combination of scorching temperatures, high humidity, and rising air pressure trapped Manhattan in a sweltering heat wave. The mercury had been in the high 80s and low 90s all week. "It was hot, hotter, hottest," the *New York Herald* reported, complaining about "the utter absurdity of expecting any family this side of pauperdom to endure the prostrating and enervating heat." Air conditioners had not yet been invented. Suddenly "a brisk breeze began to blow from the north-west," and the temperature plunged quickly.[23] At midnight, the famous thermometer outside Hudnut's Pharmacy, in the New York Herald Building on Broadway, read 65.[24] Folks could finally *sleep*. Despite the expertise of the Signal Service Bureau, a forerunner to the National Weather Service, authorities were bewildered by what had happened. "The cool wave, if such it can be called, appears to have dropped from the clouds," concluded a *New York Times* reporter.[25] Maybe it was the birth of William Anthony Madden, whose personal style in adulthood would be nothing if not cool.

Another enormous development, two months after Will's birth, changed the way America was being built, when the colossal Pittsburgh-based steel-making corporation Carnegie Bros. & Co. bought out its major local rival, Bessemer Steel, pioneers of a faster, cheaper production technique. This acquisition launched the rise of giant steel as an industry, which would impact the construction of railroads, bridges, and buildings for a century to come.

Will's childhood home was located in the worst part of Little Africa, situated in the shadows of the elevated tracks of the Manhattan Railway Company's Sixth Avenue Line. Completed in 1878, it stretched from West Fifty-Ninth Street by Central Park South down to South Ferry Station at the bottom of Lower Manhattan, carrying colossal steam-powered locomotives that belched thick black smoke while creating a constant "roar and shriek and hiss on the rails overhead." But although they were considered marvels of engineering, these two-hundred-ton monsters were terrifying and dangerous for people at street level thirty-five feet below, who were bombarded with burning chunks of coal, hot oil, and loose rivets, as well as a continual rain of sparks and ashes.[26] The grinding of wheel against rail created rusty steel dust, invisible bits of iron that caused "welder's lung" from constant exposure.[27]

Meanwhile, for the trains to achieve maximum speed, their tracks were built along Manhattan's wide north–south avenues. But they inevitably had to turn sharply left or right to go briefly across town before turning sharply back again, uptown or downtown. These crosstown sections were considered the worst places in the city to live. Wherever municipal planners located them, "white people began to sell out and rent to Negroes."[28] There were seven such blocks, and Will's was one of them.[29] Because of this quirk, his family and neighbors had to suffer up to "nineteen hours and more of incessant rumbling day and night" caused by the locomotives. Good sleep was impossible. "No experience of noise can enable you to conceive of the furious din that bursts upon the senses," one pedestrian shared about the engines and their wooden passenger cars rounding those sharp corners up above. "The noise is not only deafening, it is bewildering."[30]

At street level, there was a large livery stable on the block, adjacent to workshops that repaired carriage wheels, axles, gears, and lamps.[31] This meant that unhitched horses constantly lined both sides of West Third. With no underground sewers, animal waste flowed and stagnated openly in the street, attracting vermin and disease.[32] Meanwhile, the destitute living conditions attracted the needy as well as the seedy. Hookers, thieves, and beggars lurked in the shadows. "Half-naked women sat in the windows as piano music played inside" while male passersby were "called and insulted."[33] A teenage boy walking along Will's block said he was propositioned "some nights by between seven to ten different women, belonging to as many houses." Vice cops warned that Thompson Street, just around the corner, "swarms with negro prostitutes" and was "notorious for interracial sex." This is the same street that a former police reporter named Jacob Riis would visit a few years later to witness living conditions there. With a camera and notebook, Riis revealed the squalor that existed among New York City's poorest residents through photographs and personal observations. In one multilevel tenement on West Third, he recorded "a colored family of husband, wife, and baby in a wretched rear rookery," suggesting it was as packed as a birds' breeding colony.

"Their rent was eight dollars and a half for a single room on the top-story, so small that I was unable to get a photograph of it even by placing the camera outside the open door," Riis wrote.[34]

These circumstances were examples of the unseen, grim side of the so-called Gilded Age, a period after the Civil War during which the lavish materialism of ultra-wealthy tycoons and bankers, coupled with the glow of astonishing technological advances, was like a layer of gold plating that covered over the increasingly horrible social problems plaguing urban America.

Riis published his disturbing findings in *How the Other Half Lives*, a book that shocked the country and sparked a nationwide anti-poverty movement committed to improving living conditions in the country's slums. "The half that was on top cared little for the struggles, and less for the fate of those who were underneath," he concluded, "so long as it was able to hold them there and keep its own seat."[35] But to the families in the bottom half, life on these streets was a necessary part of their striving. That's how it was for the Maddens in 1883.[36]

Will's father, a railroad porter named William Wilson "Willie" Madden, was from Ellicott City, Maryland, a picturesque mill community near Baltimore.[37] After the town was severely flooded in 1868, Willie headed for Manhattan to build a new life, and by the late 1870s, he was in Little Africa living in a three-story "colored" rooming house at 81 West Third Street.[38] Rain or shine, railroad porters left home early each morning for the Grand Central Depot, the city's main train station, on Forty-Second Street at Fourth Avenue. It served close to fifty thousand passengers a day.[39] Loading, transporting, and unloading travelers' trunks, suitcases, parcels, and travel bags for around $30 a week was among the best-paying occupations available to unskilled African American men.[40]

Will's mother, Maggie, had become a trained schoolteacher and still lived on York Street with her parents, Anthony Harder and Ellen Corbett.[41] Anthony now hauled freight around the city as a truckman. In 1880, well-paid truckmen could earn $20 a week doing work that required brute strength as well as finesse because they were personally liable not only for their horse-and-wagon rigs but also for any lost, stolen, or damaged cargo.[42] Ellen was the embodiment of grit. She had arrived in the United States from Ireland in 1851, alone and illiterate as a thirteen-year-old survivor of the Great Irish Potato Famine, after a month-long voyage aboard a transport ship.[43] She never learned how to read or write and worked as a servant well into her older years. Will would inherit and display a great deal of his grandparents' strength, finesse, and tenacity in adulthood.

He would also inherit his mother's intellectual stamina. Maggie was "unusually brilliant and very beautiful," according to Will's description of her many years later.[44] Her teacher training had been at the Normal College of the City of New York, a tuition-free all-girls institution later renamed Hunter College after its founder and first president, an Irish-born educator named Thomas Hunter. Few women sought higher education, but Hunter had famously insisted that Normal College have an admission policy where "rich and poor, high and low, should be placed upon a common platform."[45] Maggie received her coveted teaching degree in June 1880.[46] That's around the time she met her future husband, Willie, and they fell in love. They were married in December of that year, when the twenty-three-year-old would-be-teacher bride was already four months pregnant with Grace, who was born in May 1881.[47] Using her new diploma, though, was another story. Although the college would graduate fifty-six Black students during the following ten years, including Maggie, the New York City Public School System would hire not a single African American educator until 1896. So, despite possessing elite teaching credentials, Will's mother would work for the rest of her life as a dressmaker, cleaner, and homemaker.[48] Maggie's own children would be her best and only pupils. But she remained determined to change the family's educational trajectory.

In October 1883, two months after Will's birth, as if to make emphatically clear that African Americans were excluded from the giddiness and promise of the times, the U.S. Supreme Court nullified the 1875 Civil Rights Act by declaring it unconstitutional in an 8–1 decision. Originally signed into law in March 1875 by President Ulysses S. Grant, its intent had been to ensure that White people in the South would obey the Thirteenth, Fourteenth, and Fifteenth Amendments to the Constitution. These amendments had protected former enslaved people by guaranteeing them free access to public facilities, voting rights, political representation, land and business ownership, jury duty, elected offices, and other basic rights of citizenship. The nullified act had stated that all citizens "shall be entitled to the full and equal enjoyment of the accommodations, advantages, facilities, and privileges of inns, public conveyances on land or water, theaters, and other places of public amusement," and that this should apply to "citizens of every race and color, regardless of any previous condition of servitude." Anyone denied "on account of race would be entitled to monetary restitution under a federal court of law" rather than in state courts.[49]

By 1875, Black males had had eight years of suffrage and most had joined the Republican Party of President Abraham Lincoln, then the dominant political wing of the federal government and state legislatures in the South. A total of seven African Americans had been elected to the U.S. House of Representatives. All were Republicans from former slave states, and all voted for the bill. "Every day my life and property are exposed, are left to the mercy of others, and will be so long as every hotel-keeper, railroad conductor, and steamboat captain can refuse me with impunity," one of them, Representative James Rapier of Alabama, had said, later adding that "either I am a man or I am not a man."[50] The eventual legislation was compromised under pressure from Democrats, who represented Whites of the failed Confederacy. They wanted to reestablish White supremacy, demanded racial segregation, and sought to regain control of their own state governments. That meant the new law specifically left out a prohibition on racially discriminatory schools and the right of Congress to define the racial composition of juries selected for state courts. It also included some amnesty provisions that were meant to help former Confederate territories rebuild in order to reunify with the rest of the country.

Despite those federally mandated legal enforcements and compromises, Whites throughout the South continued to openly resent the fact that Black people had any rights at all. As the 1875 election season approached that fall, Republicans held a large rally in the town of Clinton, Mississippi, near Jackson. It was a picnic-style event attended by an estimated two to three thousand Black men and their families. Speeches were to be given and about seventy-five White people were also present. But they included a handful of local Democrats, who "went there for the express purpose of creating a disturbance and of killing as many as they could," a White female witness testified later.[51] After instigating fights with African Americans in the audience, the White attackers drew their weapons as choreographed. Then, in formation, they began firing at the crowd, killing five Black people, including two children, and wounding almost thirty other attendees. Three of the White assailants were shot to death, but they had been sacrificed in the name of their real agenda.

In the aftermath, Whites reversed the narrative, claiming through widely read newspaper accounts that hundreds of African Americans had murdered Whites at the rally and were gathering to attack the town. In response, a White vigilante mob was rounded up, whose members rampaged throughout the region for several days indiscriminately killing every African American man in sight. GENERAL SLAUGHTER OF NEGROES, read a *New York Times* headline, adding, "The Chivalrous Vicksburg Militia Shoot All the Blacks They Can Find."[52] But they were far from done. The Clinton Massacre, as it came to be known, kicked off the notorious "Mississippi Plan," a reign of terror devised by the state's Democratic Party to regain political control, which included the assault and murder of more African Americans, Republicans, and their sympathizers. The plan succeeded. Democrats won control of the state legislature on election day, November 2, when many Black voters stayed away out of fear for their lives. Today, a historical marker in the area states accurately that the massacre "served as a pretext for the return of white rule and the end of Reconstruction in Mississippi."

The Mississippi Plan provided a road map for the other Southern states, which paved the way for the Supreme Court's 1883 nullification of the 1875 Civil Rights Act. The court ruled that it was unconstitutional because while the federal government could regulate the behavior of states, it had no such right concerning businesses or individuals. Protections for African Americans in the former slave states, at the time numbering more than 90 percent of the country's total, were undone by the ruling. After that, widespread deadly violence against Black people throughout the South would escalate with impunity, since any prosecution was left up to locals. The door to modern systemic racist oppression of Black people had been opened wide, enabled by the Supreme Court and by President Grant, who denied requests for federal intervention to protect Black citizens in Mississippi and throughout the South. Southern-born African Americans had been migrating northward since before the Civil War, but now that steady flow accelerated into a mass exodus. Hundreds of thousands more would relocate before 1900. In those seventeen years alone, the Black population would expand from 60,000 to 86,000 in the District

of Columbia, triple from 20,000 to 60,000 in Manhattan, more than triple
from 6,000 to 20,000 in Pittsburgh, and multiply nearly fivefold from 6,500
to 30,000 in Chicago.[53] That was just the beginning.

On November 24, 1883, exactly three months to the day after Will Anthony
Madden's birth and two hundred miles south of New York City in Washington, D.C., the future "Grandfather of Black Basketball" was born. His name
was Edwin Bancroft "EB" Henderson. Life on the impoverished street of his
birthplace was similar to Will's experience in Manhattan. But in contrast to
the tenacious Greenwich Village youngster with ambitions to emerge from
the bleakness of Little Africa, EB's family background and location would give
him earlier and better access to privilege, distinction, opportunity, and grace.
Described in adulthood as "a quiet man of wisdom, humor, and kindness" as
well as "receptive" and "modest," he was also blessed. Destiny would make him
one of Dudley Allen Sargent's most important physical training students at
Harvard, and a future member of the Naismith Memorial Basketball Hall of
Fame.[54] And like Will, EB came from a family of survivors.

With just over sixty thousand people of African descent and growing,
Washington had the largest Black population of any city in America. "Colored"
residents made up more than one-third of its total population. Though some
African American migrants from the South were "free Negroes," most had been
formerly enslaved and arrived "desperately poor." They chose the District of
Columbia because it offered government jobs, and its public school system
was not only accessible but better than those of other cities. It became known
that "Black Washingtonians" were thought to be "more educated than typical
urban blacks, and more cosmopolitan and sophisticated than their southern
contemporaries." The city developed its own African American aristocracy.
"It was not uncommon, on any given Sunday evening, to see well dressed
black residents strolling down Pennsylvania Avenue or riding in horse-drawn
carriages."[55] Washington's annual Emancipation Day parade, traditionally
celebrated in the District on April 16, was originally organized in 1883, a
few months before EB was born. That first parade was led by marshals in
"black suits, black silk hats, purple sashes, white saddle cloths trimmed with

purpose, and purple rosettes," followed by Black military organizations such as the Capital City Guards, Sumner Mounted Guards, Baltimore Rifles, and Lincoln Light Infantry. Trades were also represented, including the Hod Carriers' Union and the Brickmakers' Union. And citizens "four abreast" as well as carriages "two abreast" were allowed to join the march. The procession would begin in front of City Hall at Judiciary Square, go around the Capitol, up Pennsylvania Avenue, through the grounds of the Executive Mansion, home to President Chester A. Arthur, then up Seventeenth Street to Farragut Square, before looping around back to City Hall and disbanding.[56]

But there was a hidden side of Washington, D.C., that wasn't visible to parade marchers. This showmanship of middle- and "upper-class" Black people did not accurately depict the way things were for most African Americans in the District, who longed to be validated but struggled to keep up with those appearances. In his book *Up from Slavery*, Booker T. Washington would lament that the children of Washington's poor Black people too often cared more about "dressing well" than with raising their actual socioeconomic status. This "front" played out in real-life terms.

Behind most of the structures on the city's residential blocks, there was enough room for alleyways, and as the District's population grew, opportunistic owners and developers began seeing the potential for erecting residences in those spaces. Washington's alley-building boom was at its peak when EB was born, but although alleyway homes provided more housing, they were "hidden from white and upper crust black residents." This meant few respected citizens noticed at first that these living spaces were built so cheaply and crammed so tightly together that they attracted the city's poor and became dangerously overcrowded.[57] Too often, these were tiny, dilapidated tenements, even shacks. They were gaslit and coal heated, so one mistake could spark an inferno. This housing also lacked basic amenities like plumbing, running water, or sewer connections. Enclosures for horses and carriages were often added at one end of an alley, making the settings even more hazardous. Housing reformers reported "the stench of the alleys caused by decomposing rats and cats and horse manure from the stables." In 1897, the D.C. police department would count 237 blocks that contained inhabited alleys, in all housing about 11 percent of the District's entire population, with Black residents making up 93 percent of that total.[58]

Ultimately, the Committee on Housing of the Civic Center concluded that "many of these alley houses are unfit for human habitation" and that "typhoid fever and other infectious diseases cause a considerable mortality in these alley houses as a result of such insanitary conditions."[59] That struck home because Black people in Washington were more than twice as likely to die as Whites. But this declaration did little to help a woman of color named Eliza Hicks Henderson, EB's mother, who gave birth to him in such an alley, within "a shabby little house" his grandmother had owned in the Southwest section of the District, also known as South Washington.[60] Her journey to that point had been remarkable.

Southwest was a mostly working-class and poor community that was home to large numbers of formerly enslaved Black migrants and European immigrants who lived in hundreds of closely spaced row houses built after the Civil War. Its borders were The Mall and the United States Capitol to the north, the Potomac River Channel and its wharfs to the west, the U.S. Arsenal to the south, and South Capitol Street to the east. Eliza's humble home was a fifteen-by-seventy-five-foot, two-story wood-frame structure on School Street SW, a narrow, one-block-long backstreet that ran between Sixth Street SW and Four-and-a-Half Street SW, to the rear of a large lot where the massive Thomas Jefferson School building stood.[61] Racial segregation in housing had been outlawed in the District since 1872, but most African Americans in Southwest lived in their own clusters and pockets. One of them was School Street, where out of 169 residents, 143 were listed as Black, including EB's grandmother, 22 as White, and four described as "Mulatto."[62] Known as Union Alley until 1871, School Street was only thirty-three feet wide and its name didn't fool anyone. This was still effectively an alley. And still a mess. Washington's superintendent of city property found the street "in such wretched condition as to occasion serious public annoyance."[63]

According to EB, his grandmother, Eliza's mother, was herself the granddaughter of a Powhatan Indian chief named John Logan. The chief had led a tribal settlement in an area near Washington, D.C., that is now Falls Church, Virginia, within the bounds of the White-owned Mordecai Fitzhugh plantation. The chief and his wife were both killed around 1755 when a band of British colonials raided their homes to run them off the Fitzhugh land. A papoose survived the massacre: the chief's baby boy, who was "picked up" by one of the Englishmen and given to the Fitzhugh family to raise.[64] The child was given the full name of that soldier, Andrew Hicks, eventually growing up to marry a woman named Elizabeth Mimetou Foote, a cousin of Chief Logan described as "almost pure Indian, with some white blood," though she was also said to have had African American lineage.[65] Their children lived on the plantation and were not slaves but were not permitted to leave either, since "those who attempted to run away when caught were sold south."[66] That's what happened to Andrew and Elizabeth's daughter Eliza, who was shipped off to Vicksburg, Mississippi.

Vicksburg was one of the South's most important commercial cities, and she joined about fourteen hundred enslaved Black residents who were there by the start of the Civil War.[67] Around that time, at about fifteen years of age, Eliza gave birth to a son named William, who would be EB's father. Records indicate that William's father was a man named Shadrick Henderson, but history offers no confirmation about where he was from or what ever became of him. On the Fourth of July 1863, Vicksburg surrendered to Union troops under General Ulysses S. Grant after a forty-seven-day siege. That victory, considered Grant's finest military achievement, was a turning point of the Civil War, giving the Union Army control of the entire Mississippi River and splitting the Confederacy in two.

During the siege, the general had had several thousand Black soldiers under his command, who played important roles in the city's surrender and the aftermath. They were from the United States Colored Troops, a volunteer deployment initiated by President Abraham Lincoln in 1863 that eventually numbered 175 regiments, each led by White officers. This totaled 178,000 servicemen, about 10 percent of the entire Union Army. As these soldiers approached Vicksburg, the city's enslaved Black residents secretly celebrated each Confederate setback, knowing that a Union triumph meant their effective emancipation. Indeed, large numbers of African Americans reportedly stood along the roadways of Vicksburg cheering as Grant and his troops, including the Black soldiers, marched victoriously through the city. At some point, either during the Union Army's lengthy blockade of Vicksburg or in the aftermath of the city's fall, Eliza made her way to Washington, D.C., with William. According to Henderson family lore, she escaped the war zone with her son hidden in a trunk.[68] The fact that the young mother had been able to return to the North with her child at all, after being quite literally "sold downriver" into slavery, was profoundly dramatic.

Once in D.C., Eliza soon reunited with her relatives in the area, and "in due time she bought the house on School Street" in the alleyway where William grew up, while his mother ran a grocery store that she had set up on the ground floor.[69] In May 1874, at around age fifteen and standing all of five feet, three and a half inches tall, he left home and joined the U.S. Navy, enlisting as a "First Class Boy" aboard the USS *Gettysburg*, a 950-ton side-wheel gunboat attached to the North Atlantic Blockading Squadron. By the time he was honorably discharged for the last time in September 1880, William had served six tours on four ships and been promoted to landsman, coal heaver, second-class fireman, and seaman.[70]

Such frequent transfers were not necessarily unusual in the navy, but records now kept by the U.S. Department of Veterans Affairs reveal a possible reason. Throughout his naval service, William seemed to endure continual acute ailments that included bronchitis, adenitis, and intermittent fevers, possibly stemming from a hernia injury he reported while heaving coal aboard the *Tallapoosa*, his second ship.[71] These conditions bothered William for years after he left the military. It's possible that EB's love for his father and an ongoing mystery about the underlying causes of his father's ailments influenced the future Black basketball pioneer to develop his profound interest in the vital role that physical training could play in one's overall well-being.

At some point after his final discharge, William returned home to School Street and met a young Virginia-born woman from the same block named Louisa "Lulu" Mars. The daughter of an enslaved Black woman and a White slave-holding plantation owner in Williamsburg, Virginia, she was very light-complexioned and listed as "Mulatto." Lulu could have passed for White but did not. Instead, she leveraged her skin tone. "To be a mulatto almost always identified you with a powerful white family," one observer remembered, about the importance of complexion within the city's Black social hierarchy. "Those children had more opportunities."[72]

Lulu lived with her sister and brother-in-law, a storekeeper named Hubbard E. Brown, and their children in a two-story brick building right around the corner from William at 405 Four-and-a-Half Street SW.[73] Like many shop owners who resided above their small businesses, they inhabited the upstairs while the grocery that Hubbard kept was on the ground floor.

Known as Fourth Street SW today, Four-and-a-Half ran down the center of Southwest halfway between Third and Sixth Streets, resulting in its quirky name; there was no Fifth Street. It was the area's hub for business and culture, with shops, offices, drugstores, craftsmen, tradesmen, and suppliers, as well as cafés, restaurants, and saloons. The cobblestone street was always busy with a rich mixture of people. Black people shopped among Irish, German, Polish, and Italian immigrants. The well-kept storefronts on Four-and-a-Half belied the alleyway interiors of their respective blocks, as was the case throughout South Washington and much of the District. In contrast to William, who lived only two hundred feet around the corner, all of Lulu's neighbors were White, showing just how different life in Washington's presentable front-facing buildings was compared to the deplorable tenements on its backstreets and alleyways. This wasn't just visual. Four-and-a-Half residents included shoemakers, musicians, store clerks, sales ladies, restaurant keepers, apprentices, and dressmakers, while School Street had laborers, waiters, servants, bricklayers, drivers, brickyard workers, a blacksmith, and a junk dealer.

Looking past these differences, William and Lulu found enough common ground to begin a courtship and were married on February 22, 1883, the month following Dudley Allen Sargent's important physical training article. The groom was twenty-three, the bride was twenty, and the couple's first child, EB, was born thirty-nine weeks and three days later.

A month after that, in December 1883, the Intercollegiate Athletic Conference met in New York City for a pivotal meeting. It was "the first joint attempt by college faculty representatives to impose some regulations on athletics, which were beginning to present formidable problems of student participation, sports rules and regulations and amateurism that individual colleges could not solve alone."[74] They sought to restrict college teams from playing with or against professionals, limit a student's playing time to four years, have faculty supervision of all competition, and require the home court or field of one of the teams to be used for a given game. But this early attempt at control failed because out of the nine participating institutions, only Harvard, Princeton, and Cornell agreed to the proposed rules. Needless to say, collegiate authorities would keep trying for generations to come.

Meanwhile, William and Louisa Henderson shared the same promise of the times that 1883 offered to the rest of the world. The young couple added

another child, William Jr., in 1885, and Louisa taught EB how to read at home
before many children who were enrolled in schools even knew the alphabet.
Just like the newlywed Poseys, who had recently moved there from Ohio, the
Hendersons had heard about Pittsburgh, a progressive industrial city full of
opportunities. So, when he was five years old, EB and his family moved there
to seek a better life than what School Street in South Washington could offer.

CHAPTER 4

PITTSBURGH PEDIGREE

PITTSBURGH WAS RIPE WITH AN intoxicating array of economic and social opportunities when Captain and Mrs. Posey moved to the area in 1884. Because of its location at the point where the Allegheny and Monongahela Rivers unite to form the Ohio River, the city became an enormous commerce hub with the emergence of the steamboat in the 1820s, which transformed its three rivers into accessible, reliable, inexpensive transportation routes that were navigable year-round. These waterways connected Pittsburgh west via the Ohio River to the Mississippi River and ultimately to the Gulf of Mexico, east into Upstate New York via the Allegheny, and south to Morgantown, West Virginia, via the Monongahela. Because of its accessibility, the city became one of the America's most efficient locations for importing and exporting raw materials and finished products. Pittsburgh also sat on "exhaustless supplies of iron" and "unfathomable wells of oil" in addition to vast deposits of bituminous coal, of which it had become simultaneously the country's top supplier and its leading consumer. "Coal meant light, heat, and power," a local handbook from the late-1800s explained, fueling enormous growth in manufacturing.[1] The nonstop burning of coal as fuel throughout the entire region was so intense that locals began to realize "our city would give out an appearance of greater neatness, cleanliness, and beauty than it does now, were it not for the dense cloud of smoke always resting upon it."[2] Pittsburgh had earned its nickname, "the Smoky City," and its buildings had become covered by so many layers of dark soot that they would remain for generations to come. Yet this environmental and architectural spoiling was rationalized because "it meant industry and progress."[3]

Pittsburgh's population had grown to more than 150,000 residents as the city became a center of movement not only for trade but also for people and ideas. Racially segregated schooling had been abolished there since 1874, so Black children and White children were learning side by side. Access to quality education for African Americans meant jobs and self-worth, which translated into entrepreneurial success. Along with industrial smoke, there was opportunity in the air for everyone. That's why a steady stream of Black families like the Poseys and the Hendersons were coming to Pittsburgh. There were already more than six thousand African American residents living there by the time EB and his family arrived from Washington, D.C., triple the number at the beginning of the Civil War.[4] Many were Black migrants from the farmlands and small towns of the South, where wages for African Americans averaged less than $3.50 per week. That went up to $9 a week in big Southern cities like Louisville. But in the urban North, the average weekly wage for Black employees was as much as $14 per week, and no Northern city was more financially promising than Pittsburgh, which was entering its golden age and poised to become the most powerful industrial force in America.[5]

The city's Black community was centered in an area called the Hill District, "the Hill" for short, located on a slope overlooking Pittsburgh's downtown from the east. Originally populated by Jewish, German, and Irish professionals after the Civil War, more than half its residents were African American, and the rest were an ethnically diverse mixture of German, Irish, English, Scottish, Welsh, Italian, Syrian, Greek, and Polish immigrants "from Europe's ghettos."[6] But they found common ground, having come to the city to seek a better way of life.

Six miles southeast of Pittsburgh and across the Monongahela, there was a bend in the river containing a thousand acres of level land that backed into gently sloping hills. It was an area "favorably situated for the location of industrial establishments, and for dwelling places for workingmen," a contemporary description explained.[7] A settlement called Homestead had sprung up there, which was incorporated in 1880 and inhabited by several hundred residents by 1884 when the Posey family relocated there.

Though few outsiders yet envisioned it, the area had immense potential.[8] For one thing, Homestead was strategically located along the tracks of the Pittsburgh, Virginia & Charleston Railroad, which ran through the section and connected with the far-reaching Pennsylvania Railroad network in nearby Pittsburgh. It also linked with the extensive Baltimore & Ohio Railroad at Wheeling, West Virginia, to the south, as well as with the widespread Pittsburgh, McKeesport & Youghiogheny Railroad, which itself connected to the entire Lake Erie system that extended all the way to Connecticut.

Homestead's population tripled within twelve months of its incorporation and doubled again a year later after a group of area steelmakers formed the Pittsburg Bessemer Steel Company and began construction of a huge mill in the center of town, on the banks of the Monongahela River. Its massive projected annual production capacity of eighty thousand tons of steel rails and structural materials attracted legions of highly skilled, well-paid steelworkers and craftsmen. Homestead also drew in whole communities of miners because it rested above the renowned Pittsburgh coal seam, a high-yield deposit that wound through the Monongahela Valley. One of the town's biggest coal mining and shipping operations was owned and operated by the family of Captain Hays, Posey's employer and mentor, on land that the Hays's owned. That growth was accelerated further with the October 1883 buyout of Bessemer Steel by Carnegie Bros. & Co., Andrew Carnegie's corporation that had already built its own steel mills and other industrial operations in the region.[9] Little known outside the area at the time, "Carnegie" and "Homestead" would soon become household names, as would the Posey surname among rivermen, at first, and then in the world of sports.

Only after he settled into Homestead did it become clear that Captain Posey's connection with Hays was much more than just a mentor relationship. The Poseys' high socioeconomic ambitions also revealed themselves. First, they purchased a plot of land in the town, acquired from Hays.[10] The one-tenth-acre lot was at the northeast corner of McClure Street and Eighth Avenue, diagonally across from the front lawn of the enormous estate of Abdiel McClure, the grandson of another one of Homestead's original settlers. But this was strictly an investment property, because the Poseys' actual residence was a rental house on the Hays family estate, known as Harden Station, where Captain Hays and his father lived.[11] That was located alongside the PV&C Railroad at Six Mile Ferry on the Monongahela River, and it's where the couple's first child, a girl named Beatrice, was born in 1885.[12] Within two years, Anna gave birth to their first son, named Seward, after Hays's middle name.

In 1888, when Edwin Bancroft Henderson's parents moved to Pittsburgh with five-year-old EB and his younger brother, William, they rented an apartment on Wilson Street in the lower section of the Hill District, a predominantly Black neighborhood.[13] Many of its African American residents were single male laborers from the South, often with experience in Southern steel factories. "Wherever the Negro has had a chance to acquire the necessary skill," *Iron Age* magazine wrote during that time, "he has shown himself capable." This was being proven in Pittsburgh, where strikes by White steelworkers at the Pittsburgh Bolt Company, Black Diamond Steel Works, and Solar Iron Works were being broken using imported African American workers. "In every instance they were men trained in the mills of the South," the publication reported.[14] Ending labor disputes like this was so routine that management labeled the African American workforce as "strike insurance."

The trouble at Solar Iron was typical. A year earlier, the steelmaking giant Carnegie Bros. & Co. had announced that it was building a gigantic new rail mill as an add-on to its Edgar Thomson Steel Works in Braddock, a town on the Monongahela River across from Homestead. At a cost of $1 million, or more than $27 million today, this addition would make Edgar Thomson the largest steelmaking operation in the world. America's railroads were expanding so fast that the company had more orders for tracks than what Edgar Thomson and the Homestead Works could produce. This would ramp up its production capacity to four hundred thousand tons of rails a year, or about a third of the total output in the entire United States. The move was reportedly "intended to introduce a new manufacturing process in the mill which will cheapen the cost of production considerably."[15] But it would also displace Solar Iron Works, a manufacturer with a five-hundred-man workforce that produced hoop iron and cotton bale ties, to a different part of Braddock. In the process, the puddlers at Solar Iron went on strike "out of a demand for higher wages and dissatisfaction with some new regulations," which effectively shut down the entire plant.[16] Represented by the Amalgamated Association of Iron and Steel Workers, puddlers were highly skilled laborers who worked as two-man crews that stirred molten pig iron through doors in an open-hearth furnace heated up to 2,800 degrees Fahrenheit, producing steel that could be molded into bars for rolling. This essential work was extremely dangerous, and puddlers often died before reaching thirty years of age.

This strike was still dragging on when the Hendersons got to the Hill District. EB's father didn't have steel industry experience, but after settling the family, he soon landed a job that was listed as "laborer." Their new place was just four blocks from the highly regarded Franklin Public School, where EB started kindergarten in the fall of 1888. Franklin School, at the corner of Franklin and Logan Streets, housed 250 students and was racially mixed. According to EB, attending this school for the next five years helped him realize how excellent his homeschooling had been. "One white teacher of the third grade had me read before her pupils and gave me a quarter, one-fourth of a laborer's pay in those days," EB would later recall.[17] There was no doubt that he was an advanced learner.

The place where EB and his family lived was also just one block from the corner of Wylie Avenue and Fulton Street, a bustling intersection that the Harlem Renaissance poet Claude McKay would nickname the "Cross Roads of the World" for its character as an epicenter of African American culture.[18] But just like life in New York City's Little Africa, the surrounding streets were notorious for their vice and crime. In 1888, the year EB started at Franklin, the *Pittsburgh Daily Post* ran an investigative report on its front page that found eighty-three "gamblers' dens" in the same vicinity, of which forty-two were used to operate "policy" games, a highly popular though illegal form of lottery gambling.[19] "The colored gentlemen of the Hill District, who have a weakness for squandering their nickels and dimes playing this game, give each place good support," wrote another local newspaper.[20] Yet it was an Irish "retired butcher," who lived with his wife and two sons a couple of blocks away on Diamond Street, that was "the reputed head of policy in Pittsburgh."[21] The man, Irvin "Irv" Redpath, was "a well known gambler" who owned "many fine thoroughbreds" and was "intimately acquainted" with the city's chief of detectives.[22] Then there was Daisy Moore, an African American woman who kept a saloon on Wylie. She also ran a "disorderly house" at 32 Bedford Avenue that "was a resort for a very tough element of colored people," one of many such establishments within blocks of the Henderson's residence. "Four young white girls found in the house were taken with her to Central Station," where Daisy was fined $100 plus costs and released.[23] The block where the Hendersons lived had been further sensationalized as the family home of Edward Coffey, a thirty-one-year-old Irish "bully" convicted of first-degree murder for the killing of a Pittsburgh police officer. After a lengthy trial, with attempts by many friends to have his sentence commuted, Coffey had been set to be executed in early 1888 but instead cut his own throat and died before the fateful day arrived.[24]

Despite these scenarios, Pittsburgh remained a promising land of opportunity for enterprising and adventurous African Americans like the Poseys and the Hendersons. That puddlers' strike was resolved a year later when Solar Iron Works announced it had "whipped the Amalgamated Association before" and planned to do it again. "There is a rumor afloat that the firm will fill the places of the strikers with colored men from the South," the *Pittsburgh Daily Post* reported on its front page.[25] "There will likely be some lively scenes," it said prophetically, "before the trouble is over." The union tried inducing "colored puddlers" to join the strike, but the effort was in vain because the Amalgamated Association otherwise had been treating its Black members unfairly up to that point. This was not to be the last time the Amalgamated union would pay a heavy price for its systemic racism.

During this time, Captain Posey had begun establishing several businesses related to hauling coal and building the boats for the job. Some of these firms were in partnership with Captain Hays, his longtime mentor, real estate supplier, and friend. Both of the rivermen had their offices at 99 Water Street in downtown Pittsburgh. Much of the coal they hauled came from the large mines owned and operated by the Hays family on their estate overlooking the Monongahela.[26] These businesses were lucrative, as proved by Posey's purchase of a forty-acre parcel of land adjacent to Homestead in October 1889 for $6,000, or about $168,000 today.[27]

When the up-and-coming Poseys had their third and last child, Cumberland Jr., on June 20, 1890, also at Harden Station, his birth brought the couple an extraordinarily fertile period of optimism and growth. In addition to their real estate holdings, Captain Posey was "the only colored steamboat owner of these waters," the *Pittsburgh Dispatch* pointed out just weeks after Cum's birth.[28] Five months later, he and Hays formed the Pittsburgh Sand Company, with a charter to mine, excavate, and transport sand, gravel, cobble stones, and other materials from the surrounding region.[29] The company would eventually construct an incline railway at the foot of Twenty-Fourth Street, on the South Side, to carry its inland yields down the side of Mount Oliver to the Monongahela and onto the company's steam-powered sand boat, the *Cascade*, which Posey had built through one of his other businesses, the Delta Coal Company.

Delta Coal would ultimately build and sell forty-one steamships in all. Serving as its general manager and treasurer, Posey supervised the acquisition, construction, refurbishment, and operation of his vessels with meticulous care, so they were exceptional in quality. And the entrepreneurial captain had a natural special touch with the press in promoting his operations, knowing what rivermen wanted to read. Often 120 feet in length, containing three decks, and able to tow ten or more barges full of coal, the steamboat itself was literally the biggest thing in the lore of river life, symbolically as essential as food and shelter and even family. Reporters speculated for weeks on the name Captain Posey might choose for one of his upcoming vessels, seemingly as excited as the girlfriends of an expectant mother. "The owners have not yet decided on a name for the new boat," the widely read *Pittsburgh Daily Post* reported in April 1891, as one of his new paddle wheelers was nearing completion, "but THE POST would suggest that 'C.W. Posey' would be the best name they could find." Having created a mystery, he got double the mentions when it was resolved a month later. "Captain Posey has named his new sand boat Pittsburgh," the *Daily Post* shared. That newspaper was so enamored with "the very handsome appearance" of his steamship, the *Delta*, that it called her a "little beauty" and "so light she could float on morning dew" after the vessel got extensive repairs that included new boilers and a new coat of paint.[30]

Posey took the publicity about his *Delta* a step further and challenged the captain of a rival steamboat, the *J.S. Neel*, to a race. Paddle wheel steamboat racing was a thing. But it was extremely dangerous because no matter how attractive a vessel looked, if its boilers weren't properly built or carefully tended while going full speed, they could become overheated and over-pressurized, resulting in a spontaneous, spectacular, catastrophic explosion. Such blasts were so frequent that people practically came to expect them. That's partly why these races were so thrilling, for onlookers as well as for the passengers themselves. Congress even had to enact special legislation specifically prohibiting this activity, and to this day, Missouri still has an anti-steamboat racing law on its books. But in May 1892, the *Delta* and the *J.S. Neel* raced upstream on the Monongahela through Pittsburgh Harbor to see which vessel could be the first to cross under the Smithfield Street Bridge.[31] The steamboats had "a nice little race," and although the *Delta* had a sizable lead approaching the finish line, Captain Posey slowed her down until they were "neck and neck." A reporter believed "the Neel was just about passing her" when they went under the bridge.[32]

Though rivermen risked their boats, their passengers, and their own lives, they stood by their workmanship and skill. That was part of the lore, and Posey was both literally and figuratively the captain of his own ship. The whole steamboat race spectacle might have been designed to build up the Delta Coal Company's value, because soon afterward Posey sold his stake, promptly forming another venture, the Posey Coal Dealers and Steam Boat Builders Company. And the Poseys kept investing their proceeds. Over the next few years, they would buy more than a dozen additional plots of real estate from Hays, as well as nearly twenty more properties from other local landowners. These included a set of eight lots in downtown Homestead, on the north side of Second Avenue between McClure and Dickson Streets, which the couple purchased for a total of $4,321, or around $122,000 today. Each of them measured twenty-four feet across and one hundred feet deep, creating a street-facing side-by-side presence so impressive that the entire block was listed in the official *Homestead Directory* as "Posey's Row."[33] Set back less than two hundred feet from the Monongahela River, these properties were next to the renamed Carnegie Steel Company's massive Homestead Works, which employed about five thousand men, more than half of the town's population, which made the Posey's Row homes ideal as rentals to laborers employed at the mill.[34] All the while, fueled by technological breakthroughs, Carnegie Steel kept expanding the plant and eventually acquired the section of land directly across the street from Posey's Row to use for its operations.

But the same innovations that had fed the mill's expansion also made its skilled workforce, represented by the Amalgamated Association of Iron and Steel Workers, feel increasingly insecure about job security. Those advances had allowed Carnegie Steel to hire more unskilled labor, and in response the union sought to renegotiate its terms, which in turn caused the corporation to order a wage reduction. In June 1892, a month after Posey's steamboat race, the union's negotiations with the company broke down, causing the mill to lock out the workers. Outraged, union men and their supporters equipped themselves with firearms, clubs, and other devices, vowing to keep out management and any strikebreakers. In response, Carnegie Steel hired hundreds of armed private security operatives from out-of-town offices of the Pinkerton National Detective Agency to protect the company's property and reopen the mill. On hearing of this, thousands of workers and Homestead townspeople angrily waited for their arrival. Then, on July 6, 1892, as two barges full of the "Pinkertons" were towed up to the mill, a gun battle broke out in which thirteen men were killed and twenty-three others wounded. Eleven of those who died were from Homestead.

With that, following a proven model, Andrew Carnegie authorized the company to bring in Black laborers as strikebreakers. The union's previous policy had been to exclude African American laborers from its ranks or restrict their opportunities. These new men were eager to work in better jobs under improved conditions. They arrived at the Homestead Works under the protection of 8,000 armed soldiers from the Pennsylvania State Militia, and the mill was back in operation less than two months later with more than 1,700 nonunion workers, including large numbers of African Americans. These strikebreakers were subjected to so much violence by townspeople on the streets of Homestead that Carnegie Steel built sleeping quarters, a barbershop, and even a saloon inside its heavily fortified mill yard for their use. By mid-November, the Amalgamated union ran out of funds and gave up the strike. This was a crushing defeat because Carnegie Steel was western Pennsylvania's largest employer. For the first time, Black iron- and steelworkers had gained a solid economic footing in the industry that would last for generations to come.

Ironically, one of those two barges full of Pinkertons that landed at the Homestead Works on that fateful night in July 1892 had been towed to the mill by the steamer *Little Bill*. Although her pilot, engineer, second engineer, deckhand, and mate would later testify under oath that they did not know who was on the barges or their mission, that steamboat, built by Captain Hays, would forever be "hated by the strikers with a bitter hatred."[35] In some ways, however, by association, this further cemented Captain Posey's legendary and unassailable stature among Black people in Pittsburgh.

Through the Poseys' hard work, their surname had been made famous and well respected not only within the city's African American community but also throughout the entire Ohio River Valley region. Captain Posey, a "portly and well-dressed colored man," had "prospered in a way that is rare for one of his race," the *Cincinnati Enquirer* wrote in 1894, when Cum was four years old. "But it was a reward for qualities which will bring wealth to any one, black or white."[36] And Anna Posey, always "a guiding hand and safe counselor in the business success of her husband," was just as prominent with social causes in Black Pittsburgh as Captain Posey was as a riverman in the valley.[37] She became involved in literary pursuits as a charter member of the Aurora Reading Club in Pittsburgh, an African American women's improvement organization that advocated betterment through reading. Founded in 1894 with the motto "Lifting as We Climb," the club still exists today as the oldest organization of its kind in America.

Meanwhile, the Poseys had tucked away some land to use for their own home, on which they built a set of residences during the mid-1890s. The property consisted of three lots on the upper side of Thirteenth Avenue in Homestead, "one of the most prominent streets" in the town because of its elevation atop the hill overlooking the Monongahela River Valley and the Carnegie Steel mill on its banks.[38] "This colored man owns considerable property," an African American sociologist named Helen Tucker would write in her much-admired turn-of-the-century study of Blacks in Pittsburgh. "He lives in a large comfortable house and owns one on either side which he rents."[39] Their own home, a centered-gable Gothic Revival with a full-height porch, was "tastefully, but not extravagantly, furnished" and adorned with Anna's own exquisite art. Multitalented, she produced items that included "hand-painted china, oil paintings, watercolor sketches, fine silk and lace," the *Pennsylvania Negro Business Directory* reported a few years later. "Many pieces of her handiwork adorn the homes of some of Homestead's wealthiest people."[40] It was believed that some of her creations had found their way into Andrew Carnegie's art collection.[41]

Although the Poseys were not interested in making a large display of wealth, Tucker still pointed out that their residence "might have been the home of a prince."[42] Indeed, that prince would be Cumberland Willis "Cum" Posey, Jr.

CHAPTER 5

RITES OF PASSAGE

IN 1888, THE SAME YEAR Edwin Bancroft Henderson entered kindergarten at the Franklin School in Pittsburgh, Will Anthony Madden became a kindergartner at Primary School No. 13 for Boys and Girls in Greenwich Village. P.S. No. 13 held about eight hundred students and was on Downing Street near the corner of Bleecker, a short walk from Will's home.[1] Willie and Maggie, his parents, had added a third child by then, Florence, born in 1886.[2] Just as EB's mother, Louisa, had done with him, Maggie had homeschooled Will, and he was a precocious learner.

The fact that the Hendersons and the Maddens had been able to enroll their sons in kindergarten at all gave both youngsters an extraordinary advantage. According to a 1905 report by the Department of Commerce and Labor, the nationwide illiteracy rate for African American preteen boys ranged from 40 to 70 percent throughout the 1890s, ten times more than that for White children.[3] This outcome was not surprising considering that literacy itself had been *illegal* for the vast majority of Black people less than a generation earlier; in other words, the parents of those youths. Despite the abolition of slavery, African Americans had been systematically deprived of educational opportunities ever since. White educators seemed to recognize this, though delicately, with a mix of hope, goodwill, and built-in denial. "As the proportion of illiteracy decreases for one race it usually decreases for the other also," one such expert stated in that report, "indicating that the negro, like the white man, responds to the influence of improved conditions."[4]

But conditions rarely improved for Black youngsters in the impoverished, overcrowded cities of the North. Will faced even tougher odds than EB did, because New York led all cities with the highest proportion of children from any race who couldn't read or write. Fortunately, Maggie recognized his gifts and focused on educating Will rather than finding outside work. To make ends meet, his father, Willie, had a side job selling produce from a grocery pushcart in the neighborhood. Will would later describe this part of his father's career as the "days when there was plenty of money to be made" in Greenwich Village.[5] Willie's produce cart was stationed at a licensed sidewalk location around the corner from his home on a small but infamous alleyway called Minetta Lane.[6] Having a pushcart license at all was an improvement over most cities in the South, where White supremacy prevented Black proprietors from obtaining those credentials just to do business.

This crooked little cobblestone street sliced through the "Minetta District," a notorious predominantly Black section adjacent to Little Africa, which was so overcrowded and treacherous that one newspaper described it as a "pest spot."[7] With eighty-five buildings crammed into less than four acres, its hidden entrances, dark alleyways, and jumble of streets were a refuge for villains. Minetta Lane "swarmed with the most dangerous people in the city," wrote the young reporter and novelist Stephen Crane. "Even a policeman in chase of a criminal would probably shy away instead of pursuing him into the lane," he added. "The odds were too great against a lone officer."[8] Jacob Riis portrayed the African American cellar dives of the Minetta District as dangerous and risky environments where "when a fight breaks out during the dance a dozen razors are handy in as many boot-legs, and there is always a job for the surgeon and the ambulance."[9]

"Artists and poets, daubers and scribblers infest the district," it was said, mainly because it was void of noisy traffic and the old houses had big rooms with many windows.[10] Still, public officials wished to replace the whole Minetta District with a children's playground. That's because the surrounding area had virtually no open playing space for the ten thousand youths of all races and ethnicities between ages four and eighteen who lived just in Greenwich Village at the time. A "mass of humanity" occupied "every available square foot."[11] So many of these "poor waifs of the city" were being mistreated by adults that the New-York Society for the Prevention of Cruelty to Children had been established to protect them.[12] Hordes of abandoned, homeless, unschooled, deprived juveniles who had turned to crime or delinquency roamed the area looking for trouble. A poor, small, scrawny lad like Will had to negotiate many unpredictable and potentially threatening encounters with these misfits just to claim a spot on which to play.

Fifty blocks uptown from Little Africa, a man named John Davison Rockefeller left his home each morning and headed to work. He was not just rich; he was the richest. Not just on top, but at the top of the "top half" by himself.

Rockefeller was an oil tycoon who ran an enormous corporation called the Standard Oil Trust, which he had founded as a single company, Standard Oil, in Ohio in 1870 and built into one of America's most powerful businesses by taking over most of his competitors by 1882. As the nation's leading producer of oil and its essential by-products, including gasoline, petroleum, and kerosene used in ordinary household lamps, Standard Oil was central to the country's growth. Through some of history's shrewdest and most innovative of business practices—a few of which were illegal—the company had gained control of more than 90 percent of the market. In other words, Standard Oil had become a monopoly. And it had made Rockefeller into the world's richest man, the equivalent of a multi-billionaire today.

In 1885, the business relocated its headquarters to New York City, into a newly erected ten-story structure at 26 Broadway, facing Battery Park in Lower Manhattan. This early office tower came to be known as the Standard Oil Building. Rockefeller himself moved to Midtown Manhattan and purchased a fine Victorian brownstone at 4 West Fifty-Fourth Street, just off Fifth Avenue, on a site occupied today by the Sculpture Garden in the Museum of Modern Art.[13] On a typical weekday, the oil tycoon would catch the downtown-bound Sixth Avenue Elevated Railway at its Fiftieth Street Station. This was the main commuter train for businessmen employed in the city's Financial District. Other frequent riders included the railroad executive Russell Sage, the banker Jacob Schiff, and the financier John Pierpont "J. P." Morgan. These men, themselves multimillionaires, all lived near Rockefeller and often commuted to work together.[14] Despite being known as "the Richest Man in the World," the Standard Oil chief was "a plain, ordinary man in appearance," according to an 1890 report in the *New York Evening World,* and rode the train like a regular commuter.[15] Traveling down Sixth Avenue pulled by locomotives that pounded forward relentlessly at twelve miles per hour, the executives rode in "light and airy" passenger cars with cushioned wooden seats and floors covered by braided matting.[16] It would take Rockefeller about twenty-five minutes to arrive at the Rector Street Station in Lower Manhattan. From there, it was a three-block stroll to the Standard Oil Building—which still stands today, facing the famous *Charging Bull* sculpture in Bowling Green.

About halfway into each of these trips, the Sixth Avenue train would hit that sharp curve of elevated track at the corner of West Third Street and pass directly above the unfortunate section where Will, his family, and their neighbors lived in its shadow. Though only a few feet separated the commuting "richest man" from the rooftops and front windows of the poor folks residing on the block below, they could not have been further apart. Yet, in their wildest dreams, neither John D. Rockefeller nor the Maddens could have known that one day, Will would travel to the same building, enter the same lobby, ride the same elevators, stride along the same hallways, walk into the same offices, and pass the same boardrooms that Rockefeller and his fellow Standard Oil executives used to build their fortunes. In fact, Will and the Rockefellers would become coworkers on a first-name basis. This rarest of connections spoke to the striving determination of this young native of Little Africa and the kind of person he was meant to become.

By 1890, the year Cumberland Posey, Jr. was born, the Maddens had outgrown 99½ West Third and were eager to leave Little Africa behind. Will was seven, his older sister, Grace, was nine, and his younger sister, Florence, was four. The plan was for Maggie's parents to move in with the family so they could all pool their combined wages to afford a bigger residence. That's how they got into a three-story brick dwelling with a basement on Waverly Place, in the Christopher Park section of Greenwich Village, just off Sheridan Square.[17] Affordable freestanding homes in Manhattan were extremely rare, but the family's timing was perfect; 1890 was "the year of greatest activity in the building of houses for single families," during which plans for 835 of them were filed with the city.[18]

Though only a few blocks away on the other side of Sixth Avenue, Waverly was a world apart from West Third. Will's new block was quieter, cleaner, and safer with fresh air, sunlight, and civil decency. He was also able to remain enrolled at Primary School No. 13. Across the street from his home was the Northern Dispensary, a respected hospital established in 1827 as a free clinic for "the worthy poor."[19] (Edgar Allan Poe was treated there once, for a cold.)

Two doors down, at the corner of Grove Street, was the wood-frame building that housed Abyssinian Baptist Church, the second-oldest Black congregation in New York City.[20] Their neighbors represented a rainbow assortment of skills, trades, professions, and personalities. These included cigar makers, machinists, policemen, clergymen, a bootblack, a physician, waiters, feather curlers, collar makers, a riding instructor, a bartender, and an artist.[21] All were first- or second-generation immigrants from Europe and the Caribbean, as well as American migrants from Virginia, Pennsylvania, New Jersey, Maryland, and Georgia. This aspect of the city's racial, ethnic, cultural, and occupational diversity would later prove formative for Will's outlook on life: Differing kinds of people could live and play side by side.

That same year, in the western New England town of Springfield, Massachusetts, a man named Luther Halsey Gulick, Jr., was learning the ropes as the newly promoted director of the School for Christian Workers, a local YMCA-affiliated academy that trained men for non-clergy Christian work. He had been there since October 1887 as a physical education instructor. Gulick's prior background had included coursework at Oberlin College, as well as a year as director of the YMCA Gymnasium in Jackson, Michigan, and at the time he was also taking classes toward a medical degree in 1899 from the New York University Medical College. Most importantly, he had completed six months of studies at the increasingly popular Sargent Normal School of Physical Training in Cambridge, Massachusetts, during the winter term in 1885–6.

By then, that school's founder, Dudley Allen Sargent, had expanded his views on muscular Christianity to include competitive sports, believing these could help strengthen the concept's spiritual virtues. "Some of the specific mental and physical qualities which are developed by athletics are increased powers of attention, will, concentration, accuracy, alertness, quickness of perception, perseverance, reason, judgment, forbearance, patience, obedience, self-control, loyalty to leaders, self-denial, submergence of self, grace, poise, suppleness, courage, strength and endurance," he wrote. "These qualities are as valuable to women as to men."[22] Sargent thought highly of Gulick as his student. "He is a young man of excellent moral character and good intellectual attainments," the instructor wrote in a letter of recommendation for the

Michigan job. "He has considerable enthusiasm for Physical Training and a fund of mirth and vivacity that would enable him to inspire others with an interest in the work."[23]

A year later, Sargent was persuaded by Harvard University to teach an intensive, condensed version of his physical training curriculum in the university's Summer School of Arts and Sciences. The result was a five-week physical education course, which debuted in July 1887. As it happened, when Sargent stood in front of his inaugural class and looked around the room, he saw that Booker T. Washington was one of his students.[24] Washington had been reluctant to attend at first, because he was a self-confessed workaholic who later admitted, "I think I would now be a more useful man if I had had time for sports."[25] But his wife, Olivia, had wanted him to go, despite the arrival of their newborn baby. "For some time past," she wrote to a girlfriend earlier that year, "I have felt that Mr. Washington's present mode of life is unfavorable to his health." She thought Sargent's course would do him some good.[26] Her nudging made a difference: Washington embraced its principles and formed many of his later opinions about wellness while taking those classes. "We need, as a race, a good strong public sentiment in favor of a sounder, healthier body, and a cleaner and higher-toned morality," he later proclaimed.[27] Washington's promotion of fitness would not only reinforce physical training as essential for African American survival and social progress, but also inspire a generation of Black sports pioneers to take these ideas one step further.

That fall, Gulick began working in Springfield. In those days, the city was an industrial center that specialized in precision manufacturing, with its Springfield Armory producing the majority of arms for the United States military until it closed in 1968. The locale was known for its forward think-ing, which is why the YMCA had established one of its first North American branches there. Springfield was a good proving ground for the social ministry, good citizenship, and wholesome recreation that the organization wanted to promote among urban workers. With a population of about twenty thousand, greater Springfield was big enough to have spawned some big-city morality-based problems—such as alcohol abuse, gambling, and prostitution—yet small enough to be able to explore different solutions. Seeing these conditions, Gulick envisioned that the School for Christian Workers could play a more meaningful role. So, in 1891, he changed its name to the International YMCA

Training School and revised its mission to produce workers specifically for placement within the worldwide YMCA network.[28]

To staff this new school with appropriately experienced instructors, Gulick recruited in Montreal, the site of North America's first YMCA branch, and found an ideal candidate there. His name was James A. Naismith, and he was the superintendent of athletics at McGill University. Naismith had all the right qualifications, including a bachelor of arts degree in physical education from nearby Presbyterian College, so Gulick hired him to join the International Y faculty as a physical education teacher. The newcomer arrived in Springfield in time for its 1891–2 academic year.[29]

Meanwhile, still a "fund of mirth" about the principles of physical culture, Gulick had begun to notice that many International Y trainees, especially those who had competed in the fall in high-exertion sports such as football, were so bored by their gymnasium activities during winter that they totally lost interest in working out. This was unacceptable. "We degenerate from the top down," he later wrote. "Therefore, bodily vigor is a moral agent, it enables us to live on higher levels, to keep up to the top of our achievement."[30] Fully engaged, it was Gulick who subsequently designed the YMCA's triangle logo incorporating its mind, body, and spirit philosophy. With morality at stake, he assigned the challenge of how to make indoor fitness exciting again to his rookie teacher, Naismith. In a subsequent faculty meeting to discuss the issue, the new teacher suggested that the problem was not with the students but with the outdated indoor fitness routines that the school was using. Everyone sat in silence. "The only indoor games that we had at that time were three-deep, prisoners' base, long-ball, and games of this type," the Canadian later explained.[31]

Three-Deep was a tag game in which a player chases a runner in a circle around the inside of two concentric circles formed by stationary inward-facing players, usually everyone in the entire gym class, who are standing "two deep." The runner being chased can stop in front of any two players, thereby making them "three deep," and forcing the player in the outer circle to become the new runner being chased.

Prisoner's Base was also a running and tagging game, which involved dividing a class into two teams that would face each other, separated by a line drawn with chalk. A large square, the prison, was also drawn about thirty feet behind each team. Then each team sent one of its players, usually the

fastest runner, to the other team's prison. The goal was for each team to free
its prisoner by sending a teammate to run and dodge past the opposing team
and bring back the teammate without getting caught or tagged. If caught, that
player would also become a prisoner in need of rescue. Each team would be
busy rescuing its own players and protecting its prisoners; at the end of the
period, the team with the most prisoners would win.

Long-Ball, the last game Naismith mentioned, was a bat-and-ball game
that, combining elements of cricket and baseball, required catching, throwing, and batting. "It is easy to see now why it was impossible to interest grown
men in the games that even the youngsters of today fail to enjoy," Naismith
remembered.[32]

That's when Gulick ordered Naismith to devise "a new game to exercise
our students," adding that it should be "a competitive game like football or
lacrosse," but had to be played indoors.[33] In other words, it needed to be a challenging activity requiring so much skill, sportsmanship, and physical exertion
that it would lead not only to student engagement but also to spiritual growth.
This would apply in Springfield and in YMCAs everywhere.

Several weeks went by as Naismith examined the best parts of other
sports and attempted mashing together every combination of them. He tried
to modify some of the most popular existing games, with no success. "I then
left out the idea of any individual game and began to think of the fundamental
principles of all games," Naismith later recalled.[34] Nothing happened. Then
one day, he snapped his fingers and shouted, "I've got it!" A ball was needed.
"I discovered that in all team games some kind of a ball was used," Naismith
said. Appreciating that football was too "rough," Naismith concluded that
running should be prohibited. "If the offense didn't have the opportunity to
run with the ball, there would be no necessity for tackling and we would thus
eliminate roughness." Next, he wondered what the offense should do with the
ball. At first, Naismith considered "putting goals on the floor at each end of
the court through which the ball would be thrown." However, this would have
made throwing the ball "with great force" and accuracy the most important
skill, which wasn't appropriate for an indoor game. Besides, players would
clog up the area around the goals. Then it occurred to him that "if the goals
were so placed that the ball had to be thrown in an arc, the premium would be
taken off sheer hard throwing." And if the goals were elevated, then "players
couldn't interfere with the ball once it was launched." Also, getting the ball

into a position from which to launch it would require players to move, and for the ball to be passed from player to player.

As legend has it, the game would have had square goals except that the janitor at the Springfield gymnasium "apparently had a box fetish." He collected them. So when Naismith requested two such containers to put on poles, he was refused. Instead, this custodian went home and retrieved a pair of peach baskets, which they nailed to the balcony at each end of the gymnasium.

More time passed. Further tweaks added a jump ball at center court after each made field goal, and stepladders to remove the ball from the baskets. In all, Naismith developed thirteen rules. Brilliant in their simplicity, these were so basic that twelve of them are essentially still in use today. Finally, at the next faculty meeting, in December 1891, Naismith showed his colleagues the new game he had invented. It was called "basket ball."

Will Anthony Madden was scrawny, but he was also brainy. After completing primary education at P.S. No. 13 in 1893, he began fifth grade at Grammar School No. 35, a prestigious public all-boys institution on nearby West Thirteenth Street at Sixth Avenue. Once again, Will was in privileged company there, as it "boasted of being the most bluestocking school in the city," according to the *New York Times*, using a turn-of-the-century term for the educated elite.[35] "More politicians have been turned out of Grammar School No. 35 than any school in the city," William Lafayette Strong, the mayor of New York City, said later.[36] Indeed, its graduates included a future governor and U.S. Supreme Court justice, a future senator, and future mayors, as well as countless doctors, bankers, and businessmen.[37] But the most beloved figure ever linked with Grammar School No. 35 was its first principal, Thomas Hunter, who went on to found the Normal College of the City of New York after leaving that office. Hunter ran the Normal College while Maggie was enrolled there, and the two had something in common since both of their mothers were Irish.

That same genealogy was on Will's side as he navigated the streets around his neighborhood, thanks to his Irish grandmother, Ellen Corbett, and her lucky surname. A popular Irish American boxer named James "Gentleman Jim" Corbett was the world heavyweight champion at the time. Will was known to state that he and Jim Corbett were related, "as far as could be traced."[38] Known today as the "Father of Modern Boxing" for mastering technique rather than brute force and willpower, Corbett had knocked out the great John L. Sullivan in 1892 to win the heavyweight title, becoming the only man ever to defeat that legendary Irish American boxer. Though he would later be labeled as a "well-documented racist," Corbett was appreciated by some Black people for agreeing to fight Peter "Black Prince" Jackson, a Danish West Indies native who was the reigning Australian heavyweight champ, when no other White fighters would. That bout had ended in a draw after sixty-one rounds.[39]

Kinship—or even a hint of family ties—with such a man would have commanded a certain level of respect and street cred for anyone, and this would have applied even after Gentleman Jim lost the title in 1897, the year Will entered ninth grade at the racially integrated Boys' High School, which replaced Grammar School No. 35 in the same building when the school for younger students moved to a new location. Boys' High later was renamed DeWitt Clinton High School, subsequently moved uptown, and eventually produced a vast array of famous alumni in basketball as well as other disciplines.[40]

Even though Edwin "EB" Henderson couldn't brag about a world heavyweight boxing champion in the family, his own athletic skills and fighting spirit would soon become renowned. And EB's schooling kept giving him advantages. In 1893, the same year Will Madden entered fifth grade in New York City, EB started fifth grade back in the District of Columbia, where his parents had returned after living in Pittsburgh for five years. By then, William and Lulu had added two more children, Charles and Annie, and moved the family back into EB's grandmother's old alleyway home on School Street in South Washington. Eliza had relocated out to Falls Church, Virginia, where she had acquired some land, leaving the place in Southwest for her son and his growing family to use. William found local work as a waiter and then a porter, and they would live in that home on School Street for the next ten years.

During this time, EB would attend a series of schools in the city's racially segregated public education system. For fifth grade, he enrolled at the Eliza G. Randall School, one of seven intermediate schools "for colored pupils" in the District, located at the intersection of Delaware Avenue, H, and First Streets, ten blocks from the Henderson's household. But there were some issues. The school's one-story brick structure, with ten rooms and seating for 280 students, was originally a military barrack, so it had "very limited conveniences."[41] Also, Randall was the only such school in South Washington, the section with the most African American residents, so it was always over capacity. Finally, according to EB, he got into an altercation on the first day of classes there, with a kid who "teased him" about his "western twang," which might have been the "Pittsburghese" accent he had been around during the last few years. Seeking a change for sixth grade, his parents transferred EB to the Anthony Bowen School at 9th and E Streets SW, less than four blocks away from their home. They may have believed it would be a better learning environment for him, but it wasn't.

The school for first through sixth graders had been built in 1867 with the noblest intentions by a formerly enslaved District resident and community pioneer named Anthony Bowen, who had devoted his life to the education of African American children. After purchasing his freedom in Maryland in 1826, he accumulated substantial savings as the first African American clerk in the U.S. Patent Office and purchased two side-by-side two-story brick houses on E Street, which he combined to operate as the schoolhouse. After the Civil War, every male resident of Washington, D.C., including all Black men, was taxed one dollar for the support of its schools, even though no schools were available for "colored" children. Unstoppable, Bowen petitioned Congress for funds to build free schools for African Americans throughout the District, which were finally approved. That's when the Bowen School was built.

Years earlier, in 1853, Anthony Bowen had founded the very first Colored Branch of the YMCA. Though it did not have a formal home, offered little more than Bible study meetings, and never evolved beyond club status, this breakthrough would become a marker for future African American community leaders to follow.

By the time EB arrived at the Bowen School, which had never been upgraded, it was desperately in need of renovations, containing just eight classrooms for about four hundred pupils and ten teachers. And overcrowding was only one concern. "Being one of the oldest buildings in the District, we suffer for the lack of those modern conveniences in the way of ventilating, heating and lighting of school rooms with which our modern schools are supplied," the school's Virginia-born African American principal, Julia C. Grant, wrote in a letter to the editor of the *Washington Times*. The structure, she said, was kept warm in the winter by ten stoves, "from which gas escapes, permeating the building and causing pupils and teachers to complain seriously." Even worse was that the school had to cancel its mandatory fire drills and "some of the physical culture exercises on account of falling plastering." Bowen School had become dangerously unsafe.[42] Miss Grant's letter resulted in a visit by a *Times* reporter, who confirmed the horrifying situation. With sunken floors, bulging walls, cracked ceilings, and a bare stovepipe that rose through the wooden floorboards of the landing to the steep stairwell, which was the only way down from the second floor, he labeled the school a "death trap for children."[43]

EB was smart but also a self-described "typical delinquent" to teachers with his "pranks and incessant talk."[44] Luckily, his academic abilities got him promoted to the next grade level, allowing EB to escape the Bowen School just before it was condemned by the school board—to attend seventh and eighth grades at the Bell Colored Public School. (Congress subsequently granted appropriations for reconstructing the entire Bowen School building, to include safety provisions and modern amenities while preserving the original site.) Still, despite his short stay there, EB remembered Miss Grant fondly, and she may be the reason why, in later years, he would leverage the transformative power of letters to editors so effectively.

The Bell School was even closer to the Henderson home. Like the Randall School (and in stark contrast to the lack of space for Greenwich Village youths like Will Madden), the Bell School had its own playground, which was constantly in use. That's because the original layout for the District of Columbia included plenty of open areas and urban parks for the public. Within city limits, there were twenty-six squares, circles, and triangles between one and twenty-five acres in size, and 275 similar areas ranging from one acre down to 405 square feet. These were conceived from the start to "provide an agreeable appearance to passers-by and shade and pleasant surroundings for those who resort to the square for recreation."[45]

The school also stood directly across the street from the front of the United States Capitol grounds, approximately where First Street SW and Southwest Drive intersect today near the Garfield Monument. This allowed EB to visit the galleries of the U.S. Senate and the House of Representatives as well as the adjacent Library of Congress whenever the opportunity came up. "I knew many of the great statesmen around the turn of the century by sight," he later recalled. EB also remembered a racist legislator "of particularly ill-repute" to him, Senator Benjamin Tillman of South Carolina, an outright White supremacist, defender of lynching, and founder of Clemson University, who, he said, "often referred to 'damned niggers' on the floor."[46] Balancing these viscious perspectives, EB was able to spend his school vacation away from the city with his grandmother Eliza, in the countryside of Falls Church. "In those summers I enjoyed the best days of my life," he reminisced. It's where EB had the freedom and space to be like any other kid. "Every boy used a bean shooter, threw stones at telegraph pole glass insulators, took fruit from nearby farms, and occasionally visited somebody else's cantelope [*sic*] or melon patch," he said.[47]

These experiences were of great value in shaping EB's views about what could be done to help Black people address and overcome the racially motivated and systemic social, economic, and political challenges they faced.

In 1898, he enrolled as a freshman at M Street High School, one of the District's two racially segregated options for academically high-achieving African American students. Built in 1891, M Street High was located at 128 M Street off New York Avenue in Northwest. EB was one of 124 students in his graduating class. M Street offered a broad range of rigorous study, including physics, geometry, Latin, chemistry, biology, and music. Once again an eager student, he walked there daily from School Street, just under two miles, missing only two days of classes in four years. Known as "the Colored High School," M Street had "a splendid corps of teachers," EB remembered, because it employed brilliant Black faculty who, though educated at the finest universities, couldn't be hired by D.C.'s White high schools. "There was no recreation," he said, and "because there were no automobiles, no green and red lights we played all sorts of games in the streets and on the vacant lots." In terms of basketball, EB remembered the M Street women's physical education teacher, who taught the girls to play "under the ten girls' rules." Her name was Anita Juburness Turner, one of the first Black women to graduate from the Sargent School. "However, no boys were introduced to the game."[48]

On the streets of New York City, Will Anthony Madden was gaining a different kind of wisdom, using another survival instinct in his repertoire. During adulthood, Will would become known for his elegant appearance and dandy style. A flair for fashion, as it was for many with poor backgrounds, often had its origins in growing up knowing that better clothes meant "better advantage," according to ads for fine apparel. One could tell the privileged from the needy by what they wore. Better-off lads sported ankle-high, lace-up leather boots and dark-colored woolen knickers, which were like baggy pants cut and tightened just below the knees to form a bloomer look.[49] With a matching jacket, the entire knicker suit went for $5.50. In 1901, that's how much a master plumber could earn per day.[50] Less fortunate boys, on the other hand, settled for ragged, hand-me-down versions of those out-of-reach styles, typically topped by floppy newsboy caps.

But there was still a way that a needful youth without the finest wardrobe could aspire to better advantage, at least as portrayed by the best-selling children's book novelist Horatio Alger, Jr. He wrote motivational "city stories" published during the late 1800s, in which underprivileged urban street kids became champions because of their admirable character traits. In a typical Alger plot, a poor yet hardworking teen uses humility, smarts, and courage to get noticed by a wealthy benefactor whose generosity lands the boy with a stable, respectable job. Alger's protagonists were "inspiring examples of what energy, ambition, and an honest purpose may achieve, even in their case."[51] A generation of youngsters Will's age enjoyed reading these vivid tales. They grew up believing that merit and charisma alone, regardless of race, religion, or social status, could give them a chance to "rise above their station in life" and prosper.

This idea was so convincing to the general public that Alger became known as "the Father of the American Dream."[52] And his favorite heroes were New York City telegraph boys, also called telegraph messengers, messenger boys, or simply messengers.[53] They were a familiar sight in every city, delivering all kinds of letters, documents, telegrams, financial transactions, parcels, and messages back and forth across town, all day, every day. Messengers typically came from poor backgrounds, worked hard, and fit the Alger script by encountering many different kinds of people in the most dramatic urban circumstances.[54] For an aspiring teenager, the keys to getting this desirable job were integrity, wit, and grit. "You think you're a gentleman just because you're a telegraph boy," says a low-class bully to the star of Alger's bestseller *Adventures of a New York Telegraph Boy*. "I could be a telegraph boy myself if I wanted ter."

As the turn of the century neared, African Americans found it hard to believe the so-called American Dream of Alger's narratives. For most Black folks, even those who W. E. B. Du Bois would call the "talented tenth," White supremacy and systemic racism, legalized all the way up to the U.S. Supreme Court, prevented their unobstructed access to that mythical ideal. Yes, Alger's tales contained inspirational qualities, and, in years to come, iconic African American achievers were publicized as evidence that that dream could work for all. Heavyweight champion boxer Joe Louis would be referred to as "the modern Horatio Alger of the prize ring." Harry Belafonte's successful entertainment career, resulting from a five-minute audition, was seen as a "Horatio Alger life story."[55] But the harsh reality was literally evident in black and white on the pages of his books, where every single one of whose rags-to-riches heroes was White.

Still, there was hope. Black youths like Will and EB couldn't help but see some elements of themselves in the fictitious hero of Horatio Alger's novel *Mark Mason's Victory; or, The Trials and Triumphs of a Telegraph Boy*, who asks, "Plenty of poor boys have risen, why not I?"

CHAPTER 6

SATAN'S CIRCUS

IN JANUARY 1900, THEODORE ROOSEVELT, THEN the governor of New York, hired a professional fitness trainer to be on his Executive Mansion staff in Albany. "There seems to be a veritable craze for some sort of physical culture this winter," a reporter for the *New York Times* informed readers that month. Though the governor's move may have helped the trend, the journalist concluded, "probably the very general advice of physicians nowadays, 'You need exercise, not medicine,' is more responsible."[1]

But that was not true for everyone. Black people facing White supremacy and systemic oppression often had access to neither. The biggest threat to their health was racist violence. A year earlier, the African American author, civil rights activist, and historian James Weldon Johnson had been moved to write the poem "Lift Ev'ry Voice and Sing." Later set to music by his younger brother, the singer and songwriter J. Rosamond Johnson, this composition would become known unofficially as the "Negro National Anthem." Its words, deeply stirring to African Americans, were needed more than ever. "The status of the Negro as a citizen had been steadily declining for twenty-five years," Johnson would point out in his 1930 retrospective book, *Black Manhattan*. "In the decade ending in 1899, according to the records printed in the daily press, 1,655 Negroes were lynched, many of them with sadistic savagery, even by mutilation and by burning alive at the stake in the presence of great crowds."[2] Waves of African Americans had been fleeing the South, with no signs of slowing down. Between 1890 and 1910, the combined Black population of New York City, Pittsburgh, Chicago, and the District of Columbia was doubling from 132,000 to 264,000.[3] "And these debauches in bestiality aroused no action on the part of the country nor any general protest," Johnson added. "The outlook was dark and discouraging."[4]

As their pace of migration speeded up, African American newcomers from the South were joined by more than twenty thousand newly transplanted, foreign-born Black people of similar backgrounds and predicaments, nearly all from the Caribbean, who had relocated to America by 1900. They swelled the already overcrowded "Colored" sections of Northern cities, only to find new forms of systemic disadvantage. Lack of education, underemployment, poverty, municipal neglect, social mistreatment, and civic obstruction had led not only to increased rates of mortality, stillbirths, and illness, but also to despair, moral decay, and crime. There were no Black elected officials, and White officeholders ignored these issues, instead prioritizing the problems caused by European immigration. While the African American population of New York City more than doubled from thirty thousand to sixty thousand between 1890 and 1900, the city simultaneously added nearly 1 million new residents, the vast majority from Europe. This was a staggering 40 percent increase in the city's population. In fact, New York City alone had absorbed more than 20 percent of *all* United States immigrants since 1896.[5] Of that total, about four hundred thousand ended up in Manhattan, and of those, around 120,000 settled into the Lower East Side. This inflow crowded out the Black residents of Greenwich Village, forcing them up into Midtown Manhattan. So by 1900, an area from West Fourteenth to West Fifty-Ninth Street and between Sixth and Eighth Avenues had become the city's largest "Negro ghetto," while the Little Africa of Will Madden's childhood had been reduced to fewer than two thousand African American residents.[6]

The flood of Black newcomers to Midtown at the turn of the century created a blossoming of racial empowerment, creative expression, and entrepreneurship that had a major social, cultural, and economic impact. The epicenter of this vibrant new scene was a section of the blocks along West Fifty-Third Street between Fifth and Eighth Avenues in Midtown, considered to be "the most attractive and the most culturally stylish" African American section of Manhattan.[7] It was "to the Negro colonies what Fifth Avenue is to white society."[8] Sometimes called "Black Bohemia," the area became an enclave for the country's leading African American writers, artists, entertainers, and intelligentsia.

Anchoring the street were two fashionable Black-owned hotels, the Marshall and the Maceo. The lounge of the Hotel Marshall, housed in two connected brownstone buildings at 127 and 129 West Fifty-Third Street,

between Sixth and Seventh Avenues, was "the place to be" for a who's who
of Black celebrity. "There gathered the actors, the musicians, the compos-
ers, the writers, and the better-paid vaudevillians," James Weldon Johnson
later explained. Johnson would have known all this, because he lived at the
Marshall.[9] So did his talented brother Rosamond and the renowned Black
musical theater actor Robert Allen Cole, Jr., who together made up the famous
vaudeville act Cole & Johnson.

The Hotel Maceo, at 213 West Fifty-Third Street, had opened in 1898 with
"first class accommodations ONLY," and the place was "illuminated throughout with electricity," a distinct convenience in the days when gaslight was the
norm.[10] These hotels weren't the only African American institutions on that
strip. St. Mark's Methodist Episcopal Church, one of several Black churches
in the section, was at 233 West Fifty-Third. Its members included "solid men,
solid of morals and in the estimation of their fellows," which was a tribute to
the church's minister, the Reverend W. H. Brooks, a native of Maryland who
was known to scold self-defeating behavior by saying, "Go now, go find your
man-part."[11] And there were dozens of complementary Black-owned small businesses that provided tailoring, printing, deliveries, meals, and other important
community services. That was just on this street. By one count, the surrounding
area contained twenty-six "Negro" restaurants and lunch counters, seventeen
hotels and lodging houses, and ten billiard rooms, to name a few.[12] There were
scores of popular after hour cafés, lounges, saloons, cabarets, taverns, dance
halls, and other night spots, including Barron Wilkins' Café, Percy Brown's,
the Douglas Club, Chadwick's Novelty Café, Nail Brothers' Saloon, the Little
Egypt Nightclub, Edmond's Cabaret, the Banner Club, and Diggs' Place. These
businesses and others like them provided solid jobs to African American men
while still others operated without official liquor licenses. Regardless, they
were the places to be, on any given night of the week. But there was a cost.

That flood of new African American residents caused Midtown's wealthiest homeowners to flee farther uptown, leaving behind hundreds of high-
quality apartment buildings, brownstones, town houses, and even some
mansions. These were once "the decorous homes of the old Knickerbockers,
the proud aristocracy of Manhattan in the early days." They had graceful,
neatly shuttered facades with handsome lamps, flower boxes, and colorful
canopies.[13] To cover the steep rent on their premium properties while oppor-
tunistically exploiting the poor, landlords soon subdivided these spaces into

cheap apartments and rooms for rent. The number of these tenements built in the city nearly tripled in the three decades before 1900.[14] Plots of land and buildings were partitioned into ever smaller units and along back alleyways. These often lacked windows, ventilation, or other access to outside air. It was common for several families of men, women, and children to occupy a single room measuring barely two hundred square feet, where "waste was removed to the street in a bucket."[15] Only the most desperate souls moved into them, except that African Americans were charged more. "Property is not rented to negroes in New York until white people will no longer have it," *Harper's Weekly* reported in 1900. "Then rents are put up from thirty-five to fifty percent, and negroes are permitted to take a street or sometimes a neighborhood."[16] White real estate agents had hit the jackpot. "We would rather have negro tenants in our poorest class of tenements than the lower grades of foreign white people," said one. "We find the former cleaner than the latter, and they do not destroy the property so much."[17]

To make matters worse, most African American migrants from the South were from rural backgrounds. On arrival in New York City, they were strangers in a strange land, not only poor but also undereducated, unskilled, and unfamiliar with the basics of urban living. It was no wonder that the death rate from tuberculosis and pneumonia alone among the city's Black residents was nearly 25 percent.[18] In contrast, modern mortality rates there are less than 1 percent for all causes of death combined. As underprivileged migrants from the South and immigrants from Europe kept arriving, saloons kept opening up. They were owned by Black people as well as Whites, and the liquor continued to flow. Known as "the poor man's club," drinking establishments were seen by progressive reformers as having the biggest negative effect on the lives of the impoverished. "The saloon problem" was continuously in the headlines. "The drink habit, roughly speaking, causes about one-quarter of the poverty, about one-half of the crime, and is one of the greatest enemies of the home," stated a *New York Times* editorial in 1906. Drunkenness, it was said, prepared the poor for crime, impaired their reasoning, and put them into dangerous contact with "the vicious class." It was a gateway to vice, a steady progression into the company of gamblers, pickpockets, robbers, and worse.[19]

Meanwhile, the more those racially mixed nightspots kept popping up, the more popular they became, and the more attention they began to receive as a group, becoming known as "black and tans," often "to the horror of more conventional folk."[20] That's precisely why they were so attractive to patrons of both races. In the backlash, a calculated effort was made by segregationists to shut those places down, mainly because White women found these hotspots appealing. Characterizing this paranoia as a saloon problem, they got support from City Hall and, by correlating interracial contact of any kind with degraded behavior and prostitution, made racially mixed social interaction immoral in and of itself. In their eyes, White women at these "pleasure resorts" had to have been prostitutes, and the Black men in their company must have been pimps. In one of many surveillances targeting black and tans, undercover vice patrol notes described Wilkins' Café as a "rathskeller and dance hall (swellest club in town)." It was a "rendezvous for white and colored people" that was "open all night" and "very popular." [21]

Vice squads repeatedly tried to find wrongdoing at the Hotel Marshall. "Supposed to be a high class restaurant for colored people," one report stated. "Is patronized largely by white women and colored men." Not finding any misconduct didn't stop the investigator's imagination. "Very hard to get, because of its popularity and the discreet manner in which it is run," the vice sleuth reported. "Most questionable orgies and revels are held there nightly," he continued. "Perhaps most popular place in town."[22]

When a nightspot was labeled "hard to get," it meant investigators couldn't find evidence that might stick. The truth was, many of these establishments provided safe havens for underground economies like gambling, backdoor liquor sales, sex work, and other hustles that benefited unemployed or disenfranchised African Americans. "We don't let white men in here unless we know them," a Black porter at Chadwick's Novelty Café openly stated, before sending a would-be infiltrator away.[23]

At the height of this anti-saloon activity, civic leaders seemed much more concerned with ending interracial nightlife than with immoral drinking, and even then, the police looked the other way. Cops with the Twenty-Ninth Precinct Station House at 137 West Thirtieth Street, in the heart of that vice area, pocketed so much cash for payoffs that in 1885, when a new captain named Alexander Williams was transferred there from the less lucrative Lower East Side to take over, he famously declared, "I guess I'll live on tenderloin now," in contrast to the rump steak he had previously tolerated. From then on, Captain Williams's new command was referred to as the "Tenderloin District," and, not shy with his nightstick, he would become known as "Clubber" Williams, the Czar of the Tenderloin.[24]

As liquor flowed freely, the illicit nightspots of the Tenderloin targeted, attracted, and relied on an endless throng of naive Black newcomers. Frustrated morality inspectors watched helplessly as those folks lost their hard-earned cash, or worse. These grim realities of slum life in Manhattan were described by the Black novelist Paul Laurence Dunbar in his turn-of-the-century book *The Sport of the Gods*. According to Dunbar, one Tenderloin nightspot, the Banner Club, was "a social cesspool" continuously "reeking with the stench of decayed and rotten moralities," where "parasites came for victims, politicians for votes, reporters for news."[25] That's why Booker T. Washington chimed in about vice shortly after Governor Roosevelt's personal trainer made the news in early 1900. "There is little question that one of the Negroes' weak points is physical," wrote Washington, who was a faithful student of Dudley Allen Sargent's ideas. "But in almost every case this physical weakness can be traced to ignorant violation of the laws of health or to vicious habits."[26] He would later warn his daughter, Portia, then a lively twenty-one-year-old attending an all-girls junior college who was planning a visit to Manhattan, "If you go to New York at all, I prefer you to be in the home of some family with whom I am acquainted."[27]

The widespread filth, unchecked lawbreaking, and rampant immorality controlling the Tenderloin District were widely considered so perverse, degenerate, depraved, and unsafe that social reformers began calling it "Satan's Circus." Social service providers, aid societies, and relief agencies were overwhelmed. The situation was dire. "The Negro himself had in a large measure lost heart," James Weldon Johnson concluded. Yet, as Johnson had poetically and prophetically written, though the road was stony, there would be continued hope among a resilient people. That's why the location of St. Philip's Protestant Episcopal Church, an all-Black congregation at 161 West Twenty-Fifth Street between Sixth and Seventh Avenues, was perfect. This was in the heart of Satan's Circus, and its minister, a Baltimore-born African American named the Reverend Dr. Hutchens Chew Bishop, was perfectly suited to preach there.

Founded in 1809 as the Free African Church of St. Philip on Centre Street in Lower Manhattan, the church had moved near Little Africa in 1857 and then onto West Twenty-Fifth in 1886. By the early 1900s, under Bishop's leadership, it had become New York City's largest African American congregation and "the wealthiest non-white church in the city."[28] Everyone who was anyone in Black Manhattan belonged to St. Philip's. That's because Bishop practiced what he preached. "Every man should have an ideal," he insisted. "Talk about ideal things and stand up for them."[29]

True to his word, the clergyman had painstakingly created an array of community service programs aimed at providing spiritual morality to counteract the Tenderloin District's powerful negative influences.[30] The church also offered classes in literacy, liberal arts, and industrial skills, staged plays and music recitals, and held social functions to encourage networking. These efforts made it easier for a lot of folks just to get by. One of Bishop's most promising initiatives was the St. Christopher Club, which he had originally set up in 1896 as a Bible study group. It was named after the patron saint of safe travel, who carried an infant that turned out to be the baby Jesus securely across a dangerous river. The goal of the club was to "throw the mantle of protection around our boys and save them from the many enticements to wrong doing which surrounded them." To join, a young man had to pay a 50-cent initiation fee and monthly dues of 10 cents. According to its constitution, "all members pledge themselves to observe the habit of prayer both morning and night, to attend at least one service at Church each Sunday, to cultivate a spirit of reverence in the Church at all times, to render a read obedience to those in authority, and to observe gentlemanly demeanor."[31] Within the decade, his wisely chosen "St. Christopher Club" name would become nationally recognized as representing the most elite African American basketball team in the country.

Meanwhile, though, rather than Bible study alone as offered by the St. Christopher program, Booker T. Washington believed that Black Southern migrants arriving in Northern cities were so inexperienced with tools of simple hygiene like toilets, showers, bedding, kitchen appliances, and garbage cans that what they needed foremost was "the gospel of the toothbrush," which, he said, was part of the Tuskegee creed.[32]

Washington and other Black community leaders began to recognize that overall wellness was linked to personal health. They looked at the ideas that social reformers in London had used in response to the Industrial Revolution, concepts that Dudley Allen Sargent had adapted into his physical culture movement. Building on the pioneering steps taken by Anthony Bowen, there were already sixty active "Colored" YMCA branches in America by the time the U.S. Supreme Court issued its "separate but equal" ruling in *Plessy v. Ferguson* in 1896, the same year the St. Christopher Club was organized. None of these early African American YMCAs had athletic programs, let alone exercise equipment or their own facilities.[33] Even the New York City YMCA Colored Men's Branch, organized in 1899 by the Reverend Charles T. Walker of Mount Olivet Baptist Church in a leased building at 252 West Fifty-Third Street, had no gymnasium. Still, these branches could continue teaching scripture while adding programs that covered health, hygiene, and physical efficiency, which was about how to move one's body optimally during day-to-day activities.

Even as these physical culture ideas were being considered, in August 1900, a young African American man named Arthur J. Harris saw a White out-of-uniform police officer grab and mistreat his wife while, according to his account, she was standing on a sidewalk in the Tenderloin District waiting for him to come out of a store where he was buying a cigar. The cop assumed she was a soliciting prostitute, and Harris assumed his wife was being assaulted, so he confronted the attacker with a blade, causing a gash wound that proved fatal. As news of the officer's death spread, mobs of angry Whites formed, seeking revenge on any African American citizens they could find, racing "up and down Broadway, 7th and 8th Avenues, and the side streets from 34th to 42nd Streets in pursuit of Negroes" while angry cops "stood by and made no effort" to restore peace. Policemen even "ran with the crowds in pursuit of their prey," according to witnesses.[34] While "a stream of bloody colored men" reported their critical injuries, the true toll was never known, as many Black residents "preferred to remain in their houses, being afraid to trust themselves to the mercy of the crowds on the streets while on the way to the police station or hospital."[35] No wonder, when by nearly all official accounts it was New York Police Department billy clubs that were responsible for the most brutal beatings that night, some in the precinct station house.[36]

A week after that incident, which was labeled a "race riot," Will Madden celebrated his seventeenth birthday. Will had become a slender, handsome, dark-complexioned young man. Still, he was the opposite of tall, never standing higher than five feet, seven inches, with features that made him look youngish even into adulthood.[37]

Two weeks after the police attacks in the Tenderloin, in his sermon at Mount Olivet Baptist Church, the Reverend Walker shouted, "What we need is a place that shall be known to every young man in the South as a home where he can come and find friends."[38]

Yet, not even the largest African American enclave in the North was safe for Black people. Neither exercise nor medicine was accessible, and the brutality they faced was as bad as in the South. That year, many African Americans began moving out of the Tenderloin District, up to Harlem and out to Brooklyn.

By the time Brooklyn was added to New York City in 1898, it had become the equivalent of America's fourth-largest city. Though the majority of residents in the growing and prosperous borough were of German, Irish, and Italian descent, Brooklyn was also a thriving hub for African Americans. Hardworking and industrious, the Black community had grown from about five thousand residents in 1870 to more than eighteen thousand by 1900, representing about 2 percent of the total population.[39] Most had settled in Crown Heights, Fort Greene, Bedford, Stuyvesant Heights, Bushwick, and Brownsville. Upwardly mobile middle-class Black families had been moving out of Manhattan into Brooklyn for decades, ever since the New York City Draft Riots of 1863. "As soon as Negro men amass a comfortable fortune," the *New York Times* had explained in 1895, "they move from this city across the East River, because they can find in Brooklyn more economical and satisfactory investments."[40] As a result, Brooklyn had become known for its many prosperous, educated African Americans who held down "white-collar" jobs, blossomed as entrepreneurs, and thrived in skilled trades. They included teachers, merchants, clergy, caterers, barbers, clerks, tailors, and other professionals. They were strivers. Many had the means to own residences on all-White blocks in their neighborhoods, where typically the only other African American residents were servants.[41]

For religion among Brooklyn's prosperous Black residents, "everybody except for the few Catholics or Methodists" attended St. Augustine Protestant Episcopal Church."[42] This was a large African American congregation, second only to St. Philip's in Manhattan in terms of its overall prestige in the greater New York City area.[43] The church was founded in 1875 at a site adjacent to Fort Greene Park, on present-day St. Edward's Street near Myrtle Avenue.[44] Its rector was the Reverend George Frazier Miller, an energetic, activist South Carolina native trained at Howard University and the General Theological Seminary in Manhattan. Over the years, St. Augustine's became a "fortress" of "elite black Episcopalianism."[45]

Being a center of African American affluence and culture, Brooklyn had also developed its own class of "Negro intelligentsia." These pioneering individuals included the newspaper publisher T. Thomas Fortune, the inventor and scientist Lewis H. Latimer, the educator William L. Bulkley, and the physician Susan S. McKinney.[46] Fortune had organized the Brooklyn Literary Society in 1883 and was the founder of the *New York Freeman* and the *New York Age* newspapers. Latimer had patented the carbon filament for incandescent light bulbs and had been associated with the inventions of Thomas Edison and Alexander Graham Bell. Bulkley had become New York City's first Black principal of a racially mixed public school. And McKinney had been the first African American female doctor to practice medicine in New York State.

They also included an inventor, manufacturer, educator, Civil War veteran, civic leader, public servant, and self-made man named Samuel Raymond Scottron. After arriving in Brooklyn following the war, the Pennsylvania-born entrepreneur used ingenuity and sheer will to obtain several patents. Among his inventions were the common curtain rod, an adjustable system of opposite-facing mirrors that barbers could use to see both sides of a client's head at once, and a leather hand strap that standing streetcar riders could grasp to keep from falling over. He licensed these out and invested the royalties to form Scottron Manufacturing, which produced a variety of additional goods. Its annual business income soared to $25,000 per year, or the equivalent of about $770,000 today, with retail customers that included Wanamaker's, Macy's, and Abraham & Straus, regarded as among the finest department stores in the world.[47] Scottron became Brooklyn's leading African American manufacturer and a man of considerable wealth. But he didn't stop there.

Though not a "man of letters," he contributed regular columns to Black publications. To help encourage others with learnedness, he formed the Diversity Reading Club, the Philosophical Reading Circle, and the Semper Fidelis Reading Club.[48] No wonder Scottron was appointed to the Brooklyn Board of Education by three successive mayors from 1894 until Brooklyn became part of New York City in 1898, the only African American among forty-five board positions.

By 1900, Scottron had become the most famous and influential Black person in New York City. "The Negro has advanced rapidly and seemingly beyond all comparison," he later exclaimed, "but it remains for him to show that he is contributing to the force that moves things!"[49] Yet although he was

was an outspoken advocate of "self-uplifting," Scottron also understood and fought against systemic racism as an active member in the Colored Citizens Protective League and the Committee for Improving the Industrial Condition of Negroes in New York.

Socially, Scottron was well-connected as a thirty-third degree member of the Free & Accepted Masons of Brooklyn, Carthaginian Lodge No. 47, a secret all-Black fraternity for which he was a former Grand Master.[50] Scottron also was "an intimate acquaintance" of Frederick Randolph Moore, the soon-to-be owner and publisher of the weekly *New York Age*, the most widely circulated Black newspaper at the time.[51] And he was a close ally of Booker T. Washington, who later wrote, "Perhaps no man of the Negro race has shown such versatility in the field of invention as Mr. Samuel R. Scottron, of Brooklyn, N.Y."[52]

In other words, Samuel Raymond Scottron of Brooklyn was a force. In many ways, he *was* Black Brooklyn.

As the new century began, Pittsburgh had eclipsed all possible industrial expectations. It was the global leader in the manufacture of iron, steel, glass, electrical machinery, steel cars, tin plate, air brakes, firebrick, white lead, cork, and aluminum, producing half the country's steel, 60 percent of its rails, the majority of its manufactured copper and lead, and most of its nuts and bolts. The city even hosted the world's largest pickling and preserving plant. Many of these goods were stored in the biggest warehouse on earth, a local facility that covered an astounding twenty-three acres of floor space, the equivalent of more than seventeen football fields.[53] As a result, total cargo transported in and out of the Smoky City exceeded Boston, Chicago, and New York City combined, making it "incontestably the greatest shipping point in the world."[54] Pittsburgh's factories were churning day and night, all week long, year-round. Marveling at the unmatched panoramic views of industrial might from the tops of the city's surrounding hills, visitors could see "the red glare of fire and furnace, the gaunt and shadowy figures of the half-dressed workers darting here and there, and seemingly at play with great lumps of molten metal."[55] Even decades earlier, witnessing the abundance of "fire, noise, sparks, steam, and panting machinery in every direction" from that vantage point had prompted a journalist from the *Atlantic Monthly* to describe the scene as "Hell with its lid off."[56]

CHAPTER 7

1901

A SERIES OF SEEMINGLY UNRELATED incidents in 1901 touched off a chain of events that would turn Harlem into the mecca of Black basketball.

On February 25, articles of incorporation were finalized to enable the sale of Carnegie Steel Company, the giant Pittsburgh-based steel manufacturer, to the United States Steel Corporation in a $492 million transaction, more than $15 billion today. Of that, $226 million, over $7 billion today, went directly to the company's founder and owner, a diminutive Scottish-born industrial tycoon named Andrew Carnegie, pushing him ahead of John D. Rockefeller as the richest man in the world.[1] He immediately announced plans for the construction of an eighty-room mansion in Manhattan, at the corner of Fifth Avenue and Ninety-First Street, so enormous that its sub-basement furnace room could store two hundred tons of coal.[2] Carnegie had been born into poverty, a handloom weaver's son who lived in a one-room cottage before moving to the United States. American newspapers knew that their readers couldn't get enough about the enormity of Carnegie's wealth, gladly painting it as heroic because the steel tycoon was everyone's favorite real-life Alger-style rags-to-riches champion. He was the idol of every young man with ambitions to succeed, especially diminutive lads, like Will Madden. Standing just five feet tall, Carnegie had been a penniless kid who started out as a telegraph boy.

Three weeks later, sadness struck at Will's home. On March 16, 1901, his maternal grandfather, Anthony Harder, passed away at age sixty-nine. The official cause was listed as "pulmonary congestion and exhaustion."[3] He had worked himself to death. It was time for Will to help the family by going out to make a living. His parents, Willie and Maggie, had prepared their son with "paternal practicability and experience and maternal culture and intellectuality," according to a later profile by the newspaper columnist Floyd G. Nelson. These were at Will's disposal when he "came into the world."[4]

Later that same day, amid metallic clangs and the clatter of hoofs a few minutes before midnight, a platoon of New York City police officers in horse-drawn patrol wagons pulled up to Waldron's Dance Hall, a notorious and lucra-tive nightspot near Columbia University.[5] An ambitious forty-nine-year-old Bavarian-born police captain named Max Schmittberger, who would one day be New York City's chief of police, was in charge.[6] "I'll arrest the first person that waltzes a step, and I'll take you in, too," he directly warned the owners of the establishment, two Jewish entrepreneurial brothers named Louis and Eddie Waldron.[7] Neither proprietor was intimidated. Both in their mid-thirties, they were the sons of a cigar maker from Berlin, and Louis, a former advertising, theatrical, and boxing agent, had a known history of getting into fistfights.[8] That they were Germans squaring off wasn't a big coincidence, considering that nearly 40 percent of the city's 3.4 million residents were foreign-born, and of those, the largest portion, about 10 percent, were from Germany.[9] Defiant, the brothers continued "urging and inciting people to dance."[10] So, at precisely twelve o'clock and true to his word, Captain Schmittberger had the two proprietors arrested. Dozens more arrests were made, among them the patrons who were dancing, the waiters who served them, and the managers who ran the place.

Though this single act of defiance spelled the beginning of the end for Waldron's Dance Hall, it would lead the brothers to create an entirely new business that became a gateway into Harlem for Black basketball.

Located on at 216 West 110th Street, also known as Cathedral Parkway, between what was then called Broadway Boulevard and Amsterdam Avenue, just down the street from the Cathedral of St. John the Divine, Waldron's was a large "concert saloon" that served wine, liquor, and lager beer at a bar in the front while a back area with a piano contained floor space for dining, music, other entertainment, and dancing.[11] The sizable property included a bar and dance area with an overlooking balcony, as well as a two-story brick structure with rooms for rent, which technically made Waldron's Dance Hall a hotel. Installing rooms at a saloon was a work-around for sidestepping the Raines Law, a rigidly enforced piece of New York City anti-vice legisla-tion that prohibited establishments other than hotels from serving alcohol on Sundays.[12] For cheery Columbia students, this was the place to be. On a typical weekend night there, six hundred hatchecks had already been taken by eleven o'clock.[13] But for police at the nearby West One Hundredth Street station house, it was nothing but a skimpy cover for wholesale prostitution.[14] One investigator swore in his signed affidavit that no less than one hundred female sex workers were crammed into the establishment on any given night. Neighborhood associations and social reformers referred to Waldron's, in shock, as a "finishing school in vice for girls."[15]

Hundreds of such establishments dotted Manhattan. In fact, so many of them were adjacent to Waldron's Dance Hall that the block was nicknamed "Little Coney Island," after the amusement park in Brooklyn. But when cops had previously tried nabbing Louis and Eddie Waldron, they could never pin anything on the enterprising brothers. In frustration, detectives instead declared that their concert saloon was in violation of Section 277 of the Penal Code of the State of New York, enacted in 1881, which made conducting, allowing, promoting, or encouraging a dance in "theatrical and other performances" on a Sunday illegal.[16] Armed with this rationale, police raided Waldron's not just once, but for seventeen straight Sundays during one stretch. Each encounter resulted in a tense standoff and arrests, but each time, magistrates at the West Side Police Court would dismiss all charges and let everyone go since the dancers were ordinary couples, not entertainers. This eventually went all the way to the New York State Supreme Court. "The case is looked upon as the most important that has yet come up affecting the dance halls of the city," reported the *New York Times*.[17] When this didn't work, state legislators passed the "Little Coney Island Bill," prohibiting public dance halls with liquor from operating within a half mile of any cathedral. It was promptly vetoed by Governor Benjamin Odell, who called the measure unconstitutional since it had merely targeted one specific establishment.[18] But by then, Louis and Eddie Waldron had had enough.

With neighborhood opposition mounting, weary of courtroom battles, and desiring more freedom, the entrepreneurial pair decided to leave. Their back-and-forth legal saga had lit up newspaper headlines around the country for months, making them celebrities. So in 1902, they closed Waldron's Dance Hall and looked to build a new and even bigger facility in the remote northern outskirts of Harlem, away from churches, neighborhood protesters, and constant police harassment. The brothers found the perfect site in a vacant plot of land on the southeast corner of Eighth Avenue and West 155th Street, across the street from where Holcombe Rucker Playground, aka "Rucker Park," is located today.[19] There, the Waldrons constructed a massive venue they called the Manhattan Casino, which opened in 1903.

This new place wasn't just a dance hall; it was an all-out amusement complex on the scale of a city park, a monument to the immensity and scope of Louis and Eddie Waldron's vision. With a capacity of six thousand patrons a night, the Manhattan Casino contained a symphony-sized performance stage with four dressing rooms, private function areas, a saloon, a small hotel, a beer garden, and an outdoor picnic ground. Incredibly, the brothers constructed a dedicated ballroom with a six-thousand-square-foot dance floor beneath a colossal crystal chandelier under a sky-blue painted ceiling, and encircled by a second-floor balcony packed with fifty-one velvet-lined luxury boxes that spectators could reach by ascending a gold-banister staircase.[20] The mere spectacle alone was breathtaking. They even had an ice machine air-conditioning device installed, joining the Victoria, Knickerbocker, and Madison Square theaters as the only venues in Manhattan to have one.[21]

The entrance to the Manhattan Casino was directly below the last stop of the Metropolitan Elevated Railway Company's new Ninth Avenue Line, whose rail cars traveled up Eighth Avenue before terminating at the West 155th Street Station to release passengers. Their place was also diagonally across the intersection from a baseball stadium called the Polo Grounds, home field of the New York Giants, then one of the lowliest clubs in the major leagues. But fortune was smiling on Louis and Eddie. When they built their venue, no one knew that a seemingly second-rate Giants pitcher named Christy Mathewson would soon win more than thirty games for each of three consecutive seasons, or that an apparently washed-up hurler named Joe McGinnity was about to join the team and win an average of twenty-eight times in each of his next four campaigns. Throngs of baseball fans began swarming the area and flooding the Manhattan Casino before, during, and after regular season games. Fans would leave the Polo Grounds through the center field gate, its main exit, which deposited them right onto Eighth Avenue, headed toward the Waldrons' place. Always promotion-minded, the brothers even advertised their venue on the stadium's outfield wall, visible to everyone packed inside. This windfall of clientele continued into postseasons, when the Giants captured two out of the next three National League pennants and won the World Series in 1905. Fans who didn't have tickets could share in the action, for a 25-cent fee, by visiting the facility's saloon for up-to-the-minute "accurate results by Special Wire from the field," making the Manhattan Casino one of America's first live sports bars.[22]

Then the brothers made two moves that would prove pivotal to the advancement of African American basketball. First, they staged an "international cake walk" competition, with publicity stating that it would "call forth the leaders of all races."[23] The cake walk was a dance that had originated with enslaved people on antebellum Southern plantations, in which couples would promenade in a square around a large decorated cake to the delight of their White masters (without the owners realizing they actually were being mocked). "The men walked with stately and soldierly step, and the women with considerable grace," James Weldon Johnson later explained.[24] As determined by expert judges, the couple who danced the best would "take the cake."

This public promotion by the Waldrons was a signal to African Americans and Black West Indians throughout New York City that the Jewish brothers could be approached as friends; their doors would be open to everyone. That was meaningful because more and more of the city's Black residents had been moving up to Harlem.[25] Assembly District 23, for example, which included streets in the West 130s between Fifth and Lenox Avenues, contained just over three hundred residents listed as Black or "mulatto" out of almost 1,700 total inhabitants, or less than 20 percent.[26] But even these few, as well as other pockets of African Americans in surrounding areas, became the target of a methodical, organized, aggressive campaign by some White property owners in Harlem to have them removed, as well as to end the "colored invasion" of the community altogether. Including "all races" in their cakewalk publicity seemed to be the Waldrons' intentional response to rumors that White landlords in Harlem were plotting a massive, coordinated action to evict Black people all at once by refusing to renew any of their leases. When word got out about this, one newspaper predicted that as many as seven hundred families might be at risk.[27] It prompted an African American real estate broker and entrepreneur named Philip A. Payton, Jr., to establish a property management business called the Afro-American Realty Company, which focused on placing Black renters uptown. Payton and his wife, Maggie, already lived on West 131st Street. "The idea that Negroes must be confined to certain localities can be done away with," wrote Payton in the company's prospectus.[28] His move helped encourage African American investors of all types to begin acquiring buildings in the neighborhood, even if they were occupied entirely by White tenants.[29] Efforts like these made the call for Black migration into Harlem not just rhetoric but an actual, ongoing, organized movement. The floodgates had opened. Soon, entire buildings were owned or managed by African Americans. "Beautiful Homes for Colored People," read an advertisement by the Black-owned Benjamin G. Howell Realty Company. "It is no longer necessary for our people to live in small, dingy, stuffy tenements," the promotion continued, promising "plenty of God's air and sunshine, with steam heat, hot water supply, open plumbing, tiled bathrooms, porcelain sinks and bathtubs, beautiful entrance and every modern improvement."[30]

All of this also meant business for the Waldrons. Gladly accepting their open invitation, African American organizations gradually began booking the Manhattan Casino for their affairs. But this was only the beginning. Louis and Eddie would just keep taking the cake.

On a typical early morning during May 1901, Will Madden left his home on Waverly Place and headed for school. This was his last year at DeWitt Clinton High School, and there were about six weeks left until graduation exercises.[31] He was in good company with his fellow students. Clinton's principal, John T. Buchanan, insisted that "better boys than they, and more happy and loyal, could not be found, and that no report of their bad conduct had ever come to his ears."[32]

Will's older sister, Grace, now twenty years of age, had become a dressmaker. Their little sister, Florence, was now fourteen and attending Wadleigh High School for Girls, a few blocks away on East Twelfth Street.[33] Walking to school up Sixth Avenue, Will would have passed the covered stairway leading up to the Eighth Street Station platform, and its newsstand displaying morning papers and all the latest magazines. "Why Young Men Should Begin at the Bottom" was the cover article featured in the current *Saturday Evening Post*, America's most popular illustrated weekly publication. *McClure's Magazine* promoted the first installment of Jack London's new book, *The God of His Fathers*, a tale about the ruthlessness of life in Alaska that explored humankind's inborn urge to survive and thrive. These titles were signs of the times, providing a road map for career and life success to young men like Will.

Having life ambitions was not a given.

Many youths wondered daily whether showing up for classes was over-rated, especially if their families needed money. Even the earnings from unskilled low-paying jobs—elevator boys, houseboys, office boys, newsboys, cashboys, errand boys, boot shine boys, hotel boys, train boys, kitchen boys, messenger boys—could help out at home. "They say we ought to be in school," said one cashboy in San Francisco in the summer of 1900, "but I'd jes' like to know what 'ud become of the folks if we didn't."[34] The store where he worked paid $3 a week.

However, Clinton High was very strict with attendance. Skipping class had severe penalties. That's because in 1901, the city's public schools were so crowded that more than two hundred thousand school-age youngsters could not be enrolled at all. They were simply left behind.[35] "Those children unable to obtain admission will have to wait for vacancies or until new schools are organized," School Superintendent John Jasper had said in 1897, when Clinton (then called Boys' High School) first opened with only five hundred spaces available for seven hundred applicants.[36]

Consequently, every New York City public school's attendance was tabu-lated daily and sent to the Department of Education. This data was carefully examined for the slightest excuse to replace uncaring students with eager learners from the citywide waiting list. The department even assigned special inspectors. "Last year there was a total of 34,180 cases of truancy investigated," the *New York Times* reported in 1901. Of these, "4,220 were picked up on the streets and sent back to school."[37] Others weren't so lucky. Truant boys or girls of any age could be sentenced to the New York Juvenile Asylum in Upper Manhattan, remaining incarcerated for as long as it took to reform them, even if that ended up being several years.[38]

These factors were crucial in deciding whether to stay in school or drop out. Some unskilled positions were better than others. But on this day, histori-cal events would show that messengers were the most consequential of all, not just in New York City but throughout the entire financial industry. This was a job that would change Will's life forever, by leading him into a series of connections that vaulted him out of poverty, into the elite company of Black America's who's who, and onto a throne at the top of the Black basketball world. A classic Alger-style tale was about to unfold.

On the morning of May 9, 1901, throughout the city, students like Will were headed to school when suddenly, packs of youths could be seen sprinting in the direction of downtown. Others were running as fast as they could to the nearest elevated train. Some grown men were dashing too. Confusion and excitement filled Lower Manhattan. Word was spreading that the Financial District had completely run out of messenger boys and was frantic for more. Emergency calls had been made to all the uptown messenger service offices. Agents from the American District Telegraph Company, New York City's largest messenger service, "were sent out into the streets" to hire extras. One manager was "out searching the highways and byways for more boys." Those already employed who normally earned $4 a week were being offered $5 for the day. "Clerks from all the big brokerage houses, and in some instances the brokers themselves," were out recruiting new couriers.[39] Some who couldn't wait were so desperate that they carried their own dispatches.

This would be an epic day for Horatio Alger's favorite protagonists, the city's messenger boys. Swarms of investors and throngs of spectators had been crowding the entrance to the Produce Exchange Building since before dawn while droves more congested all of Lower Broadway. The massive Produce Exchange just below Bowling Green in the city's Financial District, was serving as the temporary location of the New York Stock Exchange and its trading floor. The Stock Exchange had been trading there for only eight days, ever since it moved from Wall Street so that its outdated home there could be torn down and replaced by a new structure.[40]

"When the down town office of the American District Telegraph Company in Exchange Court opened at 7 o'clock there was already a long line of men at the door waiting to employ messengers," the *New York Times* observed that Thursday morning.[41] The company, known as ADT, was the country's leading messenger service and normally had "about 150 boys" in its Lower Manhattan office. The Postal Telegraph Company's downtown bureau, on Broadway next to City Hall Park, provided similar numbers. So, too, did the Bankers and Brokers' Messenger Exchange on New Street, which specifically served the financial exchanges.[42]

Wall Street utilized messengers because every financial transaction was done using actual touchable, certifiable papers that had to be hand-carried from place to place. Shareholders actually *held* the shares they owned, physically possessing the authentic engraved and embossed paper stock certificates, and ownership of a stock was transferred to someone else by handing it to him or her, like cash. The location where actual stock certificates were exchanged for cash, and vice versa, was called the Stock Exchange, because that is literally what happened there. An order to buy a share of stock was written at a stockbroker's office and handed to a messenger, who rushed it by foot over to the trading floor of the Exchange. He would give the order to a trader with a form of payment in return for the stock certificate itself, which was then hand-delivered back to the broker's office. Sell orders worked the opposite way, with sold stocks delivered to the trading floor in return for payment. Messengers handled all of this, which meant that the daily ebb and flow of America's financial markets was entirely in the hands of street teens.

Messenger boys had New York City's most thrilling occupation. That's what made the job so desirable to young men like Will. The work demanded flawless integrity because, rain or shine, they carried outrageous fortunes through the side streets and back alleys of Lower Manhattan. Stocks and bonds. Payments and collateral. Gold notes, bank checks, treasury bills, family valuables. An incalculable number of confidential letters, contracts, telegrams, memos, and hastily scribbled notes. And, of course, ridiculous amounts of cash. Besides fighting temptations to run off with the loot, it was also dangerous. Messengers were frequently robbed at gunpoint. Or harassed. The job required fast thinking, fast talking, and fast feet. But not *too* fast. A messenger boy could be "killed, crippled, or incapacitated" by an automobile, a team of horses, or a streetcar. "WALK across a street—never run," the ADT training manual warned. "A sudden dash may mean death."[43]

Part of the allure was that a messenger's morality was always at stake, since he had to cover all neighborhoods including Little Africa, Satan's Circus, Little Coney Island, and every other New York City red-light district. Here, "hundreds of such boys" knew many of the prostitutes "by name," according to one child labor reformer. "In answering calls from houses of ill-repute messengers cannot avoid being witnesses of scenes of licentiousness," that crusader warned. "He smokes, drinks, gambles, and, very often, patronizes the lowest class of cheap brothels." Indeed, "by presents of money, fruit, candy, cigarettes, and even liquor, the women make friends of the boys, who quickly learn all the foul slang."[44] Reformers believed messengers represented "an exceedingly large proportion of cases of juvenile delinquency," especially in big cities, so much so that Jacob Riis insisted flat-out that messenger services "ought to be prohibited with the utmost rigor of the law."[45] To help prevent these excesses, messenger boys were to appear "neat, speedy, polite, and responsible" with "clean hands and face, uniform pressed and spotless," and "cap squarely on head," according to the training diagram of one messenger service company.[46] Personal charisma was key, since a boy might be sent on a private errand, like escorting an unaccompanied lady to the theater. She could be the daughter of a millionaire.

Meanwhile, by 9 A.M. that Thursday, the Produce Exchange was "crowded as it has never been crowded before," according to the *Evening World*.[47] The market had fallen badly the day before, but no one knew why. Desperate investors woke up fearing the worst, demanding answers. "Inflamed and angry thousands filled the brokerage offices in the Stock Exchange district" as stockbrokers and their clerks scrambled to prepare for the avalanche of buy and sell orders they knew were coming.[48] MARKET FAILS AND PANIC SOON REIGNS read a front-page *Times* headline.[49] An early bird newsboy shouted, "All about the panicky Wall Street!"[50]

But the value of one stock in particular was rising conspicuously. Behind the scenes, two rival groups of powerful industrial tycoons were battling for control of the Northern Pacific Railroad Company. One side was led by Northern Pacific's majority owner, James Jerome "J. J." Hill and backed by J. P. Morgan, the financier. The other faction was headed by Edward Henry "Ned" Harriman, who controlled the Union Pacific and the Southern Pacific railroads. His backers were William K. Vanderbilt, a grandson of the railroad titan Cornelius "Commodore" Vanderbilt; William A. Rockefeller, the younger brother of John D. Rockefeller; and Jacob Schiff, the influential banker. Unknown to the public, these rivals were purchasing hundreds of thousands of Northern Pacific shares, which was making its stock price skyrocket.

When trading began at 10 A.M., Northern Pacific opened at 170, ten points higher than the night before. Simultaneously, a large portion of the stocks those millionaires had purchased were sold to them "short," a risky selling practice used by opportunists to make a profit if the price of a stock went down rather than up. Short stocks were sold to buyers at their current price, with a promise to deliver the actual certificates to them at a later date. If the price fell, the opportunistic seller could buy those certificates at the lower price, hand them over to the buyer as promised, and pocket the difference as profit. As collateral, short sellers had to put aside enough cash for the buyers so that they could purchase those shares on their own, at whatever the current market price was, in case the seller didn't or couldn't show up with the promised certificates. This set-aside cash, called the margin, was held by a third-party broker in what was called a margin account. If the Northern Pacific stock price went up instead of down, short sellers had to add more cash to their margin accounts to cover that increase. Whether or not the price dropped, sellers had to turn over those stock certificates when due, no matter what, or else lose all of the cash their margin accounts.

The problem with this scenario was that all of those in-the-know tycoons had purchased so much stock in Northern Pacific that by Thursday morning there were no more shares left for anyone else to buy. The millionaires had cornered the market. And instead of cash, they now insisted on getting the actual certificates owed to them. No one knew where those certificates were, or who had them. Speculators scrambled to find that paper. But since the stock supply approached zero, its price zoomed toward infinity. The result was a financial catastrophe. Tens of thousands of risk-taking short sellers were "placed in the position of having to deliver stock that they did not own, and which they could neither buy nor borrow."[51] To cover their margin accounts, they were forced to liquidate entire portfolios. "Securities were being dumped on the market altogether without regard to value," the *Times* stated.[52] This happened so fast that "many fortunes went into the vortex thus formed and were sucked out of sight in a twinkling."[53] Then "prices elsewhere began to fall off—not slowly, as the day previous, but with fearful, heart-breaking rapidity," the newspaper exclaimed.[54] "The panic was on!"

The scene on the trading floor "resembled, more than anything else, a football field, with 600 determined players striving for the goal," the *Times* reported.[55] "Men climbed over each other to buy and sell." That's because "a second's delay might mean thousands of dollars."[56] Top brokerage houses pleaded with these tycoons to accept cash on loan instead of the actual stock certificates, but they wouldn't "yield an inch."[57] It was a slaughter. Investors "went around with ashen faces, wild-eyed, and haggard looking," a reporter observed. "A moment before they had been rich," the *Times* continued. "Now they were paupers."[58] Fortunes were "swept away in a breath."[59] The losses were beyond staggering, not just millions but tens and even hundreds of millions.[60]

In a matter of minutes, the drop in the value of United States Steel alone was $100 million, equivalent to more than $3 billion today.

In Troy, New York, an investor and brewery owner named Samuel Bolton, Jr., disappeared during the intense single-vat heating process necessary for sterilization of the draft. "About noon his hat was seen beside the vat of boiling beer and an investigation brought to light his body in the steaming liquid," a reporter explained. "It is said that Mr. Bolton had lost heavily in stocks."[61]

Meanwhile, a steady stream of stoic gray-coated messengers "poured in and out of the Exchange" at a rate of "at least one a second," according to reports. They carried sell orders or devastating telegrams announcing that an investor's margins had been wiped out.[62] The number of orders being handled was "unparalleled in Wall Street history."[63] Still, the transactions kept speeding up. "Boys were given as many as twenty-five messages each to deliver."[64] A conservative estimate put the number of messenger boys at "between 2,500 and 3,000, and yet this huge force was entirely inadequate to meet the unprecedented demands made upon it."[65] Nearly two thousand more youths were rounded up, from all over downtown Manhattan.

Finally, after being threatened by an injunction filed with the New York State Supreme Court, the millionaires agreed to relent, and at 12:30 P.M., the Stock Exchange sent notice "that delivery of Northern Pacific stock would not be required."[66] The corner was "broken," the panic stopped, and the company's share price fell from 1,000 to 325.[67] But the damage was done. By the time trading stopped, "there were many physical wrecks on the floor and in the gallery," said the *Evening World*. "Clothes were torn, hats were battered and trampled on, and the well-groomed broker of 9 o'clock was a mess by 3 o'clock."[68] Outside, the streets were cold and wet. "There was a scarcity of cabs in the trading districts, and many men of millions were compelled to tramp through the rain," said the *Times*. "Sorrow, fear, and expectation were depicted on nearly every face."[69] But not the messengers. They had been elevated to hero status. "In and out through the surging multitude of brokers and 'lambs' moved, in the even tenor of his way, the messenger boy," the *Times* pointed out the following day. He was the only soul "throughout that whole district who was not racked with doubt and fear," the newspaper continued, and "was in a small way the master of the situation yesterday."[70]

The Panic of 1901 made it clear that firms doing business on Wall Street had to operate their own full-time, in-house messenger staffs. In fact, quietly, there was a preference for African American youths in that position. "The white boys are more difficult to control than negroes," some prominent messenger service managers in Atlanta later revealed, adding that "the latter are more attentive to their duties."[71]

When the dust settled, Will Madden had become a messenger. That's when he "launched out for himself," approaching his work with seriousness and purpose. The ambitious teenager even began calling himself "Will Anthony Madden." It sounded more official. For the next several years, working on various assignments and "getting out of them any value there was to be gained, he acquired and developed considerable experience." There was little doubt that Will was daring and confident. In fact, he wished to be "a sort of 'Soldier of Fortune,' keeping his eyes open for whatever turned up."[72]

Three weeks later and nearly two thousand miles south of New York City, another seemingly unrelated development enabled the emergence in Harlem of one of the greatest basketball minds the sport has ever known.

On the morning of May 24, 1901, in the picturesque port city of Basseterre on the Caribbean island of St. Christopher, popularly called St. Kitts, a local eighteen-year-old Black West Indian named Robert Lewis Douglas made his way down to the harbor. Standing five feet, eight inches tall with brown hair and brown eyes, he was getting ready to board the SS *Madiana*, an iron-hulled passenger and cargo steamship preparing for a thirteen-day voyage to New York City.[73] Nearly as long as an American football field and with a capacity of about one hundred travelers, the *Madiana* was promoted as an "elegant passenger steamer" and was "specially fitted with electric lights, baths, and all improvements," making her ideal for service as a vacation ship.[74] The cost of a round-trip voyage out of New York City ranged from $185 to $255, up to more than $8,000 today, and the ship would sail to numerous Caribbean destinations, including St. Kitts, then return to Manhattan stocked with merchandise picked up from various West Indian ports.[75] Emotions at the Basseterre dock that day must have been bittersweet. Robert was saying goodbye to St. Kitts, leaving his home and his family behind to look for a better life. And traveling to the United States was a pioneering, sometimes solitary journey that took courage and grit for anyone, especially at eighteen years of age. But it was for good reason, and his departure was emblematic of why West Indians were deserting the Caribbean overall.

Located southeast of Puerto Rico, St. Kitts had golden sand beaches, tranquil bays, gorgeous climate, and rocky peninsulas that made the island an idyllic vacation spot. Belonging to the British West Indies that were governed by the United Kingdom, the island had become a lucrative business hub, exporting cane sugar, rum, limes, cacao, and coffee on the strength of "some of the most effectively cultivated sugar plantations in the West Indies." Along with Antigua, a neighboring island, St. Kitts produced twenty-five thousand tons of sugar the year Robert left, a 38 percent increase over 1899–1900.[76] Imports had also grown over the prior year, and the island's public debt had been reduced.[77] Yet, these financial advances hid a terrible truth. Demand and prices for Caribbean sugar had been plunging since the mid-1800s, as the newly developed process for crystallizing beet sugar, a cheap alternative to cane, became more widespread.[78] The sugar beet could be grown in Europe and North America, didn't need a tropical climate to thrive, and yielded white sugar that was indistinguishable from the original Caribbean cane version. To survive, sugar plantations, all White-owned, slashed wages for Black workers. Since their livelihoods and daily bread were tied closely to the plantation system, this caused anger, despair, and a decline in living conditions so sharp that malnutrition, rising infant mortality, and even starvation set in.[79] "What this must mean to the labouring class," a White observer wrote in a dispatch, "can be better imagined than described." One visiting White American writer in the late 1890s complained that there was "only a shadow of the old prosperity throughout the island." Another White American during this period confirmed that conditions on St. Kitts were "indeed deplorable, far worse than any of the other islands," lamenting that his traveling party was "almost mobbed" by beggars when they landed.[80] What was a matter of optics to White visitors, was a matter of life and death for local Black residents.

When the White ruling class failed to address the grievous inequities that workers of color had to endure, many Black people opted to abandon St. Kitts. It was time to go. Robert was saying goodbye to St. Kitts, yet an epic adventure awaited the young man.

Though most turn-of-the-century working-class Caribbean émigrés went to Panama, other parts of Central America, or Cuba, those who were educated, skilled, professional, and entrepreneurial preferred the United States, which was enjoying an economic expansion at the time. America offered higher wages, improved labor conditions, richer opportunities, and a more optimistic spirit in business. This self-selection effectively ensured that only the best and the brightest West Indians made it to America. And they overwhelmingly favored New York City over all other U.S. destinations, especially the South, since word had spread about horrible violence against African Americans in the former slave states. After arriving in Manhattan, Caribbean immigrants often found that they were more educated than European newcomers—and disproportionately more literate than American-born Whites.[81] As a result, many West Indians in the United States were self-confident, diligent, and thriving. Success was not only understood but expected.

In the days leading up to Robert's departure for the United States, only limited reports about the devastating stock market crash and resulting financial disaster had reached St. Kitts, and on board the *Madiana*, there was even less news from the outside world. So when he arrived at the Port of New York on June 6 and disembarked onto Pier 47 at the foot of West Tenth Street, Robert had no clear idea what to expect.[82] Like many immigrants, he arrived with little more than hope and vigor. His first overnight stay might have been with St. Kittian acquaintances in the San Juan Hill section of Manhattan, which stretched from West Sixty-First to West Sixty-Fourth Street between Tenth and Eleventh Avenues. The heavily industrial area wasn't attractive—geographically, it surrounded the New York Central & Hudson River Rail Road Freight Yard and the open livestock pens of the Union Stock Yards, which were adjacent to the Hudson River.[83] But the neighborhood was a favorite destination for newly arrived West Indians because there were numerous large, multistory tenements on its streets that were entirely occupied by Black residents, including strong concentrations of Caribbean immigrants, some of whom just didn't want to mess with the Tenderloin District a few blocks to the southeast.

Of just over ten million foreign-born residents in America, less than fifteen thousand were West Indians, or about one-tenth of 1 percent.[84] Of those, less than five thousand foreign-born Black people lived in New York City at the time. So the Caribbean immigrant community stuck together. They had to, establishing numerous aid organizations to provide their newly arrived compatriots with social, political, economic, health-related, and even financial support through churches, associations, and sports clubs.[85] In 1901, the most prominent of these was the West Indian Benevolent and Social League, which held picnics and festivals throughout the city.[86] Such activities were perfectly suited for young immigrants like Robert, who "was in this country 4 months before he knew anyone," according to what he told the *New York Age* sports columnist Carl Nesfield, more than fifty years later.[87]

Wherever they were from, Black people sought out folks from their own island, or their own home state if they were from the South, in order to fit in as quickly as possible. People helped one another, and Robert soon found work as an elevator man.[88] Meanwhile, the handsome, friendly, outgoing, proper young man with athletic abilities was an eligible bachelor and a desirable catch. He soon met a woman named Sadie May Perry, whose parents were also from the British West Indies. She was born in Savannah, Georgia, was a year younger, and worked as one of eight Black female servants in a multifamily home at 320 Manhattan Avenue, adjacent to Morningside Park in Harlem.[89] Before long, the two developed a romantic interest.

Nearly seven months after Robert Lewis Douglas's arrival in America, and on the other side of Central Park from San Juan Hill, one more apparently unconnected action would enable an explosion of basketball on the Lower East Side, spawning a generation of Jewish players and coaches who dominated the game with "scientific" efficiency—one of whom would help bring Will Anthony Madden national success, fame, and acclaim in the sport.

On the evening of December 30, 1901, the Central Board of Education of the City of New York assembled a meeting in the new Hall of Education Building at Park Avenue and East Fifty-Ninth Street.[90] It was two days before the official end of Mayor Robert Van Wyck's four-year term in office, and the board was rushing through one last order of business, not only to get it on the books for fiscal reporting reasons, but also, more importantly, to get a jump on the education crisis now facing Mayor-elect Seth Low. The city's scholastic infrastructure, neglected under Van Wyck's administration, was simply unable to keep up with the massive, years long, unyielding waves of immigration. Nowhere was this of more concern than on the Lower East

Side of Manhattan. It was during Van Wyck's four-year term that more than 20 percent of the total number of all U.S. immigrants had settled in New York City, causing acute overcrowding in that neighborhood, an area roughly 1.5 square miles in size, which was already inhabited by some five hundred thousand people, the vast majority of whom were poor Jewish immigrants from Europe.[91] By the late 1800s, "often and sometimes contemptuously referred to as 'The Ghetto,'" the Lower East Side was said to be the most densely populated place in the world, even more crowded than the slums of Bombay, India.[92]

Meanwhile, the shortage of classroom space in New York City was so extreme that some seventy-eight thousand registered students had been forced into part-time schooling, the most in city history, while thousands upon thousands of would-be pupils were already being turned away outright. This was abhorrent to most New Yorkers, especially on the Lower East Side, where hopeful Jewish parents who had fled Europe for better lives in America made education a priority for their children's sake, as the primary pathway toward better opportunities in life. So, in that Board of Education meeting, no resistance was reported when the Finance Committee resolved to appropriate $383,000 from the city's corporate stock holdings for a large new school to be built in the heart of the Lower East Side. Less than a month later, on January 21, 1902, with newly inaugurated Mayor Low presiding, the Board of Estimate and Apportionment met and approved the spending. With that, construction of Public School No. 188 was officially set in motion, scheduled for completion by the fall term of 1903.[93]

When it opened, P.S. 188 was dubbed "the largest school in the world."[94] But it was way beyond just large. The five-story, H-shaped structure, designed by the famous urban education architect Charles B. J. Snyder, then superintendent of school buildings for the Central Board, was of "bright red brick and limestone amid the gloom of its surroundings," and it took up the entire city block bounded by Lewis, East Houston, Manhattan, and East Third Streets. With a six-thousand-student capacity, one hundred classrooms, four kitchens for cooking instruction, two assembly rooms, two libraries, a carpentry shop, two glass-covered rooftop playgrounds, and two ten-thousand-square-foot natural-light courtyard gymnasiums, it was *titanic*.[95] The school even had public baths "with hot and cold water" in the basement, since "it has been found by the school authorities that baths in connection with schools are one of the most desirable adjuncts" of education. P.S. 188 was immediately embraced by educators around the country as a model for urban school design and the adaptation of education to special city needs.[96]

It was such a big deal that visiting foreign dignitaries were taken there for tours to show off American ingenuity. Snyder envisioned schools as urban enclaves and was known for his concern about the health and safety of school-children, expressed through his revolutionary innovations in ventilation, lighting, classroom ergonomics, fireproofing, efficient evacuation, and related areas. His signature H-shaped design plan was inspired by the Hôtel de Cluny in Paris, near the Cathedral of Notre Dame.[97] "You will see, side by side, the children of the poor, the well-to-do, the ignorant, the enlightened, the criminal and the law-abiding classes," the school's first principal, Edward Mandel, explained. "All are learning out of the same books; all are to be American citizens."[98] Every pupil even had a desk. They represented "nearly every country of Europe, the children of American-born parents being a small minority," newspapers reported. "The Russian predominates, closely followed by Hebrews and Hungarians."[99] Though the public narrative was about the certainty of these pupils attaining American citizenship one day, existing American citizens who were Black got no such consideration. The difference was that no matter how foreign the foreign-born European newcomers at P.S. 188 might have been labeled, they could someday be considered White Americans, and so could their parents. In line with White supremacy ideology, this was not the case for people of African descent.

Meanwhile, regarding the school's athletic facilities, no one on the Lower East Side had ever seen or even dreamed of anything quite like what now was available. They were considered engineering masterpieces. "The chief feature is, of course, the open-air gymnasiums, with their equipment and dumbbells, Indian clubs, parallel and horizontal bars, flying rings, and horse, buck, and spring boards," a *New York Times* reporter explained.[100] Among the school's first appointments, after its teachers and administrators, were the staff who would supervise these progressive recreational spaces, men and women who were known in those days as *gymnasts*. These were experts familiar with gymnasiums, the various athletic apparatus, and their uses for physical fitness, often becoming coaches for the school's sports teams. Gymnasts were considered so essential that, like regular teachers, they had to be carefully certified, licensed, selected, and appointed by the Board of Education and its special Board of Examiners. So when P.S. 188 hired a twenty-two-year-old Lower East Side native named Augustus Edward "Jeff" Wetzler as one of its gymnasts for physical training and athletics, that in itself was a big deal. Wetzler, born in New York City around 1882, was the son of German immigrants. His father was a stonecutter and his mother a "janitress." He grew up in a tenement on Sheriff Street, just two blocks and around the corner from where P.S. 188 now stood. Sherriff was notoriously known as the roughest street on the Lower East Side, before it was cleared in 1898 to make room for the four-acre Hamilton Fish Park, which opened in 1900 with a play center that included a gymnasium. This was part of an initiative by the Playground Association of America to create open spaces and introduce sports to immigrant youths living in densely populated urban settings. The same concept had been proposed for the Minetta District adjacent to Little Africa. The difference was that Minetta would have been cleared to build a park for use primarily by European immigrants while displacing its large number of Black residents, who understandably resisted the idea.

A majority of the Lower East Side's predominantly Jewish labor force worked in the disgracefully low-paying garment industry, in factories that were mainly Jewish-owned and contracted their piecework to supervisors operating crowded workshops in homes and tenements. They employed workers, sometimes entire families, who were driven to toil for long hours under dreadful, even hazardous conditions. "It is not unusual to find a dozen persons—men, women and children—at work in a single room," wrote the social reformer Jacob Riis.[101] These dimly lit and frequently unsanitary spaces with poor or no ventilation, excessive heat, and inadequate or no plumbing became known as "sweatshops."

Nevertheless, poor Jewish immigrants, often uneducated, unskilled, and with few other options, found this seemingly inescapable line of work tolerable because it allowed them to learn a new trade, earn desperately needed income, observe the Sabbath, and keep their families intact within the community. But the flip side was that crime and delinquency were rampant among males in the neighborhood's "teeming juvenile population," many of whom weren't cut out for the garment trade or any other legal profession. "Detectives last night rounded up 18 men said to be members of East Side gangs," the *Brooklyn Daily Standard Union* reported on the same day that P.S. 188 first opened its doors in September 1903. "Two of the prisoners had revolvers and one had 'knockout drops.'"[102] Strategically, P.S. 188 had been placed directly into the center of the area that presented the Lower East Side with its most difficult trouble spots for juvenile misconduct. Such intense overcrowding of socially unassimilated masses had resulted in widespread squalor, infestation, and disease. These aspects of everyday life were challenging, especially for school-age children.

Taking cues from Dudley Allen Sargent and even Governor Roosevelt, progressive educators and community reformers believed that the best remedy was to place a premium on physical fitness and competitive athletics. This provided a way for students to burn off youthful energy, find structure, and keep their minds occupied. As this idea evolved, they turned to basketball as a natural vehicle for bringing all those useful elements together in a practical way.

"I am sure that no man can derive more pleasure from money or power than I do from seeing a pair of basketball goals in some out of the way place," wrote the game's inventor, James Naismith, in 1941, fifty years after its birth in 1891. "The spread of basketball has been both extensive and rapid," he continued.[103] The new sport became popular so quickly, according to his account, because during its first dozen years basketball was taught with evangelical enthusiasm throughout the entire extensive YMCA network, and most of its branches had their own gymnasiums, though it must be pointed out that that did not yet apply to the organization's numerous "Colored" branches. Naismith explained that descriptions of basketball and its rules were printed in *The Triangle*, the organization's newsletter, which was distributed to branches throughout the United States in 1892. Since these facilities were "looking desperately for some activity that would interest their members, they quickly accepted the game."

Soon afterward, the inventor began receiving letters "from widely scattered points," and one of the first was from the Central Branch of the Brooklyn YMCA, which stated that members there were "more enthusiastic about the game than one could imagine." Their basketball team had already scheduled games with other Y branches. Philadelphia was another hot spot where the game "became so popular that it threatened to disrupt the formal gymnastic classes that were carried on by the Association." So many teams were formed there, and in other branches throughout America, that it left "little time for other work." According to Naismith, the Philadelphia branch dropped basketball in 1897 because it had created "a monopoly of the floor." As a result, many of its members quit and formed their own teams. "Games were held in warehouses and even in dance halls supplied with goals," he explained. That's when crowds of spectators began to show up, which opened the door for professionalism, and to the best of Naismith's recollection, the first pro team was based in Philadelphia. Still, through its own surveys, the YMCA determined that basketball was beneficial after all, because it increased membership and built loyalty toward the association among its existing members. So, they doubled down on efforts to teach "thousands of boys all over the country." More gyms were built.

Basketball was also spread throughout the country and even around the world by the students of the YMCA International Training School in Springfield, who "took the game with them" as instructors after graduating. Students from France and Japan were in the school's 1893 graduating class, Naismith explained. From there, the game spread to the Amateur Athletic Union, to high schools, to athletic clubs, and to colleges, many of which began playing around 1894. Churches, too. Then theological colleges. "It will never cease to be a wonder to me when I hear some athletic event announced from the pulpit." Naismith believed that they "realized the necessity for some activity that would keep young people interested," and at very little cost.

Soon afterward, he shared, Jewish organizations like the Young Men's Hebrew Association began taking up the game, thanks to the introduction in the late 1890s of what were called settlement houses, which social reformers and philanthropists helped establish in New York City and Chicago to provide accommodations and community services in neighborhoods congested by newly arriving immigrants. Clark House, Educational Alliance, the Henry Street Settlement, and the University Settlement Society, all predominantly Jewish and on the Lower East Side, were the most well-known of these facilities. They were actually small tenement buildings that provided temporary shelter for a few families at a time. These organizations quickly outgrew their original structures, so around 1899 they upgraded into full-fledged multistory buildings, designed by architects, with the help of philanthropic support. This was a key moment for the growth of basketball on the Lower East Side. Those new buildings, while still accommodating a few residents, now became the headquarters for dozens of community-based, cause-related programs, clubs, and societies for all ages. Most importantly, these facilities included gymnasiums with courts and equipment. They began organizing their own basketball squads. And that's when the game took off in that neighborhood.

Even before the turn of the century, basketball had become the most popular athletic activity for Lower East Side youth. This was not easy, as players from these organizations had to develop their games "in places where some teams would refuse to play, such as lofts with low ceilings, empty storerooms, back yards and in fact in any place where two basket ball baskets could be placed."[104] But from those "disadvantageous places for practice of team work and basket throwing" came squads that could "defeat any team of their weight in New York City or vicinity." In 1903, these programs collectively organized the Inter-Settlement Basket Ball League, which allowed them to compete against one another in compliance with the YMCA, the YMHA, and the Amateur Athletic Union, or AAU, whose officials were considered the highest authorities in the sport.

Though there was also a growing number of "Colored" settlement houses in the North and South, often funded and run by White philanthropists, they did not yet have the same opportunity for basketball immersion. No settlements had yet been established in Chicago, Maryland, Washington, D.C., Missouri, New Jersey, Buffalo, Brooklyn, or Milwaukee. Those that existed did not have a gym. Though the Eighth Ward Settlement House on Locust Street in Philadelphia, organized in 1895 for "social work among Negroes," was set up "in a thoroughly criminal neighborhood," they offered public baths, a women's club, and dancing classes while "a broom brigade of a dozen boys cleaned alleys three times a week." The Calhoun Colored School and Settlement in Calhoun, Alabama, established in 1892, housed twenty women and three men "in the midst of 30,000 plantation Negroes." The Doe Ye Nexte Thynge Society, established in 1901 at 18 Leroy Street in Greenwich Village, served the "Irish, Italian, French, Jewish, and colored" with activities that included sewing, cooking, basketry, and play hour while housing two residents.

Eventually, the St. Cyprian's Settlement on West Sixty-Third Street in Manhattan, founded "to give the nation a shining example of what to expect from the sober, sane, and charitable treatment of its colored people," would get its own gymnasium, "the only one in the city for colored people." But not until 1905.[105]

On the Lower East Side, the University Settlement team practiced on the rooftop court of its handsome five-story building at the corner of Eldridge and Rivington Streets. It was "far from ideal" because, exposed to the elements during basketball season, "the rain and snow often made the court slippery and the ball hard to handle, when it did not stop the game entirely." For that reason, the league ruled out their location for any games, which left University Settlement teams with "both the disadvantage of playing on strange courts and against gymnasium-trained players." But at least the players had a dedicated space, and the settlement's Middle and Junior basketball teams went on to capture the Intersettlement Cup for four straight years starting in 1901.[106]

Another important reason for basketball's popularity on the Lower East Side was that the AAU believed basketball to be a great vehicle for social progress, specifically for Americanization, especially for European newcomers. So the amateur sports organization pushed the game for that purpose, signing up participants and setting up leagues. "The habits of obedience to authority and of respect for the law and order, which are developed by our excellent rules and efficient officials, lead many to useful civic careers," AAU leaders argued. "The intermingling of immigrants around our courts unconsciously acquaints them with our American customs and helps to teach them, through use, our language and laws."[107]

In contrast, the city's Black community, whose inhabitants were already American citizens, had no such consideration, consistency, or advocacy for basketball in their corner. The AAU, despite its stated ideals, would prohibit African American membership until 1914. This meant any AAU member team that competed against a Black club risked disqualification from further amateur competition. African American squads would not be allowed to enter the AAU's New York Metropolitan District Championships until the late 1910s.

But one White man from the Lower East Side would use his privilege to help counteract that situation. Leading up to the 1904–5 season, P.S. 188 appointed Augustus Edward "Jeff" Wetzler as its first basketball manager, and after that the game would never be the same.

CHAPTER 8

PHYSICAL CULTURE

AFTER GRADUATING FROM THE ACCLAIMED M Street High School as an honor roll student in 1902, Edwin Bancroft Henderson wanted to teach. So he enrolled at Normal School No. 2, a highly respected two-year teacher training academy also known as the Colored Normal School.[1] (Normal School No. 1 was the equivalent school for White aspiring teachers.) By early 1904, EB was completing his studies as one of thirty-seven students at Colored Normal. The school had no formal athletic program, so he and some classmates took up bicycling and long-distance walking for exercise. "I would on occasion walk forty-five miles to Highland Beach, Maryland, to Baltimore or Great Falls, Virginia, frequently," EB remembered.[2]

He met a woman there, a fellow honor roll student named Mary Ellen "Nellie" Meriwether, who also wanted to become a teacher. "Until then girls were taboo," EB recalled. "So when at a recess period she sat in a seat in front, leaning toward my desk and asked for advice, I gave her nothing but academic attention." But eventually, he "was invited to call some Friday evening." Calls, he later explained, "were only allowed on Friday nights and possibly Sunday afternoon."[3] EB and Nellie began going together, and they both soon became schoolteachers.

Around this time, the city commissioners in Washington, D.C., were developing a belief that their valuable park system could be made even better by converting some of those spaces into dedicated playgrounds. That was significant, because their enthusiasm would lead to a "playground movement" aimed not only at serving "little children" with "swings and teeter boards," as well as shallow wading pools, but also at providing older youths with "regular outdoor gymnasia, with apparatus for jumping, vaulting, climbing, swinging, and the like, with tracks for running and spaces for the lesser athletic contests, such as putting the shot." The lack of playgrounds, it was thought, "drives the youth of the city into the saloons, poolrooms, and other improper places and, finally, frequently into the Police Court and the prisons."[4]

For the next several years, D.C. continued its advocacy for playgrounds, adding the idea that "there should be provision for the larger games, whether the schoolboys' games of tag and prisoners' base and scrub or the organized games of baseball and football between regular teams," according to a 1902 report.[5] Though basketball was not yet popular enough in the city for it to have been mentioned in those remarks, the District's public playgrounds committee had in its possession seven sets of basket-ball goals and posts, to be divvied up among nineteen public playgrounds. Seven of those nineteen were dedicated for use by African American youth. (The committee's inventory also included seventy-three swings, eighteen seesaws, ten sandboxes, two sets of parallel bars, two trapezes, two climbing ropes, five horizontal ladders, thirteen sliding poles, eight Indian clubs, and two baseball sets.)[6] By then, Theodore Roosevelt had become the twenty-sixth president of the United States. "I am delighted to hear that you have succeeded in establishing certain playgrounds in Washington," President Roosevelt wrote in a personal letter to the city's parks committee the following year. "It would be a national misfortune if the Capital City were developed without proper attention being given to the well-being of those of its citizens least able to protect themselves."[7]

Proper attention came in the form of a field day, intentionally a "conspicuous final event of the year" staged by the District's playground committee, in which teams from each neighborhood playground competed against one another for prizes and awards. The event, spanning two days from September 10–11, 1904, was held at Coliseum Park, a large track and baseball stadium with a grandstand and bleachers that took up the entire block bordered by East Capitol, B, Fourteenth, and Fifteenth Streets NE. Black participants competed on the first day, and White students the following day. Contestants in each set of final games received gold, silver, and bronze medals in events that included the twenty-five-yard dash, the sixty-yard-dash, the hundred-yard-dash, the running high jump, and the running broad jump. "Five hundred laughing, cheering, happy youngsters sat in the grandstand or swarmed over the field" at the meet, which was considered such a success that a repeat was planned for the following year.

Regardless of race, D.C. made it a priority to ensure that its playgrounds would be "under the constant charge of a trained and competent director," and many teachers-in-training, especially those like EB with a love of athletics and concern for Black wellness, heard opportunity within those words.[8] But the District of Columbia's proactive playground commitment was in stark contrast to the lack of playing spaces and expertise available for African American youngsters in New York City, Chicago, and Pittsburgh. The New York City Colored YMCA Branch still did not have a gymnasium. Brooklyn's first Colored Y had opened in July 1902 with the help of a White millionaire investment banker and philanthropist named George Foster Peabody. An early organizer of railroads and utilities, Peabody contributed funds as well as a three-story brownstone on Carlton Avenue, near Fort Greene Park, to house the new branch.[9] With two hundred pledged members, it contained sitting and reading rooms, a game room with billiards, overnight accommodations, and social assimilation programs—but no gym. And in Chicago as well as in Pittsburgh, it would be several years before any public gymnasiums were open to African Americans.

Yet, White communities throughout America were already capitalizing on the exercise trend and its commercial possibilities. "Such a wave of physical culture has spread all over the land that it is not astonishing to find the huge Madison Square Garden given over to the exploitation of its advantages this week," a *Brooklyn Life* magazine reporter boasted in early January 1904 about the "Mammoth Physical Culture Show" being staged in that venue.[10] Even though the *Sunday New York Times* on February 7, 1904, quoted new statistics that showed "the death rate from consumption among the negroes far exceeds that among the whites," experts knew so little about consumption, called tuberculosis today, a highly contagious disease that spreads via airborne transmission, that they thought "the best curative agents are fresh air and sunshine, good food and rest, and sobriety." Italians seemingly had the lowest rate of infection among White people, so it was believed they were immune because "the carnivorous American may underrate the dietary value of macaroni and cheese."[11]

Black people were alarmed. Many believed what Booker T. Washington had stated, that "vicious habits" were to blame. Two weeks later in Brooklyn, the beloved African American community leader Samuel Scottron spoke at the Carlton Avenue Colored YMCA about the wellness of the race. "From what and unto what shall a leader lead us," he asked, "now that the shackles have dropped from the arms and feet of our four million slaves?" The sixty-one-year-old Scottron reminded the African American audience "to fit themselves for the race of life" and to acquire the means by which they would obtain "strength and stability, to conquer the respect of their neighbors."[12] When this man spoke, folks listened. But many others were confused and didn't know what to believe. Three days after Scottron's speech, the *New York Times*, again on a Sunday, published "ten rules of healthful living" in a typical advice column. "If your work is hard manual labor," one rule stated, "nothing will do you more good than two or three glasses of beer a day." On the other hand, athletes and "brain workers" were advised they "should never touch alcoholic liquor of any sort."[13]

For an earnest and forward-thinking twenty-three-year-old Jamaican-born immigrant in Harlem named Conrad Norman, enough was enough. He believed that high infection rates among Black people were "not due to unsanitary living, for the colored woman is an excellent housewife." Instead, Conrad insisted that lack of fitness was the cause. "As there were no opportunities among colored people in New York for physical exercises tending to develop and strengthen the chest and lungs," he explained, "the disease germs found them ready victims." In discussions with others, Conrad began questioning why proper recreational facilities for Black folks were so blatantly missing. "Although there were seventy thousand colored people in New York at the time, and the big city fairly teemed with athletic clubs of all kinds, recreation centers, playgrounds, settlements, schools, Turn Verein halls, and colleges, each provided with a gymnasium, there was not a single one devoted to colored people," he recalled later.[14]

Within weeks of the *Times'* morbidity statistics, Conrad and his two brothers, Gerald and Clifton, took the initiative and founded the country's first African American athletic club, which "would afford some opportunity to our people of scientific physical training." Being the first, they called it the Alpha Physical Culture Club. This was a mammoth move. "To men less determined," an observer later wrote, "the obstacles would have been insurmountable." The way Conrad saw it, the problem wasn't just about unwise behavior, uncleanliness, and lack of gymnasiums, but also the lack of awareness about how these were connected. Closing this gap became the club's mission. Those who joined were taught how to exercise for fitness as well as medical health, and the organization also staged active social events such as picnics and dances. Dues and membership were so restrictive that "none was admitted who would in any way retard its progress."[15] Most were West Indians. In addition to Gerald, Conrad, and Clifton Norman from Jamaica, other Alpha Physical Culture Club founding members included William Simms from Jamaica, Clarence Hutchinson from Barbados, and Archibald Thomas from the British West Indies.[16] But the club was open to everyone under the motto "A Square Deal for All!"[17] Not by accident, this was a play on the "Square Deal" domestic policy platform of President Theodore Roosevelt. "When I say that I am for the square deal," Roosevelt explained, "I mean not merely that I stand for fair play under the present rules of the game, but that I stand for having those rules changed so as to work for a more substantial equality of opportunity and of reward for equally good service."[18] Again by no accident, these ideas did not extend to a "square deal" for the Negro.

The efforts of the Alpha Physical Culture Club, Conrad later said, were "helping our race by fortifying the bodies of our people in this, the struggle for existence, where only the fittest survive."[19] In putting it that way, the club founder was referencing a famous phrase that had been coined in the mid-1800s by the influential philosopher, biologist, sociologist, and political theorist Herbert Spencer, who theorized that the same breakthrough science of the evolution of species as pioneered by the fellow biologist Charles Darwin also applied to the development of human culture and societies. "This survival of the fittest," Spencer had written in 1864, "is that which Mr. Darwin has called *natural selection*, or the preservation of favoured races in the struggle for life."[20]

But that way of thinking took a dark turn. By the 1890s, Spencer's theory had been distorted into "social Darwinism," the ideological justification for hard-nosed business dealings, military aggression, and, of course, White supremacy, to justify the annihilation of entire peoples. "Survival of the fittest" had become a slogan for single-minded ruthlessness. And even while skeptics saw it as encouraging a dangerous return to the unenlightened Dark Ages, the phrase naturally found its way into sports as a mantra employed to rationalize winning by any means necessary. A perceptive newspaper columnist pointed this out just prior to the third modern Olympics, suggesting that the question of whether college students who participate in athletics were "likely to live longer than the bookworms" was up for debate. "Who will exemplify most clearly the survival of the fittest, the boys of brawn or the boys of brain?"[21] It turned out that basketball would require a lot of each, and Black folks were down for both. Though the Alpha Physical Culture Club began humbly with "five or six members" in an extra room of the Mount Tabor Presbyterian Church House on West 134th Street, across the street from where the Norman brothers lived, it would soon grow to become a driving force in the power structure behind the birth and early growth of Black basketball in New York City.

Meanwhile, that mammoth physical culture show in January at Madison Square Garden would be outdone in April 1904 with the opening of the Louisiana Purchase Exposition, informally known as the St. Louis World's Fair. Scheduled to last eight months, its spectacular scale alone went beyond what anyone had ever seen. The immensity of the fairgrounds was unimaginable, covering 1,200 acres on which dozens of pavilions, palatial in scale, displayed all the world's latest and greatest technological, industrial, medical, artistic, military, social, and commercial advancements in the form of countless machines and devices. Forty-one states and forty-three countries constructed entire buildings to display their pride. Amazingly, an enormous Hall of Physical Culture was built "for the first time in the history of expositions." This facility contained a special "model gymnasium," erected at a cost of $200,000, nearly $6 million today, which was outfitted by a "display of athletic goods and paraphernalia for all sports and pastimes" manufactured by A. G. Spalding & Bros., the nation's leading fitness and sporting goods supply company.[22]

What made this world's fair even more incredible was that starting in May, it also hosted the 1904 Summer Olympics, known as the III Olympiad— and the game of basketball was introduced for the first time ever as a men's exhibition sport. There were four regular team competitions: lacrosse, soccer, tug-of-war, and water polo. In and of themselves, these Olympic Games were a sensational boost for physical fitness. One journalist had already predicted in January, "The revival of the Olympian games is a single feature that will arouse national interest in sports and pastimes."[23] Another newspaperman declared that this was "the greatest athletic meeting of modern times."[24] Many folks could not attend, even though cities and towns throughout the country were arranging special affordable train service directly to the fairgrounds. That included EB, who was too busy with schoolwork, trying to stay on the academic honor roll at Normal School No. 2 and getting ready to graduate.

But even people who wouldn't make it there in person had been getting excited about basketball. Way back in March, after winning the intercollegiate national championship, Columbia University had announced that it was "going to send her basket-ball team to St. Louis this summer to compete for the world's championship."[25] Still earlier, at the end of January, Spalding & Bros. had published *How to Play Basket Ball*, a groundbreaking primer not only on the rules and strategies, but also on the character with which the sport was to be conducted. The booklet was written by the future Basketball Hall of Fame member George T. Hepbron, then secretary of the AAU's National Basketball Committee.[26] "The book is something that has long been wanted by those who have been anxious to play the game correctly," the *Brooklyn Daily Eagle* reported. It included articles about the qualities demanded in a successful team, the grounds, ethics of the game, character in the sport, referee backbone, passing and goal throwing, and the complete basket ball outfit. The book was "more interesting than any publication of its kind ever issued, owing to the fact that its many page illustrations, taken especially for it, show how to play the game." This was "something in basket ball that has never been attempted before."[27] *How to Play Basket Ball* even had solid advice about conduct and teamwork. "There is no game that offers the opportunity for rough playing, and which is more exciting to the temper," Luther Gulick warned in its pages. "It can only be by united action," he continued, "that the game can be kept from degenerating."[28]

In June, EB graduated from Colored Normal at the top of his class and was quickly appointed to a first-grade teaching position in the District's public school system, which was still racially segregated. [29] But this appointment was short-lived. Instead of elementary school classroom instruction, EB decided to become a gym teacher. Within days, he was a student again, taking courses in Dudley Allen Sargent's Summer School of Physical Education at Harvard University.[30]

Not explaining his abrupt move at the time, EB later admitted it was "at the urging" of Anita Juburness Turner, the M Street High School women's physical education teacher when he was a student there.[31] She had since become the assistant director of physical culture overseeing all the Colored Divisions of the District of Columbia's public school system, which was adding several new schools. There were nine White and three Black divisions in the city. This, the *Washington Evening Star* reported, "necessitated the creation of a thirteenth division, colored."[32] That also made Turner, thirty-four years old, very influential in light of the District's prevailing playground movement, because more Black gym teachers would be needed. She was now responsible for all "school playgrounds for colored children."[33] Also, since Turner had spent four summers in Sargent's program—in 1896, 1897, 1898, and 1900—she could share her firsthand experience with EB, probably explaining that very few Black trainees had ever enrolled in it. Sure enough, upon arriving, EB discovered that he was one of only two African American students out of 114.[34] Enrollees could obtain "a first-class certificate" when they earned enough credit points completing state-of-the-art physical training courses such as Elementary Fencing, Swedish Free Exercises, Gymnastic Games, Voice Training, Swimming, and Basket-ball.[35] This could take four summers, with a focus on "both the theoretical and practical instruction," according to Harvard's academic catalog.[36] It was the same course Booker T. Washington took in 1887, except now "basket ball" had been added to the curriculum. Sargent's students learned, practiced, and played the game at the original Hemenway Gymnasium, which was demolished in 1938 and replaced by the current Hemenway Gymnasium that now serves as the Harvard Law School's fitness center. Classes for the 1904 program began on July 1. By then, the 1904 Olympic basketball competition had begun in St. Louis. Even as EB was learning the game in Cambridge, the sport itself was displayed on a global stage for the first time, with more than six hundred athletes from twelve nations competing in all the Olympic events. The basketball games took place outdoors on eight grass courts set up in the infield of a modern one-third-mile oval cinder track at Francis Field, the III Olympiad's official stadium.[37] Playing outside was typical in those days. The gold medal was awarded on July 12 to a YMCA team from Upstate New York known as the Buffalo YMCA Germans, who defeated the Central YMCA of Chicago 39–28.[38] This is when EB might have gotten hooked on the game, recognizing its great potential for promoting physical culture among African American youth on a wide scale. And even though he previously had "never been involved in a formalized physical education program," the future gym teacher, who was muscular and athletic, would soon become an outstanding basketball player in his own right.[39]

On the Lower East Side that year, excitement about basketball continued to grow when University Settlement, the Inter-Settlement Basket Ball League champions of 1903, added to its advantage a brand-new gymnasium "built upon the surface of the old roof," made possible on the strength of a $50,000 charitable gift. The state-of-the-art space was "modern and thoroughly equipped" under twenty-foot ceilings, and all of its gymnastics equipment and exercise apparatus were "on movable stands so that they can be readily moved off the floor for basketball games." Complete with 350 lockers and "modern showerbaths," this was a dream facility at the time. In addition, the subsequent *new* roof was fitted up with a second basketball court "by covering it with an iron cage."[40] University Settlement would retain the league title in 1904 and win again in 1905. It was just the beginning for the team.

That enthusiasm kept building as P.S. 188 planned the organization of its first sports teams for the 1904–5 academic year. With a student body close to five thousand strong, its basketball manager, Jeff Wetzler, was in the uniquely privileged position of having an enormous pool of student-athletes from which to choose. And, having grown up on the school's surrounding streets, he knew the neighborhood and its people well, which may have helped him identify the best players. Indeed, P.S. 188's basketball programs realized immediate success in the city's most competitive forum, the Public Schools Athletic League. Wetzler's top squad won the PSAL's coveted Senior Division (up to fifteen years old) championship for the 1904–5 season in its first year of existence as a program, a historic accomplishment and still the only time that has ever been achieved in the league's history. The PSAL title game, subsequently won by Wetzler's squad, would be considered so important that it was officiated by the *How to Play Basket Ball* author, George T. Hepbron, himself. The unwritten headline was that Augustus "Jeff" Wetzler, a neighborhood boy with a neighborhood team, had brought great pride to the Lower East Side. But he would keep going. After being eliminated in 1906, Wetzler and his P.S. 188 heavyweights would come back strong to capture back-to-back PSAL Senior Division Basketball Championship titles for 1906–7 and 1907–8. Yet he was still just getting started.

Up at Harvard, EB finished Sargent's program in August and returned to Washington so he could prepare for the District's examinations to certify physical training teachers. These were given every fall. Meanwhile, the Summer Olympics were still underway, and on August 31, 1904, an African American hurdler from the University of Wisconsin named George C. Poage became the first Black athlete from the United States to compete in an Olympic Games. Not only that, he secured a medal, winning bronze in the 400-meter hurdles. Poage bronzed again the next day, winning third place in the 200-meter hurdles.[41] This was a pivotal moment in sports that reinforced and inspired fitness-minded African Americans everywhere, from Booker T. Washington to the Reverend John Wesley Johnson of St. Cyprian's to Miss Turner—and to EB, who, two weeks later, passed the District of Columbia public school gym teachers' exam, one of just seven candidates to do so.[42]

By the time the new academic year began the week after the exam, EB had accepted a $500-a-year job as an instructor in the city's physical culture department, under Miss Turner.[43] Armed with knowledge, passion, and confidence, he began teaching and promoting basketball to students in the city's Colored Divisions. Since hardly any structured cold-weather athletic activities existed for African American schoolchildren after the football season ended around Thanksgiving, EB believed that his restless pupils would readily embrace the game. It was new, physically challenging, mentally engaging, and competitive. But the rookie teacher's assumptions weren't exactly right. He later explained that among the hard-edged Black kids of Washington, D.C., basketball was "at first considered a 'sissy' game."[44] Still, this was the earliest introduction of the sport to African Americans on a wide-scale organized basis. And it marked the beginning of the Black Fives Era.

CHAPTER 9

ST. CHRISTOPHER

ON MAY 31, 1905, A TWENTY-NINE-YEAR-OLD Danish West Indies native and recently ordained priest named Everard Washington Daniel showed up in Satan's Circus. There were only two possible reasons why a young Black clergyman would appear in the middle of a place with such a nickname and reputation: he was weak, or he was strong. Fortunately for the future of African American basketball, Daniel was the latter, and this was his first day of work at the venerable St. Philip's Protestant Episcopal Church.[1] The newcomer would soon be appointed as its first athletic director, revamp and reorganize the congregation's St. Christopher Club Bible study program into the church's physical fitness arm, then develop an all-Black basketball team and lead it to national fame, leaving a legacy of having been "one of the most brilliant and energetic priests" ever to serve the parish.[2] Energetic also meant fiery.

A majestic figure who stood about six feet, four inches tall with an athletic build, chiseled features, and a clean-cut face, Daniel had immigrated to the United States with his parents as a toddler in 1878.[3] After attending St. Augustine's College in Raleigh, North Carolina, he pursued the ministry.[4] By 1899, the young man had made his way to New York City and become a candidate for Holy Orders at the General Theological Seminary on West Twenty-First Street, a White-run training center for the Protestant Episcopal Church.[5] This was no easy task, because the Episcopal Church was known to discourage its Black workers from striving for the priesthood, preferring that they settle instead for deaconship or other less influential positions. "The Church seems to labor under the delusion," Daniel would lash out later in a sermon, "that all colored men and women are in the kindergarten stage of development." Over the years, this would be his chief complaint about the denomination.

"She must not forbid to the Negro the right," he would insist, "to any higher aspiration even though that aspiration may lead to the Episcopate."[6]

Daniel graduated with a bachelor of divinity degree in May 1902, as one of thirty-three graduates.[7] By church law, he was required to complete a mandatory tour of duty, and for that, Daniel was assigned to a remote mission in the "Negro section" of St. Paul, Minnesota. Normally, it could take up to two years and sometimes as many as six or seven to be advanced to the priesthood, especially for a Black candidate.[8] But through persuasion and willfulness, Daniel successfully lobbied his bishop back in New York City to compress that window to seven months.[9] He was ordained as a priest by the Diocese of Minnesota on December 17, 1902. From then on, he would be Father Daniel. One personal reason for his eagerness to get on with it was that while at the seminary, Father Daniel had met a school worker and piano teacher named Marceline Mundy, from Manhattan. They were married in January 1903, a month after his ordainment, and Marceline had a baby boy in October. After serving faithfully in Minnesota, Father Daniel was approved in March 1905 for transfer back to the New York City diocese. He was sent back to Manhattan, where the diocese assigned him to serve as an assistant minister to the Reverend Dr. Hutchens Chew Bishop, pastor of St. Philip's. Bishop who had specifically requested Father Daniel, because the young priest previously made a good impression at the church as a volunteer.[10]

Looking for a place to live in Midtown, Father Daniel relied on his West Indian roots, possibly out of necessity, by renting a room in a four-family boardinghouse on West Sixteenth Street. It was occupied exclusively by fellow Caribbean-born Black people from the Danish West Indies, Bermuda, and Jamaica while being just several blocks from St. Philip's.[11] This building was a resource within the same circle of educated, professional, first-generation West Indian immigrant families as the Alpha Physical Culture Club founders Conrad, Gerald, and Clifton Norman. In fact, the brothers had lived in this same place as teenagers. By then, just over a year since its founding and with Conrad Norman still in charge, the Alpha PCC had grown from a handful of founders to thirty-five eager, dues-paying members. The organization had set up a clubhouse at 79 West 134th Street equipped with the latest gymnasium apparatus that was "scientifically arranged so as to use and develop every part of the body." Individuals could wrestle, box, or fence, and the facility had a piano as well as electricity throughout. They included physicians, dentists, lawyers, teachers, musicians, clerks, government employees, real estate men, brokers, and students.[12] Proud and determined, these men belonged "to the best class of colored people in New York and surrounding cities," the *New York Age* later reported.[13]

Apparently, Father Daniel already understood the benefits of "bodily vigor," as Luther Gulick referred to it, because soon after arriving at St. Philip's, he targeted the St. Christopher Club as an opportunity for physical culture programming, and Bishop appointed him as the church's first athletic director. As a Bible study group, its activities had gotten stale, and membership had dwindled to just ten participants. To breathe new life into the gathering, Father Daniel first recruited more attendees and restructured the St. Christopher Club into three divisions organized by age, size, and ability: seniors, intermediates, and juniors. He then orchestrated social activities, such as dances, songfests, a choir, and a theater group, in order to build the club's popularity. Next, the new athletic director added competitive sports, forming teams in boxing and track. But it wasn't until after Father Daniel launched a basketball program that the St. Christopher Club began its trajectory toward making national headlines. Although his teams weren't that good at first, within a decade they would be winning national championships while featuring future Basketball Hall of Fame talent.

As for Satan's Circus, the Tenderloin District could present temptations even to the most morally disciplined of men. But long before he could be considered for graduation from the seminary, Father Daniel had been thoroughly examined by an eight-person standing committee of chaplains and laymen as to whether the would-be priest had been living "piously, soberly, and honestly," so this risk was considered minimal. According to ecclesiastical law, that rigorous scrutiny had involved direct observance and evidence of his habits, as well as testimony from their personal knowledge and that of others over a three-year period. This review determined that during the entire time, he had been clean of any "error in religion or viciousness of life."[14] Father Daniel was strong, all right. But as some in the evolving world of Black basketball would soon find out, he could go too far with his righteousness.

Several blocks north of the Tenderloin and west of Central Park, the San Juan Hill neighborhood kept evolving to meet the needs of its growing African American population, and this was especially true among its West Indian immigrants. It was well-known that Caribbean-born Black people from the British islands overwhelmingly stayed loyal to the traditions of the Episcopal Church. Its authority was respected, and there was a "sharp line" separating "church goers and nonattendants," according to one observer, a local African American student at Columbia named Garrie Moore. Certain pleasures were "tabooed by the church," he explained, such as card playing and dancing. West Indians also preferred their Sunday services to be conducted with dignity and grace rather than being "more emotional, at times bordering on disorder," as they believed was the case at Union Baptist Church on West Sixty-Third Street, San Juan Hill's first Black congregation.[15]

But their loyalty to Episcopalian worship became a problem for the city's all-White Episcopal churches as soon as too many West Indian congregants began showing up. Their quick fix was to place Caribbean immigrant church-goers into separate pews, but this left White clerical leaders open to charges of hypocrisy. So instead, the Protestant Episcopal City Mission Society of the Diocese of New York built a brand-new "colored" place of worship in San Juan Hill, known as St. Cyprian's Chapel. Located at 177 West Sixty-Third Street near the corner of Amsterdam Avenue, it opened in 1905 and had as its vicar an African American native of Virginia, the Reverend John Wesley Johnson.

The following month, in keeping with the active lifestyle that was intrinsic to West Indian upbringing, and consistent with the national trend in physical culture awareness, New York City opened a new state-of-the-art public playground just below San Juan Hill, called DeWitt Clinton Park. No other buildings, parks, or recreational facilities had previously existed anywhere in the vicinity. Taking up the entire block from West Fifty-Second to West Fifty-Third Street between Eleventh Avenue and the Hudson River, it served the adjacent predominantly Irish American neighborhood known as Hell's Kitchen, the large neighboring African American enclave centered on West Fifty-Third Street, and the Black and West Indian streets of San Juan Hill, just blocks away. The park's opening ceremonies in November 1905 were attended by "nearly all of the residents of the district," at which "boys and girls of the neighborhood gave exhibitions of dumb-bell exercises, running, jumping and other games."[16]

About six months later, in May 1906, the Episcopal Mission Society jumped on the physical culture and muscular Christianity bandwagon as well by announcing that it would add a five-story parish house, which would include the latest in fitness concepts.[17] The new building was to be erected on vacant property the mission owned adjacent to the chapel, which stretched one hundred feet from the church to the corner of West End Avenue. When completed, the facility would have a six-hundred-seat auditorium, rooms for clubs and classes on its upper floors, a day nursery, an outdoor playground, and apartments for the parish staff. Of great importance to the community, it would also include "a large gymnasium with lockers, showers, and the like" in the basement.[18] Johnson recognized that "there are several ways by which young men and women can be brought into the church."[19] In his mind, they could visit the new, well-equipped gym, "thereby keeping off the streets and resorting to other forms of amusement not so beneficial."[20] The clergyman's visionary plan was bound to work, especially after his own nine-year-old son, an athletic lad named John H. Johnson, became interested in basketball. Once the new court was ready, the reverend believed, more church youths and others from around the way would stop by. Soon the Reverend Johnson's program began to take shape. It was in this setting that Robert Douglas would have first picked up the game. Years later, Douglas told *New York Age* columnist Nesfield that he discovered basketball while walking down Eleventh Avenue in 1906 and coming across a group of other young men playing the game. "They were throwing a round ball through a hoop in a 52 St. playground," he remembered. But the only playground at that intersection that year was DeWitt Clinton Park, which did not yet have any basketball court, backboard, or rim.[21]

During this time, the young St. Kitts immigrant proposed to his sweetheart, Sadie, and in July 1906, they became husband and wife. Their wedding at St. Cyprian's Chapel was officiated by the Reverend John Wesley Johnson.[22] His blessings, the matrimonial rites, and their nuptial vows were in contrast to the twenty-three year old groom's own parents, who were never married.[23] The newlyweds soon moved into an all-Black apartment building in Harlem, at 21 West 136th Street near Lenox Avenue, that was already home to numerous British West Indian immigrants. The rental property was a sign of how quickly the area's population was shifting from predominantly White to predominantly African American. The building itself was exclusively managed by a Black entrepreneur, illustrating the vast amount of business opportunity now available for African Americans in Harlem. This did not escape Robert Lewis Douglas.

It was Thursday, September 7, 1905, and Will Anthony Madden's father, the fifty-seven-year-old laborer, had been seriously ill for more than two weeks with failing kidneys. William Wilson "Willie" Madden died that afternoon of chronic nephritis.[24] He was buried on a hilltop overlooking New York City in the historic Cemetery of the Evergreens in Brooklyn.[25] Suddenly, the only man left in the Maddens' home was Will. At twenty-two years old, his carefree days as "a sort of 'Soldier of Fortune,' keeping his eyes open for whatever turned up," were over.[26]

Will Anthony Madden and his family had coveted their single-family home on Waverly Place. But the rent on such rare and desirable units kept going up. So, within a year of her husband's death, Margaret Ann relocated her mother, her children, and herself to a six-room flat "for colored people" in a nearby two-story building, at 269 West Fourth Street. This was still on the "good" side of Sixth Avenue. But with the weekly earnings of Will's grandfather and father gone, the Maddens made ends meet by renting some of their new space to two Bermuda-born gentlemen, William Taylor, a thirty-year-old barber, and Henry Swan, a twenty-four-year-old employed as a manservant. By then, Will's older sister, Grace, had become a seamstress, and Florence, the youngest Madden, was working as a "lady's maid." Although these were humble pursuits, their combined income also helped close the gap in wages. But ultimately, it was Will's earnings that brought security, allowing Margaret Ann and her mother, Ellen, to stay home doing "housework."[27] Messengers were paid a piece wage, an hourly wage, or a weekly salary. But even at a per-message rate of 2 cents, a boy could earn $2 or more a week.[28]

At this point in his messenger career, Will had begun using his "considerable experience" to get ahead, and that perseverance paid off in spectacular fashion. Out of all the messenger jobs in New York City that were filled in 1905, he landed arguably the best one. It was at Standard Oil, controlled by John D. Rockefeller. Will joined the company's messenger department at its headquarters in the Standard Oil Building, at 26 Broadway in Lower Manhattan.[29] Originally ten stories high but with six more levels added in 1895, the Standard Oil Building was one of the tallest structures in the city, with magnificent views overlooking New York Harbor in all directions.[30] Standard Oil employees were fond of calling their building "26," and it was a splendid work setting, with interior spaces unmatched in their luxury. Merely seeing the building in person was a hot ticket for tourists.

Will's job at "26" was remarkable. He was assigned to the building's ninth floor, especially opulent because the company's executive suites and its boardroom were once located there.[31] This is where Rockefeller would appear whenever he was in Manhattan.[32] Yet, the atmosphere that greeted Will when he walked through the ornate glass revolving door entrance into the building's lobby on his first day of work was thick with secrecy. The oil tycoon's private office had been moved to the fourteenth floor, and although it was reported that he no longer appeared at headquarters, no one could be sure.[33] "Rockefeller's doings are never heard of," one newspaper had observed in 1904. "When he gets to his office at 26 Broadway, New York, not even his clerks are aware of it."[34] Sneaking in and out undetected was easy. "He employs 25,000 men and not more than 300 of them ever saw him," the frustrated reporter complained.[35]

Rockefeller's mysteriousness was intentional. Standard Oil had gotten into deep trouble due to a highly incriminating exposé that revealed the company's widespread, intricate, deep-rooted, and illegal web of collusion and abusive business practices. This bombshell report was painstakingly researched and written by a pioneering investigative journalist named Ida Minerva Tarbell.[36] Tarbell showed the world what ordinary people had suspected all along: Rockefeller intentionally ruined many small businesses and hardworking people's lives using blatantly unfair tactics. "I judge him by the golden rule," she declared in the summer of 1905.[37] Her revelation caused so much public outrage that it led the government to prosecute Standard Oil for violating the Sherman Antitrust Act of 1890.

President Theodore Roosevelt, inaugurated in January, had been elected to a full term in office promising to continue his "Square Deal" policies that ensured fairness to average citizens. So, with full public support, he ordered the federal government's Bureau of Corporations to begin an official investigation of Standard Oil. That was followed by a string of indictments and lawsuits at the state level. "No one should have any pity for Standard Oil in the mauling it is about to receive at the hands of President Roosevelt," wrote a popular businessman and author, Thomas W. Lawson. "Rockefeller sees the handwriting on the wall and is now genuinely frightened, that the disintegration of Standard Oil is beginning."[38] By mid-June 1905, the company's stock value had dropped from $840 to $600 a share, a paper loss of around $200 million, or about $5 billion today. It was no surprise when Rockefeller's son, John D. Rockefeller, Jr., who was his father's heir and successor, experienced a "temporary breakdown in health."[39]

As one of Standard Oil's newest employees, Will knew he had to do his job really well. The company's very existence was at stake, so every document was closely guarded. In any highly volatile business situation, certain correspondence was so sensitive that nothing less than person-to-person hand delivery was considered safe. Only the most trustworthy, reliable, and personable couriers got those assignments. In addition, there was so much civic resentment against the company that its messengers were openly targeted. On a roadway near Richmond, California, in March 1905, armed holdup men "jumped out of a clump of brush at the side of the road" and robbed a Standard Oil messenger of $10,000 at gunpoint.[40] But he got zero sympathy. That amount was nothing "compared to the millions which the Rockefeller outfit has extorted from the public," wrote the *Los Angeles Times*.[41] ROCKEFELLER FEARS FOR HIS PERSONAL SAFETY, another headline blared in July of that year, noting that heavy security had been set up at his residences.[42]

In November, the New York State Supreme Court issued subpoenas for the tycoon and his executives to give testimony in a suit filed by the State of Missouri against the Standard Oil Company. Their official response was to assure stockholders that "your directors are entirely convinced that the company's position is unassailable from both a legal and a moral standpoint."[43] But history proved them wrong. Though it would take two years for the Bureau of Corporations to unravel the whole scheme, it found so much incriminating evidence that the government was able to file an antitrust lawsuit against Standard Oil in November 1906, which led to the company's eventual breakup in 1911 into thirty-two different business units.

Through all of this drama, Will performed his duties faithfully and won friends on all levels, from the lowly streets to the stately suites. Before long, everyone called the diligent messenger by an informal version of his first name, including the Rockefellers themselves, John and John Jr. To them, he was "Billy," the "colored" messenger.[44] Working in the same skyscraper only a few floors apart from one of the wealthiest men on earth was as close to the top as a kid from Little Africa could ever have imagined climbing. Horatio Alger may have been right—a poor boy really could rise.[45]

The country's most popular touring theatrical production in 1905 was a Black-owned-and-operated minstrel-style vaudeville comedy called *The Smart Set*. Promising "more hearty laughs than ever seen with any colored show before," its ensemble of fifty African American performers included "a chorus of 30 dusky maidens." The company's tour dates in January alone had included the Rhode Opera House in Kenosha, Wisconsin; the Illinois Theater in Rock Island, Illinois; the Grand Opera House in Des Moines, Iowa; the Oliver Theater in Lincoln, Nebraska; the Krug Playhouse in Omaha, Nebraska; the Lyceum in St. Joseph, Missouri; and the Kansas City Auditorium, following a "remarkable run" at the Fourteenth Street Theatre in New York City, where it was based. Ticket prices ranged from 25 cents to $1. The production actually went beyond minstrelsy though, because instead of portraying "negroes" in stereotypically demeaning, "traditionally Southern" terms, it dared for the first time ever to depict modern, recognizable African American characters who were relatable to Black people on their own terms. Ironically, that made the production even more popular among Whites, even while African Americans were frequently prohibited from sitting in the audience. As a commentary on race through a Black cultural lens, *The Smart Set* was revolutionary, later hailed as "a singular vehicle for constructive change on the American stage."[46]

The entire elaborate stage production, which had premiered in 1896 and would run for more than two decades, was a parody of the popular term "smart set," which referred to the most fashionable and elite elements of society. The highly successful *Smart Set* magazine had derived its name from that phrase when it launched in 1900. Popular among White literati as "the cleverest of magazines," the publication was in the vanguard for years, running society news, essays, political satire, and short stories by promising young authors such as Jack London, Dorothy Parker, D. H. Lawrence, and F. Scott Fitzgerald.

So when Samuel Scottron reminded his audience of African American friends and associates at the Carlton Avenue Colored YMCA in February 1904 to acquire whatever means necessary to "fit themselves for the race of life," he was speaking in terms that were just as revolutionary, directly to Brooklyn's own Black smart set.[47] Insisting that more than words were needed, Scottron let his actions do the talking by cofounding a new African American social and physical fitness organization. Fittingly, it would be called the Smart Set Athletic Club of Brooklyn. Most of its founding members were either directly related to Scottron, part of his extended family through marriage, or linked to him through family friendships and business connections.[48] They included the elder Scottron; his sons Oscar and Cyrus; his grandson Charles; Charles's pals Errol Horne, Edwin "Teddy" Horne, Jr., Ferdinand Accooe, and Frank Holbrook; Samuel's granddaughter Edna Louise Scottron; and a host of others in what some termed the borough's affluent African American elite.[49] Theirs was a tight-knit circle, so intimate that Teddy Horne and Edna Louise would eventually marry and have a daughter—Lena Horne, the future world-renowned entertainer. "The club concentrated on wholesome family-oriented get-togethers," Lena's daughter, Gail Lumet Buckley, later explained.[50]

Inside the Smart Set AC clubhouse, at 44 Troy Avenue between Atlantic Avenue and Herkimer Street in Bedford (across the street from a neighborhood green space known as Harmony Park in today's Bedford-Stuyvesant neighborhood), activities would encourage camaraderie toward Black cultural advancement. That meant debate about social issues, athletics, politics, education, and business as well as recitals, skits, readings, art reviews, and, of course, music and dancing. These individuals weren't just prima donnas, though. The organization was about to lay the groundwork for how basketball was to be played among African Americans and would soon become a powerful force uniting other Black athletic organizations throughout the New York City area.

John D. Rockefeller was not the only mysterious person in the Standard Oil Building in 1905. Walking its hallways was a tall thirty-seven-year-old African American executive messenger named James H. Woods. He was Will Anthony Madden's boss. But as Will discovered, there was more to his supervisor than that.

Woods' coworkers knew him as James H. Woods, the way his name appeared in the *New York City Directory*. But after work, when Woods was among family, friends, peers, and associates or at his Brooklyn home, on MacDonough Street in Bedford, he was "J. Hoffman Woods"—one of the most influential and admired African American figures in New York City. Woods was also one of the other cofounders of the Smart Set Athletic Club. He even served as the organization's president and general manager. In fact, the club's athletic programs were under Woods's leadership. This was Will's direct connection into the emerging world of Black sports.

Woods had an improbable climb to prominence. The son of a "mulatto" ship's cook from London and a Black native New Yorker who kept house, he was born in Brooklyn in 1868 as the youngest of eight children and grew up in the borough's Crown Heights neighborhood. In 1894, at twenty-six, he secured employment as a clerk at Astral Oil Works, a kerosene refinery in the nearby Williamsburg section of Brooklyn.[51] Astral had been founded in 1867 by a petroleum industry pioneer named Charles Pratt. Pratt's business became so successful that Standard Oil purchased it in 1874, keeping its founder on board and allowing Astral to retain its original name. Pratt went on to become one of Standard Oil's top executives, collecting a fortune as the corporation grew into a monopoly. In 1886, he invested that wealth in his own community by establishing and endowing the Pratt Institute in the Clinton Hill neighborhood of Brooklyn, a college known today for its top-ranked programs in architecture and design.

Woods would become much more than just a clerk at Astral. From the outset, he exhibited "a graciousness" and "a courtliness that has no counterpart," rising quickly through the company's administrative ranks to become an accountant and then a messenger before being promoted to executive messenger. Through hard work, reliability, and loyalty, he made himself invaluable. "The name of Woods is familiar to everyone in the building," the *Baltimore Afro-American* wrote in a 1931 profile. He was "known as a friend of his fellow workers," it was said. "Their troubles are his troubles." Woods was one of only fifty Black men employed in the Standard Oil Building, and his true significance became evident when Pratt's son, a twenty-three-year-old recent Amherst College graduate named Herbert Lee Pratt, joined Astral in 1896. Woods, three years older than Herbert, was selected to assist the newcomer, helping him get acquainted not only within the organization but also, as it turned out, within the scheme of life as a kind of mentor.[52]

The two began a unique, long-lasting bond that went beyond the call of normal duty. "It is hard in these times to approximate, explain or understand the relationship of J. Hoffman Woods and Herbert L. Pratt," a *New York Age* newspaper columnist wrote in 1948. Woods was an usher in Herbert's wedding in 1897, and he subsequently attended the nuptials of each of Herbert's five children. Woods even did the man's personal shopping, "whether it be the sheerest of linens, the rarest of vintage wines, or the perfection of the special-made Havana cigars."[53] So, as the younger Pratt moved up within the Standard Oil hierarchy, Woods went with him. Even after Rockefeller's monopoly was broken up by the U.S. Supreme Court, Woods continued his role at the newly formed Standard Oil Company of New York, known as Socony, the largest of the court-ordered corporate fragments. Herbert would stay on, too, eventually becoming the company's president while its headquarters remained at 26 Broadway. Woods would have his own office there, in the boardroom suite two doors down the hallway from Herbert. "In my thirty-five years with the company, I have never had but one messenger, James H. Woods," the younger Pratt would say in 1931, the year his company merged with the Vacuum Oil Company to form the Socony-Vacuum Corporation.[54]

All of this was worth it to Woods, whose influence at Standard Oil gave him what seemed like carte blanche leverage to hire and mentor African Americans within the messenger department. Several members of the Smart Set AC would eventually be employed there. But his intimate relationship with Herbert Pratt also opened a door for Woods into an aristocratic circle where sociability and an appreciation for finer details were the norm. The young executive messenger was already so talented as a dancer that he had belonged to the Metropolitan Association of Dancing Masters for years, even inventing "a very pretty *varsouvienne* called the Lenox" in 1894. (The varsouvienne, or varsoviana, was a slow, graceful dance that originated in Poland and combined elements of the waltz, mazurka, and polka.)[55] These qualities made him stand out as a highly attractive bachelor as well. Before long, Woods was courting a nineteen-year-old Brooklyn girl named Marie Rosena Van Dyke. She was the heiress to a fortune that had been earned by her father, a highly successful African American catering entrepreneur named John Frederick Van Dyke, who was said to have been a distant descendant of the original Dutch settlers of New Amsterdam by that surname. Chivalry paid off for Woods when, on

June 21, 1899, he and Marie were married. The ceremony was at St. Philip's Church, to which the Van Dyke family belonged, and was officiated by the Reverend Dr. Hutchens Chew Bishop.[56]

The couple temporarily moved in with Marie's mother, John Van Dyke's widow, Mary, who lived at 217 Stuyvesant Avenue in the Stuyvesant Heights section of Brooklyn, a predominantly White neighborhood at that time. Woods was already well connected within the borough's Black community, but even more now that he lived right around the corner from the incomparable Samuel Scottron and his family, who were on Monroe Street, and both men belonged to Carthaginian Lodge, No. 47.[57] In short, Woods hung out with New York City's topmost Black society. All of these connections opened doors, which he and his wife used to give back by devoting themselves as volunteers to local charities such as the Willing Workers' Circle of the King's Daughters.[58] That organization staged elaborate events, led by Woods as its popular master of ceremonies, to raise money in support of the Brooklyn Home for Aged Colored People. One of his Willing Workers' fundraisers, during that summer of 1905, included tennis, boating, croquet, dancing, and an orchestra, as well as a baseball game between the Carlton Avenue Colored YMCA and New York City YMCA Colored Men's branches.[59]

These upscale worlds of Black and White refinement were previously inaccessible to Will Anthony Madden, who, though well-read and well-schooled, was ultimately from Little Africa, with all its perceptions. Breaking through into these ranks would have required a social pedigree, which the messenger simply did not have nor could ever obtain—that is, until he met James H. Woods, aka J. Hoffman Woods, at Standard Oil.

CHAPTER 10

GREAT STRUGGLE FOR VICTORY

IN EARLY JANUARY 1906, BOOKER T. Washington sent his eighteen-year-old son Booker Jr., some gifts from New York City, where he was preparing to deliver a speech at Carnegie Hall in celebration of the twenty-fifth anniversary of the founding of his Tuskegee Normal and Industrial Institute. "The Negro in many ways has proven his worth and loyalty to this country," the tireless race leader and social activist would state in his fundraising appeal, saying he had faith that the opportunity for the African American to serve even more efficiently in the future "will be given to him."[1] Washington was considered "one of the greatest men of the present generation, in the world, irrespective of race." But an entirely new genre of Black voices was being heard, more ready and willing to call out systemic racism and oppression. "The chief criticism of Dr. Washington is with respect to what he leaves unsaid," the *Baltimore Afro-American* had explained a year earlier. "With respect to the suffrage matter and the civil rights of the Negro, Dr. Washington has been most cautious and exceedingly careful in his public utterances."[2]

Black folks were torn. But not Washington, who waged his battles wisely in public as well as in private. He publicly regretted not having had "time for sports."[3] And his advocacy for African Americans to strive for "a sounder, healthier body" continued. Now he was putting those words into action, if not for himself, then with thoughtful presents for his next of kin, Booker Jr. "My dear Papa," the teenager wrote back, from Tuskegee, Alabama, "I received the things that you sent me, the skates, the basket ball, and the fruit."[4] Evidently, the hardwood sport had made a believer out of the elder Washington.

At the same time in Brooklyn, instigated by Samuel Scottron and under the leadership of J. Hoffman Woods, the Smart Set Athletic Club was beginning to develop sports teams for competition against other organizations.

Responsibility for that initiative was put into the hands of a nineteen-year-old Smart Set club member named George Lattimore, Jr., who lived in Bedford at 243 Halsey Street, a short walk from Woods's home at 257 MacDonough Street.

George Jr., was born in New York City, where he grew up with his two younger brothers, Robert and Matthew. All three had a knack for business. Their father, George Sr., had been an ambitious office clerk who taught himself the necessary skills to become a stenographer. Stenography was a valuable talent that enabled upward mobility, especially for African Americans. Using elaborate shorthand and speed typing techniques, they were responsible for much if not all of a business executive's inbound and outgoing correspondence, which included preparing the mail itself. Most were male. At a time when even college-educated Black men often had no choice but to accept employment as postal clerks, stewards, porters, and similar service jobs, African American stenographers were part of a well-respected and influential brotherhood. Often considered more loyal, reliable, and dedicated than their White counterparts, they were in constant demand by high-profile corporate executives and politicians, whose communications frequently contained confidential information. "WANTED—A COLORED STENOGRAPHER WHO can take dictation and write on a Smith Premier typewriter," read a 1903 want ad in Washington, D.C. "None other need apply."[5]

George Sr., was so trusted that he eventually became the private secretary of none other than Robert Pinkerton, who, along with his twin brother, William, was a coprincipal of the Pinkerton National Detective Agency, the pinnacle of secrecy, which had coined the term "private eye." George Sr., had such high regard for his employer that he gave his second son, Robert, the middle name "Pinkerton."[6]

As kids, the Lattimore brothers had lived in the Tenderloin District, as well as in San Juan Hill, and then on Gold Street in Brooklyn, until their father died suddenly in 1893, the year George Jr., turned six. Robert Pinkerton, their late father's former employer, who was the son of the agency's famous cofounder Allan Pinkerton, also lived in Brooklyn.[7] The boys' widowed mother, Evelyn, was remarried to a socially prominent African American bank clerk named Fredrick B. Watkins, employed in the auditing and accounting department at the New York Trust Company. Watkins, a lifelong resident of Brooklyn, lived in Bedford and was a trustee of St. Augustine Protestant Episcopal Church, where many members of the Smart Set social circle worshipped. So his stepsons became part of that same clique.

George Jr., had a take-charge mindset, and although described as "a most prominent worker for clean athletic sport among young men" in general, he would become the driving force behind the Smart Set's specific push into basketball.[8] Yet that wasn't enough. "Lattimore and his Smart Set fellows led the fight to get colored athletes recognized by the A.A.U.," the *Baltimore Afro-American* sports columnist Leon Hardwick later wrote. "Prior to that time, colored star athletes in track and field, as well as basketball, were almost unheard of," Lattimore explained. "When we first applied for membership, we were flatly refused."[9]

Through their stepfather, Fredrick, all three Lattimore sons got business experience working as office clerks. George Jr., followed in his late father's footsteps to become a stenographer. His younger brother Robert became a superb athlete who would play basketball for the Smart Set Athletic Club and later become a successful Park Row attorney specializing in immigration. And the youngest sibling, Matthew, would become a partner in a printing shop. During the 1910s, George Jr., would become an officer in the New York Branch of the National Association for the Advancement of Colored People (NAACP), as secretary of the organization alongside its founders, Mary White Ovington, James Weldon Johnson, John E. Nail, and Arthur Spingarn.[10] But all of this was only the beginning of his fascinating legacy.

Meanwhile, J. Hoffman Woods was connected to St. Philip's Church through his pastor, Bishop, and that gave him and the Smart Set access to the St. Christopher Club, where the athletic director, Father Daniel, was looking to expand onto the hardcourt as well. This allowed the two groups to spark a collaboration. "Three years ago little was heard and less was known of the science of basketball among the colored athletic associations in this vicinity, at which time the Smart Set Club of Brooklyn organized the first team, and shortly after the St. Christopher Club of New York entered the field," the *New York Age* recalled in 1909.[11] By then the "St. C" club membership had shot up to several hundred youths, so many that Father Daniel launched a monthly newsletter. To oversee the new publication, the priest assigned a young man he had gotten to know, who worked as a messenger at Standard Oil and possibly had been recommended by Woods. This person seemed capable, educated, and responsible as well as talented in "literary research work."[12] His name was Will Anthony Madden, and Father Daniel made him the editor of the St. Christopher bulletin, which was christened *The Red Raven*.[13]

In turn, Father Daniel and the Alpha Physical Culture Club founder Conrad Norman had apparently been bonding within their familiar West Indian circles. This allowed a collective relationship to sprout among Woods, Father Daniel, Norman, and their people, which meant a Black entrepreneurially athletic mindset now connected Brooklyn, Midtown, and Harlem. Something similar was happening in the District of Columbia.

Shortly after Edwin Bancroft "EB" Henderson returned from the Summer School of Physical Education at Harvard in 1904 and secured work as an instructor in the city's physical culture department, his father moved from the family's old home in the District of Columbia out to Falls Church, Virginia, joining EB's grandmother Eliza, who had already relocated there. EB got a raise at year's end from $50 to $52.50 a month, which was substantial enough, more than $1,500 today, to help him fund a new apartment at 760 Harvard Street NW just off Seventh Street, right across from Howard University.

EB kept promoting and teaching basketball to African American students throughout the District, but he soon found that their schools, and others like them in the area, did not have a way of competing against one another in that sport. This was because the AAU did not recognize them; they had "very modest means" and did not have the funds nor alumni who could contribute the sums needed.[14] To explore solutions, he enlisted the help of five other African American physical education teachers in the area. They were W. J. Decatur and William A. Joiner of Howard University, Garnet C. Wilkinson of M Street High School, Robert N. Mattingly of Armstrong Manual Technical Training School, and Ralph Cook of the Baltimore Colored High School. In early 1906, after discussing the situation in Joiner's office at Howard University, they cofounded a new African American sports organization called the Inter-Scholastic Athletic Association of Middle Atlantic States, or ISAA. Its membership would consist of intercollegiate and interscholastic athletes from the surrounding area. With an original focus on track and field, these men pooled $400 of their personal funds to build an oval on the Howard

University grounds, because the college's trustees declined to pay for it. Just a few months later, the association staged its first event, a track meet at the college, on May 30, 1906. About a hundred athletes competed, representing Howard, M Street, Armstrong Tech, the Baltimore Colored YMCA, Baltimore Colored High School, Wilmington High, the Washington Colored YMCA, and "several local athletic clubs." On the business side, entry fees collected from "the largest crowd that had ever gathered on the University campus" covered nearly all of the ISAA's total prior costs.[15]

There was also an exhibition basketball matchup staged between players from Armstrong Tech and M Street High School, along the lines of an intramural game.[16] This planted the seeds for the ISAA to form its own basketball league the following season.

In the summer of 1906, nearly two months after the ISAA track meet at Howard University, the relationship that connected J. Hoffman Woods, Father Everard Daniel, and Conrad Norman brought Black athletes from Brooklyn, Manhattan, and Harlem together for the first time in head-to-head competition. To pull this off, the gentlemen devised a fundraising effort to support the Mother's Day Nursery, an African American charity at 129 Willoughby Street in Fort Greene, with a mission of "caring for the colored children of Brooklyn, whose mothers were forced to go out working daily." Led by the Alpha PCC, they did it by staging a picnic on July 20, 1906, at a Brooklyn-based family resort called Ulmer Park, located along the shores of Gravesend Bay between Bath Beach and Coney Island. Considered "one of the finest picnic grounds in all of Brooklyn," it had been opened in 1893 by William Ulmer, founder of the nearby Ulmer Brewery, with "all the first-class accommodations" including bowling alleys, shooting ranges, a dance hall, a hotel, and "spacious grounds for games."[17]

Promotional newspaper ads for the occasion promised "something new," namely, "athletics." In addition to a friendly baseball game, the afternoon would feature a track and field meet. Woods, president of the Smart Set, would be the master of ceremonies for the event and also perform duties as one of the meet officials. In response, "more than 1,500 persons were present," an astonishing number of supporters for a first-of-its-kind effort.[18]

Most had been able to hop on a Third Avenue Line streetcar or catch an elevated train on the Fifth Avenue Line out of downtown Brooklyn directly to the park. After paying the 35-cent admission fee, they were welcomed by the S. L. Painter Orchestra, an African American ensemble known to have "a good supply of excellent music." The meet included competitors from the Alpha PCC, the St. Christopher Club, and a new outfit, the Marathon Athletic Club, a Brooklyn-based organization affiliated with St. Augustine's Church. There were numerous young athletes in that congregation who weren't members of the Smart Set Athletic Club but did belong to the nearby Carlton Avenue Colored YMCA. That branch's president was a serious-minded African American stenographer named Clarence E. Lucas, who lived in Fort Greene.

As a stenographer, Lucas worked for George Foster Peabody, the millionaire chief benefactor of the Carlton Avenue Colored YMCA branch who had donated the building itself. A resident of Brooklyn Heights who grew up in Fort Greene, Peabody was active in social causes and an advocate for advancing educational opportunities for African Americans as a director of the American Church Institute for Negroes, the Negro Rural School Fund, and the General Education Board. He also was an eventual trustee of the Hampton Institute. Lucas taught classes in his stenography craft as well as physiology, hygiene, and vocal music at the branch, which offered programs designed to provide meaningful culture, education, training, and moral uplift to its members. On one typical Sunday afternoon, "Miss Mary M. Gray delivered an instructive lecture on the 'Effects of Narcotics Upon the Human System,'" after which "Mr. S. B. Williams presided at the piano and Mr. Clarence C. Clark sang a baritone solo."[19] The stenographer had a whimsical side, too, as an active member in a fraternal group of Black theatergoers called the Serene Unique Antlership Constituency of the Beneficent Philanthropic Order of Roebucks of America and Elsewhere, Incorporated. He served as its Supreme Obelus-Roebuck in the Supreme Lodge. "Just as beauty in art cannot be comprehended by a mathematical formula, so Unique Antlership cannot be obtained by mechanical means," explained a report about its ability "to comprehendingly judge a Negro production."[20]

In the Ulmer Park meet, there were medals and points awarded for placing, and beyond that, a healthy spirit of one-upmanship and a sense among the African American and Black West Indian organizers and athletes that they were part of something bigger than themselves. Conrad Norman tied for first place in the high jump, and his brother Clifton won the 220-yard sprint, contributing to 18 points for the Alpha PCC, enough to win the meet. They were followed by St. Christopher with 15 and the Marathons with 3 points. Yet for one individual, there was also a large dose of pride on the line. Father Daniel, the *New York Age* reported, "had his feelings badly hurt at the very outset because he and his boys, who were to take part in the athletic games, had to pay their way into the grounds" while the Alpha Physical Culture Club runners were admitted for free. But that was because the Alphas had paid for the officials, "whose services were worth nearly $20 to the meet." It got worse. "Rev. Daniel's passions were also exasperated at the end of the 220-yard dash," the event that Clifton won. One of the clergyman's St. Christopher runners would have placed second if he hadn't slowed down going through the tape, which allowed a Marathon AC runner to win second place. "Rev. Daniel nevertheless protested," the *New York Age* said, since for whatever reason the priest thought he saw it differently, "but the judge, J. Hoffman Woods, firmly disagreed." Finally, enough was enough for the St. Christopher athletic director. "Having had his temper thus irritated, Rev. Daniel decided that he hadn't had his money's worth," the newspaper explained, at which point he "proceeded to the entrance and for a half-hour wearied the lady in charge with demands for his money." The frustrated priest kept trying. "At last, however, he had to go off without it."[21]

African American athletes such as the sprinter George C. Poage, who had won two bronze medals at the 1904 Olympic Games, were making great strides in track and field. "But seldom do we have an athletic meet," the *New York Age* argued, "conducted solely by and for Afro-American athletic clubs." Not only that, but "all the officials were Afro-Americans, and the meet was conducted according to the rules of the Amateur Athletic Union of the United States." Yet the takeaway narrative was that "the crowd was treated to the entertaining spectacle of an irate clergyman loudly demanding his money back out of the funds raised for charity."[22] The fact that one man, especially a man of the cloth, made his own grievance more important than the event's significance, its worthy cause, and all the effort that had gone into staging it, must have been disappointing. In contrast to his pre-graduation assessment while in seminary, this behavior was certainly not clean of any "error in religion or viciousness of life."

Regardless, as winter approached, Woods and George Lattimore, Jr., built on the Ulmer meet's otherwise positive momentum by taking steps to assemble a basketball team for the Smart Set Athletic Club. This was the first formally organized, fully independent, stand-alone, all-Black basketball team in history. There had been previous African American squads that were found on playgrounds, in schoolyards, in gym classes, and in intramural groups. They had had affiliations with churches, schools, colleges, YMCAs, or other entities, each one restricted by its own obligatory institutional guidelines. On the other hand, this Smart Set basketball program was free to conduct its business any way it wished. That alone was powerful. And the squad's actual roster was more than just solid.

Charles "Charlie" Scottron, a midsize and muscular seventeen-year-old known for his "brilliant shots," was the team's captain. Samuel Scottron's grandson, he grew up on Kosciusko Avenue in Bushwick and was a student at Public School No. 26 on Gates Avenue. Chester Barton Moore, a brawny shipping clerk, was twenty years old and lived in Bedford near the corner of Gates and Marcy Avenues. One of the team's tallest players, Chester was also confident about the basketball rulebook. Robert Barnard, a Texas native who was also twenty, lived on West 148th Street in Harlem. Known as "a fast sprinter," he had won the 100-yard dash at the Ulmer meet and was connected with the well-known athletic teams of the Clark Settlement House on the Lower East Side.[23] Harold "Harry" Brown, another twenty-year-old and a track athlete, was "a very fast man at any distance from 300 yards to one mile." He worked as a printer and lived on Chauncey Street, in Bedford. George Cooper Trice was a sixteen-year-old cross-country runner, also a student at P.S. 26 and resident of Bedford, who lived on Van Buren Street. Robert Lattimore, the younger brother of George Jr. and eighteen years old, was experienced in track and field and had "done well as a sprinter, hurdler, and broad jumper."[24] Finally, Alfred D. Groves was a rising athletic talent. Though only a role player with the Smart Set basketball team, Groves would eventually prove his physical prowess at the organization's annual track meet of 1909, outscoring Smart Set teammates Charlie Scottron and Robert Lattimore to win the club championship.[25]

What made the Smart Set Athletic Club so special was that its membership stretched from the veteran activists of the 1800s like Samuel Scottron, in his sixties, to its teenage voices like George Lattimore, Jr., who would be a changemaker for decades into the 1900s. To bridge this span, the group added its own monthly publication called the *Junior Smart Set*, which contained "all the spot news of the younger set's doings." George Jr., was "prominent on the editorial staff," while his brother Robert became the publication's business manager.[26] Like the St. Christopher Club's *Red Raven* newsletter, the main goal of the *Junior Smart Set* monthly was to stay in touch. And, brilliantly, it offered something for everyone. "The Smart Set was to grow into one of the most important organizations in the whole bourgeois network, uniting all generations," Gail Lumet Buckley later explained, "and it definitely stressed sports."[27]

Now it was Father Daniel's turn. In late 1906, when the athletic director began constructing a basketball program for St. Philip's, demand for roster spots was so high among the many St. Christopher Club members that he had to form two teams. The first was called the St. Christopher Big Five, where the term "Big" (or "Senior") was an official Amateur Athletic Union designation for any team with an average player weight of 125 pounds or more. The second squad was the St. Christopher Juniors, where "Junior" was used for rosters whose average player weight was below 125 pounds. When completed, Father Daniel's inaugural lineup for the St. Christopher Big Five, nicknamed the "St. C's," was stacked with athletes, all from Manhattan.

The team was captained by Clarence Fleming "Pop" Lewis, a sixteen-year-old who lived on West Thirtieth Street near the St. Philip's Parish House. The son of a well-known Tenderloin barber, he would later star in basketball at Howard University before moving to the South Side of Chicago to manage a famous African American hostelry there called the Vincennes Hotel; later he would run the 113 Club, a popular Bronzeville café.[28] George Frederic Clayton was an eighteen-year-old student at DeWitt Clinton High who lived on Park Avenue in Manhattan. He would graduate with honors from Columbia University's College of Pharmacy in 1910 and become a well-known druggist in Harlem. Shelton Hale Bishop was the eighteen-year-old son of the Reverend Hutchens Chew Bishop, the rector at St. Philip's, and lived in the church's Parish House on West Thirtieth, two doors down from teammate Clarence Lewis. Shelton would eventually succeed his father to lead the church as its pastor from the 1930s into the late 1950s. Charles W. Bradford was a former football and basketball player at the Hampton Normal & Agricultural Institute in Virginia Beach, known today as Hampton University. He would become a popular community leader, at one point representing Harlem as a New York City alderman.

Will Anthony Madden, hailing from Greenwich Village and Little Africa, wasn't an athlete and would never make any sports roster despite his innuendo about kinship with heavyweight boxing champ Jim Corbett. But he was determined to be involved with the club's basketball program some other way. That's how the St. C Big Five made him their "mascot." Mascots were to basketball teams as the ornate figureheads decorating the bows of tall sailing ships were to bringing good luck to their crews. This embedded Will among the players not only figuratively but also literally when he posed in front of the team for its official studio photograph. This poor boy had become a messenger and the editor of the *Red Raven*, then an insider connected with one of the country's most respected and socially prominent African American churches. Surely this proved "what energy, ambition, and an honest purpose may achieve."

In early 1907, the men of the St. Christopher Big Five and the Smart Set Athletic Club scheduled a string of games between their basketball squads, to begin in November. They called this series the Olympian Athletic League, perhaps inspired by the ideals of the III Olympiad. But the organizations needed a third team in order for the OAL to be a true league. The Reverend John Wesley Johnson and his St. Cyprian program didn't have a team yet because their gymnasium-equipped parish house was still under construction. A logical choice would have been the Alpha Physical Culture Club, with a roster of its members managed by Conrad Norman. But any of their plans to form a squad had to be cut short in mid-January after a deadly earthquake demolished most of Kingston, Jamaica, the Normans' hometown, killing more than eight hundred residents.[29] It would be two years before the Alpha PCC was ready to debut a basketball team.

To fill this void, St. Christopher and Smart Set officials approached the Marathon Athletic Club of the Carlton Avenue Colored YMCA proposing that they form a squad. The Carlton Y having its own basketball team was an opportunity not only for camaraderie and competition but also for its president,

Clarence E. Lucas, to promote and reinforce the solid work being done by his YMCA membership. That the Carlton facility lacked a gymnasium was no obstacle. Lucas set up a basketball squad anyway, and the Olympian Athletic League was rendered complete.

The first Marathon AC roster included several notable athletes.

Among them was Ferdinand Accooe, an eighteen-year-old from Fort Greene, with a large wingspan and a long build, who was exceptionally athletic and had a bright future in the sport on several other important all-Black squads. The surname Accooe was already famous because his father, a Pennsylvania-born clergyman named John H. Accooe, was the pastor of the Bishops Chapel Methodist Episcopal Church on West 135th Street in Harlem. Ferdinand was also the younger brother of the late Willis J. Accooe, who, before his untimely death in 1904, had been the brilliant writer, producer, and musical director for African American theatrical pioneers Bob Cole, Bert Williams, J. Rosemond Johnson, and Will Marion Cook. There was also Earle Smith, a well-known long-distance runner who had won the one-mile race in several open track meets, at guard.[30] He worked as a clerk and lived on Monroe Street in Bedford, not far from the Carlton YMCA. And nineteen-year-old Alonzo F. Chadwick, Jr., lived on Fulton Street in Bedford. James L. Kingsland, also nineteen and from Stuyvesant Heights, was a stocky and muscular guard.

As exclusive as they seemed, the Black social, athletic, academic, and community organizations of New York City and Washington, D.C., did not keep to themselves as isolated factions. They were well acquainted with one another and supportive of each other's efforts through ongoing events, in which they often participated together to raise money for causes that benefited the greater, higher good. Their collaborative behavior would become the model for clubs in Chicago and Pittsburgh, where such support systems for African American physical culture organizers would soon emerge.

In the District of Columbia, EB and his ISAA collaborators had begun staging track competitions for their members. A three-mile cross-country run through Rock Creek Park on April 2, 1907, during the gorgeous peak of the city's cherry blossom season, featured contenders from M Street High, Armstrong Tech, and a local African American group calling itself the Oberlin Athletic Club. It was officiated by a volunteer from Howard University.[31] The runners from M Street won the event with 17 out of a possible 25 points. Athletes from these clubs and schools would soon form the nucleus of a new basketball league that the ISAA was planning.

Then, in July 1907, St. Augustine's Church staged an afternoon and evening fundraiser at Ulmer Park similar to the one held there the previous summer. This one included the St. Christopher Club, the Marathon AC, the Alpha Physical Culture Club, and the Smart Set AC, all volunteering their services. One member of the Alpha club brought a special guest, his friend, the African American arctic explorer Matthew Henson, who would soon be credited with being the first human to set foot on the North Pole.[32] After the daytime activities, the individual social clubs staged a "Grand March" at midnight to the musical accompaniment of Walter E. Craig's Full Orchestra, a popular all-Black ensemble "conceded to be the best ball room orchestra in New York barring none white or black."[33] Overall, that picnic was considered an enormous collaborative success, with a newspaper estimate of one thousand African Americans attending. And the funds raised that day were essential to those New York City organizations, because some of the total would go toward their upcoming 1907–8 basketball season.

Soon, the Smart Set Athletic Club, the St. Christopher Big Five, and the Carlton YMCA Marathons—the three teams of the Olympian Athletic League—were trained and ready. The "round robin" league arrangement called for each of the three squads to play one another three times. The first game of their inaugural series was scheduled for mid-November. Now it was time to play ball.

On the cold and rainy Wednesday night of November 13, 1907, a lively crowd of African American citizens was gathered in the predominantly White section of Brooklyn known as Bushwick, deep in the heart of the borough. They were inside a handball facility called the Knickerbocker Court for a sporting event that was scheduled to begin "promptly at 8:40 P.M."[34] The venue, a twenty-five-foot-wide and eighty-four-foot-long building located on Gates Avenue just off the corner of Knickerbocker Avenue, was a high-ceiling one-story wood-frame gravel-roofed structure "lit by electric light." Originally built as a handball court in 1900 at a cost of about $1,000, the facility was home to the Knickerbocker Handball Club of Brooklyn. "The new court is well constructed and has a finely polished floor of selected hardwood," the *Brooklyn Daily Eagle* had reported when it opened, adding that, "a gallery is being built around the court capable of accommodating three hundred spectators."[35] Handball had been the borough's most popular athletic activity, especially among immigrants from Ireland, and was affectionately called "the oldest Irish pastime known."[36] Brooklyn was dotted with courts like these, nicknamed "handball alleys."

But these "more than 100 enthusiastic persons" hadn't come to witness handball. As they began to settle in, only a few tense moments remained before the tip-off of the first official game ever played between two fully independent, formally organized all-Black basketball teams. That night, the Knickerbocker Court was the perfect venue for the occasion.

This would be a historic duel. Seated and standing, onlookers and rival clusters of vocal fanatical supporters known as "rooters" surrounded the basketball court at floor level and in raised bleachers. League organizers had selected the Marathons as the home team to host the St. Christopher Club. This created a Manhattan versus Brooklyn scenario. The rivalry between the two boroughs was no secret. Not to mention that the Black congregations of St. Augustine's in Brooklyn, which backed the Marathons, and St. Philip's in Manhattan, backing the St. Christophers, were facing off in a kind of church skirmish for bragging rights.

In many ways, Brooklyn had the edge. For years, it was viewed as New York City's attractive residential enclave for buttoned-up African American affluence and influence in business, politics, academia, religion, and politics, while Black people in Manhattan seemed left with hotels, vaudeville, music, nightlife, and vice. Two of the three Olympian Athletic League teams were based in Brooklyn. And although Brooklyn's total population reached a historic high in 1907, the flow of European immigrants into greater New York City, with its resultant overcrowding, showed no sign of slowing down as travel to America kept getting cheaper and easier. The night of the Marathon vs. St. Christopher basketball game, a transatlantic steamship named the RMS *Carpathia* wired ahead that she was midway through an eighteen-day voyage from England to the Port of New York, on schedule to arrive in a week. Only four years old and carrying 2,273 passengers, *Carpathia* was the first such vessel built exclusively for second- and third-class travel. A one-way cabin rate from Liverpool to New York City was $12.50.[37] Ellis Island would process a record number of newcomers the same year, with 1,004,756 arrivals.[38]

Basketball was gaining interest among African Americans, but in contrast, EB's promotional efforts to expand the game in Washington, D.C., had been limited to scrimmages on playgrounds, in schoolyards, during physical education, and in intramural competition, not against outside squads. So, the African American crowd at the Knickerbocker Court that night was about to experience a refreshing and worthy milestone.

It was game time. Chester Moore, the muscular twenty-year-old shipping clerk, was the referee. Holding the basketball, he strolled to the middle of the hardwood court and blew his whistle. Officials literally looked official, wearing a white short-sleeved button-down shirt with a bow tie and a black armband, like an accountant. Everything was done according to the precise procedures regarding rules, equipment, and conduct as outlined in *Spalding's Official Amateur Athletic Union Basket Ball Guide for 1906–07*, the game's bible. In fact, A. G. Spalding, with branch offices in every major American city, was the official supplier of the sport itself, making not only uniforms, jerseys, shorts, footwear, socks, and knitted warm-up tops, but also basketballs, backboards, rims, scorebooks, and even referee whistles. The company was so pervasive that the game's rulebook included AAU Rule II, Sec. 3, which stated that the "Official No. M Basket Ball" manufactured by A. G. Spalding "shall be the official ball."[39] The "Official No. M" was made of leather and had laces on one side that protruded like those on a football. Its maximum allowable circumference of 32 inches was larger than today's regulation size balls, which measure just 29.5 inches around. There was no needle hole, so inflating the sphere meant undoing the laces, unfolding a hose attached to its interior rubber bladder, blowing air into the hose with lung power until the proper pressure was reached, folding the hose back down, and then re-lacing the thing. If its pressure was not quite right after bounce testing, then these steps had to be repeated. In addition, AAU Rule II, Sec. 4 warned, "The official ball must be used in all match games." This regulation was so strict that the referee was empowered to void any game in which it was violated.[40]

As the starting players for both teams left their respective benches and grouped around the referee at midcourt for the center jump to start the game, there was more than pride at stake. Like any innovation, new endeavor, or

milestone accomplished by African Americans, this game was seen as progress for the race. The athletes got into position, and then Chester tossed the
basketball high into the air above the center circle. The momentous game
was underway.

Moments later, the Spalding "Official No. M" whipped back and forth
as St. Christopher and Marathon players sprinted to various spots on the
floor, according to their positions. "Guards should be particular to remember
that it is their function to guard first, last and all the time," the sport's most
knowledgeable experts advised. The left guards and the right guards played
near their own baskets, with the exception that whether on offense or defense,
"there should be one guard in the backfield all of the time."[41] Despite the
emphasis on hard-nosed defense, players were warned, "the rules are strict
against roughing it, not with the idea of making the game ladylike, but to make
it as skillful as possible." Once a team got possession of the ball, the guard
advanced it with a pass up court to the left or right forward, his teammates
on offense who played near the opponent's basket. Each field goal resulted
in a stoppage of play and a jump ball at center court. A center didn't need
to be tall, but his or her vertical leap was a major factor because the main
responsibility was to win this tip, in order to control as many possessions as
possible throughout the game.

The action was fierce. "It's your business to play ball every minute until
the whistle blows," was a common basketball coaching reminder.[42] Surrounding the court, loyal rooters cheered every conceivable accomplishment. A
completed pass, a few dribbles in a row, and, above all, any field goal, were
considered outrageously spectacular. Unfortunately, it didn't take long for the
Brooklyn fans to realize that things were not going well for the Marathons. "It
was to be seen that the St. Christophers outclassed their opponents entirely as
to size and weight," wrote a twenty-eight-year-old African American reporter
for the *New York Age* named Lester Aglar Walton.[43] Most of that clout came
from Charles Bradford, who played center with brute force. "His herculean
strength gave him the advantage," Walton wrote, "but he has much to study as
to the science of the game." Regardless, St. Christopher led 11–0 at halftime.[44]
The situation didn't improve afterward. "The Marathons were unable to steady
themselves during any part of the second half, and the red and black jerseys
of the St. C's were all over the court."[45] Those uniform colors were relevant

because the St. Christopher Club had earned a new nickname, "The Red & Black Machine."

Walton, the young journalist, was originally from St. Louis, Missouri, where he had been a reporter with the *St. Louis Post-Dispatch*, one of America's most highly regarded newspapers, owned by Joseph Pulitzer, the eponym of the Pulitzer Prize. Walton's reporting in the *New York Age* was published in the newspaper's "Music and Stage" column because basketball and athletics in general among Black people fell into the category of amusement. As far as the game itself though, it was no joke for the Marathons of Brooklyn. They lost embarrassingly, 31–1. Their one point came from a made free throw.

But despite its lopsided outcome, Walton recognized this had been more than just a game, especially in light of the national debate about "the Negro problem" being waged in White newspaper headlines around the country. Every single African American achievement mattered. Just two days after the historic St. Christopher versus Marathons basketball game, Andrew Carnegie gave a speech at Howard University, sharing the stage with President Theodore Roosevelt for the college's fortieth anniversary celebration. "The problem was 'What shall we do with the Negro?'," the world famous "Ironmaster" exclaimed, after receiving a "Chautauqua salute" from the vast audience. "Now the problem is 'How can we get more of them?'" In response, the outright racist legislator Ben Tillman, who EB Henderson thought was "of particularly ill-repute," had his own commentary. "He is welcome to them," Tillman said, of Carnegie. Tillman went on to say, "I hope, however, that he will import his negroes direct from Africa so he will understand how much the South has done for the race."[46] The former South Carolina governor who promised to keep the state's Black population permanently inferior and cofounded Clemson University, had once said, "When you educate a Negro, you educate a candidate for the penitentiary or spoil a good field hand."

Fortunately, Lester Walton's readers, the audience inside the Knickerbocker Court venue that night, and many others disagreed with the White supremacy leader's words. This basketball game was so sensational in the trajectory of Black cultural and social progress that the actual result was beside the point. Evolving and growing was the point. Everyone was still learning, even newspapermen, so it felt like all those involved were winners.

And there was something else. The roll call at Knickerbocker Handball Club meetings included surnames like Shea, O'Donnell, Sheehan, and Murphy, among others. The facility was owned by an Irishman and former saloonkeeper named Peter Shannon. During the handball craze, in a true measure of its all-consuming popularity, Shannon had torn down and replaced his own once-popular Irish pub, Shannon's Saloon, with the Knickerbocker facility. The grand opening of the new pastime paradise on July 10, 1900, was said to have been "the largest that has ever taken place on any hand ball court in this city."[47] Yet by 1907, throughout New York City, four-wall indoor handball had begun losing its bounce. A single-wall outdoor version of the game played on asphalt and cement courts was taking over as the new fad, which endures today at most city playgrounds. Facing shrinking demand for indoor handball, the Knickerbocker Court began renting to outside groups like the Irish American Democratic Union, the Ladies Liberty Association, and now, the African American basketball teams of the Olympian Athletic League.

Considering the long and deadly history of Irish immigrant violence perpetrated against Black New Yorkers, renting his space to African Americans at all seemed like a bold step. Maybe demand for the sport had outmaneuvered White supremacy. Or perhaps the financial pressures on Shannon were too great. In any case, that night the economic leverage available to Black basketball players, teams, organizers, and fans emerged as a permanent socially empowering aspect of the game.

In fact, thanks to an emerging countrywide telegraphy network, many of the country's more than 250 total African American newspapers, which reached in excess of half a million readers, were connected to one another. So, this historically important event made national headlines. The *Indianapolis Freeman* included a version of Walton's article from the *New York Age* under its own headline illustrating the massive extent of exhilaration and pride that the game at the Knickerbocker Court in Brooklyn had inspired among Black people everywhere:

COLORED BASKETBALL TEAMS IN BIG CONTEST
New York Teams Engage in Great Struggle for Victory

If a 31–1 score was seen as a "great struggle for victory," then imagine the scale to which excitement about the sport would grow and expand in the days and months and years to come.[48] The mood was jubilation. Basketball had caught fire.

CHAPTER 11

A REAL CORKER

FANS OF THE ST. CHRISTOPHER BIG Five were still glowing with smiles of victory two weeks after their team defeated the Marathons in Brooklyn. That is, until November 29, 1907, the night the St. C's played their next game. This was when they hosted the Smart Set Athletic Club in their first home appearance on the basketball court in the cramped basement of the St. Philip's Church Parish House in Manhattan.[1] "The game was by far the most interesting and exciting of the season," the *New York Age* reported. But this time the tables turned on the Red & Black Machine, and they lost 24–6. "Bradford, the big wonder, was so completely dazed and out-generaled by Chester Moore that he had to be taken out of the second half," said the *Age*. St. Christopher also got out-toughed. "Both Lattimore and Hammond need to be carefully watched by the referee," the newspaper explained, "as neither one's methods can be styled as genteel." Yet, even in defeat, the fact that the event was witnessed by two hundred spectators on a Friday evening in the Tenderloin District, double the attendance of the first Olympian Athletic League game, was a promising sign for the St. Philip's athletic director, Father Daniel.

That validation from spectators continued into late December, when the St. C's played a rematch with the Smart Set back at the Knickerbocker Court in Brooklyn. "About 200 persons were present, mostly the followers of the Smart Set," reported Lester Walton.[2] But although "great enthusiasm was manifested," the result for the church team was even worse, losing 35–4. "It would be well for the St. Christophers to spend more time in the practice of team work," the *New York Age* sports reporter suggested. "Great skill was exhibited by the Smart Set in shooting the baskets, the result no doubt of much practice," while loyal fans of the church team "left looking very disconsolate." This was a wake-up call for Father Daniel.

By the time St. Christopher met the Smart Set squad again in early January, the clergyman had used his Episcopal diocese network to arrange a neutral site for the game, the third-floor gymnasium in the parish house of the Church of the Incarnation on East Thirty-First Street. That turned out to be a wise move, and it made all the difference. With only a few minutes left, the St. C's were in a close game and winning 14–12. Brooklyn had possession when suddenly, "Mr. Robert Lattimore dribbled the ball down the court and made a pass resulting in a goal."[3] The referee, knowledgeable Marathons player Alonzo F. Chadwick, Jr., allowed the points, which tied the game. But not so fast. St. Christopher team captain Clarence Lewis immediately protested, running up to Alonzo and citing Rule 11, Section 15 of *Spalding's Official AAU Basketball Guide*, the no-dribble regulation that prohibited a player from attempting a shot after he or she had already dribbled.[4] "A player who has dribbled may not score a goal until the ball has been played (that is received and batted or thrown) by another player," the rule clearly stated. "If the ball is thrown into the basket at the end of a dribble it shall not be scored and the ball shall be thrown up at center."

Clarence's objection was correct. This was the wrinkle the AAU had added to its rulebook in 1900 to encourage more passing and increase the pace of the game. If it were to be applied in modern times, then dribbling to the basket and making a layup would be illegal and the basket would be waived off, resulting in a jump ball at center court. The ref had blown the call. But then he made the situation worse by preventing St. Christopher from calling time-out to discuss the play. Arguing a call was also prohibited, under AAU Rule 12, Section 7: "There shall be no protest against the decision of the officials except in regard to interpretation of rules." Even when the St. C captain insisted that stopping the action to understand or clarify a regulation was allowed, Alonzo wouldn't buy it. While the St. Christopher players were at their bench deciding what to do, they failed to realize they had to return to the court within the allowable five minutes to resume play or forfeit the game to the Smart Set. And that's exactly what happened. Alonzo blew his whistle to end the game then and there, with the Smart Set winning, 17–14.

That touched off weeks of protests and newspaper coverage. "Interest continues to grow in the basketball games which are played weekly between the St. Christopher Club of Manhattan and the Smart Set of Brooklyn," said the *Brooklyn Daily Standard Union*.[5] It showed the level of passion the game had aroused among African Americans as well as how seriously they took the rules of basketball, following them to the letter. The whole topic became irrelevant after that season, though, when the Collegiate Basketball Rules Committee dropped the no-dribble regulation in July 1908. "This is a sweeping change," the *New York Times* would declare, "and one calculated to make the game more popular."[6] Every modern-day baller able to create his or her own shot off the dribble owes a debt of gratitude to that rules committee for its revision. Meanwhile, the AAU stubbornly kept its no-dribble rule in place until 1915.[7]

On the strength of its undefeated record, the Smart Set Athletic Club went on to capture the inaugural Olympian Athletic League championship title. This moved the sports journalist Lester Walton to recognize that, for the public's sake, there needed to be an official designation for the best African American basketball team in the country. So, borrowing a term from boxing and baseball, he began using variations of the term "Colored Basketball World's Champions," and bestowed that label on the Smart Set for the 1907–8 season. With the inaugural 1907–8 Olympian Athletic League title captured, Smart Set officials quickly reached out to ISAA president William A. Joiner, asking if their squad could challenge one of the D.C. area teams to a series of games. That idea didn't work out because the timing wasn't right for the ISAA, but this correspondence paved the way for another try the following year, in April 1909, enabling what would be the first intercity game between two African American basketball teams.

Basketball's popularity kept growing, but to Father Daniel, all those losses to the Smart Set Athletic Club had become a problem. For the St. Christopher team, basketball bliss had become hardwood humiliation, under his watch. The athletic director wanted better results and needed help. Then, as if to answer the clergyman's prayers, one of the members of his own congregation at St. Philip's Church surfaced as a potential savior. That person was a twenty-two-year-old African American military veteran named Major Aloysius Hart. It would turn out that there was a lot in this man's name.

"Major" was his name, not his rank. He was born along the west bank of the Chattahoochee River in Eufaula, Alabama, the cradle of the state's White supremacy ideology. Major had the same surname as the descendants of one of the town's original settlers, an enslaver and cotton shipper named John Cleveland Hart, who had owned a large plantation, a dry goods store in town, and many dozens of enslaved Black people, whom he sold for "more than $75,000" just prior the Emancipation Proclamation.[8] Even though Major was so light complexioned that he could have passed for White anywhere, that was not the case in this vicious town, the site of the Eufaula Massacre of 1874.[9] Major left, just like another Black teenager and Eufaula native William Henry Harrison Hart had done before him. After surviving that slaughter, which White newspapers called an "election riot," William Henry had fled Eufaula by foot, walking all the way to the District of Columbia, where he eventually became a prominent attorney and a criminal law professor at Howard University.

Major ended up in New York City just after the outbreak of the Spanish-American War. One day, in early July 1899, barely fourteen years old, he strolled down to the War Department Quartermaster's Dock at the foot of Wall Street and signed on to serve as a captain's boy aboard the U.S. Army Transport *Kilpatrick*, a thousand-ton military supply ship.[10] Major was "connected with the War Department" for several years and "traveled all over the world in that service." He kept advancing, finally arriving in Hawaii with a detachment of officers from the U.S. Army Quartermaster's Department to help them survey the construction of a new military post at Kahikinui on Maui. "M.A. Hart is the rodman for the party," the *Hawaiian Star* newspaper reported, referring to his responsibility for carrying and setting up survey equipment as well as holding, sighting, and reading its leveling rod.[11]

A year later, Major had become a clerk to Captain Charles F. Humphrey, Jr., quartermaster at the Honolulu supply depot, who was the son of the quartermaster general of the entire U.S. Army.[12] He also became a highly competitive speed skater. At the time, ice speed skating was "having the greatest boom in its history" and had become a national craze. Oahu even had an ice rink. HONOLULU ON SKATES read a front-page headline in the *Honolulu Advertiser* in 1906 after the rink opened.[13] Major picked up the sport and instantly became a sensational star. Speed skating races were typically a half mile or a mile in length, around a rink course that was sixteen laps to the mile.[14] Events began at around 9 P.M. and a band played music during the entire evening. In a one-mile race against five other contestants on April 11, 1906, a week before the San Francisco earthquake, "Hart took the lead and finished strong" to win in front of "a large crowd."[15] The young Black military clerk and speed skater became so popular in Honolulu that his decision to leave the military and return to the mainland made local headlines. MAJOR HART LEAVES TODAY read the *Pacific Commercial Advertiser*. "His departure will be much regretted by a large circle of friends."[16]

Major's voyage to New York City aboard the *Kilpatrick* was an epic swashbuckling tale. The transport steamer sailed to the mainland via Manila, a forty-one-day journey that included Hong Kong, Singapore, the Indian Ocean, the Suez Canal, and the Straits of Gibraltar.[17] It cruised directly into the path of the 1906 Hong Kong typhoon, whose wind and swells were so intense that three of her sailors were washed overboard.[18] The storm claimed up to ten thousand lives in the British-controlled port.[19] Next, the ship docked in Morocco just as its countrymen were in open revolt against colonialist subjugation by France. "Major says that he was in Tangier during the recent trouble there with the French Government," a Hawaii newspaper reported. "He says he saw the soldiers trying to quiet the mob after the French consul had been killed."[20] Finally, the *Kilpatrick* was rerouted to provide relief for the people of Kingston, Jamaica, which lay in ruins following that major January 1907 earthquake, the same catastrophe that had diverted the attention of Conrad Norman and his fellow Jamaican-born organizers of the Alpha Physical Culture Club away from their efforts to establish an all-Black basketball team.[21] Two months later, Major was sighted in New Orleans, registering as a guest at the elegant St. Charles Hotel, "having just come in from Honolulu." He was on his way back to New York City, the place where his nautical adventures had begun eight years earlier.

Major had a lot of heart.

Once he got to Manhattan, the young veteran and bachelor settled into a Fifth Avenue apartment on the edge of the Tenderloin District in Midtown and began worshipping at St. Philip's Church.[22] That's where he first became tight with Shelton Hale Bishop, one of the rector's sons and a member of the St. Christopher basketball team. Major's military background and tales of high-seas adventures were riveting. And his connection with Shelton was compelling. But for Father Daniel, Major's most valuable quality was his experience competing as an elite athlete. The clergyman athletic director was so impressed that he asked the former speed skater to become his personal secretary. Then, ahead of the 1908–9 season, Father Daniel appointed Major as the first full-time head coach, manager, and promoter of the St. Christopher Big Five basketball team. The assignment brought valuable intangible characteristics to the program, like discipline and camaraderie as well as competitiveness and toughness. Also, he looked the part. With stern eyes, a solid physique, and a square jaw, the former U.S. Army man seemed like a drill sergeant. St. Philip's Church would eventually recognize Major as an "immortal" in the long athletic history of the St. Christopher Club.[23]

Meanwhile, this was also a perfect situation for Will Anthony Madden, because he and Major were around the same age. Before long, the young Standard Oil messenger, *Red Raven* editor, and St. C basketball team mascot was working closely with the squad's new program director.

The basketball league that Edwin Bancroft Henderson envisioned for the Washington, D.C., area had gotten a boost in late December 1907, when the ISAA staged another citywide competition, this time an indoor "athletic carnival."[24] The post-Christmas event took place at a venue called True Reformers' Hall, a five-story building located at the corner of Twelfth and U Streets adjacent to Howard University, an area that had become one of the city's most vibrant Black neighborhoods. Built at a cost $46,000 by the United Order of the True Reformers, an African American self-help organization, the distinctive-looking structure had an exterior of beige and red brick under a regal ornamental frieze and was embellished with pairs of eighteen-foot arched windows. This was Washington's most powerful symbol of Black ingenuity to date because it was financed, designed, and erected entirely by African Americans. "It can be said without any exaggeration," the *Washington Bee* had declared when True Reformers' opened in 1903, "that it is the best office, store, hall, and lodge room building that the Negro owns in the United States."[25]

Most importantly for EB was that the building had a second-floor ballroom space that could be used as a basketball court, and it would accommodate about seven hundred spectators in an overlooking balcony that surrounded the floor below.

The focus of that ISAA event had been on demonstrations of acrobatics, fencing, wrestling, short sprinting, and boxing. But they also staged an exhibition basketball game between a team from Howard University and a "picked"

squad of players representing M Street High and Armstrong Tech. EB even
demonstrated his own court skills, playing for the high school squad, possibly
giving them some much-needed experience, and the victory, 12–5. Though it
was just one game, this was as much of a breakthrough in Washington, D.C.,
as the St. Christopher versus Marathons game at Knickerbocker Court a few
weeks earlier had been for New York City, and beyond. Out of the entire event,
the Howard University student newspaper observed, "the basket ball game was
probably the most interesting number on the program." That's because since
the end of the football season for "several evenings a week," all of the players
involved, as well as other ISAA members, had been practicing basketball in
the armory at M Street High School. None of them "had ever seen a basket ball
game played" before they began, but "in a short while three teams at Howard
University were formed and one at each high school."[26] This was gratifying to
EB, who had been their coach during that time.

After the success of its December 1907 exhibition, the ISAA's basketball
efforts really took off. "Athletic clubs of young men began to form all over the
city and ask for the privilege of playing under the protection of the Association," cofounder Robert Mattingly would explain. Soon the region's "wild-cat
athletics," as he termed it, "began to give way to organized control, and the
high ideals of the manly sports were held before both public and participants."
Some of their female counterparts also became aroused and let it be known.
"The young ladies of M St High School wish to play a series of basket ball
games with the young ladies of Howard University, and to this end are willing to make arrangement for them to practice for same," they indicated in
the *University Journal.* "Let us hope to see these games pulled off in the near
future," the school newspaper advised.[27]

A week later, the ISAA announced its basketball league participants,
and games began on January 18, 1908. There were teams representing M
Street High, Armstrong Manual Technical (nicknamed the "Techs"), Howard
Academy, the college prep arm of the university (nicknamed the "Invincibles"
or the "Preps"), Howard Medical (nicknamed the "Medics"), which included
students enrolled in the college's medical school, and Howard College (sometimes called the "Hilltoppers"), composed of regular undergraduates at the
college. In addition, the Crescent Athletic Club, the Oberlin Athletic Club, and
LeDroit Park were independent squads from the neighborhoods surrounding
the Howard campus. Games were to be played every Saturday night in True

Reformers' Hall, with tip-offs at 8 P.M. The public was always welcome and general admission was twenty-five cents. EB's focus as an instructor was not only on the fundamentals of how to play the game but also on the business management aspects involved. The ISAA kept proper records of receipts and disbursements and was innovative with its promotion. "Basket ball is the recognized leading indoor game of the winter season," its advertisements stated, "and when played by such men as those belonging to this league it is really fascinating." That also meant accounting for social interests, which meant featuring music by the Lyric Orchestra, known as "the leading orchestra in the city," which furnished music for the Howard University upperclassmen's annual informal prom.

EB taught one day a week each at M Street and Armstrong, and three days in grade schools, but the focus of his work was now increasingly with the ISAA league. Though he rode his bike "from school to school" during those days, he still decided to get a new apartment on Eleventh Street NW near U Street, just two blocks from True Reformers' Hall.[28] His attentiveness paid off. "Great credit is due to the I.S.A.A. for its successful management of the basket ball season," the *University Journal* reported on its front page. It ended with M Street High winning the league championship by defeating the Howard Medics. The association's marketing savvy also helped. "The attendance at first was small but after a few nights interest picked up and crowded houses were the result," the *Journal* said. It's because they realized, "wherever the young ladies go, there you will find the young men also." So they "cheerfully" issued free tickets to the women of Howard, M Street, and Armstrong, "and it worked like magic." After that, people who had never attended an ISAA basketball game were often seen in the front row. "It's safe to say," the campus paper concluded, "that basket ball among the schools and athletic clubs has won a permanent place."[29]

In mid-November 1904, a City of Pittsburgh ordinance was passed, granting to the Duquesne Light Company the right to "enter upon the streets, alleys and highways of the city" for the purpose of "using thereon and therein its poles, conduits, wires, cables, and other apparatus" in order to supply light, heat, and power to citizens and businesses "by means of electricity."[30] After taking more than a year to plan and prepare, the company began their work in early 1906 only to be met with an outcry of resistance from Pittsburghers "doing their utmost to prevent unsightly overhead wires and poles that disgrace any resident neighborhood."[31]

But one young individual living on East Thirteenth Avenue in Homestead didn't mind at all. It was sixteen-year-old Cumberland Willis Posey, Jr., and that year he fastened "an iron basket ball hoop" to a Duquesne Light Company pole that had been erected on his block. This was no ordinary rim. "Every boy in the third ward of Homestead has at some time 'shot a basket through this hoop,'" Cum would remember fondly almost three decades later, after it was finally removed by the same utility company.[32] "Some gained basketball fame," he would continue, "some, whom we thought were good, dropped into oblivion."

Those neighborhood kids included "Dutch," "Skimmers," "Yutch," and "Jimsy," White boys who were characters from surrounding blocks and neighborhoods that "played in the street" on East Thirteenth with Cum and his older brother Seward during countless Saturday afternoon "free for alls," not only that summer but every season of the year. And these youths in particular were more than just characters. On this "special hoop," Walter "Dutch" Wohlfarth, James Francis "Skimmers" Campbell, Eddie "Yutch" Dolan, and James "Jimsy" Brown were developing into the finest basketball players that would ever come out of Western Pennsylvania. All were current or former Homestead High School students and all but Cum would turn professional right after graduating. Dutch, who played guard, had graduated that spring alongside Cum's older brother Seward in Homestead High's class of 1906 before joining the Homestead "Young Americans" in the Central Basket Ball League, where he would be described as "sensational to the extreme." As a forward, Jimsy would soon be considered "the best floor shot in the east." Yutch would go on to be called "the greatest center of all time" in local press. Skimmers, another forward and the youngest of the bunch, would have a twenty-year career in pro ball that included an Eastern Basketball League championship, three EBL scoring titles, and multiple seasons in the American Basketball League, earning local praise as "one of the greatest players of all time."

There were kids on the street who idolized these teens. One of them was a boy named Charles Davies, nicknamed "Chick," ten years younger than Cum, who lived on Thirteenth Avenue a few doors down from the Poseys. Chick

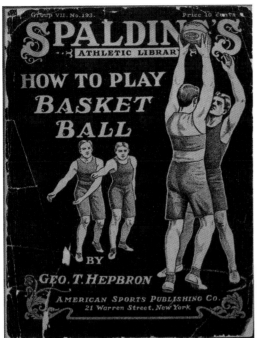

The first basketball how-to book, published in 1904 by the American Sports Publishing Company for A.G. Spalding & Bros., then the leading supplier of athletic equipment

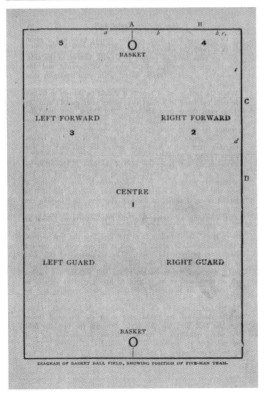

A vintage court diagram, circa 1905, shows the locations of the players by their positions.

TOP LEFT: Typical clothing styles of the late 1900s and early 1910s included knickerbocker pants and lace-up boots.

TOP RIGHT: Most young men and youths wore hats.

ABOVE: A team photo from 1931 shows the NCTS basketball team, identity unknown, standing next to a motor vehicle possibly used for traveling to games.

TOP: Youths with a basketball, circa 1908, wearing the styles of the times

ABOVE: Early streetball scenario; men in street clothes with basketball, circa late 1920s

TOP: The Smart Set Athletic Club basketball team, with J. Hoffman Woods, standing center, and Hudson Oliver, seated far right, circa 1910

ABOVE: The Alpha Physical Culture Club basketball team, 1912

TOP: The St. Christopher Club basketball team, with Will Anthony Madden, standing back row far right, and Coach Jeff Wetzler, standing back row center, circa 1913

ABOVE: The Howard University varsity basketball team of 1911, with Hudson Oliver, seated third from right, and George Gilmore, standing far right

TOP: Vintage laced leather basketballs had to be unlaced, inflated by lung, and relaced before being bounce-tested to see if the pressure was just right.

ABOVE: The Twelfth Street Colored YMCA basketball team, nicknamed the Twelfth Streeters, with Hudson Oliver, seated center left, and Edwin Bancroft Henderson, seated center, holding the basketball, 1910

TOP: The New York Girls basketball team, with Conrad Norman, standing center, and Dora Cole, standing to his left, 1911

ABOVE: An unidentified African American women's basketball team, circa 1910

LEFT: Edith Trice of the Younger Set, an African American women's basketball team based in Harlem, circa 1912 (Trice Family Archives)

BELOW: An unidentified African American women's basketball team, 1930

TOP: The Philadelphia Tribune Girls, with future Basketball Hall of Famer Ora Washington, standing third from right, circa 1937

ABOVE: An outdoor basketball game between two unidentified African American women's teams, with a crowd of Black spectators, circa 1910

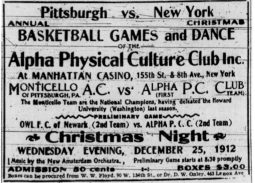

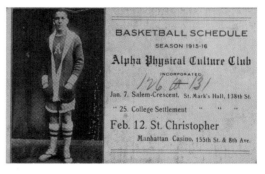

CLOCKWISE FROM ABOVE:
The Standard Oil Building at 26 Broadway, circa 1910s, where Will Anthony Madden and J. Hoffman Woods were employed as messengers

The exterior of the Fourteenth Regiment Armory in Park Slope, Brooklyn, circa 1910

A newspaper ad promoting a basketball game between the Alpha Physical Culture Club of New York City and the Monticello Athletic Club of Pittsburgh, 1912 (*New York Age*)

This early Alpha Physical Culture Club basketball schedule shows games with College Settlement, an all-Jewish team from the Lower East Side, and the St. Christopher Club of Harlem, for the 1915–6 season.

The evolving look and fashion style of Will Anthony Madden, nicknamed "Little Napoleon," in 1917 (top left), 1920 (top right), 1963 (above left), and 1970 (above right), three years before his death in Greenwich Village

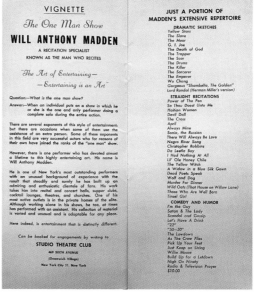

ABOVE LEFT: A gilded gold medallion with silk ribbon and pin, the earliest known in-arena promotional fan giveaway, for a 1915 game at the Manhattan Casino, between Howard University and the St. Christopher Club

TOP RIGHT: A typical first prize "loving cup," for a 5½-mile handicap road race staged by the St. Christopher Club and sponsored by the Lafayette Theater, 1917

ABOVE RIGHT: A pamphlet promoting Will Anthony Madden's theatrical talents and the Studio Theatre Club he ran at his home for several decades beginning in the 1940s

BASKET BALL

Will Anthony Madden's
"INCORPORATORS"

are the recognized colored basket ball champions of the world and have been during the seasons 1914-15-16. The big Incorporated team has a percentage of 1000, which is the very highest percentage that can be reached. To gain this unquestioned record the "Incorporators" have defeated practically every team of note in the United States and stand ready at all times with an open challenge to any team in the world, regardless of size, weight, age and ability.

The next appearance of
MADDEN'S "INCORPORATORS"
will be at
MANHATTAN CASINO
155th Street and Eighth Ave., New York City

FRIDAY NIGHT, MARCH 2nd, 1917

when they will meet

FRED D. POLLARD
and his
PROVIDENCE COLLEGIANS

in the most sensational basket ball game of the season.

Note: Pollard of Brown University is the football marvel of the Age and defeated both Yale and Harvard. Come and see him play basket ball.

ADMISSION - - - 50 CENTS

WILL ANTHONY MADDEN, Manager,
269 West Fourth St., New York City.   Tel. 718 Chelsea.

Other "Incorporators" games at Manhattan Casino: Thursday night, March 29th, 1917—Chicago Y. M. C. A. Friday night, April 13th, 1917—Lincoln University. Bookings open for season 1917-18 for both home games and road games. Address all communications direct to manager.

Mention THE CRISIS

BASKET BALL
CHICAGO
— vs. —
NEW YORK
THURSDAY NIGHT, MARCH 29, 1917
MANHATTAN CASINO

WILL ANTHONY MADDEN, Manager
269 W. 4th St., N. Y.   Tel. 718 Chelsea

Grandest Event of the Season!

10th Cavalry
Basketball Team
The Champion Basketball Team of the U. S. Army
WILL COMPETE AGAINST THE CELEBRATED

New York All-Stars
Basketball Team

LINCOLN'S BIRTHDAY
(MONDAY EVENING, FEBRUARY 13, 1911)

at 71st REGIMENT ARMORY 34th Street & Park Avenue
NEW YORK

The Preliminary Game will be Played Between the
SPARTAN (GIRLS) **A. C. & EXCELSIOR** (GIRLS) **A. C.**
OF BROOKLYN

NOTE.—The proceeds will be divided and presented to the Hope Day Nursery, the Lucy Laney League, and the McDonough Hospital.

COUNTERCLOCKWISE FROM ABOVE: Will Anthony Madden promoted the 1917 basketball game between Bronzeville's Wabash Outlaws and his New York Incorporators as CHICAGO VS. NEW YORK. A four-time winner of the Colored Basketball World's Championship with two different teams (St. Christopher Club, Incorporators), Madden also introduced to Black basketball the hiring of expert coaches, intercity rivalries, team nicknames, in-arena giveaways, marketing via editorial coverage, stylish uniforms, an annual All-American list for top African American players, an annual Black All-Star team, and long road trips.

A magazine advertisement in *The Crisis: A Record of the Darker Races*, for a basketball game that never took place between Will Anthony Madden's Incorporators and Fritz Pollard's Providence Collegians

An advertisement placed in 1911 by Major Hart, for a game between his New York All-Stars and the 10th Cavalry Regiment basketball team, an all-Black squad visiting from Fort Ethan Allen in Vermont

TOP: The St. Christopher Club basketball team, with Charles Bradford, standing third from the left, and Father Everard Daniel, standing far right, circa 1912

ABOVE: The St. Christopher Club basketball team, featuring Paul Robeson, second from left, Irving Rose, sixth from left, and Clarence Jenkins, second from right, circa 1919

TOP: The New York Incorporators of 1916, featuring Walter Cooper, standing back center, Will Anthony Madden, standing middle row center, and team mascot Ralph Cooper, seated

ABOVE: The Duquesne University Dukes varsity basketball team, featuring Cumberland Posey, Jr., standing third from left, 1917

Union Labor Temple,
Webster Avenue and Epiphany Street,
Pittsburgh, Pa.

CLOCKWISE FROM BELOW:

The front entrance to Carnegie Steel Company in Homestead, Pennsylvania, circa 1910, the year after Cumberland Posey, Jr., graduated from Homestead High School

Homestead High School varsity basketball team photo, with Cumberland Posey, Jr., seated and holding a ball, 1909

The Union Labor Temple in the Hill District of Pittsburgh, circa 1910, longtime home court of the Loendi Big Five

developed a love of basketball on this block that would one day blossom into a pro career, first as a player, then as a nationally renowned college coach.[33]

These young men were nearly unstoppable in their efforts to enjoy the game. "The boys of Homestead are sore at the burgess and members of the police force, who they accuse of interfering with their rights as free born Young Americans," the *Homestead Messenger* reported. They had written a letter to the newspaper's editor demanding to know "why they cannot play basket ball on the street."[34] Because of them, Homestead became known as "the basket ball foundry of the country." But as great as these players were, they would all be eclipsed by Cum, their East Thirteenth Avenue playmate, who was eventually to be enshrined in the Naismith Memorial Basketball Hall of Fame more than a century later.

Going into his senior year at Homestead High School in the fall of 1908, Cumberland Willis Posey, Jr., could have followed in the footsteps of his father to become a riverman, a steamboat builder, or even a real estate maven after graduation. A vast world of opportunities to work with his dad awaited the eighteen-year-old. After all, Captain Posey was unquestionably Pittsburgh's most outstanding African American citizen. His reputation and stature extended throughout the Ohio River Valley from Homestead to Louisville and beyond. He and his wife, Anna, had kept the Posey name in the news. And since the mid-1890s, riding Pittsburgh's unbroken wave of prosperity, the couple's fortunes had multiplied. In fact, Posey had become arguably the most successful and well-connected Black entrepreneur in American history.

During this time, Homestead's population had grown from a few hundred, when the Poseys first relocated there from Ohio, to more than ten thousand residents. As construction boomed across America, Carnegie Steel's earnings had soared. To feed that growth, the company kept acquiring additional land adjacent to its Homestead mill, gobbling up any available downtown tracts so that it could expand in size. Posey had held on to his "Posey's Row" properties, aware that eventually Andrew Carnegie would need to buy those lots. He was right. In 1897, the riverman sold them to the Carnegie Steel Company Ltd. for $18,000, about $560,000 today, adding to his substantial fortune.[35]

The same year, Posey had followed his wife's example and leapt into public service himself at the urging of a prominent local African American barber and news page editor named George W. Hall, who suggested that Pittsburgh's prominent Black men form a private progressive social organization. As a result of Hall's "untiring effort," twelve individuals including Posey had gathered for an August 1897 meetup at Brown's Café on Wylie Avenue to formalize the project, which they modeled after the city's swanky Duquesne Club. It would be called the Loendi Social & Literary Club, reportedly named after a rich and cultivated tributary in Mozambique mentioned in the journal of White explorer Stanley Livingstone (this was actually the Lugenda River). It was incorporated later that year with the Homestead riverman elected as one of its founding officers.[36]

The club's charter was "to improve its members in literary, social and moral culture" as well as to cover the burial cost "in case of the death of any member in good standing."[37] Its clubhouse was located in the Hill District at 68 Fulton Street, just two blocks from the Franklin Public School that young Edwin "EB" Henderson had attended, and a block away from the "Cross Roads of the World" intersection at Wylie.[38] Its interior was "magnificently furnished throughout, at great expense" and included a front and rear parlor, a dining room, a billiard room, a card room (although no games of chance of any kind were allowed), and steward's quarters.[39] Membership in the Loendi Club was reserved for "men of the race of wide reputation and ability."[40] These were accomplished gentlemen "identified with the higher walks of life" and hand-picked by the organization's board of governors. "As men advance in thought and refinement," *Colored American Magazine* explained in 1901, "the desire for congenial contact often finds expression in the formation of clubs."[41] Pittsburgh had become a leading center of African American cultural thought and vision. "There is a bright future ahead for the Loendi and its promoters," the *Pittsburgh Press* had predicted at its 1897 opening.[42] Indeed, the organization would quickly become "one of the foremost negro social clubs in the country," and would soon sponsor an African American hardwood squad that became Black basketball's first great dynasty.

Cum's mother, Anna Posey, was very well connected herself. She had stayed continually active in community causes like her Aurora Reading Club, and when Ida B. Wells-Barnett visited the city from Chicago in 1899, Anna had presented the distinguished civil rights activist with "some artistically decorated Sevres china" that was her own handiwork.[43]

Pittsburgh had remained a coveted destination for African American workers and their families. Black migrants from the South had kept arriving. "There is here a chance, such as perhaps few other Northern cities give, for the industrious Negro to succeed, and he is improving his opportunity," sociologist Helen Tucker would write.[44] By 1900, more than six thousand Black workmen were employed in the city's iron mills alone. Carnegie Steel had hired so many African American laborers that Andrew Carnegie himself reportedly enlisted Posey's influence to help with employee relations. The steel titan may also have rewarded the riverman with lucrative hauling contracts, and the two men remained close associates, even to the point where William N. Page, a thirty-one-year-old Virginia-born Black man who was Carnegie Steel's trusted long-time chief stenographer, overseeing the corporation's entire fourteen-person stenographic staff, lived with the Poseys on Thirteenth Avenue as a boarder.[45]

Carnegie Steel net profits had increased "by extraordinary leaps and bounds," climbing from $3 million in 1893, the year after the failed Homestead strike, to $40 million in 1900, the equivalent of growing from $92 million to more than $1.2 billion today. During those same years its steel production had tripled.[46] Until the day that Andrew Carnegie and his business partners, Henry Clay Frick, George Lauder, and Henry Phipps, Jr., sold Carnegie Steel to United States Steel in 1901, they believed that "this magnificent record was to a great extent made possible by the company's victory at Homestead."[47] And that victory had been made possible by African Americans. This truth was not lost on Carnegie, who had a deeply held moral conviction about equality. After cashing out, he would become the first industrialist to make major charitable contributions to Black social causes. Carnegie would have a particularly meaningful relationship with Booker T. Washington, whom the steel tycoon had called "the combined Moses and Joshua of his people," later making a $600,000 donation, equaling $17 million today, to the Tuskegee Institute.

In 1901, Posey sold his Posey Coal Dealers and Steam Boat Builders Company to form yet another new firm, the Marine Coal Company, which was reported to hold capital stock of $500,000. "Mr. Posey's career has been one of brilliant success," *Colored American Magazine* wrote that same year. "He is reputed to be one of the best steam-boat builders in the country," the monthly publication continued, "and a careful investigation of his works would more than substantiate the assertion."[48] By 1902, the captain had expanded his other entity, the Diamond Coke and Coal Company, to include a coalmine with a capacity of 12,000 tons daily. The operation was said to employ a thousand-man workforce of Black and White laborers who reported to ten supervising managers.

In other words, when Cum became a graduating senior at Homestead High School in 1908, he could have been voted by classmates as "most likely to work for his father."

But that year, something else had a powerful grip on Western Pennsylvania, and on Cum's mind, besides the region's powerful commercial interests. Though a nighttime panoramic view made Pittsburgh look ablaze, a closer gaze through the smoke and haze into the city's individual neighborhoods would reveal that the hottest thing happening was basketball. Those shadowy half-dressed figures darting here and there were at play not only with "great lumps of molten metal" but also with "Official No. M" Spaldings. "The floor game has always been popular in this section," the *Pittsburgh Daily Post* pointed out. "It is a clean and healthful branch of athletics, and a contest between two well-matched fives is always productive of a large amount of excitement." And there was no place in the area where those proclamations were truer than in Homestead, known as "Steel Town," where the opening of the 1908–9 basketball season for the newly formed National Basket Ball League of Western Pennsylvania was celebrated on November 7, 1908, with a Saturday night pregame parade. Led by a brass band, open horse-drawn carriages carrying players from the local Homestead "Young Americans" and the visiting Carnegie "Hans Wagners" rolled through the streets "amid cheers and red fire," followed by speeches from the magistrates of each town.[49] "Red fire" parades, where marchers ignited and held up red-flame-emitting powder sticks made of nitrate of strontium, sulfur, and chlorate of potash, looked like a massive moving line of fire so visually powerful that they were reserved for only the most special of occasions, like the Fourth of July.[50] "Homestead was basket ball crazy," the next morning's *Pittsburgh Daily Post* diagnosed.[51]

In the opening game itself, the Hans Wagner Five from the neighboring town of Carnegie featured the Pittsburgh Pirates shortstop and future Baseball Hall of Fame member Johannes Peter "Hans" Wagner, sometimes known as "Honus," at guard. Despite the major league ballplayer's notoriety and elite athleticism, Carnegie still lost to the Young Americans, 52–18. Homestead was for real. Their manager had "left nothing undone to make this the greatest opening of any basket ball game in this section." The league also featured squads from nearby Southside, Wilkinsburg, Freedom, and Butler, industrial centers whose people, with their tireless work ethics, deeply appreciated the grit and passion of hard-nosed sports competition. Since each of the localities in the NBBL of Western Pennsylvania would be stocked with its own talent rather than imported players, the rivalry will be far greater and the game more interesting than ever before," the *Pittsburgh Daily Post* predicted. "As each player will fight desperately to maintain a high position in the race for the honor of his home town," the newspaper continued, "this alone makes for fast basket ball."[52]

But the Young Americans weren't even Homestead's only pro hoops team. And the NBBL wasn't the region's only professional basketball circuit. There was another one, the Central Basket Ball League, which featured teams representing the South Side, Uniontown, East Liverpool, Ohio, McKeesport, Greensburg, and Homestead, whose other pro squad was also called the Young Americans but was referred to as the "Homies." This was the team with Dutch Wohlfarth on its roster, literally one of the East Thirteenth Avenue utility pole homies. Dutch was considered "the most sensational young player of the league."[53] And in a preseason Central League update, the nearby *Uniontown Morning Herald* hailed Homestead as the "prime mover in basket ball in Western Pennsylvania," calling it "one of the gamest little sporting cities in the United States."[54]

This was no surprise. A study of the town's steel mill families and their behaviors around that time revealed not only that basketball was very popular among all ages but also that those who preferred watching the sport most were "the older men and those whose work is hard."[55] Homestead's enthusiasm for the sport and the town's status as a "basket ball foundry" was embedded in the town's identity. It was practically impossible to grow up there and not get fired up about the game. That's why even little Homestead High, with its 1909 graduating class of fifty-four students, the largest in school history, dominated against every Western Pennsylvania opponent.[56] They had Cumberland Willis Posey, Jr., a senior three-sport letterman who starred in football, basketball, and baseball. Heading into the that 1908–9 season, there was no better emerging interscholastic athlete in the region. Even at five feet, nine inches tall, often the smallest player on the field or the court, he was unstoppable as an athlete, possessing a rare combination of speed, agility, strength, toughness, and mind power.

In football, playing right halfback, Cum scored almost at will in nearly every game. A week before that basketball parade, he had helped Homestead

High defeat rival Wilkinsburg with a touchdown. His two touchdowns against Union High of the city's Knoxville neighborhood had led to a Homestead win in October. Another of Cum's touchdowns the same month had helped shut out Braddock High School. And the halfback had reached the end zone twice in a September win over Duquesne High.

Cum was just as impressive in baseball, where he played centerfield and became known for reaching base, stealing bases, and stretching singles into extra-base hits.

In basketball, playing left forward, Cum would routinely hit five, six, or seven field goals a game, an enormous production in the days when twenty-four points or even less could be enough for a win. Recognizing his own size, he developed superior ballhandling skills and an exceptional outside shot that would become his signature threat.

But it was Cum's visionary mindset and iron-willed temperament that were the key to his overall game. Like the borough of Homestead itself, he was the embodiment of grit, passion, and charm. "His was a flaming spirit that brooked no interference," his longtime friend Alvin J. Moses, a newspaper columnist, would explain. As is typical of youngest children, the riverman's son "would rush at a giant," said Moses, "just as quickly as he would a man of his own size, fists flying and cussing like a South Seas Islander, but never taking a mean advantage."[57] As an adult, Cum would carry a blackjack in the breast pocket of his coat, with its handle ominously left hanging out for all to see. But he was not just bluffing. One time, Cum was on an official tour of the county jail with his adolescent nephew, Evan Posey Baker, when an inmate suddenly reached toward the boy through the bars of his cell. Cum broke the man's arm.[58] Yet, as a teenager he could socialize with debutantes over tea. "Posey was friends of the riff-raff as well as the uppity class," according to a longtime friend.[59]

Cum's high school pals would say that despite the Poseys' wealthy background he was "likeable" and that there was nothing "out of the ordinary" about him.[60] That's because Pittsburgh itself, by its very nature, molded and shaped its young athletes a certain way. The city had been built on top of a multitude of irregular hills surrounded by countless numbers of steep gorges, gulches, trenches, hollows, and ravines. When those geological rises became settled, the challenging terrain had acted as natural boundaries separating the neighborhoods that evolved. Industrialization had produced so much work that Pittsburgh's population exploded from 86,000 in 1870 to more than 520,000 by 1908. These jobs had been filled by all kinds of folks from all kinds of places. "Nationality and color probably play less part here in the matter of employment than in any other city," sociologist Helen Tucker reported at the time. "The prime questions are: Do you want to work? and can you put out the goods?" Newcomers chose to live with their own kinfolk based on place of origin, race, ethnicity, religion, culture, or other factors. In this unique setup, Pittsburgh's geographies became known by their people. Polish Hill was settled by the Polish. The South Side was Slovenian and Lithuanian. The Strip District was Irish, as was Lawrenceville. Bloomfield and Oakland were mostly Italian. Jewish people lived in the Hill District and in Squirrel Hill. Germans populated Deutschtown, Spring Garden, and Mount Washington. Hazelwood was Hungarian. There were African American enclaves in many of these areas, but the majority lived on the Hill as well as in Homewood, Brushton, and Beltzhoover. Some sections like Homestead and Allegheny City, called the North Side today, were mixed with of all of the above.

In fact, the metaphorical vision of America as a "Great Melting Pot," where many sorts of people come together to form a new unified nation, was originally conceived in reference to steelmaking as it applied to Pittsburgh's social setup. In that process, vast quantities of iron, ore, alloys, and by-products that are at first completely different from one another are melted together in giant cauldrons. Then, after being subjected to enormous and indescribable amounts of heat and hard work, something brand-new is produced that has a unique identity and is unquestionably stronger than the sum of its ingredients. Pittsburghers were proud and appreciative of their differences because they understood how that strengthened the whole, just as it did in steelmaking. For most Black people this "Great Melting Pot" ideal was as far-fetched as the "American Dream" concept. Still, it was meant to portray the country's collective strength made possible through its citizens' individual differences, showing that if Pittsburgh could do it then so could America. As a result, though the chasms separating the city's diverse hilly communities were so steep, deep, and wide that no roads could be constructed, its people were unstoppable in their efforts to traverse them anyway. By the early 1900s, 446 bridges had been built, more than any other municipality in the world, earning Pittsburgh a second nickname as the "City of Bridges." And if they couldn't cross the abysses, they went down into their depths and up the other sides, resulting in the construction of 712 public stairways containing a total of more than 24,000 vertical feet of steps, the most of any American city.

In other words, Pittsburghers tried really hard to get together and stay connected. They had already found common ground through industry, working side by side in the mills. But there was another way. Through sports. As these neighborhoods organized their own formal and informal teams, finding competition literally meant seeking other hills to conquer. As a result, an elaborate sandlot sports culture evolved as scores of squads and clubs emerged. But precisely because of its hilly terrain, Pittsburgh did not have a single municipal playground. Instead, brought together by gamesmanship, neighborhood athletes practiced and competed anywhere they could. That meant on the city's streets, in its alleyways, and across its vacant lots. The reputations of up-and-coming ballers were forged this way. It was treacherous, and only the scrappiest survived. One of them was a Jewish sandlot player from the Hill District named M. R. Goldman who was active in those days.[61] "There is no record of any fatality," he recalled fondly, "but there were many sequelae of black eyes, bruised shins, brain concussions and accidental groin contusions." Nothing stopped them. "Seldom were there any calls for an ambulance or a neighborhood physician," Goldman continued. "The warriors just slunk home to lick their wounds and get ready for the next day's fracas."

Then, in 1904, Washington Park had opened in the Hill District as Pittsburgh's first public playground. The seven-acre level open space with athletic fields and bleachers was a sandlot player's dream. Instantly popular, the park extended from the bottom of Bedford Avenue to Grant Boulevard between Elm and Fulton Streets.[62] It replaced the former site of the Bedford Avenue Reservoir, a basin that had supplied water to downtown Pittsburgh. The park was dramatically located immediately below Central High School and in the shadow of Union Station, the Pennsylvania Rail Road's colossal Pittsburgh hub. Most importantly, being centrally located in the Hill District allowed access from all sides of the city, so Washington Park quickly became a quintessential proving ground for Pittsburgh's entire sandlot sports community.

Yet, the city still did not have a single fully equipped publicly available indoor recreation facility. Though newspapers had reported that the Pittsburgh YMCA was considering adding a "Negro" branch on Wylie Avenue in the Hill District, this talk did not include mention of a gymnasium. That meant basketball players had to innovate. But *sandlot* wasn't just a community. It was a lifestyle, even if no hoop was available, like the one Cum had put up on East Thirteenth Avenue in Homestead. "The arena was any place available in the streets or yards," according to Goldman. "The banking board was any fence, a barrel hoop served as the basket, the playing ball any fairly round and firm contrivance, be it a football bladder stuffed with paper or a bundle of tightly tied rags," he explained. "From these humble beginnings came the nucleus for some of the outstanding basketball teams of the area."[63]

Within those scrappy, gritty ranks, Cumberland Willis Posey, Jr., emerged as the best of the best, excelling in football, baseball, and basketball. "Unheralded and unsung came this debonair rapier of Smokeytown, storming the citadels of the athletic greats in three branches of sport," longtime *Inter-State Tattler* columnist Alvin J. Moses would reminisce.[64]

Finally, during the summer before Cum's senior year at Homestead High School, a field house was completed at Washington Park. The $25,000 two-story brick structure covering a 50-by-135-foot area contained an assembly room, men's and women's baths, a swimming pool, classrooms, a nursery, and a gymnasium with a full-size basketball court.[65] The gym was free for use by all races, ethnicities, and religions. It was open only two nights a week for two hours, Cum would later complain, which put "every colored boy in Allegheny County who owned a pair of rubber soled shoes on the floor at the same time."[65] But one can best believe that he was in there working on his game to be ready for the upcoming basketball season. Those efforts paid off when Cum led Homestead High School to win the 1908–9 city basketball championship title.

Looking forward to his graduation in the school's June 3 commencement, Cum had some choices. Working in one of his father's businesses was still an option. The same month as Homestead's festive basketball parade, the senior Posey had given notice of his intention to incorporate yet another firm, the Beaver Valley Coal, Sand and Supply Company, whose purpose would be "buying, selling and dealing in coal, sand, gravel, brick, stone, cement, lime, plaster, lumber and a general line of builders' supplies."[67]

He could also find employment at one of the Carnegie Steel plants. Work in the mills was tempting, at 75 cents to $1.15 per day starting from as early as age twelve. But this was extremely dangerous. Just during his junior year in high school there had been 526 workplace fatalities in Allegheny County, including 195 steelworkers, 125 railroad men, 71 miners, and the rest in equally hazardous related jobs, of which 82 of them were below age twenty-one. More than half of the men killed were making less than $15 a week.[68] And there were no age limits for labor, so some of the victims had been as young as fourteen years old.

Besides, Homestead itself had a dark side resulting from Carnegie Steel's incredible success. The majority of its residents were males, and of those, 35 percent were unmarried, and 10 percent were under twenty years old. "This large transient body of single men constitutes a serious menace to the home life of the people," the Pittsburgh Council of Churches of Christ would warn.[69] The council found that less fortunate African Americans and the least fortunate Whites lived in crowded tenements, hovels, shacks, and shanty villages on unpaved back streets and back allies surrounding the Homestead mill and along the Monongahela River. Less than 40 percent of Slavic and Black families in the town had running water compared with twice that for "native whites." African Americans and foreigners rarely had indoor toilets, they said, and sewers were frequently exposed or out of order. "One child out every three born among Slavs dies; one child out of every seven among English-speaking Europeans; and one out of every five among the native white and colored," their study revealed, noting that many of these deaths were from malnutrition.

The Hill District had a similar flip side. With the rapid increase of its African American population, the Hill had sprung to life with business opportunities, including twenty barbershops, twelve hotels and restaurants, eight grocery stores, and four pharmacies. The Loendi Club had upgraded from its original clubhouse into a new $10,000 nineteen-room city-mansion on the same block at 83 Fulton. Having expanded from twenty-five founding members to more than 150, their old space had "become inadequate to meet the needs of a growing and enterprising institution."[70] Similarly, in 1907 the Warren Methodist Episcopal Church and its three-hundred-member African American congregation had sold their original building, also on Fulton Street, to purchase a larger church on Center Avenue with seating capacity for eight hundred parishioners.[71] Only several blocks from there, up Wylie, stood the lucrative and well-equipped beauty parlor of Madam C. J. Walker, "one of the most successful business women of the race." The ambitious and visionary pioneer of Black hair-care products had moved her fledgling brand to the Hill in 1907 so that it could take root. She would move to Indianapolis in 1910 once her enterprise was flowing, glowing, and growing.

Just like the Black sections of other northern cities, the Hill District had developed significant social challenges. In 1900, out of five thousand total residents on the Hill, less than three hundred were African Americans, despite the fact that the city's total Black population had grown from two thousand in 1870 to over twenty thousand in 1900. They had dispersed into African American pockets throughout the city. But from 1900 through 1909, some eighty thousand newcomers moved to Pittsburgh, with thirty thousand of them relocating to the Hill District, and of those, ten thousand were African Americans. That meant the Hill had gone from 1 percent of the city's Black residents in 1900 to more than 40 percent by 1909, the year Cum graduated from high school. The district became known as "Little Hayti" due to the large number of Black and brown faces on its streets. "The poorer Negroes live in a network of alleys on either side of Wylie Avenue," sociologist Helen Tucker explained that year. "There are respectable people living here, but the population consists chiefly of poor Negroes and a low class of whites," she continued. "As a result, there is much immorality in this section—speak easies, cocaine joints, and disorderly houses abound." Her research left no block unexamined. "I think I never saw such wretched conditions as in three shanties on Poplar Alley," she reported, of a back street right next to Washington Park.

Considering these aspects of Black life in Pittsburgh, Cum ultimately chose to leave town and go to college. That fall, he enrolled at Penn State University as a chemistry student in the Class of 1913. But although he had left the Smoky City, left Homestead, and left his father's house, it would soon become clear that Cum had not abandoned basketball. In fact, paraphrasing the scripture in Genesis 12:1, the sport seemed to be telling him, "Go to the land that I will show you."

On the afternoon of November 26, 1908, Thanksgiving Day, a large audience of around eight thousand people, "many of whom were of the Caucasian race," assembled in Washington, D.C., at a site on Twelfth Street NW between S and T Streets to witness the laying of the cornerstone for a $100,000 building that would soon become the new home of the city's Colored Branch of the YMCA.[72] Though they did not yet know it, this was the beginning of a new chapter for Black basketball in the District. The crowd, which filled the entire block in front of the location, was waiting for the man who would be giving the principal speech for the ceremony. Their wait was not in vain. He arrived on time. It was President Theodore Roosevelt.[73]

"I cannot too heartily commend the action of those colored men who are responsible for the starting of this building," Roosevelt stated. "When completed it will be a tribute to the advancement of the colored race, and also a monument to the advancement of the city of Washington." The outgoing president had been a friend to African Americans during his two terms in office, so nearly every sentence he spoke was met with an ovation. "As for the white man," he told his audience that afternoon, "let him remember in this as in all other matters, that to do justice to the colored man is demanded, not only by the interest of the colored man, but by the interest of the white man also." His booming voice reportedly carried from one end of the block to the other. "Sooner or later in the community every class of citizen will feel the effect of the raising or degradation of any other class," Roosevelt continued. "'All men up' is a much safer motto than 'Some men down.'" The sacred cultural meaning in the honorable placement of the cornerstone, which determined the position of all other stones in the entire structure, was not lost. People who witnessed his speech that day were so moved that the weekly *New York Age* said, "it will take rank with any utterance that has fallen from the lips of any President of the United States since Abraham Lincoln."

The Washington YMCA Colored Branch had purchased this plot of land measuring 63 by 165 feet on Twelfth Street in 1907 because it had outgrown its offices in True Reformers' Hall around the corner and needed a dedicated space. The branch had already counted nearly six hundred members when it originally moved into True Reformers' shortly after the building opened in 1903, and those numbers as well as its activities just kept expanding. Designed by the prominent Black architect William Sidney Pittman, son-in-law of Booker T. Washington, the magnificent five-story, 35,000-square-foot Renaissance-style structure would include seventy-two rooms for boarders, a swimming pool, and a gymnasium with a running track that encircled a full-size basketball court. Construction was well underway by the time of Roosevelt's speech, and the branch had already become known as the Twelfth Street Colored YMCA even though the new facility would not be officially opened until May 1912. The cost of the new facility, the equivalent of nearly $3 million today, was being covered by African American community donations from nearly five thousand citizens that had already reached $30,000, and by a $25,000 matching grant from John D. Rockefeller.[74]

Just after President Roosevelt finished speaking at that cornerstone event, he turned to "a colored bricklayer" named A. L. Harvey who was standing beside him and borrowed the workman's wooden-handled steel trowel. Then, as a choir sang "How Firm a Foundation," the president shoveled and spread out the first mortar a few moments before a giant block of granite was lowered into its place on that spot. The stone had a compartment that included a copper box, which served as a time capsule. It contained copies of local newspapers, a Bible, some Colored YMCA history pamphlets, and a YMCA pin.

During any other time, what President Roosevelt said and did that Thanksgiving afternoon would have been seen as just words and gestures. But this was at a moment in history when the slightest affirmation, the smallest reinforcement from a White leader at a national level was more than what many Black people could have expected in the course of an entire lifetime. Coming from a sitting president, this was rock-solid progress for the race, powerfully symbolic and inspiring to African Americans everywhere. It also showed that as the 1908–9 season was about to begin, Black basketball was on a sturdy footing. But although the game among African Americans was poised for growth, no one in attendance that day could imagine what that really meant.

Within a week after President Roosevelt's cornerstone ceremony at the future home of the Twelfth Street Colored YMCA, the athletic editor of the Howard University campus newspaper, a senior from Jackson, Mississippi, named Artee Fleming, urged the three basketball teams previously formed by the college's students to "get together immediately and select a captain" for the 1908–9 season so they could merge into one squad. A future Howard Law School graduate who would eventually become the first African American to argue a case before the Missouri Supreme Court, Fleming's rationale seemed to be that an all-star team using the most talented players from Howard Academy, Howard Medical, and Howard College could represent the entire university in the ISAA Basket Ball League.[75] Artee himself played for the Howard College squad. He knew something. The competition in the ISAA league would be stiffer than during the prior season. But the university's student-run athletic committee failed to take his advice.

A month later, in an early season ISAA game that had Artee in the lineup, Howard College lost by one point to the Crescent Athletic Club in front of a "wildly enthusiastic" Saturday-night audience of more than five hundred people at True Reformers' Hall.[76] The final score was 8–7. EB refereed the game and its official timekeeper was ISAA president William Joiner. That loss angered some folks at Howard, especially after learning how the gate receipts would be split. Seeing hundreds of ticket-buying spectators at these basketball games had become the norm. But the ISAA, which kept meticulous books, had to save its net income for the spring track season and other expenses. A dispute erupted that ultimately caused the Howard College team to withdraw from the league altogether. "The main and only reason offered for the action," the *University Journal* reported, was that the athletic committee, "or rather some few members thereof, are of the opinion that the I.S.A.A. are using the students to make money for private purposes." They were wrong, but that left the two other Howard squads, the Medics and the Preps, to fend for themselves.

Pulling out had consequences, because William Joiner of the ISAA Basket Ball League had made an arrangement with J. Hoffman Woods of the Smart Set Athletic Club. Whichever team won the ISAA league champion would host the Brooklyn squad in the District at season's end. This was another reason the ISAA had been saving its funds. That post-season game would be important because some of the Washington, D.C., faithful saw it as "the championship of colored teams in this part of the country."[77] The two organizations had also agreed that the Smart Set would then return the favor by inviting the ISAA league's best interscholastic squad up to Brooklyn for a game. Being absent meant that Howard University had taken themselves out of these opportunities to showcase themselves.

Woods and the Smart Set, on the other hand, were ready to show and prove. They had every reason to be so confident, even when the 1908–9 season in New York City opened with three new squads in New York City and three more in New Jersey, for a total of "six organized colored basketball teams in the field."[78] One of the newcomers, from Harlem, was a team representing the Alpha Physical Culture Club, known as the Alpha Big Five, which the Norman brothers had finally been able to assemble. To celebrate their accomplishment, the organization held a "ladies' night" reception at its club on West 134th

Street in Harlem. "The rooms were handsomely decorated," said the *New York Age*, and "the basketball team was given a rousing cheer by the members and friends for their splendid work."[79] A second new all-Black team came out of the St. Cyprian program Rev. John Wesley Johnson had been developing in San Juan Hill, whose influence in the surrounding neighborhood had become "manifold," according to a reporter. "The young men have organized a basketball team," he explained.[80] Though they were classified as "lightweight," that is, with average player weight less than 125 pounds, this squad would rise to the occasion and soon become known as the St. Cyprian "Speed Boys" as this was "a very fitting name for them and their style of play."[81] The third newcomer, this team from Brooklyn, was the St. Augustine Guild, formed by members of the St. Augustine's Church. "Though modest in their pretentions," the very diplomatic George Lattimore of the Smart Set AC suggested, St. Augustine would give "an excellent account of themselves" that season.[82]

Regarding the Carlton YMCA Marathons, they had disbanded after the 1907–8 season when stenographer Clarence E. Lucas relocated to Washington, D.C. He became the head bookkeeper at Howard University after enrolling in law school there, and later joined the investment department of the local National Benefit Life Insurance Company.

Across the Hudson River in New Jersey, the Jersey City Athletic Club debuted a new African American team, as did the Owl Field Club and the Strollers Athletic Club in nearby Newark. Regardless of all these new squads, the Smart Set Athletic Club had every intention of defending its OAL and Colored World's Basketball Championship titles, so they made a very smart preseason move by snagging Ferdinand Accooe off the Marathons' roster when that team dispersed. He had been their best player. Sensing the building excitement about Black basketball, J. Hoffman Woods, who had a knack for promotional work and seemed to "know everyone," started running newspaper advertisements in the Black press to attract more spectators. "When Smart Set plays you are always sure of a good game," one of the team's advertisements promised. "It's a real corker!"[83] Charging a thirty-five-cent admission fee, they generated enough revenue to cover operating costs such as the venue rental and the adverting expense. As demand for tickets soared, the Brooklyn club outgrew the Knickerbocker Courts and moved its home games to larger facilities at Pilgrim Hall on Court Street, Avon Hall on Bedford Avenue, and the Fourteenth Regiment Armory in Park Slope. To keep in step, other all-Black basketball teams in New York City followed the Smart Set's lead with advertising and musical accompaniment for their games. Within one season, some African American floor games in New York City were drawing up to 1,200 ticket-buying onlookers.

Woods also added a new enticement for fans: music. Music before games, during halftime, and after the action on the court was over, long into the night, so that folks could dance. He belonged to the Metropolitan Association of Dancing Masters, so the Smart Set president understood the vibe that people were after. It was the same thing the Waldron brothers at the Manhattan Casino knew: They wanted to dance. Popular music was transitioning from waltzes, marches, and jigs into ragtime, a new specifically African American artform. When the phonograph record player had first become commercially available in the early 1900s, people who previously didn't know about ragtime finally realized how amazing a fully orchestrated recording could sound. Before that, a piano with sheet music in the parlor or the saloon had been the only options, for anyone who could afford a piano, a parlor, or visits to saloons. Ragtime music was so catchy and infectious that it created a dancing craze. But one couldn't put a ragtime band in their parlor and most people couldn't afford a phonograph, either. To go dancing, they had to leave the house. This created a boom in ballroom construction. Filling those ballrooms meant hiring ragtime musicians, and most were Black artists. This was the vanguard. Suddenly, phonographs had allowed African American entertainers to compose and perform on their own terms, for who they truly were, not as minstrels in "blackface" on stage for White "coon show" audiences. Positive and culturally affirming opportunities for Black talent in the entertainment industry began to replace insulting, degrading minstrelsy.

But since those ballrooms were empty some nights, enterprising and observant African American basketball promoters like J. Hoffman Woods saw opportunities as well. Needing indoor floor space for courts, they partnered these trends to produce singularly meaningful social events. That's why Woods ran newspaper advertisements with the headline, BASKET BALL AND DANCE. And that's why he hired the J. Nimrod Jones Orchestra, a popular all-Black Brooklyn-based ragtime ensemble, as the Smart Set Athletic Club's house band. More than just a bandleader, the twenty-nine-year-old Jones was an up-and-coming musical prodigy who would soon play violin in recording sessions with the highly acclaimed and pioneering African American ragtime pianist, composer, and lyricist Ford Dabney.

Embodying the views of club cofounder Samuel Scottron, Smart Set leaders were indeed "the force that moves things!"[84] That season, their program expanded its basketball schedule beyond the Olympian Athletic League and "also competed against many of the crack white teams of Brooklyn," wrote sports columnist Lester Walton. And they made a very creditable showing." This was a breakthrough in and of itself, and the club didn't joke with it. In one close "fast and rough" game during that 1908–9 season against the Sapphire Athletic Club, an all-White squad, some of the Smart Set players "when they lost their shoes never stopped to pick them up."[85] That contest ended in a 19–19 tie. They even earned a nickname, the "Grave Diggers," partly because Brooklyn at the time contained more cemeteries and headstones than any other borough in New York City—and also due to "the uncanny faculty of the team to mow down all opposition."[86]

The Smart Set Athletic Club's ambition to push its own boundaries and conquer foes beyond New York City was well-known. But this backfired midseason when they scheduled two games with the Jersey City AC. That's because Jersey City had an eighteen-year-old unknown phenom named Hudson "Huddy" Oliver, Jr. Huddy was the team captain and played right guard while his older brother Clinton, age twenty-two, played the left guard position.[87] They were the sons of an up-and-coming Massachusetts-born Black stenographer and longtime employee of Thomas Prosser & Son, the American representative of the German cast-steel manufacturing giant Friedrich Krupp AG, which was the largest company in Europe. One of the brothers' first cousins twice removed had married Frederick Douglass's son, Frederick Jr.[88] Both young men were born on West Fourth Street in Little Africa on the "better" side of Sixth Avenue, around the corner from where Will Anthony Madden had lived on West Third.[89] Will was a few years older than them, so they probably weren't neighborhood playmates, and the Olivers had moved to New Jersey when Hudson was two years old. But basketball connected them now.

The Smart Set had only scheduled that first game against Jersey City, on Wednesday, December 30, 1908, because their original opponent, Howard University, couldn't show up "owing to some complications."[90] The Grave Diggers had defeated every all-Black foe, so their fans assumed Jersey City would be "entirely outclassed" and lose as well. Besides, "no one had knowledge of their capabilities." During the first half, "this feeling became more pronounced, as the score stood 10 to 3 in favor of the Brooklyn boys." But basketball is a game of adjustments, and "in the second half the Jersey City team seemed to have gotten a line on the Brooklynites tactics and warmed up to them in such fashion as to cause consternation to the opposing team." In other words, Jersey City started catching up. This got under Brooklyn's skin. They weren't used to losing. But lose they did, by a single point, 14–13. Following basketball tradition, the trophy for the winners was a "silver loving cup."

Leveraging their unknowns and the element of surprise as strategic advantages would become the model for future African American basketball teams, a tactic that would continue to work for decades to come. But when the Smart Set scheduled a second encounter with Jersey City two months later to seek redemption, they faced problems again. This time they played in the Bedford section of Brooklyn, a Tuesday evening game on February 23, 1909, that tipped off at 8 P.M. "Both teams are exponents of scientific playing," Woods's ad specified. "The game will be well worth seeing at all hazard." It was held at Avon Hall, a large sixty-by-eighty-foot brick and brownstone facility built in 1885 on the corner of Bedford Avenue and Halsey Street that the *Brooklyn Daily Eagle* newspaper described as "a temple dedicated to harmless games and amusements."[91] Holding over a thousand spectators, a fabulous feature of this venue was that the floor of its ballroom, almost the full size of the building, had been "laid on one hundred and fifty rubber springs, giving it an amount of elasticity almost sufficient to set the casual visitor dancing." Of course, a reception with music would follow the action. People were excited, because with admission set at twenty-five cents and another loving cup at stake, "both teams were playing not only for the trophy, but for the championship of the six colored basketball teams of New York, Brooklyn, and Jersey City." Also, this was the "Last Big Pre-Lenten Basket Ball Game." This was referring to the commandment spawned by the Christian origins of the game in the YMCA, unwritten but strictly observed among Black basketball managers, that games were forbidden to be scheduled, played, or watched between Ash Wednesday and Easter, the forty-day holy period known as Lent.

Unfortunately for the Smart Set, none of these factors mattered. "Very different from the first game, the Jersey City team demonstrated clearly their superiority over the Brooklyn team" and won again, 8 to 5. The same Jersey

City team went on to trounce the St. Christopher Club, with Will Anthony Madden as their mascot, by a 27 to 13 score, and Conrad Norman's squad, the Alpha Big Five, winning 18 to 4. Huddy was behind all of these wins. "Mr. Hudson Oliver," the *Age* exclaimed, "has amazed the public by his wonderful playing and is looked upon as the best player of the six colored teams."[92]

Fortunately for the Brooklyn squad, their season was far from over, because they still had their remaining games as well as matchups against the ISAA Basket Ball League's best club and school teams in those previously agreed upon home and away games. "Under the efficient management of J. Hoffman Woods, who has done much this year to promote basketball, a game has been planned for the Smart Set Team to play the Crescent Team, of Washington, D.C.," Lester Walton reported for the *Age,* since the Crescent AC was that season's top ISAA club.[93]

After the Smart Set captured the 1908–9 Olympian Athletic League championship title in early April, their second consecutive, the club's attention turned to the Crescents. "This team," the *Washington Herald* affirmed, "has put up a sterling article of basket-ball throughout the long season, and has found favor with the fans."[94] Not taking anything too lightly this time, the Smart Set made another smart move just before they traveled to the nation's capital, boldly persuading Huddy Oliver, the popular Jersey City star himself, to join their roster.

The "Grave Diggers," with Huddy on board, left Brooklyn on the evening of Friday, April 9, and headed for Washington, D.C., by train. But this was no easy task. The Pennsylvania Rail Road was in the middle of constructing its vast as-yet-unnamed terminal building in Midtown Manhattan, which would stretch between Seventh and Ninth Avenues from West Thirty-First to West Thirty-Third Streets. The steel had been erected and much of the stonework was in place. And, a series of single- and double-track tunnels "lined with iron plates and stiffened with a concrete jacket two feet thick" had already been dug underneath Manhattan and below the East River, connecting New Jersey, Manhattan, and Long Island. But these "stupendous undertakings" would not be opened for public traffic until 1910.[95] So the Smart Set AC entourage had to make their way to the foot of Fulton Street in downtown Brooklyn, catch the Brooklyn Annex steam ferry around the tip of Manhattan to Jersey City, then journey to the Pennsylvania Rail Road's Manhattan Transfer station more than six miles west of there to board one of its New York to Washington trains. They would arrive in the nation's capital five hours later and disembark at the District's brand-new Union Station.

The following night, the Smart Set and the Crescents met at True Reformers' Hall and, as reported by the *Washington Herald,* a White daily newspaper that would eventually merge into the *Washington Post,* it was "the most exciting game of basket-ball ever played" in the venue. The game was "evenly waged" during the first half with "the two teams running neck and neck, alternating by one score, first favor of one and then the other." At halftime the Smart Set was ahead by one point, 7–6. But the second half was a whole different story as "the visitors easily demonstrated their superiority over the local boys." Quickly hitting three straight unanswered shots with all-around talent that was "something marvelous," the Grave Diggers "took all the basket-ball notions out of the Crescents" and "showed the local champs what basket-ball really is." Putting up an exhibition, the Brooklyn squad "tossed goals and confused their opponents at will." Crescent players "at times could not even touch the ball, neither in the play nor in the toss-up," the *Herald* explained, "and now they can plainly see that they did not know the game, for basket-ball in New York and the same game in Washington don't look like the same thing."

What made the event so spectacular for those who saw it was that although the Smart Set players "were lighter by far than the locals," it wasn't their size but their agility "that showed the Crescents up so badly." Their "whirlwind work" gave them the win, 27–11. Chester Moore had made five field goals while Charlie Scottron and Ferdinand Accooe had three each. Though quiet in the box score, Huddy's leadership seemed evident. This was history. And, in true sportsmanlike fashion, the victorious Smart Set Athletic Club players and managers were honored after the battle with a party thrown by several Howard University students from Brooklyn and New York City. Hosting and toasting the visiting out of town team, win or lose, became a Black basketball tradition after that.[96]

For the Smart Set's 1908–9 season finale, they returned to Brooklyn for a home game with the ISAA league's best school team, as agreed, which turned out to be Armstrong Manual Technical High. Armstrong made the journey to New York City with its players and managers as well as with a special guest. It was Edwin "EB" Henderson, who accompanied the team as their instructor. This made sense, because some Armstrong players may literally have learned how to play the sport itself from him. EB would also be the official referee for the game. The event was scheduled for the evening of Saturday, April 17, at Pilgrim Hall, a one-thousand-capacity venue on the corner of Court and Douglass Streets in what today is Cobble Hill in downtown Brooklyn. The popular venue was familiar to the Smart Set, who had been using it all season for Saturday games. But it was best known as the home court of the Brooklyn Emeralds, a popular all-White amateur lightweight team that played in the Protective Basket Ball League. (One of their rivals in the league was another Brooklyn-based White squad, the heavyweight Knickerbocker Five, who were nicknamed the "Knicks.") A unique feature of the Pilgrim court was that the baskets were attached to the backboards using "a 12-inch shank instead of a 6-inch shank," probably "the only ones of their kind in use in Greater New York."[97]

Advertised as "Washington vs. Brooklyn," the big tip-off was set for 7 P.M. with dancing to follow at 9:30 P.M., and Woods had appropriately upped the admission fee to forty cents. "Those desiring comfortable seats will please come early," his newspaper ads recommended. When a "large and fashionable audience" showed up, many were expecting a close game.[98] But the encounter "had not been in progress two minutes before it was evident to all that the Brooklyn players were much the superiors of the boys from the capital," according to Lester Walton of the *New York Age*.[99] "From the minute the whistle blew the Smart Set team started in with an air of determination and vim," Walton continued. "Not that the visitors did not put up an aggressive game, but they were outplayed from every standpoint," the sportswriter shared.[100] Ultimately, Armstrong lost 18 to 4, with Brooklyn retaining its Colored Basketball World's Champion status. Huddy had produced three baskets to lead all scorers. Leaving no stone unturned, the Smart Set Athletic Club had even brought their own "official rooter" to the game, who was listed in the box score. Her name was Alice Cordelia Scottron, a single, twenty-year-old who was a granddaughter of the late Smart Set cofounder Samuel R. Scottron. She had had her eyes on Smart Set player Ferdinand Accooe, who scored a field goal in the winning effort. They would get married two years later, connecting two of Brooklyn's most celebrated African American families.

Artee's argument in the Howard University student newspaper was right, because win or lose, the college would have been cast in a major spotlight, had they not walked away from the opportunity. Instead, something else had been proven. It was that in spite of EB's visionary leadership, the ISAA's breakthroughs, and the contagious enthusiasm of Howard's local fans, the Black basketball pioneers of New York City, specifically the men running the Smart Set Athletic Club, had been more forward-thinking, more aggressive in pushing the boundaries of what was conceivable in the sport among African Americans. Meanwhile, the on-court setbacks of 1908–9 were not the end of Black basketball in Washington, D.C. This wasn't a sign that EB had been teaching his students the wrong way to play the game. If anything, it meant he had not been spending enough time doing so.

CHAPTER 12

AS OUR WHITE FRIENDS PLAY IT

DURING THE SUMMER OF 1909, Edwin "EB" Henderson understood that the dispute between some members of Howard University's student-run athletic committee and the ISAA Basket Ball League was out of his control. He saw how the game was developing in New York City and the moves that the managers at the Smart Set Athletic Club were making to expand their horizons. Making moves like that within the ISAA league structure involved either multiple sign-offs from several different independent teams and organizations or potential criticism, or both. But these were limitations at precisely the moment when there was a window of opportunity for the District to have its own traveling all-Black basketball team. So, EB took matters into his own hands and devised an idea. The plan was to get as many of the area's best court men onto one team, effectively following the earlier advice from Artee, the Howard athletic editor.

Then, as EB was considering his roster, something amazing happened. Hudson "Huddy" Oliver, the Grave Digger star from Jersey City, enrolled in Howard University's medical program for the fall semester of 1909. Huddy was one of the game's best talents, and EB quickly persuaded him to join the new squad. The gym teacher also secured several more key players.

There was twenty-year-old Howard sophomore Edward "Ed" Gray, one of the best athletes in the city, who had been a three-sport "terror" at M Street High School before attending Amherst College, where, during his first year at halfback, he was selected as a 1908 Walter Camp All-American in football, along with future Olympic gold medalist and National Football League player Jim Thorpe of the Carlisle Indian School. Gray, at right guard, had transferred to Howard a year later, leading the university's football team to an undefeated season and the Black college national championship. The speedy running back was "as fast in a game of basket ball as he is in a game of foot ball or in a 220 hurdle race."[1] Gray was also a ferocious competitor, known to "play the game for life and death."[2] At left forward was twenty-one-year-old Howard freshman Arthur Leo "Buck" Curtis, a Chicago native whose father was the chief surgeon at Freedman's Hospital in Washington, D.C. Freedman's, known today as Howard University Hospital, had been founded in 1862 to provide healthcare to formerly enslaved people and was the teaching center for the university's medical school. Buck had played basketball at Williston Seminary, a private boarding school in Massachusetts, before enrolling in Howard's junior medicine program, where he trained to become an anesthesiologist. Backing up at the left guard spot was "F.A" Taylor, who played varsity football at Howard as a right tackle and was the manager of its track team while also in the school's Medical Department. Formerly with the Medics, he too had an unstoppable demeanor. "Taylor is a very small boy but he is so large however paradoxical it may seem," the Howard *University Journal* wrote of him, heading into the 1909–10 basketball season. Henry F. Nixon, a business manager of the *University Journal* who had played with the "Preps," was "a reliable forward" and the team's captain. Maurice Clifford, another forward, was an instructor at Armstrong Technical High who previously played for the Medics. Then there was Howard University law student Lewis E. Johnson, who was also the secretary of the Washington YMCA Colored Men's Branch. He would soon prove to be a vital connection. And finally, EB himself was the team's manager, playing center.[3]

With so many Howard students jumping to EB's new squad, the school's student newspaper began wondering out loud about "our fellows who are joining basket ball teams in the city and taking away the talent and ability necessary to aid in lifting Howard to a higher level in the athletic world." Something was up. "These men are bringing funds to somebody while they are playing primarily for the sport," the *Journal* continued. "We should consider this and provide for these men that they may represent Howard when they play."[4] It was the beginning of an argument on campus that the college should have its own gymnasium, if not actually compensate their players. This had been an ongoing issue that was up for debate, but EB had a squad with no court seeking a court with no squad. The window was now.

He found the perfect solution at True Reformers' Hall, where the Washington Colored YMCA was keeping their offices while waiting for the completion of the branch's new home on Twelfth Street. They had the building and its basketball court at their disposal but did not have a team. This was where Lewis Johnson's influence may have helped. EB proposed to bring the new squad under the Colored Y umbrella in return for permission to use their basketball court for his games. Branch officials, including Johnson, embraced the proposal because it would mean more exposure for their programming and membership efforts as well as much needed extra income from their share of ticket sales. They adopted the new squad, and it soon became known as the Washington Twelfth Street Colored YMCA, or simply the Twelfth Streeters.

Their court at True Reformers' Hall was quirky, a typical trait in those early days when few playing venues had been built with basketball in mind. Measuring about thirty by eighty feet with thirty-foot ceilings, the floor size was small compared to today's regulation courts, which are fifty by ninety-four feet. This venue also had several structural support columns standing along one sideline, which were technically in bounds. They were plainly in the way, but unmovable, which meant that a player would learn their exact location sooner or later. "Basket ball is full of hard, consistent playing and requires coolness, quickness, accuracy, good judgment and self control, all of which qualities are necessary in the rounding up of a good character," the Howard student newspaper explained. These peculiar structural attributes gave the Twelfth Streeters a distinct home court advantage that would soon help catapult them into national fame. In fact, they would become practically unbeatable. Now all EB had to do was schedule games.

In late October 1909, about 235 miles north of Washington, the Alpha Physical Culture Club held a member meeting at its Harlem quarters during which Conrad Norman gave a speech. "To be happy our motives must be high and unselfish," Conrad stated. "Alpha must mean something," he explained. "It must be an honor to belong to the club." Specifically, the club founder was bringing up an issue that concerned most of the Black basketball teams in New York City. EB was facing the same situation in D.C. "Steps are to be at once taken," Conrad directed the group, "to materialize plans for obtaining large enough quarters to permit an adequate gymnasium." With nearly fifty members, the

Alpha PCC was already outgrowing its clubhouse. "A fund is to be set aside and the proceeds from all the matinee dances, basketball games, receptions and picnics are to be added to it," Conrad continued. In his opinion, this was more than just having enough room for members to exercise in comfort. "To help the Alpha toward getting a gymnasium," he insisted, "is to help toward solving the race problem."[5] Conrad Norman was not playing around. This was the mindset of the Alpha Physical Culture Club going into the 1909–10 basketball season. And they didn't waste any time.

A week later, on Tuesday afternoon, November 2, 1909, the Alphas staged their "First Grand Matinee Dance of the Season," a fundraising event at the Plaza Assembly Rooms, a large convention space in Midtown Manhattan.[6] Admission was thirty-five cents, and the event featured music by the New Amsterdam Orchestra, with dancing from 1 to 6 P.M. It was Election Day, so Alpha PCC advertisements for the dance noted that a special voting booth for ladies would be set up at the entrance. "Each one will receive a regular ballot," their ads said, and be "allowed to vote exactly as the men are doing outside." This was a tip of the hat by Conrad to the women's suffrage movement, bringing attention to voting rights when the club could have remained silent on the matter. But just as noted in his speech, silence was complicity and unacceptable. In fact, behind the scenes Conrad was helping develop and coach the city's first all-Black female basketball team. They would debut within months as a sister organization to the Alpha Big Five squad, calling themselves the New York Girls. One of the Girls' stars would be a captivating twenty-three-year-old stage actor named Dora B. Cole, a sister of the famous performer Robert Allen Cole, Jr., of the wildly successful African American vaudeville act Cole & Johnson. She would soon help the new squad dominate all competition.

Meanwhile, the concept of the Olympic Athletic League had faded away. With more African American teams in the area, the original OAL clubs seemed content to go independent, and by scheduling games against one another anyway, they would in effect produce the same results as a circuit would have. Conrad had been busy reaching out to the other all-Black squads. "The schedule arranged by the energetic manager of the Alpha basketball teams is one that bids fair to test the playing ability of the members," an update about the club's upcoming season stated.[7] "It will no doubt furnish plenty of amusement and excitement for all lovers of clean, healthy sport." Following the lead of the

Smart Set, Conrad had scheduled a game in the nation's capital. It would be the Alpha Big Five's season opener, set for Christmas Eve against EB's new squad, the Washington Colored YMCA. And the venue would be the unique court at True Reformers' Hall.

As the Alpha Big Five headed for Washington "with several rooters" on December 24, they felt "confident of giving a good account of themselves." But even during their warmups, the long train ride on game day combined with the activity of the holidays looked like it had taken a toll. "The Alphas, stocky and good looking, took the court early in the evening," reported the *New York Age*, which had sent a journalist to D.C. to cover the game.[8] "Their practice showed accuracy in goal shooting, but they seemed somewhat slow." Pregame looks could be deceiving, so the "large and enthusiastic crowd" of over six hundred fans couldn't really tell yet what was going on. "After a few moments' practice, the Y.M.C.A. team, led by Henderson, appeared, and the game began." At first, it was a defensive struggle. "The game started with rough playing by both teams due to a close and cautious guarding." Lots of fouls were called, but no damage was done because neither squad was hitting their free throws, including EB, who missed three. This was the trend until "Nixon, after a neat pass from Henderson, negotiated a ringer" for the home team. The score "seesawed for a while" but the action had to be stopped when Twelfth Streeter left forward Buck Curtis suffered a head injury that caused him to leave the game. His departure lit a fire, because when play resumed, "the Y.M.C.A. boys threw four baskets in quick succession" to take a 17–6 lead going into halftime.

Keeping that energy going, EB's squad "played with full steam on" in the second half. "Henderson shot four pretty goals" to make up for his missed free throws earlier in the game, and Huddy also got involved. "Oliver came down the field and landed two ringers that hardly touched the cords of the baskets." Ultimately, the Washington Colored Y never looked back, defeating the Alphas 32 to 15 in a game the *Washington Evening Star* declared was "the cleanest and best exhibition of basket ball by a local colored team" to date.[9] "Ed Gray and Huddy Oliver were invincible as guards," said the *Age*, while Curtis, Nixon, and Henderson were "right on their job every minute" for the winners. The visiting Alpha Big Five, "all tall men, excelled in high passing and bewildering team work." But they were "slow on the local floor" while the Twelfth Streeters "were much faster" and "threw all sorts of goals."

That the event was described as "one of the best games of basketball ever seen in Washington" was an extraordinary validation of EB's efforts on many levels, considering this was the first team he had ever put together, that he had begun without a court, that it had been the squad's first ballgame, and that they had gotten the win.[10] Pulling this off made it clear that the gym teacher was a basketball mastermind.

Conrad Norman and the Alpha Big Five would have another shot at the Twelfth Streeters back in New York City for the home end of their home-and-away series with EB's team. Meanwhile, even in defeat, having played in the District's finest basketball games ever was high praise, a meaningful gift for Norman's squad to relish as their train journeyed back to Manhattan on Christmas Day. Despite losing, the Alpha Physical Culture Club's reputation had grown, which supported Conrad's vision that "Alpha must mean something." Their trip had also reinforced what the Smart Set Athletic Club proved during the prior season, that traveling long distances for road games was worth it.

Will Anthony Madden had been staying busy and doing all the right things to keep advancing within the St. Christopher Club, gradually assuming more responsibility and becoming more visible. In 1909, under Major Hart's wing, he had been appointed as the organization's treasurer and "acted as Announcer of the Club at various games" starting with the 1909–10 season.[11] Thanks to Major, the St. C's basketball programming had been just as ambitious as the Alphas, the Smart Set, and the Washington Colored YMCA. The military vet knew that Black basketball was on fire and kept pushing the organization with new ideas to meet the demand. That's why he scheduled a New Year's Day matinee game and dance at the Twelfth Regiment Armory, a massive castle-like structure on West Sixty-Second Street at Columbus Avenue, which none of the other African American teams had used before. With his unique military background, Major may have been able to pull some strings in order to secure the facility, which contained an enormous drill hall surrounded by elevated bleachers with wooden flooring that seemed ready-made for basketball.

The opponent Major booked for the January 1 game was the Alpha Big Five, who had just returned from their Washington, D.C., loss to the Twelfth Streeters. Alpha vs. St. Christopher was bound to be an exciting encounter, and this was Major's big chance to take the lead and stand apart from the rest, so he went all out. His team would also need to play at their best to win. Tip-off was "at one o'clock sharp," with music provided by not one but two popular ensembles, the Excelsior Military Brass Band and the New Amsterdam Orchestra. Booking two musical groups was an innovative move. It would create its own friendly competition between the bands and ensure that "the dancing was continual." All for just thirty-five cents. This event would also give Will his first opportunity to really shine in public, because he was named as the game's "official announcer." Before microphones and audio systems, this meant his voice would have to carry throughout the venue as he introduced players, reported scores, declared substitutions, and presented the bands, among other duties, in effect being the master of ceremonies. Not only that, this also meant Will would be the vocal instigator of the Red & Black Machine's rooting section. It was in this loquacious role that his confident verbosity first caught people's attention. In fact, Will's voice and words may have actually helped change the outcome of the game.[12]

Drawn by the novelty of the new location, dueling orchestras, the growing charisma of both organizations, and the promise of intense basketball, a very large and unusually diverse crowd had showed up for the matchup. "Besides those present from New York, Brooklyn and Jersey, there were also visitors from Camden, Philadelphia, Washington, Baltimore and Pittsburg," the *New York Age* reported. This made the affair "the most select gathering of the season." The teams were evenly matched, so from the opening jump ball it was "a fast, hard game, and when the first half ended the score stood 6 to 6." Folks had hoped and paid for that exact action-packed scenario. "By this time the great crowd was almost at the pinnacle of excitement because it was easily seen that the game was to be a *battle royal.*" That's because a close score guaranteed uncontainable banter and a halftime full of meaningful, memorable mingling, amid nonstop music, with yearning and learning among out-of-town guests and between city newcomers far away from home. Before most people had telephones or traveled, this was the original social networking. Events like these were about more than just basketball. They helped build communities.

Meanwhile, it seemed that Will had found his element. "The members of each club and their following kept up an almost continual line of cheering," the *Age* explained. "The St. Christopher contingent, under the leadership of Will Anthony Madden, being especially demonstrative in cheering for their team." His efforts were crucial, because their star center, Charles Bradford, had left the game with an injury during the first half "and for awhile this fact threw a damper on the feelings of St. C." But when Will announced the second half just as Bradford "again appeared on the court with his teammates ready to finish the game, the cheering that broke loose knew no bounds." This was basketball drama at its finest. "From the sound of the whistle the St. Christophers started the second half with a rush that put them several points in the lead." Although the Alphas "played and tried hard," said the *Age*, they were getting outplayed and "could not reduce the lead gained by their adversaries." St. Christopher won the game, 22–16. Father Daniel had earned back a little bit of the respect he had lost with the Alphas at Ulmer Park that time, and Will had made a name for himself.

Up in Harlem, Louis and Eddie Waldron had also been staying busy. The owners of the Manhattan Casino were working hard to make their place the go-to venue for African American events. As long as organizers charged admission, which made the affairs private, then dancing and alcohol were allowed without police interference. The venue's six-thousand-square-foot ballroom pavilion, with its "handsome, spacious and brilliantly lighted platform," was so large that thousands of people could be frolicking on it all at once.[13] And with the convenience of their own saloon and beer garden on the premises, selling liquor had become especially profitable. Over the years since its opening, if it was a gathering at the Manhattan Casino, everyone just had a really good time. Masquerade balls, musical receptions, fundraising festivals, lodge celebrations, church outings, and political rallies at the venue had become so reliably fabulous that Black folks began calling it "The People's Pleasure Palace" and the "Waldron's Palace of Mirth."[14] African American patrons felt welcome. "This beautiful park is rapidly gaining in popularity and next year," the *New York Age* predicted in the fall of 1906, "will be in greater demand by the various social organizations who appreciate the good service given by the management."[15]

The brothers did have one main uptown rival for booking large-scale African American events, a facility known as Sulzer's Harlem River Park & Casino. Built in the late 1880s, Sulzer's took up an entire city block from East

126th Street to East 127th between First and Second Avenues. "At this park for many years back have been held some of the largest gatherings of New York's colored social and fraternal organizations," the *Age* reported.[16] But in 1907, Sulzer's had mysteriously burned to the ground. After that, their previous clients, including the Colored Republican Club, Southern Beneficial League, Negro Printers' Association, Hotel Bellmen's Beneficial Association, West Indian Benevolent Society, and even the St. Philip's Young Men's Guild, one of Bishop's featured programs at St. Philip's Church, all began using the Manhattan Casino instead.

No one had thought of using that venue for basketball, though. That is, until Conrad Norman. First, he reimagined the immense ballroom as a sports venue. "Manhattan Casino, one of the largest and most commodious halls in the city, has been secured for the game with the YMCA team of Washington," he alerted newspapers, after scheduling the Alpha Big Five's subsequent home game with the Twelfth Streeters there, for February 2, 1910. Next, even though no basketball had ever been played there, Conrad advertised the venue as "The Biggest And Best Court In New York City." To make this narrative work, the Waldrons brought in basketball standards with backboards and baskets. Then, they made sure the playing surface would be safe. "The dance floor will be covered with canvas for the game," the *New York Age* explained, "making an ideal court for the players." Though this covering was advertised as a special feature, in reality the management installed the rugged cloth simply to protect the gorgeous polished wood below. Instantly, the Manhattan Casino had become the largest racially integrated basketball arena in the country. And that wasn't all. This particular Wednesday night game was filled with so many firsts that it would usher in a pivotal new chapter in the history of Black basketball.

To begin, Conrad upped the admission fee to fifty cents, the highest amount that had ever been charged for an African American basketball game. But despite this, the event drew in "nearly twelve hundred persons," the largest crowd ever to see such an event. That's because he and the Waldron brothers were inventive in arranging and promoting the event. Instead of just one game, they scheduled a triple-header, the first ever among Black fans of the sport, and called the event a "Grand Basket Ball Carnival."[17] The preliminary matchup would be between the St. Christopher and Alpha junior teams, the second had the St. Christopher Big Five facing Baltimore Colored High School, and the main event would pair the Twelfth Streeters with the Alpha Big Five, which Conrad hyped as "Washington vs. New York."

Another special feature of the game was that spectators were offered premium seating, again the first time ever for an African American basketball game. These were fifty-one velvet-lined boxes in the second-floor balcony that surrounded the dance floor, with each box containing eight plush seats at a dollar each, advertised as "best to view the game." Aside from being a luxurious way to watch the action below, these seats offered dignity and a counter-narrative as well as respite from the racist "chicken roost" or "nigger heaven" terminology that White newspapers used routinely when describing any theater balcony from California to Kansas to Maine, reminding everyone that Black folks weren't allowed to sit wherever they wished.

There was more. "Special arrangements have been made for exhibiting the scores as the game progresses," the *Age* reported. "This will serve to keep up the interest and increase the enthusiasm among the spectators." The owners had installed an electric scoreboard, never before seen in use at a Black basketball game. This "contrivance," pioneered by the Baird Electric Scoreboard Company, could be "operated by experts from the press box" and "controlled entirely by electrical devices" with which they merely had to "touch a button on the switchboard in front of them in the press box to get results on the scoreboard."[18] This too was advertised in advance, a fascinating innovation that gave patrons yet another reason to attend the game.

Finally, there was dancing afterward to music by a large orchestra under the direction of revered musician and Alpha Physical Culture Club member Professor Robert F. Douge.

In the featured game, Washington defeated New York, 35–19. "The YMCA team played as a machine," the *Evening Star*, a D.C. newspaper, reported. It was "a faster and better game than it has ever before played."[19] EB left New York City especially proud because he had "outjumped and outgeneraled the opposing center and captain." Conrad and the Alphas would have been equally pleased, once again even in defeat, because with so many novel concepts and such a large crowd, those who attended would be talking about this game and his club for weeks.

As for Louis and Eddie Waldron, they had realized a financial bonanza and opened up a whole new world of opportunities. The basketball business model for most event venues typically involved charging the home team a flat fee plus a percentage of their ticket sales. But because the Manhattan Casino had a full-fledged saloon attached as well as those luxury boxes, the brothers had options. They could reduce the rental charge, leave ticket sales alone, and make up the difference selling alcohol. Or they could increase the fee, share the liquor sales, and take a cut of the gate receipts. Basketball managers had those same choices, having to cover the costs of renting the space, booking an orchestra, printing tickets, advertising, the referee, a scorekeeper, a timer, and game equipment as well as travel and accommodations for the visiting team. But between them there was now a lot more to share. Depending on the arrangements, certain variables could work in everyone's favor. The tighter the score of the game and the better the orchestra, the more socializing and dancing, and the more of that, the more drinks were poured. Doing the math at fifty cents a ticket and one dollar for box seats, if all the boxes were sold and twelve hundred fans attended, the team could gross over $800, or almost $22,000 today. So, it wasn't just the Waldrons who had hit the jackpot. Black basketball teams began to cash in, too. Playing at the Manhattan Casino was so lucrative that even African American squads from other cities would soon begin booking home games there.

This inaugural basketball event did include a disappointing incident that turned out to be an omen of things to come. It involved the preliminary games in which the St. Christopher Club was to face the Alpha junior squad and the St. Christopher Big Five were scheduled to play Baltimore Colored High School. But when Baltimore Colored High School didn't show up the night before the games, Alpha PCC president Gerald Norman and Major Hart blamed each other publicly for their failure to appear.[20] Attempting to fix the situation, Major assembled a substitute squad of players from several New Jersey teams. But when he also added the captain of the New Jersey Athletic Club to his own lineup, Gerald wouldn't go for that. "The Alpha management, whose motto is *Fair and square deal to all*, refused to allow the strange player to participate under those conditions," Gerald explained, adding, "the Alphas were guided by a sense of right and justice." In response, Major, "in a rage, withdrew both his teams," leaving the Alphas to create two more substitution squads. It was a mess. Major's behavior, Gerald believed, was more than just a "discourtesy." It was an existential threat to basketball itself. "As soon as men are allowed to jump from one team to another to strengthen weak places, and to satisfy an unscrupulous manager," he insisted, "so soon will the game degenerate." What was really at stake, though, was that Major's conduct had threatened the city's emerging Black basketball status quo. "We ask the aid of our many friends in stamping out this shameful practice among honorable clubs," Gerald pleaded. This would not be the end of it.

Meanwhile, without fanfare, Will Madden had been at that tripleheader with the St. Christophers, observing the scene, taking it in, and seeing the possibilities for the future. Before too long, he would be back at the Manhattan Casino, making a triumphant entrance with his own team.

History was made on February 26, 1910, the date of the first recorded game between two independently organized all-Black women's basketball teams, the New York Girls and a newly organized cross-river rival, the Jersey Girls. The Saturday afternoon game was played at the Douglass Auditorium in Orange, New Jersey, in front of a "delighted audience" attracted by "the novelty of the affair." Each team had its own "large following" of fans. "It was New York versus New Jersey," the *New York Age* reported, "with Miss Dora Cole of Manhattan and Miss Goode of Orange as opposing captains." Miss Goode was eighteen-year-old right forward Brookey Goode, or "B. Goode" as she was known. Her team was affiliated with a new African American men's athletic and social association in that city called the Independent Pleasure Club.

"The players, winsome and charming in their dainty white blouses, showed up well in practice," said the *Age*, describing their pregame warmup routines. "But it was when the referee's whistle started the game that the real surprise came," the admiring newspaper gushed. "These lassies demonstrated that they could play!"[21]

At first, female involvement in basketball was as much about camaraderie and social networking as competition. A young lady might expand her world to include other African American communities and, for some, their team's affiliation with a counterpart male organization meant that playing the sport offered the opportunity to meet eligible bachelors. Dora Cole, the New York Girls' star player, was still receiving attention from her coach and soon-to-be husband, Alpha Physical Culture Club founder Conrad Norman. And it was common practice for the men and women of these clubs to collaborate in hosting social activities in honor of visiting squads, win or lose.

In this particular Saturday night game, the audience "expected to be amused," according to the *Age*. "However, they were agreeably surprised when the young women put up a clever and even scientific game." Beyond just posing, they played "fast and vigorously, as several hard falls on the floor attested." The game went back and forth with the Orange five taking the early lead. "The New Yorkers were heavier, but the Jersey girls were more familiar with the baskets," explained the *Age*. "Then the New York team by good headwork and clever passing evened up the score." Led by Dora and her "excellent" teamwork, New York turned it up a notch, playing "such an aggressive game that by the end of the first half the score was 8–2 in their favor." The New York Girls ended up winning 12 to 3, and although New Jersey lost, they "took their defeat in a most sportsmanlike spirit." There was after all, a bigger picture. The game was described as "a pleasing innovation" and considered a big success.

Both of these squads had a common rival, the Spartan Girls of Brooklyn, which was the sister team to the Smart Set Athletic Club men's squad. Subsequently, many other all-female, all-Black teams would emerge in New York City and beyond, such as the Younger Set, Mysterious Girls, the Savoy Colts, the Quick Steppers, the Tribune Girls, the Lincoln Nurses, the Club Store Coeds, the Chicago Roamers, the Gloom Chasers, the Blue Belts, and many more.

As women's Black fives became more popular and competitive, dainty white blouses and bloomers gave way to formfitting basketball jerseys and matching shorts, prompting some authorities to doubt whether females were compatible with the sport. One male physician who was presumed to be an expert on such matters would declare in 1911 that, "basket ball is injurious and should not be engaged in by girls or women." He added that "the nature of women should keep them from this dangerous sport." These kinds of male protective instincts would continue to arise. "Basketball players, especially some in Chicago, please take a bath," an African American newspaperman would beg. In a recent game, he complained, "a local squad took the floor for limbering up to practice and the odor was so fierce that several women became deathly sick." The offended reporter would issue a simple demand. "Leave the stockyards odor over in the stockyards, please," referring to the nearby slaughterhouses and meatpacking facilities on the South Side of Chicago in which many of that city's Black laborers worked. And just like their White counterparts, Black women's basketball teams would often play using a slightly altered version of the men's rules that were considered safer. There were usually five players per side, but in some parts of the country, six players would be used, three on offense and three on defense. This disparity between so-called *boy's rules* and *girl's rules* would eventually cause debate, even among men. "As long we use the other fellow's rules and his ball, net and mark the floor like he does, we might just as well cut off the sixth player and make all teams five girls each," the well-known African American sportswriter Frank Young would recommend.[22]

J. Hoffman Woods was nothing if not a promoter. And promotion of African American basketball required nothing if not one-upmanship. That meant pushing the boundaries of what was possible, as the late Smart Set Athletic Club cofounder Samuel Scottron had said, by "contributing to the force that moves things!" In this spirit, following the St. Christopher and the Alpha successes, it was Woods's turn to make a move. He did that by scheduling the Smart Set's season-ending game with breathtaking style.

The setting was the massive Fourteenth Regiment Armory on Eighth Avenue and Fifteenth Street in the Park Slope section of Brooklyn, where the Smart Set Grave Diggers would host Edwin "EB" Henderson and his visiting Washington Colored YMCA Twelfth Streeters on Thursday evening, March 31, 1910. This date was in the week right after Easter, which meant the Lenten season had just ended and the dreaded personal lockdown period of self-denial, abstinence, and restraint was finally over.[23] Woods knew that folks would be ready to burn their pent-up energy with entertainment and socializing.

By the time they got to Brooklyn, EB's squad was undefeated. They had already beaten the Smart Set earlier in the season, 24–15, on their home court at True Reformers' Hall in front of eight hundred fans, the most people ever to see a basketball game there. The action had been "fast and rough at times," so this rematch would interest sports fans on its own merits. But basketball among African Americans had taken on a bigger meaning, so Woods went much further. Instead of merely a game, he and team manager George Lattimore, Jr., organized an "athletic carnival, basketball tournament, and assembly." The event would include not only basketball but also a one-mile relay, a one-mile run, and a 440-yard dash. This was possible because the armory's two-story, balcony-lined, one-hundred-yard long, barrel-vaulted drill shed was so immense that it contained a full-size oval running track with room to spare. Built in 1891, the fortress-like structure took up an entire city block. For the game, scheduled to begin "at 8 o'clock promptly," a basketball court was set up inside the oval. And of course, there would be dancing before, during, and afterward with "enlivening music" provided by the twenty-five-piece Excelsior Military Brass Band, which was led by twenty-year-old African American cornetist W. Hartwell Hicks and "composed entirely of young men of the city." Their motto was, "give us a chance we'll make good." And they did make good.

Most importantly, Woods had assembled an "Honorary Auxiliary Committee, comprising sixty of New York's representative citizens" to help with the turnout. For weeks in advance, this group had been "lending every aid to the young Smart Set boys in their effort to make this affair a brilliant social event as well as an athletic success."[24] Woods also imposed a fifty-cent admission fee, matching the new norm. His moves paid off. The armory was "the scene of the largest and most successful public entertainment ever given in Brooklyn," Lester Walton declared in the *New York Age*. Nearly three thousand spectators showed up, a previously unimaginable number of ticket-buying fans and the most ever to attend a Black basketball game. Charles William Anderson was there, one of the city's most influential African American political leaders, as President Roosevelt's appointed internal revenue collector for Lower Manhattan, the richest tax district in America. Maggie Payton, wife of the prominent Black real estate broker Philip A. Payton, Jr., was also present, all the way from Harlem. So were orchestra leader Walter F. Craig and his bride as well as Mrs. Oscar A. Scottron, a daughter-in-law of the late Samuel R. Scottron.

In the running events, "the prettiest was the one-mile relay," Walton shared, which was won by the Smart Set tracksters. Then came the carnival's main event, and as imagined, the basketball game was thrilling and competitive. The Grave Diggers were ahead at halftime, but in the second half, "the visitors started in with a vim and made a number of baskets in succession." The Twelfth Streeters would win, 20–17, completing an undefeated season and prompting the *New York Age* sportswriter to declare that Washington "claims the eastern United States championship, which virtually holds true for the entire country among teams composed entirely of colored players."[25] The Twelfth Streeters were African American basketball world's champions.

EB's tenacity and enduring hard work had paid off. Also, New York City had lost its title.

"After the athletic program had been carried out," Walton continued, "dancing was indulged in until an early hour Friday morning." The event was magnificent. "It was claimed by those present who can boast of having resided in the *City of Churches* long before the Brooklyn Bridge became a reality, that never in the history of Brooklyn has such a galaxy of colored persons assembled under one roof."[26] The sportswriter also indicated that J. Hoffman Woods and George Lattimore, Jr., "deserve much credit for pulling off the most successful public affair ever given in Brooklyn."

Beyond the praise though, this had been another important financial win for Black basketball as a whole. Anyone could see that the sport's revenue potential among African Americans was soaring. Just three years earlier, one hundred spectators at a game had been considered a breakthrough. For this event, ticket sales had generated around $1,500, a previously unheard-of amount considering that an elegant five-room New York City apartment with electric lights, steam heat, hot water, and a bath went for around $35 a month.

During all of this, practically unnoticed while sitting courtside during the game, there had been two official scorers who were little known at the time. One was a twenty-two-year-old typewriter and Smart Set club member named Rushford "Rush" Lord. The other was Robert Louis "Bob" Douglas, the St. Kittian who had since turned twenty-six years old and become a magazine messenger. Just like Will Madden, these men were absorbing what they saw for later use. Rush would go on to become the manager of the St. Christopher Big Five during World War I, a team that featured a young law school student named Paul Robeson. Robert would soon form his own all-Black basketball team, the Spartan Braves, which would become one of New York City's best squads by the end of the decade.

The St. Christopher Club basketball program needed a boost in the spring of 1910. They had been left in the dust by New York City's other Black fives during the prior two seasons, and every effort to push beyond their own limits or put themselves into position for a title seemed overshadowed by those squads or had come up empty-handed. Even their confident chance to knock off the unbeaten Twelfth Streeters on the road in Washington, D.C., had resulted in a crushing loss, 44–15. Their pride was at stake.

In response, Major Hart scheduled a game in New York City on April Fool's Day against Lincoln University. Bringing in Lincoln, the oldest historically Black college in America, which had a large alumnae base in New York City, was an innovative idea. New Yorkers had never seen them play before. Also, the game was scheduled for the Friday night after the Smart Set's remarkable athletic carnival event in Brooklyn. Major had booked the Twenty-Second Regiment Armory on Broadway and West Sixty-Eighth Street near the San Juan Hill area, another very large military facility, probably by using his U.S. Army connections in what seemed to be a signature move. Most impressively, the St. Christophers defeated Lincoln by a commanding score, 30–10.

Yet, despite these accomplishments, something wasn't right. The answer, literally in black and white, was in the newspaper coverage Major's game received. While his St. Christopher Big Five had gotten ten lines of print in the *New York Age* for their strong victory over a new team in a new venue, the Smart Set game the night before had received 125 lines of copy for a contest the Brooklyn squad didn't even win. That was twelve times more attention. The St. Christophers were getting out-promoted. More specifically, Major was getting out-hustled. It was the money. The Smart Set Athletic Club had been out-spending everyone else. Their funding pool was deeper. They had a bigger membership, their officers had more clout, their members came from wealthier families, and, apparently, they were bigger thinkers. They even had better talent, before Huddy Oliver left. But if anyone looked at situations with patience and a long view, it was Major Aloysius Hart. Here was a man who had spent weeks at a time on board steamships that voyaged thousands of nautical miles between ports. These traits allowed him to recognize that basketball was about more than just a game, more than wins and losses, more than newspaper coverage, more than a physical culture activity, more than a social outlet for club camaraderie, and more than community-building. Quietly, Major had a vision. The former rodman and speed skater saw what some still didn't or couldn't. With all these spectators, larger venues, and increased ticket sales, there was money to be made. Major was imagining a scenario in which players would get paid to play. Beyond benefitting just the athletes, he saw the game as a profitable new business opportunity in which African Americans could thrive in order to uplift the entire race. His sidekick,

Will Anthony Madden, agreed. "The possibility of the drawing power of this athletic sport was enormous," Will believed at the time, "but efficient general organization and a concentrated effort toward a definite purpose was lacking."[27]

This concept wasn't new. It's what the all-White New Jersey Trentons team had decided to do way back in November 1896, when they rented the Masonic Temple Hall in Trenton, New Jersey to face the Brooklyn YMCA in what became the first known professional basketball game ever played.[28] The squads had agreed to split up the money they got from ticket sales, earning each player fifteen dollars, a very large sum when a high-quality custom-tailored suit in New York City went for $14.75.[29] The challenge for the Trentons at the time had been that the Amateur Athletic Union, which saw itself as the governing body for the game, was completely against professionalism. This was in line with the principles of muscular Christianity, which held that basketball existed solely to reinforce the "mind, body, and spirit" philosophy of the YMCA. Therefore, receiving pay to play the game was more than unthinkable. It was in violation of Christian virtues. Blasphemy. There had to be a sacred line separating the amateur athlete from the professional. Luther Gulick, Jr., basketball's highest authority as the man who gave Naismith his original assignment, vigorously advocated this approach. "When men commence to make money out of sport," he warned, "it degenerates with most tremendous speed."[30] Gulick wanted "every tendency toward professionalism in athletics" to be eliminated, forever, because pay-for-play "inevitably resulted in men of lower character going into the game." As a result, the AAU could impose severe sanctions on any athlete who was even mildly suspected of accepting payment to compete, in any sport. Violators could be banned from competing in official AAU events. For life.

But while Trenton players hadn't cared about those penalties, the St. Christopher Big Five as well as the other amateur African American basketball teams in New York City were trying to do right by the AAU. In their quest for racial equality, they wanted acceptance as official members. EB Henderson was a student of those same views and echoed them fully. "When men put all their wits and strength into a contest to earn a livelihood, mean and unfair tactics are resorted to," he cautioned, within months of the massive Brooklyn carnival. "Spectators are hoodwinked," EB added, since "laying down, double-crossing and faking take the place of clean playing." In that scenario, he believed, character became "a secondary consideration."[31] Naturally, St. Christopher Club athletic director Father Daniel was also intensely against any compensation for his athletes. "Our team shall be made up of simon pures only," the clergyman who also served as church curate was known to declare. If it were up to him, St. Christopher ballers would never play for pay.[32] A longtime sports columnist for the *New York Amsterdam News* who knew Father Daniel well remembered that the priest was so fanatical about this that "he would pursue his course no matter what the cost."[33]

But for Major, the situation had become more complicated on that same Easter Sunday when Lent ended just prior to the Brooklyn carnival event. During his eleven o'clock service at St. Philip's on March 27, 1910, the Reverend Hutchens Chew Bishop had told worshippers that this would be their last Easter celebrated at the church's Tenderloin District location on West Twenty-Fifth Street. The congregation was moving to Harlem, he explained, into an existing building on West 134th Street near Seventh Avenue.[34] After renovations scheduled to be completed in March 1911 at an estimated cost of $150,000, the church's new home would have a frontage of seventy-two feet and include an adjacent five-story parish house with a gymnasium that could double as a basketball court.[35]

"When completed it will be the largest and best equipped gymnasium possessed by any colored club in the country, and will be a great incentive to the members," an A. G. Spalding & Bros. publication reported.[36] The St. Christopher Big Five would have an attractive facility in which to properly train, practice, and play. Also, the court would be surrounded by a balcony that could accommodate more fans than the constricted court in the basement of the old St. Philip's parish house location on West Thirtieth Street. Greater attendance meant more income from admission fees. This development seemed like the answer to a coach's prayers. But on the other hand, the church would have to pay for all of this. Most likely, that would not leave room for Major to compensate his basketball players, even if he could persuade Father Daniel, let alone Bishop and the St. Philip's vestry, on that particular use of church funds.

As the 1909–10 basketball season came to a close, these factors placed the St. Christopher Big Five head coach at a crossroad. One thing was clear, though. The link between money and sports among Black entrepreneurs was too appealing to ignore. That summer, African American prizefighter Jack Johnson, the reigning heavyweight champion of the world, was scheduled to face White boxer James Jeffries in Reno, Nevada, on July 4, 1910, to defend his title. Jeffries, who had retired as undefeated world heavyweight champion, was urged back into the ring as the "Great White Hope" and was quoted as saying prior to the bout, "I am going into this fight for the sole purpose of proving that a white man is better than a Negro."[37] The bout itself was dubbed the "Fight of the Century." African American nightclub proprietor Barron Wilkins, who owned the popular black and tan Astoria Café in Harlem, saw opportunity. He had bankrolled Johnson for the bout and made arrangements to see the event in person. As the former owner of the Café Wilkins and the Little Savoy in the Tenderloin District, Wilkins was one of the most colorful and well-loved figures in Black New York. He had made a fortune in 1908 when the city bought out businesses, including his, to make room for what would eventually become Penn Station. Wilkins knew how to travel in style, chartering a special train to Reno for fight enthusiasts from the East Coast that he called the "Barron Wilkins Special." Then he placed heavy bets covering his guy. Johnson defeated Jeffries convincingly in fifteen rounds for the heavyweight title and received a $75,750 share of the $101,000 purse, a $10,000 signing bonus, and $50,000 for the sale of his "moving picture rights" to the fight, walking away with $135,750, more than $3.7 million today, an inconceivable fortune for an African American at the time. But the new champion's backer, Wilkins, had pocketed winnings off of his bets that were reportedly in the six figures as well, in addition to getting a cut of the champion's earnings as repayment of his bankroll. The café proprietor's swaggering success gave him legendary status in the community as history's first Black sports mogul. More importantly, his moves, together with Johnson's success, made it widely known that African Americans could profit handsomely from speculative business opportunities in sports, not just as athletes.

Considering these developments, Major Aloysius Hart was determined to make some moves of his own and began formulating a history-making path that would be revealed by the end of the summer.

Will Anthony Madden was also making moves and might have found a creative outlet that was "his thing." He had gotten involved in the St. Philip's Young Men's Guild, which among other activities had produced an annual post-Lenten musical. Its 1910 edition was held in April at the Palm Garden, a Manhattan venue on East Fifty-Eighth Street and Lexington Avenue. But with Will in the mix, and with St. Philip's Church budgets tight, the group switched up their usual practice of hiring outside professional talent for the performance and instead gave a minstrel show using their own St. Christopher Club members. Will volunteered to be the program's stage director and production manager and, with no known prior experience, was definitely taking a creative risk. But he took it seriously, identifying and nurturing a modest cast "of no mean ability." Not only that, "the entire program provoked a great deal of mirth." By the end of the entertainment, "the audience was satisfied that the Guild need never fear a scarcity of professional entertainers in arranging to give entertainments, as far worse shows have been given by professionals."[38] In the years to follow, Will would continue to seek the stage, not only in sports but also in theater, not only in the orchestration of talent but as the talent itself, and always pushing the creative envelope. This approach would be his hallmark, his signature, and his brand.

Lester Aglar Walton was more than just a showbiz correspondent. The man was the expressive voice of the *New York Age*. In late September 1910, as the 1910–1 basketball season approached, he pointed out the obvious. "From present indications basketball will be in high favor," Lester explained. "The young men who are identified with the basketball clubs of Greater New York represent the highest type of the race, intellectually, morally and physically," he added, saying that there would be "quite a number of colored quints" in the area. "What these organizations should do is to get together," he recommended, adding that "a meeting should be called at a near date and at the session a league should be formed."[39]

Before he moved to New York City in 1904, Lester's way with words as a reporter at the *St. Louis Post-Dispatch* had caught the attention of a Black theatrical lyricist named Frank Williams. Williams asked Walton to collaborate with him on bars he was developing for a new African American vaudeville play called *Rufus Rastus*, a major production that was set to include a cast of dozens. This request had been highly compelling because the composer and star of the show was Ernest Hogan, the pioneering enormously famous comedian and playwright. Hogan had been the first Black actor to star in an African American produced Broadway musical, *Clorindy, or the Origin of the Cake Walk*, which had opened in 1898. The actor had also popularized America's first organically homegrown musical art form. "Ragtime was discovered, put on paper and introduced to the people of the United States by a colored man by the name of Reuben Crowders who was known to the world as Ernest Hogan," wrote one of his contemporaries, the African American minstrel and vaudeville actor Thomas Fletcher.[40]

Walton had obliged Williams's request and subsequently "came to Brooklyn for a few weeks to help with the lyrics." At some point during this visit, the handsome, single, and charming St. Louis native met a young woman named Gladys Moore, who worked as a secretary at the *New York Age*. Popular and beautiful, she lived in Brooklyn with her father, Black publishing entrepreneur and journalist Frederick Randolph Moore, who would soon become that newspaper's owner. Something had clicked when Walton met Gladys, though she was barely fifteen years old. Yet, evidently there was substance to it. "I married her in the cradle," Walton would laugh years later, on the occasion of the couple's fiftieth wedding anniversary in 1962.

Rufus Rastus subsequently opened to packed houses at the American Theater on Broadway in 1905, where it played into 1906 before going on tour through 1907. The musical "brought Hogan to the peak of his career," which had lifted the visibility of everyone connected to the production including Walton, who was credited as a contributing lyricist. This had placed the young reporter right up among Black New York's hottest entertainment elite and made him a show business insider. That's when Moore asked Walton to contribute to the *Age* as a guest columnist, and Walton subsequently submitted a series of well-received pieces over the summer of 1907. "It is very seldom that the pioneer in any walk of life reaps the harvest from the seed he has sown," he wrote prophetically that August. "Ofttimes many of them even die without knowing the real good they have accomplished."[41] By September, he had become confident of his prospects as a scribe, writing, "I am of the opinion that I am qualified and competent to enter wordy war." Walton joined the publication full-time after Moore persuaded him to come on board as managing and dramatic editor. By mid-October, his future father-in-law had acquired the newspaper. "It is a tremendous opportunity as well as a serious responsibility," the new publisher was reminded via a letter that month from Booker T. Washington, a silent backer of the deal. Washington wished for the *Age* to target "the better element of the race" and Moore was even more direct. "If race prejudice shuts the door of hope in our face, we must turn our face in other directions," he wrote. "How can this be done better than by patronizing race enterprises?" Not long after Moore took over the weekly, Walton "married the boss' daughter" and "lived happily ever after."

In the meantime, Ernest Hogan had asked Walton to write the lyrics for a *Rufus Rastus* sequel called *The Oyster Man*, which was set to make its Manhattan debut at the Fourteenth Street Theater on November 19, 1907. This was the Monday after that first African American basketball game at the Knickerbocker Courts in Brooklyn. A month earlier, Hogan had sent Walton a telegram from the show's pre-New York road tour stating, "The Oyster Man a knockout. Chow!"[42]

All of this meant that when Lester wrote, people listened, especially since "drama" included sports. Yet no one in Black basketball responded to his opinion that a league should be formed among the African American clubs. This gave Major Hart the opening he needed. For his next move, the U.S. Army veteran took a page from *The Art of War*. (The ancient Chinese lesson book by fifth century BC military strategist Sun Tzu, which had been translated into English correctly for the first time in history just months earlier.)[43] "Let your plans be dark and impenetrable as night, and when you move, fall like a thunderbolt," the text advised. In early October, Major resigned as head coach of the St. Christopher Big Five, announcing that he had formed his own new team. It would be a for-profit venture. "That this game has taken a firm hold of our people has been demonstrated beyond a doubt," Major explained in a lengthy editorial letter to the *New York Age* that got plenty of ink. "We want to play the game as our white friends play it."[44]

Then he dropped the bombshell, in line with another *Art of War* stratagem, "Every battle is won before it is ever fought." Major proceeded to explain that his new squad's roster would be "composed of thoroughly seasoned players, having been selected from the best material in the basketball game in this vicinity."[45] He had already signed the top St. Christopher Club players to leave with him. And then persuaded all of the best African American ballers from across New York City to do the same thing. This exploded the region's Black basketball scene. Among the St. Christopher Big Five defectors was Charles Bradford, the team's former captain. Ferdinand Accooe and Charles Scottron from the Smart Set were also on board. So was Alonzo Chadwick, formerly with the Marathons. William Wiggins of the Alpha Big Five also made the leap. Major had even gotten his loyal sidekick Will Madden to join him. With the precision and stealth of a military coup, he had assembled an amazing roster, taking talent from right under his future opponents' noses. The new team owner, who humbly took the title of "manager," appropriately named his freshly minted lineup the New York All Stars.

This city takeover was a move that really took the cake, so Major anticipated immediate backlash. "This team was not formed for any spirit of revenge or to hurt any of the good clubs that are in the game, as has been rumored," he explained. "We are not trying to break up any club or to cause any hard feelings."[46] Major believed this team could be a top-notcher. "If we fail in our predictions, it will not be because we have not tried to do our best," he argued. "All we ask is a 'square deal,' both when we play and when we are talked about."

In acquiring all of that talent, the All Stars' manager was only doing what EB Henderson had done when he recruited the best players in Washington, D.C., to launch the Twelfth Streeters, who were now reigning Black national champions. The difference was that EB had not devastated any of his opponents, whereas Major had stunned New York City's entire African American basketball community. Any hope for history's first official multi-state Black basketball league had also been effectively smashed, because so much talent had been looted from the same fives that would have made up such a circuit.

Will Madden ran in stride with it, though. He became the new squad's mascot and then, in characteristically smooth style, wasted no time fitting right up into the new picture. Literally. When the All Stars posed for their promotional team photograph, Will positioned himself on the floor of the studio in front of the players, comfortably reclined with an elbow propped on a pillow, still wearing his knitted woolen St. C shawl-collar warmup sweater, the essence of swagger and cool.

With personnel issues under control, Major focused next on operational matters. "The All Star basketball team is rapidly getting into good trim," said the *New York Age* in early November 1910.[47] "Games are being negotiated with teams from Washington, Philadelphia, Baltimore, and other places, and the lovers of the game will be treated to some fine contests during the coming season." Their uniquely designed red, white, and blue sash-front uniforms also got attention. "The new suits of the All Star team have been received," the *Age* reported. "They are very pretty and durable." At the time, Spalding was the leading supplier of sleeveless athletic garments, known as *jerseys*. Theirs were produced using best quality worsted wool and available in stock colors at a cost of $2.00 each, with additional pricing for letters, numerals, and woven sashes in contrasting hues. They also made shorts, known as *basket ball pants*, that were "padded lightly" on the hips and went for $1.75 a pair. The company's high collared, pearl button shawl-collar warm-up sweaters, the same kind that Will wore in the All Stars' studio pose, were $7.00 each and used the same worsted wool yarn as their jerseys. Solid leather knee protectors that were "heavily padded with felt conforming to the curve of the knee," including a strap and buckle fastener, were available for $3.50.

Spalding's *basket ball* shoes were "strictly bench made" with a "flexible shank" and lightweight "best quality black genuine kangaroo leather." At $8.00 a pair, these were expensive but state-of-the-art. Originally, basketball shoes were high-top "Blucher" cut leather boots made out of heavy-duty cowhide that was sturdy yet clunky. To meet demand for more flexibility and lighter weight, sport shoe companies developed canvas uppers. The downside was that they lacked support and couldn't withstand the wear and tear of the game. "We cannot consistently recommend canvas top shoes for any athletic use and especially not for basket ball," Spalding warned in its catalogs. "In a game like basket ball, which is played generally on board floors, there is a strain on the feet altogether different from that in almost any other athletic game, and to support this strain, properly made shoes with leather uppers and correctly shaped soles are absolutely necessary." Kangaroo hide, introduced to consumers in the 1890s, was about ten times the tensile strength of cowhide or calfskin and remained strong even when split into layers. This allowed for a finer, lightweight, flexible leather that was also durable. Kangaroo became ideal for finely made high-use, high-wear items like gloves, bullwhips, and eventually athletic shoes. Early basketball footwear had standard leather outsoles, but these eventually proved too slippery. For better performance, Spalding's premier style included "patented pure gum thick rubber suction soles, with reinforced edges, absolutely guaranteed to give satisfaction with reasonable use."[48] That entire ensemble, not including embellishments, socks, athletic undershorts, and a gym bag to carry it all, cost $22.50 each, about $616 today.

The New York All Stars made history on the evening of Saturday, October 15, 1910, when they became the first African American pay-for-play basketball team. In other words, playing with the intention of splitting the gate receipts among its players. The game took place at a venue in Astoria, Queens, against a local all-White opponent from there called the Seneca Basketball

Club. Inside their gym, a "large and representative" audience watched as the All Stars lost, 28–19. "While the New Yorkers played a good game, they showed a lack of team work," wrote Lester Walton for the *Age*, keenly expressing one of the chief criticisms about the potential downside of paying players that is still being argued today.[49] Regardless of the game's outcome though, the pay-for-play concept adopted that evening by Major Aloysius Hart and his New York All Stars sparked a movement that would soon take Black basketball by storm. But officials from the St. Christopher Club, the Alpha Big Five, and the Smart Set saw Major's defection from their amateur ranks, with their key players, as a profound betrayal that could not be allowed to stand. Sooner or later they would have to retaliate.

CHAPTER 13

WABASH OUTLAWS

IN 1890, A FARMHAND NAMED Thomas Blueitt and his wife, a homemaker named Angelina, were married in Bowling Green, Kentucky. Between then and 1902, when the couple decided to flee the state for a better life in Chicago, the couple had seven children—four girls and three boys. During that period, lynch mobs murdered 108 African Americans throughout Kentucky while nine Black people were lynched in Bowling Green and its surrounding towns alone.[1] For the Blueitts, who lived on Second Street in the city's Second Ward, this was no place to stay. Naming their two oldest sons Napoleon, after the monumental French emperor, and Virgil, after Rome's greatest poet, spoke to the aspirations that Thomas and Angelina had for them, and how they felt about themselves. It was time to go.

In migrating to Chicago, the Blueitts joined more than 80 percent of Black people already living there who were born outside of Illinois. The city's African American population was expanding rapidly, but it hadn't always been that way. Before the early 1890s, there were so few Black folks in Chicago—less than 1 percent—that its White people were almost indifferent to their presence. The city itself had been founded by a man of African heritage named Jean Baptiste Point du Sable, credited with being the first permanent non-indigenous settler in the area. And from its incorporation as a frontier settlement of two hundred men and women in 1833, there had always been small groups of Black residents there. They were mostly formerly enslaved people and their children. The city had gradually grown into a farming center and then expanded into a Midwest metropolis built around its stockyards, steel mills, manufacturers, and rail-roads. A vast pool of European immigrant labor had poured into Chicago to support this growth, and just as in New York City, many were Irish who had escaped the Great Potato Famine of the late 1840s, and Germans who fled after their 1848 democratic revolution was defeated. By 1850, more than half of Chicago's population was foreign-born. Meanwhile, less than a thousand African Americans lived there, most settled within a narrow strip of land at the southern end of the downtown business district that came to be known as the South Side or the "black belt" and eventually, "Bronzeville," alluding to the multitude of brown skin tones represented by its residents.

After the Civil War, the city's overall population had tripled, and so did the number of its Black inhabitants. Those earlier waves of Europeans were followed by more floods of White newcomers from Scandinavian countries and then from Eastern European lands led by Poland, Russia, Italy, and Hungary. Its immense cultural diversity had shaped Chicago into a leading center for education reform and in 1874, racial integration in schools had been mandated by law. "Conflict between the races was not very great at the time the paper was started," said the African American editor of a Black tabloid called the *Conservator*, which launched in 1878.[2] Even when the U.S. Supreme Court invalidated the 1875 Civil Rights Act in 1883, removing crucial protections for African Americans in the former slave states, Chicago helped replace that law locally with the Illinois Civil Rights Act of 1885. But that federal invalidation had caused such a backlash against Black people in the South that many packed up and left, some fleeing for their lives. With its promise of jobs and better treatment, such large numbers of domestic refugees migrated to Chicago that by 1893, Bronzeville's population had swollen to more than 15,000.

By then, three-quarters of Chicago's more than one million residents were either foreign-born or their offspring. They had to compete with native-born Whites who were four times as likely to hold white-collar jobs as "foreigners" were. That meant toiling in the mills, stockyards, and factories. The lowly White workman was subject to wage reductions, unemployment, homelessness, and even starvation with no accountability from corporations. But even with all that, it was at least possible for the bottom-rung foreign-born laborer to work his way up. Within a generation, he could become "Americanized," meaning "White." He could live among his peers, gradually master English, seek education, gain access to economic opportunities, drop his old country ways, and blend in with his neighbors. At that point, he would be free to move to better communities with better schools, find better jobs, and create improved financial conditions. European immigrants in Chicago (and other Northern industrial cities) accepted this well-established socio-economic arrangement. It was a system of White privilege that worked, for them. But when "the Blacks" began showing up from the South in the early-1890s, White Chicagoans suddenly found themselves side-by-side with African Americans for housing, schooling, jobs, quality of life, and even prestige. This threatened not only the entire status quo but White supremacy itself.

An undercurrent of resentment was in place when, in 1894, unskilled railroad workers at the Pullman Company went on strike, fed up with unfair treatment by management. The walkout gained national attention when Chicago's stockyard laborers joined in solidarity. But when their collective protests erupted into violence, President Grover Cleveland sent in the Illinois National Guard, which jailed the insurrection leaders while killing thirty workers in the process. The strike had been crushed. But the ultimate reason it failed was that management had brought in African American laborers as strikebreakers. Most of them were later dismissed, but for White laborers, their propped-up sense of self-worth was at risk. A seething bitterness against "Negroes" in the workforce remained. After that, no matter how skilled he may have been, the mere presence of an African American worker in a railyard, slaughterhouse, or mill was treated by Whites as a hostile threat for which preventative or retaliatory violence was justified. Jobs, promotions, and raises for Black laborers were systematically blocked, so that by the early 1900s, African American men in Chicago steered toward service work or menial labor to avoid "trouble" from Whites as a matter of survival. But it was all relative. Conditions in Bronzeville were still better than the deadly social dangers faced by the Blueitts in Bowling Green, Kentucky. When they moved to Chicago, Thomas and Angelina were able to achieve what previously had been unthinkable to them. They settled into a mostly White neighborhood on the Near North Side called Lincoln Park, renting an apartment in an all-Black three-family house on Belden Avenue.[3] So few of the ward's residents were African Americans that Whites in the neighborhood didn't yet offer much resistance.

Soon after moving in, Thomas and Angelina Blueitt had their seventh child, a daughter. But as European immigration and Black migration into Chicago soared, so did White people's underlying fear of having to compete outright or losing their authority. This reached a flashpoint in 1904, when stockyard and meatpacking workers went on strike. That work stoppage failed once again when an estimated two thousand nonunion African American laborers were imported by management as replacements. Then, less than a year later in 1905, the city's United Brotherhood of Teamsters joined the local United Garment Workers' for a major strike. Once again, Black laborers were recruited from other cities as strikebreakers. During one of the many racist attacks that followed, thousands of unionists and their sympathizers rampaged through Chicago assaulting any Black residents or wagon drivers they could find in the streets.

Management exploitation of African American laborers was a go-to strategy for strike-breaking that had been used a total of nineteen times during the 1880s, sixteen times during the 1890s, and eleven times since 1900, with six of those in the meatpacking industry in as many cities in 1904 alone.[4] These actions had increasingly fed a narrative by Whites that Black people were a "scab race." Paradoxically, smarter White labor unions throughout the country adopted a policy of including African American workers precisely because they saw this as the best defense against management's use of Black labor for strikebreaking. Despite that label, when African American publishing entrepreneur Robert F. Abbott founded the weekly *Chicago Defender* newspaper in 1906, he promoted Chicago as being rich with employment opportunities for Black people in the South urging them to migrate north. He was right, but many African Americans did not fully realize what they would face once they relocated.

By the early 1910s, Chicago was celebrated as the mecca of African American success. The city's African American population had grown to over 45,000 strong, spread over twenty-four of its thirty-five wards. Black people had voting rights, schools, jobs, and homes. Chicago was celebrated as the mecca of African American success. There were more than 525 Black-owned businesses, including two dozen churches, a bank, a hospital, hotels, restaurants, and saloons, a nationally read newspaper, and professional baseball teams. The city's African Americans supported their own. But a problem loomed. The South Side was geographically confined by the downtown business district to the north, the stockyards to the west, steel mills to the south, and Lake Michigan to the east. With so many newcomers, Bronzeville had become dangerously congested, underserved, and impoverished. More than 70 percent of those Black-owned businesses were service-related. They included beauty parlors, churches, barbershops, tailors, undertakers, and dressmakers.[5] The large majority of African Americans labored below the "job ceiling" in unskilled work as janitors, waiters and waitresses, laundresses, mail carriers, elevator men, and messenger boys. Yet even these spots went increasingly to foreign-born Whites. African Americans were downgraded still further as "domestics," making up more than 20 percent of the city's total number of household servants.

Being financially deprived, Black families on the South Side couldn't afford to move out and weren't welcome in other neighborhoods anyway. "A Negro could never be certain of what awaited him when he entered a store, restaurant, saloon, or hotel outside of the black belt," the prominent sociologist Allan Spear wrote in 1967.[6] He was trapped, in an underserved community plagued from within by deterioration, crime, alcoholism, corruption, and vice. With nowhere else to grow, Bronzeville had to stretch its boundaries into adjoining White middle-class neighborhoods. But just as in Harlem, White property owners resisted this "Negro invasion" through an escalating series of techniques, namely "the neighborhood improvement association, the community newspaper, the boycott, and in the last resort, violence."[7] So many African American homes on White blocks were firebombed—as were those of the real estate agents, White or Black, who brokered those properties—that people began keeping statistics.[8]

Through all of this, Chicago had developed a thriving amateur basketball culture. Its sports pages included daily coverage of university, high school, settlement house, parks department, and youth league games. Dozens of local pre-college teams in every weight and age class represented all parts of the city and its surrounding communities. State, city, and league championship titles were enormously significant. And there was a history of prominent African American interscholastic basketball players who had competed on some of Chicago's most successful otherwise all-White teams. In 1901, Samuel L. "Sammy" Ransom had led Hyde Park High School to win the Cook County Basketball Championship, playing at the forward position. Described as "the greatest prep colored athlete" of his time, Sammy had also captained his school's football team to countrywide renown, leading them to win the East-West national championship title in 1902.[9] Three years later, Wendell Phillips High School, on the South Side and predominantly White, had featured Jess Wright, who was "a demon" at football and "at baseball had few his equal," while in basketball "his mates always counted on his perfect throws to stave off defeat."[10] There were others, who had only played on those teams because they were talented enough to help capture wins. But just because these outstanding young men were celebrated didn't mean that their presence was accepted throughout Chicago. "While every other class is welcome in the Y.M.C.A. dormitories, Y.W.C.A. homes, the Salvation Army and the Mills hotels, not one of these will give a negro a bed to sleep in or permit him to use their reading rooms and gymnasiums," the prominent Chicago-based Black civil rights activist Ida Wells-Barnett would write in a letter to the editor of the White-owned *Chicago Record-Herald*.[11] Among the city's outstanding young Black basketball players there was a spark and a hunger for more. But no serious independent programs could be developed without gymnasiums open to African Americans. With no flame for their spark to ignite, no fire could ever be lit. That is, until New Year's Day of 1911.

On the Sunday afternoon of January 1, 1911, inside the auditorium at Odd Fellows Hall, a Black fraternal lodge located on South State Street in Bronzeville, a middle-aged Jewish gentleman was introduced in front of a group of "500 representative colored men" who had gathered in the hall for a public meeting. These were local Black citizens interested in launching a campaign for the construction of a YMCA building on the South Side that they would be allowed to use.[12] It would be a first.

Presiding over the meeting was a YMCA official named Jesse E. Moorland. A graduate of Howard University and a former pastor, Mooreland was an international secretary for the Y, one of the few African American executives within the association. He had played a vital role in establishing the YMCA's growing network of Black branches, despite the organization's "pronounced commitment to segregation."[13] That had been an uphill battle, until now. The man Moorland introduced was Julius Rosenwald, president of Sears, Roebuck & Company, the giant catalog mail-order business. Rosenwald, a Jewish self-made man from humble beginnings who never finished high school, had joined the company in 1895 as vice president when it was doing just $750,000 a year in sales. By 1906, he had grown Sears, Roebuck's annual revenues to more than $50 million, taken the firm public that year with $40 million in stock, or $1.1 billion today, and made a fortune. Rosenwald was named Sears' president in 1908 but remained modest, once telling a friend, "I really feel ashamed to have so much money."[14] The millionaire executive handled this "burden of wealth" by pursuing social improvement initiatives, and that's why he was at Odd Fellows Hall.

"I have been considering for some time the question of the best method of assisting the colored people," Rosenwald began his speech, "particularly in our large cities, in securing such facilities for education and recreation as are afforded to others."[15] As was the case throughout the country, African Americans in Chicago were barred from entering White athletic clubs and prohibited from using White YMCA branches, yet lived in communities that weren't strong enough financially to support purchasing their own buildings. Rosenwald believed that improving conditions for Black people was in the interest of progress for the nation as a whole. "It is therefore, in my judgment, the duty of the White people of this country, irrespective of their religious beliefs, to evidence their interest in the welfare of these, their neighbors, by assisting to supply this need." And with that, he made an important announcement that would change the landscape of African American basketball forever. "It will afford me great pleasure to contribute the sum of $25,000 for such an institution in every community in which, by popular subscription, you shall raise, within the next five years the additional sum of at least $75,000, the entire sum of not less than $100,000 to be devoted to the cost of the land, building, and furnishings of such institution." It was up to Black communities themselves, Rosenwald explained, to decide which should have their own YMCA building.

In immediate response, two prominent White local businessmen each pledged $25,000 more. One was a bank owner named Norman W. Harris and the other was a fellow corporate president named Cyrus H. McCormick, Jr., who ran the International Harvester Company. Several other local business leaders also made significant donations. In total, at least $150,000, or over $4 million today, would be available if Rosenwald's conditions for local community involvement could be met.

This pledge was literally a game changer, making headlines around the nation. Strategically, syndicated newspapermen had been invited to the event so that news of the sensational philanthropic offer would hit front pages across the land the next morning. $150,000 BUILDING FOR NEGRO Y.M.C.A. read a Davenport, Iowa, headline.[16] The city's own local African American weekly, the

Chicago Defender, compared Rosenwald to Lincoln, and the importance of his challenge grant, which was unprecedented, to the Emancipation Proclamation.

What happened next was astonishing. In the subsequent community fundraising campaign, nearly one quarter of Chicago's entire Black population made donations, yielding $66,841 in all.[17] One man, a retired telephone company messenger, gave his entire life savings of one thousand dollars to the project. "Treat people fairly and honestly and generously and their response will be fair and honest and generous," Rosenwald was known to say. Officials and community leaders soon decided that the new facility would be located on South Wabash Avenue at East Thirty-Eighth Street, because this intersection was right in the heart of Bronzeville and easily accessible from all parts of the neighborhood. The proposed five-story structure would contain a swimming pool, a cafeteria, reading rooms and classrooms, an employment bureau, dormitories, and a fully equipped gymnasium complete with basketball fixtures.

President William Howard Taft applauded these developments. "There is a white Young Men's Christian Association and a colored Young Men's Christian Association," he would try explaining to an audience of African American students at Howard University in May 1911. "You are more comfortable to have your own club limited to your own race, as perhaps the white young men are more comfortable in having theirs limited to their race," claimed Taft.[18] "But they are both nevertheless all under the broad roof of charitable and uplifting Christianity, and you ought to take pride, as you do, in having contributed and labored and worked for this association."[19]

And so, Black Chicago watched and waited. "It does the followers of athletics good to see the YMCA building on Wabash avenue nearing completion," the *Defender* wrote the following year in November 1912. "It means the greatest advantage to your young boys, as we have never had such a place where we could feel so much at home."[20]

CHAPTER 14

SPORT FOR SPORT'S SAKE

PICKING UP A COPY OF the *New York Age* had become a time-honored weekly tradition among African Americans in New York City by the time that publication hit newsstands on Thursday morning, December 22, 1910. With its offices at 247 West Forty-Sixth Street in the Tenderloin District, the eight-page broadsheet had been around since 1887, along with a handful of other small, short-lived, or start-up African American papers in the city, but the *Age* was by far the largest and most widely circulated. That meant it had the most advertising, and its space on Page Six, the location of Lester Walton's "Music and the Stage" column, was normally reserved for entertainment-related ads promoting theaters, booking agencies, moving picture houses, orchestras, society balls, song shops, and record stores. So, people looking through the *Age* that day couldn't help but notice how Page Six had become dominated by three enormous bold-print basketball advertisements, each trying to out-do the other. WASHINGTON VS. NEW YORK said one, by the Alpha PCC; GREATEST OF THEM ALL claimed another, placed by the All Stars. MATINEE BASKETBALL AND DANCE, a third one placed by the St. Christopher Club announced. These games were packed into the holiday week following Christmas, on December 26, December 30, and January 2. All would feature an orchestra, box seats, admission that included a hat check, and hours of dancing. All would be held at the fabulous Manhattan Casino on West 155th Street and Eighth Avenue. This meant Louis and Eddie Waldron had arrived. It meant Harlem had arrived. It meant African American basketball had arrived. And that those ads combined with the amount of editorial ink about the sport itself took up nearly half of the *New York Age*'s tabloid-size page, meant journalistic opportunities had arrived for Black newspapermen interested in covering basketball. This was the natural growth and expansion that Major Hart had seen coming.

Black newspapers, the "Negro press," by their very existence were political, whether they were merely educating their readers or outright helping them to survive. Their views about African Americans were similar to what Frederick Randolph Moore's publication expressed. The *Age* was considered "the Republican negro organ," as the frequently racist *New York Times* had put it.[1] But, Moore had a different take. "It's against human nature for a negro to vote Democratic," he had personally insisted. Democrats were the party of out-and-out racist White supremacists such as Senator Tillman and his kind, the publisher would warn. "What chance have we against such men?" But one way to beat them would be to join them, at least theoretically. That's what twenty-six-year-old African American entrepreneur and Howard University graduate Sumner H. Lark did in 1900 when he moved to Brooklyn from Augusta, Georgia, opened a printing office on Atlantic Avenue, and began publishing the *Brooklyn Eye*, "a newspaper devoted to the interests of colored people" that soon "attracted unusual attention because of the support it gave to the Democratic party."[2] He trusted and argued that this party was "most advantageous to the Negro in the North" because it was "the poor man's party." It must follow that its principles were best suited for the "needs of the fellow farthest down," Lark believed, "excepting, of course, the sentiment of the South in reference to the race question." He could overlook that one minor detail, apparently.

In 1905, Lark hired a precocious and fiery twenty-year-old Danish West Indian native named Romeo Leonard Waldemar Dougherty as a reporter for the *Eye*, not knowing that the young Black man would become one of the most formidable sports journalists of his time. Born in Charlotte Amalia on St. Thomas in 1885, Romeo had immigrated to the United States with his family as an eight-year-old. According to his own account, at age twelve he came across a copy of the *New York Age* and vowed right then and there to become a newspaperman.[3] Two years after Romeo joined the *Eye*, Lark "inducted" him into the Kings County United Colored Democracy "as a member in good standing"—but it turned out that the words of Fredrick Moore were correct, this move was indeed against human nature. "As I grew older," Romeo would recall, "and studied the history of the race and found that whatever they used to be in politics could be traded to the Republican Party, I became a man *with Republican leanings.*"

His reporting continued, though. "I attribute whatever success I have achieved to the fact that I always stand by my convictions and let my conscience be my guide," he would say. "The people stand with me, both entertainers and sportsmen, because they know I am not afraid and because they know I am usually right."[4] But that could be taken too far, because the tall athletically built journalist began developing a reputation as a self-righteous hothead. While living in a rooming house on Fleet Place in Brooklyn in 1908, Romeo, then age twenty-three, was arrested and sent to the Court of Special Sessions after being "gravely accused" by a "young negress living in the same building" who claimed with witnesses that he "called her a 'black demon', and struck her in the face so that she lost a tooth."[5] The incident made front-page news and may have been a lesson in the power of newsprint, because Romeo left the *Brooklyn Eye* soon afterward.

That same year the *New York Amsterdam News* was founded, and the young reporter jumped at the chance to join the new African American weekly when it began operating in 1909, becoming the paper's first sports editor. His timing was perfect because Black basketball was an emerging force and New York City was its hotbed, so Romeo immediately "threw open the columns of his paper to athletics."[6] Just like Major, he instantly grasped the business side of the game. He also understood its cultural impact as a contributor and participant in the culture itself. "It will be hard for the newcomer to fully appreciate what basketball from a social and athletic angle meant to the people of Greater New York in its infancy and the years which followed," Romeo would recall during the late 1920s. "Here was the game which both sexes could enjoy, which also gave all hands their best opportunity for mingling socially." So much history was made, Romeo guessed, that "it would take this entire copy of the *Amsterdam News* to fully cover the period in which this game had its hold upon the fancy of Negroes."[7]

There were more than a few reasons why Black basketball was on fire, but one of them was not obvious to the outsider. "In those days sports, theatre and society among Negroes were hooked together in many ways," longtime journalist Dan Burley, eventually one of Romeo's colleagues at the *Amsterdam News*, would write in 1944. These diversions, according to Burley, "constituted the principal avenues of escape from the discriminatory practices which we still fight unrelentingly," using words that still ring true today.[8] "One gained some social status if he were of the theatre or the sports world."

From the perspective of Black sports editors like Lester Walton and Romeo Dougherty, the reason they covered basketball was simple. It sold newspapers and advertising. But in Romeo's case, his early coverage of the Smart Set, St. Christopher Club, Alpha PCC, and other African American fives was not only helping put the fledgling *Amsterdam News* on the map. The young journalist wasn't the owner's son-in-law like Lester, so it was also about job security and elevating his own career. That meant Romeo, who was "eternally ambitious," had a vested interest in the health, vitality, and expansion of the city's African American basketball culture.[9] "No sport event, large or small, during his heyday was complete without the presence of Mr. Dougherty who was recognized as the pioneer in his field in the East," the columnist Burley would explain.[10] So much so, that Romeo became an intense supporter of many Black causes, especially those involving sports and the arts. This made him widely admired among athletes and celebrities. "He battled against all forms of discriminations whether in the prize fight game, the athletic field or the stage." But there was a slant to Romeo's approach. He was also aggressively protective of West Indians. Right from the start, his journalism stood out for its unapologetic bias toward the basketball clubs that shared his Caribbean roots. But this would eventually go too far.

The 1910–1 season was well underway. But despite the outward appearance of racial unity among people of African descent in New York City, there was continual friction between those who were American-born and those who were Caribbean-born. A mood of mutual resentment was swirling, barely below the surface. "We were all strangers," a Panamanian immigrant during that time named Maida Springer Kemp would remember, "the black American, the black foreigner, and we did not like one another, and the white foreigner liked us less and the white American hated all of us."[11] A young poet, author, and native Jamaican named Claude McKay would soon observe, "There is a sharp struggle for place and elbow room between the educated West Indians and the native-born Negroes."[12] Descendants of enslaved African Americans couldn't appreciate why Caribbean immigrants would "flaunt their British allegiance." Meanwhile, native West Indians disliked Black people for what they considered a "lack of industriousness."[13]

Within the city's Black basketball scene, this translated into a power struggle. Two of New York City's three original powerhouse squads, the Alphas and the St. C's, had been organized and were operated by first-generation Caribbean immigrants. Father Daniel from the Danish West Indies ran the St. Christopher Club while the Alpha Physical Culture Club team had been founded by Conrad Norman from Jamaica. The St. Cyprian "Speed Boys," though not run by West Indians, represented the city's largest Caribbean church congregation. These constituencies were soon to be joined by Robert "Bob" Douglas from St. Kitts, who had formed a multisport athletic organization called the Spartan Field Club in 1908, originally conceived to draw on the huge popularity of cricket among West Indians. But, Robert quickly realized that basketball had become the sport of choice among Black people from the islands. He was about to form a hardcourt team of his own, called the Spartan Braves, that would soon make African American sports page headlines.

These individuals recognized the cultural impact that basketball could have. But beyond their Caribbean kinship, they had something else in common. All of them were strictly amateur. All were sternly opposed to professionalism in the game, and all would advocate their position to anyone who would listen. They had found their "mouthpiece" in Romeo Dougherty. The sportswriter had become dear friends with Father Daniel, his country-mate from the Danish West Indies, and was just as much against play-for-pay as the priest. "He is one of the cleanest men in the ministry, one of the most learned, one of the most outstanding," Romeo would write of the St. Christopher athletic direc-tor. He faithfully supported Father Daniel's stance that amateurism was one of "the highest principles upon which the foundation of sport is built," and nurtured the city's Caribbean-run organizations like an ally.[14] "In basketball Greater New York will never realize what it owes to the West Indian for the thrills of that period," Romeo would reminisce.[15] "He was the moving spirit in Alpha, St. Christopher and Spartan, to say nothing of a number of the other clubs which found him ever ready to bring the best he had within him to the game." It paid for Romeo to be in step with them. Their successes translated into his own. But he took that even further.

Through his weekly columns, Romeo insisted that West Indian athletic clubs were successful because they pursued basketball "with a militancy and an urge that could not be denied." This was so, he believed, because American-born Black people were in it for the money, whereas the motives of Caribbean immigrants were pure. "When the West Indian came to this country he brought with him those principles with their high appreciation of 'sport for sport's sake,' which he was taught from his earliest childhood," Romeo explained.[16] "Untouched by the commercialism which plays so great a part in every game in this country, it was easy for the West Indian in America, enjoying a better competence for his labor, to invest his money in helping to build the moral fibre which made possible the basketball clubs." In other words, they apparently did it to benefit their character and build community. This outlook, Romeo argued, came from their early exposure to cricket, which created a "natural urge" toward athletics and a cultural willingness to make "personal sacrifices" in order to enjoy that pastime. "Without hesitating even as boys, they gladly dig down into their own pockets to purchase the expensive gears necessary with which to play the game," the West Indian sporting editor would write. "Members of cricket clubs come together in putting up money for the maintenance of playing fields and the rivalry existing is truly friendly."

Romeo seemed to be suggesting that the British colonies had produced a more refined version of Black people. But this social theory hid his own direct personal role in making sure that Caribbean-run basketball clubs held on to their power. And the man did that with a vengeance. "He could write with praise when praise was due," columnist Burley would explain, "but woe unto those who tried anything underhanded—whether friend or foe."[17] Using his literary prowess and powerful newspaper platform, Romeo colluded with the West Indians in an effort to stop professionalism among African American basketball squads in its tracks. This began at the start of the 1910–1 season and it was a team effort. The clubs affected by the New York All Stars' "betrayal" refused to schedule Major's squad, while the West Indian journalist disparaged them with taunts and innuendos in his columns.

That prompted All Star player Ferdinand Accooe to respond with an early December 1910 letter to the editor of the *Age*. "Rumors have been plentiful," he said, and they had "been started by those who evidently wish us out of existence."[18]

None of this discouraged Major, at first. He scheduled two key games against all-Black teams. One was against Howard University on December 30, and the other on March 25, 1911, against the Tenth Cavalry Five, an African

American basketball team from the U.S. Army's Tenth Cavalry Regiment, also known as the renowned "Buffalo Soldiers," who were stationed at Fort Ethan Allen in Vermont.[19] The All Stars won both games convincingly, which made the *New York Age* wish for the improbable. "There is no question about the All Stars having a crack quint," the paper stated, "and lovers of the game would like to see the team and the Alphas bury their differences and play for the championship of Greater New York before the season closes." Especially since the Alpha Big Five were "playing an excellent game just now" and surely, the weekly believed, "such a contest would draw a record-breaking crowd."[20] But this was never going to happen. The boycott by the West Indians was real. And it was effective, causing Major and his New York All Stars to lose momentum despite their dominating season. They would play no additional games during 1910–1 against any of the African American fives in the New York City area.

Major had desperately needed to schedule Manhattan-based games with those clubs so he could seat enough spectators to make a profit. Instead, the All Stars manager was forced to take his team on the road, where they could find willing competition but few appropriately sized venues. Ultimately, they never recovered, faltering during the following 1911–2 season before disbanding a year later.

Today, the lucrative contracts in pro basketball make it seem as though big money has always been a part of the game. But that wasn't the case for Black players until pioneering African American basketball promoter and entrepreneur Major Aloysius Hart began paving the way. Though his play-for-pay failed, Major planted some seeds that would continue to grow and inspire a new wave of Black basketball entrepreneurs.

As for Major's sidekick, Will Anthony Madden, he narrowly escaped the controversy. As a "Little Africa" survivor from a family of survivors, Will would not be driven out of Manhattan. He wasn't going anywhere.

That game between the Alpha Big Five and the Twelfth Street Colored YMCA at the Manhattan Casino on Monday, December 26, 1910, which Conrad Norman had advertised as "Washington vs. New York," meant a lot to EB Henderson, but it likely meant more to Mary Ellen "Nellie" Meriwether, the woman he had been courting for the past six years.

Even though they were both teaching and had their own salaries, the social and cultural tradition for women in those days, according to EB, was that "marriage meant resigning from the school system." So the young physical education instructor couldn't ask Nellie to marry him until he earned a high enough income to support them both. EB was determined to increase his pay. "My first salary was $45.00 a month for ten months in the year," he would explain. Following each of those Harvard summer school sessions he would work several weeks waiting tables in Ocean Grove, a New Jersey seashore community just south of Asbury Park, which was a beach town with a predominantly Black population. "When not in summer school, I became a playground director," EB would recall. Back in the D.C. public school system, he explained, "I received several increases each year by small increments until in 1910 I think I was getting a magnificent sum of about $90.00 per month." At that point, EB discussed the situation with Nellie and, finally, "we felt my salary might support a wife."[21]

This is why that December 26 basketball game in Harlem was so meaningful. "Since I was to play the Alpha team at the Manhattan Casino in New York on Christmas night and my expenses were assured," he said, "we decided to make that Christmas week our honeymoon." To pull it off, they got married at 10 A.M. on December 24 at the Fifteenth Street Presbyterian Church in Washington, D.C., then hopped on a train to New York City, arriving later that day. After spending Christmas Eve and Christmas Day in Manhattan, EB joined the Twelfth Streeters for their game at the Waldron's place, in which they defeated the Alpha Big Five, 25–18, by scoring the last five baskets in a row with "fast and snappy" play to come from behind.

This was the last basketball game the Washington Twelfth Street Colored YMCA team would ever play. A few days later, the same lineup would regroup as Howard University's first varsity squad. More importantly, for Nellie, this was also the last basketball game in which her new husband would ever play. As if it had been a pre-nuptial agreement, EB retired from the sport following his team's win. Though he would continue to be involved in basketball as a referee and advocate, this was EB's grand finale on the court, a triumphant exit from the game as well as a proud pivot into the next chapters of his life. The newlyweds would return to Washington, D.C., and shortly afterward move in with EB's parents in Falls Church, Virginia, where he would soon begin pioneering a new path as a relentless organizer, author, and civil rights activist.

CHAPTER 15

A JANITOR'S KEY

WHEN SOPHOMORE PENNSYLVANIA STATE UNIVERSITY forward
Cumberland Willis Posey, Jr., came off the bench at the start of the second half
during his team's 1910–1 season opener, a Saturday-night home game at the
Armory on December 10, 1910, against Susquehanna University, he became
the first African American varsity basketball player in Nittany Lion history.
A week earlier, he had been plucked out of intramural basketball, playing in
the university's Interclass League as captain of the Penn State Sophomores. In
their first game of the season, he had scored eight points on three field goals
to lead his team to a 26–11 defeat of the Class of 1911 Seniors. After checking
into the Susquehanna game, Cum "played very fast and caged baskets with
rapidity." With eight points on four field goals in their 41–9 victory, he ended
up as the game's high scorer. Not a bad start.

This outcome had ensured the Penn State faithful that Cum could be
"counted upon to materially aid the varsity players in the home games." Their
assumption was that underclassmen would not be traveling for road games
since "only six or seven players can be carried." But the following Wednesday
when the team left State College for a road trip to Philadelphia, Brooklyn,
Manhattan, and West Point for games with Penn, Pratt Institute, Columbia
University, and the U.S. Military Academy, Cum was with them. He had too
much talent to be left behind. Ironically though, this was the beginning of the
end of his Penn State basketball career. He may have been too neglectful of
his schoolwork on this particular trip, because school officials prohibited him
from going on any future road games until his studies improved. Frustrated,
the young star left the program in a huff and returned to Homestead. As one
sportswriter would later explain, "he quit Penn State University flat because

the dour visaged professors refused him permission to go away on a trip in the midst of important exams."[1]

Cum had at least two other reasons for quitting PSU in 1911 and heading back home. First, he had been a tremendous baseball player in high school, so talented on the diamond that he was enticed to play with a popular Homestead-based semi-professional team that summer called the Murdock Grays. In fact, Cum earned a spot as their starting centerfielder. It was the beginning of a long association with the Grays; he would eventually become the team's owner. The following year, the Murdock nine would vote to change their name to the Homestead Grays. Meanwhile, Cum's older brother Seward joined the operation as the club's business manager, helping organize their schedule, arrange games, and keep the books. This would have given the centerfielder valuable exposure to the management side of running a sports team, from communication, salesmanship, and negotiation to expenses, ticket sales, and contracts. The sons of Captain Posey were involved in business after all. They would soon apply this know-how to basketball.

A second reason may Cum left PSU have been his neighborhood friend, Dutch Wohlfarth. Dutch was thriving as a professional basketball player and had led Central Basket Ball League guards in scoring during Cum's freshman year at college. "For real nerve none of them have anything on 'Dutch' Wohlfarth," the *Reading Times* had stated that season.[2] Hanging out with him at the East Thirteenth Avenue rim, Cum could have gained much wisdom from the pro baller, who was about three years older.

As fate would have it, in mid-December 1910, a week after Cum's debut at Penn State against Susquehanna, the University of Pittsburgh hired then twenty-two-year-old Dutch as its interim head basketball coach for the 1910–1 season, charged with getting Pitt's basketball program back up and running. Hiring one of Homestead's most famous pro stars for the job seemed like a wise idea. DUTCH WOHLFARTH IS COACHING PITT, read a local headline.[3] When the new coach held his initial workout at the Duquesne Garden amphitheater, a spacious sports venue on the other side of the Hill District in Oakland, many prospective players showed up, including "Skimmers" Campbell, the Homestead homie from the East Thirteenth Avenue rim, who had since enrolled in the college's School of Dentistry. Dutch announced that practices would be "Mondays, Wednesdays and Fridays at 4 o'clock," which allowed him simultaneously to continue playing for Homestead in the Central League. Had he not attended Penn State, Cum could have tried out for Pitt's squad under Dutch's coaching and most likely made the team, thereby legitimately staging what might have been called a Homestead basketball takeover. Instead, the PSU sophomore went on that long road trip back east that got him in trouble academically. Meanwhile, with Dutch as head coach, the University of Pittsburgh managed to pull off a season with six wins and six losses.

Going into the 1911–2 season, it wasn't too late for Cum to become a Pitt Panther. And that's exactly what he did, perhaps recruited by Dutch, enrolling in the school's College of Pharmacy in the fall of 1911. But by the time he showed up on campus, Wohlfarth had left the university and the Homestead "Homies" to play professionally for the Johnstown "Jawns" of the Tri-State Basket Ball League, which included teams from Pennsylvania, New Jersey, and Delaware. University of Pittsburgh records show that Cum enrolled in the school's class of 1913, but little is known about his time at Pitt other than that he did not play on any of the university's varsity sports teams and didn't earn a degree.

Cum didn't need a college diploma. By then, he knew enough to have something else in mind.

In May 1910, while he was away at Penn State, a startup weekly African American newspaper called the *Pittsburgh Courier* had been formally incorporated with financial support from his father, CW Posey, who was named as president of the new weekly, published every Saturday. The *Courier's* offices were located on Centre Avenue in the middle of the Hill District. This was directly across the street from the Hill District's own new Colored Branch of the Pittsburgh YMCA, which had been undergoing a facelift ever since its groundbreaking a year earlier.[4] One reason for this yearlong delay was that it had not yet received enough financial support from the surrounding community to qualify for one of those matching grants from Sears Roebuck philanthropist Julius Rosenwald. "The colored citizens of Chicago have already paid in cash over $15,000 and in Philadelphia over $10,000 towards their colored men's buildings," a local newspaper's social column complained, "while we have not paid half of our promised $12,766."[5]

Folks eventually got their funds in order and the refurbished Centre Avenue Colored YMCA was dedicated on November 12, 1911. By then, Cum had decided to organize an amateur basketball team for this branch with a roster of local African American players, and he wasted little time making some moves of his own. With himself as the squad's captain, Cum called for tryouts less than a week after the new facility's dedication ceremony. They were held at Washington Park Field House because the YMCA's gym wasn't ready yet. "The initial practice was highly satisfying," reported the *Pittsburgh Press*, a White newspaper, "and indications are that some star games will be pulled off during the present season."[6] Few if any who read this report could have known how accurate it would turn out to be. The *Press*, which ran an "Afro-American Notes" section in every issue, provided continuous dependable coverage of the city's Black community and all of its activities, including sports. "As Cumberland Posey is a well-seasoned player and made quite a reputation with the Homestead High School team by his sensational work," the *Pittsburgh Courier* added, "you may look forward to this team to make good."[7]

Cum's players were talented as well as connected. His lineup included himself and a lanky twenty-one-year-old named Walter Clark at the forward spots. Clark was the son of a teamster and worked as a laborer at CW Posey's new Beaver Valley Coal, Sand and Supply Company. He lived with his sister Sarah and her husband, a well-known African American fitness expert named Hunter Johnson who was the official athletic trainer of the Carnegie Tech (now Carnegie Mellon University) and University of Pittsburgh football and track teams.

At center was a tall and speedy twenty-three-year-old multisport athlete named Sellers "Sell" McKee Hall. Sell, who worked as a post office clerk, was one of Loendi Club originator George W. Hall's sons. A lifelong go-getter, he would eventually become a Negro Leagues baseball star with an eighteen-year career pitching for the Pittsburgh Collegians, Homestead Grays, Chicago American Giants, Cuban X Giants, and other squads, before becoming a nationally renowned jazz entertainment promoter and small business proprietor. Sell's older brother, powerfully built twenty-seven-year-old Howard "Ram" Hall, played backup guard. Cum's older brother Seward, nicknamed "See," held down the left guard position. A solidly built athlete, See worked as a foreman on one of his father's coal floats. Playing at the right guard spot was a tall and muscular twenty-year-old named James "Big Jim" Dorsey. Charles Nicholas "Charley" Rickmond, twenty-one years old and a bookkeeper in the Pittsburgh tax assessor's office, was a backup forward. His father, a railroad clerk named Howard E. Rickmond, had been an early investor in the *Pittsburgh Courier* newspaper. Playing center in a backup role was eighteen-year-old

Israel S. Lee, Jr., a student at the University of Pittsburgh who was a son of the Reverend Dr. Israel S. Lee, pastor of the popular Trinity Congregational Church. Running the team operation as its manager was a twenty-four-year-old waiter named Joseph R. "Joe" Mahoney.

There had been another reason Cum held the tryouts for the team at Washington Park Field House. It was that he didn't want to publicly reveal the squad's secret advantage, a crucial element in their incredible upcoming success to which his teammate Big Jim literally held the key. "I had the janitorial job at a gymnasium and bathhouse on the Northside," Dorsey would explain in an interview decades later. "On Sundays I would sneak a group of our own boys into the gymnasium and indulge in all the possible pastimes, especially basketball."[8] This was not just any gym; it was the Phipps Physical Culture School, a state-of-the-art athletic facility that had been built in 1902 by the philanthropist Henry Phipps, Jr., located down the street from where Phipps and childhood friend Andrew Carnegie had grown up.[9] Phipps School was fully equipped with brand-new exercise gear, fitness apparatus, a regulation-size hoops court, and a bathhouse, as well as an extensive library stocked with the latest books on physical culture and "scientific" basketball. "Over there, by the river," Big Jim would recount with a smile, "we taught ourselves all the 'modern' tricks."[10]

Those included learning plays, developing footwork, strength, and conditioning, running scrimmages, practicing free throws, and swimming in the facility's otherwise Whites-only pool. Amazingly, this clandestine basketball program at Phipps went undetected for over a year. Then one day, a church official decided to stop by. The group was busted, and Big Jim was promptly fired. But this had been a blessing in disguise because, wonderfully, the would-be janitor picked up a new job as the athletic director over at Washington Park Field House. One has to believe that Big Jim's hiring was aided by the physical culture learning he had picked up in the Phipps library. And this was a double blessing because the Washington Field House gym was known to be crowded. Yet, with Big Jim's help, Cum and his crew could practice and scrimmage there at will, for hours at a time.

Playing against all-White neighborhood squads like the United Friendship Sunday School, the Schenley Athletic Club, and the Washington Athletic Association, it soon became clear that the Centre Avenue Colored YMCA "Big Five" outclassed all their competition. This made Cum aim higher. In the early spring of 1912, the group decided to target the more experienced African American basketball teams from the East Coast as future opponents. Here is where the brilliance and strength of Cum's vision revealed itself. Like his father, he did not take baby steps. With fearlessness and artful negotiation, which also ran in the family, Cum was able to secure a home game in Pittsburgh with Howard University, the undefeated reigning Colored Basketball World's Champions. It was a massive, gutsy breakthrough. This was Howard, who had not lost a game in three seasons. Howard, widely regarded as one of the nation's most elite, exclusive, and prestigious historically Black colleges. Howard, whose players were considered "the monarchs of the courts." They seemed unshakable. To everyone, that is, except for the indomitable baller from Homestead. He had a plan.

The game was scheduled for early March 1912, at the Washington Park Field House. But long before these arrangements were made, Cum had had his sights on creating a long-term business in basketball, and he calculated that keeping his fortunes linked to the YMCA, with its jumble of AAU rules, restrictions, and formalities, might be too limiting. To solve this problem, he formed an entity called the Monticello Athletic Association, then disconnected his team from the Centre Avenue Y and placed it under the umbrella of the new organization. This had an additional benefit because it effectively made them independent. Their new association was named after Monticello Street, a residential roadway in an exclusive neighborhood called Homewood on the eastern edge of the city where numerous wealthy industrialists had originally built their estates, including Andrew Carnegie, who lived there until the late 1880s. Homewood had since become an enclave for better-off European immigrant families. But the prominent African American attorney and *Pittsburgh Courier* cofounder Robert L. Vann had purchased a home on that previously all-White street a year earlier.[11] So did Charley Rickmond's father Howard, who had since been named as corporate secretary at the *Courier*. These inspiring moves were paving the way for other successful Black families to consider the area, so selecting the Monticello name symbolized forward progress for the race.

Monticello AA officers included the elder Rickmond, who was elected as president. Their vice president was a twenty-five-year-old Pittsburgh fireman named George Washington Cole, Jr., the son of longtime city police detective George W. Cole, Sr., who had been on the force more than two decades. The elder Cole had become the police department's first African American sleuth in 1901 after his assignment to Hill District, where supervisors described him as "especially efficient among the colored race." Cum's sister Beatrice had recently married a post office clerk named Evan Edward Baker, who, at twenty-six years of age, was appointed as the entity's treasurer. Evan, who was just as entrepreneurial as the Poseys, also ran a store on Mifflin Street in Homestead that featured a large soda fountain, making it a popular gathering spot. Naturally, the *Pittsburgh Courier* was sold there, for five cents a copy. Finally, Cum persuaded Walter Clark's brother-in-law Hunter Johnson, the Carnegie Tech football trainer, to be the association's official fitness coach. Johnson was a true expert in his field and would soon train the great long jumper DeHart Hubbard to become the first African American individual Olympic gold medalist in that event, at the VIII Olympiad in Paris in 1924. "Would that there were more men like Hunter Johnson," Hubbard was to declare afterward.

Leading up to the Howard University game, the Monticello organization staged a benefit dance so they could "raise funds to defray the expenses." Host teams were on the hook to take care of the visitors' travel and accommodations, as had become customary in Black basketball for road invitations. That meant the Monticellos had to charge an admission fee, which was set at fifty cents. The venue could hold several hundred paying spectators and their attendance would matter financially, so the group devised an all-out promotional campaign to fill up the gym with fans.

First, they announced that tickets could only be purchased in advance. They wouldn't be sold at the door and nobody would be admitted without one. Newspapers reported that Howard Rickmond as well as Monticello team managers Evan Baker and Joe Mahoney had been assigned as the go-to men for pre-event sales. Next, promotional postcards were sent to local friends and out-of-town guests as well as to delegations of Howard alumnae far and wide. Then they stirred interest and excitement through local newspaper publicity. Cum described this as "the first colored game ever played in Pittsburgh."[12] Then he made it public that Pirates baseball star and basketball aficionado Honus Wagner, a local favorite, would be there.[13] "Pittsburgh's famous baseball player will referee the game," it would be announced. Charley Rickmond's younger sisters, twenty-three-year-old Ella and seventeen-year-old Josephine, as well as several other young ladies, volunteered to organize the squad's cheering section, and word was put out that "refreshments will be served by the Monticello Girls." One of them was a nineteen-year-old fifth-generation Pittsburgher named Ethel Shaw Truman, who lived in the Hill District and whose father worked at a bank. She was there because of her romantic interest in Cum, the young and dashing Homestead heartthrob. Meanwhile, the *Courier* made it practically a civic duty to attend the event. "It is a fact that quite a number of Pittsburgh's best people have never witnessed a basketball game," the newspaper teased. "Now is the time for them to come out and see a strenuous and pleasing game." Novices were given even further enticement with the promise of a postgame reception with music and dancing to honor the visitors in what was supposed to be "the social event of the season."[14]

Through an astonishing series of thoughtful and strategic moves, this young sportsman from Homestead had single-handedly lined up a roster of exceptional homegrown players, a state-of-the-art practice facility, a brand-new gymnasium, a renowned athletic trainer, cheerful neighborhood cheerleaders, widespread newspaper coverage, devoted fans, brilliant officers, nationally ranked competition, and organic funding for the entire effort. "This, it is hardly necessary to add, was in the days when the boys played because they loved the game," the longtime *Pittsburgh Courier* sportswriter W. Rollo Wilson would later reminisce. "And how we Pittsburghers loved them and hugged them to our hearts!"[15]

That perspective was only partly true. Cum's team was playing for the love of the game, *and* for the money. That's why he didn't respond publicly to those who wondered whether Pittsburgh, a humble and hardworking labor town, had any business provoking the powerful team from the nation's capital known as the "Blue & White." It had taken a large double dose of audacity for Cum to invite them, and few outside observers took his unknown band of sandlot basketball players seriously, least of all the reigning Black national basketball champions. In fact, the game was seen "in the nature of a huge joke by the authorities at Washington, D.C. who considered Howard invincible," according to one journalist. They fully believed that the good money was on Howard. "So to Pittsburgh trekked the chesty collegians, to show the Smoky City just how basketball is played in polite circles."[16] But they failed to realize that "polite" was not in Cum's game plan.

To reach Pittsburgh, the Howard University basketball team would depart from Washington's monumental Union Station, a magnificent Beaux Arts structure jointly constructed in 1907 by the Baltimore & Ohio Rail Road Company and the Pennsylvania Rail Road on a reclaimed tract of swampland near the United States Capitol. It had opened in October of that year with the ceremonial arrival of a B&O passenger train from Pittsburgh called the Steel City Express. That was the same train the Howard men would use. Pulled behind an enormous two-hundred-ton coal-burning steam-powered locomotive that could reach top speeds up to sixty miles per hour, the 350-mile journey could take half a day.

In 1910, the B&O Rail Road, whose tracks ran mostly through northern states, did not have an official racial segregation policy for passengers. Instead, according to advertisements, all paying passengers were guaranteed to ride in style aboard "a splendid train, electrically equipped, complete in appointments, of strictly modern construction, with exceptionally good dining car service."[17] This was first-rate style, matching Howard University's stature as the nation's most distinguished institution of higher learning for Black students. As the college players and their entourage climbed on board to enjoy these fine amenities, some were in for an eye-opening experience. "The American who has never visited Pittsburgh does not yet know his own country," a Smoky City travel guide warned, because "he does not yet comprehend its stupendous power and wealth."[18] The brash college boys would soon discover as well that the basketball player who had never visited Pittsburgh did not yet know his own sport.

Howard University's varsity basketball program was the brainchild of EB Henderson. He had originally approached authorities at the college before the 1910–1 season to enlist his Twelfth Street Colored YMCA players as their first varsity team, since all of the athletes were already enrolled at the school. This accomplished two things. "Heretofore the team representing Howard University has been handicapped on account of lack of facilities for practice and also by the playing of its best material with outside clubs," wrote J. H. Brown, the college's then-new varsity basketball manager. Howard's campus was electric with the news, he had said, as "every student in the university is lending his best effort in building up the team to represent the institution."[19]

Prior to reorganizing as Howard's varsity, the Twelfth Streeters were undefeated in their ten games, including three victories over the Alpha Physical Culture Club, two wins against the Smart Set, and one defeat of the St. Christopher Club. This was done in dominating fashion, with an average margin of victory of more than 22 points while opponents were held to less than 20 points a game. The new Howard team still had its original Twelfth Streeter backcourt stars Huddy Oliver and Ed Gray as guards, while adding several newcomers to get even better. These included Leo Newton "Snake" Sykes, who was also the captain of Howard's varsity baseball team and its star centerfielder, at left forward, Henry F. Nixon, who was also the team's assistant manager, at right forward, and a twenty-one-year-old Howard University student and native of Oil City, Pennsylvania, named George B. Gilmore, an exceptional talent who would become an all-time great center. This was "the most polished battle array of its history, one of the smoothest working teams of any era," the *Pittsburgh Courier* would remember a decade later. "Every man on it was All-American."[20]

The Steel City Express offered departures out of Union Station at 11 A.M., 9:15 P.M., and 12:40 A.M. at a fare of $9.00 for a one-way coach seat. Night departures included Pullman drawing-room sleeping cars, in which berths were available for an additional $2.00 fee. B&O timetables were set up to ensure that the company's trains passed "through the Allegheny Mountains during daylight" so that passengers could experience why the railroad was called "The Picturesque Route of America." Every section of the journey between Washington and Pittsburgh offered "unceasing interest." Leaving the nation's capital, this route followed alongside the lovely Potomac River to Harper's Ferry, West Virginia, surrounded by its "grand mountain scenery." Farther up the Potomac, the Steel City Express turned toward Martinsburg, West Virginia, considered the gateway to the Shenandoah Valley, then continued gradually uphill to Cumberland, Maryland, where that stretch of "wild and awe-inspiring" landscape began.[21] This section, called "The Narrows," was a thirty-mile-long natural pass along a winding creek that cut through a steep, narrow, and mountainous valley.

For $1.50 extra, these thrilling sights could be viewed from magnificent Observation Cars that were specially equipped with extra-large picture windows to enhance the experience. They featured conversation-friendly seating, private nooks with writing desks, and information pamphlets with facts about the territory along the way. In the days of the steam locomotive, this was more than just a scenic trip; it was a glorious adventure.[22] The Narrows led to a curvy one-hundred-mile uphill section of track called the Sand Patch, one of the steepest railroad grades in the world. At the top, near Mance, Pennsylvania, was the 4,777-foot-long Sand Patch Tunnel, then one of the longest in the country and a brilliant triumph of engineering. As their massive train labored up this incline and powered through the tunnel at its peak, 2,258 feet above sea level, the Howard University squad did not yet realize how much work lay ahead of them in Pittsburgh.

Now in Pennsylvania on the less steep downslope, their express glided along the Cassellman River, which winds through the mountains until joining two other waterways to form the stunning and celebrated Youghiogheny River, a tributary to the Monongahela River. The B&O tracks then continued to Connellsville, where the world's greatest coke producing region began.[23] Rich with bituminous coal deposits, it stretched all the way to Pittsburgh, still sixty miles ahead. Coke was a fuel made from coal and was essential in the making of steel. At the time, there were about 48,000 coke ovens in Pittsburgh, most of them near Connelsville. First-time visitors approaching from the east would be awestruck by the spectacle of so many furnace fires at once, which made it clear how the Smoky City got its nickname. That cloud was said to the city's "huge crown of industrial kingship."[24]

Once the train carrying Howard's team had descended out of the mountains to level ground, it would cruise alongside the Youghiogheny until it reached McKeesport, a coal mining town on the Monongahela, then follow that river into the industrial borough of Braddock, a few miles from downtown Pittsburgh. This was the site of the world's largest steel mill, the Edgar Thompson Works, which had been built by Andrew Carnegie in 1873 and was one of the first American steel plants to use the Bessemer process. Poetically, the Steel City Express traveled directly through the center of this booming Carnegie Steel plant, which was producing record tonnages of steel and iron that year. This also meant record wages paid to the laborers in the area, a factor that did not go unnoticed to entrepreneurially minded men such as Cumberland Willis Posey, Jr.

The express train would continue beyond Braddock for the passage's final leg toward the Ohio River, past Swissvale, Hazelwood, Oakland, and the bluff below Duquesne University of the Holy Ghost, before reaching its final destination, the Victorian-style B&O Rail Road Station at Smithfield and Water Streets along the north shore of the Monongahela River at the foot of the historic Monongahela Bridge in downtown Pittsburgh.

Seeing the city in person was eye-opening. For one thing, people marveled at Pittsburgh's new and technologically advanced urban transportation system, with its extensive grid of electric trolleys. Gone were horsecars on rails, which had been "shabby, dirty, slow, and uncomfortable." These state-of-the-art streetcars, operated by the Pittsburgh Railways Company, traveled a network of 581 miles of track and could reach suburban towns and communities within a one-hundred-mile radius. "There has been no aspect of social development in the territory of Pittsburgh during the last 10 years more vitally important, or which presents to the mind's eye a stronger contrast with the primitive condition than the remarkable upgrowth of the interurban trolley service," the *Pittsburgh Post-Gazette* newspaper had declared.[25]

Streetcars passed directly in front of the baggage pickup area outside the B&O station's passenger depot, able to carry the Howard entourage to their accommodations in the Hill District. The team would be staying at the Hotel Royal, a Black-owned and operated establishment at 81 Fulton Street, which meant catching a streetcar that traveled up Smithfield past the giant United States Post Office before continuing beyond City Hall and then turning onto Sixth Avenue. Next, the tracks bent at Grant Street, then crossed Webster Avenue and rolled one more block before turning left onto Wylie. The trolley then labored up the hill across Epiphany Street, past Bethel African Methodist Episcopal Church, the city's oldest African American congregation, and the *Pittsburgh Courier* newspaper offices at 1209 Wylie, until it reached Fulton, where a right turn would take the streetcar directly in front of their lodging house.[26]

Run by a thirty-two-year-old Virginia native named William G. Green, the Hotel Royal was advertised as "Pittsburgh's leading colored hotel" with "up-to-date accommodations" that were "strictly first class." Its café was "open at all hours" and the property offered special rates for theatrical companies and railroad porters.[27] Heavyweight boxing champion Jack Johnson and other Black celebrities would stay there when visiting the city because it was right next door to the famous Loendi Social & Literary Club. Most importantly, these accommodations were five short blocks from Washington Park and its Field House, where Howard would play against the Monticello Athletic Association the following evening.

After arriving at their hotel, the Washingtonians were brought next door, to the Loendi clubhouse where they were dined as guests of honor. "To meet any member," it was said of that organization, "is to meet a man who is in touch with the city's progress, and hence a type of citizen who has contributed his share to the upbuilding of this great city."[28] Meant to impress, the Loendi Club was housed in a three-story pressed brick structure that was "magnificently furnished throughout at great expense." Guests could tell that its "rich carpets, fine tapestries, beautiful pictures, rosewood piano, and the furniture and decorations" had been "selected with rare taste."[29]

Yet, after dinner, as they settled into their sleeping quarters in the Royal the night before the game, these Howard players must still not have thought much of the Monticellos. They were "the cream of the country in things basketball out to smother the ambitious Monticello lads."[30] And after all, "Howard never had a greater team than Gilmore, Sykes, Gray, Nixon and Oliver," sportswriter W. Rollo Wilson would recall. "And never did anyone else."[31]

The next day was game day, March 8, 1912, a rainy, snowy Friday, and as the 8:30 P.M. tip-off time approached it became clear that Cum's marketing drive had been a complete success. The response was overwhelming, as nearly five hundred spectators showed up at the Washington Park Field House in the Lower Hill, cramming into its gymnasium. There were no grandstands, so they packed around the court for a spot to see. It had to have been three- and four-deep.

Many of the faces in the predominantly African American crowd that night were locals. This was a chance for them to see and be seen, especially since "quite a number of out of town guests" had been predicted, thanks to the postcard mailers sent out weeks in advance.[32] Some wished to catch a curious glimpse of Honus Wagner wearing a different uniform for once. Others were lured by the possibility that James "Jim" Thorpe, the twenty-five-year-old multisport athlete from the Carlisle Indian Industrial School, might be courtside. He was in town to compete the following night in an indoor track carnival at Duquesne Garden. Staged by the Pittsburgh Athletic Association, this was a warm-up for Thorpe, who was about to leave for the 1912 Olympiad in Stockholm, Sweden, scheduled to open in two months. The "wonderful Indian" would win the pentathlon and decathlon events there to become the first Native American to capture Olympic gold medals for his home country.

A buzz of anticipation filled the building. For the Monticellos to stand a chance against the powerful Howard five, Cum devised a skillful game plan that would work if executed well. His approach was to surprise the visitors by taking advantage of their hubris while unleashing his team's own secret talents steel-town toughness, and sandlot street smarts. The basis of Cum's plan was so simple that no one could have imagined it. He would exploit a basketball rules glitch.

Weeks in advance, Cum had realized that when EB Henderson's team became the Howard University varsity, they were opted out of the YMCA hierarchy and no longer governed by the Amateur Athletic Union. The same thing had happened to him when disconnecting from the Centre Avenue Y to form the Monticello AA. But the difference was that after EB's move, Howard had been obligated to comply with collegiate policies while the Monticellos became independent of any governing body. Cum knew there were two different sets of rules, the one the AAU used, and another version formulated by the Collegiate Basketball Rules Committee. Although almost identical, these differed in several crucial ways. "The inter-collegiate rules allowed a two-handed dribble, and a shot from the dribble," Cum would explain. "Amateur rules permitted a one-hand dribble, the dribbler not permitted to shoot if he had dribbled even once," a regulation the organization had added in 1900. If a player had already dribbled, then in that case "he must pass to another man for the shot."[33]

The difference had persisted over the years because officials in both organizations refused to bring them into unison. Their reasoning, as the *New York Times* had explained back in 1907, was that "the game which the collegians play is too strenuous to be adapted for the use of men in athletic clubs and Y.M.C.A.'s who are not in constant training, and the college men do not want a less vigorous game." Instead of combining them, they "agreed to continue the present disparity of rules and to discourage games between colleges and athletic clubs." Both sides believed that "by strictly prohibiting collegians from playing on outside teams, by discouraging competition between colleges and athletic clubs, and long barnstorming trips about the country it is expected that the whole situation will be cleared up."[34] Or so they thought. Cumberland Willis Posey, Jr., didn't care about all that, nor about who governed whom.

Howard University's basketball manager, J. H. Brown, seemed to care even less, as his collegiate varsity squad had been "barnstorming" all season with victories over numerous amateur athletic club teams. That had been a mistake. It allowed Cum to set Howard up before they had even boarded the Steel City Express. He did it by persuading them to use both rulebooks. "One half of this game was played by inter-collegiate rules and one half by amateur rules," Cum would explain, almost three decades later.[35] Mastering two different versions was brilliant. Also, a collection of African American street ballers from the alleyways of Pittsburgh had no business knowing about these subtleties unless they had studied them in a private institutional athletic library, an unlikely scenario. This is what Big Jim had meant by "all the 'modern' tricks."

Under college rules, the first half would favor large, physical players who could dominate an opponent with brute force, bodying him toward the basket one dribble at a time, inside the paint. By these rules a player could dribble the ball, catch it with two hands, then dribble again. And again. As many times as needed until finally, he could simply turn to the rim and put up a shot. This was indeed demanding on the defender, and it's no wonder why basketball authorities felt that amateur teams, believed to be less physically mature, might become overwhelmed. But for the Monticellos, toughness was a given. "Posey's teams had intestinal stamina," sports columnist W. Rollo Wilson would later write. They could "stand the brunt of combat." As for CW Posey's son himself, although "fragile in appearance and innocent in looks," he could "out-rough Jim Dorsey" and "take more bumps than a Hudson River ferry slip." Heavy duty hard-charging men like Cum and Big Jim, Wilson would explain, "were necessary for the game that was played in those days."[36]

On the other hand, during the second half under amateur rules, also known as AAU or YMCA rules, the game would favor teams with quickness, ball control, outside shooting, movement away from the ball, and disciplined possessions. Then too, AAU Rule II, Sec. 15, which prohibited a ballhandler who had already dribbled from scoring a field goal, created a fundamental disadvantage for players who were used to college rules, because suddenly the double dribble was illegal.[37] In addition, shooting the ball after already having dribbled, a basic part of the game under collegiate rules, was a change-of-possession violation in the amateur ranks that resulted in a turnover.

Cum was about to finesse the defending Black national champions. "He was a natural athlete and a born leader," the sportswriter Wilson would say, later describing the Western Pennsylvania player as "perhaps the most colorful figure who has ever raced along the sundown sports trail."[38] His exploits would make Romeo Dougherty list him as "America's greatest Negro basketball player of his time."[39] But beyond basketball talent, it was the Homestead native's mental game that set him apart. Cum's mind power, deceptiveness, and charm were unmatched. "The mystic wand of Posey ruled Basketball with as much éclat as 'Rasputin' dominated the Queen of all the Russias," the popular social columnist Alvin J. Moses would later muse.[40] Any legal tactic that worked was fair game. Politeness was never considered. Before playing a team for the first time, Cum would have his squad warm up like novice country "farmers" so that heavily favored opponents would become overconfident. All the while, pregame betting odds would shift in Cum's favor. With feigned high hopes, his operatives would work the crowd, taking bets with ease. Another gimmick Cum used was the "long distance" routine. His players would do pregame warm-ups using only half-court shots, making most of them. This astounded the crowd in their favor while rattling most opposing squads. Despite these moves, Romeo would marvel, Cum was "applauded by both friend and foe."[41]

At this point, it was game time. The referees were ready, including an official to replace Honus Wagner, who had canceled at the last minute. The timekeeper was all set. The scorers and their books were prepared. The band was tuned up to perform. Looking around the Washington Park Field House, this crowd was, according to a local observer, "as large and as fine an audience of local society people as it would be possible to assemble."[42]

At exactly 8:30 P.M., the head ref took the game ball to center court and took one last glance at his watch. The starting players for both teams had left their benches, matched up, and got set for the opening tip-off. Then he tossed the basketball up between Sellers Hall of the Monticellos and George Gilmore of Howard, the opposing centers, and right from the jump it was "a clean yet furiously played game." Monticello executed exactly as Cum had envisioned, unleashing "an offensive attack that so bewildered the Howard players that Pittsburgh sprinted to a nearly insurmountable early lead." But within a few minutes, the Blue and White regained their composure and began staging a comeback, behind loud cheering from their out-of-town fans. "As there are many former students and graduates from Howard in the city, which still feel the school spirit," it was reported, "the rooting on both sides was at times quite a feature of the game."[43]

Cum had taken a calculated risk. He knew that the Monticello's brutal defense in the paint would result in numerous potentially costly fouls. This didn't matter to Posey, though, because the visitors, if fouled, still had to sink their resulting free throws. By then, however, he calculated that the overconfident college players would be completely flustered. The gambit worked. "Howard was woefully off in foul shooting and only made a showing when Gilmore was called on to shoot," the *Courier* reported. "The first half ended 9 to 8 in favor of Monticello."[44]

Going into the locker room with a halftime lead, or even within a few points of Howard, was exactly where Posey and his players wanted to be. It was important, though, for the Pittsburghers to stay intense. That's because they knew that the rules were about to change. Literally.

"In the second half Monticello seemed determined to carry the game to Howard," coming out as aggressive as before the break, and "fairly swept them off their feet."[45] The amateur rules had kicked in, allowing the game to open up with more spacing, and the college responded with more aggressiveness on offense. However, then as now, experts frowned on putting up wild shots. "It takes no headwork to throw a basket," they insisted, "but it does take headwork to get the ball to a position where it can be easily caged by an accurate thrower."[46] The ballhandler needed awareness of when to set up a perimeter shooter, the same as any modern-day point guard.

On the court, the individual toughness of each Monticello player began to frustrate the Washington team, including its most reliable stars. "Even Gilmore, Howard's crack center and always sure good shooter was held by Hall, a novice at the game."[47] At this moment, Cum busted out the secret weapon he had been waiting months to reveal. Working in secrecy during those closed practices at the Phipps gymnasium and later, on the Hill, the Monticello AA founder and his crew were developing the most fundamental of basketball skills: outside shooting. Not just from outside, from way outside. If it worked, this would be the turning point in the contest. As one of the Monticello guards dribbled the ball up court, the Howard defenders were so used to packing themselves into the paint that none of them noticed Hall, playing center, lingering behind the play. Instead of going down low near the basket, he arrived at his hot spot and calmly sank a long distance "ringer."

Hall's lengthy field goal electrified the fans and a few moments later when Cum did the same thing, folks just about lost their minds. One lady lost her large leather purse, later turned in at the complex's lost and found office. This gritty action was everything Pittsburghers had hoped to see. At this point, Washington tried to regroup and regain their composure, but for them this was the beginning of the end. The collegians were unnerved, and the building was now fully behind the locals. "Howard seemed shot to pieces in the second half of the game after two long shots were caged by Hall and Posey from back of the center to the floor"—in other words, from beyond the half-court line. "These two shots easily featured Monticello's end of the game," the *Courier* pointed out, as the Pittsburghers executed the long-distance strategy again and again. Howard had no answers. "Gray, the famous guard, Nixon and Sykes, the fast forwards could do nothing with Monticello's fast play," the paper said.[48]

All the while, Cum and his teammates had been playing relentless defense. "Howard was completely dazed and their reputed teamwork was nowhere in evidence," the *Courier* continued. "Dorsey, Clark, and S. Posey played brilliantly, breaking up most of Howard's plays."[49] This was textbook basketball, as if straight from a library. And when the final whistle blew, Monticello had shocked the heavily favored university team, winning 24 to 19. "A bunch of kids had licked the everlasting daylights out of the famous Gilmore-Gray-Oliver-Sykes-Nixon machine, and from that moment they began to make history," W. Rollo Wilson would reminisce. "When the romp was over," he continued, "Monticello's star had risen high in the athletic heavens."[50]

Leading the charge for Howard was an impressive performance by center George Gilmore, with four field goals and three free throws for 11 points. Though in a losing effort, this would not be George's last star performance in Pittsburgh. Meanwhile, Cum finished with 15 of Monticello's 24 points, on five field goals, all from long distance, as well as five made free throws. Shooting from the far perimeter, he had proven himself to be Black basketball's first known long-distance scoring ace, forty-nine years before three-pointers were to be adopted during the American Basketball League's inaugural 1961–2 season.

PITTSBURGH SHOOTERS ARE NOW WORLD'S CHAMPION COLORED BASKETBALL PLAYERS, read a center column headline on the *Pittsburgh Courier's* front page.[51] "The colored basketball world will be forced to recognize Monticello as one of the fastest colored quints," the *New York Age* proclaimed.[52] "The members of the Monticello Athletic Association desire to express their sincere thanks to the Monticello Girls for lending their assistance to the boys in the way of furnishing the lunch and refreshments and giving the proceeds to the Monticello boys to assist them in their efforts," read the team's statement in the *Courier*. "They also thank their friends and patrons who showed their appreciation by coming to the game and cheering the boys to victory," the message continued. "In beating Howard, the Monticello boys are champions of the United States."[53]

Courier columnist Wilson would write, "That victory 'made' Monticello." And like the christening of a new steamboat launched into the Monongahela, this game elevated the basketball career of Cumberland Willis Posey, Jr., into a national spotlight. He took advantage of that right away, openly challenging other leading African American basketball programs like the New York All Stars, the Smart Set Athletic Club of Brooklyn, the Owl Field Club of Newark, and the New Jersey Imperials. Monticello had the title, Cum said, and was ready "to defend it against all comers."[54] The strategy worked, *Courier* sportswriter Wilson would remember, "and soon the team was in demand in New York, then the center of the basketball universe."[55] This meant playing at the lucrative Manhattan Casino, and when the Pittsburgh team subsequently came to New York City, they "swept through the east and established a reputation which succeeding years but enhanced."

As was customary for visiting basketball teams, win or lose, the Howard University players and staff stayed in Pittsburgh for two nights as guests of the hosting Monticello organization, then headed back to Washington, D.C., aboard the same Steel City Express that had brought them. But their trip home would seem longer, because the tables had turned. The formerly "chesty" collegians "left town on Sunday evening at 10 o'clock over the Baltimore & Ohio Railroad and we suppose they are still trying to explain to their fellow students how they were defeated by the Monticello boys."[56] They may never have figured it out. Cum's gambit had paid off. "They were able to bewilder the opposition by this style of play," the Homestead native would explain years later.[57] These moves also set Cum apart as one of the basketball's most brilliant thinkers.

"In the next decade Posey's power became absolute and his teams the quintessence of excellence," Wilson would state.[58] Every all-Black basketball squad in the country "knew of the glory awaiting them by decisively defeating that team moulded [*sic*] from the original Monticellos and with the toughest of steel cast in the caldrons of their own Pennsylvania."[59] Many years later, people who were there, from players to fans to newspapermen, still fondly remembered the final score of the Monticello-Howard game as if it were played the night before. "Surrounded by stars," Wilson would recall, Cum "was and still is THE STAR."[60]

Even after thirty years, *Amsterdam News* sports columnist Romeo Dougherty was still reminiscing. "It would take a more competent and facile pen than mine to paint a thrilling word picture of those exciting days," Romeo said, when Posey "raced upon the hardwood. Though he was small, the sportswriter added, the "Little Pittsburghian" was "the man who put Homestead on the map."[61] True, but Romeo only got part of the story right. As far as African American basketball was concerned, Cum had put lasting respect on the entire city of Pittsburgh and State of Pennsylvania as well as on the notion that innovative game planning and preparation could win ball games.

CHAPTER 16

VIRGIL

ON THE NIGHT OF JANUARY 13, 1912, two months before the Monticello Athletic Association's victory over Howard University in Pittsburgh and 460 miles away in Chicago, the Seward Park Midgets tipped off against the Racine YMCA in a parks department basketball league game at a gymnasium in a section of the city's North Side known today as Cabrini-Green. Both squads were lightweight class youth teams. The visiting Racines were from Racine, Wisconsin, seventy-five miles to the north, while the Midgets represented Seward Park, a small local "recreation ground" at Elm and Orleans Streets seven blocks west of Lake Michigan. Named after William Seward, the Secretary of State in President Abraham Lincoln's cabinet, the playground had a wading pool for children, an eight-lap cinder path, a baseball diamond, and an $80,000 fieldhouse whose gym was the Midgets' home court.[1] The game was competitive at first, with the locals leading the Racines by only two points at halftime, 10 to 8. But then the Seward Park lads turned it on. Using "superior team play and condition" to "pile up a big score" they dominated the Wisconsin squad in the second half and rolled to a 40–23 win. It was the Midgets' fourteenth straight victory and their eighteenth out of nineteen. They would go on to win twenty-four games in a row, a new league record, and end that season with twenty-nine victories altogether over teams from throughout Chicago and its surroundings, including the Division Street YMCA, Cornell Square, the Elroy Athletic Club, First German Methodist Episcopal, and the Hull House Premiers.[2] Their only loss was to Armour Square, another small park with its own fieldhouse near Chicago's stockyards.[3]

When the Seward Park facilities opened on July 4, 1908, the ceremony had featured Irish, Italian, and Swedish folk songs, reflecting the ethnicity of the surrounding neighborhood. Yet the Midgets' best player was a fifteen-year-old

African American eighth grader named Virgil Finley Blueitt. Born in Bowling
Green, Kentucky, on March 18, 1896, he was Thomas and Angelina Blueitt's
fourth child. Playing the left forward position, Virgil was the only Black member of the squad. Though old for his grade, the teen was average height, yet
with a muscular physique and remarkable athletic abilities, he often scored
most of Seward Park's points. Local sports pages featured weekly updates
about the Midgets' record-breaking season. Their players even posed in uniform for a photography studio session staged by the *Chicago Daily News*. So,
Virgil's name, athletic abilities, and race were known throughout the Windy
City. That season his older brother, an eighteen-year-old high school senior
named Napoleon Porter Blueitt, born December 24, 1893, was having a similar
experience playing basketball for the Seward Park Seniors, the heavyweight
version of the Midgets. However, Napoleon's real fame came from his record-
breaking performances running with the track and field team of the Albert G.
Lane Manual Training High School, a majority White institution.

The state-of-the-art vocational school, known as Lane Tech, had opened
in 1908 just a block away from Seward Park, at the corner of Division and
Sedgwick Streets.[4] Costing $500,000 with facilities considered among Chi-
cago's finest, the school was designed to hold 1,400 students who were meant
to become "foremen and superintendents whose future plans didn't necessarily
include further education."[5] Napoleon was in Lane Tech's first graduating class.
His track teammate there was another eighteen-year-old African American
senior, a gifted sprinter and native Chicagoan named Frederick "Fritz" Pollard,
Jr., who also starred in football and baseball. Later that spring, Napoleon and
Fritz would leave their competition in cinder dust, leading Lane Tech to win
not only the 1912 Cook County Interscholastic Track & Field Championship
but also the 1912 Illinois High School Track & Field state title. Napoleon would
anchor the school's 880-yard relay team to a record-setting county title win,
then capture the individual 440-yard state title. Fritz would take home the
individual 220-yard low hurdles county crown. Both men are still listed today
on the Lane Tech all-time track honor roll.

Fritz's best sport wasn't even track; it was football. On the gridiron, he
won "so many games with his brilliant head work, both in defensive and
offensive playing, also his ability to kick field goals at such an accuracy that it
astonished all who seen [*sic*] him in action."[6] Fritz would graduate in June,

report to Northwestern University, then change his mind and leave Chicago to become the first Black football player at Brown University. He would subsequently lead Brown to the 1916 Rose Bowl before playing professionally in the early National Football League. Eventually the speedster would be enshrined in the Football Hall of Fame.[7] He was that good.

Virgil would enroll as a freshman at Lane Tech in the fall of 1912 and continue his news-making ways on the hardwood court, jumping right into the school's varsity lineup. "Cook County Basketball teams start working off their schedule, and while basketball has never proved very attractive to the average colored student we find a young man by the name of Virgil Blueitt, a brother of the runner and substitute on the Lane Tech football team, who is playing left guard on the Lane Major basketball team," said the *Defender*. "From all reports he is playing a star game."[8] Napoleon, who had graduated alongside Fritz that year, decided to stay in Chicago.

At the time, the Blueitt's third son, their youngest child, was a self-assured eight-year-old named MacKinzie. Though he didn't become a prominent athlete, "Kinzie," as he was nicknamed, would eventually outshine both of his older brothers combined as a headline-maker. After joining the Chicago Police Department as a patrolman in 1929, the year of the St. Valentine's Day Massacre, which took place in a garage a few blocks from the Blueitt's near–North Side home, Kinzie would rise to become the highest ranking African American in the force's history. NEGRO HANDLES LARGEST POLICE JOB IN THE WORLD, a front-page headline in the *Kansas City Plain Dealer* would say in 1949 after he was named acting captain of the South Side's notorious Wabash Station. This was the precinct house for the city's Fifth District, which contained the Bronzeville community that would grow to 200,000 residents by then.

Big and forceful, Kinzie understood both sides of the law and would eventually be appointed District Commander over the entire Fifth.[9] "Just about everyone on Chicago's Southside knows Kinzie Blueitt," the *Chicago Defender* would state in 1953. "But those who know Blueitt best are the criminals." The double-meaning in those words was not a mistake. Kinzie had been generous with his community and was committed to cleaning up narcotics. But he had also developed friendly connections with Ed, George, and McKissack Jones, three African American brothers who ran Chicago's multimillion-dollar-a-year policy syndicate. Known as "The Fabulous Jones Boys" and with the South

Side as their base, these men remained untouchable by collaborating with mobster Al Capone, controlling politicians, and building community loyalty through capital investment, job creation, real estate acquisition, business loans, and, ultimately, some pioneering basketball team sponsorships. It was while Kinzie was a Chicago Police Department detective, moonlighting as Joe Louis's bodyguard during the mid-1930s, that the Jones brothers would hatch an elaborate Black hoops takeover with tentacles so ambitious that they reached all the way into Harlem.

Because of the pivotal role of Black strikebreakers in Chicago's history, and because Lane Tech was at a crossroads of labor empowerment as a training ground for future foremen, African American students there were always under scrutiny as to whether they would become strike leaders or management collaborators.[10] To offset the socialized "scab race" label, Virgil, Napoleon, and Fritz practically *had* to be excellent athletes at Lane. Because of racism in the labor market, their fathers, like so many Black men in Chicago, were in service work. Thomas Blueitt was a porter and Fritz Pollard, Sr., was a barber. (Sammy Ransom's father, George, was a shoemaker despite missing three fingers on his right hand.) Still, African American barbers, shoemakers, and some porters were considered middle class strivers in Bronzeville.

Meanwhile, the families, friends, and fans of talented Black athletes who played on White teams were unwanted at their own sporting events. "All the colored people I have ever met at a basketball game or indoor track meet could be counted on one hand, and that includes the colored students from the same school from which the colored boy represents," wrote an observant African American sports and society columnist with the *Chicago Defender* named Julius N. Avendorph during Virgil's freshman season at Lane Tech later that year. "The colored athlete who is fearless enough to attempt to win a place on one of the athletic teams, and succeeds with the prejudice that he has got to contend with, he ought to at least get the encouragement from his own to the extent of cheering him on."[11] It's likely that Avendorph was talking about Virgil Blueitt. The columnist famously worked as an assistant to the president of the Pullman Company, which manufactured and operated those luxury railroad passenger cars that featured dining and sleeping compartments. Avendorph was onto something. But it wasn't that Black people in Chicago wouldn't support their own athletes, of which there were many.

Jack Johnson, who in 1908 had become the first African American world heavyweight boxing champion, came to Chicago in 1910. Originally from Galveston, Texas, the coastal city where the Juneteenth Jubilee celebration originated, Johnson had planted roots on the South Side with the purchase of a three-story Victorian house there for his mother. After that, he called the Windy City home.[12] The champ was a hero to Black folks everywhere, admired and in July 1912, he opened a five-hundred-seat cabaret called Café de Champion in the heart of the Bronzeville.[14] Considered "the city's most magnificent café," on opening night, so many South Siders waited out front for a chance to glimpse the champ's arrival that the entire block from Thirty-First Street to Armour Avenue was packed with thousands of Black people, despite knowing they couldn't get inside without a VIP pass.[16]

The city's most admired baseball player was an African American athlete named Andrew "Rube" Foster, nicknamed "the world's greatest pitcher." Born in Calvert, Texas, a tiny plantation town that once boasted of having the world's largest cotton gin, Foster had moved to Bronzeville in 1902 after signing with the Chicago Union Giants, the top Black baseball team in the Midwest at the time.[18] The club was owned by Frank Leland, a local African American court clerk and entrepreneur. The pitcher eventually split with Leland and in 1911 formed his own club, the Chicago American Giants. Then, Foster devised winning strategies on the field and partnered with John Schorling, a White tavern owner who controlled an 11,000-capacity ballpark on the South Side, eventually named after him.[19] With seats at fifty cents each, an attractive ballpark accessible from all corners of Bronzeville, and an outstanding record that made them popular, Chicago American Giants games were always packed. In one instance, more fans showed up at Schorling Park than at both the Chicago White Sox and Chicago Cubs home games the same afternoon combined.

So, the scarcity of African American fans at White high school sporting events that Julius Avendorph was talking about during the early 1910s wasn't their lack of support for Black athletes, it was their reluctance to leave the South Side. Though he was "personally acquainted with more Chicago millionaires than possibly any other Colored man in Chicago," Avendorph's influence couldn't change the way African Americans were being treated elsewhere.[20]

When the Wabash Avenue Colored Branch of the YMCA opened on June 15, 1913, completed at a cost reported to be $200,000, its Sunday-afternoon dedication was a larger-than-life event.[21] The festivities began with a full military parade led by the Illinois National Guard's Eighth Infantry Regiment and followed by representatives from all of Chicago's secret African American societies.[22] "The gleaming trappings of the guardsmen were set off by the somber black coats and high silk hats of several departments of the Masonic order which took part," the *Afro-American* reported.[23] As they marched through the heart of Bronzeville, more than five thousand spectators lined the festively decorated route, many leaning out of the windows of their homes. An overflow crowd, including "thousands of women," waited in the hot sun on the street outside the Y for almost four hours while inside, six hundred people crammed into the facility's state-of-the-art gymnasium to hear speeches from a who's who of dignitaries including Julius Rosenwald and Booker T. Washington. The city's African Americans couldn't have been prouder, and they had every reason.

When it was Rosenwald's turn to take the stage, the building's original benefactor was greeted with such an ovation that "for many minutes he could not speak."[24] This was his moment, and the recognition well-deserved. "We are here to dedicate this building to the task of removing race hatred, of which so much exists," he shared. "I believe the races are coming to a better understanding every day." But to him that wasn't enough. "To paraphrase a part of Lincoln's immortal Gettysburg address, we should here dedicate more than this building," Rosenwald urged. "We should dedicate ourselves to the unfinished work." By then, Black YMCA buildings in Washington and Indianapolis were nearly completed. Construction would begin soon in Cincinnati. And in Philadelphia, Atlanta, Los Angeles, Kansas City, and Baltimore, the required matching funds had been raised.[25] "Here is an opportunity," Rosenwald insisted, "to show that things can be done with the Negro rather than for him, and for the Negro to demonstrate to the world that what he wants is an opportunity not as a Negro but as a man."[26] Rosenwald was right. Race hatred did exist in Chicago. But its expression was one-sided. Black people were on the receiving end. Hoping that Bronzeville's new YMCA could somehow eliminate this condition overlooked White supremacy and systemic racism at the root of the matter. Washington's remarks that day were similar. "Influences growing out of this building should result in putting into the colored men of Chicago a new ambition, a spirit to live clean, upright lives and to work to save not only themselves but others," he enthusiastically imagined.[27]

Although their words were strident and packed with power, both of these men had carefully avoided mentioning what was being done *to* the city's "Negroes," namely that their already existing clean, upright aspirations were steadily being crushed. That's exactly why the South Side's enthusiasm about this outstanding new facility was so high. They now at least had their own YMCA. That, along with the mere presence of these renowned leaders in Bronzeville at all, and the inspiring words they spoke, offered a profound sense of hope.

It seemed as though every young African American athlete in Chicago joined the Wabash YMCA the instant its doors flew open in July 1913, including Virgil and Napoleon Blueitt. To no one's surprise, open racial hostility toward its members launched "by gangs of white boys" began immediately. In one case just weeks later, several Black youths conducting a "program of athletics" under the supervision of a YMCA official at nearby Armour Square Park, a twenty-two-minute walk from the YMCA building, were "assailed with sandbags, tripped, walked over, and some of them badly bruised." Not long after that when a local priest "took a group of Negro Y.M.C.A. boys to Armour Square to play basket-ball," the entire party, including the clergyman, "was beaten up by white boys, their sweaters were taken from them, and they were otherwise maltreated."[28]

That vibe continued into the fall as Virgil began his sophomore year with Lane's varsity. "In this cosmopolitan city it may seem strange, but last Friday night Evanston Academy drew the color line on Lane High School basket ball team, simply because Virgil Blueitt was a member," the *Defender* reported.[29] "Lane stood upon her manhood and refused to play without him." To his credit in what proved to be a pivotal move, the referee awarded the game to Virgil's team. That effectively put an end to any thoughts other coaches may have had about trying this tactic, which was most likely more about Virgil's talent than his skin color. Everyone knew how good he was. "There can't be a great deal in a name when five baskets are thrown by a party hight Blueitt," the widely admired satirical *Chicago Tribune* sports columnist Ringgold Wilmer "Ring" Lardner would point out after another Virgil-driven victory brought Lane closer to the interscholastic playoffs.[30] "Blueitt's sharp shooting, following numerous fouls, gave Lane Tech a place in the Chicago High School Basketball League finals and eliminated Hyde Park, last year's champion," the *Chicago Daily Tribune* reported later that season following their 18–10 win.[31] "Lane won by exceptionally clever team work," the report continued.

But the real reason was innovative thinking by Lane's coaches, who broke with long-standing protocol regarding player positions. "When the tech guards exchanged places with the forwards the Hyde Park defense was bewildered, and when several switches were made, the south siders were put to rout." Naismith's rules never specified where guards should or could play, let alone that there be a left and right side for that position. "This system of play adopted by the north siders resulted in many personal fouls, giving Blueitt a chance for free throws." That was the key to the game. "Getting eight free throws and two baskets is going some," the *Defender* added, because that was a lot for an individual player when games rarely went above twenty points.[32]

Meanwhile, the win by Lane Tech over Hyde Park High School, led by a Black player, was itself doubly sweet for African Americans in Bronzeville because their attempts to expand over the border into neighboring Hyde Park for better housing were being met with violent resistance. (Lane would have won the ensuing title game against Park High School with the same strategy, except Virgil hit only four of eleven free throws, the difference-makers in their 18–16 loss.)

Virgil also established himself as a force on the baseball diamond, leading Lane Tech to the finals in the Chicago High School Indoor Baseball League, a Windy City athletic tradition that was the equivalent of preseason spring training. He was on the mound for the school's 5–0 defeat of Medill High in the semi-final, holding them to two hits while striking out eighteen batters. "Almost perfect pitching by Blueitt, the star colored pitcher, gave Lane its shutout victory," said the *Chicago Daily Tribune*. "He also was a run getting factor with three bingles."[33]

Early bouts with racism didn't change the mood around the Wabash YMCA at all. In terms of athletic talent, this branch had *the goods* and intended to make that clear. So, in June 1914, just after the high school baseball season ended, they staged a Chicago-wide track and field meet at Schorling Park.[34] This was their first big event, and it drew 8,000 spectators. Bronzeville's support for its own was indeed special. And when Virgil and Napoleon were the meet's top scorers, collectively winning the 100-, 220-, 440-, and 880-yard runs as well as the running broad jump, and were both on the winning 4x100- and 4x400-yard relay teams, there was no question about who was who.[35]

That same summer, the Black community in nearby Evanston, Illinois, opened its own YMCA Colored Branch in a new facility on Emerson Street that was a ten-minute walk from the center of Northwestern University's campus.[36] Just like on the South Side, this Y gave African American youths a place where they could feel safe, connected, valued, and loved. One of the great features of the Emerson Street YMCA was its gymnasium. Though it was "so small that the out of bounds was the walls," the court was good enough for them to form a basketball team.

Virgil was just getting started. In the fall, the Lane Tech junior made the varsity football team as a running back, and performed so skillfully that it was said, "he looms up as one of the greatest individual players at football Chicago has ever seen."[37] During one game at Schorling Park in October 1914, Virgil handed defeat to Chicago Public League rival Wendell Phillips High School by completing a dropkick from the twenty-five-yard line "with ease" to clinch a 3–0 win.[38] Similar to a field goal and also worth three points, the dropkick is one of the most difficult of all football plays to execute, so rarely completed that there has only been one successful attempt in the National Football League since the early 1940s.

Phillips High would play a vital role in Bronzeville sports. It had opened in 1904 at Prairie Avenue and East Thirty-Ninth Street as the South Side's first public high school. (Schorling Park on West Thirty-Ninth Street and South Wentworth was Wendell Phillips' home field.) "In addition to its several laboratories, completely equipped, the building has a gymnasium, swimming pool, and lunchroom," newspapers reported when it was unveiled, as well as "open playgrounds," which were considered "indispensable appendages for the health, development and morality of city children."[39] "W.P." served the youngsters of the area's wealthy White industrialists yet was racially integrated from the outset, with thirty-seven Black students enrolled in its inaugural class. By 1907, that number had grown to ninety. As migrations from the South accelerated, so did the proportion of African Americans in the institution's total enrollment until it became Chicago's first predominantly Black high school in the mid-1910s with just over 50 percent. No one yet realize how many exceptional African American basketball players would soon be coming out of there.

Virgil made the All-Chicago Football Prep First Team that season while Ring Lardner, apparently an admirer, named him to his Collegiate All-American Second Team despite his still being in high school.[40] "Blueitt is the boy who put the 'p' in pep at Lane," the *Defender* declared.[41]

With the 1914–5 basketball season approaching, the Wabash YMCA began forming its own hardwood teams at all size levels. As one of the best and most experienced players in the city, Virgil was selected as captain of the branch's heavyweight unit. This was the Y's all-important "Big Five" travel squad. Wabash Y officials had no idea that they were about to become one of the greatest basketball stories in Chicago history.

Building the roster of the Wabash branch's 1914–5 heavyweight team, Virgil's first move as captain was to bring in his older brother to play left forward. Napoleon, bigger than Virgil and just as tough, was twenty years old by then and employed as a tanner at the Griess-Pfleger Tanning Company, a leather plant on Halsted at North Branch Street. At right forward was a talented sixteen-year-old Wendell Phillips player named Robert James "Bobby" Anderson. Playing at the left guard position was Clarence A. Cousins, a twenty-three-year-old department store salesman. Frank Giles, a twenty-two-year-old who lived and worked at the Wabash YMCA facility, was one of the centers. A youngster known as "Raze" Curry was a backcourt player who would soon be "considered the best defensive guard in the West." The other center was a nineteen-year-old Illinois Steel Company worker named Jesse James Leavell. His name proved significant because this heavyweight crew elected to nick-name themselves the Wabash "Outlaws."

Just as with Rube Foster's baseball team, newspaper headlines and glory awaited the Wabash YMCA and all of Bronzeville if the Outlaws could play well, so the team's efforts were for a higher cause from the outset. This wasn't lost on their manager, a twenty-five-year-old local African American dentist and Howard University graduate named Dr. Albert Creighton Johnson. Ambitious and visionary, Dr. Johnson organized a long-term plan that included devising a competitive schedule of basketball games against the toughest opponents he could find in and around Chicago. Over the next two seasons, these included rugged all-White teams who were known to scrap. The Dodger AC represented West Town, the city's oldest Polish settlement. The White Eagles were described as "a rough bunch of Polacks, and if they can't win a game by fair playing, they rought it." Their home court was the gymnasium of the landmark St. Stanislaus Kostka Church in the same area. The South Chicagos repped the Bessemer Park neighborhood adjacent to the city's thriving steel mills below the South Side. And the Hull House, was from a settlement community on the North Side for recent European immigrants.[42]

During that 1914–5 season, the Outlaws became so popular that they had to turn down a number of interested African American challengers because, according to the *Defender*, "they were tied up with white teams for the remainder of the season and wished to measure their skills with their white brothers."[43] One all-Black opponent that got on the Wabash schedule was the Emerson Street Colored YMCA in Evanston. "We are eagerly awaiting our first indoor athletic meet at Wabash Avenue Y.M.C.A," the Emerson branch declared.[44] But things got hectic when the teams finally met on the Outlaws' home floor in Bronzeville. It was late in the game and the visitors were winning big. Suddenly the Outlaws became hot, finally getting physical to match the Emerson Y intensity until they were down by only one point with little time left.

Wabash had the momentum and it looked like they would take the lead. Then something strange happened. Evanston walked off the court "after the Wabash team had come from behind so strong that nothing seemed able to stop them." This was not only unsportsmanlike but also considered soft. Tensions flared, "then trouble started, and the result was that the game was never finished, because the visitors would not agree to anything within reason." The takeaway was that "it simply looked as though Evanston wanted a loophole to escape defeat." That did not go over very well.

"If they would cut out some of their rough work it will make the game of basketball as popular here as in New York, where many times a game precedes a dance," a perceptive *Chicago Defender* sportswriter pointed out afterward.[45] A fundamental truth had taken hold. In the Black community, this game and its popularity was about more than just winning, about more than even the sport itself.

CHAPTER 17

MADDENING

IF HE HAD ACCOMPLISHED ANYTHING by staying observant as a push-cart vendor's son, a messenger-by-day, a basketball mascot by night, and the protégé of sports entrepreneur Major Aloysius Hart with the New York All Stars, Will Anthony Madden learned how to spot an opportunity and make a deal. As the end of the 1911–2 season approached, he was still watching from the sidelines, remaining loyal, patiently waiting and observing.

After the All Stars lost to Howard on March 22, 1912 at the New Star Casino in their last game of the season, the U.S. Army veteran asked Will to be the "official announcer" during a late-April event at the Seventy-First Regiment Armory in Manhattan. It was a basketball doubleheader between two visiting teams, the Tenth Cavalry Five from Fort Ethan Allen, Vermont, and a selected squad from West Point. The preliminary contest featured the Spartan Girls versus the New York YMCA Girls. All the while, Will kept exercising his theatrical voice, making an appearance in the choir of a musical comedy at the New Star in May 1912.

But by that summer, the New York All Stars had begun falling apart. The boycott against them had forced Major to book games with lesser teams in smaller venues. This was not sustainable. Charlie Scottron, Charlie Bradford, and Babe Wiggins, three of their brightest stars, had already quit the team. At this point, *Amsterdam News* sports journalist Romeo Dougherty would remember more than a decade later, "when things were at its height, athletically speaking, Bill Madden had just about graduated as the mascot of the famous New York All Stars."[2] Now it was Will's turn to make some moves of his own.

Scottron had returned to the Smart Set Athletic Club. Wiggins had gone to the Alpha Physical Culture Club. Bradford, arguably the best African American basketball center in the game, had not yet found a landing spot. He and Will had become friends though, and this was key. Because when he went back to Father Daniel asking to be reinstated in the St. Christopher Club, the clergyman apparently welcomed Will back with open arms, as long as he would also secure the big man, which the former mascot did. Next, with enormous nerve, Will went after an even bigger target by running as a candidate for the St. C. organization's basketball manager, an elected position in the early days of club teams. And he won. This was surprising to many, but not to Will himself. "It is said of Madden that he cherished great ambitions," Romeo would later explain. And as if to prove that point, he immediately hopped into a studio pose with the St. Christopher Club Juniors, who he called the "Tigers," for a photograph that would appear in the next season's edition of Spalding's *Official Handbook of the Interscholastic Athletic Association of the Middle Atlantic States*.

This pioneering publication was the work of Edwin "EB" Henderson, who had launched its first annual edition in May 1910 immediately after retiring from basketball as a newlywed. These handbooks, which cost ten cents apiece, included "pictures, occasions and information concerning colored athletes" and a suggestion that "every young man should have a copy."[3] Some eight thousand units of the 1910 edition were reportedly distributed "among negro schools and communities, where they have worked untold benefits." Coedited in Washington, D.C., by Armstrong Manual Training School principal and ISAA treasurer Garnet C. Wilkinson, the *1912 ISAA Handbook* was a "profusely illustrated" 174-page guide that was "neatly gotten up, is quite attractive in its typographical make-up, and furnishes much interesting information."[4] The project itself was made possible by EB's and Garnet's tremendous passion and organizational skills, having asked every African American school, college, and athletic club along the East Coast and parts of the Midwest to submit details and photographs of their football, baseball, basketball, and track teams. The fact that it was published by A. G. Spalding & Bros., the powerful and profitable sporting goods manufacturer, helped validate Black athletic organizations and African American athletes themselves.

Within weeks, Will had assumed his new managerial duties at the St. Christopher Club and all seemed to be forgiven. Father Daniel had to have been pleased because his new basketball manager brought enthusiasm and knowledge of the game as well as familiarity with the team's system of play. But there was still the matter of explaining to the leaders of the boycott against Major Hart why Charlie Bradford, who had turned semi-pro with

the All Stars, was allowed back on one of the amateur basketball teams that
had been boycotting his pay-for-play move in the first place. For that, Will
showcased his writing talent by going public in October 1912 with a letter
to the editor of the *New York Age*. "For the past two years Bradford has been
considered an outlaw in our basketball world on account of his affiliation with
that famous team—namely—the New York All Stars," the new St. C. manager
explained. "The origin of this team," he continued, "is now basketball history."
Things had changed for the 1912–3 season, Will argued. Bradford had been
"re-elected a member" of the organization and "as such will be eligible to play
with the club during the coming season, and all seasons to follow as long as
he remains a full-fledged member of the team as he now is."

By protecting Bradford, Will was also protecting himself by evading any
mention of his own defection. The main reason for sending the letter was to
avoid "any contention or disagreement" about the center's eligibility, he wrote.
Will also addressed some of the criticism the All Stars had gotten. "I will not
affirm or deny the grounds on which these contentions were based, still they
have always been distasteful to me." He was sure the public felt the same way,
since they "paid their money to witness a physical argument and not a verbal
one." Then he added, "I want to avoid all such trouble during my leadership,"
which was ironic because Will's argumentative words would soon become his
trademark. Finally, he appealed to the other amateur clubs, "trusting that all
my brother managers will look at the matter fairly and see it from the same
standpoint as myself." But although no one seemed to be questioning his stature, one could detect in this letter an attempt by Will to insert himself into a
position as their equal. Perhaps the "Little Africa" escapee, who now found
himself running the basketball program of the country's most elite African
American church, didn't truly believe that he belonged. Whatever his doubts
might have been though, Will wasted no time sweeping them aside. The new
manager "almost immediately began to apply his own policies of operation
with the result that due to his managerial ability, his unusual personality and
his great accomplishment as an ad-writer, the St. Christopher teams rose to
their greatest heights, eventually passing all the other clubs."[5]

Less than a month later, on November 11, 1912, Will was at his messenger
job inside the Standard Oil Building at 26 Broadway. It was a Monday, and
he was among those riding in the elevator headed down from the fourteenth

floor, its topmost level. But when the car reached the thirteenth étage, it suddenly plunged uncontrollably in a terrifying free fall. "The automatic safety
clutch stopped the car at the sixth floor "or everyone would have been killed,"
the *New York Age* reported. "Mr. Madden escaped injury."[6] During the years
to come, this would be Will's theme, landing safely on his feet time after time
from one dire situation to another. He was a survivor, after all.

Quietly during that 1912–3 season, the Spartan Field Club "Braves" basketball
team, owned and operated by Bob Douglas, now twenty-nine years old, had
begun playing in front of increasingly larger audiences. Just like Cum Posey, Jr.,
Bob was a player-coach on his own team, though he was not nearly as talented
on the hardwood court as the Homestead wonder, and Will Madden would
later describe the St. Kittian immigrant in print as an "ordinary guard." But the
Spartans had other interesting personnel on their roster, including a slender
seventeen-year-old Russian-born Jewish player at the left forward position
named Abraham Solomon Tischinsky. Teammates called him "Tisch," and he
was known for what the *Age* described as "his crazy long shooting." Tisch also
played for DeWitt Clinton High School on Tenth Avenue, a team he would
lead to the Manhattan borough basketball championship in 1914 as a senior.
After graduating, Tisch became a star forward at the City College of New
York, playing alongside future New York Original Celtics Star and Basketball
Hall of Fame member Nat Holman. Even while at CCNY, he would help the
Spartans as their coach until graduating in 1918. After that, Tisch would work
in the garment industry and eventually start a small clothing manufacturing
business. He would get married, have two sons, Larry and Bob, and, like many
European immigrants simplify his name, calling himself Al Tisch.

Tisch would liquidate his garment business after World War II and use
the proceeds to stake his sons with $125,000 in entrepreneurial funding. Larry
and Bob would go on to become billionaires in control of the Loews Corporation. Larry would eventually take over CBS, rescuing it from bankruptcy, while
Bob would become co-owner of the New York Giants in the National Football
League. Thanks to wide-reaching philanthropy in education, healthcare, culture, and the arts, their last name is familiar to many, but few people today

would know that it began as a nickname given to a White Jewish basketball player on an African American team led by a future Hall of Fame member during the 1910s.

Bob Douglas booked his Spartan Big Five games at the Black-owned Young's Casino in Harlem, a newly opened facility on East 134th and Park Avenue that was said to "equal any in size and furnishings that various race organizations now hire from white owners." The 85-by-125-foot brick structure was "heated by steam and lighted by electricity," which was significantly modern compared to the days of gas-lit venues with potbelly stoves, and could seat three thousand persons when including its thirty luxury boxes, making it ideal for balls, performances, and private parties as well as basketball. Young's even had its own roof garden for outdoor picnics. The business was owned by a forty-four-year-old Kentucky-born entrepreneur named Gibson L. "Gib" Young, also the proprietor of Young's Café, a popular nearby saloon. Both businesses were said to employ "all Negro help." Reportedly backed by $100,000 of Gib's own funding, around $2.7 million today, the new basketball venue was considered "the most up-to-date casino owned by the race anywhere in this country" when it opened in the summer of 1912 amid a "blaze of glory."[7]

Gib went after his nearby rival, the Manhattan Casino, by charging "25 pennies" for admission to games, which were followed by "dancing until 3 A.M.," instead of the fifty cents the Waldrons charged, and by catering to the city's second-tier squads such as the St. Cyprian Seniors, the New Jersey Imperials, and the Salem Crescent Athletic Club. The Salem Crescent AC had been organized and promoted by the Reverend Fredrick A. Cullen under the umbrella of his Salem Memorial Mission, which he had founded in 1902. (Cullen later became the foster father of Harlem Renaissance poet Countee Cullen.)

Gib also green-lighted a new women's basketball team using members of a girls' social club called the Younger Set, and used Young's Casino as their home court. All the players were attractive young ladies who were popular darlings of the city's Black social scene, and their charming team identity featured a huge red heart on the left chest of their uniforms and warm-up gear. The team's organizer was a master promoter and a showman named Henry S. Creamer. "I shall introduce to New York the Younger Set Girls' basketball team, the neatest, sweetest, likewise cleverest girls' team it has known," he announced, adding that his new team "put the word 'all' in basketball."[8] This was a girls' club, but they were also an all-star collection of New York City's best female basketball talent. Rosa Mitchell, formerly a star with the championship-winning New York Girls, was club president and team manager. Eva Miller was vice president. Mildred Gasaway was the club's secretary. Edith Trice, formerly the captain of the powerful Spartan Girls of Brooklyn, was now the Younger Set's captain and the organization's treasurer. Two of Edith's brothers, George, and Arthur, played for the Smart Set Athletic Club basketball team, which considered the Younger Set its unofficial sister squad.

The Younger Set's very first game, played in late October 1912, was at Pierson's Hall in Newark, New Jersey, against a team from there called the Crescent Girls, who the Younger Set defeated 4 to 2. The visitors, "under the able leadership of Miss Edith Trice, outwitted and outplayed the Jerseyites at every stage of the game."[9] Edith sprained her ankle in that contest and was out for two weeks but rejoined the squad in time for its next Newark visit, to face the Crescent Girls and the Criterion Girls. Though not yet fully recovered, she played in both games anyway, boasting in advance that the Younger Set would "clean out New Jersey" before returning home. They did, winning 4–2 and 10–2.[10] His team had been physically ready because, according to Creamer, under his leadership, "by hard and constant practice, the team was whipped into presentable shape" for the season.[11] After seven games, the Younger Set girls were still undefeated.

Will Anthony Madden kept making the St. Christopher Big Five basketball program more competitive by adding bona fide expertise and new star players. For that reason, he had had his eye on Jeff Wetzler, still working as head coach and head of basketball programs at P.S. 188 on the Lower East Side. Since winning the Public School Athletic League Senior Division for the 1904–5 season, Wetzler's teams had been virtually unstoppable, capturing back-to-back PSAL Senior Division titles for 1906–7 and for 1907–8. Then there was the Evening Recreation Center program, an innovative new initiative launched by the New York City Department of Education after realizing that the Inter-Settlement Basket Ball League and the PSAL were limited in their reach. Settlement houses only covered the blocks they served, and the impact of schools faded soon after a student heard their dismissal bell. But the ERC, as it became known, solved this dilemma by using existing school buildings and their gymnasiums for programming after hours, six nights a week, for anyone fourteen or older. The idea was instantly popular. Nineteen ERC sites were operating citywide by the 1904–5 season, when P.S. 188 opened its own evening center, called ERC 188.

The initiative became a major success for its social impact on the city, with more than four hundred visitors per night flocking to each ERC location on average, and the centers were especially effective in Wetzler's old Lower East Side neighborhood. That's because they rallied kids around sports. "For most of the men and boys the gymnasium is the principal attraction," one report observed. "No matter how bad a young man may be, the acquisition of 'the athlete's code of honor' is a triumph over lawlessness, the beginning of a citizen's conception of duty."[12] Eugene C. Gibney, superintendent of city playgrounds for the City of New York, observed something else. Although each site varied in size, equipment, nationality of attendees, or other individualities, "there is one feature that is omnipresent and that is basket ball."[13]

ERC's formed their own basketball teams to play in the Evening Recreation Center Athletic League, or ERCAL, which was governed by the AAU. "The aims in fostering inter-club basket ball competition within each center and inter-center competition between all the centers, are three-fold—physical, civic, and moral," said Gibney, who was a strong proponent of fitness and fair competition as a way of life. "The whole upward trend of society is toward the acquiring of freedom—national freedom, political freedom and social freedom," he would say. "We secured national freedom when we liberated the slaves, political freedom with the abolition of feudalism, but social freedom involves race, color, and creed," Gibney added. "To gain that, we must level the 100,000,000 people in this country," he continued. "The community centre will go a long way toward this."[14]

Because of the sheer number of students at P.S. 188 and the quality of its facility, ERC 188 had automatically become New York City's largest and best equipped. And with Wetzler in charge of the basketball program for both the school and the ERC, they soon dominated all competition in the Inter-Settlement Basket Ball League, the Public Schools Athletic League, and the Evening Recreation Center Basketball League, as well as the AAU's own New York Metropolitan District championships, which were open to any team from these leagues. By the end of the 1911–2 season, ERCAL officials claimed theirs was the largest basketball league in the country, serving 610 players on 63 teams in two age divisions.[15] Yet, Wetzler was winning annual ERC Athletic League titles seemingly with ease.[16]

Wetzler's most famous challenge had come in 1909 in the final of the Metro AAU Junior Division Championship, when ERC 188 defeated University Settlement, the defending titleholders, nicknamed the "Busy Izzies" for their bewildering speed and ballhandling abilities. They had featured future Basketball Hall of Fame members Max "Marty" Friedman and Barney "Mighty Mite" Sedransky as well as future collegiate and professional stars Ira Streusand, Harry Brill, and Louis "Sug" Sugarman, all in their teens.

Their 20–16 win made ERC 188 not only Metro AAU Junior champions but also the Lower East Side's new basketball kings. This alone could have made Wetzler famous, but he wasn't done.

There were no all-Black basketball teams involved in the Metro AAU, because none were yet allowed to join, nor in the Settlement league, because African American settlements were so small, nor in the ERC league, because there were no longer any formally segregated "colored" schools in New York City, so Black student-athletes were dispersed. But the fact that these leagues comprised nearly the entire basketball-playing population of New York City, arguably the best pool of talent in the world, meant Wetzler was more than just successful. His system of identifying, recruiting, training, motivating, and coaching players and teams wasn't just scientific, it was savage. Wetzler's fame grew and he appeared in the sports pages of local newspapers in Manhattan and Brooklyn as well as in nationally distributed publications.

But this prominence had its downsides. By the time Will Anthony Madden took over the St. Christopher Club basketball program prior to the 1912–3 season, ERC 188 had become so successful that, paradoxically, they posed a threat to the AAU's vision of expanding the sport at all levels. "The novice and ordinary athletes have always been discouraged by the performances of stars," said Gibney of the AAU. "This fact more than anything else retards the growth of the game and the organization of teams."[17] The amateur body had to take action beyond just scolding the coach for being "too good." So, they imposed a new rule, arbitrarily, which stated that from then on, all players who had previously won a Senior Division championship title would be ineligible to play in any future ERCAL championships. That didn't matter. Wetzler's squads weren't based on individual stars, so they kept on winning titles in both weight divisions anyway, the AAU, at their wit's end, simply just kicked him and his program out of postseason competition completely.

With that, Wetzler was a free agent. He took his championship-winning system and went looking for another team. At precisely that moment in Harlem, Will Anthony Madden was looking for expertise, leadership, and talent. So, prior to the start of the 1913–4 season, Will hired Wetzler as the club's new head basketball coach, also allowing him to bring in a promising young Jewish player from ERC 188 named Irving Rose. The husky forward was not only accepted into New York City's blossoming world of African American basketball with no questions raised, he was embraced as "a good hard player," according to Fred W. Fuhrtz, an official in the Alpha organization, writing in the *New York Age*. "All white boys are as a rule," Fuhrtz added, "they have a better chance to learn the game in the schools."[18] This was true.

At least part of the reason Will was so confident about bringing Fred Wetzler and Irving Rose into an otherwise all-Black program was that Bob Douglas and his Spartans squad had already broken the ice racially with Tisch. Still, it was not clear whether African American basketball players, their fans, and the newspaper reporters who covered them would appreciate that script. Once again, Will used his writing to get ahead of the narrative. "In my opinion, Mr. 'Jeff' Edward Wetzler is the best basketball coach in the game to-day and his record is a wonderful one," he stated. "I was after Mr. Wetzler for several seasons," Will explained, adding, "I feel well repaid for my hard work and untiring efforts to give my squad the best of everything."[19] The *New York Age* appreciated the new addition and said the boys of St. Christopher were sure to improve "under his zealous coaching."[20] By implementing a rigorous training program and introducing the latest techniques in "scientific basketball," the former PS 188 coach would quickly produce results with lasting value. His strategies, drills, and game plans implemented with the St. Christopher Club soon became known as "the famous Wetzler system."

Having these new pieces in place also helped Will discover new talent for the program's junior pipeline, including an athletically gifted African American youngster named Clarence "Fats" Jenkins, a guard whom he predicted would "in a few years become one of the greatest basketball players in the country."[21] Will was right. Fats, who had been given that nickname to distinguish him from his older and skinnier brother, Harold "Legs" Jenkins, was a one-of-a-kind talent with exceptional quickness, speed, agility, and leaping ability as well as brilliant ballhandling skills, shooting range, court vision, and basketball intellect. He was quite literally a generational athlete who would play professionally in four different decades, and ultimately earn enshrinement into the Naismith Memorial Basketball Hall of Fame. As the game's first African American superstar, Fats would be praised even by White newspapers. "He is a great basketball player as well as the colored race's standout cager," the *Hammond Times* of Gary, Indiana, would write in 1938, in the midst of Jim Crow and the Great Depression, adding that Fats was "regarded by the colored race as their Babe Ruth." This was when the Harlem star had been playing for more than twenty years. His solid physique and outstanding conditioning were due to good habits. "Fat, who doesn't drink, smoke or chew, stands only 5 feet, 7 inches tall, yet he weighs 175 pounds," the *Times* would add.[22]

Fats's career was the ultimate testimony to Will's knack for identifying and cultivating talent. And through the newspapers, the St. Christopher manager was always willing to credit any success to the coaching expertise he had brought into the St. C program. "Wetzler was responsible for the development of many famous athletes in Harlem," the *Amsterdam News* would recall. "He taught the great 'Fat' Jenkins basketball from the time 'Fat' was barely able to hold a basketball in his hands."[23]

Being well-liked and talkative, Will was also able to persuade former Smart Set Athletic Club star Ferdinand Accooe to join the St. C's. In addition, Irving, the new White player, would quickly become a dominant force for the Red and Black Machine. "It was during this season that the St. Christopher Club of St. Philip's parish reached the highest point of efficiency and its teams swept everything before them," the *New York Age* later recalled.[24]

And still, Will kept pushing, constantly looking for ways to improve and grow the St. C organization both on and off the court. He began heavily promoting the club with new advertisements that mentioned Coach Wetzler. He signed a new orchestra and introduced door prizes to enhance the experience for fans. Then he was invited to contribute as a guest basketball columnist in the *New York Age*. On a personal level for Will, this was really big. It happened because Lester Walton, the newspaper's resident sports and entertainment reporter, had left the weekly newspaper and returned to the entertainment business as manager of the Lafayette Theatre on Seventh Avenue in Harlem. The theater once had a Whites-only policy where Black patrons were restricted to the balcony. But it was sold in the summer of 1913 to new owners whose vision was to attract African American audiences. This change, plus the former journalist's promotional efforts, soon turned the Lafayette into the Black community's most popular theater.

Lester was a tough act to follow at the *Age*, but Will's educational pedigree was more than enough to handle this new responsibility. Being on staff with a newspaper also gave him a self-serving incentive to excel, because now he could provide better and more in-depth coverage of the St. Christopher Big Five, his own team. And this new role must have made his hardworking family proud. Here was this small-sized lad from Little Africa, the son of a produce peddler and a would-be schoolteacher, the grandson of an illiterate Irish immigrant, and a Standard Oil messenger by day, doing the unthinkable. He was writing for a major nationally circulated African American weekly.

By this time the Smart Set Athletic Club had lost so much basketball talent to other squads that its officers decided to de-emphasize the sport in favor of track and field. For the upcoming 1913–4 season, the club would only sponsor a lightweight floor team, which J. Hoffman Woods was elected to manage. The squad featured a talented young player named Leon Monde, who was elected captain. He would soon play a pivotal role in a series of events that unlocked professionalism among African Americans in New York City. With their major focus shifted to track and field, the Smart Set recruited some of New York City's finest runners to join their club. This was a smart move. Within a year, these athletes would be featured on the front page of the *New York Times'* sport section. NEGRO ATHLETES WIN MANY HONORS, the headline read, over a story about Smart Set runners besting White competitors and predicting how, soon, "many laurels now won by white athletes will pass into the keeping of negroes." And in a rare acknowledgement of Black athletic clubs, the *Times* recognized that "promising colored athletes" now had their own organizations to join.[25]

But the Smart Set wasn't done innovating. That season, they also announced plans to become the first African American organization to schedule an indoor tennis spectator event, an indoor basketball-tennis doubleheader to be held on Tuesday evening, March 18, 1914, at the Sixty-Ninth Regiment

Armory, a National Guard facility on Lexington Avenue at East Twenty-Fifth Street that contained a five-thousand-seat arena. The same venue would be used during the early 1950s by the National Basketball Association for some New York Knicks home games. "The beautiful indoor tennis courts of the Sixty-Ninth Regiment Armory will furnish great advantage for fast and snappy play," said the *New York Age*. The event would be sponsored by the still new National League on Urban Conditions Among Negroes, also known as the Urban League. Boxholders would include Mrs. Oscar Scottron, the widow of Samuel Scottron, Edwin F. Horne, the cofounder of the Smart Set AC, and the famous African American vaudeville star Aida Overton Walker.

The Smart Set club's effort to promote tennis among African Americans led the *Age* to predict that the game would soon become "one of the greatest attractions of the season."[26] They were right. Within two years, so many outstanding Black tennis players would develop throughout the country that an African American governing body would form in 1916 called the America Tennis Association, with its mission to develop Black talent as well as to standardize rules, organize tournaments, and establish rankings.

By the start of the 1913–4 season, Howard University's basketball team had produced so many fans that the days of them playing on their tiny, quirky, small-capacity home court were coming to an end. Its limitations had created a long-term downside. "True Reformers Hall is alright for a home attraction," Will Madden would explain, "but is hardly adequate for the making of enough money to cover the expenses of a team from New York or places of like distance."[27] To compensate, Howard scheduled four of its games at the six-thousand-seat Manhattan Casino in Harlem: Hampton Institute on Friday, January 16, the Monticello Athletic Association on Monday, February 23, the Columbia University Alumni, an all-White team, on Friday, March 13, and the St. Christopher Club on Friday, March 20.

This home-away-from-home idea made sense for the D.C. college, and it made headlines, since this had never been tried before. Making arrangements for one visiting basketball squad was already quite an effort. Doing that for two at once would require a whole new approach: a New York City front man to take care of arrangements for the hotels, the venue, the orchestras, and related details. Newspapers announced that all three games were being promoted by Nat Colvin Strong, a notorious White booking agent who previously had made a fortune brokering the use of baseball fields he controlled to African American teams in return for enormous portions of the gate receipts.

At that time, Strong was one of the most powerful yet most hated men in Black professional baseball. A native of Manhattan and a graduate of City College in Harlem, he had had a successful early business career in sporting goods before investing in sports-related real estate. His holdings included strategically located ballparks in New York City and Philadelphia, where local and visiting teams had few diamonds with grandstands available to them. Strong had particular leverage over African American owners for whom it was otherwise virtually impossible to book White-owned venues. He routinely charged them much higher fees than he charged White ballclubs, up to 40 percent of the total revenues for a game. It was primarily because of White money-gouging agents like Nat Strong that Black-owned baseball teams were not able to remain financially solvent for very long throughout the 1910s.

Strong was attempting to push his way into Black basketball because he saw how lucrative it had become, and made a bet that African American fives in New York City would soon have as much difficulty booking White-owned venues as their counterparts in baseball. Maybe he could make another fortune by inserting himself between them and their go-to venues, starting with the popular large-capacity Manhattan Casino. Being a shrewd observer, Strong sensed that Howard University's basketball program could be the perfect partner for this plan. But folks in Harlem knew when someone was trying to be slick. And the broker didn't comprehend just how powerful the forces behind Black basketball in New York City really were.

As the booking agent for the four Howard games at Manhattan Casino, Nat C. Strong was responsible for making all the arrangements. This included travel and hotel for the visiting squads, which meant four trips for Howard and one each for Hampton and the Monticellos. He was also accountable for setting up the game operations at the venue, which included securing referees to officiate the games.

Though the Hampton versus Howard game at the Waldron's place in January 1914 was the Virginia school's New York City debut, they lost 27–24. Still, it was "a fast game abounding in sensational passing and shooting" and was considered "one of the best exhibitions of basketball ever played" in the area. "The popularity of basketball in Greater New York was evidenced by the large and enthusiastic galaxy of spectators," the *New York Age* shared.[28]

On the eve of Washington's Birthday in February, Howard played the Monticellos and defeated the Pittsburgh squad, 38–12. Notably, Cumberland Posey, Jr., had not joined the team on their trip to Manhattan, while Howard University had "a host of loyal followers in New York" that cheered for them despite being on the road. "An added feature in the big game," the *Age* explained, was that every player's jersey had been numbered, and each number corresponded with a scorecard that was "issued so that each and every play can be recorded by the fans and the game scored by anyone similar to a baseball game." This was also the last pre-Lenten game of the season, an added incentive as "the last chance" for fans to dance until after Easter.

Then in early March, Howard played the all-White squad of former Columbia University stars. "The Columbia Alumni came on the canvas all nicely uniformed with a light blue A on their jerseys, and immediately each man shook hands with his opponent in the Howard line-up, which showed true college spirit to begin with," the *Age* said.[29] The first half of the "nip and tuck" game ended with Howard ahead, 13–12. It was a clash of two differing styles of offense. "Howard's players worked the ball up to their basket and shot close range, while the Alumni team made quite a few long spectacular shots which brought the enthusiastic audience to its feet." This was similar to what Cum and his Monticello squad had been doing back in Pittsburgh. During the second half, "it was plain to see that the Columbia 'Grads' knew basketball, and so did Howard." And here is where the official, "one of the most cool and gentlemanly referees in this business," made a difference. "There were no scraps, no back talk and no arguments."

There was an exemplary social culture prevailing in New York City basketball at the time, and this is what fans wanted to see, regardless of the outcome. Columbia won 25 to 19, and "immediately after the game was called the Columbia boys got off in a corner and gave their old college cry—Rah! Rah! Rah C-o-l-u-m-b-i-a! Howard! Howard! Howard! While Howard came

back with its own cry," said the *Age*, and then "Capt. Mark Hurley, of Columbia, and Gilmore, of Howard, walked off the mat arm in arm."[30] Afterward,
there was a buzz going around. "The game was one that will be talked about
for some time," the *Age* predicted. Strong had arranged one more New York
City basketball game for Howard University that season, the final move in his
gambit, which everyone was eagerly waiting to see. It would be a matchup
against the St. Christopher Club at the Manhattan Casino in late March in
what was predicted to be "the basketball classic of the season."

Meanwhile, Will had made it his mission to keep the St. C Big Five in the
spotlight, and scheduling Howard, with its tremendous popularity in the New
York City area, was a brilliant move that allowed him to hit full stride with those
efforts. He did this with an irresistible blend of media coverage, advertising,
and promotion. That formula has become commonplace in modern sports,
but it was unprecedented at the time.

First, Will hyped the game in the *New York Age* through weekly editorial columns as well as large-sized ads, explaining that previously, none of
the teams from the city and surroundings had been able to win against the
collegiate squad from the nation's capital. "St. Christopher's famous *Red and
Black Machine* expects to upset all precedents and accomplish something that
no New York club has ever done," he wrote. Will also taunted the famous university. "If St. Christopher defeats Howard at Manhattan Casino on March 20,
she will be the champion of the country," he proclaimed, instantly raising the
stakes and putting pressure on the college team. Will predicted such a flood
of loyal fans for both sides that the venue would look like "a sea of red and
black and blue and white." That many rooters would likely mean a big payday
as well as side bets among the loyalists. He also devised a unique promotion
to drive even more interest, announcing that special "miniature basket-balls
will be given to every box-holder and lady as a souvenir of this great game."[31]
These were actually round gold-toned medallions molded so that the front
face looked like a laced basketball, etched with the names of the two teams,
Howard and St. Christopher, as well as the year. Each was attached to a silk red
and gold ribbon that included a fastener pin so it could be worn like a military
decoration. The stylish gifts were produced by the prestigious sports jeweler
Dieges & Clust, which had provided the medals for the 1904 Olympic Games in
St. Louis. Will's basketball medallions were so well-received that one reporter
stated they were "without a doubt the most novel and appropriate souvenir

that could possibly be given away."[32] Historic in and of themselves, they also became the first known promotional in-arena fan giveaways in basketball. "Come early so as to be sure of securing one," Will wrote, "because owing to the expense of having them made there will a limited number."[33]

Then the St. Christopher manager announced an even bigger incentive, "a handsome silver trophy" for the winner, donated by William Henry Hunt, the first African American career diplomat to serve in the U.S. Department of State, who at the time was the United States Consul at Saint Etienne, France.[34] Hunt, who was a presidential appointee, and his wife, civil rights activist Ida Alexander Gibbs, were considered royalty within African American social circles, counting among their personal friends Booker T. Washington and *Crisis Magazine* founder W. E. B. Du Bois. The prized "Hunt Trophy," as it came to be known, was to be awarded by another highly placed Black political appointee, Charles W. Anderson, Internal Revenue collector for the Third Revenue District of New York, the district that included Wall Street, who was widely considered one of the most powerful African American men in the country.[35]

As a result of Will's multisided efforts, an enormous crowd of over three thousand showed up on Friday evening, March 20, 1914, for the game between Howard's "Blue and White" and the "Red & Black" St. Christophers. The church team's roster included Charles Bradford, Irving Rose, and Ferdinand Accooe while Howard had their power rotation of Gilmore, Sykes, Gray, Nixon, and Oliver. It turned out to be a classic, considered "as interesting and beautiful a demonstration of first-class basketball as any follower of the game would care to see," according to the *Age*. "St. Christopher plunged into the game right at the start and got three baskets in rapid succession before Howard had a chance to get herself together." But the university team dug in and tied the game, then added a basket for a 10–8 lead at halftime. When play resumed, Howard surged ahead, 16–8, with three straight field goals. St. Christopher clawed its way back into the game and with five minutes to play, was down by just two points, 16–14. That was the score with fifteen seconds left on the clock when Howard committed a foul, and after St. Christopher made the free throw, it was 16–15. "Immediately following this, both teams called time out, in order to reinforce their strength by putting in substitutes."[36]

The ball was put in play at the St. Christopher end of the court, about ten feet from the baseline at the free throw circle with a jump ball. At this point, "the real fight for victory reached its zenith." There were two seconds to play with Howard leading by one point as "the great throng stood breathlessly." The referee tossed up the jump ball. "St. Christopher got it" and quickly passed to a wing, who quick-released a hurried shot from around mid-court. As the Spalding No. M sailed through the air, the timekeeper blew his whistle mid-flight. The ball came down through the basket for an apparent St. Christopher score and victory. But no, Howard argued that the field goal was "too late to count," because they "had stopped playing in obedience to the whistle." According to AAU rules, under which the game was played, the basket counted and St. Christopher won, 17 to 16, but Howard argued that the shot hadn't been attempted before the whistle. The fact that "this all happened in the twinkling of an eye" led officials to huddle for a discussion that stretched on for about twenty minutes. Finally, the referees came back onto the court and called the game a tie, which meant the Hunt Trophy was "still without an owner," so the organizations agreed to play a tiebreaker. It was scheduled for April 17 at the Manhattan Casino.[37]

A headline in the *New York Age* on Thursday, April 9, 1914, made it clear that St. Christopher officials had their own important reason for calling the game a tie. TO PROHIBIT GAMBLING AT HOWARD "ST.C" GAME, it read. "The Rev. Hutchins C. Bishop Says There'll Be No Betting On April 17," the byline continued. WANTS GAME KEPT CLEAN. It was said that "church officials had not hesitated in showing deep resentment over several features in connection with the game." Their grievances were confirmed by a letter to the *Age* from Bishop himself, stating his belief in "keeping basketball above sordid influences." After all, the St. Christopher Big Five was connected with the church, which meant it "cannot be a party to gambling, which is a misdemeanor before the law, and anyone who bets on the game makes himself liable to prosecution."

Beyond that, the paper added, "rumors have been rife that the Rev. Hutchens C. Bishop and the vestry of St. Philip's Church had not sanctioned this match." They had been "strongly opposed" to their basketball team appearing at a big game and dance during Lent. Just as significantly, the event had been "promoted by outsiders who were in no way connected with St. Philip's Church, and that neither the church nor the St. Christopher basketball team profited financially by the large audience."[38] This was clearly about Nat Strong.

All of these trespasses could only have happened because Strong had brokered the game directly with Howard and the Manhattan Casino, leaving

St. Christopher entirely out of the financial and cultural equation. Luckily, the game had ended in a tie, giving the church a second chance to make sure such breaches would never happen again. To regain complete control, Bishop got directly involved, requiring that this time the proceeds would be used for the benefit of the St. Philip's parish home. It was a historically significant move as one of a growing number of instances where African American sports organizations leveraged their own financial power for self-determination. Although these games had been lucrative for Strong, his gamble failed, and he was ultimately kicked out of Black basketball, never to return.

Now that those church matters had been ironed out, the tiebreaker would be held April 17, post-Lent, with box seats priced at three dollars and admission at fifty cents apiece. St. Christopher seized the moment and defeated the visiting Howard squad, 29–17, and afterward Will quickly attributed his team's victory to their better knowledge of "inside scientific basketball." The Red and Black Machine, he said, had used "the best system of coaching obtainable," which was provided by Jeff Wetzler, the "best basketball coach in the game."[39] Will's knowledge of basketball was now on full display. This breakdown published in the *Age* revealed he was more than just a self-promoting guest columnist for the newspaper. Will had become an aficionado of the game itself.

On the strength of this victory, the Hunt Trophy was joyously accepted by the St. Christopher Club. That silver loving cup stood for much more than just a win. The fact that men with the national stature of Hunt and Anderson had donated and presented such a prize to the organization meant that its tiny African American church-sponsored amateur athletic club had reached the big time. More than that, it meant Black basketball itself had arrived. The young priest and athletic director Father Daniel, who had overseen this trajectory, must have felt immense pride, because this accomplishment also reflected on his own image. With this win, the St. Christopher Big Five claimed the 1913–4 Colored Basketball World's Championship. And the clergyman's close trusted aide, Will Madden, the squad's sensational manager and promoter, had led the team to capture Black basketball's highest honor. Father Daniel and Will Madden had formed a remarkable sports duo. Will had also won back the hearts of the St. C faithful and silenced any doubts about his loyalty to the organization. From the outside looking in, this appeared to be a triumphant moment. But something else was about to wash all of that goodwill away. For the second time.

CHAPTER 18

SUPREME COURTS

DURING THE SUMMER MONTHS AFTER the St. Christopher Big Five won the 1913–4 national "colored" basketball championship title, World War I began after Austrian archduke Franz Ferdinand was assassinated on June 28, 1914. Back in Harlem, the Black basketball world was about to experience its own sort of war. Word had started going around that St. Philip's Church officials, including its vestry, were still upset about those trespasses against their basketball program. Father Daniel, the St. Christopher Club athletic director, was under pressure. These had happened under his watch. Someone had to take the blame, but it wouldn't be the young priest. Instead, they had begun scrutinizing Will Madden. Maybe he had allowed or perhaps even encouraged those misdeeds in the first place.

That there was a serious problem came to light when, as the 1914–5 season approached, Will publicly announced his resignation as manager of the St. Christopher Big Five. This news came as a total surprise to the city's Black basketball community and led to breathless speculation. At first, Will would say nothing other than to characterize the cause as "individual bossism." *Amsterdam News* sportswriter Romeo Dougherty would later suggest that since Will was "flushed with the success which came from a foundation laid by others, he soon started to feel that his power should be wider spread and the constraint which had to be placed upon him was irksome." Maybe the hotheaded ways of Father Daniel could explain the suddenness of the break. Everything had seemed fine, even triumphant. "Then one fair day came the declaration of war out of a clear sky," Romeo would recount. But that was just the surface. This is what really happened.

Back in May 1914, soon after their national title, with the church vestry still concerned about the St. Christopher basketball situation, and with the club's managerial positions up for renewal, Father Daniel had begun lobbying for Will's removal as basketball manager. Since it was an elected role, all that the influential clergyman had had to do was plant seeds of doubt among the club's voters regarding Will's integrity or his intentions. Despite the fact that the manager had delivered a championship, Father Daniel's efforts prevailed. "At that time the majority of the members of the Club were opposed to Madden's candidacy for re-election and he was defeated and Arthur Johnson was elected Manager of the teams."[1] Will was more than maddened. He believed that the St. Christopher Club's basketball program had a "high reputation" and national prominence "through his efforts and through his efforts only." In fact, as he would later testify in court under oath, Father Daniel had "hampered him in his work as manager of the Red and Black Machine and that on different occasions cancelled games," that Will had set up. Based on that, the outgoing basketball manager was not planning to exit with grace. Instead, he quietly embarked on a quest to get back at his former athletic director.

Will's influence with his players had been strong, so if the church wouldn't cooperate, then he could just take them and leave. A basketball manager raiding his St. Christopher Big Five roster might have felt like déjà vu, but this time was different. Instead of merely cherry-picking the club's talent, Will would literally take the entire organization including its name and nicknames. To do this, he first persuaded nearly every man on the St. C roster to join him. These included Ferdinand Accooe and Charlie Bradford as well as a gifted young player named Walter Cooper, who many considered the most outstanding player in New York City. "There is no center that can out-jump him, and there is no center that can out-shoot him," Will would soon proclaim. "Without question he is in a class by himself."[2] Coach Wetzler decided to stay and would end up running the skeleton of the former church squad, whose roster still included Irving Rose, the hard-nosed White player, as well as Fats and Legs Jenkins, who the coach moved up from the St. Christopher Junior "Tigers" to help fill the void.

Will then acted as if the entire St. Christopher Club itself was splitting off and leaving the confines of St. Philip's Church, so he continued calling his new squad the "St. Christopher Club" and the "Red and Black Machine" like nothing had changed. Will had even stated in the *Amsterdam News* that he would organize a junior team called the "St. Christopher Tigers." To make it official, on August 20, 1914, he filed for incorporation in the State of New York as a nonprofit called "The St. Christopher Club of New York, Incorporated."[3] Their clubrooms and offices would be in Harlem at 119 West 136th Street. Founding directors for the organization were listed as Will Anthony Madden, Ferdinand J. Accooe, and Charles Bradford. Ferdinand was appointed as president. An official Certificate of Incorporation was prepared and duly approved by the state. This is when things got ugly.

Sure that he would be taking the entire organization with him, Will intentionally submitted his incorporation papers just two days before the St. Christopher Club held a large Saturday-afternoon picnic and track meet in New Jersey.[4] He had been assigned as the event's "custodian of prizes," so as soon as his Certificate of Incorporation was formally recorded with the Office of the Secretary of State that day, Will "took possession of and has ever since kept the Howard Trophy, *St. Christopher* banner, *St. Christopher Tiger* banner and certain other goods belonging to the St. Christopher Club" and then refused to give them back. In addition, he declined to turn over to the church any of his basketball-related documents or correspondence, which included important scheduling arrangements Will had made with other teams for the upcoming season as well as a valuable placeholder contract with the Manhattan Casino in the name of the St. Christopher Club for a traditional New Year's Day afternoon game there on January 1, 1915. Most hurtful of all, from the church's viewpoint, was that among the items Will had kept was the prized Hunt Trophy. It was clear he had been plotting this takeover for weeks in advance.

In the aftermath, both the original church team and the new incorporated squad used the same names, and folks were getting understandably confused. To address this, Will used his newspaper connections to frame the narrative. Believing he had a scoop, Romeo Dougherty of the *Amsterdam News* let him explain the situation in his own words with a lengthy editorial column. Incorporating the club was necessary, Will explained, to allow "a wider field of activity in every branch of its interests, such as social, financial and athletic." The club had wanted "power over its own interests" and incorporation naturally meant that the organization would have to "sever" its connection with the church. "Practically every man in the Club, either secretly or openly, has desired this independence," he stated, adding that "the matter has been brewing for nearly three years." Compared to the Smart Set and the Alphas, the St. Christophers were the smallest of the so-called "Big 3" athletic organizations, Will further explained, and that was because the other two had total independence. "We are not allowed the free scope that other clubs have, not because this freedom is wrong, but it is not in keeping with the ethics of the church."[5]

Just like Major Hart before him, he wanted to get after the money in basketball, but church principles got in the way, so those ties had to be cut. "There is no human power that can stop this movement now," Will exclaimed. "Our slogan is *Watch Us Grow.*" He also wanted the public to understand this wasn't his own "personal wild-cat move," but rather a "steady organized movement." Will also insisted there was "absolutely no ill feeling" on their part, so "there is no reason whatsoever why the Church should not, as always, give the Club the full strength of its moral support." The former St. C manager went so far as to say this movement, "without a doubt, is about the biggest movement that has ever taken place in the social and athletic history of New York."[6]

Incredibly, Will persuaded Romeo Dougherty to back his agenda despite the journalist's Danish West Indian kinship with Father Daniel. "Madden's side of the story carried such a strong appeal to this writer we immediately gave him our support," the *Amsterdam News* columnist would recall. "We had admired the spirit of Bill Madden while he guided the destinies of that machine which ran roughshod over all opposition, and when the break came we found it hard to throw him down." This caused Romeo to write up his own article under the headline MADDEN RE-ELECTED, in which he personally interviewed Will about his latest moves and plans. "At a recent meeting of the St. Christopher Club, Inc., Will Anthony Madden was unanimously re-elected basketball manager for the season of 1914–15," the piece began. "The entire basketball world knows and appreciates Mr. Madden's work as manager," Romeo wrote, "and his hosts of friends will be glad to welcome him again as head of the St. Christopher squad."

According to the sportswriter, Will had told him that his "sole ambition" was to lead the "Red and Black Machine" to its second straight championship. And there was something else. He also "stated his intention of forming a national basketball league that would include eight or ten of the biggest teams in the country, the best team in a particular place being the representative team of that City or State." This idea, which would seem logical today, was revolutionary at the time. Lester Walton had suggested that New York City's amateur squads form a local league. But this went far beyond that. It was the first known public mention of a regional or countrywide African American basketball circuit. "As basketball is continually spreading, this league arrangement seems possible," Romeo admitted. "Furthermore," the journalist assured readers, "Mr. Madden is well known in such basketball centres as New Haven, Boston, Philadelphia, Lincoln, Pittsburgh, Syracuse, and Washington." More than simply just narrative control, this was a riveting, irresistible vision. It was no wonder that Romeo admired Will's spirit. "Mr. Madden is certainly living up to his reputation as the *Johnny McGraw* of basketball," the sportswriter observed, referring to the equally diminutive and feisty New York Giants baseball team manager and future Baseball Hall of Fame member. It was through this article and its revelations about Will's ambitions that the leader of the St. Christopher Club, Inc., then thirty-one years old, was bestowed the same nickname as McGraw: "Little Napoleon."

Back at St. Philip's Church, on the other hand, they took Will's unauthorized incorporation of the St. Christopher Club so seriously, believing the move so brazen, that it was the first item on the agenda of their very next vestry meeting, held on the night of September 8, 1914. Bishop had brought the matter to the church's attorney, he explained to the assembled officials, with the intention of having Will's incorporation "declared illegal by the court." Their counsel was George B. Glover, Esq., an experienced middle-aged White lawyer whose office was at 48 Wall Street. The pastor asked for permission to take this action, and upon a motion and a second, he got "the hearty approval of the Vestry" to proceed.[7]

With that, the original St. Christopher Club, as plaintiff, took Will straight to the New York State Supreme Court, filing an injunction on September 22, 1914, that sought a restraining order to stop him from using their organizational names, citing the threat of "irreparable damage." They also filed a wrongful possession lawsuit to reclaim their property, specifically the Hunt Trophy and Will's official correspondence. Finally, the church sought damages of $1,000. The presiding justice, Thomas F. Donnelly, granted their motion and the restraining order was served the next day.

Will immediately appealed, retaining his own downtown counsel, Arthur G. Basch, a recently graduated White attorney whose practice was at 42 Broadway, just a few doors down from the Standard Oil Building where Will worked by day. In response, the court ordered the former Little Africa resident turned messenger turned Black basketball team owner to appear on September 28, 1914, 10:30 A.M. at the County Court House, Borough of Manhattan, New York City, in a special session to show cause, if any, for why his actions should not be restrained and why the plaintiff should not receive proper relief.

Basch followed up by filing an opposition to the original motion on October 3, 1914, for which each incorporator of the St. Christopher Club of New York, Inc. entity had to provide their own depositions. Will's deposition stated that the plaintiff's injunction "was brought simply to hamper and hinder and embarrass" him, not because his actions interfered with their affairs but because Father Daniel "would lose his prestige at the church." One of the players who had left the old team supported this idea, testifying that when he went to meet the angry clergyman to explain his reasons, "he was accosted by the said Daniel, who told him to 'get out and never show his face again.'" Another departing player described "the tyrannical methods of Daniel." Basch also stated his client "cannot understand" why the church "changed their name of St. Christopher Club of St. Philip's Parish to the St. Christopher Club," arguing that in all his dealings he had always known them as "St. Christopher Club of St. Philip's Parish," attaching advertisements to apparently prove it, even though these ads were originally placed by Will himself. Basch contended that the public could "easily" tell the two names apart, and that since "most of the members of the old basket ball team of the plaintiff have joined the new organization," it was actually the St. Christopher Club of St. Philip's Parish that was doing all the interfering.

Arguing with Will had to have been infuriating. But he didn't seem to care, sending out invitations for the "opening gathering" of the St. Christopher Club of New York, Inc., to be held on October 9 at the organization's new clubhouse at 119 West 136th Street in Harlem. Meanwhile, the 1914–5 basketball season was approaching fast, so he stayed on the offensive, always aware of the public narrative, and used his position as guest columnist at the *New York Age* to release yet another statement that tried to put the name issue to rest. Will insisted, "we have absolutely no desire to deceive the public or represent ourselves other than what we are," adding that his new entity "is distinctly known as the St. Christopher Club of New York, incorporated, and is an athletic and social organization that we intend to build up until it becomes one of the best known men's clubs in existence."[8]But the court didn't see it that way. Justice Donnelly's opinion delivered on November 3, 1914, read, "I am convinced from the papers submitted, that the actions of Madden and his associates tends to deceive the public and to appropriate the property right of the plaintiff to the use of the name St. Christopher Club." The church's motion was granted, and the St. Christopher Club of New York, Inc. was ordered to stop using its own incorporated name.

Public confusion surrounding the monikers of the two teams lasted until about midway through the 1914–5 season. By then, Will had begun calling his own squad the "Incorporated team" and then simply "The Incorporators." Newspapers and fans went along with that nickname, even though officials of the original St. Christopher Club were still so outraged that they refused to play them. Only the Alpha Big Five agreed, scheduling a New Year's Day game with the Incorporators. This prompted St. Christopher to refuse booking Alpha as well, charging "professionalism" in both programs. A boycott of Will's squad by the city's other amateur teams followed, similar to the one they had staged against the New York All Stars. This meant the Incorporators were only able to schedule three games in New York City that season. But that didn't stop Will. In grand fashion, he set up the team's public debut with a Thanksgiving Day matinee game at the Manhattan Casino against the Independent Pleasure Club of New Jersey. "FIRST BIG GUN of the Basketball Season," read a large ad Will had placed in the *New York Age*. The date selection was smart because there was typically no basketball until after Thanksgiving, the traditional end of the football season, so this became the only game on anyone's schedule. "Every real basket-ball lover should come out and see these boys in action," the advertisement stated. Tip-off was set for 2:30 P.M. and dancing would follow.

With theatrical flair, Will put on a show. "Madden's boys came out in brand new outfits, even to the ball," the *Age* reported. The game itself was close for a short while, until the Incorporated team pulled away for a 37–22 win. "All the boys gave a good account of themselves, Cooper especially doing some great work," the *Age* added.[9] The same day, before the smoke from the "first big gun" had even cleared, Will unveiled an ad promoting the "SECOND BIG GUN of the BASKETBALL SEASON," a game versus Howard University on December 15, and followed that with another open letter, this time in appreciation of his team's loyal fans. "On behalf of the St. Christopher Club of New York, Incorporated, I wish to thank all of our friends, as well as my personal friends, and the general public, for the hearty support they gave us at our initial affair on Thanksgiving Day," he stated. "And that in spite of a certain malicious undercurrent of opposition working against us we came out successful from every standpoint."[10] Will had applied that ages old circus maxim, popularized by Phineas Taylor "P.T." Barnum in 1879: "The show must go on."[11]

For the upcoming game between the Incorporators and Howard University on December 15, word from the college was that their squad would be "one of the best and strongest teams ever seen" in New York City. But according to the *Age*, Will was "losing no sleep over the strength of the 'Blue and White' team as he has on the 'Red and Black Machine' players who ought to be able to hold their own with any team in the East." Putting showmanship into action, the Incorporators boss invited the popular tax collector Charles W. Anderson to appear at the game to deliver a speech and give away a solid gold watch, "which the club will present to some lady present." Will also brought in James Reese Europe's Lady Society Orchestra to "furnish music for the evening."[12] But when the scheduled tip-off time arrived, Howard allegedly refused to play until they received and counted the $250 dollars (more than $6,500 today) that they were due. Apparently, the *Age* explained, the visiting team's management had had some trouble getting paid their expense money in the past and were adamant they "would not undergo the same ordeal." Finally, the game got underway in front of about a thousand fans. But despite all that fussing, "Will Madden's incorporated team played rings around the boasted Howard aggregation of basketball tossers," the *Age* stated, winning 33–13. People were surprised by the result, but Howard's manager and coach admitted that "the incorporated boys simply outplayed their team."[13]

"WHO IS WHO? In New York IN BASKET BALL 'Big 5' or 'Incorporators,'" read Will's next advertisement for his team's January 1, 1915, date with the Alpha Big Five. "Everybody knows what to expect when these teams meet," said the ad, "so come early and see these teams fight it out."[14] Just scheduling this game in the first place represented a major victory for Will. He had been left with neither a New Year's Day opponent nor a venue after the New York State Supreme Court made him give the Manhattan Casino game agreement back to Father Daniel. The incorporated squad's manager had needed to secure a prominent adversary, successfully reaching an agreement with the Alpha Big Five just two weeks earlier.

Will still needed a place to play, ideally on the same date, and now the afternoon slot at Eddie Waldron's place was taken. So, re-arranging the script, he opted for a night game, switching to a 9 P.M. start. But getting fans to attend so late in the evening could present a challenge, the *New York Age* pointed out, since this would be the last scheduled game of five total African American basketball contests in the city on January 1, "each one bidding for the prestige and support of the public." That many games, the newspaper suggested, was "too much basketball for one day and night, so the whole matter narrows down to this one point and that is, that the organization staging the best attraction will likely have the biggest crowd." People yearned to see quality matchups. "The consensus of opinion is that the game staged by the Incorporators with the Big 5 on New Year's night will be the best game of all," said the *Age*. "Each team has been undefeated this season and is going at top speed," the newspaper continued. Then too, Will was behind it, and to a showman, everything was a show. "There will be plenty of dancing until late in the morning," the *Age* reminded readers, with live popular music performed by Professor Robert F. Douge and his orchestra.[15] It was almost as if he had written the column himself. One had to give Will a lot of credit for his grit and unstoppable spirit. He had his finger on the pulse of the game, and knew what basketball fans were after, almost before they did. Once again, he had turned multiple challenges into a blessing. And with all this behind-the-scenes action, the real drama was about to unfold on the basketball court.

To start the much awaited "who's who" game, the Incorporators jumped to a 7–1 lead. But they allowed an Alpha run that tied the game at halftime, 8–8. "The teams were too evenly matched," Lucien H. White of the *Age* exclaimed. Coming out of halftime, "the Alphas for a few minutes played the Incorporators off their feet," and took a commanding five-point lead with two minutes remaining. For the fans of both teams, said Lucien, "it was all over but the shouting." Then something clicked. "Madden called his boys to the western end of the court and talked to them for a few seconds," wrote the *Age* journalist. "After that the game took on a new phase, the Incorporators putting up the most desperate fight ever witnessed on the court of Manhattan Casino, trying to overcome the Alpha's lead." It was, he said, "one of the gamest and best exhibitions of basketball seen in this town for many a season." Finally, with only seconds left to play, the Incorporators had climbed to within one point, down 20–19. Then, in a critical mistake, the Alphas fouled Incorporators left forward Harry Williams. As he walked to the free throw line, Lucien shared, Harry called his teammate, right forward Edgar "Perky" Perkinson, to his side, telling him that he planned to miss the free throw on purpose. Perky was to be in position, "ready to jump for the ball before it struck the floor and try for a field goal." As planned, Harry shot the ball and "it struck the rim of the basket, bounded into the air, and as it fell 'Perky' jumped for it, caught it and caged the goal." Perfect execution. "As the ball passed through the basket the whistle blew for the ending of the game." A one-point win for the Incorporators, 21–20. With that, Perky and Harry were "elevated to the shoulders of their club and teammates and carried around the hall in a triumphal procession." But not before pausing their "jollification" to cheer for the Alpha Big Five, "their defeated but not disgraced opponents." In a post-game interview, Will was just as gracious. "Alpha has a great team and played my team to a standstill," he explained, "but my boys scored baskets when the points were sorely needed."[16] This was what folks had wanted. It was a magnificent result for the Incorporators boss. A BASKETBALL CLASSIC, read the *New York Age* headline afterward, adjacent to a large portrait photograph of Will, the first known appearance of his likeness in print. Posing with a relaxed, slightly stern, slightly amused expression and close-cropped hair, he wore a dark tailored suit, white shirt, high collar, dark cravat with center pin, fitted waistcoat, and a white carnation on his left lapel, a final sartorial touch that would become his signature look. Will's portrait, the only image on the broadsheet newspaper's entire dramatics and athletics page, presented him as a dashing, heroic, culturally important figure. And he was.[17]

The New York Incorporators would go on to capture the 1914–5 Colored Basketball World's Championship with an undefeated season while beating Black and White teams alike. Though he had lost the brutal court battle, Little Napoleon had won the war.

Will Madden's controversial getaway from the St. Christopher Club of St. Philip's Church—with their best basketball talent, some gear, and some contracts—was one thing. But taking the Hunt Trophy with him on his way out while insisting he and his players earned it had been unforgiveable to Father Daniel. For the proud clergyman and athletic director, this hard-fought prize was more than just a trophy. It defined his program. It defined his own identity. And now that the 1914–5 season was over, Romeo Dougherty of the *Amsterdam News* couldn't help but agree. The journalist seemed to grow increasingly more outraged with Will's trespass against his fellow Danish West Indian. Romeo was also such a fan of sportsmanship, camaraderie, and honor. "To the man without real red blood coursing through his veins and who had failed to thrill at the exploits of the red and black machine this perhaps does not mean so much," the sportswriter would later explain, about the Hunt Trophy heist, "but to the youngsters of those years not so very long ago it meant a great deal."

Father Daniel had no choice but to press onward. And he did have some bright spots. Before that season had even begun, star center Charles Bradford, one of the players who deserted with Will and signed those incorporation papers to become an Incorporators officer, changed his mind and decided to remain with the original St. Christopher Club after all. That meant Coach Wetzler had Bradford, Irving Rose, and young Fats Jenkins secured, giving the team at least a baseline of solid talent. On the other hand, without their other stars who had left, the St. C Big Five couldn't compete with New York City's top-tier clubs. And without Will, they didn't get the newspaper coverage they previously had. That meant booking games with emerging squads like the Spartan Braves, which was still run by Bob Douglas, now 32 years old and still their player-coach at the guard spot. Will had written about the Braves in December 1914, suggesting they were "fast but lacked the teamwork which would make them winners." Little did he or anyone else realize that this was the beginning of Bob's remarkable Hall of Fame basketball career.[18]

Meanwhile, to the credit of St. Philip's Church and St. Christopher Club officials, the old Red and Black Machine would soon be back in championship form. But that evolution had to pause when, in May 1915, just weeks after the season finale, a German submarine sank the British merchant and passenger liner *Lusitania*, killing 1,198 passengers and crew. This compelled the United States to prepare for war in Europe. By the time the 1915–6 basketball season began, all athletic activities had been cut back while armories and other large venues previously used for those events were outfitted in support of World War I.

CHAPTER 19

LOENDI

WHEN THE U.S. POSTMASTER GENERAL reorganized the Railway Mail Service and its more than 18,000 mail clerks in early 1912 by orders from an act of Congress, they announced the opening of a new division in Pittsburgh, which had previously been ignored. This gave the city its own railway mail headquarters, allowing quicker and better local service as well as "proper recognition from the postal authorities."[1] It also provided 250 new jobs, one of which was filled by twenty-two-year-old Cumberland Posey, Jr., fresh off of his basketball team's thrilling win over Howard University. Requiring civil service examinations, Cum's position was coveted because the pay was better than for post office clerks and city letter carriers, and this was important for him because by then, his romantic interest in Ethel Truman, secretary of the original Monticello Girls, had become mutual and more serious. They were spotted together frequently at social events all year long, most famously at the fifteenth anniversary of the Loendi Social & Literary Club in November 1912, where she appeared in pink silk with crystal trimmings.[2]

By then the 1912–3 basketball season was underway and African American fans back in New York City eagerly anticipated the arrival from Pittsburgh of Cumberland Posey, Jr., and the Colored Basketball World's Champions, the Monticello Athletic Association, a team they had so far only heard or read about. Key players Cum, his brother See, Big Jim Dorsey, Sell Hall, and Charley Rickmond were all still in the lineup and had gotten even better. "Dorsey has developed into a first class shooter and will soon be on a par with Capt. Posey," the *Pittsburgh Press* reported.[3] Two new players, Israel Lee and Austin Norris, were "showing a marked improvement in their manipulation of the ball," the paper added. But regardless of what was on paper, the Monticellos were unproven in Gotham, so Cum had scheduled a series of games in late December against two of the city's strongest teams, the Alpha Big Five and the Smart Set Athletic Club. The first was set for Christmas Eve at the Manhattan Casino against the Alphas. A few nights later, they would face the Smart Set in Brooklyn at Saengerbund Hall, a spacious facility with a large gallery at the corner of Smith and Schermerhorn Streets in what is Boerum Hill today. The "mirror-like waxed floor" at Saenngerbund was a basketball player's dream, compared to the flooring with uneven planks, splinters, or nails that they often encountered. Regardless of venues, as the *New York Age* put it, both New York area teams vowed to "send the Monticello A.C. back to the Smoky City in mourning."[4]

But the Homestead hero had other plans. For him, victories in these games were crucial for financial success. By having booked two of the city's largest basketball facilities, Cum was already guaranteed a healthy cut of gate receipts. To survive for the long run though, a traveling squad had to be invited back. Return trips often meant more spectators wanting to see the rematch, and leverage for the visiting team to negotiate better terms. The potential advantages of winning were too important to squander. That's why, despite the lights and distractions of the big city and the local teams' bravado, the Monticello Five went about their business. Using "a fast, consistent game," they beat the Alphas decisively, 40–24, and then trampled the Smart Set by a score of 27–14. This caused the *Age* to paraphrase Julius Caesar by exclaiming that the Pittsburghers "came, played, and conquered."[5] The win was notable because the Smart Set had strengthened their lineup with Ferdinand Accooe, the brilliant guard formerly with the New York All Stars, and with Leon Monde, the lanky young rising star who previously played with the Smart Set's junior team. Cum and the Monticellos would return jubilantly to Pittsburgh, but not before being entertained by the young ladies of the Younger Set.

Meanwhile in Washington, Howard University was also on the hunt for the Black national title. They still had the fabulous combo of Gilmore, Sykes, Gray, Nixon, and Oliver on the roster. Their plan included scheduling Monticello for at least one game so they could have a head-to-head outcome against the reigning champions and see who was who. Cum agreed to play them in the District on January 17, 1913, and based on that, Howard's assistant manager of basketball, aspiring journalist Clarence W. Richardson, sent out contracts and began advertising the game, as he put it, "on a large scale." But it was only when the Monticellos got the agreement in hand that they learned

Howard was proposing its same old home venue, True Reformers Hall on U
Street NW. According to Richardson, the contract was returned unsigned with
a note stating that "the court in the True Reformer's Hall was unsatisfactory."
Frustrated, Howard's guy went public with an accusatory complaint letter to
the sporting editor of the *New York Age*.[6] "The Monticello basketball team of
Pittsburgh, since its sham victory over Howard University last year at Pittsburgh, has been pretending that it is anxious to meet Howard in Washington," wrote Richardson. "With regard to the True Reformer's Hall, it is by no
means an ideal court, but it is the best we can procure," the Howard assistant
manager added. "Furthermore, it is better than the court on which Howard
played Pittsburgh in that city last year." There was something else going on,
though. For whatever reason, Howard was still holding a grudge about last
year's game. They believed that the referee "deliberately handed the victory
to Pittsburgh," Richardson charged. "Pittsburgh realizes that it 'lucked' out
a victory over Howard last year which it did not earn and deserve." He wrote
this, even though the game was a decisive win, 24–19 for the Monticellos, and
it didn't come down to a final shot or just one call. "Rather than meet Howard
again it chooses to sneak out of the contest," Richardson went on. "In other
words, it has cold feet." Howard had been forced to play lower-character non-
collegiate squads such as Monticello, he then explained, because there weren't
enough Black schools in the area.

Among men of honor, these were very serious claims.

Richardson was wise, though, to concede some room for negotiation. "If
Pittsburgh really hasn't the yellow streak which she seems to possess, and if
there are any methods under the sun by which we can obtain some binding
agreement, we will meet her anywhere." He was open to counterproposals.

But this back and forth tone was too petty for Cum, so he had Monticello's
assistant manager, nineteen-year-old J. Austin Norris, reply on behalf of the
team.[7] "Since Howard has torn the veil of privacy from our negotiations by a
letter that was the consummation of falsehood and unsportsmanship, in order
to preserve our own dignity and good name before the public eye, and to show
the masquerader in his true light, it is necessary to give the uncolored facts,"
Norris began. "Mr. Richardson dedicated part of his letter to the belittlement
of Monticello's victory over Howard," he continued, but "these statements
are so ridiculously untrue that we who know are touched to laughter rather
than anger." He went on to repeat the complaints about True Reformers, and

confirmed that the Monticellos were "as desirous as Howard seems to be to play her a game on neutral ground." That's how they settled on the Manhattan Casino as the site of their rematch. Although everyone knew that more money could be made playing in New York City than in Washington, neither Richardson nor Howard University yet recognized that the days of basketball games at True Reformers Hall were over.

Before the Monticellos left for New York to meet Howard's squad, Cum scheduled a game in Pittsburgh against the New York area champions, the Alpha Big Five. The game was played at the South Side Market Hall, an aging facility with a large open floor on South Twelfth Street on Pittsburgh's South Side, built in the 1870s for the wholesale produce, meat, and poultry trade. The court was surrounded by netting that "kept fans of both teams from encroaching on the players, when things became exciting," the *Pittsburgh Press* reported. Though it was an old venue, the event "drew a large and brilliant assemblage of men and women of the race," according to the newspaper. They had pennants, noisemakers, and even a brass band "to help disturb the atmosphere." Smoky City fans knew how to represent, and they had reason to cheer, because the odds heavily favored Monticello. But the Alphas had come to the city "with blood in their eyes" and were ready to stage an upset. The large audience, the *New York Age* reported, "expected to see the unbeaten team dispose of the New Yorkers handily, but lo! they were doomed to bitter disappointment."[8] Trailing the game early, the Alphas came from behind to beat Monticello, 24–19, avenging their early-season loss. Cum scored thirteen of his team's total points, but it wasn't enough. "The teams decided to play National rules (dribble and shoot) the first half and A.A.U. rules the second half," the *Age* continued, but eventually, "they were outplayed at their own game." Afterward, in keeping with tradition, Cum and his teammates hosted a reception in honor of the Alpha Physical Culture Club. They reportedly "outdid themselves" as hosts and "set a mark for hospitality and generosity that will be hard to equal." The Monticellos and their local network of friends were so complimentary of the New York squad, according to the *Age*, that "among the many to congratulate them was Hans Wagner of baseball fame and a basketball player of many years' experience."[9]

Next it was time for the Monticellos to disprove Howard's "cold feet" accusation. But in New York City a few weeks later, their energy was flat, and they promptly lost the much discussed and highly anticipated game, 33–17.

It was a disappointing showing, and the *Age* confirmed that Monticello "did not put up their usual snappy game."[10] Their teamwork had suffered, relying too heavily on Cum, who, the newspaper continued, was "the strongest individual colored basketball player in the game to-day." Not to be outdone in terms of hospitality and good sportsmanship, the Alpha Physical Culture Club hosted a large reception for Monticello at Cosmopolitan Hall on Fifth Avenue at West 132nd Street in Harlem before sending them off on their journey back to Pittsburgh.

As the debate over who could claim the 1912–3 Colored Basketball World's Championship heated up, it became clear that both Howard and Alpha deserved the title. And since they did not compete against one another that season, most observers concluded they had finished in a dead heat. In that sense, Howard University regained the crown they had lost to Cum and the Monticellos the prior season, while Conrad Norman and his Alpha Physical Culture Club attained their first Black national champion honors.

The season was over and Cum was back in Pittsburgh, but with his new job and his dating life, Cum was too busy for school, so he left Pitt in the spring of 1913 after two years there. By then, he and Ethel had become so close that they decided to wed, getting their marriage license at the Allegheny County Office Building on June 18, 1913. They married the following week, and it wasn't long before the newlyweds were expecting their first child. "He loved his wife, because she was a fine woman, understood him, and did such an excellent job in rearing his four daughters," wrote the longtime *Pittsburgh Courier* sportswriter John Clark, who was one of the couple's best friends. The young Poseys would name their girls Ethel, Mary, Anna, and Beatrice.[11]

With the added financial responsibility of a family as a catalyst, Cum saw that he and his older brother Seward could apply their sports business know-how from baseball toward the money-making opportunities they recognized in basketball. As the sons of a renowned local entrepreneur, this was a natural step, and their plan was smart. During the summer of 1913, while Cum was still a newlywed, the brothers split the Monticello Athletic Association into two separate teams. The idea was that the first squad would continue under the Monticello AA banner so that it could comply with the Amateur Athletic Union. "Monticello's application for admission to the AAU has been accepted," the *Pittsburgh Press* would report the following January, "and it is now the only Afro-American club in the middle division so advantageously situated."[12]

This was a great move on their part "for protection and cleanliness in athletic sport," the newspaper suggested. The second team would be set up openly from the jump as a play-for-pay venture, using the best players from the original Monticello roster as needed while adding new top talent attracted by the money they could make. Importantly, Cum and See got their for-profit offshoot sponsored by the prestigious Loendi Club, whose honorable reputation and respected name were known far and wide, and where it couldn't have hurt that their father held an elected position as the organization's president. The brothers also got approval to use the Loendi name, and the team subsequently becoming known as the Loendi Big Five.

Importantly, their efforts were also fully supported by the *Pittsburgh Courier*, where the elder Posey was a cofounder. See would look after back-office operations like bookings, travel, and finances while his brother would take care of recruiting players. Cum's penchant for obtaining top talent was legendary. It was said he could "lure a melting snowman into Hell."[13] He also secured a large hall called Union Labor Temple, which had a five-thousand-person capacity, for usage as the team's home court. It was perfectly located at the corner of Webster and Washington Avenues in the Lower Hill District, just a few blocks from the Loendi clubhouse on Fulton. The Labor Temple would remain at the center of the city's Black basketball world until the mid-1920s, when it began to fall into disrepair. For now, though, with the promotional strength of the Loendi brand, newspaper reinforcement, the Posey name, an immense home venue, and the attention of top players, this effort was sure to be a success. In effect, the two brothers were doing exactly what Will Madden had wished St. Philip's Church could have done with the St. Christopher Club—to remove amateur restrictions on his players, opponents, compensation, and related matters, rather than split with the church. Except that Cum and See hadn't taken another organization's name and prized trophies without permission, nor ended up in litigation.

That season, the Loendi Big Five aimed to prove themselves by scheduling a visit to Washington, D.C., for a game against Howard University on January 9, 1914, a Friday night. Howard was considered the Black national champion, so the Loendis were reportedly "practicing vigorously in an effort to get into the very best possible shape." And scheduling them in the first place showed that the District of Columbia collegians "esteem the Pittsburgh boys as worthy foemen."[14] There was mutual respect, and this time Cum agreed to play at True Reformer's Hall without an argument because he knew that, regardless of the outcome, a rematch was already scheduled in the Smoky City for February 6. "This will give a great stimulus to local colored basketball," the *Pittsburgh Press* projected. Cum and his team left for Washington "in splendid condition" and, with little effort, defeated Howard, 27–14.[15]

This set the stage for the college squad's February "return game" in Pittsburgh, for which they were "banqueted" at the Loendi Club rooms the evening before, shortly after arriving in the city. This was just like that time Howard first came to the city in 1912. It would be "a basketball game worth going miles to see," predicted the *Press*. Labor Temple was not always available, so the contest itself was played at St. Peter's Lyceum, a gymnasium facility on the North Side. "So numerous was the attendance that the space for play was very limited," the *Press* reported, "and the players were often badly handicapped by the ball going into the crowd which lined up on every hand." One can imagine Pittsburgh's finest African American citizens in their best attire, spilling onto the court from all sides. In fact, the game had its own official "patronesses," which included Capt. Posey's stately wife, Anna. This is why many basketball venues were still using wire or mesh caging to enclose the game action on the court.

"It was a lively bit of ball-tossing right from the start," the newspaper stated about the close game. "The referee had his hands full every minute of the time, and some of his rulings were provocative of a good deal of feeling among both players and spectators."[16] Even the halftime was competitive, as "there was an attempted guitar and mandolin contest," wrote the *Press*. "No decision was reached by the judges as to the victor." Ultimately, the Loendi Big Five won the basketball game, 15–14.

Though the Monticellos and the Loendis were supposed to be two distinct teams, in reality they swapped and borrowed from each other's rosters. But another reason why the teams were said to have split up was some friction reported between Cum and teammate Sell Hall, the son of Loendi Social & Literary Club cofounder George Hall. The two younger men were similar figures both on and off the court. They not only played together in basketball, football, and baseball, but were also close acquaintances who grew up in similar social circles and toughed it out on the same city sandlots. Cum was considered the more athletically gifted of the pair, while Sell was known as a master of hype who had a penchant for spontaneous street corner philosophy.

"Sell Hall was a 'Plato of the Pavement,'" recalled longtime Pittsburgh cultural historian Frank Bolden, who knew him personally. Playing to their strengths, Cum managed the basketball teams while Sell doubled as the publicist. The friction arose because "both of them were prima donnas," according to Bolden. Always colorful, Sell "loved to argue with anybody, about anything, anywhere, and at any time." He was always trying to upstage Cum, but the Homestead native edged out Sell in almost every category. On the basketball court, Bolden reported, Sell would sometimes resort to hogging the ball, showboating, or taking ill-advised shots in attempts to steal attention away from the team's main star. The only way Sell would outshine Cum, Bolden mused, was that Sell had "more mouth," which was saying a lot.[17]

Whatever conflict existed between the two individuals or clubs was resolved in the last week of September before the 1914–5 season got underway, when the Monticellos and the Loendis held "a get-together meeting" at Big Jim Dorsey's residence on Wylie Avenue in the Hill District. This was a year after they had split up. By consensus vote, "it was arranged to consolidate the clubs for the good of both," the *Pittsburgh Press* reported. "This will give to this city a team able to compete with any first-class team in the country."[18] Their collective squad now counted Big Jim Dorsey, Sell Hall, Walter Clark, Seward Posey, and Cumberland Posey from the original Monticello team, as well as talented local newcomers who were "the pick of the colored basketball players around Western Pennsylvania." These additional all-stars included Archibald "Arch" McClanahan and Oliver "Ollie" Lucas, who were "ranked among the best in basketball circles, as well as Frank Bell and Charlie Catlin who were "second to none on the team."[19] Big Jim was elected captain and Cum was voted in as manager of the new collective, which publicly debuted its renewed bond by staging a dance and reception on the following Friday evening, October 2, at Arcade Hall on Center Avenue in the East End, known today as Shadyside.

At first, the combined crew called themselves the Loendi Athletic Club in an attempt to appear officially amateur. This was because, ultimately, they were trying their best to finesse the Amateur Athletic Union to avoid getting penalized by them. But the AAU was close to figuring out what was going on, sensing that officially registered amateurs from the Monticellos had been making appearances with the pay-for-play Loendis, who in turn were showing up as ringers in Monticello lineups. These manipulations backfired in late December 1914, when the AAU announced that it had canceled the registration cards of Ram Hall, Frank Bell, and Walter Clark as well as those of Seward and Cum Posey.

That effectively turned the page on the original Monticello Athletic Association, ending the chapter on their heroic basketball contributions to Pittsburgh and to Black basketball. At this point, since there was no longer any need for an amateur athletic club ruse, all that remained was the Loendi Big Five, and under that identity, a whole new chapter began for the squad. They would dominate local basketball for the next two years, playing exclusively against all-White teams in Western Pennsylvania, West Virginia, Indiana, and Ohio. With the revenue from home games, Cum would gain financial leeway to extensively recruit out-of-town talent, becoming the first African American basketball club manager to do so. In the years to come, the Loendi Big Five would grow into a powerful team and become nearly invincible. But in the fall of 1915, Cum would step away from the squad to enroll in college yet again, this time at Duquesne College of the Holy Ghost.

Duquesne College of the Holy Ghost, known as Duquesne University today, is still located on a forty-three-acre campus atop a 115-foot bluff overlooking downtown Pittsburgh, the Monongahela River, and the city's South Side. Mysteriously, when Cum registered there, he used the alias, "Charles Cumbert."[20] Starting with that 1915–6 season, his first at Duquesne, "Cumbert" would play three consecutive years as a forward on the school's varsity basketball team, the Dukes. He would lead the squad in scoring during each of those seasons. Cum would also play varsity baseball there for three straight seasons during that period. In his freshman year of basketball, Duquesne posted a respectable 7-2 record playing against opponents such as Beaver Falls College, Lafayette College, and Buffalo University. "Cumbert and Morrissey were dead-sure shots," the *Duquesne Monthly* wrote.[21] CUMBERT SCORES OFTEN, read a headline in the *Pittsburgh Daily Post* following a 34–15 win over Waynesburg College in which Posey scored eighteen points. "Cumbert of the Dukes was the 'shooting star' with six baskets to his credit," the paper noted.[22]

It was once believed that Cum used an assumed name at Duquesne in order to pass for White. Yet, there was no evidence that Duquesne had a formal or even informal policy of racial exclusion at the time, nor that a racist aura existed there. In the early 1900s, the Holy Ghost Fathers, the college's original founders, worked closely with the local Black community in an effort to reverse declining interest in the Catholic Church. This effort continued through the 1940s, when a local basketball star named Charles Henry "Chuck" Cooper would attend Duquesne and then become the first African American player drafted into the National Basketball Association. The more probable reason for the disguise was that by 1915, when he enrolled at Duquesne, Cum's name and reputation were so well known throughout western Pennsylvania athletic circles that he had to fall back. After all, Cum had been written about in newspapers since high school, and Pittsburgh was a sports town. He was a highly regarded athlete and team manager. An alias would have helped Duquesne avoid suspicion among administrators from rival colleges on the Dukes' schedule as well as from local bureaucrats from the always-vigilant Amateur Athletic Union. This would have also allowed him to play worry-free semi-professional basketball with the Loendi Big Five using his real name. More than likely, Duquesne's own administrators, coaches, teammates, fans, and even local newspapers knew that this was an arrangement set up with a nudge and a wink. The maneuver may have been detected by careful observers of a *Pittsburgh Daily Post* newspaper article late in the 1915–6 season, which included a Dukes basketball team photograph with Cum listed in the caption as "Cumberland W. Cumbert."[23]

Neither the Homestead hero nor the team nor the school ever got in any kind of trouble. Meanwhile, despite his prolific athletic career at Duquesne, no official record has ever been found confirming that a Charles Cumbert, a Cumberland Cumbert, or a Cumberland Posey, Jr., ever enrolled in any classes there or ever received a degree from the university. Yet, he would ultimately be enshrined in the Duquesne University Sports Hall of Fame in 1988, under his real name.

Meanwhile, with or without a degree, Cum would get something invaluable from his time on "The Bluff." Duquesne's campus housed an affiliated high school called Duquesne Preparatory High School, with its own interscholastic sports programs, including a football team. While in his last year at the university, Cum would befriend a newly enrolled student-athlete at Duquesne Prep who had made its varsity football squad as a freshman running back. This kid was being called "one of the greatest halfbacks in High School circles" by *Duquesne Monthly*. "His wriggling, squirming, and serpentine runs netted at least one-half of the Dukes touchdowns."[24] Destined to leave a mark on the game, this new player was Arthur Joseph "Art" Rooney.

Following their overlapping experience on campus, Cum and Art would remain lifelong friends, always bound together by sports. After graduating from Duquesne Prep and attending college, Art would spend several years playing and promoting sandlot semi-pro football in and around Pittsburgh as one of the city's best and most rugged players. Finally, in 1933, having amassed a small fortune, he paid the National Football League a $2,500 franchise fee entitling him to form a professional football team in the city, which he named the Pittsburgh Pirates. In 1942, Art renamed them the Steelers. By then, Cum would be running his own exceptionally successful Negro Leagues baseball franchise, the Homestead Grays, during the Great Depression and war years, when a Black team having its own home field was a make-or-break financial proposition. That's when their friendship paid dividends for both men. Art's football team played at Forbes Field, an enormous and popular stadium in the city's Oakland section near the University of Pittsburgh. Rooney not only allowed the Grays to play there, but he also offered Cum excellent business terms. In return, Art benefited from the baseball team owner's candid insights, his ear as a sounding board, his savvy with recruiting, his negotiation tactics, and his competitive mindset. Arthur Joseph Art Rooney would be elected to the Pro Football Hall of Fame in 1964, and Duquesne University would rename their football field in his honor in 1993.

In February 1917, toward the end of "Charles Cumbert's" second varsity basketball season at Duquesne, the Dukes played a home game against a local all-Jewish team called the Coffey Club. The Coffeys were organized in 1911 through Kingsley House, a Jewish community settlement center and recreational facility on the corner of Bedford Avenue and Fullerton Street in the Lower Hill District. The center had been around since 1894 to provide social services and fight immorality among the less fortunate citizens of the Hill.[25] The basketball team got its name from John V. Coffey, a local newspaper distribution company owner running for political office who sponsored the squad to promote his campaign. Coffey was already immensely popular as the idol of over 500 newsboys whom he generously employed, which included the players who had made the Coffey Club's roster. The innovative candidate's promotional basketball squad ended up being so successful on the court against various local fives that they lasted beyond the campaign and began booking games outside of Pittsburgh city limits. "This team has won the Amateur Athletic Federation championships without suffering a defeat," the *Pittsburgh Press* wrote in 1913. Soon they secured their own home court, Montefiore Hall on Fifth Avenue, located south of Pitt in an area known as West Oakland today.[26]

By the time the Coffey Club got onto Duquesne University's basketball schedule for the 1916-7 season, they had been defeating teams from Ohio, West Virginia, Illinois, New York, and New Jersey. This would be the Dukes' toughest opponent of the season, so the Duquesne campus was buzzing with excitement and expectation leading up to the game. What they got as their reward was "a splendid exhibition of basketball, before the largest crowd that has seen an athletic contest in the Bluff gymnasium for two or three years, and until the last six minutes of play, the race was neck and neck," the *Pittsburgh Daily Post* reported.[27] Unfortunately, the Dukes lost that game, 45–35, despite a solid effort by Cumbert, with three field goals and eight of eleven free throws for fourteen total points.

But for Cum, there was a silver lining. The enormous number of loyal fans the Coffeys brought with them to the Duquesne court was so impressive that it inspired him to arrange a game of his own, between the Jewish squad and his Loendi Big Five, as soon as their schedules permitted. This would be easy to accomplish, because Cum already knew most of the Coffey Club guys from the playgrounds, sandlots, and alleyways of the Hill District. The names of players like "Lefty" Abrams, "Cutesy" Levine, "Buck" Gefsky, "Gimp" Golomb, "Chick" Meyers, and "Goodie" Rosenshine were well known not only within the city's Jewish community but also throughout western Pennsylvania. And they already knew Cum. He was a man "whose standing as a baseball player, football advocate, and basketball negotiator is away above par wherever he is known," wrote the *Pittsburgh Press* that year.[28] This is why Cumberland Posey, Jr., had needed a pseudonym while playing sports at Duquesne. But the Homestead hero wanted more than just one game with the Coffeys, sensing something bigger. "As Loendi progressed," Cum explained, "the colored opposition became less formidable and attendance fell off to such an extent that only the larger colored colleges and New York social clubs drew crowds large enough to cover expenses."[29] He would solve this problem by creating an epic ongoing Loendi-Coffey archrivalry that ignited players, promoters, communities, and, most importantly, newspaper writers and paying fans to become permanent supporters, producing a continual lucrative source of income.

Cum would set up similar arrangements with another local all-White club called the Second Story Morrys, whose lineup was also all-Jewish. Formed in 1920, this squad was sponsored by a clothing haberdasher named Morry Goldman. His shop, on the second floor of a building in downtown Pittsburgh, was known as "Second Story Morry," which is how the team got that name. One of the shop's mottoes was, "Clothing with a Conscience," and one of the Morrys' stars was Chick Davies, Cum's neighbor from East Thirteenth Avenue, who had become so talented that he dropped out of Homestead High School during freshman year to sign with the team. It was to support his widowed mother and his sisters, while earning up to $20 a game.

Chick would leave the Morrys in 1924 to coach Duquesne University for twenty-four seasons, copping three National Invitational Tournament appearances and one NCAA Final Four berth. While there he famously recruited Chuck Cooper, a local African American basketball talent from Westinghouse High School, who was to lead two of those NIT teams and, in 1950, become the first African American player drafted into the National Basketball Association, by the Boston Celtics.

A date for the first Loendi-Coffey clash was set for Friday night, February 15, 1918, at the Labor Temple. By this point in the season, the powerful Coffey Club had lost only two games. "It will be a battle royal for supremacy and should attract an immense audience," wrote the *Press*.[30]

But first, the Loendi Big Five would travel to New York City for a February 1, 1918, game at the Manhattan Casino with Will Anthony Madden and his self-declared "world's famous" New York Incorporators.

CHAPTER 20

OUTLAWS

IN OCTOBER OF 1915, AFTER several seasons as a contributing columnist, the *New York Age* officially added Will Anthony Madden to its staff as their full-time basketball editor. "Mr. Madden needs no introduction in the world of sports," the weekly paper proudly announced, "as he is well known and has a wide experience."[1] Now, in addition to his daytime messenger duties, Will had become an actual newspaperman. This was a powerful new role and in effect cleared Will's name. With the confidence of one of the nation's leading African American publications backing him, with a vast stage from which to reign, and with a second straight "colored" world's championship title to his credit, the Incorporators leader had solidified his place at the top of the Black basketball world. He was the toast of the town, appearing at galas alongside New York City socialites such as James Reese Europe, J. Rosamond Johnson, and John E. Nail.

Will's first column as basketball editor for the *Age* displayed what seemed to be a newfound level of self-awareness about the importance of his position, by sharing the successes, challenges, and opportunities he saw in the game. "All of basketballdom is anxiously waiting the sound of the referee's whistle that will start going the most popular of winter's sports," wrote Will. "I say most popular because it has been well proven by the great crowds that follow the game all through the long months of action." The social side of basketball was as important as any other factor. "Then again, the fans seem to take the game seriously, this being especially true of New York." Will was genuinely tuned in to the sport. "One of the things I took particular notice of last season," he shared, "was the many new people who came to see the games, some of these folks actually seeing a basketball game for the first time, and I can truthfully say that all of those with whom I came in contact had simply 'gone wild' over the game and are now 'dyed-in-the-wool' fans." Will wasn't just optimistic; he could see where this was leading, possibly more clearly than anyone else ever had. "In years to come I honestly expect to see the big basketball games witnessed by crowds pushing the 5,000 mark," he predicted. "It is a positive possibility and with the right kind of management and the right kind of advertising it can be done."[2]

But in the same vision, Will attempted to dictate what could and could not happen among the squads conducting those games, in messaging aimed at the St. Christopher Club of St. Philip's, leaders of the New York City boycott against his team. "This season all teams in the field for the championship will *have* to meet all other teams in the field who are contenders for the title," he proclaimed. "There will be no standing behind technicality and standing on ceremony and each team will *have* to be ready to meet all comers," the basketball editor continued, before aiming directly at Father Daniel. "No one man, or no one club can or ever will be able to control basketball so anyone laboring under that impression may as well give up the idea." Like many of Will's comments, that one would age extremely well. "The public has a good deal to say about basketball and they know what they want," he added. A championship title had to be earned. "It will not be handed out on a silver platter."[3] Will had even pondered the potential conflict of interest in his journalism. "I wish to mention officially to the public and particularly to all the clubs and organizations that although I am manager of the 'Incorporators' this fact will not interfere in one iota with my fairness and squareness as basketball editor of The Age."[4] Yet, he doubled down anyway, turning the matter into a public feud. "No matter what teams or how many games St. Christopher play and win," Will declared, "unless they face the Incorporators, the Parish House boys will not be one step nearer the championship."[5] The man certainly was not shy about using a typewriter.

Next, Will addressed his team's amateur status, just like Cum Posey had tried to do with his Pittsburgh teams. "The Incorporators have been registered in the A.A.U. and by doing so have eliminated any question arising as to their eligibility to play any other registered team," he wrote.[6] "Since this point has been adjusted, I wonder what excuse will be offered now." Will knew that the city's amateur clubs routinely played against unregistered teams, "but what makes me smile," he explained, "is this haggling over technicalities when it is known that it will affect practically every Negro organization in this

Metropolitan District." The basketball editor was right. Their stance against the Incorporators and similar squads would soon come back to haunt them.

Will was a self-made man with flare, style, energy, inventiveness, and the audacity to question Black basketball's status quo. His fans really appreciated that. The current African American cultural trend was to break from the previous strategy of accommodation, approval, and compliance in favor of African American self-identity. As if to close the old chapter, a week after Will's appointment at the *Age*, the author of Black accommodationism, Booker T. Washington, the man termed as "the ablest Negro in the United States," died on November 14, 1915, reportedly from "arterio sclerosis and overwork."[7]

While his popularity was soaring, Will scheduled the Incorporators for a unique season-opening, home-and-away, day-and-night basketball double-header on Thanksgiving Day 1915, against the Jersey Imperials, an all-Black team from Orange, New Jersey, recognized as the "colored champions" of the state. The first game was played in New York City at the Manhattan Casino, and the second took place at the Orange Armory. In keeping with their manager's showy style and high expectations for success, the Incorporators unveiled new red and black uniforms. "As always they were faultlessly and immaculately clad, their new shirts being a pleasure to the eye."[8] Ever promoting, Will also arranged for "special ladies" to distribute team color buttons at the games. "These novel souvenirs sold like hot cakes," the *Age* explained, "and most everyone bought one and wore it." The incorporated squad won both contests, 46–18 and 34–20, respectively.

Will's advocacy of "race matters" also played an important role in his continued popularity. Like many African American leaders, he was protective and publicly outspoken against any real or imagined encroachment upon his people. A closer look, though, hints that the Incorporators manager was also just looking out for his own team. "All through basketball circles I have been hearing rumors that white boys are going to play on some of the colored teams this season," Will wrote prior to their 1915–6 opening game. "This may only be rumor, but if it is true, I can only wonder what the idea is and await further developments."[9] Yet, it was the Incorporators boss who had brought the "white boy" Irving Rose into the St. Christopher Club of St. Philip's in the first place. Rose was still with the St. C.'s, an important part of the team and "easily the star of the game," Will would write just a few weeks later, after a St. Christopher loss to Hampton at Manhattan Casino. "In fact, Rose played his game as he alone can play it, and was all over the court playing guard as well as forward and bringing many of his accurate shots."[10]

This apparent double standard by the Incorporators manager was not limited to White players. Later that season, the Carlisle Indians, a popular barnstorming basketball squad made up of Native American players from the Carlisle Indian Industrial School, visited New York City to play the St. Christopher Big Five on New Year's Eve, and Will urged the public to attend. "If the Indians can play basketball as well as they play football," he predicted, "or if they can play as well as the Indians on Hampton's basketball team, they will undoubtedly make it interesting for the Parish House boys."[11] But he also let it be known that "the result will have no bearing on the championship," the rationale being, "White teams, Indians, and all other novelties do not and can never figure in a colored championship."[12] St. Christopher promptly defeated the Indians, so that point was rendered moot, but Will's message about the definition of the word "colored" was loud and clear.

And his stature kept growing, because Will was a players' manager, putting them first in all regards. Like in November 1916, when he revealed that the Incorporators had added two new features to their team facility that would improve their overall fitness regimen: a swimming pool and a handball court. "The place now is complete in every particular, as it has every known convenience and accommodation for the perfect training of the boys," he reported, adding, "The showers are a joy forever."[13] One must note that bathing—with a pitcher, basin, and washcloth—was by far the norm, since plumbing technology would not advance enough for showers in most homes and facilities until the 1920s.

All the while, Will was continually taunting St. C.'s management for refusing to face his Incorporators. "St. Christopher could play Alpha, Smart Set, and Salem-Crescent and then play Howard, Lincoln, and Hampton," he argued. "After this they could play Yale, Harvard, and Princeton and win each of all these games yet at the end of this great record they would be no nearer the championship than at the time they started." They had to beat the Incorporators, too. "This big 'Incorporated Machine' is the stumbling block of all teams and in the case of St. Christopher the 'Incorporators' seem to be the big 'boog-a-boo' between St. C. and the championship."[14] Will was relentless in throwing everything at the parish house leaders, including knocks on their courage, or lack of it. "There is no yellow paint on the Incorporated machine," he asserted in his *Age* column, "its colors are red and black and non-fading."[15]

This behavior was surely hostile. Yet, in his own reporting, Will pushed back on those he claimed were out of line. "The basketball columns of the *Age* will not countenance personalities that incline to be antagonistic, unless there is sufficient warrant for same, so our contemporaries are wasting time if they think to draw us into worthless controversies," he remarked, in seemingly targeted commentary. "Co-operation and harmony is [*sic*] the watch-word of these columns and not antagonism and dissension."[16] Will just kept up his tireless assault, going back and forth with call-and-response arguments through the Black press. But people gradually began to notice another side of Will Anthony Madden.

With the 1915–6 season drawing to a close, various championship-lobbying efforts were initiated by African American basketball authorities and sportswriters to advocate for their favorite teams. For the *Baltimore Afro-American* it was Hampton Institute. "Hampton has demonstrated her superiority on the basketball court by decisively defeating every team she has met both at home and on the road," the respected newspaper stated.[17]

Will understood that his knowledge of basketball, his proven winning record as a manager, and his platform as basketball editor for a leading publication now placed him as one of the country's foremost authorities on the game. It was time for him to use that clout, and his response was swift. Though the Incorporators had lost several games that season, Will made an extensive argument in support of his own team. He reasoned that the win-loss record of "big league," or ranked, teams in games played against one another was the only factor worthy of consideration in determining that season's champion. In his estimation, only Alpha, St. Christopher, Howard, Lincoln, Hampton, Monticello, and his Incorporators fit that description. Will explained that both Hampton and the Incorporators were undefeated against such prominent squads and therefore, he argued, both of those teams had a record of "1.000." Any losses suffered against "unranked" African American teams like the Washington, D.C., Hiawatha Cardinals, the Atlantic City Vandals, and the New Jersey Independents, he argued, "could not have any particular bearing on a championship." Therefore, Will concluded, Hampton and his Incorporators were tied for any such consideration. And, since a tie would go to the

previous championship titleholder, following the accepted practice in boxing, he reasoned that the Incorporators had retained the Colored Basketball
World's Championship title.

Going a step further, Will used the *New York Age* to publish his own
"Colored All-American" basketball team for that season and named the *entire*
Incorporators team and its lineup as the 1915–6 All-American squad. An "All
American" team, he said, was any combination of players that formed "the most
perfect working machine," and since the world champs were the best team,
that must therefore be the Incorporators as a whole. One certainly had to give
Will credit for trying, and for the do-or-die support he showed his players.[19]

He also named his 1915–6 All-Star selections, which in Will's mind were
the best *individual* African American players. In this effort, he was more
gracious, rightfully including members of other teams, not only the Incorporators. His picks were, "Clarence Jenkins, forward, St. Christopher; 'Cum' Posey,
forward, Loendi Big Five; Walter S. Cooper, center, Incorporators; Ferdinand
J. Accooe, guard, Incorporators; and George 'Headacheband' Capers, guard,
Alpha Physical Culture Club." Will also gave Irving Rose, his forward on the
Incorporators, "honorable mention" status, describing him as a "hard, strong
player with plenty of grit," but regretting that he couldn't very well name the
"white boy" Rose to his All-American "colored" basketball team.

All these arguments were sounding like wordplay. Any other sportswriter
considering how to rate a given team would put weight on the number of games
they had played against ranked opponents and factor in the relative strength
of its schedule. Hampton had played and won four "important" games. But
the Incorporators had played and won only one such contest. Not only that,
but the squads that Will argued were "unranked" each had multiple victories
over "big league" teams, including wins over the Incorporators. There was a
growing sense that his self-serving interpretation of the results hardly seemed
fair and that Hampton, not the Incorporators, deserved consensus Black
championship honors that season. This discontent was echoed by Edwin
Bancroft Henderson, the preeminent pioneer and scholar of African American
basketball, when he voiced his views on the matter in the June 1916 issue of
Crisis Magazine.[20] "Hampton Institute basket ball team can, without successful contradiction, claim the National Championship," Edwin confirmed. "The
lads of the Virginia school have applied brains to brawn in so telling a fashion
that the city and college teams with whom they played could at no time quell

CLOCKWISE FROM ABOVE:
A group of Monticello Athletic Association rooters, 1910 (Swain Family Archives)

Nearing the end of his pro basketball career, Cumberland Posey, Jr., formed a Homestead Grays hardwood team, circa 1923.

The Monticello Athletic Association basketball team, featuring Cumberland Posey, Jr., front row second from left, Sellers Hall, front row second from right, James "Big Jim" Dorsey, second row left, Seward "See" Posey, second row center, and Evan Baker, standing right, 1912 (Swain Family Archives)

TOP: The New York Renaissance prepare to face the Whiting Five (Whiting, Illinois), with pre-handshakes by the team captains, circa 1939.

ABOVE: The Loendi Big Five basketball team, featuring Cumberland Posey, Jr., standing second from left, William "Pimp" Young, seated center, Ulysses Young, seated far left, and James "Pappy" Ricks, seated far right, 1921

THURSDAY, JAN. 25, AT 8:00 P.M.
PRELIMINARY GAME BEFORE BIG GAME

Philadelphia Giants B.B.C.
COLORED CHAMPIONS
—VS—
Northboro A. C.
Giants Record, Won 400 Games in 5 years
Biggest Attraction in Basket Ball   **Drawing Capacity Crowds**
ADMISSION - 40 Cents

BILLY LEONARD, 246 HUNTINGTON AVENUE, BOSTON

COUNTERCLOCKWISE FROM ABOVE:
A post-fight group poses with reigning world featherweight champion Albert "Chalky" Wright, standing third from left, after his title defense against Lulu Constantino at Madison Square Garden in 1942. William "Pop" Gates is seated at center table across from his wife, standing.

The New York Harlemites, an all-Black barnstorming team, featuring Donahue Goins, standing front and right of the center circle, prepare to face the Calgary Neilsons basketball team in Calgary, Alberta, Canada. (Donahue Goins Family Archives)

Poster showing the Philadelphia Giants Basket Ball Club, featuring Jackie Bethards, standing far left, circa 1929

CLOCKWISE FROM TOP LEFT:
New York Renaissance owner Robert "Bob" Douglas, circa 1940

New York Renaissance players position themselves for a rebound, with John Isaacs at lower left, 1943.

New York Renaissance basketball team, circa 1939 (left to right): William Smith, Charles "Tarzan" Cooper, John Isaacs, William Gates, Clarence Bell, Eyre Saitch, Zack Clayton, and Clarence Jenkins

Zachariah "Zack" Clayton of the New York Renaissance, circa 1939

TOP LEFT: John Isaacs in front of the Renaissance Ballroom in Harlem, 2006

TOP RIGHT: New York Renaissance player Charles "Tarzan" Cooper, circa 1939

ABOVE LEFT: Clarence "Fats" Jenkins in New York Renaissance uniform, circa 1939

ABOVE RIGHT: William "Dolly" King of the Long Island University Blackbirds, 1941

PRESS

NINTH ANNUAL
WORLD'S CHAMPIONSHIP
BASKETBALL TOURNAMENT
HERALD AMERICAN
CHICAGO STADIUM
SAT. APRIL 5 8 P. M.
1 9 4 7

N? 11

PRESS
GATE 6½
WOOD STREET
N? 11

NEW YORK RENS	B.	FT.	P.
1 WM. "Pop" GATES			
2 EDDIE YOUNGER			
3 DOLLY KING			
4 SONNY WOODS			
5 GEORGE CROWE			
6 JIM USRY			
7 TOM SEALY			
8 NATHANIAL CLIFTON			
15 DUKE CUMBERLAND			
ROBERT L. DOUGLAS, Manager			

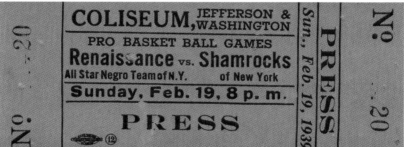

COLISEUM, JEFFERSON & WASHINGTON
PRO BASKET BALL GAMES
Renaissance vs. Shamrocks
All Star Negro Team of N.Y.   of New York
Sunday, Feb. 19, 8 p. m.

PRESS

Sun., Feb. 19, 1939

N? 20

N? 20

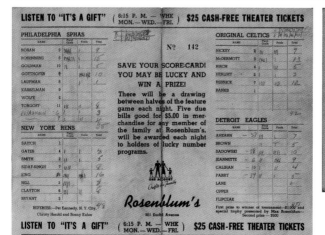

LISTEN TO "IT'S A GIFT"   (6:15 P. M. — WHK)
(MON. — WED. — FRI.) $25 CASH-FREE THEATER TICKETS

PHILADELPHIA SPHAS

NAME				Total
BORAN				
ROSENBERG				
GOLDMAN				
GOTHOFEN				
LAUFMAN				
KASSELMAN				
WOLFE				
TORGOFF				

NEW YORK RENS

NAME				Total
SAITCH				
GATES				
SMITH				
SIDAT-SINGH				
KING				
BELL				
CLAYTON				
BRYANT				

REFEREE—Pat Kennedy, N. Y. City.
Christy Harold and Sonny Kuhar

N? 142

SAVE YOUR SCORE-CARD!
YOU MAY BE LUCKY AND
WIN A PRIZE!

There will be a drawing
between halves of the feature
game each night. Five due
bills good for $5.00 in mer-
chandise for any member of
the family at Rosenblum's,
will be awarded each night
to holders of lucky number
programs.

Rosenblum's
921 Euclid Avenue

ORIGINAL CELTICS

NAME			Total
HICKEY			
McDERMOTT			
BIRCH			
HERLIHY			
RESNICK			
BANKS			

DETROIT EAGLES

NAME			Total
AHEARN			
BROWN			
SADOWSKI			
JEANNETTE			
CALIHAN			
PARRY			
LANE			
OPPER			
FLIPCZAK			

First prize to winner of tournament—$1,000 and
special trophy presented by Max Rosenblum—
Second prize—$500

LISTEN TO "IT'S A GIFT"   (6:15 P. M. — WHK)
(MON. — WED. — FRI.) $25 CASH-FREE THEATER TICKETS

AISLE 4   TIER 3   BOX 14

CHICAGO STADIUM
1800 BLOCK WEST MADISON STR.
6th ANNUAL WORLD'S CHAMPION:
BASKETBALL TOURNAMEN
HERALD-AMERICAN
Established Price $2.27 · Federal Tax
BOX

$2.5

SUN. MAR. 20
7:00 P.M.

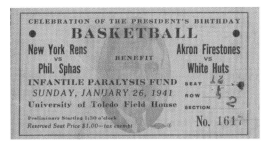

THIS SPREAD, CLOCKWISE FROM OPPOSITE, TOP LEFT:

A press ticket for entrance to a 1939 basketball game between the New York Renaissance and the New York Original Celtics (alias Shamrocks of New York), played at the St. Louis Coliseum in St. Louis, Missouri

A page from the tournament program for the 1948 World's Championship of Professional Basketball shows that season's edition of the New York Renaissance aka "Rens."

A ticket for basketball games benefiting the Infantile Paralysis Fund, 1941

The Basketball Hall of Fame enshrinement plaque for the New York Renaissance team that won eighty-eight straight games during the 1933-4 season, which was inducted collectively in July 1963

A placard promoting a New York Renaissance game, 1946

Ticket fragment from the 1944 World's Championship of Professional Basketball

A scorecard from the inaugural Max Rosenblum Invitational Professional Basketball Tournament in Cleveland, 1941

A rare press ticket to a game between the New York Renaissance and the New York Shamrocks, aka New York Original Celtics, played at the Coliseum in St. Louis, Missouri on February 19, 1939

THIS SPREAD,
CLOCKWISE FROM RIGHT:

A souvenir scorecard for a late-1943 game featuring the reigning world's pro basketball champion Washington Bears shows ads for recent film releases, for Edwin Bancroft Henderson's "Negro in Sports," and an an honorary roster spot for the late Wilmeth Sidat Singh.

Promotional flyer for the Chicago Crusaders, featuring Donahue Goins, far right, Dave DeJernette, far left, and Clarence Jenkins, center, 1940

Postcard of Wendell Phillips High School on the South Side of Chicago, circa 1919

The back side of a postcard from 1938 seeking to schedule game dates with the Milwaukee Colored Panthers basketball team reveals the business model used by many barnstorming programs. (Sandler Archives)

Mayor Michael Bloomberg declared February 10, 2013, "Black Fives Day" for the City of New York with this proclamation.

Newspaper headline from 1937 describes the New York Renaissance victory over the Oshkosh All Stars in the deciding Game 5 of the World Series of Basketball.

Promotional flyer for the New York Harlemites traveling basketball team, 1935 (Donahue Goins Family Archives)

MILWAUKEE PANTHERS NEGRO BASKETBALL TEAM   C-92

TOP: The Savoy Big Five, with manager Dick Hudson, far right, circa 1927

ABOVE: Postcard promoting the Milwaukee Panthers Negro Basketball Team, 1938 (Sandler Archives)

TOP: American Legion Post 272 (Akron, Ohio), City Basketball Champions of 1944-5

ABOVE: The West Virginia State University basketball team, featuring Earl Lloyd, soon to become one of the first three African American players in the NBA, meets with Governor Earl Warren (future chief justice of the US Supreme Court) in 1950.

ABOVE: The Chicago Studebakers of the National Basketball League helped racially integrate that league in 1942 by signing six African American players.

RIGHT: The Franklin (Indiana) High School Tiger Cubs varsity basketball team, 1938–9, featuring George Crowe, who was Indiana's first "Mr. Basketball" that season. Crowe later played for the New York Renaissance and the Dayton Rens.

OPPOSITE, TOP: Nathaniel "Sweetwater" Clifton of the New York Knicks in a Coca-Cola advertisement, circa 1950

OPPOSITE, BOTTOM: Industrial teams such as the Missouri Pacific Colored Booster basketball team of Kansas City, 1947, employed by the Missouri Pacific Railroad, helped popularize the sport with new generations of fans.

OPPOSITE: Jackie Robinson of UCLA leaps to score a field goal in a basketball game against the University of California in 1940. Robinson led the Pacific Coast Conference Southern Division (now Pac-12) in scoring in 1940 and 1941.

TOP: Colorized image of the 1943 Washington Bears, World's Pro Basketball Champions

BOTTOM:: Duquesne University star Charles "Chuck" Cooper, soon to become one of the first three black players in the NBA, with head coach Chick Davies, 1950

Descendants of William "Dolly" King, including then-New York State secretary of education John King, pose by a mural depicting Dolly, inside the concourse of the Barclays Center in Brooklyn, 2013.

the Hampton spirit, nor outwit the athletes on the court." The authority had spoken, and his only mention of the Incorporators was in the same breath as a number of other teams that he felt "were good in their localities."

It was a flat-out rejection of Will's self-promotion and, seemed to cost the Incorporators chief dearly in terms of credibility and respect. The following season would be his last as basketball editor for the *New York Age*. But there was one thing people kept underestimating. Will Anthony Madden was a survivor. He wasn't quite ready to give up his Black basketball throne. Instead, Will just set his sights on distant lands to conquer and charted a course for the following season.

While the drama surrounding Will Anthony Madden and his Incorporators was unfolding in New York City at the close of the 1915–6 season, the Wabash Avenue Colored YMCA Outlaws, with twenty-year-old left forward Virgil Blueitt as captain, were quietly building momentum as a local powerhouse. Without much fanfare outside of Bronzeville, they had won the 1916 Cook County Colored Basketball Championship as well as the 1916 Illinois State Colored Basketball Championship by defeating numerous talented squads, both Black and White, throughout Chicago and the Midwest. These included the Chicago Hebrew Institute, the West Chestnut Street Colored YMCA Branch in Louisville, the Ninth Street Colored Y in Cincinnati, and the Senate Avenue Colored YMCA Branch in Indianapolis.

Continuing the momentum of those triumphs, the Outlaws returned for the 1916–7 season in fine form. Even though the Wabash Avenue Colored Branch included a state-of-the-art gymnasium, few people a year earlier could have expected its heavyweight basketball squad to become so competitive so quickly. But that was then. This season, their own expectations were higher. Virgil, who played professional baseball during the spring and summer as a second baseman and pitcher with the Chicago Union Giants, a local all-Black team, was ready to get back onto the hardwood with his teammates. And, they picked up where they had left off. "Blueitt was enough to spell defeat for the white boys," the *Chicago Defender* reported, after a victory over the powerful Harrison Maroons heavyweight squad. "Virgil was a team by himself and although the Maroons tried hard to keep him covered he shot seventeen baskets."[21] In a win over Eckhart Park, "the white lads were no match for the fast machine-like precision" of the captain and his YMCA crew.[22]

But there was at least one person outside of Chicago who did in fact take notice of the Wabash Outlaws' success. It was Will, and back in New York City he was creating a vision for how to take their basketball program, and his, to historically unprecedented higher heights.

In early 1916, the *Chicago Defender* had assigned a special eastern correspondent and representative named William White to cover New York City and Brooklyn, stating that he was highly regarded for his talent and integrity.[23] About midway through the 1916–7 season, White was covering the city's Black basketball action when he began noticing that some of the local sportswriters were beating up on Will Anthony Madden, who seemed to be having a hard time. He had scheduled a basketball game on March 2, 1917, at Manhattan Casino between his Incorporators and a team from Rhode Island called the Providence Collegians. This squad was a collection of college athletes led by Brown University football star and Chicago sports hero Fritz Pollard, who had organized the unit to tour the East Coast on the strength of his fame. A year earlier as a freshman running back, Fritz had led Brown to the 1916 Rose Bowl, becoming the first African American to play in that New Year's Day game. And as a sophomore, leading up to the this basketball season, he had powered Brown to an 8-1 record, which included wins over both Harvard and Yale in the same season, the first time any college had ever done that.

Having orchestrated this Collegians-Incorporators game at all was a triumph for Will. He had a knack for knowing that in the big picture, it wasn't the team with the best record that won, it was the one with the best headlines. FRED D. POLLARD OF BROWN UNIVERSITY, WILL PLAY BASKET BALL WITH THE PROVIDENCE COLLEGIANS VS. INCORPORATORS, COLORED WORLD CHAMPIONS 1914–15–16, read his bold-type advertisement in issues of the *New York Age*.[24] "The biggest game of them all and the most wonderful attraction ever staged in New York basketball history," Will pronounced in his column. "The conqueror of Yale and Harvard in football says he can conquer the 'Incorporators' in basketball," the basketball editor added. "March 2 will tell." But the March 2 game would never happen because, inexplicably, Fritz canceled his appearance.

Defender correspondent William White explained that it was "because the faculty of Brown set their foot down on the matter, as did the AAU officials here."[25] But actually, that was only after a pressure campaign launched by Will's rivals, Cyril V. Briggs, the *Amsterdam News* sports columnist, and Romeo Dougherty, through contributions to the *New York News*. Together, they "not only knocked the game but branded the scheme as a money making proposition," then contacted Brown University about it. It was sabotage. It was foul. And it was, arguably, the most unmanly deed ever committed within Black basketball ranks. Dougherty, thirty-two years old by then, and Briggs, a twenty-nine-year-old native of Nevis, the island neighbor of St. Kitts, were deeply loyal to fellow Caribbean Islanders and specifically to Father Daniel. Just as importantly, they resented that Will had been refusing to advertise in their newspapers. Briggs, who would become renowned as the founder and publisher of the *Crusader*, a seminal magazine of the Harlem Renaissance period, and as the organizer of the African Blood Brotherhood, a group dedicated to Pan-Africanism, was a hothead, just like Dougherty. He would famously sue and cause the arrest of fellow West Indian civil rights activist Marcus Garvey for criminal libel, charging that Garvey "had defamed his character" by asserting that Briggs was "actually a white man posing as a negro to gain the good will of the negro subscribers of the *Crusader*."[26] Briggs and Dougherty not only disparaged Will's character, but also threatened to have Fritz's amateur status suspended if he played in a game with the for-profit Incorporators. They were haters.

Many people saw the jealousy. Will was good at what he was doing, confident about it, successful, and pursuing his vision through new and innovative means that disrupted the status quo. He was so confident that, back at the start of this 1916–7 basketball season, he took the step of *incorporating* the name "Incorporators" under the laws of the State of New York. This move, he announced, "protects the use of the name and avoids any infringement upon its rights by any other organization."[27]

Will didn't seem to care about all the nonsense. He just rolled with the cards he had and, without missing a beat, substituted Lincoln University of West Chester, Pennsylvania, for the empty March 2 date. That night, one of the worst snowstorms anyone could remember "did not interfere with the true lovers of basketball" who packed Manhattan Casino "to its capacity."[28] Will's personal brand was at stake, so before the game tipped off, White explained, the Incorporators' boss asked the referee to "read a long statement, evidently written by Mr. Madden, vindicating himself before the public."[29] Will also shifted the blame to Fritz, the correspondent said, "for signing a contract on his word of honor and not keeping it." Regardless of this intrigue, spectators got a great game as "it was to be seen that each team was playing for all it was worth." But the Incorporators won with ease, 38–19. "Despite the knocks and biffs and bangs that a bunch around this town have been trying to hand Billy Madden's Incorporators, the famous 'bunch' handed the Lincoln University quintet one the neatest trimmings they have ever received," White wrote afterward.

On the court for Lincoln's varsity in that game were a twenty-two-year-old right guard named William Pennington Young, nicknamed "Pimp," and at center, his older brother, Ulysses S. Young, twenty-three years old and known as "Lyss" "Lyss." The sons of a garden laborer and a laundress, they grew up in Orange, New Jersey, and would become, as *Pittsburgh Courier* sportswriter W. Rollo Wilson would put it, "the most feared pair on ANY floor five in the country!" Both brothers would later play for Cum Posey's soon-to-be-famous Loendi Big Five team of Pittsburgh, and both men would also make significant pioneering contributions off the court. Lyss would eventually return to Lincoln, serving as head coach of the school's legendary varsity football team and as its athletic director, from 1923 until his untimely death in 1927. Pimp would ultimately become the Secretary of Labor and Industry for the Commonwealth of Pennsylvania and a pivotal delegate to the 1964 Republican National Convention.

On top of that, when these men were little kids, their Virginia-born parents rented a room to another young couple from Virginia, the Ricks family, who had a newborn son named James. Over the years, the Young brothers embraced little James as if he were their own kin. The older boys attended Orange High School where they starred in football, basketball, and baseball, then began playing semi-pro basketball for the Imperial Athletic Club, a local African American squad that competed against other all-Black teams in the area such as the Newark Strollers, the Montclair Athletic Club, and the Jersey City Colored YMCA. Their attraction to basketball got their young protégé hooked on the sport too, and James soon developed his own incredible talent.

James Ricks grew up to become superstar baller James "Pappy" Ricks, who, along with Pimp and Lyss, would be recruited by Cum Posey to play professional basketball for his Loendi Big Five squad in Pittsburgh. This threesome of childhood playmates would spark the Loendi's subsequent domination of Black basketball, with a dynasty that was to include four straight Colored Basketball World's Championships from 1919 to 1923. After that remarkable run, Pappy would leave Pittsburgh to become one of the founding members of a new team, the New York Renaissance Big Five. He would be on that squad's 1933–4 roster, which was eventually enshrined collectively into the Naismith Basketball Hall of Fame. Pimp would also play as a catcher for Cum's baseball team, the Homestead Grays. After the Loendis disbanded, he would stay on with the Grays for over a decade as a player and a catcher's coach, helping develop Josh Gibson and Roy Campanella into Baseball Hall of Fame catchers.

Meanwhile, during that 1916–7 season, Will was not only surviving, he was thriving. The man was gifted at coming up with big ideas, and his next one was the biggest yet. He invited the Wabash Avenue Colored YMCA Outlaws of Chicago to visit New York City for a game against his Incorporators. "When the big team from the Wabash Branch of the Chicago Y.M.C.A. steps out on the court, it will be the first time a basketball team has traveled such a distance to compete in a game and old New York town will see the finest product of basketball in the western world," Will explained. The date was set for Thursday night, March 29, 1917, at Manhattan Casino. BASKET BALL, CHICAGO VS. NEW YORK, read his newspaper advertisement in giant bold print. This was a triumph for the Incorporators owner and manager. "In sending a basketball team all the way from Chicago to meet one of the New York teams is proof conclusive as to what extent the game has developed," Will wrote in his weekly *New York Age* column.[31] "Years ago it was a big thing for a Brooklyn team to come over to New York to play or for a New York team to go to Brooklyn, but now teams travel back and forth from practically every city in the United States." This was precisely what his vision had been all along, and why he felt that a national African American basketball league was possible. Will was justifiably proud of this historic milestone, and by mid-March 1917, the upcoming Outlaws-Incorporators game was the hottest ticket in Harlem.

Even more significantly, this would be a barometer for whether it could *pay* for Black fives to travel such great distances for intercity games. The increased travel costs alone meant gate receipts had to be that much higher. But the Incorporators boss seemed to relish those higher stakes, according to a twenty-four-year-old *Chicago Defender* reporter named Roscoe Lee, who the Bronzeville-based newspaper hired to assist William White. "While the sporting writer of the *Amsterdam News* continues writing about Pollard, and

Dougherty of the *New York News*," Lee taunted, "Will Anthony Madden, the eastern Napoleon of basket ball, and responsible for the world's famous Incorporators, who this same writer keeps abusing, is making great preparations to entertain the Wabash Y.M.C.A. of Chicago here on March 29, seemingly not very much worried about the recent sensation that was caused by the non-appearance of Mr. Pollard and his Providence Collegians."[32] The only people worried about Will's actions, Lee stated, were "a few of those chesty New Yorkers who have a personal grievance against Mr. Madden." He was right.

Will stayed focused because his Incorporators still had several games to play before meeting up with Chicago, including one with the talented Salem-Crescent Athletic Club scheduled for Friday night, March 9. But this game was also never played, for an entirely different and peculiar reason. Though both squads showed up, Will and his Incorporators, according to the *New York Age*, "objected to the presence of a white player in the line-up of the Salem-Crescents, maintaining that he was not a member of the A.A.U. and was looked upon as a professional."[33] The church squad refused to substitute, and the Incorporators refused to yield, so the event organizers had to call off the game. That meant "several hundred basketball enthusiasts lost their temper, some showing a desire to participate in boxing exhibitions without the sanction of the State Boxing Commission." Even though many fans were given their money back at the box office, the controversy made the front page of the *New York Age*. BASKETBALL GAME ENDS AMID EXCITEMENT, read the banner. One thing had to be said about Will: He knew how to make headlines. But this incident was merely a forerunner of things to come.

When the Wabash YMCA Outlaws left for New York City on Monday, March 26, 1917, for their Thursday-night game, the team had nearly the same core roster as when they were first organized. By now, forward Napoleon Blueitt was twenty-three years old and married, but still employed at the Griess-Pfleger tannery. Virgil, just shy of twenty-two years old and an apprentice drug clerk, was still the team's captain and played guard.[34] Bobby Anderson was still at right forward with the squad, now age eighteen and working as a trucker for the Chicago Junction Railway.[35] Defensive specialist Raze Curry was also still on board as a guard, as were twenty-four-year-old Frank Giles, the star center from Council Bluffs, Iowa; Giles's backup, Jesse James Leavell, age twenty-one, who worked at Illinois Steel; and twenty-five-year-old guard Clarence Cousins. New to the team were former Lane Tech all-state interscholastic center Edward Thomas; former Normal, Illinois, Public High School star George Duff, age twenty and described as "a lightning forward"; Thornton Winters, a minister's son; and twenty-year-old Carl Blair, a Chicago stockyards butcher who was "conceded to be the best utility man East or West." Dr. Johnson was still their manager.[36]

"The weather was perfect for the event," the *Chicago Defender* correspondent William White stated, regarding the game-day conditions. He would be the newspaper's courtside reporter for the game. Though it was cold and windy outside, the sky above was starry and clear. Perfect-weather evenings were always a delight at the Manhattan Casino since, in addition to the dance pavilion, small hotel, and saloon on its grounds, there was a picnic park out back, as well as a beer garden that overlooked the Harlem River. Because of those features, music played a vital role in creating the right pregame atmosphere at the venue. "Prof. Douge's Perfect Orchestra was very much in evidence," White continued, "playing all the latest and popular airs, which worked as a tonic upon the crowd and left them in a jolly mood until the teams appeared for practice."[37]

That tonic was just what the doctor ordered, because many patrons were worried about the imminent winds of war sweeping the country. Debate and concern had been swirling for months about whether the United States should enter the conflict raging in Europe. Weeks earlier, Germany had announced a policy of unrestricted submarine attacks, which threatened American shipping. The enemy was potentially anywhere. Unofficial sources told of German "under-sea boats" off the shores of Long Island. Some people legitimately wondered if they could navigate up the Harlem River. SEARCHLIGHTS TO SCOUR N.Y. SKY IN NIGHTLY HUNT FOR ZEPELLINS! read a sensational evening edition headline just hours before tip-off.[38] Manhattan Casino spectators, known to enjoy its famous outdoor grounds, could have looked for enemy subs and blimps except there was a basketball game to watch.

Will Anthony Madden's promotional hunger had struck a chord for folks wanting to escape their anxieties. "Get down to the game, it ought to be a hummer," Roscoe Lee had written, under the *Defender* headline, CHICAGO VS. NEW YORK IS THE SENSATION OF BASKET BALL SEASON, in a piece that ran on

St. Patrick's Day.[39] There was a buzz of excitement and appreciation in the building for all the Chicagoans who made the historic journey and many others who were transplants now living in Harlem. That's when someone in the crowd first spotted the Wabash players filing onto the court for their pregame warm-ups, led by manager Dr. Johnson, and the wild cheering began.

"The Windy City boys were first to appear," White reported, and they "received the most tremendous ovation ever accorded a visiting team in Gotham."[40] This was everything the Incorporators' manager could have dreamed. "They appeared to be in first class shape, the way they went through practice," wrote the courtside reporter, watching the Outlaws conduct their rituals from press row, "especially Thomas, the big center, and Blueitt, the phenomenal guard, Giles, Winters, Duff and Anderson also showing up well."

Now it was Will's turn. To a consummate showman, everything is a show, and this was showtime. Just like in modern times, a hint of the game's importance was the courtside presence of star athletes from other sports. These included catcher Louis Santop and first-baseman Bill "Zack" Pettus of the New York Lincoln Giants who, according to White, "received a great ovation."[41]

Just then, emerging from their locker room, "the Incorporators appeared, led by little Ralph Cooper, mascot of the team, and brother of Walter Cooper, the star center." Ralph, then just nine years old, liked being front and center so much that he would grow up to become a Black Hollywood matinee idol, movie director, radio personality, film producer, and an entertainment entrepreneur as the creator of "Amateur Night at the Apollo," which premiered in 1934. As that show's master of ceremonies for many years, Ralph would introduce each act with his famous command, "Open up them curtains!"[42] He might have acquired some of his showmanship instincts from Will.

Now, both teams were on the court warming up with "the usual demonstration" of skill, drill, and thrill. Spectators loved these pregame routines. When the players finally headed to their benches, Professor Douge's Perfect Orchestra broke out on cue with "There'll Be a Hot Time in The Old Town Tonight," a favorite saloon anthem, with "the crowd joining in the song to the lively tune."[43]

At this point, it was game time. The referee, a White insurance claims adjuster by day named Thomas "Tom" Wachenfeld, Jr., had been officiating basketball since 1903 and was highly regarded as "one of the fairest referees in the business," according to the *New York Age*.[44] He was ready. His whistle was in place. He checked with the scorer's table. Their books were prepared. Each player's name and number were inscribed. The timekeeper and official game clock were all set. Next, Wachenfeld strolled to center court and waited patiently until "the excitement had quieted down to normal," then he summoned out the captains of both teams, Blueitt and Perkinson, for his final instructions.

In one last bit of housekeeping, Wachenfeld took the unusually transparent step of announcing to the audience that Will "had especially instructed him to caution them" about not getting too feisty toward "these boys so far away from home."[45] It was a touching gesture. On stage at the far end of the court, Professor Douge's ensemble was all warmed up to play during time-outs, throughout halftime, and to accompany the dancing that would follow the game. Ticketholders were in their seats. Judging from the size of the gathering, it was clear that, as Roscoe Lee of the *Defender* had predicted, "All roads lead to Manhattan Casino."[46]

Wachenfeld blew his whistle. Here, on the home side of the scorer's table, were the New York Incorporators "in the pink of condition." There, on the visitor's side, were the Wabash Outlaws of Chicago, giving "a good account of themselves."[47] The remaining starters for both squads left their benches on the sideline and strode toward the center court circle to gather around, match up on defense, arrange themselves into position, and get set for the opening tip-off. The spectators on the edges of their seats around the Manhattan Casino symbolized the eagerness of African American communities everywhere. They wanted simply to achieve progress, as a race. This was history in the making.

Taking one last glance at his watch, Wachenfeld noted that it was exactly 9:15 P.M.—game time. Holding a Spalding "Official No. M" game ball, he checked that all players were set in their spots, then tossed it high in the air above and between guard Virgil Blueitt of the Wabash Y and center Walter Cooper of the Incorporators, the two players selected by their teams for the jump ball.

Blueitt left his feet faster, elevating quicker to outjump the taller Cooper. "Thomas got the tap," White reported, "and, catching the ball, missed on a long-range shot."[48] There was a mad scramble for the rebound. "In the mix-ups that followed," the journalist wrote, the Incorporators center got possession and was fouled. However, he then "missed two free shots in succession." Wabash was the first to score, finding the open man with quick, unselfish passing. "Thomas to Giles to Winter to Blueitt scored the first real point of the game on a long-range shot," White shared. That heated up the action. "The game at this point was fast and furious," he continued. "The consistent team work of the Wabash boys seeming to bewilder Madden's team."

Putting this much detail into a newspaper account was the correspondent's own idea. During an era when most folks did not own a radio, his descriptive game reporting was novel for the *Defender*, which only four years earlier barely had an athletics section, as well as for sports journalism overall. This was as near to play-by-play as was possible for a weekly newspaper.

Unnoticed in the press hype leading up to the event was any mention by the Chicago writers about that unusual practice by the Manhattan Casino management, namely, to cover up its wooden flooring with heavy duty canvas. Local fans wondered what the visitors would do with such a surface. The answer proved pivotal. "It was plain to be seen," White noticed, "that the strangeness of the court was to be Chicago's downfall, if beaten, for time after time they were missing what appeared to be easy shots."

New York was gaining momentum. "Cooper at this stage of the game was shooting baskets with ease for the Incorporators," the *Defender* reporter explained, "while Blueitt was missing chance after chance." Virgil became flustered, but Wabash needed their feisty captain to regain his composure. "The little guard's team mates gathered around him, patting him on the back and uttering words of encouragement," White related, "causing him to settle down to the point that the game really turned into a battle between Blueitt, for Wabash, and Cooper, for the Incorporators."[49] This is what the fans had come to see.

"The first half ended 18 to 15 in favor of the Incorporators," said the sideline reporter, who stayed on the job during halftime, even though it was an attraction not to be missed. For some rooters, the intermission was their highlight of the event. While many spectators spilled into the beer garden, others stayed indoors to enjoy the orchestra.

After the break, the game resumed. "In the second half team work on both sides featured, but Blueitt was up to his old tricks—couldn't see the basket," wrote White. "More than once," the reporter added, "he ducked through the whole Incorporator team, only to get to the basket and miss." Wabash struggled even when they got to the free throw line. "Many fouls were missed," White lamented.[50] At the Wabash bench, Dr. Johnson saw the game slipping away and made a substitution. He put in Bobby Anderson, who one day would become "one of the greatest all around athletes ever developed in Chicago."[51] "Anderson, now playing in place of Duff, braced up the team a bit," the *Defender*'s sideline man shared. "A triple pass, Anderson to Blueitt to Giles to Winters, brought the spectators to their feet." White, at courtside, was thrilled with the hustle play. "Winters was going at such speed," he wrote, "that in making the basket he jumped clear across the press table."[52]

Meanwhile, the Incorporators were relentlessly plowing forward, proving why previous Madden-managed teams were called the Red and Black Machine. Though by now they were sure to win, the home squad played until the final whistle. "Just before the ending of the game Perkinson made a spectacular basket from the middle of the court, said to be one of the longest made on the court this season," wrote White.

Finally, the timekeeper fired his starter pistol into the air to signal that the clock had ticked down to zero. "The score, 34–23, in favor of the Incorporators, ended the most sensational game seen this season," the *Defender* correspondent admitted. Regardless of the outcome, he was pleased for the greater, higher good.[53] White felt that his satisfaction was echoed by the Wabash Outlaws, as expressed in the graciousness in their post-game interviews. "The canvas floor bothered the western lads a bit," the visitors admitted, but still they "plainly stated that Wabash lost because the Incorporators were a better defensive team." Today's coaching truism that defense wins games was just as true more than a century ago.

Meanwhile, referee Tom Wachenfeld had been noticeably terrific, according to Wabash. "In New York they were given fair and square decisions," the *Defender* confirmed in a separate column, noting that the YMCA squad applauded the Incorporators for their sportsmanship.[54] Will, for his part, returned the admiration, observing, "The Windy City boys played a wonderful game and showed that they have the goods and next season will be a mighty big attraction."[55] Taking advantage of the limelight, Will used his *New York Age* column to share a few points he wanted to make clear. His team had originated the title of "world champions," he claimed, and had always held it "and will continue to hold it until one or more of the seven big teams register a victory over them." Refusing to play the Incorporators, he said, "will not and cannot help the situation." Specifically, he was calling out the St. Christopher Club for their "continual hiding behind technicalities and imaginary principles," which, Will stated, were doing them no good. The "great public" didn't care about how teams felt toward one another. "All the public wants or cares about is the game," he said. And this was even more true outside of New York City. "The game is the thing," Will emphasized mimicking Shakespeare, "and nothing else matters one iota."[56]

Meanwhile back in Chicago, the man known as Little Napoleon was being elevated to the status of a hero. "Madden's reputation is sky high in the east, a clean sportsman and a man who has led team after team to the championship laurels," the *Defender* said. What he had pulled off, though, was more than heroic. Will Anthony Madden had become "king of the basket ball world and Beau Brummel of New York City."[57] Like the real George "Beau" Brummell, that well-loved influential dapper chap of the early 1800s who used personal fashion forwardness to charm his way into the inner social circle of England's future King George IV, Will had willed himself into becoming the central figure in African American basketball.[58] Using that momentum, Will immediately arranged a return game in Chicago with the Wabash Outlaws, scheduled for Christmas Day, 1917.

"The public can look forward to the year 1917 with great expectation of enjoying some of the finest entertainments that it is possible to stage," he had predicted when it began.[59] And this had already come true. But 1917 was hardly over. In fact, as Will and the country would soon find out, it had hardly begun.

CHAPTER 21

DEMOCRACY LADS

THE DAY AFTER THE NEW York Incorporators defeated the Wabash Colored YMCA Outlaws at the Manhattan Casino on March 29, 1917, legislators in Washington began debating how and when to join the conflict in Europe. HOPE OF AVOIDING WAR ABANDONED, read that Saturday's headline.[1] The following week, the United States Senate and House of Representatives passed resolutions declaring a state of war with Germany, which President Woodrow Wilson approved, officially plunging the United States into World War I. Millions of able-bodied American men were called on to serve their country, and Black leaders urged African American men to participate as well. "Out of this war will rise an American Negro with the right to vote and the right to live without insult," wrote W. E. B. Du Bois, in his highly influential publication, *Crisis Magazine*. Inspired by Wilson's catchphrase, "The World Must Be Made Safe for Democracy," hundreds of thousands of African Americans immediately enlisted for military duty. Several million more registered for the draft. These included Black basketball players, too.

On Tuesday, June 5, 1917, a little over two months following that epic game, numerous athletes and personnel from both squads were obliged to report for registration at their respective local draft boards in New York City and Chicago. These included Walter Cooper, Perky Perkinson, and Ferdinand Accooe of the Incorporators as well as Napoleon and Virgil Blueitt, Frank Giles, Thornton Winters, and Dr. Albert Johnson of the Wabash Outlaws. They all reported patriotically and were registered the same day, which became known as Registration Day. A total of 2,290,527 men of African descent would ultimately be signed up on several different reporting dates, representing nearly 10 percent of the entire pool of eligible Americans. Of those, over 370,000 ultimately served in the U.S. military during World War I.

Despite these numbers, Wilson's "safe for democracy" slogan still did not ring true with the vast majority of Black Americans, for whom the year 1917 would be a bitter mixture of progress and despair. "Darkly I gaze into the days ahead," Claude McKay would later write, with words that captured their prevailing mood.[2]

In the North, tens of thousands of African Americans who had relocated from the South felt helpless, frightened, and enraged, just worrying about their kinfolk back home. Black people there could be murdered with impunity for any reason, or for no reason. In 1916 and 1917, African American men in Southern states were lynched for "accidentally bumping into a white girl as he ran to catch a train," for "annoying white girls," for "striking a white man" in self-defense, and for grounds "unknown."

This was why Black people were fleeing the South. Yet, many White folks there were angered by this or actually baffled as to the cause. "Take some of the sections from which the Negro is departing and he can hardly be blamed when the facts are known," the *Houston Chronicle* had to explain in 1916. "He is kicked around, cuffed, lynched, burned, homes destroyed, daughters insulted and oftimes [*sic*] raped, has no vote nor voice, is underpaid, and in some instances when he asks for pay receives a 2 x 4 over his head." It was obvious. Yet, this was Jim Crow, a lifestyle so common that it had become normalized. In February of 1917, *Crisis Magazine* announced that a study of "Negro problems" had been added to the curriculum at Howard University, taught by esteemed sociologist Professor Kelly Miller. But many wondered why the topic was not about the real issue, "Caucasian problems."

Black people needed anything that spelled relief: a sign of progress, someone with a smile, or any cause concerned about "the betterment of the race." If even one young African American man got a job in Chicago's business district, known as the "Loop," it was front-page news. If a small group of Black men got their jobs back at a Whites-only hotel in Milwaukee where they'd been Jim Crowed, it made headlines. And if an African American basketball team represented a Black community, then every detail was considered heroic. Sports offered a sense of refuge and progress that was missing from daily life.

But sports couldn't solve the bigger problem. Due to the war, European immigration to the United States had dropped by nearly 90 percent, creating a vast labor shortage that provided unprecedented job opportunities for African Americans. By June 1917, *Crisis Magazine* estimated "about 250,000 colored workmen have come northward" during the past six months. This was just as White workers in many areas of labor were striking for better conditions. Their hatred of African American strikebreakers seethed.

This frothing hate erupted on July 2, 1917, in East St. Louis, Illinois, when mobs of White men, women, and children numbering in the thousands proceeded to roam the city's streets hunting, attacking, and murdering every Black person they could find and catch. Their victims were bludgeoned, stabbed, mutilated, kicked to death, shot, hung, or burned alive inside their own homes, many of which had been boarded up by the mobs before being torched. Congressional investigation confirmed that in addition to men and women, many of the dead were children and infants, some thrown into the flames after being shot. TWO HUNDRED NEGROES KILLED IN RACE RIOTS WHICH SWEPT OVER EAST ST. LOUIS, read a North Carolina newspaper headline the next day, labeling the event in typical socialized fashion as a disturbance rather than an outright massacre of African Americans.[3] "Men were killed simply because they were black, and the only limit on the slaughter was the ability of the crowd to find negroes," the more honest *St. Louis Post-Dispatch* reported.[4] Some tried blaming the "riot" on White people's anger about Black replacement workers, but as African Americans knew all too well, the scapegoat was not "jobs" because the American economy was booming. "Manufacturing business aggregated $2,500,000,000, an increase of 35 percent" compared to 1916, the *Minneapolis Morning Tribune* reported in January 1917.[5]

President Wilson was as much to blame as anyone. In February 1915, he held a White House screening of the sociopathic film *The Birth of a Nation*, despite widespread protest about its violently racist views and deplorable depictions of African Americans as well as its glorification of the Ku Klux Klan. "It's like writing history with lightning," said Wilson afterward. "And my only regret is that it is all terribly true." Nothing about East St. Louis was ever heard from Wilson. Meanwhile, during the same month, July 1917, the first African American military units began mustering out to military installations for duty. By custom and by law, these troops were obliged to remain racially segregated, though their commanding officers were always White. "If we must die, O let us nobly die," Claude McKay would write. This was the situation.

In mid-July, Will branched out professionally by managing the promotion of a talented up-and-coming African American singer from Boston named Roland W. Hayes for a recital at the Manhattan Casino. Also, the basketball manager was so interested in theater and singing that he had been performing at private events under the pseudonym "Jimmy Valentine" since 1911. Will was even a founding member of the Harlem-based Amathesp Club, which presented dramatic and musical productions. This was more than just a hobby. In excess of 1,100 ticketholders turned out for Hayes's concert, and within a few years the young vocalist was being praised as "America's greatest tenor" in front of audiences as large as ten thousand.[6] This would not be the last of Will's personal interest in the performing arts.

As a response to the East St. Louis massacre, one of the country's most impactful acts of protest took place in New York City, where African American church and community leaders organized a "Great Silent Parade" on Saturday, July 28, 1917.[7] An estimated eight thousand citizens were said to have marched down Fifth Avenue in silence, many carrying signs and placards that gave voice to their voiceless protest, led by women and children dressed in white followed by men wearing black suits. Though the East St. Louis tragedy had instigated the event, it was also "a mute but solemn protest against the atrocities and discriminations practiced against the race in various parts of the country" as well as "the failure of the proper authorities to provide adequate protection and redress" to Black citizens. The Reverend Dr. Hutchens Chew Bishop of St. Philip's Protestant Episcopal was deeply involved with the event as president of its planning committee while the Reverend Frederick A. Cullen of Salem Methodist Episcopal was appointed vice president. Father Daniel was also active, with St. Philip's Church itself made available under his management for the planning committee's use. Black people in Bronzeville were particularly horrified and outraged because this had happened in their own state, the land of Lincoln, and reports indicated that Illinois National Guard troops sent to restore order instead participated in the slaughter, stood by and watched, or arrived late, if they arrived at all. African Americans everywhere were terrified that they could be next. This was a blot that "can never be wiped out," wrote the *Tyrone Daily Herald*, a White-owned Pennsylvania newspaper, recognizing the depravity of what happened.

The ups and downs of Black life in 1917 continued when, in August, African American labor activist A. Philip Randolph launched a new magazine called *The Messenger*, a breakthrough publication that advocated forcefully for the rights of workers and all oppressed people. Yet that same month, in Houston, a Black woman was accosted in her home by a White police officer, touching off violence that prompted Black soldiers from the U.S. 24th Colored Infantry Regiment stationed nearby to protect her honor and the lives of African American residents in the area. "The primary cause of the Houston riot was the habitual brutality of the white police officers of Houston in their treatment of colored people," an NAACP investigation concluded. Regardless, thirteen Black soldiers were found guilty of "mutiny" and sentenced to death by hanging, while forty-one others were sentenced to life in prison.

In basketball at the beginning of September 1917, Will Madden and the Incorporators suffered a major setback when their best player, Walter Cooper, abandoned the team, taking with him its two biggest stars, Ferdinand Accooe and Perky Perkinson. In a cruel twist, Cooper began calling his new squad "Walter Cooper's Original Incorporators." This ruined Will's lineup with barely any time left to react before the start of the upcoming 1917–8 season. It was an existential crisis. War restrictions had significantly cut back travel and uses of facilities, making it hard to schedule new games, and challenging to attract new players on short notice. It also opened the Incorporators manager to potential ridicule by those same jealous New York City newspapermen, raising questions about why Walter Cooper, Will's own All-American, would desert his manager. It also put the Chicago game at risk. Backing out of that booking would be disastrous, not only for his brand but also for Black basketball as a whole.

Making matters worse, on September 26, Will's grandmother from Ireland, Ellen Corbett Harder, passed away at eighty-one years of age. "She is reputed as being wealthy and leaves a daughter, Margaret Madden, and four grandchildren," said the *Defender*, even though Ellen had been a cleaning lady for her entire adulthood. But the Incorporators founder must have been thinking, "The show must go on," because Will figured it out.

First, he got his official secretary, a sergeant in the 15th New York Infantry Regiment, to issue a warning "threatening a lawsuit against any persons or person who uses or threatens to use the name of the Incorporators." This was being done, the *Chicago Defender* reported, "to let the general public know that there is but one bona fide organization known as the Incorporators, and that one is managed by Will Anthony Madden."[8] The newspaper even backed him up. "At this stage of the game, the name Original Incorporators means practically nothing and stands for less," its correspondents reported in late September, a few weeks after Cooper's split. Using that name "would be ridiculous and laughable," the weekly said.[9] "Mr. Madden is more of an Original Incorporator than anyone else concerned."

Then, once again, Will displayed an uncanny ability to land on his feet. He rallied, showing that his knack for securing top basketball talent could rival anyone's. By the end of September, Will had assembled a new roster of highly skilled players built around three solid stars who remained with the team. These were Grenier Turner, Hobart "Hobie" Johnson, and Frank "Strangler" Forbes.

Grenier was "a fast little forward," according to the manager, and Hobie was a "big utility man" with talent. But his biggest keeper was Forbes, a powerful guard who had earned the nickname "through his tactics on the basketball court." Originally from Philadelphia, he had been a three-sport star at Southern Manual Training High School before enrolling at Howard University for the 1911–2 academic year to focus on baseball. Forbes was so talented as an infielder that the following summer, while home after freshman year, he was signed by the semi-pro South Philadelphia Giants, an all-Black team. Never returning to college, Forbes then played professionally with the Philadelphia Colored Giants, the New York Lincoln Stars, and the New York Lincoln Giants, which were African American squads owned by the entrepreneurial brothers Ed and Jess McMahon, two White sports promoters who were based in Harlem. The infielder joined the Lincoln Giants in 1915 to replace future Baseball Hall of Fame member John Henry "Pop" Lloyd, still considered the greatest shortstop in Negro League history. Forbes would play with that team for the next four seasons, and during this time, he became interested in returning to basketball. That's when Will added him to the Incorporators lineup.

"Much new material has been added to the squad, which will be developed around these three veterans, thereby producing another champion team," the *Defender* predicted, adding that when the Incorporators showed up for this year's Thanksgiving afternoon game, "all the eyes of the basketball world will be centered on Madden's team." Will scheduled that game against the Jersey City Athletic Club, known as the "Jersey Blues." Always fun-loving, the Incorporators manager added special touches like enlisting a "galaxy of pretty girls" to sell pennants, buttons, flags, and other novelties, according to the *Defender*.[10] And then of course, Douge's Perfect Orchestra would provide dance music.

Pulling this off would be an ambitious task for Will, considering everything that had happened. While some New York City newspapers were still being critical, he had a friend at the *Chicago Defender* in J. E. Patterson, another of the weekly's eastern correspondents. Patterson advised these haters in the media to "take into consideration that the public in general wishes genuine basket ball news, etc. and not the personal grievance you have against some individual involved in the game, whether he be manager or player!"[11] This notion was indicative of the growing number of Black basketball teams, and their growing number of African American fans. The success or failure of Will's entire 1917–8 season would all come down to how many of them showed up on Thanksgiving Day. Fortunately, that was apparent before tip-off. Looking out at the Manhattan Casino audience, Will knew he was back. 5,000 PEOPLE SEE WORLD'S FAMOUS INCORPORATORS DEFEAT THE JERSEY BLUES, a headline blasted, afterward. It was "the largest crowd of basketball fans that ever witnessed a game in Gotham," the *Defender* correspondent Patterson marveled. Plus, "the game was bitterly fought from beginning to end and kept the crowd in a frenzied state of excitement until the final whistle blew." And the Incorporators won, 46–29. But for Will, and for others too, this victory stood for much more than merely a win. There were levels to it.

This crowd included a host of A-list Harlem celebrities and socialites, from "Lift Every Voice and Sing" composer J. Rosamond Johnson to arts patron A'Lelia Walker Robinson, the thirty-two-year-old daughter of Madam C. J. Walker, who ran the Harlem office of her mother's hair care business. Will's own luxury box was adjacent to that of influential Danish West Indian immigrant Casper Holstein, a forty-one-year-old self-described "gambler" who would soon establish one of the largest "numbers" operations in New York City history.[12] His policy was so lucrative that Holstein used the revenues to set up numerous legitimate businesses that paid employees generously and made him, as the *New York Times* put it, "Harlem's favorite hero."[13]

Even prior to the game when the Incorporators "emerged from their dressing room at 3 o'clock" to stretch and warm up, "their appearance brought forth applause as no team has received in this city, in the history of the game," said the *Defender* reporter. That was because Black communities across the country were looking forward to the start of the 1917–8 basketball season with

so much anticipation. There was a war going on. African American men—
many of them teenagers—had been sent to Europe, rations had been imposed,
facilities had been closed and re-purposed. The scene at the Casino that night
gave many people back a sense of normalcy that had been missing for months.

And from the players' perspective, enormous ovation they received was
also "encouraging to the youngsters in their initial appearance." There was
pride and excitement in it, as the Incorporators must have felt the whole
community behind them.

Then, the roster itself was "a surprise to the public in general," Patterson
said, "as they had not expected to see an entirely new team." Not entirely
new, because Will had retained Greneir, Hobie, and Forbes, which paid off
because, according to the reporter, they ran the pregame drills "like old timers,
with no stage fright, and showing they were game to the core." Of the actual
new players, three were the most significant, starting with a fifteen-year-old
Barbados-born center named Hilton Slocum. Hilton was phenomenal, and
guarding him was a disaster. "With a game or two more under his belt, he will
be the equal of the great Cooper, last year's popular center," Patterson observed.
Will had discovered a young player so exceptional that in 1923, he would sign
as a founding player with the New York Renaissance all-Black professional
basketball team and star with that club during its first ten seasons. But it was
two other new players who created the biggest part of the public's surprise
reaction. They were forwards Spike Cooke and Barney Klatt, "Hebrew boys
from the College Settlement team of New York," according to the *Pittsburgh
Press*.[14] These guys, in Cooke's words, were "the only white men on that team."[15]
Klatt was a remarkable free throw specialist who would make twenty-three of
his team's twenty-four chances during an important game later that season as
the squad's designated foul shooter. Free throwers were difference-makers in
the early game, until a new rule was established in 1924, requiring the player
who was fouled to attempt their own free throw. Spike and Barney would
soon become difference-makers of a different kind, in ways few could have
conceived. For some reason, no one seemed to remember that it had been
Will Madden who, just two years earlier, heard rumors about "white boys"
on "colored teams" and wondered why. But at this stage, it was either that or
forfeit the game with no team. Will clearly had a growth mindset.

Coming back from the brink of sure personal and organizational failure
to win this game in such fashion in front of so many people was one of the

most gratifying accomplishments any basketball manager could ever have achieved. Best of all, those who had prayed for Will's downfall were publicly exposed. There would be no death knell. Will Anthony Madden was a survivor, from a family of survivors.

By the beginning of December, even as the *Defender* covered that Thanksgiving Day basketball game in New York City, the newspaper complained about the foot-dragging by local, state, and Federal officials responsible for investigating and prosecuting the Caucasian defendants from the East St. Louis massacre, under the December 8 headline, RACE LOSING CONFIDENCE IN TRIAL OF RIOT CASES. Simultaneously, those thirteen African American soldiers in Houston who had been sentenced to death for protecting Black citizens from local police abuse were executed.

Days later, on December 12, the enthusiastic 369th Colored Infantry Regiment of Harlem shipped out of Hoboken, New Jersey, headed for combat in Europe, following a farewell party for them and their families at the Manhattan Casino given by millionairess Madam C. J. Walker, who was in town for the occasion. Black communities questioned how it was possible for the government to ask African American men to fight against injustice around the world, a request patriotically endorsed by race leaders and heeded by Black folks in hopes that their fight would help eliminate lynchings and discrimination, only to have that same government hang those same soldiers for fighting to defend their own people against injustice at home.

As the holidays rolled around, Christmas couldn't come soon enough for many African Americans. This was especially so for Will, who hoped that the upcoming Christmas Day return game in Chicago between his New York Incorporators and the Wabash Outlaws would be an epic gift in and of itself. This was how the year 1917 led up to the game Will had scheduled between his New York Incorporators and the Wabash Colored YMCA Outlaws on the South Side of Chicago on Christmas Day.

It was Christmas 1917, a Tuesday afternoon. Game day.

INCORPORATORS OF NEW YORK INVADE CHICAGO, the *Defender* headline shouted on the prior Saturday. "'Tis a long ways to come, Bill, but we wish you well," the newspaper had playfully taunted. Will may have had a "sky high" reputation. But that was back home, the paper teased. "Now he comes into the lair of the Chicago lads." With most of the Wabash players returning, the *Defender* insisted, especially Virgil Blueitt, "it is an assured fact that Mr. Madden and his men from the center of Harlem will not have a walkaway." True, the Incorporators had won last time, but "can they do it again?" One thing for sure, they advised, was that the Outlaws were "leaving no stone unturned to make this one of the grandest affairs that has ever been held in Chicago." Seats for local soldiers, for various clubs, and for "society in general" had already been reserved for the 1:30 P.M. game in the regal and cavernous Eighth Regiment Armory, with dancing to follow. "Come and root for your team, as any bunch that is game enough to travel 1,000 miles to play basketball is worth paying 50 cents to see play," the weekly said.[16]

The immense armory itself, which stretched almost the entire two-block length between East Thirty-Fifth and East Thirty-Seventh Streets, had been built in peacetime to house the Eighth Regiment of the Illinois National Guard. Inside, a four-story-high arched roof covered a massive drill floor designed for formations, parades, and military exercises, as well as for training on equipment and machinery. This space was ringed by ornate wrought iron balconies and walkways from which onlookers could review the activities below. But over Christmas of 1917, it was transformed into a basketball court and dance floor surrounded by seating to accommodate thousands.

The game had been advertised for weeks already, in the local and national editions of the *Defender*, the *New York Age*, and other publications. The annual campaign of the Wabash YMCA, which ended a few weeks earlier, had netted 329 new members, bringing the total to more than fifteen hundred, the most of any other Colored Y branch in the country. This Y was a symbol of Bronzeville's determination to lift itself up. The name "Wabash" was famous and meaningful in Black communities throughout the country. That was why its basketball team, the Outlaws, had gotten such a large ovation in New York City when they played there back in March.

Now, after making the seven-hundred-mile train trip from Manhattan to Chicago on the New York Central Line of the Pennsylvania Railroad, Will, his players, and Incorporators team personnel finally had the chance to see the actual Wabash YMCA facility in person. This is where they spent the night, as guests of the branch and its basketball program, still managed by Dr. Johnson, the dentist. Waking up here on Christmas Day was literally *like Christmas.* The building had everything, and it was all brand new. In addition to the swimming pool, gymnasium, and fitness equipment available to them, this Y had its own cozy basketball court, on this occasion a perfect space for a walk-through or the fine-tuning of set shots and free throws.

That morning, there might have been Christmas prayers, a celebration, and even some gift giving. But the real joy and preoccupation was the game. The Eighth Regiment Armory was a few blocks' stroll away, through the heart of Chicago's famous "Black Belt." This was in the same vicinity as many institutions the visitors may have read or heard about as a source of African American racial pride. The Appomattox Club on South Park Avenue was an organization of leading Black professional men. The Binga Bank on the corner of East Thirty-Sixth and South State was where thousands of African Americans had opened savings accounts. And the offices of the weekly *Chicago Defender* were on South Indiana near East Thirty-Fifth Street. By 1917, its circulation was up to ninety-eight thousand copies a week. There were African American proprietors everywhere. They owned barbershops, smoke shops, newsstands, and pool rooms as well as eateries, saloons, and hotels. There were undertakers and pharmacies as well as hat makers, shoemakers, and cleaners. There was even a taxi, limousine, and tour company as well as a Sinclair service station. There were numerous after-hours spots but the Incorporators didn't indulge. They had to leave for Cincinnati first thing in the morning to play the Ninth Street Colored YMCA that night, followed by games in Columbus, Pittsburgh, Harrisburg, Baltimore, Washington, Philadelphia, and Atlantic City.

As the tip-off for the big game neared, people were already standing in line waiting to get in at the formal archway that marked the main entrance to the Eighth Regiment Armory. Then it was time for warm-ups. Up until then, everything had been cordial and gracious, from the arrangements to the correspondence to the accommodations. But when the New York Incorporators finally trotted out onto the basketball court in the middle of the facility's drill floor to begin their warm-ups, there was a problem. "It was announced before the game that the promoter would protest it, as Madden had two white men," the *Defender* reported.[17] This was referring to Cooke and Klatt, who had traveled with the team. But for the local players and most of their fans inside the armory that day, with all that had happened in 1917, this was hard to accept. Will had also brought the White official Tom Wachenfeld, Jr., along, "one of the best referees in the business." It was common for a visiting squad to bring their own ref, a practice "which insures both teams and the general public a square deal all around." The game hadn't even tipped off and there was already a heated confrontation. People must have wondered what Will would do. They didn't yet realize that what happened next would change the future of basketball. Not just Black basketball, but the game itself.

This was Will Anthony Madden, Little Napoleon, a players' manager, a survivor who didn't back down. He was there to win. So of course he brought Cooke and Klatt. According to the *Defender*, Will made it plain, stating "there was nothing in the contract that prohibited him from playing his team as it was" and that he "would play an Eskimo, if he wanted to and the man knew basketball." This was Will at his best. "Madden is democratic," the newspaper voiced, in his defense. "We say so—why Jim Crow basket ball teams anyway, when one can break it up." These words coming from the *Chicago Defender* were historically profound. "Go on Bill, we are with you," said the race's leading weekly. "As for protesting—to whom," the paper asked. "It's a joke."[18]

As if to prove how little these complaints mattered to him, Will started Cooke and Klatt. And no sooner did the game get underway then the Outlaws found themselves being outhustled and outplayed on their own home court. They had star player Virgil Blueitt, but one star couldn't make a team, and the visitors were so well prepared that Wabash was getting "swept off their feet," according to the *Defender*, which covered the action closely. Virgil was able to get fouled, but that didn't help. "His free throws were the poorest in his history, he missing five in a row." At first it looked like a walkaway after all. "Some fast teamwork and clever passing brought the New York boys within striking distance, and Slocum started the scoring with a pretty basket, making a difficult shot." Just as the crowd settled down from that, Turner of the Incorporators brought them to their feet again with another basket, "causing the New Yorkers to gain not only courage, but they displayed more pep." Will's plan was working. "At no stage of the game did the local lads have a show," the *Defender* admitted. "From the time the first whistle blew till the final the New Yorkers dazzled along with brilliancy that baffled the Chicago boys and caused many of the fans to root for the visitors to win." The Outlaws were no match. "It was simply too much New York." The old Wetzler system. Will's eye for talent. "His team is all stars, yet none try to outshine each other," the newspaper explained. Pulling this off with a lineup that had to start nearly from scratch was extraordinary. "Madden deserves a lot of credit."

Finally, Virgil found his groove. "Blueitt got away from his followers and by some eel like squirms, worked the ball within shooting distance and shot it into the basket for Chicago's first score." Then the ball went right back to Turner again, who "ended the half going the whole length of the floor for a basket, evading the entire Chicago five with some of the prettiest zig zag work ever seen on a basketball floor."

That's when the Wabash Outlaws began living up to their nickname. "Seeing themselves outclassed, Chicago started a rough game, which caused many of the spectators to get disgusted."[19] Their frustration had turned to anger.

Inside the Eighth Regiment Armory, the locals were getting upset. The referees were losing control. Eventually this reached a boiling point and "Winters and Slocum started to mix it up." That was the minister's son beefing with the Incorporator's new fifteen-year-old center, who was having a solid game. "A moment later Virgil Blueitt and one of the New York players got into a mixup," the *Defender* reported. Then all hell broke loose. "Crowds swarmed on the field, which was enough for New York to have been handed the game." Virgil's older brother, who had been drafted into the Eighth Regiment by then, was watching from the sidelines. But when the fighting began, Napoleon, "in the uniform of a non-commissioned officer, was out there, too, and for several minutes it looked as though it was a free for all fight." It was hectic. Everyone seemed to jump into the action, many "using abusive language" so foul that the *Defender* recommended, "rooters from both sides are to be censured." In other words, this was not a good look. Not for Bronzeville, not for Black basketball, and not for the sport itself.

In the aftermath, the Chicago *Defender*'s bold headline read, MADDEN'S INCORPORATORS BEAT CHICAGO, 25 TO 15, with a sub headline stating, LOCALS NO MATCH FOR "DEMOCRACY LADS."[20] That nickname, which referred to the team's multi-racial, all-inclusive roster, was heartwarming and fitting. But not everyone liked this outcome. Seven hundred miles away from Bronzeville, in Harlem, Romeo Dougherty, the dual-threat sports columnist with the *Amsterdam News* and the *New York News*, was still obsessed with bringing Will down, and wasted no time relentlessly criticizing him. This went on for weeks. Finally, the *Defender* stepped in again, letting readers know they had Will's back and calling Romeo out by name.

WE WILL NOT AND MUST NOT STAND FOR ANY COLOR LINE IN ATHLETICS, read the February 1918 headline above an editorial by the newspaper's own "Mr.

Fan," a pseudonym. "Romeo Dougherty's Fight on Will Madden Uncalled For and Totally Unwarranted," was the sub line. Wabash's objection was all uncalled for, he wrote, and "the bringing up of this color question" shouldn't have marred the game. "Recently, Romeo L. Dougherty, sporting writer and dramatic critic, took Will Anthony Madden to task for playing a white lad," the editorial read. "This is not only unfair to the Race, but puts Dougherty in a bad light."[21]

A question comes to mind, said Mr. Fan, "Is Dougherty sore because Madden cannot or does not see fit to give him the amount of advertising he thinks he should get?" He was getting right into it. "If so, he should not make a proverbial ass out of himself by jumping on Madden through his columns, leading the people along in a false impression." Instead, the columnist explained, Romeo should face Will directly "as a man and state his grievance." This was brutal honesty. There was no escaping it. Besides, the columnist argued, if he was to "coincide" with Romeo, then that would mean numerous African American athletes, including Fritz Pollard, Paul Robeson, Howard Drew, and others, "would never be permitted to run in white meets." The AAU and amateur athletics have done more to "open the existing bridge between the white man and us than any other thing in the world," he continued. Chicago University had changed not only because champion African American sprinter Binga Dismond attended there and "won laurels for his school," but, as their campus newspaper the *Daily Maroon* would say, because "he gave them a different conception of a Colored man." It was that simple, said Mr. Fan. "The door wide open to us in the schools and the universities, the door being pushed open in the world, and now comes an educated ass advocating that we draw the color line on the white people." It was a scathing lecture. Not getting "a certain amount of advertising out of a man" doesn't entitle a sportswriter "to condemn him and his policy of broadness," he added. Mr. Fan concluded with a final admonition. "Wake up, Mister Dougherty, wake up from thy slumber."[22]

Will had stood firm. He had rebounded from the brink of failure to the glory of national triumph. Yet, this was a bittersweet moment. Time would show that Will Anthony "Little Napoleon" Madden was on the right side of history. He was just way ahead of the times. It was also true that his personality got the best of him.

Will and Romeo Leonard Waldemar Dougherty were both powerfully influential. Yet they were too different from each other, on too many levels, for them to ever reconcile and work together. This was unfortunate. Where once Romeo was championing Will's vision of a nationally organized multicity professional African American basketball league, now their public feud prevented its formation, which could have happened before the dawn of the Harlem Renaissance.

CHAPTER 22

THE FUTURE OF BASKETBALL

LIKE ANYBODY ELSE IN PITTSBURGH, Cumberland Posey, Jr., his organi-zation, his players, and their followers could read the headlines of the *Chicago Defender*, *Amsterdam News*, *New York Age*, and other out-of-town African American newspapers. Through them, they could keep up with the headlines about Will Madden's World-Famous Incorporators, the crowds they were getting, what sportswriters were saying, the drama that was unfolding, and most importantly, how they were doing on the court. This made the upcom-ing basketball game between Cum's Loendi Big Five and Will's Incorporators scheduled for February 1, 1918, at the Manhattan Casino in Harlem one of the most highly anticipated matchups of the 1917–8 season. The city's own local newspapers that covered Black cultural topics were reporting, too. Even though it didn't have a dedicated New York City sports correspondent, the *Pittsburgh Press* knew "both teams were out for blood" and would take advantage of "every trick and device to improve their chances of victory."[1]

The Loendis departed Pittsburgh via the Pennsylvania Rail Road the day before their Friday evening matchup with the Democracy Lads in New York City. "They took with them a string of their best, most dependable and fastest players," the *Press* reported, adding that all of them "were in the pink of condition, and feeling quite sanguine of their ability, even before a New York audience, to take Billy Madden's tossers into camp."[2] Those in the party included brothers Cum and See Posey, brothers Sell and Ram Hall, and *Pitts-burgh Courier* sportswriter W. Rollo Wilson, as well as other players and a few extra guests, like team manager Evan Baker and his bride.

Against the Loendi Club, Will used the same Incorporators rotation that had been working so well on his club's recent road trip to Chicago and back. Slocum, Turner, Forbes, Cooke, and Klatt had not lost during their eight-game journey back to New York City, and they continued that trend. Will had advertised the matchup at the Casino as "Pittsburgh vs. New York," and as billed, the game was a competitive thriller, with the Incorporators winning, 28–25. This was when Klatt, the Incorporators' designated foul shooter, hit twenty-three out of his twenty-four total free throws, contributing 82 percent of his team's offense from the charity stripe. Cum made ten of ten foul shots in the losing effort. Though it was a difficult loss, the Loendi Big Five now headed back to Pittsburgh for their first-ever matchup with the popular Coffey Club.

To improve his chances against the Coffeys, Cum borrowed a ringer from the St. Christopher Club of Harlem and brought him back to Pittsburgh. He was the gifted young forward Fats Jenkins. In the highly anticipated game, several thousand fans filled the Labor Temple. "It was a fast and scientific exhibition of toss, dribble, block, and team work by both teams," the *Pittsburgh Press* reported. "The playing was at all stages full of clash, vim, and good head work." And it came down to a last second shot by George Gilmore, which gave Loendi a one-point victory, 32–31. Cum led the scoring with seven field goals and ten out of fifteen free throws, followed by Gilmore's six baskets. This was an enormous victory. A heated, sustainable Loendi-Coffey rivalry was born.

In the years to come, the Loendi Big Five and the Coffey Club would play numerous times per season, with each game decided by only one or two points. The names of Loendi stars were well-known not just in Pittsburgh but throughout every Black community that had an African American newspaper with a sports section. The crowds kept coming, and more spectators meant more gate receipts. "We used to get $25 a game when we played little teams," Loendi player William "Greasy" Betts would say in 1973. "But when we played the big teams, like Coffey and the Original Celtics"—a celebrated White team based in New York—"we got as high as $75 per game."[3] A monthly income of $300 or $400 per player was possible, a large amount of money in the late 1910s. Furthermore, players could supplement these payments with other jobs during the weekday and in the off-season.

Cum was single-handedly building a Black sports economy in Pittsburgh. His pioneering approach was to schedule teams of different races, ethnicities, or religions against one another with the arrangements masterfully orchestrated from behind the scenes by both clubs in collaboration to maximize revenues. This approach was so successful that within a couple of years, it would become the business model of choice for New York City's other emerging

Black basketball entrepreneur, Bob Douglas. With epic results, Douglas would match his New York Renaissance team against the New York Original Celtics, the Oshkosh All-Stars, and other great clubs at multiple locations per season in what could be called traveling archrivalry road shows.

It was while riding the wave of these competitive games with the Coffeys that Cum and the Loendi Big Five began their stretch of four consecutive seasons without a loss to another African American five, and a streak of four straight Colored Basketball World's Championships. This was a true undisputed basketball dynasty, earning Cumberland Posey, Jr., a place as the second rightful king of Black basketball. The Loendis would dominate all African American competition until the early 1920s, when a bold series of strategic and opportunistic moves by Bob Douglas would take over the African American basketball landscape.

By early 1918, the winds of war had drastically changed America's basketball landscape. The United States was sending nearly ten thousand newly trained soldiers to Europe daily in support of the Allied fight against Germany. This was an all-out effort. As a result, basketball activity among Black teams dropped off almost entirely, except at the collegiate level where White colleges and African American schools like Howard, Hampton, Shaw, and Lincoln continued to operate on a scaled-back basis. One of Lincoln's star players was a twenty-one-year-old, six-foot, seven-inch center from Paterson, New Jersey, named James "Stretch" Sessoms, who would later be called "the tallest man in basketball." Stretch had played with the Paterson Royals and New Jersey Invaders, local all-Black squads, becoming one of the best pivot men in the country while battling against the region's best African American centers, including George Gilmore of the Alpha Big Five.

Another big man who Stretch went up against was a nineteen-year-old center for the Tempo Athletic Club of Brunswick named Paul Robeson. Robeson was still a student at Rutgers University and had been emerging as a star athlete at the school, especially in football, where, just before Christmas 1917, he had become the first Black player to be named as an All American. At around six feet tall, Robeson was so massive that his nickname was "Tiny." Now, coming off his football season, he began playing basketball with the

St. Christopher Club in Harlem. Robeson was the team's most imposing player, and he competed alongside some exceptionally talented future greats. These included Fats Jenkins and Georgie Fiall, who would join the New York Renaissance within a few years.

Though the second half of the 1917–8 basketball season was all but lost for most African American squads, the war was about to end, and the action picked up again right after Armistice Day, November 11, 1918. A week later, 1918–9 preseason reports said that Rushford "Rush" Lord, the new manager of the St. Christopher Five, was already focused on a winning campaign. According to Rush, all of his players were ready except for the "giant" Robeson, who was still "playing football at Rutgers but would be present when big things start to happen."[4] Rush and his longtime coach Jeff Wetzler even expressed surprise that every single player from the previous year's lineup had reported for the new season.

Not one to break his word or to let teammates down, Robeson came through for them in epic fashion. A week after Rush's comments, Tiny was playing football for Rutgers against Syracuse at the Polo Grounds in Harlem, in the last game of his college gridiron career, while the St. Christopher Big Five were preparing for their basketball season opener across the street at the Manhattan Casino. Immediately following the football game, which Rutgers lost, Robeson rushed out of the Polo Grounds' center field exit gate onto Eighth Avenue and into the popular dancehall's dressing room, where he quickly changed into his St. C. basketball uniform and stepped onto the court just in time for the tip-off against their archrival, the Alpha Physical Culture Club. The Alpha Big Five had been weakened when George Gilmore, the former Howard University star center, moved to Pittsburgh to play with the Loendis. But they were still powerful. "I had no time to hope or be sorry for the sad events of the early afternoon," Robeson would say, years later.[5] Maintaining his positive attitude, the football All American made the most of his special day by helping to beat the Alphas. "So here I was at the Manhattan playing forward for St. C.," he would reminisce. "I was fast for a big six footer and played near the edge of the court while little Fats Jenkins dribbled them silly." Fats would often score most of his team's points in their quick moving offense. "It was hard to follow the ball," Robeson said. "And so this November day we went home to shower and dress and come back for a wonderful few hours of dancing." This was basketball during the Black Fives Era.

Meanwhile, many African American players were still in the military, which allowed the popularity of Black college basketball programs to keep growing as an alternative to watching diluted squads. There was also the dancing craze that had started in the early 1910s and was still going strong, ensuring that entertainment remained a vital feature when basketball games were played. For a Christmas Day 1918 contest between the junior teams of St. Christopher and the Spartans, spectators were promised "an elaborate souvenir program score-book, which will have among its many features a very handy and convenient dance order."[6] The game, played at the Manhattan Casino, also had a pleasant surprise in the form of Madam C. J. Walker, who made an unannounced appearance. Walker had by now amassed a fortune, and her residence on West 136th Street was only a short ride away from the Casino. "Mme's entrance was the signal for an ovation," according to one of Walker's houseguests who also attended the game, "and she was at once requested to throw the ball from her box."[7]

A few days later, on December 28, 1918, St. Christopher beat Alpha again in front of 3,500 people at the Manhattan Casino, marking the return of big-time basketball to New York and confirming that the war and its restraints had really ended.[8]

A month after that, possibly looking to leverage Paul Robeson's notoriety, the Red and Black Machine of St. Christopher entered its club team into the 145-pound (or junior) class for the AAU Metropolitan District Basketball Championship. The tournament spanned two months, from January 19 to March 28. There were nine entrants in total, including two other African American squads: the Salem-Crescent Athletic Club of New York and the Titan Athletic Club of Orange, New Jersey. The remaining entries were little known White amateur fives including the Rutgers Place Gym, the National Turn Verein, the Bronx Church House, and the Union Settlement Athletic Club. Rutgers Place won first place honors while St. C. came in fifth place and Titan AC finished last with no wins. But the fact that the AAU had opened its doors to Black club teams was a breakthrough signaling the extent to which the White mainstream amateur basketball world had accepted, or at least respected, the viability of those African American organizations.

Bob Douglas continued to improve his Spartan team and kept winning. With an eye on the future, he hired City College of New York head basketball coach Joe Deering to fulfill those same duties for the Braves on a part-time basis. Deering was no stranger to talent, as his new assistant at CCNY was Nat Holman of the Original Celtics. Nat's brother "Mussy" Holman was a star guard on the team as well, and Nat himself would eventually become CCNY's head coach, leading their 1950 squad to become the first and only team ever to win both the National Invitation Tournament and the NCAA tournament in the same year. By the end of the 1918–9 season, Bob's squad had improved so much that they seriously threatened St. Christopher for Colored Basketball World's Championship consideration. But his Braves ultimately lost to the Red and Black Machine, who earned a repeat title.

On February 12, 1919, the 369th Colored Infantry Regiment arrived back in New York City from France. To honor the occasion a few days later, James Reese Europe and his all-Black military syncopation band led the triumphant regiment in a parade up Fifth Avenue.[9] An estimated one million New Yorkers watched as they marched in tight formation up to Harlem, where family members, sweethearts, and children rushed into the street to embrace and march and dance alongside their hero soldiers.

But the exuberance was short lived. Within months, ignited by their own hatred and insecurity, White people would launch more than two dozen massacres of Black citizens, shedding so much blood that James Weldon Johnson would call it the Red Summer of 1919.

When aspiring poet Claude McKay wrote his stirring sonnet "If We Must Die" in response, it in effect galvanized the reclaiming of African American self-identity that had become known as the "New Negro Movement."

At the end of February 1919, Bob Douglas and his Spartan Braves, the "Green and Gold Juggernaut," faced Rush Lord and his St. Christophers at Manhattan Casino for the Black national basketball championship. "The Spartan boys started off as if they were going to slaughter the Machine," racing out to a 10–0 lead. But with "cool and steady playing," St. C. gradually crept up and eventually surged ahead, leading 18–16 at halftime. "Their accuracy in making baskets and clever teamwork bewildered their tired opponents." St. Christopher kept the lead for good, winning, 36–21. "They have practically cinched the championship, having won every game so far this season," the *New York Age* predicted.[10] Winning the 1918–9 title was an exceptional accomplishment for Rush Lord, considering that the St. Christopher Club had twice been victimized by walkouts, yet were able to rebound for two championships in a row. It was also remarkable for St. Kittian immigrant Bob Douglas to have come this far, to the title game, despite his team ultimately losing.

Now it was Will Madden's turn to test his team's post-war prowess. He was able to schedule and win a game with Howard University in March 1919, yet the event was anticlimactic because it lacked consequence. In the past, contests involving the Incorporators meant championships were at stake. But the times had changed. WWI and the boycott were costly. Little Napoleon had lost his powerful grip, and after this game, things began to go downhill. Something else besides war and sabotage had played a role, though. HAS FOUGHT HIS LAST BATTLE, read an April 1919 headline in the *Chicago Defender*, above an update about Will by the newspaper's New York City correspondent, William White. "Strange as it may seem," White shared, "when you take into consideration that he won his last battle with Howard at Manhattan Casino, Friday Evening, March 21st, Bill Madden, better known in the basket ball world as 'Little Napoleon,' has fought his last big battle and is practically dead, dead forever." White offered that although he would "venture to say that Bill has done a whole lot for the game in the East," there was another truth to be aired. Will was accomplished and successful, the correspondent explained, "but he was too smart and knew too much about the game." This, White said, "has caused his downfall."[11]

There was a difference between knowing a lot and being a know-it-all who always had to be right and have the last word, regardless of the facts or commonly understood norms. "At Manhattan Casino his best friend was the proprietor, Eddie Waldron," White explained. And although Waldron and Howard University had "stuck by Madden for years," the newspaper man revealed that "the attendance at the recent game has caused them to change their minds for 1920." It was true that spectator numbers were down, but some other underlying tension seemed to be at play. Romeo Dougherty of the *New York News* had once said, "Madden has been successful at camouflaging sporting writers." White reminded his readers of this, with his own wistful opinion on that statement: "The writer believes you were right, Romeo."

Late that year, right after Christmas 1919, White announced that the final nails in the coffin of Will Anthony Madden's basketball career had been hammered. Will, he said, "is lost to basketball forever, so far as being the prominent factor he was a few years back, when his name was known from coast to coast." The former king of Black basketball had drawn a miserable crowd on that prior Thanksgiving afternoon "against a team dug up somewhere over in Jersey," and this, White said, had "sounded his death knell" once and for all. Will had already "been in disfavor with the Gotham public" and after this latest awful showing, the *Defender* correspondent expected him to give up basketball and "solicit membership in the down and out club." If there was a single thing that led to Will's downfall, that game in Chicago against the Wabash Outlaws had been "the ending of Mr. Madden's heyday, although at that time he was not aware of that fact," White suggested. "It was the handwriting on the wall."[12]

Not fully counting him out, people were still looking forward to what Little Napoleon would come up with next. But in the 1919–20 season, his efforts were "so weak that you don't hear of him any longer," White lamented. Will was a "has-been," the sportswriter said, adding that "no one other than Bill himself is responsible for his present predicament." White wouldn't venture to elaborate, other than "there is plenty of evidence that something is and was wrong." He ended by asking, "What is it, Bill?"[13] And with that Will Anthony Madden disappeared from active involvement in basketball.

Some clues about what White was hinting at might be found in longtime *Pittsburgh Courier* columnist Floyd Nelson's bio of Will a decade later.[14] "Upon his withdrawal from activity in the basketball field, he devoted his attention to a variety of all kinds of entertainment," Nelson wrote, adding that Will coined the expression "The Art of Entertaining" and eventually became the city's "premier promoter and producer of entertainment." He had a broad repertoire, staging "carnivals, dress parades, literary and musical concerts, vaudeville shows, midsummer nights dream and that popular and most famous institution known as the 'Saturday Night Assembly,'" which, according to the columnist, was a subscription-only supper-dance with entertainment that catered to exclusive New York society. Just what the exact nature of those events was may never be known. And whether he was pushed out of basketball after losing his footing or pulled into the world of show business, was subject to speculation.

Will did reappear a year later though, with a January 1920 basketball commentary in *Competitor Magazine*, a new monthly publication for African American readers issued by *Pittsburgh Courier* newspaper cofounder Robert L. Vann. Entitled "The Future of Basketball," this column was historically significant as perhaps the most revealing glimpse into the world of early Black basketball that was ever written. Will's insights about the current state of affairs, the debate about professionalism, and the public's love of the game foretold what would prevail for generations to come.

"There are two branches of the game," he wrote, "namely, amateur and professional, and the unique part about it is the fact that both branches are so closely interwoven that it is almost impossible to separate them." But although basketball started as a purely amateur pursuit, Will noted, "the power of the dollar crept in" once clubs began generating income. "There is no power on earth that can prevent this situation," he explained, "because the very success of the thing creates the idea of commercialism, which in turn is bound to create professionalism."[15]

Will knew that amateurism was fine "for young boys" in academic settings at the high school and college level, where school spirit and ideals are often the overriding priority. But, among men who play "in the social clubs, athletic clubs, and independent teams scattered everywhere across the country," he explained, "it is entirely another proposition." Will urged that big time amateur organizations that stubbornly remained amateurs should give up their status and join the professional fold before it was too late, preferably in a league that "will not stop merely at a local formation, but will form a national league stretching from New York to St. Louis or from New York to Washington." This was the vision he had shared with Romeo Dougherty before the war. If the "brains and money of the men interested in this project" were pooled and the circuit became a reality, then, Will believed, "it will be goodbye to amateur basketball," meaning that the forces behind amateurism would no longer be able to control the game.

Will's resentment toward the Black amateur clubs of New York City was longstanding. He felt that the men behind them were self-righteous and hypocritical. They were willing to criticize professionalism, yet, Will felt, none truly adhered to the strict amateur guidelines they promoted.

Will further warned that any attempts by the amateur clubs to form their own amateur league would simply fall prey to the professional clubs, who could easily steal their best players. Furthermore, due to their financial power, pro clubs or a pro league would be in a position "to get control of the best halls, casinos and other places in all the different cities where the game would be played," he claimed, "to say nothing of buying up all the choice dates."

For the amateur clubs to change their status, though, was next to impossible. Their leaders wished to stay in control, and their charters bound most of them to remain amateur. While some of these clubs saw the advantages of going pro, most opposed a Black pro league and instead preferred their own circuit. As they saw it, Black basketball was meant to remain amateur in status, and therefore needed a governing body. As none existed, they aimed to create one.

Yet, most of these same clubs faced a major philosophical dilemma. Basketball had become the main source of revenue for their entire organizations. Not just basketball—winning basketball. In turn, there was serious competition for the best players, and, as Major Hart, Cum Posey, and Will Madden all knew, financial rewards had to be offered. "This perfecting of the team, with the strong desire to have a winning combination, is the crucial point upon which the future of basketball will depend," the former Incorporators boss astutely noted. It was "the very thing that opens up the floodgates of professionalism."

Will also pointed out the lack of cooperation between the various organizations, both pro and amateur. The teams, although closely interwoven, operated too independently of one another. They were, for the most part, only concerned about their own survival and not about the overall state of basketball. This prevented Black fives from using their sizeable collective economic leverage when it really counted. It was this lack of solidarity that Will saw as the most dangerous menace to African Americans in the game. So, he reluctantly agreed on the need for a governing body, even if that body was to be amateur in principle. A league was the answer in any case, "otherwise the unorganized condition of affairs that exist at present will surely pave the way for the disintegration of the game."[16]

Despite these calls to action by Will and by others, in 1920, even the prospect of starting a Black professional basketball league was daunting.

The main problem was "player jumping." Athletes in these leagues operated as independent contractors and often played for teams on a game-by-game basis. This gave the most talented players a strong financial incentive to play in as many games as possible, and this usually meant playing in more than one league.[17] Athletes had complete leverage over team management, selling their services to the highest bidder. This had made early all-White pro basketball leagues vulnerable because they were regional and often overlapping. Their teams were so close to one another that a player could decide, within hours of a game, for which team or even *league* he would play. Basketball Hall of Fame member Joe Lapchick, a dominant center with the New York Original Celtics, at one point in his career played in four different leagues at the same time."I played one manager against the other and sometimes got as much as $75 per game," he would recall. "No manager could count on his starting team from one game to the next, but it was not considered illegal for a player to jump from one team to another for a game," Lapchick explained. "When there was a clash of dates I took the best offer."[18] But this caused fans to lose interest, which led to smaller crowds, dropping ticket sales, and, eventually, lower salaries. It was a downward spiral because teams that couldn't afford salaries couldn't get the best players, which led to fewer fans. The regions themselves, dependent on farming or manufacturing, often faced economic uncertainty. By the beginning of the 1916–7 season, the Central and Hudson River Leagues had folded due to waning fan support, with the latter collapsing after four of its teams deserted the circuit. In their places were three new all-White leagues: the New York State League, the Pennsylvania State League, and the Interstate League, which fielded teams from New York, New Jersey, and Connecticut. But World War I interrupted their operations.

The Original Celtics were the first to solve this problem when they introduced full-season guaranteed player contracts in the late 1910s. Pro salaries were so high that a player could become legitimately affluent by most measures. By locking in their stars, the Celtics soon became one of the most dominant teams in the game, a trend that would last through the 1920s and 1930s.

Will Anthony Madden undoubtedly had observed the Celtics model closely. Other organizers in Black basketball, such as Bob Douglas, were surely also aware of the factors that led to their success. These men must have realized that the biggest obstacle to the formation of a Black professional league was that it was often better to remain independent and not join such a league in the first place. An all-Black pro basketball league would have to be financially stable enough to keep its best teams while having enough leverage over each of them to maintain order and authority.

In his commentary, Will would make any argument for why African American semi-pro clubs like the Loendi Big Five should join a league rather than remain independent. But it was understood from the times that Black unity would also be a key reason. There were men and organizations ready and able to give it a try, but history shows that no such league was ever formed.

Basketball's future, Will noted, "is safe as far as its entertaining possibilities are concerned because it is a fast open game and much more easily understood than either baseball or football." It also had advantages as an indoor game that could be played during the winter because it mixed well with music and dancing. But the visionary sports entrepreneur wondered who would ultimately control the game—"real amateurs, fake amateurs or professionals."[19] At the dawn of the Roaring Twenties, this remained to be seen.

Back in Pittsburgh, Cum Posey was making ambitious moves to begin the 1919–20 season. He called for Loendi Big Five practices to begin on October 5, earlier than any Black team had ever ventured to start, owing to the football season, and he signaled that all his players were returning. "The Gold and Blue have scheduled some of the best and fastest race teams in the country and will have to go some to emerge at the top of the heap," the *Pittsburgh Press* announced. Those included two big matchups with the repeat champion St. Christopher Club, one at the Union Labor Temple during the Christmas holidays and the other at the Manhattan Casino on January 29, 1920. These games would be for 1919–20 "colored championship of the United States," so to make sure that St. Christopher would have no complaints, Cum had the Pittsburgh branch of the AAU issue all of his players registration cards to make them officially eligible. Loendi's roster included Posey and Gilmore at forwards, Sessoms at center, and Young and Betts at guards, forming the nucleus of the powerful squad.

The first contest, before "the largest crowd that has ever witnessed a basketball game in Labor Temple," was full of action and excitement for the fans. "The easterners through dazzling floor work and brilliant passing, rushed into a lead of 13 to 2 before the local lads warmed up to the task," the *Press* reported. But eventually, the Loendis crept back into the fight and were down just one point at halftime, 23–22. Then the locals' onslaught began, with Pittsburgh outscoring New York 18–4 in the second half to win 40–27.

Anticipation was high for their rematch in New York City, just days after Prohibition had gone into effect, outlawing the manufacture, production, use, and sale of intoxicating beverages such as liquor, wine, and beer throughout the United States. Some people didn't yet realize the impact this new law would soon have on the business side of sports. But at the Manhattan Casino, Eddie Waldron knew. Like other venue operators who sold alcohol, he was about to alter, singlehandedly, the entire trajectory of Black basketball. For now, the biggest constant nagging question leading up to the contest was why these matchups were never refereed by Black officials. "Hardly any big game has been staged," wrote *Competitor Magazine*, "that has not drawn some comment as to why the white referee?"[20] The *New York Age* was asking of African American team managers, "Do they not trust their own?" Officials could earn five to twenty five dollars per game, so it wasn't the pay. The problem was that refs had to be certified by the AAU, and there wasn't a single individual who was officially sanctioned. But that changed in early 1920, when a native of Dutch Guiana (now Suriname) named Chris Rudolf "Dutch" Huiswoud became the first AAU certified basketball referee of African descent.[21]

The fact that this issue was raised meant that as African Americans evolved in the sport, their teams became so serious about the game that they demanded *official* officials, preferring White ones over Black ones. "This is certainly meant as no reflection upon the brave colored men who have tried the exacting role of a basketball referee," the *Competitor* wrote. But there was always some degree of skepticism. And there was another dynamic at play whenever a Black official showed up. "The moment he comes on the court, even to referee a preliminary contest, the young players bawl at him," the monthly magazine explained, adding that "the crowd would expect more, if anything, from a colored referee who is just starting or trying to start than from a seasoned white veteran."[22]

For his debut, Dutch couldn't have picked a more intense and pressure-packed contest than the upcoming Loendi versus St. C. matchup. This would be trial by fire. "It seemed that the entire sport loving population of Harlem, Brooklyn and New Jersey, along with a host of loyal Pittsburgh rooters" showed up for the Thursday night game. "The stage, the stairs and every bit of available room where one could get the least peek at the basketball court, was taken up long before either team made its appearance on the floor," the *New York Age* reported. The over-capacity crowd was so big that "special policemen" were required to usher each team's players out onto the court.

Loendi went through their usual psyche routine of warming up by shooting half-court shots, and "the crowd was brought to its feet in applauding the wonderful aim these stars had on the basket." Dutch started the game with a jump ball, and barely ten seconds later called a foul on Loendi. St. Christopher took an early 4–2 lead and "the Red and Black cheering squad was in tumult." But then, according to the *Age*, Pittsburgh "produced a brand of basketball seldom witnessed around these parts of the country" and began running up the score to take a 12–4 halftime lead. St. Christopher started the second half with enthusiasm until George Gilmore scored a basket, "followed by one from Posey from the center of the floor, and things began to look hopeless." Trying to respond, Coach Wetzler switched Fats Jenkins to guard Posey and subbed in Paul Robeson with the clear message for them to get tough. "Fats Jenkins deliberately punched, tripped and fell upon Posey whenever opportunity permitted and Paul Robeson seemed to think he was back on Rutgers' football team from the way he ploughed through his much smaller visitors." This tactic backfired though, because St. C. had returned from their loss in Pittsburgh complaining about "rough treatment" and promising to play clean in the return game, according to the *Age*'s sporting editor, Ted Hooks. Much worse was that the Harlem squad only "resorted to rough and unfair tactics after she saw she could not win." The Red and Black Machine lost many followers by their actions, he said, "not only the kind that is always with a winner, for they are not worthwhile, but the kind that loves good sportsmanship, which means it must be a good loser as well as a good winner." Loendi won the game, too, in a 32–15 blowout.

"We certainly congratulate Mr. Huiswoud upon his signal success in measuring up to the required standard in this Blue Ribbon clash," *Competitor* wrote afterward. "He was tried and proved equal to the occasion."[23] This game was the launch of a very successful career for Dutch.[24] For the next several years he was a fixture in virtually every important basketball game involving a Black team, traveling the country as a kind of barnstorming basketball official, becoming so famous that he was mentioned on game tickets as part of the attraction. Within a few years, Bob Douglas would hire Dutch to be the permanent "house ref" for his team, the soon-to-be-formed Renaissance Big Five, in what was to be literally a gamechanging move.

As for the Loendi Big Five, *Competitor* considered them so exceptional that, "it was hardly possible to pick a basketball team from all the colored players of the country that would have a ghost of a chance to beat that Pittsburgh five."[25] Meanwhile, the *New York Amsterdam News* tried claiming that the 1919–20 Black national championship remained with St. Christopher on account of Loendi being recently declared professionals and suspended by the AAU. Few others shared this view, and the *Age* as well as the *New York News* dismissed it as laughable.

Although the "colored" basketball title had once again eluded Bob Douglas, within only a few years he would become one of the most successful basketball managers in the history of the game. The Spartans were fast becoming "without a doubt the most popular team in New York to-day."[26] Beyond his great smile, Bob was a great manager and, as newspapers were eager to point out, "knowing how to cope with men has had much to do with the Spartan manager's success." The methodical Braves had since added the talented Frank Forbes and George "Headacheband" Capers to their lineup. Forbes was formerly with the Incorporators and Capers, named an All-Star by Will Madden, was formerly with Alpha. Bob may have found it fitting to recall the title of the song "You Can't Keep a Good Man Down," released that year by Mamie Smith as part of the first blues album ever recorded.[27] It might as well have been his theme.

In early September 1920, the Black basketball world was rocked by the loss of George B. Gilmore, who became a victim of the "White Plague" and died of tuberculosis at his home in Pittsburgh. The former star center for Howard University, the Alpha Big Five, and the Loendi Big Five was thirty-one years old. Gilmore was widely acknowledged as "the greatest negro basketball player ever turned out."[28] He had just moved to Pittsburgh a year earlier to join the Loendi Big Five on a full-time basis, where Cum Posey had set him up with a mill worker job at Carnegie Steel in Homestead. Gilmore was an integral part of the team. It was his last-second shot as a ringer in 1918 that had given

Loendi a one-point win over the Coffey Club to kick off that rivalry with the all-Jewish team.

In the Loendi's 1919–20 season finale at Labor Temple in Pittsburgh on March 25, 1920, they lost to the Coffey Club by six points, 36–30, with Gilmore in the lineup. He was already stricken by then, and this was to be his last basketball game. Although he played poorly, his exceptional athleticism concealed the illness from all but a few observers, one of them being Cum Posey himself. When it was confirmed days later, the team immediately scheduled a benefit game to raise funds for the ailing star, who was one of the squad's most popular players. Writing about that loss to the Coffey Club almost two decades later, Cum admitted he "always contended it was the totally surprising weakened condition of Gilmore, who died from lung trouble a few months later, which kept Loendi from an easy victory."

"Ye gods, there'll never be another Gilmore," the *Pittsburgh Courier* would write a few years later, still lamenting his loss and capturing the sorrow of all African American basketball fans. "Blessed memory."[29]

As the 1920–1 season approached, the future of the Alpha Physical Culture Club's basketball team was uncertain. People were writing the *New York Age* office asking, "what has to be done, what is being done or what is to be done," the paper said, adding, "Big Five of years gone by has left an immortal impression on all Negro lovers of basketball." In truth, there was a rift between Hobie Johnson and Walter Cooper, the former Incorporators stars now with the Alphas, which would soon cause Hobie to quit the team. The St. Christophers were also having "internal trouble," according to reports. Under new management, they were expected to regroup but, in a move no other club had yet dared to make, they opted out of all their dates at the Manhattan Casino "owing to the large increase in rental of that place since the dry laws went into effect." They booked the much smaller New Star Casino in East Harlem instead. But the damage had already been done.

Eddie Waldron, the Manhattan Casino owner, had built his business around providing the public with maximum mirth. Though he and his brother Louis, who passed away in 1912, had left Little Coney Island to avoid vice squad harassment there, Eddie turned a blind eye to some immoral elements that followed him uptown and took root in and around his establishment. When a Western Union Telephone and Telegraph office opened across the street from the Manhattan Casino in 1903—one of only thirteen in the city–the ready access to money wires, the small hotel on the ballroom's premises, and the venue's location away from reformers made it a prime setting for solicitation by prostitutes. Though they incurred no recorded morality violations at first, by 1911 the freewheeling brothers' establishment at 2926 Eighth Avenue had made the vice committee's "Protest List" at "Level B" status.

Trouble came in the early morning hours of September 24, 1915, at the annual Summernight's Festival hosted there by Tammany Hall's popular 11th Assembly District Leader Thomas J. McManus for his friends and supporters. While some two thousand guests danced in the ballroom and six hundred more patrons socialized in the beer garden, a fight broke out in the barroom and gunshots were fired. Two off-duty New York City policemen in the dance hall rushed to the bar, and as they fought through the crowd, more bullets flew. One hit Officer James Bishop in the shoulder and entered his lung. Another bullet struck Officer George Dapping in the head, entering his eye and piercing his brain. Both men were rushed to Harlem Hospital, where Dapping died several hours later. Bishop later recovered. A small-time White hoodlum named Thomas Bambrick was apprehended at the scene and, according to McManus, the shooting was "not the result of a political feud." Ironically, the arresting officer was charged with "failure to enforce the excise law when it was violated in his presence at the bar of the Casino."[30] Bambrick was subsequently tried, convicted of murder, and electrocuted at Sing Sing Prison in 1916.[31]

Manhattan Casino business continued to boom, as such incidents only added to the venue's notoriety. Prostitution thrived there until reformers eventually began to investigate. By 1918, they had upgraded the ballroom to "Level A," which meant Eddie's liquor license would be suspended unless he took steps in the name of "decency and order."[32] No dances could be given on Sunday nights, no girls "under, or apparently under, the age of 18" could be admitted unless accompanied by a parent or guardian, no "breaking of couples" could be allowed on the dance floor, and no waiters could "knowingly permit soliciting by immoral women in the place or offer to secure a woman for any man."

Eddie broke all of these rules within months, causing one frustrated vice reformer to complain directly to the Commissioner of the New York State Department of Excise.[33] "Considering that the vast majority of the girl patrons of the place average about nineteen years of age, at the risk of being sensational I can designate the Manhattan Casino in no other way than as a manufacturing place for prostitutes," he wrote in September 1918, "and hence I seek your co-operation in bettering conditions." He didn't have to wait long. Just weeks later, the Eighteenth Amendment to the United States Constitution was ratified, prohibiting the production, sale, and transport of "intoxicating liquors," which ultimately went into effect in early 1920 as the National Prohibition Act. After that, business at the Manhattan Casino began to dry up and the place fell into disrepair. "During an affair one rainy evening some of the dancers were drenched owing to a leaky roof," a saddened journalist wrote, adding that "the place to my recollection has not been properly heated all winter."[34] Unable to turn a profit off the sale of alcohol, Eddie had to boost the basketball rental fee from $50 to $200, and then again in 1922, up to $500, a desperate amount. "The People's Pleasure Palace" had lost its mirth. Eddie was unable to keep up his mortgage payments and would soon be forced to relinquish the individual lots of the block he controlled, one by one, until his crown jewel, the Manhattan Casino itself, went into receivership later that year. The legendary ballroom, Black basketball's mecca for over a decade, would finally be repossessed by the Dollar Savings Bank of the City of New York in 1923.

Prohibition would cause the demise of many ballrooms and saloon-style dancehalls. Their collapse would give rise to a new Prohibition-era institution that became a central ingredient to the emergence of the Harlem Renaissance: the speakeasy.

Meanwhile, the city's African American basketball managers were forced to a crossroad: rethink their business models or fold. That's why clubs like the Alphas had begun switching to other venues. Yet, an even more profound shift was needed, and this was when Bob Douglas quietly began formulating his own ideas for how to move forward.

On the evening of Saturday, January 15, 1921, a new "moving picture house" called the Renaissance Theatre celebrated its grand opening at 2341 Seventh Avenue between West 137th and West 138th Streets with "a very excellent bill."[35] The new facility, described as modern, beautiful, and spacious, gave "the colored people of Harlem" their second theater "owned, operated and controlled by members of the race," the other one being the famous Lafayette Theater, managed by Lester Walton.

Built at a cost of $175,000, the Renaissance housed an auditorium that seated 950 patrons at ticket prices of eleven cents, seventeen cents, and twenty cents for moving picture shows.[36] The venue, which could also be used for lectures and stage performances, included space for offices, six retail storefronts, and a second-story pool parlor. One of the building's shops, instantly popular, was the Dunbar Cigar Company run by Puerto Rican immigrants who had developed a new brand of cigars they named the "Dunbar."[37] Their shop contained a small newsstand while also selling cigarettes and tobacco.

The building was financed, built, owned, and operated by a Black West Indian immigrant from the island of Montserrat named William Roach. After arriving in America with practically nothing, Roach formed a business in 1918 called the Roach Cleaning Company that cleaned homes and offices. The proceeds were so lucrative that he started buying property throughout Harlem the following year. By the early 1920s, his real estate holdings included numerous multistory residential buildings uptown. These were reportedly "among the best apartments occupied by Negroes in the city." Roach's theater venture was just one of many Harlem businesses set up by Caribbean-born immigrants, who were particularly proud that one of their own was behind the effort, and whose kinship and community-based self-help networks allowed rapid assimilation for new arrivals. These social, political, and business alliances were extensive and highly effective. For example, in 1914, Roach helped found the Montserrat Progressive Society, whose purpose was to unify the people from that tiny island now living in New York City, and to assist in their social, moral, physical, and intellectual well-being. By the mid-1920s, that organization had 750 members, owned a meeting hall, and provided medical benefits.[38]

Black pride and the New Negro Movement were at their peak. African Americans eagerly supported projects like the Renaissance, advertised as the first and only theater in New York City "built by colored capital."[39] Roach had apparently learned that the first rule of real estate was location, location, and location. His building would become the northernmost anchor of Harlem's fashionable Seventh Avenue, which thrived between West 125th and West 138th Streets. And that he had called this venue the *Renaissance*, possibly after the famous Théâtre de la Renaissance in Paris, even before the New Negro Movement came to be known as the Harlem Renaissance, was quite remarkable. Remembering the 1920s years later, the African American poet Langston Hughes would remark that, back then, "The ordinary Negroes hadn't heard of the Negro Renaissance." But this theater was only the first phase of Roach's development plan. He eventually wanted to build a large two-level ballroom on the adjacent vacant lot, forming a block-long entertainment complex that featured even more shops as well as banquets, concerts, and dancing. That additional portion of the venue would not be completed for another year, but it would soon play a leading role in the evolution of Black basketball.

In an ironic twist of fate, on Friday night, January 21, 1921, two days after the grand opening of the Renaissance Theatre, a group of representatives from leading amateur basketball teams held a meeting in Harlem to discuss the formation of a league comprised of Black squads from the Metropolitan District of the AAU, a territory that included New York City, Brooklyn, and New Jersey. This conglomerate was to be known as the Metropolitan Basketball Association, or MBA. Reps from the Alpha PCC, the St. Christopher Club, the Borough Athletic Club, and the Titan Club of New Jersey were there, and Gerald F. Norman of the Alphas was elected as president. "The different clubs have expressed their willingness to join such a league in order to stamp out professionalism from this popular sport," the *New York Age* reported.[40] With confidence, the group stated that they "should have the continued support of all athletic clubs of the city, as well as the hearty support of the public." However, this would turn out to be wishful thinking.

Will Madden's insightful remarks exactly one year earlier about the unstoppable financial power of professionalism in basketball being the future of the game were ahead of their time, but not by much, and they were literally on the money. His article may even have encouraged the MBA to take action. "Professionalism has grown to such an extent," Will had warned, "that very serious talk has been made and is being made relative to the formation of a league." He believed this was "something the so-called amateur forces should have done long ago," adding that "unless they get busy on this matter they will find themselves losing ground before the rapid advance of the 'pro' ranks."[41] This new amateur association aspired to be less a league and more like the AAU, a governing body set up to control amateur African American basketball by regulating its otherwise corruptible member teams. The founding MBA clubs were the St. Christopher Club, Alpha Physical Culture Club, Borough Athletic Club of Brooklyn, St. Mark's Athletic Club of Harlem, the Titan Athletic Club of New Jersey, and the Spartan Field Club. Other all-Black clubs from the Metro District were expected to join, and by April 1921, the association was up to nine member organizations.

Under its constitution, the MBA established strict rules and regulations to prevent professionalism or even the hint of compensation within its ranks and, according to reports, the group felt it was "in position to enforce its mandates to promoters of games." Fines, suspension, or expulsion would be the penalty for failure to comply. Players were forbidden from participating in unsanctioned games and only the MBA could decide which games were sanctioned or not. This was to prevent so-called "All-Star" games over which they would have no control. No player from one member team could play for another MBA club during the same season, to prevent "jumping." Member clubs were forbidden to use any player who had been paid to play any sport, even if not basketball. Member teams were not allowed to book games with non-member clubs without the MBA's prior review and approval. "This means that Loendi, the Chicago clubs, and other such basketball clubs must satisfy the games committee that they are amateur clubs before member clubs of the M.B.A. will be allowed to book games with them," the *New York Age* pointed out, even though those were the best teams in basketball at the time.

Furthermore, it was at the MBA's sole discretion to dictate the maximum amount a player could be reimbursed for expenses, which would only include "meals, the cost of medical attention for accidents incurred while playing, and pay for the actual time lost by players." No other reimbursements or pay would be allowed.[42] Yet, as would soon be seen, the best players had other options. The MBA meant well, but their restrictions were so strict that even their own founding members found them challenging, even unrealistic. Every member team was now on high alert for any of its own players who may have been "tainted" by professionalism. The MBA's position was that each athlete was to be individually investigated at length, and they warned that the review process could be a long one. It was unclear how the investigations were to be conducted, or by whom. Still, despite the risks to their own rosters, of the amateur clubs in the New York City area were eager to join the new association. Little did they know that, exactly as Will had predicted, the forming of the MBA would spell the beginning of the end for big-time amateur club basketball.

Believing they had sorted everything out, the MBA now looked to expand the reach of their power further West, targeting the Loendi Big Five for being "a menace" to the game. But the forward momentum of the basketball was too strong to be slowed down by quibbling about amateur principles. As if oblivious to the news from back East, Cumberland Posey, Jr., and his Loendi Big Five had not lost to another African American squad in four straight seasons. Loendi's chief offense, in the eyes of the MBA, was that they were in the practice of importing players from anywhere they could, often for just one game, and that these players were compensated for their play. These allegations were of no surprise to anyone, especially in Pittsburgh. Loendi *was* a semi-professional team. Of course, since Loendi played all kinds of teams, Cum could not yet admit this openly without potentially affecting his schedule, as most amateur and college clubs booked dates with pay-for-play teams at their own risk of AAU or Intercollegiate Association sanctions. Still, his results were undeniable, and enviable too. Now the MBA was putting Loendi's violations on record. But they were really just trying to block Cum. It couldn't be done, because this was going to affect African American livelihoods far and wide, controlled by fancy proper dudes from New York City, and Pittsburgh wasn't having it.

As the 1921–2 season ended, the *New York Age* recognized the Alpha Big Five as the best MBA-certified team in the East. Bob Douglas and his Spartan Braves might have gotten that distinction had they not lost to Loendi three times. The Loendi Big Five were in the so-called West, which extended as far out as Chicago, but the *Age* seemed to ignore them.[43] The Chicago Forty Club, a new team from Bronzeville, had emerged as the strongest competition to Loendi in the West, with a roster that included Solomon "Sol" Butler, a local star athlete who had been the first Black varsity basketball player at Dubuque College. But the Forties were still no match for the Loendis.

Cum and his team were clearly the best African American squad in the country, having beaten not only the best Black fives but also many of the country's outstanding White teams while winning the 1921–2 Black national title, their third straight. Though they were a source of pride, Loendi's brand of "out and out professionalism" was feared for what it could mean to the future of amateur basketball.[44] Despite their success, many African American sportswriters felt it was an omen of bad things to come. Despite this, the team earned unshakable respect. Many years later, Romeo Dougherty, the archrival of professionalism, couldn't help but reminisce fondly about the legendary Loendi Big Five.[45] All of the Black teams in New York and New Jersey "knew of the glory awaiting them by decisively defeating that team moulded from the original Monticellos and with the toughest of steel cast in the caldrons of their own Pennsylvania," he would write. "There they stood, strong as the Rock of Gibraltar, thumbing their noses at New York and defiantly sending word from the 'City of Smoke' that they could always make the Gay Gothamites do the Pennsylvania Polka to the tune of Betts, Gilmore, Rickmond, Hall, 'See' Posey, 'Pimp' Young et al!"

Having waited all summer and then through several lengthy delays that lasted into the 1921–2 basketball season, the MBA finally issued its report on the eligibility of its players on December 12, 1921. Then, just as Will Madden had predicted, this backfired on the association's own member teams. Bob Douglas and the Spartan Braves took a major hit when their star guard, Frank "Strangler" Forbes, was refused his amateur rating on grounds that he had tried out for a professional baseball team in the off-season with intentions to play. Leon Monde, the former Smart Set star who by now played for the Borough Athletic Club in Brooklyn, was refused for the same reason.[46]

The MBA's hard line on professional sports was essentially emulating the strict guidelines of the AAU and the Intercollegiate Association of the United States. For years, these institutions had been fanatical in their efforts toward "the correction of the summer baseball evil," stating their intention was for it to be "rooted out completely."[47] Douglas was ordered to remove Forbes from the Spartan Braves roster or else be suspended from league play.[48] Monde was barred from playing with the Borough A.C. as well.

Despite the sensational headlines about the MBA's report, it was generally conceded that their sanctions would not hurt the Braves financially since they already had big games on their schedule with non-MBA teams, including the Loendi Big Five, the Pittsburgh Puritans, and the Forty Club of Chicago. Knowing this, Bob proceeded with his schedule anyway, and with Forbes on the roster. Although the *New York Age* speculated about various possible reasons for his outright defiance, the real purpose was that Bob and his team were merely trying to survive. This put the MBA in a tough spot since the St. Kittian immigrant was a well-respected and well-liked rising star in the West Indian community. Naturally, he "resented the dictatorial attitude" of the association.[49]

Finally, after a great deal of internal debate that caused several resignations, the MBA relented and allowed the otherwise well regarded Spartan Braves to continue playing. The association didn't really have any choice. But to help everyone save face, Bob promised not to use Forbes for the remainder of the season and to disqualify Stretch Sessoms, the former Paterson Royals, New Jersey Invaders, and Lincoln University star who had jumped to the Spartans mid-season from Loendi. These were crushing blows to their lineup that reduced the Braves to a second-rate team, and they went on to lose most of their remaining games. Worse, the Spartans relinquished their Eastern championship status, which had belonged to them for two seasons. Bob had been in the right place at the wrong time. But although he stayed low key for remainder of the 1921–2 campaign, the Braves manager kept at it. Bob Douglas wasn't about to disappear. In fact, he would soon use Will's predictions about the future of basketball as the template for his own future in the game.

CHAPTER 23

OUT-AND-OUTERS

AS THE 1922–3 SEASON APPROACHED, it seemed outwardly that the collective of club managers who created the Metropolitan Basketball Association had succeeded in masterminding a Black amateur basketball cartel in the New York City area. It appeared they had ensured amateurism would prevail over professionalism by securing healthy revenues for their clubs as gate receipts rolled in without concern about paying players' salaries. By attempting to make examples of even its most reputable teams that stepped out of line,—clubs like the Spartan Braves and the Borough Athletic Club—the MBA had sent a clear message that they meant business. And they blocked any clubs that couldn't prove they had *not* been tainted by compensation. The association invariably and conveniently targeted any organizations that did not want to join its cause, as well as teams that posed too much of a competitive threat to its member teams. Most of this activity was kept from the public, so ordinary basketball fans naturally believed that the MBA was acting for the greatest, highest good of the game. The association earnestly believed this too. But they didn't yet realize that New York City's traditional amateur African American basketball power structure was about collapse.

What the Metropolitan Basketball Association failed to see was that Black identity itself had been changing, giving rise to new ways of thinking that sought to untangle African American aspirations from previously accepted White standards of approval. The accommodationist views of Booker T. Washington had become old school. The vanguard was Black nationalism and economic empowerment alongside unapologetic African American cultural expression through art, literature, and music. This awakening, previously established as the New Negro Movement, had its epicenter in Harlem. And it only made sense that the natural extension of these ideas overflowed into all areas of Black business, including basketball. This is what the entrepreneurial Jewish brothers Eddie and Louis Waldron had understood so early on, making their Manhattan Casino available to African American basketball entrepreneurs before Harlem became Black.

As this was unfolding, Jess and Ed McMahon, the White sports promoters who had controlled the Harlem-based New York Lincoln Giants and New York Lincoln Stars, two popular all-Black baseball teams, decided to divest from those nines so they could pursue opportunities in boxing and wrestling. The brothers had recently opened a ballroom at West 135th Street and Madison Avenue called the Commonwealth Casino and Sporting Club. Through their earlier experiences with baseball, the McMahons knew the importance of controlling their own venue. They were also keen observers of the African American basketball world, and seeing the opportunity in the wake of the MBA's moves, they seized the moment.

Acting swiftly, the brothers organized a new all-Black basketball team named the Commonwealth Five, and they used the financial security of guaranteed contracts to lure New York City's best African American players away from their amateur squads. Just like that, the MBA was sunk. The Commonwealth Five became the first fully professional all-Black basketball team, and the first White-owned African American squad. This form of ownership arrangement was commonplace in Black baseball, so it was nothing new to Jess and Ed for the realm of basketball. Their control of the Commonwealth Casino broke the mold of reliance on venue rentals, a change that would enable higher team profits, allowing salaries at levels that had been unheard of for most players, Black or White, just as Will Madden had said. The Commons, as they were called, featured a powerful lineup that included Legs Jenkins, Fats Jenkins, and Georgie Fiall, all formerly of St. Christopher; Hilton Slocum, the former Incorporator star; George Capers, the former Alpha Big Five and Spartan Braves star, who Will had once named as an All Star"; Strangler Forbes, who had been banned by the MBA; Creed "Hops" Hubbard, a guard formerly with Wilberforce University, the Wabash Outlaws, Chicago Forty Club, and Chicago Defender Five, who was one of the best players in Chicago; and the banned Leon Monde, formerly of the Borough Athletic Club. Players were put under contract and were to be paid every two weeks during the season.

The final blow of defeat for the MBA was the formation of yet another professional all-Black squad, the Monarch Five. This was a sign of how much demand for top notch "colored" basketball existed, and how enormous the association's miscalculation had been. The Monarchs represented the local Monarch Lodge No. 45 of the Improved Benevolent and Protective Order of Elks, the second largest African American body of Elks in the city, boasting over 1,300 members, a beautiful clubhouse on West 137th Street in Harlem, and a relatively large bank account. The Monarch Elks' exalted ruler was none other than Huddy Oliver, now a prominent uptown physician better known as Hudson J. Oliver, MD.

The Elks were not ingenious, they simply jumped on the pro basketball bandwagon for a quick profit. But their lineup was as formidable as the Commonwealth Big Five roster. They signed the great Cumberland Posey, Jr., of Loendi, Stretch Sessoms, formerly of the Spartan Braves, and Ferdinand Accooe, formerly of the Smart Set, Incorporators, and of late, the Borough Athletic Club. Like the Commons, the Monarch Elks also played at the Commonwealth Casino.

The idea of a basketball governing body that could dictate amateur-only terms for member teams and place restrictions on individual players in the face of money-making opportunities was far-fetched from the beginning, because there were few if any benefits to joining. When the four all-White pro leagues that had survived the post-war years—the Pennsylvania State League, the Interstate League, the Eastern League, and the New York State League—tried to set up a governing body to control salaries, player jumping, attendance, rules-making, and dispute settlement, their efforts failed due to backlash from players.[1] By the end of the 1920–1 season, only two leagues remained: the Eastern League and the New York State League. Both of them would collapse into ruin during the 1922–3 season. Basketball was increasingly popular, but the structure of the game was a mess.

As the Roaring Twenties began, the overall economic picture for the country as a whole was prosperous, but this was not the case for everyone. In 1921, precious few Black people were in the "middle class" or held what would be considered white-collar jobs. After the end of World War I, most African American men were disillusioned by the failed promise of democracy. Thousands upon thousands of Black factory workers who had supported the war machine were systematically removed from their jobs when White soldiers returned to the labor pool. That year, a two-year-long market collapse in steel, iron, coal, cotton, and other raw materials forced many workers, both White and Black, into unemployment lines. Between 1919 and 1924, more than one million Europeans, mostly from Italy, Poland, and Russia, entered the United States along with nearly one hundred seventy-five Mexicans. The vast majority of these immigrants settled in urban areas of the Northeast and Midwest, primarily in New York and Chicago. White supervisors were all too glad to give jobs to the new White faces from overseas, who were willing to start at any level. Black and Brown workers at the bottom of this labor chain were the last hired and first fired; they now struggled even harder to support their families.

Black basketball had changed dramatically as well during the fifteen years since its introduction to African Americans by EB Henderson in 1904. The once dominant old-school Black athletic clubs had been counterbalanced by waves of ambitious and hopeful African American migrants and immigrants from the South and the Caribbean, whose numbers included new basketball talent. These players were looking to make a living off the game from day one. Although the MBA's ideals of team spirit and moral strength through amateur pursuits were valiant and important during their day, they were born in the age of muscular Christianity and physical culture, which, by 1921, were as outdated as Black accommodationism.

Ultimately, there had been few other options for the MBA to consider, as they could not very well have granted membership to pro and semi-pro teams, nor could they ask its amateur member teams to turn pro in order to attract the best talent. Had they stuck to supporting amateurism rather than going after professionals—in other words live and let live—then they might have survived. This could have resulted in a more cooperative overall arrangement where financial commitment from professional teams may have been enough to secure a permanent playing space for all the squads in the New York area, including the amateurs. The specific petty animosity toward teams like the Incorporators and Loendi had been a mistake. Finally, in the early 1920s there were not yet enough African American basketball entre-preneurs, such as Cumberland Posey, Will Madden, and Bob Douglas, who understood the game as a business. This was the same challenge that former baseball star and entrepreneur Rube Foster faced, until he finally founded the Negro National League in 1920, after having lobbied for a league as far back as in 1910. But this was more than fifty years after Black people first began playing baseball. In any case, the opportunity for orchestrating a Black pro basketball league was never riper than in the summer of 1922.

But despite all these obstacles and warning signs, and even though their teams had been gutted by the raiding of the Commons and the Monarchs, the MBA went ahead with its plans anyway, for an amateur league that was to debut with the 1922–3 season. Things did not go well, and at the end of January 1923, the official MBA standings revealed that only four league games had been played to date.[2] Bob Douglas and his Spartan Braves were conspicuously missing from them. Bob had tried to hang on and support the cause, but ultimately dropped out of the MBA to pursue his own destiny. Staying just didn't make sense. To remain in business, the Braves continued to schedule games, including one contest with a new team from the West sponsored by the *Chicago Defender*. The paper hoped to cash in on the basketball turmoil in the East while increasing its exposure and subscriptions there by forming a team called the Chicago Defender Five, which featured former Dubuque star Sol Butler and former Wabash star Virgil Blueitt.[3] Douglas's squad lost this game, standing little chance against the talented new team while the remaining five MBA member teams—St. Christopher, Alpha, Borough AC, St. Mark's AC, and Titan AC—performed poorly against approved non-league clubs, yet continued to operate.

Also missing from the MBA membership was the pioneering Smart Set Athletic Club of Brooklyn, whose basketball team had already become so weak that they were no longer competitive. Though they would continue as a viable social club, their days in athletic institution were over.

Meanwhile, Cum had played in only one game for the Monarchs to start the season. He probably joined merely for some extra cash and maybe for a bit of inside recruiting, before hastily returning to his role as manager and player for the Loendi Big Five. Stretch Sessoms was also done with the Monarchs, and Cum promptly snatched him back for the Loendi roster. The Monarchs quickly folded, becoming Black basketball's version of a one-hit wonder. Without their own court, they would have had trouble remaining profitable for very long while having to deal with the McMahons for court privileges. Bob Douglas, who had plans of his own, happily scooped up the rest of the Monarch's available players. These acquisitions breathed new life into Bob's team, and into the man himself—because right around this time, he began to be called "Smilin' Bob."

In contrast to the declining level of play and lower attendance for amateur MBA games, the management of the Commonwealth Casino expected to bring some of the best pro teams and biggest crowds, both Black and White, into their place. The Commons' season opener was against the only other openly professional African American team at the time, the Monarchs. But since the Monarchs had apparently not had enough time to practice together, Commonwealth won easily. After several more such victories, the Commons became almost invincible by adding yet another star to their lineup, the hulking Paul "Tiny" Robeson. They then began racking up wins, including a 52–24 trouncing of the Chicago Defender Five.

The Commonwealth Big Five Commons were now "the thing" in Harlem, a must-see attraction. The players themselves, who had become familiar to the public over the years and were bona fide stars, were what drew the crowds. It had taken a White-owned team to break the ice, but suddenly, professionalism in Black basketball didn't seem so bad after all. That they did not receive any criticism in the African American press or otherwise perhaps had less to do with the owners' skin color and more with their forthrightness from the inception. The Commons were never meant to be anything but pros. They were set up that way from the jump, announced publicly, and hadn't pretended to be amateurs or circumvent the AAU in order to cop lucrative dates with the big clubs. It didn't hurt either that the Black sporting public in Harlem happened to like the McMahons, who had given African American prizefighting title contenders chances to challenge White titleholders. This was something Tex Rickard had never allowed under his unwritten but well-known color ban at Madison Square Garden.

Suddenly, Black New Yorkers and their newspapers appeared to be caught up in a pro basketball craze.[4] "If they had a representative professional team of color in New Jersey, it is dollars to doughnuts the game would receive a boost in the mosquito towns," wrote Romeo Dougherty. Finally, just as Will Madden had predicted, everyone seemed to realize there was money to be made.

With a new angle this time, the *Chicago Defender* tried to capitalize on the old rivalries between East and West by splitting the Defender Five squad into two lineups, with the second one supposedly representing the East and called the New York Defender Five. The two teams then staged a "rivalry" with each other, in a game played in New York City, with Virgil Blueitt representing Chicago and Sol Butler representing New York. The "New York" team won 29–25, but the game was poorly attended because savvy fans considered it nothing more than an intra-squad scrimmage and just didn't take it seriously. The New York Defenders continued playing, though, and won three straight games, including another defeat of the Spartan Braves, proving that their first win was no fluke. The other two contests were victories over Howard and Lincoln. Though the games were financially disastrous, the New York edition of the team got praise for their auspicious start as a new squad. They had notably signed Legs Jenkins, the former St. Christopher player; Hobie Johnson, formerly of the Incorporators and Alpha; Walter "Hackie" Rhone, an up-and-coming guard who formerly played with the St. Marks Church Bears in Harlem; and former St. Christopher and New Rochelle Orientals player "Zan" Anderson. Rhone and Anderson would both be playing for "Smilin' Bob" Douglas within a year.

Around the time that the Spartan Braves went missing from the MBA standings in January 1923, the *Amsterdam News* began goading Cum Posey to arrange a three-game series between his Loendi team and the Commonwealth Big Five. Even the *Pittsburgh Courier* called for a series between the clubs, warning that the season could not end without such a matchup. Cum refused at first, it was reported, because he felt certain of defeat. A few weeks later he claimed that he had never been made an offer, although evidently a very lucrative proposition had been laid out. Then he claimed, as Will Madden would have, that since Loendi had not lost to a Black team, they retained the championship title. In reality, Cum, the consummate businessman, was simply negotiating for more favorable terms and stalling for time while he lined up the necessary ringers to ensure on-court success. But his antics backfired. As the Commons kept winning, his finessing became labeled as outright fear and eventually inspired something close to loathing. FORMER BASKETBALL STAR A MOST PATHETIC FIGURE, read an *Amsterdam News* headline after they had apparently had enough.[5]

There was more to this bitterness than just impatience over the terms for one matchup. Behind the scenes, the real reason was that Romeo Dougherty harbored a longstanding resentment toward Cum, believing the Pittsburgh prodigy was to blame for the disastrous condition of basketball in 1923. But it turned out to be even more petty than that. Romeo was still pissed about a Monticello versus Spartan Braves game at Manhattan Casino when, with time running out, a Pittsburgh "fan" snatched the timekeeper's watch and set it to zero just as the Braves were about to score the game-winning basket, sealing the victory for Cum's team. This came to be known as the "watch grabber" incident, and it almost caused a riot among incredulous spectators. Romeo never got over that, and now, a decade later, he wanted to make the Pittsburgher into a pariah.

Meanwhile, the McMahons kept cashing in. Apparently hell-bent on squeezing every last potential barnstorming dollar out of their windfall opportunity, the brothers arranged a previously inconceivable schedule of almost one hundred games for their team through only the beginning of March. Although they did lose several games, the Commonwealth Big Five had a twenty-four-game winning streak to that point and had lost only one game on their home court. By the time they played the "world famous" New York Original Celtics on March 3, 1923, the Commons were already calling themselves "Colored Champions" and went into the game with soaring confidence. It was even reported that the McMahons, flanked by a group of leading citizens, visited the New York City mayor's office to request that a legal holiday be granted if their team were to beat the Celtics. But beating a team that featured future Basketball Hall of Fame members "Dutch" Dehnert and Nat Holman would be no small task. With tickets for the game at the Commonwealth Casino selling at $1.10 each, a crowd of three thousand Black spectators with "a good sprinkling of whites" witnessed history as the Celtics beat the Commons by a score of 41–29. The game marked the first known contest between two recognized basketball world's champion teams, one all-Black and one all-White. "Although outplayed and beaten in both halves of the game," the *New York Age* reported, "the fans appeared well pleased with the showing of the colored team."[6]

In attendance at that game was Cumberland Posey, Jr., who, bowing to the considerable pressure calling for him to play the Commons, was scouting the game ahead of the potential contest with his own club. Cum knew that although Loendi had an impressive record with only one loss to that point, all claims to the title "Colored Champions" were still up for grabs. Having avoided a game with the Commons all season long, Cum, perhaps spotting a weakness, was now convinced of the possibilities of head-to-head competition. He quickly scheduled a two-game home-and-home series with the McMahon brothers, to be played only if certain conditions were met. Black newspapers in New York City ridiculed Cum's terms as outrageous and self-serving. But he was a businessman, a shrewd negotiator with supreme confidence and a well-known chip on his shoulder. Cum had laid out fourteen conditions regulating everything from referees to gate receipts to game time, all in service of protecting the Loendi Big Five and their business interests. Audaciously, he even included a clause forcing terms for games to be played the following season. All of this was in print for the public to see. The fact that Cum was dictating the terms, essentially strong-arming a White-owned team, was unprecedented, but it was what a businessman with leverage was supposed to do. His open letter to Jess McMahon calling out the Commons owner for working the press and interfering with his schedule, which he cheekily excused because it was the McMahons' "first year in basketball," would have been inconceivable as well as possibly suicidal had it been published in the South. But it was moves like this that made Cumberland Posey, Jr., a debonair hero, because, at the end of the day, the letter ultimately illuminated his diplomacy in getting everyone on the same page.[7]

This was proven when the Commonwealth Sporting Club owners bowed to Cum's conditions, not because they were naïve but because they knew the road to the mythical Black basketball championship went through Pittsburgh and Loendi. There was no choice but to deal with Cum. But this is where the Homestead hero so thoroughly outshone others. Quietly, amid all the chaos around the terms, there was one condition that seemed innocent on its face but in fact would be the difference between winning and losing. Cum told the McMahons that the games would be played under intercollegiate rules, which the Commonwealth Big Five players had been playing under "all their life," and the owners bought it. The Commons usually played under professional rules that still allowed the double dribble, which required a completely different strategy and preparation, especially on defense, than when playing under college regulations. Teams that weren't used to this were more likely to be unprepared and play out of sorts for most of the early part of a game. The intercollegiate rules also created a more wide-open game, giving Loendi's quicker, faster men a decided advantage. Perhaps overconfident, or "new to the game" as Cum had put it, the McMahons somehow agreed to this condition for both games.

Romeo Dougherty didn't waste any time making fun of "Posey's Fourteen Points," but his relentless antagonistic position toward Cum merely revealed the sportswriter's grievances, not to mention his contempt for business, negotiation, and strategic advantage.

Finally, the haggling had been completed and all eyes were on the Loendi-Commonwealth series. Pittsburgh papers predicted victory for Loendi, while New York whipped up frenzy among Commonwealth followers, with the *Amsterdam News* even guaranteeing its readers that it would be first with the news of the results. Giving a new meaning to the term "newsflash," the *New York News* even promised it would flash a red light in the windows of its office building on Newspaper Row across from City Hall if Loendi won the game, and a blue light if the New Yorkers won.

Adding to the anticipation, in their last game before their series with the Commons, Cum's team lost a game to a little known all-Black team representing the John Roan American Legion Post in Xenia, Ohio. "We wonder if the American Legion Five which defeated the Loendi team of Pittsburgh last week will now be referred to as 'world's champion'," Romeo asked derisively. "They make me laugh."[8]

But unfortunately for the locals, that blue light never did come on, because Loendi crushed the Commons not once but twice, by scores of 51–27 in Pittsburgh and 43–33 in Manhattan. These results were so astounding that they caused a sensation. The ever-present *Age* exclaimed, "all doubt as to which team is colored champion of the world was dispelled."[9] Loendi played a faster and "more scientific" game. Cum had done his homework on that scouting trip; this is what separated him from other managers. He got the last laugh.

Then again, Romeo perhaps still got the last laugh, stating publicly that after realizing what rules would be used, he immediately put out the word, bragging that "those who ordinarily bet on these games took our hint and very few dollars were put up on the event."[10]

But there was one other thing about Cum: His pettiness game was savage.

When the McMahons scheduled one last game, against the Original Celtics for a prize of $1,000, the famed barnstorming team was favored, having beaten the Commons once already. To improve their odds, the brothers announced a secret weapon. Trying to be slick themselves, they had signed Stretch Sessoms to play for them against the Celtics, a move made possible since the Loendi season was over. But when game time arrived, Stretch never showed up, and Commons forward Fats Jenkins suddenly fell ill. A lot of Commonwealth fans, and probably Romeo Dougherty too, lost money that night. Cum had the last laugh after all. More importantly, his Loendi Big Five won the Colored Basketball World's Championship for the 1922–3 season, undisputed, and their fourth such honor in a row.

CHAPTER 24

THE NEW NEGRO

BY THE SUMMER OF 1923, the African American cultural renaissance in Harlem was well underway. It was a period of tremendous change and expression. W. E. B. Du Bois had helped plant the seeds for this flourishing back in 1903 with the publishing of his classic work *The Souls of Black Folk*, and he then inspired further progress with the launching of the Black activist magazine *Crisis: A Record of the Darker Races* in 1910. The collective effort behind the idea of the "New Negro" was a concerted attempt to change White stereotypical views of "colored folks" as "sambos," "mammies," and "pickaninnies" that had pervaded and prevailed for decades.

There was also a gradual expansion of sociological factors significant to African Americans that led up to the 1920s, which included the formation of the NAACP, the Pan African Congress, the Universal Negro Improvement Association, the Associated Negro Press, the National Negro Baseball League, and the first Black-owned motion picture and record companies. These were closely linked to an explosion of economic opportunities as well.

But if "ordinary Negroes" didn't yet know what was going on, as Langston Hughes would say, then White people in Harlem knew it even less, including Ed and Jess McMahon, owners of the Commonwealth Sporting Club. While the brothers were no strangers to attracting Black patrons for their Harlem venue, it was simply a business to them, and they were just as eager to seat increasing numbers of White visitors from downtown who might want to begin their uptown evenings with a Commonwealth Big Five basketball game.

So, it only made sense that leading up to the 1923–4 season, the McMahons began referring to the Commons as "New York's only colored professional team." The brothers announced they had strengthened the squad by signing

Stretch Sessoms, the "crack" center who evidently finally did show up, and Pappy Ricks, both formerly of the Loendi Big Five. The organization was well run, their drawing potential now commanded considerable respect with other big-name teams, and they had already scheduled a five-game series with the New York Original Celtics. Their openness about professionalism inspired other African American basketball managers to give the pro ranks a try—so many that some wondered if this "professional craze" was going too far. One paper advised its readers that it was "still looking upon some of the would-be teams as the huge jokes they will turn out to be before the end of the next basketball season."[1]

Basketball was just as much a part of the cultural awakening of African Americans as any other aspect of the blossoming of Black self-identity and expression that was happening, not just in Harlem but throughout America. Yet no one was hearing anything from the old amateur clubs anymore, nor did people know what those early programs would do now that the basketball landscape was changing. The *Age* hoped, perhaps in a bout of wishful and wistful thinking, that "certainly there is room for an organization which offers wholesome recreation to the growing boys of the community, which at the same time aids in the development of their bodies."[2] The irony of this statement was not lost, for the pursuit of muscular Christianity and physical culture, not big time revenue producing basketball programs, was exactly why the original pioneering African American athletic clubs were formed in the first place. But in 1923, those ideals were out of place, having lost much of their relevancy. A few of the early amateur clubs did remain on the scene with track and field teams, including St. Christopher and Salem-Crescent. But their basketball teams were practically nonexistent, getting very little press and insignificant crowds.

One man never believed that the professionalism craze in Black basketball had gone too far. He was the thirty-nine-year-old St. Kittian immigrant Bob Douglas. After reportedly nearly quitting basketball, Bob was "uncovered by his friends and brought back." He had been waiting and watching patiently for an opportunity to return to the game, or rather for the game to come to him.[3] It had to be a certain way. So when the Spartan Braves leader resurfaced in October of 1923, it was with a bold plan. Bob had observed the business and marketing model the McMahons were using so successfully with the Commonwealth Big Five, and now he intended to duplicate their success while staging his own epic comeback. It was more like a takeover. He was confident about creating an equally successful team and encouraged by the support of many friends who believed in his vision and abilities. Bob would make one slight modification to the template created by the McMahons, though. He insisted that his team, like the Renaissance Theatre, be "built by colored capital and owned and managed by colored people." This was the small but major detail that the McMahons could not have seen coming.

Bob first secured the loyalties of a few former Spartan Braves players, now on the Commons, with whom he had kept in contact. One of them was Frank Forbes, and he was willing to jump back to Douglas's new venture if Bob could match his pay from the McMahons. Forbes was disgruntled and set to leave anyway, ever since the owners stripped him of his team captaincy the previous season. The Strangler had created his own problems with the Commons, though, when he refused to bench himself in favor of Leon Monde, who was a better player at that position and whom the public demanded to see. It was felt in Black basketball circles that Forbes should have bowed out and run the team from the sidelines in as big a fashion as he had played the game. The *Amsterdam News* even made their assessment known, writing, "This is a professional outfit and not an amateur aggregation and no man is big enough in professionalism to refuse to heed the calls of an insistent public, for with them it is business first."[4]

In contrast to his intimidating nickname, Forbes was known off the court as a courteous, charming gentleman. His career in sports would last well beyond basketball, as he would become involved in Negro League baseball as an umpire, coach, manager, and promoter before pursuing an interest in boxing. Strangler would be so persistent with the ring sport that he eventually became the first African American member of the New York State Boxing Commission as a referee, officiating many important fights including the Joe Louis–Billy Conn heavyweight bout in 1946. By the 1950s, he would be so well regarded as a sports ambassador that when Willie Mays moved to Harlem after joining the New York Giants in 1957, Forbes became his mentor.

Leon Monde, the other former Spartan on the Commons, was already available to Bob Douglas because he had been let go allegedly on account of one too many "beefs" with referees, and the McMahons did not want such a source of distraction on their team. The *Amsterdam News* could say only that Monde "was not fully alive to what harmony means."[5] In truth, that was likely just a pretext, because he wasn't getting much playing time anyway and it didn't make sense for the owners to carry his salary.

Regardless of the drama, Bob wanted Forbes and Monde anyway. He struck deals with the players in principle but secretly lacked the funding to provide his prospective lineup with competitive professional salaries. He also lacked control of a home court where the Braves could play. For years, the only affordable "big-time" basketball venue in New York City had been the Manhattan Casino, but Eddie Waldron had jacked up his fees by 1,000 percent. And the Commonwealth Club was unavailable, being the McMahons' own home court.

Bob was resourceful, though, and unstoppable. He had the close-knit West Indian community of Harlem at his disposal, which enabled him to approach William Roach, the owner of the Renaissance Theatre, with a win-win idea. By then, Roach had opened the second phase of his entertainment complex, the Renaissance Casino, which he built adjacent to the theater at the corner of Seventh Avenue and West 138th Street. The new structure contained a ballroom, which Bob envisioned as the Spartan Braves' new home court. He asked Roach for permission to use that dance floor for basketball, offering him a percentage of the ticket sales. The building owner at first rejected the idea, fearing that the "rough" play of basketball might wreck his establishment. So, as a clincher, Bob offered to rename his team after the new facility to help promote it far and wide. Roach agreed, and that's how the Renaissance Big Five basketball team was born.

With that venue deal in hand, Bob had all the necessary ingredients for financial viability and promptly offered his prospective new players full-year, full-time contracts, making the New York Renaissance Big Five the first Black-owned, all-Black, openly professional basketball team in history.[6]

After learning of these plans, the *Amsterdam News* was impressed, writing "we are forced to believe that another bona fide professional team will soon be going on the court."[7] Bob was well liked, his reputation was impeccable, and having come from the amateur ranks, he was instantly adopted as a shining example of the upstanding, principled, talented people that could be developed at that level. By coming to the papers and openly announcing his plans to field a professional squad, Bob had taken a page from the McMahons' playbook to sidestep any potential criticism. Sure enough, Romeo Dougherty, the longtime critic of pay-for-play, did an about-face for his fellow West Indian countryman, writing, "If we must have professionals, let them be out and outers." From that point on, Black newspapers encouraged their readers to attend Renaissance Big Five games, and Bob's new team was immediately dubbed the "Big R" Five, later to be called simply the "Rens."

At first, the New York Rens lineup was labeled as "not so formidable as the Commonwealth." Their initial players included Forbes, Monde, and another former Commons star, the young center Hilton "Kid" Slocum, as well as Walter "Hackie" Rhone and Zan Anderson, both formerly with the now defunct Chicago Defender Five. One more talented young player, Harold "Hal" Mayer, was committed but had not yet come to terms with the Rens' owner. In one further move, Bob hired the popular AAU referee Chris Huiswoud as the Rens' official referee. With players, an official, and their home court in place, the West Indian basketball entrepreneur began to build a schedule. Among his intended victims were the McMahon brothers and their Commonwealth Five.

The McMahons, in the meantime, got right back into it with Cumberland Posey, stating publicly that the crowd attracted to the prior season's Loendi game was not big enough to warrant bringing them to New York again for a game this season. Games with White teams were attracting enough spectators, they claimed, so they didn't need the expense of bringing a team from Pittsburgh.

For many African Americans, direct competition with Whites through sporting events was perhaps the only healthy, constructive outlet for pent-up frustrations and despair that would not go away. The forthright *Amsterdam News* even commented, "mixed basketball, like mixed bouts at the Commonwealth, will do much to keep up the interest, at least, of the colored fans."[8] To put their money where their mouths were, the McMahons announced that the very popular and talented Coffey Club of Pittsburgh, Loendi's archrival in Western Pennsylvania, was booked to play the Commons in New York. It may not have occurred to the brothers they would likely have to play Loendi to claim the championship title. To clarify matters, Cum wrote a letter to Romeo Dougherty, who published it in the *Amsterdam News*.[9]

October 7, 1923

Dear Sir:

Despite rumors, hopes and fears, Loendi will be on the court this basketball season. Each season Loendi is threatened by opposing all-star organizations, but the result is "a new star uncovered by Loendi."

We are leaving the once-a-week realm of basketball behind. This season Loendi will tour Ohio and Indiana, playing once a week in Cleveland and every other Wednesday in Detroit. Celtics will be met at least ten times this season in various Ohio cities.

The makeup of the Loendi team this season is a small item. We will still have the same backbone which has carried us successfully over six campaigns. We have three undisputed All-American men in Young, Posey, and Capt. Betts, and the best utility players in the game in Pete Johnson and Jimmy Gayle. Edwards, the former Puritans and Hampton star, will arrive in Pittsburgh from the Pacific Coast this week. U.S. Young of Lincoln University, the present coach of Lincoln, will appear in all of Loendi's home games and all games against colored clubs. Despite rumors to the contrary, Pappy Ricks has signified his intention of playing with Loendi. It can be safely said that Loendi will have either Ricks, Fiall, Moton, or Slocum to line up with the before-mentioned men.

Loendi has been signed to appear in New York twice this season, which will probably be their only Eastern appearance.

I hope your position this season will not be so antagonistic to Loendi, who, after all, are the undisputed "champs."

Yours,
C. W. Posey, Jr.

This almost seemed as though Cum was informing the New York public of his intentions to steal one or more of their players. They were probably on his wish list, though he must already have known about Slocum's signing with the Renaissance Five.

Back in New York, in addition to the Coffey Club, the Commons set up an ambitious schedule that included the mighty Madison Square Whirlwinds (also known that season as the Italian Catholic Club), lined up for a three-game series. The Whirlwinds at the time were the only team in the New York area that challenged the Celtics for dominance and popularity. At the end of the 1920–1 season, the Whirlwinds had split a two-game series with the Celtics to decide the unofficial championship of the New York area and had drawn eleven thousand fans. Two weeks later, the Celtics signed two of the Whirlwinds biggest stars, Nat Holman and Chris Leonard, who then played as Celtics for the following season.[10]

So, when they met the Commons in 1922–3, the Whirlwinds were not what they used to be, but they were good enough to hand the Commons their first defeat of the season, 33–26. The Whirlwinds' strong passing attack was credited with the victory. A couple of weeks later, the Commons lost to the Whirlwinds again, 29–28. Despite the losses, these were considered decent showings against a very good team.

Yet some still felt that the McMahon team's chemistry was not clicking. It had been known for some time that Stretch Sessoms wasn't at his best and did not quite fit in with the Commonwealth team. "There are tricks of the trade," the *Amsterdam News* felt, commenting on the former Loendi player, "which Posey injected into the men surrounding him that seem to leave them at a loss when they are not in the Loendi lineup and that is the obstacle that Sessoms will have to study hard to overcome."[11] So the McMahons and Sessoms's teammates were relieved when he finally decided to quit, returning to Pittsburgh to play for Loendi. "Specs" Moton, a forward, also quit the Commons and left for Loendi, but his departure was criticized since he never formally resigned. With Moton, whom he had named in his letter to Dougherty, Posey once again had gotten his man. Still, the McMahons must have been pleased, since they no longer had to pay those players' salaries.

After rehabilitating their lineup, the Commons team vibe evidently improved, and they quickly won several subsequent games, including two on the same day over the Hudson County Five of Hoboken, New Jersey, an all-White squad. In fact, the guys must have gotten along pretty well because several of the squad's players, it was reported, showed up at a surprise birthday party for Fats Jenkins, thrown by his wife in Harlem.

During this time, the Commonwealth Big Five began to adopt the rapid passing attack on offense used by Cum Posey. This style of play was apparently still rarely seen outside of Pittsburgh. One paper noted that the Commons "displayed some of the form exhibited two weeks ago [. . .] by passing the ball up and down the court in criss-cross fashion. This style made a hit with the fans and they applauded generously."[12]

They continued their streak by beating the Whirlwinds for the first time on December 22 by a score of 26–19. This victory was just what the McMahons needed to boost public interest (and gate receipts) for the Commons upcoming contest in February against the Original Celtics, who had by then won 108 of 110 games they played that season.

When the Celts came to the Commonwealth Casino, three thousand fans were disappointed as the world's champion White team, playing with future Hall of Fame members Joe Lapchick, Nat Holman, and Dutch Dehnert, beat the Commons 40–28.

The Rens, in the meantime, started the season winning their first game ever, against the all-White Collegiate Five, and lost only once through the beginning of December. By mid-season, people were calling for a game between Harlem's new neighborhood rivals, Commonwealth and Renaissance, whose home courts were only a few blocks apart. By the end of February, uptown basketball wishes came true when Bob got dates to play the Commonwealth Five in a three-game series for the championship of New York, the first matchup to be set at the Renaissance Casino on February 24. It was a sign of things to come that Douglas was able to get his first game date with the Commons at the Renaissance instead of at the McMahons' rival Commonwealth Casino. When the teams finally met, the short, slippery court at the Renaissance Casino probably benefited the Rens at first, much as Howard University and then the Twelfth Streeters had found an advantage with their peculiar floor at True Reformer's Hall more than a decade earlier. The *Age* explained the playing conditions:

Renaissance Casino was never meant to be a basketball court as the floor was slippery as ice. More than one player found himself sprawled on the floor as he tried to get away from an opposing player. Another bad feature, and one that was to cause groans from both sections, was the construction or rather the erection of the baskets. They were shaky, and frequently time had to be called to allow the supports to be tightened. Many otherwise good shots were spoiled when the baskets swayed as the ball was thrown. These defects were overlooked by the fans who were enjoying the game too much to take these details into consideration.[13]

Despite the Rens home court advantages, the Commons prevailed and won with a score of 38–35. But the game was very evenly matched and, with such a performance against a first-class team, everyone present felt that the Rens had arrived in the big time. The game also drew a large crowd of about three thousand, which was of primary interest and importance to Robert Douglas. In the return game at the Commonwealth Casino in front of the largest crowd of the season, the Commons won again, this time more convincingly, 31–21.

By then, the biggest news coming from the amateur ranks was a fabulous grand reunion held by the old St. Christopher Club. Dozens of current and former members of the club as well as other special guests met up at the St. Philip's Parish House in Harlem, where "songs, cheers, smokes, and rousing talks completely captivated the happy gathering."[14] Among other things, a committee was formed whose goal was to revive the spirit of the old club, which had been out of action for several years. Romeo Dougherty was there and made a rousing speech, as did Charles Bradford, the old center who was chairman of the new committee. A further comment on the event revealed the conflicting activities that were apparently considered good, clean, healthy fun in those days.

After the dinner a basketball game was held in the gym, and smokes were abundant. Between halves of the game many of the old timers swarmed upon the floor and after teaming off, delighted themselves at a rough little game of "muscle-stiffening."

Will Madden had been invited to the reunion, but newspapers didn't
mention whether he attended. The former St. Christopher and Incorporators
manager was keeping a low profile during this period, which may have been
a wise choice. A year earlier, Romeo Dougherty was still openly voicing his
disdain for Will.

> Madden was driven from basketball years ago and he could
> not today find three colored boys who would play under his
> management. The other day the "Little Napoleon" for whom
> we found a St. Helena after furnishing him with his Waterloo,
> expressed a desire to return to the game via managing the Com-
> monwealth team and this raised such a laugh among the players
> they almost lost a game, suffering with cramps from the effects
> of Madden's desire.[15]

Meanwhile, there were two new African American squads of note that
emerged "out West," the Cleveland Acmes and the Eighth Regiment of Chicago. After many years as a sporting town, the city of Cleveland was finally
getting more serious about its Black basketball. The Acmes were one of the
main reasons Cum Posey had scheduled so many visits to Cleveland for his
Loendi team.

The Eighth Regiment of Chicago, the "colored" infantry battalion of
the Illinois National Guard, formed a strong team that would soon take the
national spotlight. The "Fighting Eighth," as they were known, played their
home games at the huge Eighth Regiment Armory on Giles Avenue at Thirty-
Fifth Street in Bronzeville. Its lineup included Sol Butler and Virgil Blueitt,
both formerly of the Chicago Defenders, and Wu Fang Ward, an illustrious
former star in basketball and football at Wilberforce University.

Toward the end of the season, Loendi visited Chicago to face the Eighth
Regiment. The game took on great meaning, since the championship of the
West was at stake and a win by Chicago would eliminate Cum's team from title
consideration. Though the Loendis were considered unbeatable, they were
defeated 29–22 in what was hailed as the biggest upset in Chicago's "colored"
basketball history, in front of almost one thousand spectators.

Despite the win, there were still some doubts as to the Eighth Regiment's
championship claims. In order to remove those doubts completely, they still

had to play and beat another local team, the Evanston Big Five, who also had an outstanding record and who were tied in their series with the Regiment team that season. To settle the question, a tiebreaker game was scheduled for April, which the Chicago team won.[16]

Back in New York, the Rens' final game of the season was a one-sided victory over the St. James Crowns, 33-28. Despite their nice start, the Rens ended the season with a 15-8 record. Overall, Bob Douglas's inaugural 1923-4 season was relatively basic, not only in their record but also in the number of games they were able to book. The Rens played only twenty-three games, compared to other top teams such as the Celtics and Commons, who played upwards of one hundred games a season. Yet, Bob must still have looked up and seen the whole basketball universe in front of him. The Roaring Twenties had begun. Upper Manhattan was in the middle of an explosion of Afro-centric culture that would be called the Harlem Renaissance. Black leaders and business-men advocated a "buy from your own" policy of economic self-empowerment. Sadly, the heyday of amateur African American basketball was over, replaced by Black professionalism. But, Smilin' Bob was finally in sync. In fact, he was aligned with the stars.

The Commons had the best record among Black fives in the East, and the Eighth Regiment had the best record in the West, but they had not played each other, so the 1923-4 season may have ended in a tie.

The 1924-5 season started with a shock in Pittsburgh when the esteemed Loendi Social and Literary Club announced it would no longer sponsor a basketball team. This stunning turn of events suddenly left Cum Posey with-out a backer.

In an article headlined DISBANDING OF LOCAL FIVE, WORLD CHAMPS, CRE-ATES SENSATION, the *Pittsburgh Courier* reminisced about the greatness of the Loendi Big Five, singling out the 1920-1 season during which not one player missed a single practice.[17] But the column implied that the team had lost some of its form as a result of revelry—Cum himself was apparently well known for it—and the criticism was harsh. Although they had lost the edge against some of their stronger White opponents like the Coffey Club, Loendi had won four championships in a row, and they probably deserved their share of celebration and good cheer.

In what was more likely the reason for the withdrawal of its support, the Club charged it had lost money on the squad during the last season, likely the result of decreased attendance. Pittsburgh, being as far away from the other popular clubs as it was, simply could not attract enough important game dates to pay the bills. The *Courier* went on to observe that the basketball situation in Pittsburgh was not lucrative enough to support a team made up of full-time athletes, noting that the best teams of the past were composed of players who worked daily at other regular jobs. Cum's players had evidently been asking for more money than the social club could afford. But instead of questioning the validity of the business model that the Loendi Club had chosen to use, or even questioning Cum's leadership skills in selecting talent that would ulti-mately make such demands, the *Courier* instead blamed the team's demise on the players themselves. They had failed to be self-supporting on their own, the paper wrote.[18] Cum's efforts though, were precisely to make his players financially sound through basketball. Perhaps the Black press in Pittsburgh did not clearly understand the business of the floor game, even with examples from baseball's Negro Leagues from which to learn.

The McMahons certainly understood the basketball business, but the Commonwealth Five were also on the verge of failure—their gate receipts had been dwindling since the prior season. The new campaign had barely gotten underway, when reports emerged that the Commons were under new management and would play their remaining games at the Palace Garden on Seventh Avenue at West 140th Street in Harlem.

The cause of the Commons impending failure was not obvious, but speculation focused on their repeated inability to beat the best White rival teams such as the Celtics and Whirlwinds. With disappointing losses such as those, the public's enthusiasm declined. The McMahons had failed to real-ize that to keep the Black sporting public's interest—and therefore remain profitable—African American basketball teams had to win against White teams as well as the top Black fives. As was well known, opponents had to be chosen wisely and local loyalties had to be painstakingly built before the public would embrace a team.

But there was something else even more compelling working against the McMahons: competition from Bob Douglas and the Renaissance Ballroom itself. Although the Rens did not have an outstanding record during their first season, Bob's partnership with William Roach had been profitable. Within a few months of launching, the Rens were taking large numbers of spectators away from the McMahons and their venue.

The team owner's formula for success was simple. As a Black resident of Harlem, he was part of the community and was more able to get a read on what his audiences desired than were Jess and Edward McMahon. Just like Cum and Will before him, Bob realized that the public wanted more than just basketball, they craved entertainment. Harlem in 1923 was a cabaret society in the jazz age. The entertainment that its residents, as well as White visitors, wanted most was music and dancing. Douglas's secret formula was simple. So, instead of staging two basketball games, as the Commonwealth and most other clubs had done in the past, the Renaissance Casino offered only one game, with festivities added as a powerful draw. "Good orchestral music, an occasional song, Charleston contests, and uncensored dancing are the features," explained the *New York Age* in describing the nightly action at the Renaissance.[19] The key word was "uncensored," as Harlem had become a frolicking, teeming nightclub scene. So much so, that the conservative *Age* couldn't help but add, "This writer has no objection to this form of entertainment for grown ups but he does believe that it is bad for the children and there were at least 200 boys around 14 and 15 years of age in the hall."

Despite losing his sponsorship backing, Cum was determined to stay in the game. At first, he named his new team Loenda, then *Leondi,* in order to capitalize on the fame he had developed over the years using the Loendi name. Even the newspapers were confused for a while, and, although they might have preferred that he had gone back to using the old Monticello name for sentimental reasons, they were supportive of the plan, since, as far as basketball, it was the players who'd brought fame to the name, not the Social Club.[20]

Without the same financial backing, Cum tried lowering the team's salaries and his overhead while increasing revenues. His goal was to sign only local players, reckoning that out-of-town talent simply cost too much to entice, to move, and to accommodate. He also sought to attract more spectators by hiring a new band for his games—Billy Page's Broadway Syncopators—and added one hundred new bleacher seats to the Labor Temple. Cum also hired a dedicated publicity manager, Harry Washington, who must have been effective because the press was abuzz with the news of these moves. It *was* news, because Pittsburghers loved their great basketball teams, and Cum promised a roster of "topnotchers." In a final action, Cum patched things up with his old friend Sellers Hall and installed him as team manager. In wishing them well, the *Courier* waxed, "To Loenda we tilt the battered and dusty felt and bespeak the new organization all the success and none of the ill-fame, which was a portion of the old."[21]

Meanwhile in Manhattan, Bob Douglas suddenly had a windfall opportunity on his hands with the decline of the Commons. He now set his sights on doing to the Commonwealth Five what they had done to him two seasons earlier: raid their remaining players. As news of his professional innovations in Black basketball spread, Bob systematically signed one formidable ex-Commons star after another, adding to Forbes, Slocum, Mayer, and Monde, whom he had already signed, Fats Jenkins, Georgie Fiall, and Pappy Ricks. In addition, the Rens' owner picked up utility players Hy Monte and Louis "Six" Garcia. All of this amounted to a coup, having signed the best Black players from the New York area. These were proven stars, and they formed the nucleus of the Rens for the next several years, giving Bob a solid foundation on which to build. Soon afterward, the once-dominant Commonwealth Five team was forced to fold, as they were no longer able to remain competitive.

At first, Pittsburghers failed to recognize the Rens' newfound strength, and in a bit of wishful thinking the *Courier* suggested that the squad was not even as impressive as the previous season's Commonwealth Five team—even though in effect the Rens *were* the old Commons. But Douglas knew what he was doing, and his squad promptly started the 1924–5 season with a win over the all-White Newark National Turners, who billed themselves as "New Jersey champions."

Meanwhile, Loenda won its first contest, 49–22 over a local Homestead team. In the game a new player, Sammy Hampton, formerly of Oberlin College, emerged as a star at center when he hung up Loenda's first seven "two-markers." Although they had the same familiar faces as the prior season, it was explained to the crowd before the contest that the new Loenda team had nothing whatsoever to do with the Loendi Social Club. In their next game, now playing as Leondi, Cum's team trampled another all-White team, the

Attawa Club of Homewood, 72–23. So far, it appeared that the naming trick had worked, as these two games easily outdrew the first two contests of the previous season.

Then on December 23, 1924, at Clarksburg Auditorium in Clarksburg, Virginia, Leondi beat the Clarksburg Five, 42–18, in what was thought to be the first game ever played between a Black five and an all-White team below the Mason-Dixon line. No incidents were reported. Clarksburg's squad was made up of former West Virginia University players and had Don Potter, an ex-Carnegie Tech star, at guard. Leondi's one-sided victories did not seem to keep their opponents from trying to triumph. In one game in Erie, Pennsylvania, they suffered their first loss of the season when the St. Moske's Cadets made an improbable half-court shot with no time left on the clock to win by one point, 29–28.

About midway through the 1924–5 season, it became apparent to Cum that the Labor Temple was no longer the best place to play. The hall was worn down after fifteen years of use and taken its toll on the grand structure. Spectators openly complained about the cleanliness of the place—and the three flights of stairs that had to be scaled in order to get to the court. Furthermore, the Labor Temple's location in the lower Hill District, where living conditions had deteriorated dramatically, was considered a problem. Even the newspapers called for Leondi to move, insisting that the city's Black citizens simply did not want to see games there.

CHAPTER 25

CHICAGO CRUSADERS

EVEN THOUGH WENDELL PHILLIPS HIGH School in Bronzeville had become Chicago's first predominantly Black high school during the mid-1910s, their varsity basketball team had only two African American players on its roster for the 1919–20 season. Reginald Waddell and Adolph Simms, Jr., were starters and would travel with the squad, but not without friction. After a February 1920 loss to nearby Tilden Technical High School, an all-White rival also on the South Side, "the Phillips five found every exit jammed with Tilden students and outsiders who were intent on giving them a beating," the *Chicago Defender* reported. Someone in the Tilden mob allegedly "drew a knife and threatened to use it on Waddell and Simms for coming to their gym."[1] One of the White players on Phillips had to call the local stock yards police, "who responded and escorted the team to safety." The presence of two Black athletes on a Phillips varsity roster was seen as progress, since the school had been continually making headlines for the racist policies of its White principal, Charles H. Perrine, who famously tried enforcing "Jim Crow" seating arrangements at WP's commencement exercises that year. By then, folks had had enough. So many complaints were sent to the city's board of education that Perrine was removed from his principalship.[2]

Something else was plaguing Wendell Phillips. The school's once-mighty athletic standing "seems a thing of the past," a *Chicago Defender* columnist complained. One of the issues was funding, since the most that schools were allowed to charge for admission to games was twenty-five cents. Another reason was just plain civic disinterest. "Last fall when the coaches issued a call for football candidates, only nine reported," the journalist said.[3] But the basketball situation at the school was completely different. A slow and steady influx of young up-and-coming African American players that had been matriculating into Phillips was about to reach a critical mass on the roster of its junior team.

At the beginning of the 1920–1 season, Bronzeville was eager for more Black basketball. And since the Wabash YMCA Outlaws had disbanded after World War I, their former coach and manager, Dr. Albert Johnson, organized a new African American squad called the Forty Club, which was sponsored by an exclusive Black social organization in Chicago of the same name, for which he served as president. This squad was essentially the old Wabash Outlaws team, with many of its former players, including All Cook County star guard Virgil Blueitt as captain, forward George Duff, who had since made the All-State team while attending Illinois State Normal School, and Thornton Winters of Englewood High. They also had key new players Sol Butler, who had made the 1920 U.S. Olympic track team and traveled to Antwerp that summer only to be sidelined by a tendon injury, and Creed "Hops" Hubbard, known as "probably the fastest man on any of the local floors," as well as Bobby Anderson. Practicing at the Wabash YMCA gymnasium on Tuesdays, Thursdays, and Saturdays, they wanted nothing less than the Black national championship.[4]

After an undefeated record at home, the Forty Club and its entourage hit the road for games with a dozen all-Black squads in as many cities—the Harrisburg Scholastics, the St. Christopher Club of New York, the Baltimore Athenians, the Washington Alcoes, the Cleveland Pioneers, the Cleveland Acmes, the Cleveland Swastikas, the Springfield, Ohio Colored YMCA, the Cincinnati Colored Y, the Indianapolis Colored Y, the Atlantic City Vandals, and the Loendi Big Five. For these contests the "40" just overwhelmed their competition. For example, in beating the Athenians at the Richmond Market Armory, according to the *Baltimore Afro American* newspaper, they "outplayed, out-passed, out-generaled, and out-shot the locals, showing themselves the speediest five that has ever visited the city."[5] Virgil Blueitt was easily the Forty Club's best player. "His dribbling and change of pace was dazzling, his passing and accurate shooting was bewildering," the paper said. "He simply could not be stopped, and by scoring ten double deckers, did more than any opposing individual has ever done against the locals." Meanwhile, at guard, Hops Hubbard was "a jumping jack."

Midway through this road trip, in front of two thousand fans at the New Star Casino in Harlem, including Virgil's wife sitting in one of the boxes, the

"40's" mauled the St. Christopher Club as well. It was such a beat-down that the St. C.'s reportedly admitted after the game, "the visiting club displayed the greatest knowledge of basketball of any of the teams that have come to Gotham in the last decade."[6] This was a nod to the days of Will Anthony Madden and Coach Jeff Wetzler, as far as the standards they had set. The Forty Club dominated in every city, despite not having a single player on the bench. "The visitors are doing a mighty dangerous thing by having only five men on such a strenuous trip, but their wonderful physical condition enables them to withstand the strain," the *Afro American* reported. This eventually caught up to the Chicago team, resulting in losses to the Vandals in Atlantic City and to Cum Posey's Loendi squad in Pittsburgh before returning home. Still, a 10–2 tour to twelve cities with five players would be unthinkable today.

At season's end, in a sign of things to come, the team's manager, Dr. Johnson, gave a presentation at the Wabash Y in which he reportedly "told of the adventure of the Forty Club on the road and of their business possibilities."[7] As hinted by Johnson, the club was taken over by the Defender Athletic Club in the fall of 1921. The newspaper-backed organization, with *Chicago Defender* owner Robert S. Abbott as president, absorbed the entire "40" operation including its players and manager. Though they had a new name, the team kept winning. But they now had additional funding because the weekly paper was banking on converting the team's fans into new subscribers.

Meanwhile, with its matriculating African American players, the Wendell Phillips lightweights had been crushing their competition, and in a March 1921 game they defeated cross-border arch-rivals Hyde Park High by "the walloping score of 23 to 9" to reach the city championship semi-finals.[8] This junior squad would ultimately win the South Side division title, but it was only when those same players made the WP varsity in the fall for the 1921–2 season, that the school's basketball program would finally turn around. As that season began, the *Defender* reported "the heavyweight squad is made up of five of our boys, while the lightweight squad has only one white lad on it." This was not the old varsity. These were brand-new heavies who represented a complete racial turnaround at Wendell Phillips. But the race of the team's players was just part of the story. "You will be surprised at the quality of basketball these youngsters put up—fast, snappy, accurate passing and a plenty of pep in the game," the *Defender* shared while encouraging fans to attend, adding that it would be "a good chance for women folks to get away from their household duties and learn the game."[9] All that pep led to Phillips High winning the Chicago City High School League's Central Division title on February 14, 1922, with a victory over none other than Tilden Tech, on the losers' home court. Two weeks later, WP defeated Parker High in the city championship semi-final to earn a spot in the Public School championship final against Lane Tech.

Phillips High ended up losing in the final by one point, due to several missed free throws. But their impact as well as those of other African American basketball teams in Bronzeville was vitally important for the neighborhood's Black community. A social services report published in May 1921 showed that although there were eleven thousand "colored boys" living on the South Side, they rarely used the area's parks and playgrounds. "The white boys are said to keep them out," its findings showed.[10] "Many a boy who has only the street or the alley for a playground," the report declared, "plays his way into crime." The idea of "building for a better tomorrow" with material gains, its experts argued, would lose its meaning if the city's Black youths weren't given a chance to develop character today. For that reason, the survey recommended "better park and playground provisions and boys' clubs for Negro boys." Any positive distraction that could offer African American youths in Chicago a path away from delinquency was seen as invaluable, and basketball was being enlisted in that effort.

This way of thinking continued into the 1922–3 season, with all Bronzeville excited about their newest all-Black squad, Wendell Phillips, which was out to repeat as Central Division champs. "The followers of the institution look for them to uphold the standards of the race," the *Defender* explained, "as the rapid change in the color of the students of the school leaves Phillips without a white boy on the heavyweight squad."[11] Adding to the thrill of cheering for WP was that they had appointed the ambitious and visionary former Wabash Outlaws head coach Dr. Albert Johnson to handle those duties for the school.

Meanwhile, the WP lightweight "all-Colored quintet," led by a seventeen-year-old Mississippi-born player named Walter "Toots" Wright, Jr., at right guard, made it to the finals of the city championship, which resulted in a triple-tie for the title in a round-robin-style playoff. This was "the first time in years the old spirit that existed here when ninety-seven per cent of the students were white is back," the *Defender* declared, "and we all know the complexion of the school has changed owing to the majority of the people in this ward being those of our own." For the Wendell Phillips basketball program to have reached the city finals was cause for a celebration. A banquet was held at the Wabash Avenue Colored YMCA Branch with an A-list of speakers that included Ida B. Wells-Barnett, representing the women's clubs, Rube Foster, president of the Negro National League, future U.S. Congressman Oscar Stanton De Priest, who was a real estate dealer and city council member at the time, and Binga State Bank owner Jesse Binga. "When the student body finds that the businessman and the professional man, the citizens of the community are back of them and their school, they'll make better students, better athletes and that means better citizens," the *Defender* suggested.[12]

For the following 1923–4 basketball season, Toots Wright moved up to the Wendell Phillips heavyweight squad, where he was joined by a new teammate at right forward named Thomas "Tommy" Brookins, a seventeen-year-old St. Louis, Missouri, native whose family lived on the same South Side block as the Wabash Avenue YMCA. Adding this combo of Wright and Brookins to the roster of WP's returning stars was good enough to lead the school all the way to the South-Central Division title in the Chicago City High School Basketball League, earning Wendell Phillips another trip to the city championship final against Lane Tech, winners of the Northwest Sectional. Lane would defeat WP in that final, in front of twelve thousand fans at Loyola University gymnasium on the North Side in a game attended by correspondents from all the major African American newspapers. It was a stinging loss for Chicago's entire Black community. But win or lose, *Chicago Defender* columnist A. L. Jackson reminded readers that for the African American team to have made it to the final again, with a win over an all-White squad from Englewood High, was "far more important than most of us are apt to realize."[13] From his point of view, "the white man's creed of racial superiority will need some tinkering and readjustment for many folks who saw or heard of that contest." Even the White-controlled *Chicago Tribune*, which Jackson labeled "our old, persistent and subtle enemy," paid tribute to Wendell Phillips, suggesting that "the effect of the game itself reached beyond the sport department." The promise they showed in basketball, in the columnist's opinion, would translate for them into "more and larger successes" in other fields.

But not just for WP. Their success in Chicago created a paradigm shift within Black high school basketball everywhere. Having won the city's Central Division, Wendell Phillips issued a challenge to high schools throughout the country for a chance to face them, and specifically requested a game in

Washington, D.C., against Armstrong Manual Training or Dunbar High. "The Chicagoans can easily get permission from the board of education for such a trip," said the *Defender*, which advocated for Phillips, adding, "the business men in Washington could make the trip worth while by having dancing following the contest, which will over offset the cost of bringing the Chicago boys to the city."[14] Two all-Black high schools answered WP's challenge, and plans were set for games in April 1924 with Lincoln High School in Kansas City and with Armstrong Manual in D.C.

"Word comes from Kansas City that a record-breaking crowd is expected, as railroads have planned special trains from nearby cities," the *Defender* reported on its front page.[15] Wendell Phillips would defeat Lincoln, 23–13, completely outplaying them in every way. But despite this loss, something much bigger had taken shape for the Kansas City locals. According to the Bronzeville newspaper, they had been "boiling over with enthusiasm" and Black folks came out to the event in full force not just from Kansas City but also from throughout Missouri as well as Kansas. With a total of 7,091 paid admissions, the game was "a decided success and brings about a friendly relation between Lincoln high of this city and Phillips high of Chicago."[16] This was a much-needed form of Black civic activation and connectivity, which gave African American communities throughout the country a reason to gather, compare notes, make acquaintances, rekindle relationships, create plans, share opportunities, and otherwise have a good time. All of this, despite Jim Crow.

The matchup in D.C. between Phillips and Armstrong Manual was scheduled for "Easter Monday Night" from 8 P.M. till 4 A.M. at Convention Hall, a large facility at Fifth and L Streets, Northwest, said to accommodate fifteen thousand. It was heavily promoted as "Washington's First Great Basket Ball DeLuxe and Gorgeous, Stupendous Brilliant Easter Carnival" and would feature music by New York City's famous thirty-piece Clef Club Orchestra for dancing before and after the on-court action.[17] "Call Douglas 0697 or 0698," said an ad for a special telephone number the *Defender* had set up in Chicago for anyone back home wishing to get the final results of the road game right away. As the Wendell Phillips High School Five caught the Baltimore & Ohio Rail Road to the nation's capital, they were following in the pioneering footsteps of the Wabash YMCA Outlaws as well as Will Anthony Madden and his New York Incorporators, who had arranged those first long-distance road trips between Chicago and New York. Before them, the Smart Set Athletic Club, the Crescent Athletic Club, and Howard University, between New York City and D.C. More than seven thousand spectators would show up to witness Wendell Phillips top Armstrong, 17–10, and again the event was a rousing cultural success. The visiting team was put up at Howard University, fed at the school's new dining hall, and toured around campus. "Howard students made the Chicagoans feel at home and were loud in their praise of the conduct of the team," the *Defender* correspondent in D.C. reported. This was free national publicity for the Black college, and in fact three Phillips players were planning to attend there in the fall. The visitors even got to see U.S. President Calvin Coolidge with the help of U.S. Congressman Morton D. Hull, representing Chicago.[18]

But there was also an overarching storyline connected with why Phillips High was so superior to Lincoln and Armstrong. It clearly demonstrated the benefit of Chicago's racially inclusive high school athletic league, the *Defender* argued, because "all season Phillips has been up against stiff competition while Lincoln has had to look for 'Colored' schools to play." The same held true for Washington, D.C., and other racially segregated school systems. There was nothing like the toughness, grit, and single-mindedness developed by players accustomed to competing against the best talent regardless of race, regardless of racist audiences or biased referees.

Naturally, plans were immediately made for a rematch between the two high schools the following season, this time in Chicago at the Eighth Regiment Armory. "The public is warned to get tickets in advance," the *Defender* stated. The event was scheduled to tip-off at 9 P.M. on Lincoln's Birthday, February 12, 1925, accompanied by jazz music for dancing, to be dished out by Joe Jordan's Famous Red Hots, a sixteen-piece orchestra featuring two pianos.[19] The Wendell Phillips Band, fifty-four pieces in all, would also perform. The game was all anyone was talking about, according to the newspaper. "Aren't you going? Won't you be there? Certainly you couldn't miss the biggest event of the winter season, could you?"

Wendell Phillips was way too strong for Armstrong, winning once again, 25–15, in front of 4,500 fans that included "businessmen, doctors, lawyers, society matrons, debs and near debs, school teachers, Young Women's Christian Association workers," and anyone else who could get in to see the game. As many as two thousand ticketless would-be spectators were left outside standing in the cold. They never got to see the "pretty girl ushers, daintily attired in their evening gowns" who were flanked by male ushers in formal attire, all serving "the elite of Chicago's social and business world" seated in fifty-five luxury boxes surrounding the court, all decorated alternately in the orange and blue of Armstrong Manual and the red and black of Wendell Phillips. This was the kind of scene that would have made Will Anthony Madden proud, only it was even more spectacular. The event was also a financial success "far beyond the fondest hopes" of its organizers. The total receipts from sales of tickets, programs, and the check room for hats and coats were $3,384.30, around $53,000 today. Total costs including the armory rental, music, advertising, publicity, entertainment of the visitors, room, and board, as well as travel to and from Washington, amounted to $2,636.59. That left a net profit of $747.71, about $12,000 today. Since they could have nearly doubled that with a larger venue, a commitment was made to book the more spacious Chicago Coliseum for a 1926 version of this new tradition, dubbed the "Winter High School Basketball Classic," with talk of bringing Lincoln High School up from Kansas City next time.

As passionate as Bronzeville basketball fans were about Wendell Phillips, they also had the newly minted Defender A.C., the Forty Club, the nearby Evanston Arrows, the Eighth Regiment Five, the Grenadier Five, and the Appomattox Five. In fact, so many new all-Black teams had emerged in Chicago and beyond since World War I, that African American newspapers could hardly keep up.

In the rest of the Midwest, Cincinnati had the Comets, the Dunbar Flashes, the Peerless Club, and the Ninth Street Colored YMCA while Cleveland had the Acmes, the Pioneers, and the Swastika Athletic Club. Indiana had the Indianapolis Colored YMCA.

Pennsylvania now had the Morgan Club, the Scholastic Five, the Homestead Five, the Edgar Thompson Works Five, and the Holy Cross Athletic Club in Pittsburgh. Harrisburg had its own version of the Scholastics, while Philly had the Philadelphia Panthers, Quaker Reserves, the Hog Island Colored YMCA, the Claver Catholic Club, the Wissahickon Five, and the Germantown YMCA Hornets, a women's squad.

In the South, Memphis had the Comets featuring "Jelly" Brice at center while Atlanta had its Colored YMCA quintet. "What Norfolk fans need is more basket ball to enable them to have an appreciation for the game," wrote *Norfolk New Journal and Guide* sports columnist Willey A. Johnson, Jr., in the African American newspaper's Theatres and Amusements section in 1924. "We have been discussing possibilities long enough why not some realities now or instead? MORE BASKET BALL."[20]

On the East Coast, Washington, D.C. had the Carlisle Field Club and the Alcoes while Baltimore had the Athenians, the Red Circle Five, the Harmony Five, the Yannigans from the Sharp Street Community House, and the Roosevelt Athletic Club as well as the Oriole Girls, a women's unit. New Jersey had the Owl Field Athletic Club, the Brotherhood Athletic Club, the Tuxedo Athletic Club, the Imperials, and the Orange Puritans as well as the Mysterious Five, a women's team. Finally, new squads in New York City included the Borough Athletic Club, the St. Marks Flashes, the Grand Central Red Caps, the 369th New York Infantry "Hell Fighters" Five, the New York American Legion Five, and of course, the Renaissance Big Five as well as the Blue Belts, the Tattler Girls, and the Twentieth Century Girls, all women's teams.

Numerous new nationally competitive Black college fives had also begun to sprout and blossom, including Morehouse, Clark University, Morgan State, Wilberforce, Johnson C. Smith, Storer College, North Carolina A&T, Shaw, Fisk, Morris Brown, Atlanta University, and Tuskegee joining the traditional power schools Howard, Hampton, Langston University, and Lincoln. This trend received a major boost of support in February 1924 when Wilberforce announced that its student athletes would receive academic credits toward their degrees for participation in the college's varsity sports programs, which emboldened other Black colleges to do the same.[21]

But of all the squads in Chicago, there was something special about a new team called the Giles Post American Legion Five. They were formed under the umbrella of the George L. Giles American Legion Post, No. 87, which had been organized in 1919 and named in memory of Second Lieutenant George Louis Giles, an African American soldier and the only officer in the Eighth Colored Regiment who gave his life during World War I. The twenty-three-year-old son of a Bronzeville junk shop laborer had been killed in action in October 1918 at Grandlup-et-Fay, Departement de l'Aisne, Picardie, France, thirteen days before the war's end. (Foster Avenue, site of the Eighth Regiment Armory itself, had also been renamed to Giles Avenue in his honor.) Giles Post was located at 3201 South Wabash and its mission was to "enlist the interest and attention of every Colored ex-service man in the city."[22] For this purpose, the post would stage musical performances, balls, vaudeville shows, and other events. Its members also began "conducting an aggressive house-to-house campaign to round up the ex-service buddies of the neighborhood and sign them into the Legion."[23] These new legionnaires included several former Wabash Avenue YMCA Outlaws players as well as other basketball stars. Soon the idea of forming their own basketball team made sense, and the Giles Post Five was born.

At first, they used the Eighth Regiment Armory as their home court, with games that were followed by music and dancing. "The Giles post team is something new in Windy City basketball and promises much," the *Chicago Defender* had reported in January 1922. "They have a few trained men in their lineup who, after some more coaching in passing, will be in fine shape to do battle."[24] Prophetically, after spending a couple of years in Chicago's basketball trenches, this prediction would come true as Giles Post stormed the city to occupy its hardcourt territory. But it wasn't so much with more coaching as with better management in the form of a mysterious African American sports figure on the scene who had come to Chicago from Minnesota around 1925, calling himself "Dick" Hudson.

On the afternoon of Sunday, June 12, 1910, while everyone else in the small town of Newton, Iowa, was watching the Odd Fellows parade on Main Street march past the public square, an eleven-year-old African American lad named Leonard Lloyd Hudson and his friend, a White boy named Harold Morgan, the same age, broke into the Chicago & Northwestern Rail Road freight depot on the other side of town behind the factory of the Maytag Company, manufacturers of washing machines, corn shredders, and self-feeders, then dismantled the lock of the cash drawer and stole two checks, one made out for $5.30 and the other for $118.[25] Leonard was the son of a laborer who did odd jobs around town, and Harold's father was a local farmer. The youngsters cashed the smaller check at a candy store, but the two aroused suspicion later while attempting to tender the much larger amount at a bakery, where they were arrested and confessed. NEWTON BOY BURGLERS, said a front-page story the next day, one of many that would appear across two states for weeks to come. ELEVEN-YEAR-OLD LADS, ONE A NEGRO,

BREAK INTO C. & N.W. DEPOT. Though townspeople didn't know it at the time, Leonard's subsequent life and career would be marked by his penchant for making newspaper headlines.

Both kids were sent away to the Eldora Industrial School, Iowa's notorious reformatory for delinquent boys, fifty miles away, for what must have seemed like a life sentence. In 1910, Eldora confined about five hundred male "students" from twelve to eighteen years of age, with around ten percent being African American youth. They were typically held until reaching adulthood. This incident in Newton was sensational because just a week earlier, Leonard's older brother, Tracey, age seventeen, had "attempted to kill his father with a revolver." Another older brother was already serving time at Eldora, and yet another elder sibling was confined in the Minnesota juvenile reform system. FAMILY A BAD ONE, a headline stated, since this made four brothers from the same household "to be restrained."[26]

Eldora, now known as the Iowa Industrial School for Boys, offered "services and programs" designed to "control the offender for his own benefit and the protection of society," amid reports of abuse, foul conditions, and shockingly harsh disciplinary methods, such as restraining devices that strapped students to a bed in solitary confinement for twenty-four hours or more at a time. Its occupants were continually trying to escape, right up into modern times. (In 2018, a judge finally labeled this treatment as "torture," and in 2020, the state of Iowa lost a federal lawsuit charging that these restraints violated students' constitutional rights because they were "cruel and unusual.")

Despite this setback, or maybe because of it, Leonard was determined to make good. Five years later, on May 24, 1916, the sixteen-year-old was among a small group of Eldora students to complete the institution's classroom curriculum and graduate in its first annual commencement, only because this was the year their studies were finally officially recognized by the state. Finishing his reformatory term was a major accomplishment for Leonard, and this time the headlines he got were much more positive. NINE BOYS COMPLETE EDUCATIONAL COURSE, one newspaper reported.[27]

Returning to Newton, Leonard registered for the World War I draft and then moved to nearby Des Moines, where he enrolled in West High School and began playing football. With athletic talent and imposing size—his military registration listed him at well over six feet tall—Leonard soon became so dominant that in 1919, the school selected him as its starting fullback, the "first time in many years that a colored boy has been thus honored at west high school."[28]

Increasingly prominent, the nineteen-year-old made headlines again in February 1920 when a thirty-nine-year-old African American woman whose soldier husband was serving in the Philippines accused him of rape. HEINOUS CRIME CHARGED, read the article title. But the charges wouldn't stick and a month later, Leonard was released from jail, making another headline. GRAND JURY FAILS TO FIND BILL AGAINST COLORED BOY, the *Evening Times-Republican* stated. "Testimony presented did not warrant holding the youth and today he is expected to resume his studies at the high school," the paper said.[29] "Hudson has made a good impression among men who have met him and has tried to earn his way thru high school by attending to two or three odd jobs." He had also reportedly spent "most of his spare time" at the YMCA, where his conduct was declared to be "exemplary."

After graduating from high school in Des Moines, Leonard took his football to another level, reportedly playing end and halfback at nearby Creighton University in Omaha, Nebraska between 1920 and 1923. Enrollment, academic, and athletic records at Creighton University do not show that he ever attended the college or played for their football team, the Hillmen. Yet somehow Leonard's talent got the attention of the Rock Island Athletic Association Independents, a founding franchise in the National Football League, because they offered him and two other players professional contracts that fall, which each of them accepted.[30] SIGN TRIO MEN TO REPORT AT DOUGLAS PARK, the Rock Island Argus headline read in September 1923, after the Independents had secured "E.W. Glaver, halfback from Georgia Tech, Leonard Hudson, end from Creighton university, and Alex Gorgal, backfield man from Peru, Ill." This press release also claimed Leonard had played professional football for several years "on the same team" with Eddie Novak and "Shorty" Des Jardien, two early White gridiron stars, and pioneering African American player Robert "Bobby" Marshall. This meant Leonard had been with the Minneapolis Marines, another early NFL franchise that was Rock Island's biggest rival. Marshall was a sports superstar, having been the first Black football player in the conference that would later become the Big Ten, and as one of the first two African American players in the NFL, along with Fritz Pollard. Yet again, historical documentation cannot confirm whether Leonard ever played with the Marines during that period.

Hyperbole by White newspapers regarding African American sports stars, whether local or with visiting teams, was an important element in their writing because building up acceptance of Black athletes as superhuman or exotic to make them worth witnessing was essential to drumming up large crowds. This was as important to local promoters as it was to the visiting squads. But there was often outright falsification involved. That was the case with the reporting of Leonard's football background, and this soon became evident. First, even though he reported to the Rock Island Independents training camp that fall, they released him prior to the season opener "due to a surplus of high-class material." Luckily, as a ball carrier, Leonard was noted "for his powerful line plunging on the offense."[31] So he was quickly scooped up by the Minneapolis Marines. Yet, local newspapers there introduced the football star as if Minnesotans had never heard of him before, describing Leonard as a total newcomer who had never been in the Twin Cities, having recently moved there from Rock Island, even suggesting that the Marines' opponents would be "in for a surprise." That mystery was deepened when, upon moving to Minnesota, Leonard changed his name in what seemed like an attempt to break clean from the past. MARINES SIGN DICK HUDSON FOR BACKFIELD, said the headline in the *Minneapolis Star* on November 1, 1923. Exactly where and how the facts went astray would never be known, but the hype worked out to Hudson's advantage. This was a taste of how it worked.

Regardless of his new identity in a new city with new advantages, the Iowa native was still a magnet for trouble because he fit the description of a large Black man. Then as now, a widespread and societally conditioned presumption of guilt and dangerousness unfairly made young African American males the targets of police harassment and aggression. "Dick Hudson, giant Negro fullback, is held without charge in jail today as Minneapolis police seek to identify him as the Negro who in the past two weeks has robbed three taxicab drivers in the Twin Cities in holdups." He and another man were arrested "when they were found acting 'suspiciously,'" the *Minneapolis Star* reported.[32] Weeks later, Hudson was exonerated yet again and back with the Marines football team by October 1924 as their "big punch on the offense."[33]

But the big man soon had enough of Minnesota and moved to Chicago during 1925, where he settled into a home in Bronzeville. As a prominent former elite athlete, Hudson was quickly secured to work with the Giles Post

American Legion basketball team as their manager, promoter, and coach. And right from the start, he had a long-term vision for the squad. Hudson couldn't help but stand out on the South Side either. Arranging parties and making contacts around town, the tall and physically fit Iowan, who was attractive, personable, and reported to be a great dancer, became a prominent figure within the city's Black athletic and social circles. Among his favorite contacts were dancehall and ballroom directors because they knew what was happening socially and controlled the event venues. One connection Hudson developed was with a Jewish entertainment impresario and World War I veteran from New York City named Isadore Jay Faggen. Walking in the footsteps of Louis and Eddie Waldron, the twenty-seven-year-old had become wealthy and famous there as manager of the palatial four-thousand-capacity Arcadia Ballroom on Broadway, nicknamed the "Million Dollar Ballroom," where he presented bands, dancing acts, and other stage events. It was "the ball room where good taste and good manners are an inherent part of a good time," said a *New York Times* advertisement. But in January 1925, Faggan bought out the Arcadia's owners to gain complete controlling interest and a month later sold the facility for $32,000, about $500,000 today.[34]

The entrepreneur, who also controlled the Roseland Ballroom in Manhattan and the Rosemont in Brooklyn, was competing with other headline-making monster venues that were all the craze, with each one trying to outdo the next, like the Cinderella Ballroom in Miami, scheduled to open April 15, 1926, in Miami, designed "to hold 10,000 dancers comfortably."[35] A month later, in May 1926, Faggen took over the Savoy, a "colored dance palace" in Harlem on Lenox at West 141st Street. The ballroom mogul knew that although more people were listening to music on their radios, this was "no good for dancers," as confirmed by experts cited in *Variety* magazine. "Something in the microphonic transition mars the tempo and distorts the perfect dance rhythm," they claimed.[36] Dancehalls with live orchestras were here to stay.

Looking elsewhere for more opportunity, Faggen had begun visiting Chicago and in early summer of 1926, he was rumored to have been staying at the lavish twenty-three-story Hotel LaSalle with a group of White investors from New York City. They envisioned constructing a large new ballroom that would cater to the lucrative African American community in Bronzeville. This was confirmed in June 1926 when a want ad seeking builders, investors, and brokers appeared in the *Chicago Tribune* listing Faggen as the contact.

"We will lease large plot, over 201,000 sq. ft., heart of colored section, for amusement project," it said.[37] There would be plenty of backing, the advertisement promised.

Meanwhile, after taking a season off to be away from football, Hudson would get back on the field again in late 1926 with the nearby Indiana-based Hammond Pros, yet another NFL team. Their roster included exceptional African American stars Fritz Pollard, Sol Butler, and former Brown University player J. Mayo "Inky" Williams. Following that season with Hammond, Hudson would retire from the gridiron but remain close friends with his former teammates, especially Pollard, who had finished that season with the Providence Steam Roller, a new NFL franchise, before returning to Chicago and opening a coal distributorship. According to the former Brown University star, Hudson would stop by his business often to "shoot the breeze" with him. "It was in that office that the idea for forming an all-colored basketball team was conceived," Pollard would recall.[38] They were talking about turning the Giles Post Five into a sponsored professional squad. The future Pro Football Hall of Fame member would further explain that lots of sports stars visited his office. This was known, so there was this one Chicago parks department basketball coach, a twenty-five-year-old London-born Jewish immigrant named Abe Saperstein, who always "happened to drop in at the time to see the outstanding athletes" when they came around. "Could Dick Hudson possibly have dreamed," Pollard would ask years later, that Saperstein "would some day capitalize on his idea and make an all-Negro basketball team the sensation of the country?" At the time, Hudson's idea was just a "never-to-be-realized pipe dream," Pollard said, until the former juvenile delinquent from Iowa "took it out of the dream stage" shortly afterward by "persuading I.J. Faggen to back a colored team, taking Saperstein along with him as a partner."

Faggen eventually secured land at East 47th Street and Michigan Avenue, where construction of the new Savoy Ballroom began in late 1926, promising to be ready by September 1927 with a space that could accommodate four thousand and would book "all the 'name' colored orchestras."[39] All the while, Hudson had been leveraging his clout to ensure that when the 1926–7 basketball season tipped off, his Giles Post Five squad would be stacked with talent. The twenty-six-year-old had secured former Wendell Phillips and Wabash Outlaws star Bobby Anderson, former WP heavyweights Lester Johnson and Randolph Ramsey, former Phillips lightweight stars Toots Wright and Tommy

Brookins, and an all-state high school football and basketball player from Mason City, Iowa, named Joseph "Joe" Lillard, Jr. Lillard was a hometown hero, considered by many locals there to be "the greatest athlete ever to wear the Mason City high school colors."[40] Hudson even planned to insert himself into the Giles Post lineup as a player for some contests.

Next, he arranged a long road trip against local teams from numerous small towns throughout Wisconsin. This was reported in several of the state's important newspapers, including the *Sheboygan Press,* which labeled the squad as "national colored champions" based on announcements the publication said they had received from the Giles Post management.[41] It was also reported that Sol Butler, a hero in Wisconsin by way of Beloit College and the Olympics, was now the team's coach.[42] Hyperbole was at work again, because Hudson was now listed as having played not only for Creighton but also for St. Mary's College in Winona, Minnesota, and for the Providence Steam Roller, which was at best a case of him getting mixed up with Fritz Pollard.[43] Lillard, still in high school, was called "the Iowa university star," while Brookins was transformed into a Colgate University graduate and Ramsey turned into a University of Southern California player. Adding exaggerated or even fake backgrounds may have become a signature move Hudson gradually embraced, knowing from experience how effective that could be. But it could also backfire. Upon reading about Butler coaching the Giles Post Five in Wisconsin, *Chicago Defender* sports columnist Fay Young decided to do some fact-checking. Three days later, he wrote in response, "Sol IS NOT and HAS NOT been coach of this team and his name is being used without his permission." Young also checked with the commander of Giles Post No. 87 and discovered that Hudson had not been authorized to use the post's name. "The post has nothing to do with the team," the columnist stated.[44] He cautioned his readers that Hudson could ruin the prospects for legit all-Black basketball teams that might want to visit Wisconsin in the future.

It was clear, though, that some of the hype was also coming from local promoters, as in a Wisconsin Rapids advertisement that stated, "The Giles Post Team is the Greatest Colored basketball squad ever assembled."[45] Meant to boost attendance, such advance hype was also useful to local oddsmakers, because some White hometown squads were talented enough to defeat visiting African American teams. Race ego was also at play, since it would be triumphant to win or stay close in a game with the "world's greatest" Black team. This was the case in Marshfield, where "fans had their first chance to see a colored basketball team in action" when Giles Post, with Hudson playing right guard, faced the local Company C squad for a late-February contest and experienced "a decisive trouncing," losing 40–24. "The visiting team was composed entirely of 'cullo'ed gen'men' and they showed plenty of basketball ability but not enough to effect the prowess of the home team," said the *Wisconsin Rapids Daily Tribune*. "Hundreds of fans were turned away from the armory so big was the drawing power of the colored team."[46]

Ironically, all that exaggeration and deceit were hardly necessary. Except for an occasional loss, the on-court talent the Giles Post Five displayed was real. White fans were described as "satisfied far beyond their expectations by the classy and clever playing."[47] They were winners. "The fake passing, clever dribbling and dead-eye shooting of the Giles Post team" would be on display one minute, then, "using trick plays and stalling somewhat," they would wait for "an opening," and then "the ball would be whizzed down the floor for a basket."[48] According to the *Appleton Post-Crescent* newspaper, this was "America's best colored cage squad."[49]

Back in Harlem, New York Renaissance owner Bob Douglas and his team would have begged to differ with that "America's best" description. They had gone from fifteen wins in their inaugural 1923–4 season to sixty-seven wins during 1924–5 to eighty-one wins during 1925–6. In 1927, the Rens finally defeated the New York Original Celtics, twice. The first win was at the Renaissance Casino, which the Celtics protested was "really too small for a big game." To that, Bob graciously scheduled a rematch at the Manhattan Casino, where four thousand fans saw his team do it again, winning 44–22. That was the night the Rens came "into their own as a great pro basketball aggregation," he would reminisce years later.[50] By late December of the 1927–8 season, they had defeated an array of the area's best all-White squads including the Original Celtics, again; the New York YMHA; the Brooklyn Dodgers, twice; the Visitation Triangles; and the New York Cahoes, and would achieve 111 wins in all by April 1928.[51]

That season had begun with a major announcement in late-November that African American representatives from cities and towns on the East Coast had agreed to form the Eastern League of Associated Basketball Clubs, an all-Black circuit. The ELABC would be composed of teams representing New York City, Philadelphia, Asbury Park, Atlantic City, Baltimore, and Washington. This was an exciting new development, which was revisiting the vision that Will Anthony Madden had first laid out during the 1910s, and which was attempting to pick up where the Metropolitan Basketball Association had failed. The ELABC would tip-off on Thanksgiving night with two games, one in Manhattan with the St. Christopher Club of Harlem hosting the Alcoes of Washington, D.C., and another in Asbury Park, where the local Capitol Club would host the Atlantic City Vandals. Philly would be represented by the Briscoe Club and Baltimore by the Athenians. This would be a strictly amateur league, designed to stamp out "wild-cat tactics"—where clubs would import ringers for key games—a practice that "became disgusting," according to the new association, making it "impossible for visiting teams to get a square deal." The ELABC champion would be awarded the "Amsterdam News Cup," said to be "a magnificent trophy two feet in height, exclusive of the pedestal." The runner-up would receive a cup sponsored by the *Baltimore Herald-Commonwealth* newspaper. That the ELABC initiative was for the good of the sport, the league commissioners stated, could not be denied. "The public, after all, must be served."[52]

But serving the public was precisely what men such as Douglas, Hudson, and Faggen—and Hart, Madden, and Posey before them—were aiming to do. So, the announcement of the launch of the Eastern League of Associated Basketball Clubs in New York City was overshadowed that same week by the Thanksgiving 1927 opening of Faggen's new Savoy Ballroom in Bronzeville. With two house orchestras instead of just one, a beautiful dance floor that was "a joy to glide over," and "draperies of gold and of red damask," the *Pittsburgh Courier* called the Savoy "magnificent" and the *Chicago Defender* wrote that it was "one of the prettiest show places and one of the finest conducted in the Windy City."[53] One reason for the strong public interest in the Savoy and its subsequent success was Faggen's prior track record. But another factor was the advancement of music technology. Just as the phonograph had led to demand for ballrooms and live orchestras, which led to more venues for Black basketball teams, now it was the radio and live broadcasting that created new opportunities.

By this time, practically every city and town in America had a radio station, and their broadcast schedules were listed in syndicated newspapers. WSB Atlanta would air Negro Spirituals at 11:45 p.m. on Tuesday nights and live music from the Invincible Colored Quartette on Wednesdays in the same time slot. WFAN Philadelphia would broadcast Philadelphia Quakers basketball games on Tuesdays at 7:30 P.M. The Quakers, also known as the Phillies, were in the American Basketball League, an all-White circuit, and would eventually become the Philadelphia Warriors.[54] Most importantly for Faggen, radio station WCFL Chicago had agreed to broadcast his dueling house orchestras for four hours of live performances from the Savoy Ballroom starting at 8 P.M., nightly. WCFL, the "Voice of Labor," had been formed a year earlier by the Chicago Federation of Labor as a listener-supported station serving the labor movement and working-class communities with entertainment, news, and public affairs programming. Broadcasting from the Navy Pier in downtown Chicago with ten thousand watts of power—and approved for an increase to fifty thousand watts—WCFL's signal soon reached listeners up to 250 miles away.

Meanwhile, the Giles Post Five were not yet sponsored, but this didn't stop Dick Hudson from scheduling more games in Wisconsin. Some local newspaper ads still there included hyperbolic descriptions of the team, such as "Colored Champions of Chicago," and the squad was still said to have been "traveling through the country," to have beaten the best teams "from Dixieland," and to include "a galaxy of stars."[55] In an early-December 1927 game against the Sheboygan Eagles, the "dusky visitors" lost 45–35 but put up "a fine fight" and managed to "include enough trick shots and clever passes to draw the approval of the crowd on numerous occasions."[56] The term "trick shot," previously used almost exclusively for pool or golf, was becoming more common in basketball, thanks to the Giles Post Five. This meant simply that players were running plays and making baskets in ways that White townspeople had rarely seen before—certainly not "tricky" by any stretch today, yet even into the 1940s, making a "long distance forward pass goal" or sinking shots while "standing on one foot" were worthy of world record claims.[57]

But something else was happening. The connecting of a dominant all-Black hardcourt squad with trick shots, hyperbole, and "cullo'ed gen'men" on the sports pages of Wisconsin newspapers was a mixture of ideas that would soon lead to a fork in the road for the future of African Americans in the game. On account of their superiority, Black players were about to be superhumanized as primitive savages with unbridled physicality *and* exoticized with magical or godlike skills. These subtle forms of "othering" would ultimately be seen as dehumanizing.

Soon after the Savoy Ballroom opened, someone convinced I. J. Faggen to stage basketball there. The first game ever played in the venue tipped off at 8:30 P.M. on Wednesday night, December 28, 1927, when Clark University, a historically Black college in Atlanta, Georgia, faced "a colored amateur team" called the Evanston All Stars from nearby Evanston, Illinois.[58] This was also the first time that a "Negro" collegiate championship team had ever visited Chicago. Their coming to the city "created such a stir in the social as well as the sport world" that more than three thousand spectators showed up, including Mayor William Hale "Big Bill" Thompson.[59]

Clark won the game, 38–30, but something much more important than the result had been achieved. From then on, Faggen knew Black basketball was a thing. And at that moment, Dick Hudson stepped in with an offer to make his squad the ballroom's permanent hardwood team. The men agreed, and the Giles Post Five began playing at the Savoy right away. At first calling themselves the Savoy Legionnaires, they started with a series of home games in January and February 1928 against reputable opponents that included Wilberforce, Fisk, Lincoln, and Howard universities in front of sizable crowds of enthusiastic fans. The "dusky Savoy artists from Chicago" also added a series of games in Wisconsin, which to them was familiar territory. Newspapers there soon reported that Lillard, Brookins, and Ramsey were the stars of the Legionnaires, and that even when Coach Hudson substituted for the starters with his second stringers, opponents were still unable to stop them.

This was working out well. Hudson's squad became known as the Savoy Big Five, and everyone wanted to visit Chicago to play them at the new ballroom, including Cum Posey, whose revitalized Loendi Big Five were scheduled to meet the Savoys there in mid-February 1928. "Manager Hudson of the Savoy Club is placing big time basketball in Chicago," Cum declared with admiration before his arrival from Pittsburgh. He was right, because the Savoy Five manager was making the Savoy Ballroom into what the Manhattan Casino had once been. The hero of Homestead still had wisdom to share. "Basketball is practically the same as it was 15 years ago," Cum explained, adding, "the games are still won by the players who watch their men, move around the court continuously, have accurate eyes for the basket and practice or play at least twice a week."[60] Hudson's team promptly defeated the Loendis not once but twice on the shiny Savoy ballroom, gliding to scores of 36–19 and 30–24. But this was not the same dynastic team of old. Loendi had not been able to keep in step with better teams because, Cum explained, there was no suitable place to play in Pittsburgh and securing the best talent was not as easy as in years past. But this narrative backfired. "As it was they lost Saturday night and Sunday night and lost a lot of prestige and a lot of friends in around Chicago," the *Defender* complained afterward. The squad was "worn-out," according to the newspaper. "Cum Posey will learn some day that you can't be young always," said the weekly, with all due respect. "When men get old they ought to quit playing basketball games, or better yet, quit trying to play."[61]

Meanwhile, a diminutive young African American player named Albert "Runt" Pullins had led Wendell Phillips High School to win Chicago's city high school heavyweight basketball championship title. This was the first time an all-Black squad had won that honor, so the accomplishment made national headlines and made Pullins a star.

Chicago had become the mecca of Black basketball.

The "cullo'ed gen'men" concept introduced in Wisconsin sports pages in early 1927 was derived from the "Zip Coon" character of minstrelsy, the staged performances by White actors in blackface that depicted African Americans in ways that reassured White audiences of their superiority over Black people. Using intentional iconography and structure originated before the Civil War, the "Sambo" character represented under-educated enslaved or formerly enslaved rural African Americans, while the genre's "Zip Coon" persona represented urban Black migrants from the South exemplified by their gaudy clothing and failing attempts to seem sophisticated through manners and speech. These characters, along with others, always comedic, were meant to leave the audience "roaring in laughter" and nostalgic for the good old days of plantation life. There was so much money in it that even Black actors, such as the iconic Bert Williams, made fortunes performing with burnt cork rubbed on their faces. Sadly, those stereotypes became socialized as the norm.

By the late 1920s, the New Negro Movement had swept Black America upward to new heights of self-determination, self-pride, ownership of identity, and freedom of expression. Black minstrelsy was a thing of the past. But not with White people, who patronized and applauded movies depicting those racist typecasts. In early 1926, several months before Dick Hudson formed the Giles Post Five, a White comedic duo named "Sam 'n' Henry" had debuted on radio station WGN in Chicago performing an audio "comic strip" as two "two forlorn and laughable colored boys from Birmingham."[62] This new show was such a hit that within days they earned a regular slot, every evening at 10 P.M. Their immense popularity could have given Dick Hudson every reason to introduce comedy and entertainment into his Giles Post games. Yet nothing of the kind was mentioned in newspaper reports from the road while the squad was touring Wisconsin during the early half of the 1926–7 season. But in January 1928, the *Sheboygan Press* wrote that the Giles Post Five had "delighted the fans in many places during a tour of the state, by their comical antics on the floor."[63] Other newspapers in Wisconsin began writing similar commentaries. Hudson's squad would bring an entire "colored orchestra" on the road with them, to furnish music for a dance after each basketball game, reports said. And within weeks, by mid-February 1927, a paper in Marshfield, Wisconsin reported that star player Tommie Brookins was "a jazz piano player of considerable renown" and that he would be heard playing during an upcoming game.

A year went by and in February 1928, "Sam 'n' Henry" left WGN to sign with rival Chicago radio station WMAQ, controlled by the *Chicago Daily News* newspaper, and reappeared as the same act under a new name, "Amos 'n' Andy." Their first show aired on March 19, and this began a thirty-two-year run as one of the most popular radio shows of all time, supposedly about Black people, yet created, written, and voiced by the White actors Freeman Gosden and Charles Correll portraying minstrel stereotypes as "two happy but luckless darkies."[64] Right as "Sam 'n' Henry" were leaving WGN, Wisconsin newspapers began describing the Giles Post Five as a humorous attraction with more conviction than ever. Their "comical actions" were well worth seeing, wrote the *Sheboygan Press* in late January 1928.[65] "It is the comic antics of the Dixie boys that make them the big drawing cards they have proved to be everywhere they have played," the *La Crosse Tribune* wrote."[66] Another headline read, ENTERTAINMENT WITH GOOD GAME IS ASSURED FANS, with the subtitle, "Clowning Colored Boys Are Opponents of Papermen Here Next Week."[67]

What had changed was that during these same days, Abe Saperstein made his first appearance in a Giles Post lineup, as a guard, alongside Tommie Brookins, Willis "Kid" Oliver, "Fat" Long, and a former Lane Tech star named Willian "Bill" Watson. "The Giles team was a little short of players and Manager Abe Saperstein was forced to get into the game," the *La Crosse Tribune* reported. "His handling of the ball drew an occasional laugh out of the crowd."[68] All of this turned out to be brilliant. "The dark skin boys are already the talk of the town and many local people are planning on seeing them in action," said the *Chippewa Herald-Telegram* before their next game.[69]

Hudson regrouped the Savoy Big Five in Chicago and added a new player, Lawrence "Rock" Anderson, a star from Cincinnati. But then, after a series of disputes, several players quit the team, led by Brookins, and that faction eventually formed a new team called the Globe Trotters. In the fall, during the ensuing 1928–9 season, this new squad decided to tour, and in doing so, secured the services of Abe Saperstein as their booking agent. The original Savoy Big Five reorganized around a new coach, an African American sports columnist from the *Chicago Defender* named Al Monroe. Meanwhile, the Globe Trotters' touring efforts resulted in another dispute, after which Brookins departed, and Saperstein took over.[70] It was a fork in the road, and from that point on, the Globe Trotters would become known for their touches of comedy, while the original Savoy Big Five would continue playing "straight basketball."

In the years to come, Globe Trotter rosters would always feature a player who newspapers promoted as the team's "showman" or "clown prince." This image became so powerful that African American squads were virtually expected to have a comedic element. But back in Harlem, Bob Douglas was having none of that. He vehemently opposed clowning—not for money, not for acceptance, nor any other reason. The Renaissance Big Five would entertain through their talents, knowledge, and teamwork; the recipe for wins. He believed their fans "wanted to watch a game of skill and not an exhibit that belongs in a circus sideshow," according to *Amsterdam News* sports columnist Dan Burley. Bob selected his players "strictly on basketball merit," Burley would explain. "They must have height, speed, nerve and the ability to shoot," he added. If they could "clown" then that was an added bonus, but "with Saperstein the reverse seems true."[71] It was during this period that Bob began building the Renaissance Five to another level, into arguably the greatest team of the century, starting with his signing of a twenty-two-year-old

Philadelphia native and future Basketball Hall of Fame member named Charles Cooper in 1929. Previously with the Philadelphia Panthers, who toured as the Colored Giants and then the Quaker City Elks, Cooper was six feet, five inches and 215 pounds, earning the nicknames "Stretch" and "Long Boy." He was described as "reminiscent of George Gilmore at his best" with "the physique of Paul Robeson" before being noticed by the Renaissance owner in 1928. After joining the Rens, Cooper became known as "Tarzan."[72] His debut with the team was against the New York Original Celtics on March 24, 1929, in front of ten thousand spectators at the Seventy-First Regiment Armory in Manhattan. Cooper and the Rens lost, 38–31, but this was the start of a new chapter for the team.[73]

Despite large crowds for the biggest games, Bob knew that there was more money to be made on the road, and their schedule now approached 130 games.[74] During the 1931–2 season, showing how significant the addition of Cooper had been, they achieved a 115-23 record that included nine wins over the Original Celtics. Billing themselves in advance as the Colored World Champions, they were considered the best team in basketball. But for the 1932–3 campaign, Bob took a pioneering new step. Basketball programs at historically Black colleges had continued to expand and improve. As a result, more African American players were enrolling in those schools, and the Rens owner wanted to see how good they were. There was another reason. He could expand the team's travel into the South. It was during this season that the Renaissance Big Five won eighty-eight straight games during an eighty-six-day period. This was enabled by their signing of a towering six-foot, six-inch twenty-one-year-old center from Cleveland, Ohio, named William "Wee Willie" Smith. Willie had been playing for the Slaughter Brothers Undertakers Five, an African American squad in Cleveland, when Bob noticed him during a preliminary match-up prior to a Rens game there. Their winning streak doubled the prior record of forty-four-straight set by the Original Celtics and ran from January 1 to March 27, 1933. The Renaissance Big Five would win 2,588 of 3,117 games for a staggering 83 percent winning percentage over a twenty-five-year span from 1923, when Bob founded the team, to 1949, when he dissolved them as a business. They were just getting started.

Meanwhile in Chicago at the beginning of the following season, Dick Hudson retook the reigns of the Savoy Big Five. The team's nucleus of players

included "Cooney" Brown, who would later break racial barriers with the
Chicago Studebakers and who was splitting his time with the amateur Old
Tymers Athletic Club; former Giles Post and original Savoy player Joe Lillard,
who was a star with the National Football League's Chicago Cardinals at the
time; "Hops" Hubbard, formerly a star with the Wabash Outlaws, Forty Club,
Defender Five, and Commonwealth Big Five; former Wendell Phillips High
School and Giles Post star Randolph Ramsey; and former New York Rens
players Harold "Hal" Mayer, "Kid" Slocum, and Joe "Red" Mills.

To make ends meet for the Savoys, who were no longer connected with the
Savoy Ballroom, Hudson secured financial backing from a source previously
untapped in Black basketball: numbers racketeering. Edward, George, and
McKissack Jones were African American siblings popularly known as "the
fabulous Jones Boys." Though they had only been at it for a couple of years,
by 1934 the Joneses had become Chicago's biggest policy kingpins, annually
taking in over $1 million from "numbers" operations that, by the mid-1940s,
would grow into a $25 million-a-year syndicate. They were "the brotherly
outfit that controls the team," it was said.

The Joneses were considered heroes on Chicago's South Side. By investing
huge sums of money back into their community through real estate and commercial ventures as well as by ensuring the availability of capital, the pioneering
brothers created hundreds of jobs and enabled further entrepreneurship in a
Bronzeville grievously stricken by the Great Depression. They also exploded
the prevailing myth that Black businessmen couldn't operate competitively
with Whites. "Just how the Jones boys got their 'stake' is a story yet unknown
or untold," is how Black newspapers left it.

Hudson further strengthened his roster with powerful six-foot, seven-
inch center Jack Mann, an all-state Indiana high school sensation and former
Wilberforce University star who barnstormed briefly before signing with the
Savoy squad. For quickness and sharpshooting, Hudson added five-foot, nine-
inch Harry Rusan out of Detroit, but he lasted only a couple of games before
Saperstein lured him away to the 'Trotters. Still, the Savoy Big Five were good
enough to defeat John Wooden's Indianapolis Kautskys and the powerful Duffy
Florals of the Midwest Professional Basketball League that year.

As the 1934–5 season approached, the Jones brothers had ambitious
plans for strengthening the Savoys even more and also planned to rename
them. Rumors surfaced in September that they wanted to sign additional

Rens players, targeting Willie Smith, Tarzan Cooper, and Bill Yancey. They represented the heart of Bob's roster. This move, predicted the *Defender*, would give Chicago "one of the strongest teams ever assembled." McKissack "Mack" Jones was named as the point man. He was reportedly back East "lining up the star ball tossers," because his new wife was the beautiful former Broadway actress and Cotton Club performer Jean Starr, who still spent much of her time there with friends. One can imagine the big money and other temptations that might have been flashed at Smith, Cooper, and Yancey in efforts to persuade them. But the deal fell through.

Hudson instead signed Al "Big Train" Johnson, formerly a star with the original Savoy Big Five and the Old Tymers Athletic Club, and the son of Dr. Albert Johnson, the dentist who had managed and coached the Wabash Colored YMCA basketball team of the 1910s.

Hudson also recruited three sensational young players from Philadelphia: Jackie Bethards, Zack Clayton, and John Yancey. Bethards and Clayton were previously stars with the Philadelphia Panthers, where they had played alongside Tarzan Cooper before he joined the Rens. Bethards was an amazing ball handler who was often called "the Satchel Paige of Negro basketball." Clayton had gotten his start at the legendary Wissahickon Boys Club in Germantown. It was the country's first African American boys club, having opened in 1885, and organized Philadelphia's first independent all-Black basketball team in the early 1910s. Clayton was a lefty but could shoot with either hand and "from all angles," wrote Jack Saunders, eventually a longtime *Philadelphia Tribune* sportswriter, who had played with him. "He is a demon guard, and is a dead-shot from the foul line." The third player was John Yancey, "Philadelphia's greatest guard," who was the brother of Bill Yancey, the talented New York Rens player.

In December of 1934 the Savoys got a new name: the Chicago Crusaders. Their uniforms were spectacular—bright red jerseys with white and black trim tucked into black shorts with matching trim, and matching red leather belts with buckles. The jerseys were adorned with bold black CHICAGO team lettering with white trim, in the font style used by the famed Chicago American Giants of baseball's Negro Leagues, arched across the chest over a player number in matching style.

The upgraded organization was impressive even to White newspapermen. "These colored boys never loaf on the floor," the *Sheboygan Press* declared. "Authorities rate the Crusaders along-side with the New York Renaissance quintet."

Now, backed by the capital generated by the Joneses' policy syndicate, Hudson was able to create split squads to play more games and also formed an all-Black women's team called the Club Store Co-Eds. They were backed by an African American cooperative shop by that name, located at East 47th and Wabash Avenue, and this store in turn was funded by the Jones's seed capital. "We might mention the fact that Mr. Hudson is one of the best behind-the-door chatters we have," the *Chicago Defender* teased. "So proficient is he in the art that each season he has ten or twelve teams playing something, whether it's basketball or policy."[75]

The Co-Eds featured an all-star lineup that included a six-foot, seven-inch center named Helen "Streamline" Smith and played their home games at the South Side's renowned Eighth Regiment Armory. Hudson envisioned a national stage for the Co-Eds and shortly after forming the squad he took them on an extensive West Coast tour with stops in Wisconsin, Minnesota, Iowa, and Colorado as well as Canadian stops in Alberta and British Columbia, making them the first all-Black female barnstorming squad in history. On the road, they were nicknamed the Chocolate Co-Eds, and Smith was promoted as the "tallest woman in the world." But this was not a comedy act. Playing straight basketball, they became so dominant that other women's teams refused to play them, so Hudson scheduled games against men's teams instead. At one point, the Co-Eds defeated forty-one all-male squads in a row, and in a typical season they traveled over ten thousand miles, covering dozens of states while scheduling up to one hundred games. The success of the Club Store Co-Eds helped expand the image, definition, and realm of the African American female athlete while also promoting race relations, gender equity, and economic empowerment for Black women overall during a time when these concepts were new to most Americans.

Meanwhile, the Crusaders were truly a great team, but Black Chicagoans hadn't caught on yet as shown by the low attendance at their games. After a season-opening victory at home over the undefeated Sheboygan Ballhorns, a team "that only real class could defeat," columnist Al Monroe of the *Defender* reminded fans that the Jones brothers had "gone to considerable expense and worry in an effort to give Chicago a winning team and their efforts should be rewarded." Unfortunately, Monroe complained, though "there must have been about five hundred out—the attendance should have been five grand."

Regardless of crowd size, after the new-name Crusaders achieved a 114-15 record for 1934–5, including a ten-game winning streak and a barnstorming tour of New England, winning 24 out of 25 games, they called themselves Western Colored Champions. "The situation is this, folks," wrote Dan Burley for the *Associated Negro Press* in describing the team that season. "Chicago's South Side is proud of its basketball players as are certain Indiana, Ohio, Michigan, New York and Pennsylvania cities where the game is played for blood."

By December 1936, the Crusaders had a four year record of 431-34. This trend would continue through 1940, and during that time, no other team was as much of a conduit for major African American basketball stars. The all-time Crusaders roster would include Jackie Bethards, Agis Bray, Hillary "Cooney" Brown, Zack Clayton, Dave DeJernett, Al "Big Train" Johnson, Byron "Fat" Long, Roosevelt Hudson, Jack Mann, Harold Mayer, Joe "Red" Mills, Bernie Price, Randolph Ramsey, Harry Rusan, Hilton "Kid" Slocum, Eddie "Bricktop" Wright, and Clarence "Fats"Jenkins, all of whom played for the Rens or Globe Trotters, or both, as well as Donahue "Donnie" Goins, Creed "Hops" Hubbard, Joe Lillard, and John Yancey who played for other elite all-Black squads.

The Chicago Crusaders were surely on their way to an eventual "colored" basketball world championship title. But there was something haunting them that would eventually get in the way of that dream.

CHAPTER 26

"TRUE WORLD CHAMPIONS"

FEBRUARY 19, 1937, was a big night in Oshkosh, Wisconsin. That's because the Oshkosh All-Stars, a local all-White basketball team, were on the eve of playing in a "World Series of Basketball" that would put the small city and the state of Wisconsin on the national professional hardwood stage.

Their opponents were the all-Black New York Renaissance Big Five. One would think that in the Midwest, during the Great Depression, and during Jim Crow, that the appearance of an African American team in an all-White town would be of concern. But actually, the Rens were universally considered the champions of basketball, and Wisconsin residents were some of the country's most passionate basketball fans. So they eagerly welcomed the visitors.

Wisconsin was not new to interracial basketball. The Renaissance Five had begun visiting Wisconsin in 1934. That year the Milwaukee Raynors, an all-Black club, barnstormed the state from their home base of Milwaukee. The Milwaukee Colored Panthers were also popular, and the all-Black Chicago Crusaders toured through Wisconsin during the mid-1930s.

Formed in 1931, the Oshkosh All-Stars had played the Rens for the first time in February 1936 in a two-game series. The games drew so many spectators that local promoter and Oshkosh team manager Lon Darling decided to do it again in 1937. This time the two squads staged a five-game series to be played in Oshkosh, Racine, Green Bay, Ripon, and Madison. Darling declared that the winner of the series, which the papers dubbed the "World Series Of Basketball," would be considered the world's champions of basketball.

"It was a money-maker," recalled former Renaissance Five star and future Basketball Hall of Fame member John Isaacs. Each venue saw huge attendance, and in local newspapers, race as a point of difference was rarely mentioned. It seemed to matter only as a descriptive term. Prejudice was, if not trumped, at least mitigated by love of the game. According to Isaacs, on this trip the Rens were able to stay in hotels and eat at restaurants like everyone else. "We had trouble when we first started with all these white All-Americans, and when we first started playing them, damn near every night we had to knock one or two of them out," said the Rens travel secretary and road manager, Eric Illidge, many years later. "For two or three years straight, two or three jaws were broken," he continued. "Every night, every GAME we played, we had a fight, not with the customers but with the players themselves—they couldn't stand us beating them," said Illidge, whose only concern was keeping the score down so they would get invited back. "I had two fighters on the team, they broke about four or five different jaws, Pop Gates and Wee Willie Smith" he explained. "And we kept doing it until everybody respected us." Illidge had no regrets. "My job with the Renaissance was easy and I'll tell you why, we had the best team at that time in basketball," he said. "We was the biggest drawing card in basketball." His duties included making sure players would "leave on time, be at the game on time, check the gate receipts, collect the money, give them their lunch money, in fact, I took care of all the business." Yet, Illidge was always prepared for inevitable trouble. Often, the cash accumulated so fast that he had to wire it back to Harlem using Western Union, unless it was close to payday. "All this goddamn money in my pocket," Illidge said. "One time in Louisville some guy came and grabbed me and tried to take my money off of me, but, he was so scared," Illidge laughed. "I had my pistol in my pocket, and I stuck it in his jaw, and he flew!"

While the Rens faced all kinds of challenges on the road, none were as bad as what happened to the New York Harlemites, an African American barnstorming squad based in St. Louis. While driving toward Chester, Montana, on February 6, 1936, for a scheduled game, they encountered a blizzard. Their car broke down and "the entire party was forced to get out and walk to a farm house three miles away," according to the *Fort Benton River Press*. "The lowest reading of the thermometer was approximately 42 degrees below zero" that week, the paper reported. They were rushed to nearby Shelby for medical attention treatment of "frozen faces, feet and hands." They continued playing on schedule into March, when it was reported that the players, whose frostbite injuries had "necessitated their playing with their hands taped, are again able to play without bandages." About 260 people showed for the game, which the Harlemites won, 44-43, and "the colored artists performed perfectly despite the loss of their classy forward who died at Shelby when gangrene set into his hands after they were frozen near there during the recent blizzards."[1] The twenty-six-year-old professional basketball player, Benson Hall, had lost his life after being sent home "because his mother back in St. Louis refused to let them amputate parts of his body," according to the daughter of Donnie Goins, one of his teammates.[2]

Getting back to the Rens, just in case, their team bus, a custom-made REO Speed Wagon, had two potbelly stoves on board for heat. These also served to dry their sweat-soaked woolen uniforms when it was too cold to let them air-dry with the windows open. "The bus was your home, when you come to think of it," said Isaacs in 1986. "The hard part wasn't the playing, it was the traveling."[3] Still, according to Isaacs, the Rens' game strategy was always the same. "Get ten points as quickly as you could, because those were the ten points the refs were gonna take away."

Meanwhile, the Oshkosh All-Stars were trying to build a case to join the National Basketball League, a proposed new circuit of teams from the Midwest representing both large and small companies, from the Akron Firestones and Akron Goodyears to the Indianapolis Kautskys and Richmond King Clothiers. This league was still only just an idea at the time. The All-Stars lost that 1937 series with the Rens, three games to two, but Bob Douglas agreed to a return engagement, a two-game series in March 1937.

Ever the shrewd promoter, Darling declared that those two extra games would extend their previous "World Series" to seven games. In other words, if the All-Stars won both, they would be the new world champions, instead of the Rens. The All-Stars managed to pull it off, and the following season the NBL added Oshkosh as a founding member.

Beyond delighting Wisconsinites, the series between the All-Stars and the Rens served a purpose for basketball fans around the country: It helped to determine which top-notch team was truly the best. For a long time, any team (like Will Madden's Incorporators) could claim they were "world champions," and often the public was understandably confused. Behind the scenes, promoters took notice. A team's won-loss record might speak for itself. But no hard stats could prove the greatness of a barnstorming team without a doubt. Which was why Edward W. Cochrane, a *Chicago Herald-American* sports editor, came up with the idea for a World Championship of Professional Basketball. "At the time there were no less than a score of professional basketball teams, all advertising themselves as world's champions," Cochrane remembered in 1941. The annual tournament was born "out of the chaos of these conflicting claims," he said. So, they decided to settle the chaos once and for all. The clear-sighted inclusion by the *Herald-American* of all-Black teams from the outset gave legitimacy to the tournament as well as to pro basketball itself.

Twelve teams were invited to the inaugural tournament in 1939, the best pro teams in the country, including the New York Rens, Oshkosh All-Stars, Harlem Globe Trotters, and New York Celtics. It tipped off on March 26, at the 132nd Regiment Armory in Chicago, a cavernous drill hall, where eight thousand fans saw the Rens defeat the New York Yankees 30–21. The following day, the Rens took down the Globe Trotters, 27–23 at Chicago Coliseum, a historic structure that had been the site of six Republican National Conventions and the home of the Chicago Blackhawks early in their existence. Bob Douglas and his Renaissance Five had made it to the final, which was played on March 29 against their familiar rivals, the Oshkosh All Stars. New York triumphed, 34–25, making headlines across the country. But when championship jackets were awarded to the players, star guard John Isaacs famously borrowed a razor blade from a teammate and carefully removed the stitches that attached the word COLORED off of the back of his, so that it read, simply, WORLD CHAMPIONS.

John William Isaacs, aka "Boy Wonder," a bruising, powerfully built six-foot, three-inch, 190-pound guard, was a star player from East Harlem. He led his Textile High School squad to the 1934–5 Public School Athletic League championship, with a defeat of New York City powerhouse and defending PSAL champion DeWitt Clinton High School. Following a successful 1935–6 season, Textile lost in the city PSAL playoffs when Isaacs, being twenty years old, was ruled ineligible to play in high school."[4]

Being ineligible had its perks. Isaacs played games with the St. Peter Claver Penguins, a Brooklyn-based "colored" team that featured Puggy Bell, a future pro teammate, and in the fall of 1936, he appeared with the New York Collegians, another all-Black squad.[5] These brief stints not only proved that Isaacs could play at the next level, they also caught the eye of Bob Douglas. The Rens owner, a keen observer of talent, invited him to a team practice and was impressed. Years later, even after signing a generation of other basketball stars, including future Hall of Fame members, Bob would say, "Isaacs had the most natural ability of any man ever to play for me."[6] After that single workout, he immediately offered the young man a three-year contract. Only there was a catch—the twenty-one-year-old first had to get permission from his mother. That's because, for the 1936–7 season, the Rens would play all of their games on the road. It helped to know that her son would be making a guaranteed salary of $125 per month, including medical coverage and meals. This was standard in Bob's player contracts.

The Great Depression had taken its toll on Harlem, and Bob knew that the Rens could draw bigger crowds elsewhere as the visiting team. Isaacs was the last key piece he needed to make his roster complete. The team would need every bit of talent, going into that 1937 series with Oshkosh.

Their four-month road trip began immediately after Isaacs was signed. "The Rens tour included thirty-two games in as many cities in the thirty-one days of January," according to historian Susan Rayl, a professor with the State University of New York at Cortland. It took them to "small towns and large cities in Pennsylvania, Ohio, Kentucky, West Virginia, Virginia, Illinois, Michigan, Indiana, Wisconsin, Iowa, and Missouri." By the time they arrived back in Harlem for the team's only home appearance of the season in April 1937, the Rens had played 110 games in ninety-seven days, winning 102, "traveled 18,000 miles by bus, played to a total of 89,000 spectators, and averaged 800 spectators per game."[7]

Local promoters invited the Rens not only because fans wanted outstanding basketball action, but because hardworking families sought an entertaining diversion from their daily grind, and thrill-seekers craved the exotic novelty of seeing African Americans in athletic motion. They also saw the Rens, as with all African American teams, as a mobile economic stimulus. People would come from miles around to spend money in bars, restaurants, shops, and hotels, as well as on side bets that backed their homegrown team within a given spread. Nevertheless, for strategic reasons, Black teams still let White audiences know their race prior to arriving in town. These race-signaling squads included the Zulu Cannibal Kings of Chicago, Chicago Hottentots, Cincinnati Lion Tamers, Iowa Colored Ghosts, and of course the "Harlem" Globe Trotters. Therefore, whenever the Rens were on the road they were billed in advance as "Colored World Champions."

"Johnny Isaacs, a local boy, played his first game with the Rens before a home crowd," the *New York Age* reported after their first home game. "His playing was a pleasure to watch. Big and fast, he handles himself with the greatest of ease, playing the ball off the backboard well, never making a bad pass or taking a foolish shot. He's a player to be watched."[8]

Isaacs promptly led the Rens to season records of 122-19 and 121-19, establishing himself as a playmaking floor leader with crisp passing, uncanny court vision, hardnosed defense, and tenacious rebounding. He was a ferocious competitor and in addition to a crushing brand of physical toughness, Isaacs also introduced the pick and roll to the Rens, a play he learned playing at Textile.

Throughout this time, Isaacs had a high school sweetheart named Ruby Stevens, whom he would marry following his second season with the team, in April of 1938. The couple was expecting their first child by the end of the 1938–9 season, after Isaacs powered the Rens to a 127-15 record and an invitation to the inaugural World Championship of Pro Basketball in Chicago in 1939.

In November of 1939, basketball superstar Clarence "Fats "Jenkins of the New York Rens announced his retirement and was immediately signed as the Chicago Crusaders' new manager, promoter, and coach. He was known throughout the country as perhaps the finest basketball player ever. Though officially retired, he was listed as a "playing manager," and it was said Jenkins "means to show the world he still has plenty of basketball in his system."

There was no doubt that teams such as the Rens and Crusaders were in the game for the money. The idea was to play as many games—and get as many return engagements—as possible. A select few teams would be invited to the recently created World Professional Basketball Tournament in Chicago. Just being invited would mean not only a chance to win cash but also the ability to leverage that honor in the booking and promotion of more games in the future. The fact that this tourney was won by an African American team, the New York Rens, in its first year, was a wake-up call for Dick Hudson, the Jones brothers, and all of Chicago's Black basketball fans. Their new mission was for the Crusaders to gain an invitation to compete in the new tourney, with the advantage of playing in their home city, possibly as local fan favorites. But the Crusaders also had to be noticed. Therefore, the added expense of hiring Jenkins and placing him publicly at the center of the team, creating new attention-grabbing marketing materials, and expanding bookings and related promotional activities was worth it.

As the 1939–40 season began, Jenkins started at guard in some games but soon realized his limitations. Toward the end of a win over Kentucky State University on January 27, the player-manager "benched himself in favor of Agis Bray," the much younger and more athletic choice, who had now scored a total of forty-nine points in his last three games.

Toward the end of February, less than a month before the second annual World Championship of Pro Basketball was to begin, optimism among Crusaders fans ran high for an invitation. "In the tournament will be such teams as the Harlem Globe Trotters, the Chicago Bruins, the San Francisco Seals, the Chicago Crusaders, and other outstanding pro fives of the country including the Celtics," the *Chicago Defender* wrote confidently.

But there were hints of disfavor behind the scenes. Though the Crusaders were celebrated as "a combination which should have a chance in the national pro tournament," it was also said that promoters of the world championship event were "trying to sidestep" Hudson's team. And they were never invited. On March 5, even as tournament officials were considering the brackets, the Jones brothers, bankrollers and controllers of the Crusaders, were indicted on three separate counts of income tax evasion by a special federal grand jury, charging they owed the government over $1 million in taxes going back to 1933. Edward, McKissack, and George Jones surrendered in federal court a few days later.

Investigators, including Detective Kinzie Blueitt, Napoleon and Virgil's younger brother, had been "conducting probes" on the South Side for several years, but during the prior month a stream of "big and little shots" who were involved in the numbers had been "paraded before the special grand jury" for examination. What was previously Bronzeville's "widely known secret" was laid out for all to see.

Policy-making was not a federal offense, it was a state matter that was easy to overlook in the case of the Joneses because of their strong financial support of legitimate tax-paying local businesses. "The pennies, nickels and dimes placed on the policy bets have been the foundation for some of the

Southside's biggest business institutions," the *Atlanta World* related. But federal tax evasion of this magnitude was a different matter.

In a subsequent deal, Edward Jones agreed to plead guilty and was sentenced to twenty-eight months in prison, while the government dismissed charges against McKissack and George, and gave them back over $800,000 they had paid, the equivalent of over $15.4 million today.

Because of these legal issues and their implications, the Chicago Crusaders weren't invited to appear in the 1940 World Championship of Professional Basketball, a tournament they might have won. This failure and the subsequent legal difficulties of the Jones brothers caused their players to disperse, which meant that one of the finest African American basketball teams of its time was forced to dissolve.

CHAPTER 27

WORLD SERIES OF BASKETBALL

THE WORLD PROFESSIONAL BASKETBALL TOURNAMENT continued through the years of World War II. In that 1940 edition, the Rens, led by future Basketball Hall of Fame member William "Pop" Gates, were defeated in the second round by the Globe Trotters, who went on to win it all, taking home the nation's highest basketball title. The following year the Rens placed third, with the Detroit Eagles as the champions.

Wartime rationing of gasoline and other travel necessities caused Bob Douglas to cut the schedule for the barnstorming Rens, which impacted his ability to pay top salaries consistently. As a result, many of his players jumped to a new African American squad in the nation's capital for the 1941–2 season. They were called the Washington Bears.

On the freezing cold Cleveland, Ohio, night of Friday the thirteenth in March 1942, the New York Renaissance looked like they were out of luck. Playing in their first-round game of the Max Rosenblum Tournament, a $5,000 pro basketball invitational competition, the Rens trailed the Fort Wayne Pistons by fourteen points, 51–37, after three quarters. The crowd, "6,000 frenzied fans cheering to the roof-top," were there to see the "hustling colored hardwood artists" who commanded a special place in the hearts and minds of sports fans.[1] Similar to heavyweight boxing champion Joe Louis, the "Brown Bomber," who would make his twenty-first title defense at Madison Square Garden the same month, the Rens had endeared themselves not only to African Americans, but to all Americans. Their victories meant more than just mere wins; they symbolized the progress of the race, and perhaps something even greater still—the progress of America.

Fort Wayne, a future National Basketball Association team, was in control and "well on its way to a big upset." They were ahead the entire game, and at the start of the fourth quarter, the Rens trailed 51–37. The Harlem team faced certain defeat. But not if Zachary "Zach" Morris Clayton had anything to say about it. The star from Philadelphia, who had made waves during two seasons with the Chicago Crusaders, debuted with the Renaissance in 1935, and after stints with the Harlem Globe Trotters during parts of the 1937-8 and 1938–9 seasons, Clayton came back, helping the Rens to win the inaugural World Championship of Professional Basketball in 1939, where he was named to the All-Tournament team.

Being former world champions, losing in the first round of the 1942 Rosenblum Tournament which some considered a side event, was not an option. Then, in the fourth quarter, "with the suddenness of a tornado, the Rens struck back with a vengeance," the *Pittsburgh Courier* recounted.[2] First, brilliant shooting guard Hillery Brown hit three field goals in a row "to start the big bronze court machine rolling." The teams exchanged baskets but clutch defensive stops down the stretch by the Renaissance cut the Pistons lead to one with fifty seconds left. The score was 61–60.

"At this crucial point Zack Clayton, the 'Philly Phantom,' shot the 'money' basket of the tournament," the *Courier* exclaimed. "Standing on the side near mid-court with the clock ticking away precious seconds, Clayton took a pass and 'set' himself for the shot that cinched the ball game, the one that eventually sewed up the tourney for the Rens." It was nothing but net, and the Renaissance Big Five took the lead, 62–61. Fort Wayne had to foul, and a moment later Brown hit a free throw to ice the game. After surviving the opener, the Rens went on to win the tournament by defeating the Chicago Bruins and the East Liverpool All Stars.

The nickname "Philly Phantom" was nice, but after that first round game, newspapers began calling Clayton by a new handle: "The Black Bomber."

Clayton played with the Rens for the 1942-3 regular season and then signed with the Washington Bears for the post-season to help them in the 1943 World Championship of Pro Basketball in Chicago. In that tourney final, the Bears defeated the defending champion Oshkosh All-Stars, 43–31, to take home the $15,000 cash prize. Clayton earned co-MVP honors for the title-clinching game.

In the following years, he continued playing basketball with the Renaissance while also playing numerous side games with teams including the New York Forty Acre Barons, Tarzan Cooper's Bears, the Philadelphia Firemen, and, most notably, the Harlem Globetrotters during their visit to Hawaii in 1946.

"We were able to beat the white teams because of our quickness," Clayton remembered years later. "I think the Harlem Globetrotters, Renaissance, and the Bears paved the way for Blacks by defeating the best white teams for the world championships," he added. "That was a major accomplishment for Blacks in the sport of basketball."[3]

Clayton also played professional baseball in the Negro Leagues as a brilliant first baseman with the Philadelphia Stars, Bacharach Giants, New York Black Yankees, and Philadelphia Giants. After retiring, he began to officiate prizefights, where he was so highly regarded that he was appointed as commissioner of the Pennsylvania Athletic Commission. In 1952, he became the first African American to referee in a heavyweight world championship, in the title bout between Jersey Joe Walcott and Ezzard Charles at Philadelphia's Municipal Stadium. Twenty-two years later, in 1974, he was the referee in the famous Muhammad Ali vs. George Foreman heavyweight championship fight in Kinshasa, Zaire, known as the "Rumble in the Jungle." Clayton also became a career firefighter with the City of Philadelphia Fire Department, where he would serve more than thirty years, and directed community athletic programs for youngsters at the Christian Street Y in South Philly as well as through the Salvation Army, all the while scouting prospects for the Harlem Globetrotters.

The Bears, often called the Washington "Lichtman" Bears, were sponsored by Abe Lichtman, a successful businessman who owned a chain of "colored" movie theaters around D.C. They played home games at Turner's Arena, which stood on the northeast corner of Fourteenth and W Streets. D.C.'s main basketball venue, Uline Arena, prohibited African American teams from playing there, so Joe Turner, the White owner of Turner's Arena, allowed the Bears to use his erstwhile wrestling facility. Lichtman's movie houses were among the few where Black customers were allowed to patronize freely. Since his theater business kept him afloat, Lichtman had cash to spend during the lean years of World War II, which is how he could afford to sign his amazing lineup of star players.

The Bears were not at the 1942 World Professional Basketball Tournament, where the field had expanded to sixteen teams. But in 1943, they were stacked. The roster included future Basketball Hall of Fame members Pop Gates, Tarzan Cooper, Zach Clayton, and John Isaacs, and the team went an astounding 41-0, winning the World Championship in Chicago handily, 43–31 over Oshkosh at Chicago Stadium. *Herald-American* sports editor Leo Fischer, who was also the chairman of the tournament, wrote effusively about the Bears. "Winning the World's title, the Washington team performed a feat that NO PREVIOUS WINNER HAS RECORDED. They finished the 1943 season with a perfect record having won every one of their 41 starts. THIS IS THE FIRST TIME SINCE THE TURN OF THE CENTURY THAT A PROFESSIONAL BASKETBALL TEAM HAS ENJOYED A SEASON WITHOUT A SINGLE DEFEAT." In the days when using ALL CAPS in print really meant something, this write-up said a lot.

Winning the championship was hard enough but going undefeated was an especially difficult accomplishment when one factors in all the challenges the Bears had to face, both on and off the court.

"Yes sir," wrote *Chicago Defender* sports columnist Eddie Gant, "the Bears are the best."

CHAPTER 28

THE MISSING NBA TEAM

IT WAS THE EVENING OF Saturday, April 10, 1948, and Robert Louis "Bob" Douglas was at the Hotel Grand, a "Negro hotel" on South Parkway and East Fifty-First Street on the South Side of Chicago. His basketball team, the New York Renaissance Big Five, was staying there. They were perfectly fine with not using the Morrison Hotel on Madison Street in the Loop, where most of the White teams entered in the tenth annual World Championship of Professional Basketball were housed.

Though the Morrison was much closer to Chicago Stadium, where they would play in the tournament's title game the following night, the Rens preferred to lodge in the part of town where they were welcomed and embraced as heroes: Bronzeville. Besides, the Grand was one of Black Chicago's most fashionable hotels. Quiet yet ritzy, overlooking the bronze statue of George Washington at the entrance to Washington Park, it was the hostelry of choice for the country's topmost African American entertainers, athletes, and business owners. It's where the Rens always stayed, ever since they won the tournament's inaugural championship in 1939.

The tournament had become a yearly classic—"the greatest parade of basketball stars ever seen in one meet" the official program boasted.[1] Douglas felt confident. His squad had amassed a record of 110-10 that season, and at one point went on a twenty-two-game winning streak.[2]

It had not been easy, though. As an independent team, the Rens did not have the luxury of a regular schedule. They had to travel near and far to generate income, and their barnstorming took them to Connecticut, New Jersey, Pennsylvania, Ohio, and Illinois, as well as to West Virginia, Kentucky, Missouri, Tennessee, and Georgia, where Jim Crow laws and customs severely restricted their access to basic travel resources like lodging, restaurants, and gas stations. Getting back to the South Side and the Hotel Grand for the annual championship was an incentive and a reward in and of itself.

Earlier that day, news had arrived from Germany that the Nuremberg War Crimes Trial was over and that fourteen Nazi SS officers were sentenced to hang for the murder of millions of Jews. Wire service reports said they were guilty of leading special brigades of "triggermen" ordered by Hitler to "wipe out Jews, gypsies and others tagged by the Nazis as racial undesirables."[3] For many African Americans, this news seemed hypocritical because those war criminals sounded very similar to White lynch mobs. Black folks were asking, What about them?

Bob Douglas was asking and answering this question in his own way, through basketball, and he had every reason to be proud. Since founding the team in Harlem in 1923, the diminutive St. Kitts native had achieved more success than he ever could have dreamed. The Rens utterly dominated basketball, and despite the travails of the times, Douglas had achieved these successes with unwavering honesty, cheerfulness, and charm.

However, something was gnawing at the man. For him, tomorrow's title matchup against the top-seeded Minneapolis Lakers, the leading team in the National Basketball League, had far-reaching implications that made it more than just a must-win championship game.

Yes, winning this tournament signified basketball supremacy; it would bring praise and would certainly be an honor. Additionally, the champion would get the event's $5,600 prize, a relatively large sum considering that a brand-new Cadillac could be had for less than $3,000 and in New York City the rent for a three-room apartment with a Frigidaire in a quiet neighborhood was $26 a week.[4]

But there was an even bigger reward. Douglas yearned for equality. He was tired of the "Colored Champions" label. He wanted the New York Renaissance to belong to a top professional league so they could be called, simply, Champions. This would also provide the financial stability for which he strived.

The strategic owner believed he had an angle. The best pro clubs played in the NBL and in the younger, less established Basketball Association of America. Less than a year earlier, the BAA voted to deny Douglas's effort to join, despite advocacy from Joe Lapchick, the star of that league's most important team, the New York Knicks. Yet, both the NBL and the BAA were struggling with gate receipts. They had begun scheduling doubleheaders that used the Rens and the Harlem Globetrotters for the front-end games to entice more ticket buyers for the main event. However, this caused a backlash. "The lily-white BAA will gladly use the Globetrotters or the Rens to draw in the crowds, but draws a rigid line on Negro players or Negro teams playing in the league," one African American publication voiced.[5] Still, though these were Whites-only leagues, Douglas hoped that economic necessity might make them overlook prejudice. Or maybe they would just overlook prejudice, period.

He was encouraged in this way of thinking when the American Basketball League, a small-town circuit that was well established though not as prominent as the NBL and BAA, began signing Black players, including Cleveland Indians baseball star Larry Doby, who was hired by the Paterson Crescents.[6] The ABL was even reportedly courting Smilin' Bob himself. However, Douglas was holding out in hope of first winning another outright World Professional Championship title, which he could then leverage for a greater negotiating position with all of these leagues.

Of the eight professional teams invited to compete in that 1948 Chicago tournament, five belonged to the NBL—the Anderson Packers, Fort Wayne Zoellner Pistons, Tri-Cities Blackhawks, Indianapolis Kautskys, and Minneapolis Lakers. Another team, the Wilkes-Barre Barons, belonged to the ABL. The two African American teams—the Rens and the Globetrotters—were independent barnstorming clubs. Teams from the BAA were not invited.

To win the championship, Douglas went "whole hog" to stack his team. That meant padding the existing Rens roster with any new ringers he could sign. They would be needed. Minneapolis had been almost unstoppable that season and was heavily favored. Their high-powered offense featured two future Hall of Fame players in six-foot, ten-inch center George Mikan of DePaul University, the game's first true big man, and six-foot, four-inch small forward Jim Pollard of Stanford.

Douglas had seven players on his official Rens tournament roster. At point guard was future New York City Basketball Hall of Fame member Eddie "The Rabbit" Younger. Roscoe "Duke" Cumberland, an all-time great former Globetrotters player, played shooting guard. So did Sonny Woods, a veteran of the Washington Bears team that had won this tournament in 1943.

The front court had Jim Usry, a former Lincoln University star, at small forward; future Long Island University Sports Hall of Fame member William "Dolly" King at power forward; and team captain Pop Gates at center. King and Gates were also members of that 1943 world pro champion Bears squad. George Crowe, who was Indiana's first "Mr. Basketball" and is enshrined in the Indiana State Basketball Hall of Fame, was a versatile utility player. Importantly, in 1946, Crowe had played alongside Jackie Robinson with the Los Angeles Red Devils, a pro squad that split a two-game series with the Chicago American Gears, an earlier NBL team that featured Mikan as a rookie.

In the past, this could have been more than enough talent to win. But that was before Mikan. No one on the Rens roster was taller than six feet, four inches. They still needed a true big man, and that's where Douglas made his shrewd move. He signed a highly talented six-foot, seven-inch, 220-pound center named Nathaniel "Sweetwater" Clifton as his eighth player.

This was a coup. Everybody wanted Sweetwater, who was "conceded to be one of the best pivot men in the business."[7] Clifton was a fine rebounder at both ends who could handle the ball and run as well as defend in the pivot. "He is one of the greatest 'bucket men' we have seen in some time," wrote the *Woodstock Daily Sentinel*, an Illinois newspaper.[8] Some sportswriters felt he was as good as Mikan, yet there was nothing flashy about him. "He is the stolid, silent, Joe Louis type of athlete," reported the *New York Age*, referring to the notion, which many people believed regardless of their race, that the more physically dominating a Black athlete, the more docile, friendly, funny, or even subservient he ought to appear.[9]

Born and raised on Chicago's South Side, Clifton had been a highly publicized star at DuSable High School, located just five blocks from the Hotel Grand. He averaged nearly thirty points a game during four years as a starter and even scored twelve points in an AAU game against the DePaul University Freshmen, a squad led by George Mikan.[10] "Sweetwater Clifton will enroll at DePaul in the fall," wrote a local columnist after the senior's last official high school game in 1942. "He hopes to be a doctor."[11]

Instead of DePaul, Clifton turned up at Xavier University in Louisiana, where in one 1943 game against Benedict College he scored forty-two points before setting a new scoring record in the Southern Intercollegiate Athletic Conference post-season championship tournament.

After serving nearly three years as a United States Army staff sergeant in Europe, he returned to basketball and reportedly signed a contract with the Harlem Globetrotters in 1946, appearing in a press release for their season-opening tour of Montana. Globetrotters owner Abe Saperstein was thrilled about acquiring Clifton and would later say, "He can do more tricks with a basketball than a monkey can do with a peanut."[12] Saperstein was also plagiarizing the Harlemites' tragic story, claiming in an elaborate fabrication that he had crawled through snow drifts in a Glasgow, Montana blizzard in 1929 (later he changed it to "Haxby, Montana," 368 miles away), after the team's car got stuck, and been rescued by a sheepherder, when not a single newspaper account throughout the state could corroborate that fiction. This same week, though, Saperstein's excitement turned to fury when Clifton never showed up. The center went to New York City instead and signed a contract with the Rens. His professional basketball debut was on November 5, 1946, in a home game against the Bridgeport Bullets at the Renaissance Ballroom in Harlem.

Saperstein was so upset that he filed a lawsuit charging that Clifton was "rightfully his property." But even while that case was in court, Clifton no-showed again, this time ditching the Rens and reappearing as the first Black player for the Dayton Metropolitans, a team originally with the National Basketball League that had quit and joined the new National Professional Basketball League, a small-town loop in the Midwest looking to capitalize on the NBL's name.

He played a few games with the Mets until, one day in January 1947, a newly created franchise, the Detroit Gems of the National Basketball League, announced they had signed Clifton to a two-year contract reportedly worth $1,700 per month. However, the big man played just one game for the Gems, only to vanish again.

He resurfaced back with the Dayton Metropolitans, whose owner, a local businessman named Elwood Parsons who ran the Metropolitan Clothing Stores chain, insisted, "He's my property." Simultaneously, Rens owner Douglas roared, "Clifton is my player!" Meanwhile, Globetrotter's owner Saperstein staked his claim to the superstar by stating for the record, "I'll take the case to the Supreme Court of the United States if necessary." Not to be forgotten,

Detroit Gems owner C. King Boring chimed in. "We brought him here from Dayton and signed him to a two-year contract," the entrepreneur insisted. "We'll go to court if he isn't returned." Renowned *Pittsburgh Courier* sportswriter Wendell Smith called it "The Strange Case of Sweetwater Clifton."[13] At this point, Clifton's pro career was barely three months old.

With the 1947 World Pro Tournament approaching, Douglas declared that the Rens, a top draw at the box office, would withdraw from the event unless the rangy center played for his team. This settled the matter of Clifton's allegiance, for the time being. He wore the navy and gold uniform of the Rens, who lost in the first round.

Despite his contract jumping, Sweetwater's game was beyond reproach as he began the 1947–8 season. Rens manager Eric Illidge marveled that Clifton "can shoot like blazes and handles the ball like it's a golf ball."[14] He remained "the people's choice."[15]

Douglas saw the upcoming 1948 World Championship as a showdown between his Rens and the seemingly unstoppable Lakers. But he knew they could be defeated because they had been before. In front of a mid-February sellout crowd of 17,823 fans at Chicago Stadium a few weeks earlier, Mikan and his team suffered a dramatic loss to the Harlem Globetrotters on Ermer Robinson's long-distance swish that just beat the timekeeper's gun. The contest had been billed as the "Game of the Year."[16] The Rens took note of how the Trotters had pulled off that win, by double-teaming Mikan to the point of frustration.

After defeating the Bridgeport Newfields and the Tri-Cities Blackhawks in the preliminary rounds behind twenty-eight and then nineteen points from Clifton, the Rens were ready, and the stage was set for the Sunday-night championship showdown with the Lakers at Chicago Stadium.

The game got underway with a 9:30 P.M. tip-off in front of 16,892 fans, but the Rens double-teaming strategy quickly backfired when both Clifton and King drew three fouls apiece just a few minutes into the first quarter and had to be benched. That left George Crowe, an all-around athlete with a reputation for outstanding defensive skills, to guard Mikan. He got help from Duke Cumberland. The plan worked well. Even though Mikan had fourteen points, the first quarter ended with the Rens down just 18–17.

The Lakers ran their offense through Mikan, but they had many scoring options, so he responded by looking for assists. This forced Clifton and Cumberland to back off, which allowed Mikan to attack. Out-of-position defenders had to foul him or allow easy buckets, so the Lakers' center began racking up free throws, ten altogether in the second quarter. Minneapolis surged ahead and Mikan had twenty-eight points as the Lakers went into halftime leading 43–35.

To start the second half, the Rens fought and scrapped on every possession, holding Mikan to just five points in the third quarter, until they were down by just one basket, 57–55, at the end of the period.

Then it was Sweetwater Clifton's turn to take over the game. The Rens pushed ahead, 58–57. The Lakers answered with four straight field goals by Jim Pollard and a basket from former University of San Fransisco star Paul Napolitano required another Rens comeback. It was a tremendous seesaw battle, until, with one minute to play, the Rens were down 73–71.

The Lakers had possession in a half-court set, attempting to milk the clock while the Rens frantically pressured on defense. Time was running out when suddenly, Sonny Woods stole the ball. Turning, he spotted Clifton, who had been guarding the pivot spot and was now racing up the middle of the court. Woods hit Clifton with a pass in stride and instantly, the big Rens center was leading a three-on-one fast break with two teammates streaking up ahead to his left and to his right in perfect position to tie the game. This was textbook basketball, as basic as a two-handed chest pass taught to six-year-olds first learning the game.

But what happened next stunned everyone in the stadium. Clifton, the sure-handed, fundamentally sound, undemonstrative center, threw a behind-the-back pass—straight out of bounds. Teammates and spectators were speechless.

The Lakers had the ball back with only seconds left in the game. They inbounded to Mikan, who iced it with another field goal for the win. Final score: Minneapolis 75, New York 71. The Lakers were world champions.

"Clifton threw the game," Crowe said point-blank in 2009, when asked about that play, more than sixty years after the fact. By then, having suffered a stroke, Crowe was living in a nursing home, the last surviving New York Rens player. Sitting on his bed in a sparsely decorated room wearing pajamas, he literally had little to protect or hide. Those comments echoed what Crowe had shared in 1991 with Ron Thomas, author of *They Cleared The Lane: The NBA's Black Pioneers.* "He threw that ball away and that cost us the World Championship," the fiery former Rens guard said then. Though his speech had slowed down, Crowe was sharp, witty, and conversational. It was clear that he was still bitter about that incident and was not mixing up the facts. After all, no one in Chicago Stadium watching the game that night had a better view of what happened than Crowe—he was on the court trailing that fatal, final fast break, directly behind Clifton.[17]

The pass was shocking not only because it was such a bad breach of fundamental basketball, the kind of needless antic that would get any modern-day AAU player benched, but also because it was completely out of character for the Harlem-based team. Douglas despised showmanship.

In addition, the Rens missed twelve free throws that game. This was curious, since two nights earlier, they had hit their first seventeen attempts from the charity stripe, and twenty-one out of twenty-four total. Six of the free throw misses in the loss were by Clifton, which were a difference maker. RENS BLOW FREE THROWS AND NATIONAL PRO CAGE TITLE, read that week's *Chicago Defender* headline.[18] Rens owner Bob Douglas was devastated.

Afterward, no one could tell whether Clifton had merely blown or outright *thrown* the game. Newsmen voted him to the All-Tournament team, but circumstantial evidence raised doubts. There was no question Clifton was in basketball for the money, and perhaps he was in need of a financial cushion, having been married in February as the tournament was approaching.[19] As if to confirm suspicions that cash ruled him, just weeks later, on July 31, 1948, newspapers reported that Clifton "became one of the highest paid Negro athletes in history yesterday when he signed with the Harlem Globetrotters for a reported more than $1,000 a month."[20]

These reports may have revealed just who had had the most to gain by the Rens losing that night. It may have been Saperstein. The entrepreneurial Globetrotters owner had not only financial ties to the NBL and the BAA, forged behind the scenes in unwritten backroom agreements, but also a strategic stake. The leagues were struggling with gate receipts while his team was rolling in profits. Saperstein wanted to keep it that way. So, he agreed to help the circuits boost attendance using the Globetrotters in their doubleheaders, but only if they agreed never to sign any Black players.

This was an unwritten rule. But it was ironclad. "There might have been an understanding, but nobody would ever dare put it in writing," longtime Philadelphia Warriors employee Harvey Pollack remembered.[21] Saperstein wanted an exclusive lock on African American basketball talent. BAA and NBL owners were so afraid to lose the 'Trotters as their sure-fire draw that they allowed themselves to be bullied into complying with Saperstein's wishes.[22] "They were afraid that if they took one of his players, Abe Saperstein would tell them to jump in the lake, which would cost them hundreds of thousands of dollars," recalled Carl Bennett, then general manager of the Fort Wayne Pistons.[23] But the Globetrotters owner got a double financial benefit. He not only could claim a cut of the gate receipts but, by controlling the supply of African American hoopsters, could negotiate lower salaries with them.

The reason the Globetrotters were so profitable was that they clowned first and played first-rate basketball second. This is something that Douglas refused to ever do. He was in it "for the betterment of the race," as the Colored YMCA Branch fundraising posters of the 1910s used to say. But this refusal cost him. The Rens couldn't compete with the salaries Saperstein offered, even when he kept contracts artificially depressed. In addition, Saperstein's back room understanding with those league owners obliged them to block Douglas from booking large capacity arenas they controlled, like Madison Square Garden, which seated eighteen thousand, Minneapolis Auditorium, with capacity for ten thousand, or Philadelphia Arena, which could hold eight thousand.

The 1948 tournament would be the last edition of the annual World Championship of Professional Basketball, which had enjoyed a decade-long ride. The basketball landscape was changing. The BAA and the NBL, despite being the leading professional hoops circuits, were unsure which franchises would remain in their respective leagues. This uncertainty was the result of continual fighting between them over the rights to top college recruits, and the player salary bidding wars that followed. This animosity started when the BAA was formed in 1946 and promptly began raiding the franchises of the NBL—which was founded in 1937—of their best players and venues.

The vulture-like BAA, as well as the reeling NBL would face difficult choices during the 1948 off-season.

NBL owners were scheduled to meet in early May, but even before they could convene, the Minneapolis, Indianapolis, Fort Wayne, and Rochester franchises bolted from the league to join the BAA. The BAA now had twelve teams while the NBL was reduced to seven, with only three franchises in its Eastern Division. With the 1948–9 season approaching fast, the frantic NBL hastily added a team called the Detroit Vagabond Kings, a new creation of former Detroit Gems owner C. King Boring, who at one point thought he had signed Nat Clifton.

With this move, the NBL had its eight teams to start the season, but soon realized that the Vagabond Kings were bankrupt. Now more desperate than ever, they invited the New York Rens to replace Detroit. Rens owner Douglas would have been better off had the invitation been made before the season began. Instead, out of options, he agreed to move the Rens to Dayton, change their name to the Dayton Rens, and worst of all, assume the Vagabond Kings' record of 2–17, last place in the league standings.

Still, on December 19, 1948, at the Dayton Coliseum, the Rens made history by debuting in the National Basketball League. "This is the first time a Negro quintet has ever played in the NBL and is considered a forward step by those who have followed the pro basketball situation over the years," wrote the *New York Age* on Christmas day. "Now, the unpublicized bar is completely removed," the Syracuse, New York, *Post-Standard* exclaimed, "not by admitting individual Negro players, but by taking in a complete Negro team!"[24]

However, it was a Faustian bargain, because the Rens were out of playoff contention before they ever even suited up. Making the post-season would have meant winning every single remaining game, forty contests in a row. Not impossible, but unlikely.

Importantly, Dayton's basketball fans didn't even support their own new all-Black home team with ticket sales. Attempting to maintain revenues, Douglas was forced to split his squad so that a version of the "old" New York Rens could keep touring, despite a half-roster, while the other half played on as the Dayton Rens. This strategy had regrettable results, with the Dayton version of the team posting only a 14-26 record in their remaining games.

As the 1948–9 season ended, the NBL and the BAA began discussing a merger to form a new league called the National Basketball Association, which was to be in place for the 1949–50 season. Representatives of both leagues and their teams met on July 1, 1949, in separate conference rooms at the Morrison Hotel in Chicago, to plot out the details. "All nine teams in the

NBL were represented at the meeting and appeared ready and able to field teams," initial reports said. "It was indicated that all teams in both leagues desiring to continue in pro basketball would operate in any merged organization," newspapers further reported. "It would mean at least a 21-team circuit."[25]

The first casualties were three financially struggling BAA clubs, the Indianapolis Jets, Providence Steamrollers, and Washington Capitols. Four NBL teams were also rumored to have withdrawn due to lowly business results, including Bob Douglas's franchise, the Dayton Rens.

"The Dayton team of the NBL had a poor financial season last year and finished the campaign as a road team," it was reported, as the alleged reason they opted out.[26] They had not even been welcomed in their own city. Yet every pro franchise was struggling. "The majority of the teams of both leagues reportedly lost money in their last campaigns," it was said.[27] Besides, Douglas was no stranger to lean years, having kept the Rens afloat even during World War II, with all of its cutbacks and rations. Despite these rumors, Dayton still appeared to be in the running for inclusion in the forthcoming NBA. Douglas was on the doorstep of triumph.

When the NBL owners submitted the list of their own league's teams that they wished to have included in the merger, Dayton was still on it. However, when this proposed list reached BAA president Maurice Podoloff, he rejected it. "We turned this down because our owners felt such a group would be too unwieldy for schedule purposes," he said.[28]

That was a fair concern, but some questioned whether that was the real reason. If he had wanted an even number of squads, Podoloff merely could have encouraged Providence, which was rumored to be ready to withdraw anyway, to just go ahead and leave. This would have resulted in eighteen clubs, a balanced number for scheduling since it would allow for three divisions of six teams each. Or he could have added another team to make a round twenty, which could be split into four divisions of five.

Ike Duffey, president of the NBL and owner of the Anderson Packers, took the BAA's rejection at face value, walked away from the negotiating table and announced, "The NBL will operate again this winter as a nine-team league, with the Indianapolis Olympians replacing Dayton, which has dropped from the league."

However, something did not add up. It was later learned that the NBL had "pulled a fast one."[29] In its desperation to acquire college stars, they had concocted the Olympians in order to snatch up four seniors from the prior season's NCAA national champion University of Kentucky team all at once— the four had played on the gold medal–winning 1948 U.S. Olympic team in London. It was soon revealed that the Olympians were so confident of their inclusion in the NBL that they had already leased the Butler Fieldhouse for their games.[30] This move made sure that the facility's former occupants, the struggling Indianapolis Jets of the BAA, would lose their home court and be forced to go out of business. The talks were far from over, and a lot of behind-the-scenes negotiation was still in progress.

With the new Olympians of the NBL in, and the Jets of the BAA out, the upcoming NBA now stood at eighteen teams, without Dayton. It was not likely true that the Rens voluntarily "dropped from the league," but instead that this had been a premeditated ouster designed to provide cover for the "sure-fire" Olympians.[31]

Waiting for the other Chuck Taylor to drop did not take long.

PRO BASKETBALL LEAGUES UNITED, read the astonishing headlines by month's end, without advance notice. "Big time professional basketball now is just one huge happy family of eighteen members," wire services reported.[32] All along, the leagues had been holding secret meetings in Indianapolis, where they finally reached agreement. No mention was made of the Dayton Rens.

The newly organized National Basketball Association would include ten out of the twelve former BAA teams (all but the Indianapolis Jets and Providence), and seven out of the nine NBL teams (all but Hammond and Dayton), plus a new franchise, the Indianapolis Olympians. By now it was exceedingly clear that the new league never meant to include Douglas and the Rens. They wanted not only an eighteen-team circuit, but also the removal of the African American team. This was no supposition as evidenced by a shift in the way the Dayton omission was characterized once the merger became final in early August 1949. Whereas previously it was said that "they dropped out," implying it was by choice, reports began stating the franchise was affirmatively "dropped" and "eliminated" and "wiped out."[33]

Moreover, the vaunted eighteen-team arrangement never actually materialized because the Oshkosh All-Stars were also summarily "dropped from the NBA," just weeks before their season opener, because, as news accounts explained, "no one in Oshkosh offered payment of the league dues before last Saturday's deadline."[34]

This was why the NBA began with just seventeen franchises when its 1949–50 season began. It was an awkward number, with three uneven divisions: East, Central, and West. The fix was obvious once NBA commissioner Maurice Podoloff told the Philadelphia Basketball Writers Association, "the present setup of 17 teams divided into three divisions is unwieldy," and that he was considering applications for new franchises from Grand Rapids, Cincinnati, and Cleveland for the 1950-1 season, but not from Dayton.[35]

It certainly would have been an opportune moment to invite the Dayton franchise back into the equation, thus rounding the number back to eighteen. But that didn't happen. For the NBA, the Rens card was never even in the deck.

At that moment, Bob Douglas was, in effect, ruined. The New York Rens organization folded, its players disbanded, and Douglas walked away from his life's work. Meanwhile, Abe Saperstein re-signed Nat Clifton to another $10,000 contract with the Harlem Globetrotters for the 1949–50 season.

Looking back, there are numerous possible outcomes that may have happened if Sweetwater Clifton's pass in the 1948 World Championship of Pro Basketball had been accurate. The Rens could have scored on that fast break to tie the game, with momentum in their favor. A win would have meant African American teams had captured four of the ten world pro titles, including the first and the last. Douglas would have had a stronger position from which to negotiate with the BAA and the NBL.

He may not have joined the NBL, nor felt compelled to do that so deep into the 1948–9 season. Instead, that league could have invited the Rens as its first choice from the outset. Douglas might have passed on the NBL's invite completely and waited for an offer from the BAA. As 1948 world champs, they may not have stooped to the rescue of the desperate, weakened, and inferior NBL.

Instead, they might have joined the NBL on Douglas's terms, from the beginning of the season, with a clean slate, in a city and arena of their choice. Douglas could have secured Clifton under contract, rather than lose him to the Globetrotters. With reliable gate receipts, the Rens owner could have kept his squad intact, enabling them to easily take the NBL 1948-9 NBL title. This would have made the Rens impossible to ignore in NBL-BAA merger discussions.

In the first NBA Finals, the Minneapolis Lakers would defeat the Syracuse Nationals in six games. Had the Rens been in the league and reached the finals, there's every possibility they could have defeated Minneapolis in that best-of-seven series.

The NBA consolidated to eleven teams before its second season, an awkward number. Had the Rens been included in the merger, there could have been twelve franchises in total, resulting in a nicely balanced schedule with six clubs in each division.

Meanwhile, the NBA would have launched without a color barrier. With no need for players to break it, owners could have been moved to stock their rosters with star African American players from the start. For that matter, little would have kept Douglas from trading his players to other teams in return for the best talent, whether Black or White. The numerous precedents of White players joining predominantly Black squads went all the way back to his own player on the Spartans, Tisch Tischinsky, in the 1910s, and the "White boys" on the Incorporators. So much more of the history of the NBA could have been different, with the lives of so many Black players set on alternate trajectories.

Also, a certain number of Harlem Globetrotters stars may have abandoned that organization and jumped to the NBA, as did Chuck Cooper, the first Black player that league drafted, in 1950. Abe Saperstein was pulling out the stops to keep his players secure with tours of Mexico and Europe, lead roles in his motion picture deal, and bigger salaries. Yet, those temptations did not stop Cooper from quitting his 'Trotters contract to join the Celtics, so it stands to reason others would have followed suit.

No doubt, the path would not have been easy. But, Rens owner Bob Douglas may have thrived if given a fair chance in the newly established NBA. He could have shared his own brand of genius with the league during its infancy as a fellow owner and general manager alongside greats like Ned Irish, Les Harrison, Leo Ferris, Danny Biasone, and Eddie Gottlieb. Just maybe, Douglas's wisdom and popularity, as well as his formula for success and knack for spotting talent, would have helped the league avoid its early struggles to become better sooner.

Alas, none of that came to be. Nat "Sweetwater" Clifton's errant pass sailed into the sideline din, leaving the basketball world with what might have been.

CHAPTER 29

VINDICATION

AS HE WAS NEARING THE end of his life, Will Anthony Madden, the first rightful king of Black basketball, made it his business to become acquainted with an African American sportswriter at the *New York Amsterdam News* named Howard "Howie" Evans. Will needed the journalist to understand who he was, what he knew, and why that throne had been his.

Howie had first met the man once known as Little Napoleon nearly a decade earlier, during the mid-1960s, though the journalist didn't know anything about him or his background at the time. That was when Howie, a recently graduated former collegiate athlete, was a well-known baller on New York City's playground courts. He was becoming passionate about Black causes in sports and had begun organizing recreational activities for inner-city youth. Howie also had a hidden talent as a writer, and no one yet knew that he was to become one of the longest-tenured columnists in the history of the *Amsterdam News,* which itself was one of the country's oldest African American newspapers. Howie would eventually become the weekly paper's senior editor, and as it had been for Will, it was basketball that first put him on the road to journalism. They had that in common, but Will wasn't contacting Howie to socialize. There was something else. Will Madden believed that Howie, through his written words in the popular Harlem newspaper, could give him back his rightful crown.

Since vanishing from the Black basketball scene in the late 1910s, Will had immersed himself into creative pursuits—interior design, readings, drama critique, theatrical studio operation, and stage production as well as poetry and short story writing. All the while, he continued to work as a messenger. During the 1920s and 1930s he remained at Standard Oil, staying there as it became Socony, then Exxon. He quit that corporation during the 1940s to work at the renowned New York law firm of Phillips Nizer Benjamin Krim and Ballon LLP as a messenger.

"When I joined the firm in 1960, Mr. Madden was already an employee," wrote its late highly esteemed senior litigation partner George Berger, in 2007, responding to an inquiry. "I recall that he was quiet and by that time, somewhat hard of hearing," Berger continued. "I was told that at prior Christmas parties, he entertained. One of my other partners recalled that he had written a book of short stories. At some point, I heard that he died. That is the total recollection of those of us still alive, who had any contact with Bill."[1] In the late 1940s, Will set up the Studio Theatre Club, a venue at 69½ Jane Street in Greenwich Village with a staff and artists in residence, including a pianist, a guitarist, a poet, and himself, as a diseur. That's when he began a twenty-years-long correspondence with world the famous Harlem Renaissance poet Langston Hughes. Between 1947 and 1967, Will sent numerous letters to Hughes inviting him to his poetry readings of the poet's own works. Hughes never obliged, but he did send Will autographed copies of his books, notices of his upcoming shows, circulars about new projects, and passes to his readings, including one in March 1960 to his show, "Shakespeare in Harlem," as well as constant regrets that he couldn't attend Will's programs. The last letter Will wrote was one on April 15, 1967. Hughes died just over a month later.[2]

The books of short stories Will wrote were the vanity press imprints *Two And One* in 1961, *Five More* in 1963, and *Let's Read a Story about Princess Carolyn* in 1970, all by Exposition Press. "Perhaps Will Anthony Madden spreads himself too thin," wrote *Baltimore Afro-American* book critic Saunders Redding in his review of *Five More* in 1963. "He figures prominently in Greenwich Village society and to figure prominently in that society ain't easy—and he's an actor, and an entertainer, and a playwright," Redding continued. "He is also a storyteller, although 'Five More' doesn't prove it."[3]

At some point during the late 1960s, Will became ill and moved or was moved into the Village Nursing Home.

Howie Evans began playing organized basketball as a young teen during after-school recreation center sessions in the early 1950s. He was athletic, fast, and quick. The game came to him easily, and at five feet, nine inches tall, he became a point guard. A sharp student, Howie attended Morris High School, an elite educational institution in the Morrisania section of the South Bronx, where he soon became a starter on Morris's varsity basketball team. "I was playing, and in my junior year I started getting a lot of accolades." During the 1954–5 season, his senior year, Howie was named team captain and recognized with All-City honors.[4] That got his name into local newspapers and also got the attention of basketball coaches at nearby New York University.

NYU played in the Metropolitan New York Conference against top-ranked teams like St. Francis, Manhattan, St. John's, Fordham, and City College. But its basketball program had been struggling, with only one winning season since 1952, when they went to the National Invitation Tournament and lost in the first round. NYU offered Howie an athletic scholarship. "My parents couldn't afford college," he would explain,[5] gladly accepting the offer and enrolling. That's when the shenanigans started.

Before team practices officially began for 1955–6, NYU men's basketball head coach Howard "Jake" Cann invited Howie and two other incoming African American freshmen to a scrimmage against the university's starters, White players who were all upperclassmen. Coach Cann apparently expected the freshmen to lose, but the young man from the Bronx had other ideas. He led his squad to an overwhelming win. "We kicked their ass," Howie remembered, with a laugh. "Three days later I got a letter stating that they were not going to honor my scholarship anymore." The reason seemed obvious. "They didn't want Black players," he believed.[6] "I really didn't understand any of it at that time. I was eighteen years old," Howie would remember.[7]

Howie was in a jam. His scholarship had gotten pulled mid-semester, forcing him and his family to scramble for a new college with late enrollment, or else risk missing the entire academic year. Fortunately, Howie had an uncle who knew one of the assistant football coaches at Maryland State College, a historically Black institution in the Central Intercollegiate Athletic Association. The football coach connected him with their athletic director, Vernon "Skip" McCain, who was also a mathematics professor at the school. McCain didn't like the situation, but did like that Howie had also been a speedy running back at Morris High, and he found a spot for the young New Yorker. Howie enrolled, caught up on his classes, and when the basketball season began, he made varsity. The team was exceptional, finishing the 1955–6 regular season with a 27-0 record, including wins over quality teams like Hofstra University, Adelphi University, and Morgan State.[8] Labeled as the nation's "top ranked Negro team," Maryland State then defeated North Carolina A&T and Winston-Salem Teachers College to win the CIAA Tournament Championship, before losing in overtime in the first round of the National Association of Intercollegiate Athletics Playoffs.

That spring, Maryland State's commencement address was given by renowned Harlem congressman Adam Clayton Powell, Jr., the first African American from the State of New York ever elected to the United States Congress. Howie was there and would remember it vividly. "I was like mesmerized by the speech that this guy gave," he said.[9] The young student-athlete couldn't wait to go back to his dorm room and write about it. "I was so inspired by what this guy said," Howie would continue. "So, I sent the story to the *Baltimore Sun*, in Baltimore and they published it!" This was his first byline, but it wouldn't be his last.

During summers, Howie had a job at Public School No. 99 in the Bronx, which was a block from his parents' home, and after work he would sharpen his basketball skills at highly competitive Mount Morris Park on West 120th Street and Madison Avenue in Harlem, known today as Marcus Garvey Park. "That's where all the so-called players played," Howie would say.[10] He had been showing up there since high school. There would be players from every borough in the city. "Brooklyn guys would come up and they'd be sitting on the side, and they always had their knives out, like, y'all fuck up there's gonna be a rumble in here, I mean you had to have heart to play," he would reminisce. "It was amazing that nobody ever got killed in that park!" Meanwhile, older ballers with roots in the community, like former professional stars William "Pop" Gates and John "Boy Wonder" Isaacs, were always on hand to critique and mentor the up-and-coming players.

Something special was going on there. Even out-of-town players knew about Mount Morris Park. One of its well-known courtside figures was a staff member at the St. Philip's Protestant Episcopal community center named Holcombe Rucker. According to Howie, Rucker was spending much of his time at Mount Morris Park even though he was also the playground director at the nearby St. Nicholas Houses, a public housing project which had been built to replace tenements as part of New York City's "slum clearance" strategy.[11]

Then in June 1954, during the summer right after Howie's junior year in high school, Rucker organized an ambitious round robin basketball tournament for junior high, high school, and college players at the St. Nicholas Playground courts at Seventh Avenue and 128th Street. Three hundred forty players on thirty-six local and out-of-town teams from every New York City borough and as far away as North Carolina competed. In future years, he added more teams, more kids, and more age groups, and the program would become known as the Rucker Tournament, then "The Rucker," and then simply, "The Ruck." Soon, even professional basketball stars would participate. Holcombe Rucker had created an opportunity for the best playground ballers from every corner of New York City as well as from around the country, to showcase their talents on a prominent new stage.

After graduating from college, Howie first returned to the Bronx to continue his work at P.S. 99. People gravitated toward him, and he was a natural at organizing events. So, when the *New York Age* staged its 1960 Inter-Boro Basketball Tournament at P.S. 99, Howie was appointed as its organizer. Soon he was helping out at The Ruck and before long, the Maryland State grad had become an instrumental behind-the-scenes figure in the planning of the Rucker Pro League, an offshoot of the Ruck that included professional players. Howie became so well known and trusted as an insider to New York City's hallowed basketball circles that he began submitting authoritative sports write-ups to the *Amsterdam News*, which eventually published his summary of the 1963 National Invitation Tournament as a contributor.

In 1965, frustrated by the treatment of Wilt Chamberlain—who Howie was friends with from playground games—Howie wrote a defense of the star, and a call to "appreciate him while he is here."[12] According to Howie, his editorial was so well received that the *News* made him a full-time offer.[13] "The editor asked me, 'Do you wanna write a column?' 'A column?' I said, 'What the fuck is a column?' That's how I started writing."

A few weeks later, on March 20, 1965, the beloved playground director Holcombe Rucker died of lung cancer. He had been a chronic smoker, but his death was a blow to everyone, including Howie, who was the first to write about his former coach, mentor, and boss in print. "No man gave more of himself, no man asked less of others, no man had a heavier load to carry and perhaps this above all others hastened his untimely death," the *Amsterdam News* columnist remembered in a tribute.[14] Rucker was never seen formally as a civil rights leader. "Yet, somehow," wrote Howie, "you can say Holcombe Rucker did as much or even more than all the others combined in his one-man crusade to bring to Harlem an image of respectability and decency."

That summer, having outgrown its original "St. Nick" housing projects playground, the Ruck, without Rucker, was moved to the Public School No. 156 basketball playground on Eighth Avenue at West 155th Street, right across the street from where the old Manhattan Casino had been located. By then, everyone in New York City was reading Howie's column, and he began using his platform not only to support additional African American athletes still playing but also, and especially, to advocate for those earlier Black basketball pioneers he had gotten to know. The way he viewed it, that list started with men like Bob Douglas, Tarzan Cooper, Pop Gates, John Isaacs, Fats Jenkins, Zack Clayton, and others.

Nothing irked Howie and Harlem more than the omission of the New York Rens by the Basketball Hall of Fame. Through his words in print, he was almost singlehandedly responsible for the eventual 1972 induction of Douglas, and, later, other Rens players. "We had to go to war for three of them," Howie explained, of his tireless efforts to gain recognition for Bob Douglas; Tarzan Cooper, who was inducted in 1976; and Pop Gates, who was enshrined in 1989.[15]

"To this day, I have never seen a team play better team basketball," said legendary coach and Hall of Fame member John Wooden about the Rens. Wooden faced the barnstorming Rens often during the mid-1930s while a player with all-White pro basketball teams in Indiana, including the Indianapolis Kautskys. "They had great athletes, but they weren't as impressive as their team play. The way they handled and passed the ball was just amazing to me then, and I believe it would be today."

Today, in addition to Douglas, Cooper, and Gates, four additional former Rens are enshrined in the Basketball Hall of Fame: Nat Clifton, John Isaacs, Zack Clayton, and Clarence "Fats" Jenkins.

Howie's column got Will Madden's attention, and soon the old-timer was knocking on the journalist's door. "He used to come by the paper all the time," Howie recalled during an interview in a coffee shop on the corner of West 125th Street and Lenox Avenue in Harlem. "He had a problem with people," said the reporter. "He was so bitter that he couldn't even articulate, he would ramble." Howie had seen Will around but resisted dealing with him at first. "He used to show up at the playground, wearing a winter coat

in the middle of summer, man," Howie shared, seeming to regret the picture he was painting. "He would lean against the fence and watch games
and scrutinize the players as if he were their coach, critiquing about 'that's
not how you're supposed to do it,' insisting that 'they don't know a thing,' to
anyone who would listen."

The "playground" to which Howie referred was no ordinary basketball
court—it was the Holcombe Rucker Playground on Eighth Avenue and West
155th Street in Harlem. And it was during a time when this court featured
midsummer basketball tournaments in which legendary basketball players
like Connie Hawkins, Nate "Tiny" Archibald, "Pee Wee" Kirkland, Ollie Taylor,
Earl "Magic" Monroe, and Wilt Chamberlain—and local stars with nicknames
like "Knowledge," "T.V.," "Goose," and "Shoestring"—were welcoming newcomers.[16] "There's this new dude," Hawkins said then, "they call him Doctor
Somebody."[17] That was Dr. J.

In addition to his *Amsterdam News* gig, Howie was a senior staff writer for
Black Sports Magazine, host of the "Right Now" television program that aired
in New York City on Channel 9, host of a radio show, on the Board of Directors
of the City-Wide Athletic Council, director of the Bronx Youth Athletic Association, an organizer of the anti-racism advocacy group known as the Black
Sports Committee, the founder and director of the Wagner Recreation Center
in Harlem, and the president of the Garden State Colonials of the professional
Eastern Basketball Association. He also coached and scouted—as an assistant
at Fordham University and at the high school level, once taking a New York
City all-star basketball team on a four-game tour of the Soviet Union. Howie
was also the first Black sportswriter with National Football League credentials,
and he later worked in public relations with the New York Jets.[18]

One day, Howie noticed a stately looking elderly gentleman who had
been frequenting Mount Morris Park and hanging around at other uptown
basketball playgrounds. This individual, according to the journalist, was always
scrutinizing players and pointing out their lack of fundamentals like teamwork,
moving without the ball, disciplined shot-taking, defensive positioning, and
just overall disregard for scientific basketball. He always had something to
say. So much so, that the retired barnstorming legends who mentored these
ballers thought he "ran his mouth a lot." No one knew his name. But this old
guy continually had old documents and newspaper clippings with him, well
organized, that he carried around in a plastic shopping bag. And there was

something else—despite all of his talk, he seems to have been invisible. "Nobody ever paid him any attention," Howie recalled.

"He always stood outside the fence," Howie recalled. "He never came in."[19] Then one day, instead of watching from a distance, this aging fellow began telephoning the *Amsterdam News* office asking to meet with the young columnist. The mysterious gentleman's name was Will Anthony Madden.

Howie finally met with Will. "He walked around uptown with a grocery bag full of papers, photographs, newspaper clippings, documents, and what have you, always trying to show them to people." Eventually, the journalist agreed to see him. Howie explained that Will used to hand him bits and pieces of these materials, which he would just put into his desk drawer. With that, I handed Howie a photocopy of Will's "The Future of Basketball" article in *Competitor Magazine*. "He had this folded up in his vest," said Howie, looking at the words, nodding his head in recognition. It was as if he flashed back to Will sitting before him in his *News* office more than thirty years earlier. "He used to say, 'This is how it *really* happened,'" Howie said, wistfully.

Few people know that in 1971, Howie began recording oral histories of all the New York Renaissance players who were still living at the time—legendary stars like Dolly King, Puggy Bell, Fats Jenkins, Tarzan Cooper, Pop Gates, and John Isaacs, as well as owner Bob Douglas and team officials like Eric Illidge. Howie never included Will, but it seemed as though he now regretted that. "None of the Rens would have anything to do with him," Howie offered, as if to explain. "Mr. Douglas never took him in, and by then he'd made so many enemies who thought he was nuts."

Will must have demanded to know why the Renaissance were getting all this newsprint when he was the original king of Black basketball, pioneering innovator, who foretold the role of professionalism and gave that template to Bob Douglas, who ran with it. "He was jealous of everyone, Cum Posey, and everybody," Howie recalled. "He felt that *he* was the one who 'started' it all." Maybe by then, Will knew that his time was running out. "To me he seemed like an individual that life had passed by," Howie continued. "He'd begun to see things that should've happened to him," Howie suggested. "I felt sorry for him."

Howie listened to Will, though, and understood, thanks to those volu-
minous clippings, the truth about what he said and the importance of what
he had once done. Will Anthony Madden, once known as "Little Napoleon,"
formerly a sportswriter just like him, was not only a survivor; he was also a
striver. The man had played a pioneering role in the history of basketball as
one of the key figures who took a game once played in church basements,
renovated handball courts, and cramped gymnasiums in front of no more than
a hundred spectators and brought it to a stage of national glory in front of
tens of thousands. Will had pushed the envelope in terms of professionalism,
basketball operations and marketing, race relations, and sports writing itself.
Now it was time, Howie thought, for this man to get his proper recognition. It
was Black History Month, and he could include Will in a retrospective piece
and even contain some of the facts the elderly gentleman had shared with
him. Howie began to write.

On February 17, 1973, Howie's article, entitled, "Blacks Who Made History in The Basketball World," appeared in the *Amsterdam News*.[20] "Time
does not record exactly when Blacks began playing the game of basketball," it
began. "One of the first teachers of the sport was a man named Edwin Bancroft
Henderson," the article continued. Will may have been reading the article the
morning that the paper was dropped at newsstands throughout New York
City. There were some factoids about historically Black colleges and then,
this. "From 1909 until the 20's when the Renaissance Big Five got started,
Cumberland Posey, who operated in Pennsylvania and Will Madden, who
directed the St. Christopher team of New York, turned their amateur clubs into
touring pros," it stated. "They played against each other and often got the best
of their players together to go against the top white teams of the day." This was
followed—followed—by some details about Robert "Bob" Douglas, the New
York Renaissance, and that team's biggest stars. Then, under a section called
"The Rest Is History," Howie listed major athletes such as Jackie Robinson,
Bill Russell, Kareem Abdul-Jabbar, Oscar Robertson, and Elgin Baylor. No
mention of Father Daniel, or Romeo Dougherty, or any journalists, for that
matter. Will Anthony Madden had made it.

Howie remembers going about his business as usual after that and visiting the courts where he was active. "Then one day, one of the guys at the
playground, Goose Howard, asked, 'Where's that old man?' and someone
else said, 'He's dead,'" Howie remembered, picturing the parks, and their

players, who Will "coached" from outside the fences. "And that was that, until now."[21]

Will had died, nine days after the article mentioning him appeared in the *Amsterdam News.*

All that Will Anthony "Little Napoleon" Madden had on him when he died was seven silver dollars. He had been staying at the Village Nursing Home, an elder care residence on Hudson Street, less than a mile from where he'd once lived next to the elevated train tracks in Little Africa.

Will's health was declining, and he was a frequent patient at nearby St. Vincent's Medical Center. The Village Nursing Home itself wasn't in much better shape. It was a privately funded for-profit business mostly housing poor residents, and to stay financially afloat, drastic cost-cutting had left it under-staffed, overcrowded, and out-of-date. With beds for two hundred occupants, every floor was cramped and smelly. The deteriorating facility was about to be shut down. Will was there with the support of the City's Department of Social Services, which provided him with "medical aid and old age assistance" until his death on February 26, 1973.[22]

Those seven silver dollars were not all that Will had to his name. According to court documents, his total assets from saving accounts, stock and bond certificates, insurance payouts, Social Security benefits, a retirement payment, and personal belongings were valued at $8,442.37, about $45,000 in today's value.

Though no one noticed it, those assets revealed some clues about Will's life. The stock certificates included several from Exxon Corporation, the major petroleum products supplier descended from Standard Oil, and the retire-ment check he left behind was from an annuity plan purchased in 1932 that was available only to Standard Oil employees. Will's estate settlement papers did not list any furniture, clothing, appliances, keepsakes, or other household items, which means whatever of these he had were considered worthless. The historically priceless photographs, scrapbooks, newspaper clippings, letters, and files he saved—and hounded Howie Evans with—were thrown in the garbage. Will's personal effects consisted of a wristwatch and a bracelet with an "approximate unsold value of $25" as well as those coins.[23] All of this was sold by the city in a public auction to cover funeral and burial costs as well as unpaid medical bills, rent, Department of Social Services charges, and attorney's fees.

Throughout the 1800s and 1900s in America, owning seven silver dollars was a *thing*. People put the coins aside—hidden in jewel boxes, secret attic nooks, or unused kitchen pots—in case of hard times. Folks without a stash spot carried them around in their trouser pockets. Seven silver dollars took on a symbolic meaning. The clunky jingling sound conveyed confidence, prosperity, and wherewithal, even if those virtues were temporarily gone.

Post-World War II big band leader Russ Morgan romanticized this notion with a song he recorded in 1953, aptly called "Seven Silver Dollars." It's about a man who was so broke that his lucky coins were all he had left. The guy visits Las Vegas, hoping to win big at gambling. Instead, he immediately loses six of them. Then, with his last silver dollar, he hits the jackpot. It's an avalanche of winnings, but the man keeps gambling and promptly loses all but the original coins. "Just seven silver dollars to my name," he sings, as the song ends. He starts with nearly nothing and ends there, too.

That songwriter also co-composed a hit called "You're Nobody 'Til Somebody Loves You," made famous in the 1960s by movie star and romantic crooner Dean Martin.[24] "You're nobody 'til somebody loves you," Martin sings. "You're nobody 'til somebody cares."

Previously, these tunes were the woeful anthems of Will Anthony Madden's life. But he was back in a newspaper sports column, home, where he belonged. His grave has been found and marked. His journey, symbolizing the important but forgotten history of an entire sports era, has been unearthed. His soul could finally rest in peace. Will came from a family of survivors. His full story had never been told. But it survived.

ACKNOWLEDGMENTS

This book took many years to complete. It began in the days when research had to be done in actual libraries using books and microfilm readers, and ended amid a pandemic, distance learning, and remote access to digitized newspaper databases. So many roads led to the start and the completion of this book, and so many people were there along the way, like in a marathon, cheering or handing me a cup of water when I needed it most, some who I didn't even know or who didn't even realize how much they were helping me just by being there. I wish I could name everyone. Thank you just the same.

I am grateful for the research resources and their staffs that helped me, which include the Saint Kitts National Archives, the United States Library of Congress, the Sterling Library and the Beinecke Rare Books and Manuscripts Library at Yale University, the New York City Municipal Archives, the Spingarn Library at Howard University, the Springfield College Archives, the New York Public Library's Genealogy Division and its Schomburg Center for Research in Black Culture, Ancestry.com, the Lincoln University of Pennsylvania Library, the Chicago History Museum, the Kautz Family YMCA Archives, the Charles L. Blockson Afro-American Collection, the Woodson Regional Library of the Chicago Public Library, the Harvard University Archives, the Carnegie Library of Pittsburgh, the Hillman Library at University of Pittsburgh, and the University of Michigan Library. I want to give special shout-outs to Sam Black at the Senator John Heinz History Center, for his encouragement along the way, especially during the early part of this journey; Doug Stark at the Naismith Memorial Basketball Hall of Fame, for his helpfulness way back when I was just getting started; and Kate Petrov at the Greenwich Public Library, where I am a member, who thoughtfully added the invaluable ProQuest Historical

Black Newspapers database to its remote-access repertoire at my suggestion in the aftermath of George Floyd's murder.

I also want to shout out the many individuals along the way who helped me believe in my writing and storytelling abilities with publication opportunities, including Bobbito Garcia, Jesse Washington, and Alejandro Danois with *Bounce Magazine*; Susan Price Thomas at *SLAM*; Matt Zeysing with the Basketball Hall of Fame; Mike Pesca in his book, *Upon Further Review*; and John X. Miller at *The Undefeated*/ESPN.

I owe a debt of gratitude to many friends whose encouragement, passion, validation, generosity, or example helped me get started and kept me going. My earliest well-wishers included Rob and Amy Castaneda, Keith Houlemard, Glenn Hunter, Ken Sergeant, Bob McCullough, Mark Johnson, Russel Schuler, and Bobby Hunter, as well as David Aldridge, Michael Tillery, Alexander Wolff, Mark Webster, Joe Favorito, the late Monica Harris, Henry Abbott, Dave Zirin, Ray Doswell, David McCullough, Wayne Coffey, David Berliner, Stephen Edidin, and Susan Johnson. I'm sending a big thank-you as well to Bill Daughtry, Larry Hardesty, and Ray Santiago at ESPN Radio, and to many other broadcasters and media outlets over the years, for continually validating the Black Fives Era on your shows.

I'm grateful for the voices of community elders and storytellers who we have lost since I began, such as Ed Bolden, Carl Younger, Zachary "Brother Zach" Husser, Zelda Spoelstra, and John "Butch" Purcell, all of whom embraced me from the jump and added to my sense of purpose through the high value they placed on making sure our history was preserved, taught, and honored.

Since my writing for this book began, we have also lost early African American basketball players themselves, who helped me by filling in details about this history from their own experiences, including George Crowe, Carl Green, William "Pop" Gates, and John "Boy Wonder" Isaacs. I'll always remember those numerous times I was on the air at WHCR 90.3 FM, the Voice of Harlem, with host Stephanie Stepp, Brother Zach, and Mr. Isaacs, with people calling in to ask questions about this history. They trusted and believed in me, and it is to help honor them that this work continues.

A special call-out to my mentor and friend, longtime *New York Amsterdam News* sports journalist Howie Evans, whose meaningful words, forceful energy, and unconditional helpfulness over the course of many years have been a constant source of inspiration.

Thank you to the Black Fives Foundation and its board of directors, now and over the years. This would not be possible without the organization and their solid governance.

Pivotal researchers who did so much of the groundwork and provided context before I even got started were Bill Rhoden, Susan Rayl, Ron Thomas, Bijan Bayne, Nelson George, Larry Hogan, Arthur Kimmel, Joe Dorinson, Murry Nelson, Gerald Gems, Bob Kuska, Kevin McGruder, Michael Adams, Larry Lester, and my OG mentor Rob Ruck, who, when he agreed to meet with me in a Starbucks at the University of Pittsburgh more than twenty years ago, not only opened new historical vistas for me, but also helped me to believe I could write this exact book—and encouraged me to finish it, every chance he could.

And even before them, the pioneering work of researchers such as Jervis Anderson, Ocania Chalk, Bob Peterson, St. Claire Drake, Gilbert Osofsky, and Timothy Gilfoyle were crucial to understanding the context in which the Black Fives Era took place. Above all, for me, was the groundbreaking history of African Americans in sports written by Arthur Ashe, *A Hard Road to Glory*, which, after I picked up a copy at the old Barnes & Noble on Sixth Avenue at Eighth Street in the Village effectively got me started on this journey.

I am grateful for the supporters and patrons who ever visited BlackFives. org, our YouTube channel, and other social media feeds to read my articles, see what was there, or listen to updates to share their enthusiasm and feedback. In the final stretch, one amazing person who I have never met in person (you know who you are) sent devotionals and a Starbucks gift card to help me stay awake and alert not only in body and mind, but in spirit, with Philippians 1:6 being their favorite reassurance, precious indeed, that this book would be finished.

Speaking of health and wellness, I couldn't have made it without USANA!

There is no legal way to describe what John J. Tormey III, Esq., did way back when, but I cannot thank you enough and you'll see why in these pages, all these years later.

This book would not have been anywhere near complete without the input, support, and encouragement of many descendants of the Black Fives

Era, which include members of the families of Cumberland Posey, Jr., James Dorsey, Donahue Goins, James Hoffman Woods, Ferdinand Accooe, Hudson Oliver, Edwin Horne, Edith Trice and her brothers, Conrad Norman and his brothers, Zack Clayton, Charlie Isles, William "Dolly" King, Hank DeZonie, Jackie Robinson, and Edwin Bancroft Henderson.

Yes, there are a few rare individuals who never believed nor cared, but I'm grateful to you, too, as a source of motivation to keep going, and I hope you like what's in these pages after all. On that note, I need to thank the earlier version of myself, who became interested in this more than twenty years ago, who dove in and kept going despite slowdowns, setbacks, obstacles, and challenges, to eventually figure out a way to deliver the rough versions of all that work into my hands these last couple of years. People change, but history never does.

One can be the right person, with the right thing, in the right place, but it's the wrong time. But it turns out that right now, there seems to be a global yearning to right historical wrongs and to learn the true history of basketball, the game we all know and love. And here is where I credit my literary agent, William LoTurco, for sensing that well in advance of the summer of 2020. He saw an article written by previously mentioned ally Jesse Washington, with the help of a small amount of research info from me, and he told Jesse that that topic would make a great narrative nonfiction book. Jesse agreed and said, "Claude Johnson should be the one to write it." That's just beyond extraordinary. So I am doubly and even triply indebted to Jesse, because next, William called out of the blue and said he wanted to represent me for that book. He believed in me, and eventually we signed with Abrams Press, whose executive editor Jamison Stoltz expanded our vision to include not just Black basketball history from the perspective of one city, but four cities, and then managed the complexities of all those many moving parts to bring you this finished book. Jesse, William, and Jamison were and are believers; I cannot fully express my appreciation for that and how much it means.

In closing, I am so grateful for my family, relatives, aunties, uncles, cousins, nieces, and nephews near and far who always wanted to know how my writing was going, especially during the last few years. The memory of Mom and Dad blesses this book, as my mother, Marianne, had a book in her, and my father, Charles, who we lost last year, was so determined to finish his book but ran out of time. I hope this makes you both proud. My siblings, Lawrence,

Claire, Christina, and Charles (including my brother-in-law Chris Fay, an extraordinary writer, filmmaker, storyteller, and illustrator) have always been my personal sounding boards as well as my solid, unconditionally loving family foundation, always there, believing in me and offering support through thick and thin; and for whom I was inspired to finish so that we could all collective say, "We did it!" It was my brother Charles who first got me in touch with John Isaacs, through his work with Converse at the time, which enabled so many other historically informative relationships to be forged. And in conclusion, I am grateful for my sons, Cassius, Cornelius, and Carnegie. You are each amazing individuals, blessings; I admire you as people, and I am proud to be your dad. We've experienced so much together during the writing of this book. Thank you for inspiring me to keep at it (and keep at it) during every single day of this journey, reminding me to remember each moment, and always asking, in words spoken and unspoken, through your own examples, "Are you stoppable, or unstoppable?" You're the best. Thank you!

NOTES

CHAPTER 1: AN UNMARKED GRAVE

1   Burial Records, Rosedale Cemetery; Linden, New Jersey.

2   File No. 2510, Records Department, Surrogate's Court of the County of New York.

3   Funeral Records, Gannon Funeral Home; New York City.

4   Linda Lynwander, "Burying the Poor," *New York Times*, February 5, 1995.

CHAPTER 2: SURVIVAL

1   David M. Barnes, *The Draft Riots in New York, July 1863: The Metropolitan Police, Their Services During Riot Week, Their Honorable Record* (New York: Baker & Godwin, 1863), p. 13.

2   *New-York Tribune*, July 16, 1863.

3   CPI Inflation Calculator, officialdata.org.

4   Barnes, *Draft Riots in New York*, p. 13.

5   *Trow's* New York City Directory, May 1863 (New York: John F. Trow, 1863).

6   *Report of the Committee of Merchants for the Relief of Colored People, Suffering from the Late Riots in the City of New York* (New York: George A. Whitehorne, Steam Printer, 1863), p. 23. York Street extended between West Broadway and St. John's Place, which was behind St. John's Chapel, fronting St. John's Park.

7   "The Negro in the Metropolis," *New York Daily Herald*, January 25, 1861, p. 3.

8   *Report of the Committee of Merchants*.

9   Barnes, *Draft Riots in New York*.

10   Barnes, *Draft Riots in New York*.

11   *Report of the Committee of Merchants*.

12   Margaret Potter was arrested for stealing furniture from the home of Anna Maria Dickerson at 9 York Street. She was tried and convicted in the Court of Special Session and sentenced to three months in the New York City Penitentiary. Adrian Cook, *Armies of the Streets: The New York City Draft Riots of 1863* (Lexington: University Press of Kentucky, 1974).

13   *Chicago Tribune*, July 18, 1863.

14   *Trow's* New York City Directory.

15   Barnes, *Draft Riots in New York*.

16   *New-York Tribune*, July 16, 1863.

17   *Chicago Tribune*, July 18, 1863.

18   Barnes, *Draft Riots in New York*.

19   *Report of the Committee of Merchants*; "woods and fields," p. 8; "four or five white women," p. 26.

CHAPTER 3: SEEDS

1   Local civil registrations and church records identified via correspondence with the Saint Kitts National Archives; the baby was baptized on February 16, 1883.

2   Dudley A. Sargent, "Physical Education in Colleges," *North American Review* 136, no. 314 (January 1883): 177.

3   Joe William Trotter, *River Jordan: African American Urban Life in the Ohio Valley* (Lexington: The University Press of Kentucky, 1998), p. 17.

4   *Historical Sketch of the Young Men's Christian Association of Chicago, 1858–1898* (Chicago: Young Men's Christian Association, 1898).

5   On systems of physical training, Charles Franklin Thwing, *A History of Education in the United States Since the Civil War* (Boston: Houghton Mifflin Company, 1910), p. 201.

6   Sargent, "Physical Education in Colleges," *North American Review* 136, no. 314 (January 1883): 174.

7   Thwing, *A History of Education*, p. 202.

8   Ohio, County Marriages, 1774–1993, Athens County Marriage Record, p. 234.

9   *Baltimore Sun*, May 3, 1869.

10 "Crossing of the Boatman," *Cincinnati Enquirer*, March 22, 1890, p. 9.

11 *Pittsburgh Courier*, June 13, 1925, p. 2. Fireman reference, *Daily Republican*, January 8, 1895, p. 4. The *Sallie J. Cooper*, operating out of Wheeling, West Virginia, was built in 1878 and was ninety-two feet long and sixteen feet wide. The largest steamboats of the time had as many as eight boilers.

12 "Hays Farm, Near Munhall, Is Sold," *Pittsburgh Gazette Times*, July 19, 1911, p. 14. The land sold for $200,000 in 1911, about $5.4 million today.

13 From the brief obituary of Abraham Hays (who died September 10, 1887), *Pittsburgh Post-Gazette*, September 12, 1887, p. 6. See also *J. F. Diffenbacher's Directory of Pittsburgh and Allegheny Cities, 1887* (Pittsburgh: Diffenbacher & Thurston, 1887).

14 Tonnage for the steamers *Little Bill* and *Abe Hays* as listed in *Report on the Internal Commerce of the United States* (Washington, D.C.: Government Printing Office, 1888), p. 4. On the repeated sinking of the steamer *Abe Hays*, *The Louisville Courier-Journal*, April 4, 1883, p. 8.

15 1880 United States Federal Census, Athens County, Athens, Ohio, Enumeration District 3.

16 *Consolidated Lists of Civil War Draft Registrations, 1863–1865*, Ohio, 15th Congressional District, Vol. 1.

17 *Athens Messenger*, June 26, 1879, cited in Carole Wylie Hancock, "Honorable Soldiers, Too: An Historical Case Study of Post-Reconstruction African American Female Teachers of the Upper Ohio River Valley" (PhD diss., Ohio University, Athens, 2008).

18 Certificate mentioned in *Athens Messenger*, April 10, 1879, cited in Hancock, "Honorable Soldiers, Too."

19 Hancock, in "Honorable Soldiers, Too," also notes, "In 1882, Athens County was the home of 167 schoolhouses (195 rooms) that served 9,337 White students and 357 Black children." citing E. G. Beatty and M. S. Stone, *Getting to Know Athens County* (Athens, Ohio: Stone House, 1984).

20 Originally called the New York and Brooklyn Bridge and the East River Bridge, it was officially renamed the Brooklyn Bridge in 1915. *Vermont Watchman and State Journal*, May 30, 1883, p. 5.

21 The name "Little Africa" was used most famously by Paul Laurence Dunbar in his short story "Johnsonham, Junior," published in 1900.

22   Birth Certificate No. 375203, New York City Municipal Archives; *United States Census for 1900*, vol. 124, ED 100, sheet 2, line 52.

23   *New York Herald*, August 26, 1883.

24   Hudnut's Pharmacy was located at 218 Broadway.

25   *New York Times*, August 25, 1883.

26   "Route and Section Map: 2nd, 3rd, 6th, and 9th Avenue Elevated Lines," New York Transit Museum Archives; "Elevated Railways," in *The Encyclopedia of New York City*, ed. Kenneth T. Jackson (New Haven: Yale University Press, 1995).

27   Clifton Hood, *722 Miles: The Building of the Subways and How They Transformed New York* (Baltimore: Johns Hopkins University Press, 1993). The technical term for welder's lung is *siderosis*, a disease caused by iron-oxide exposure, which deposits iron particles in the lung.

28   Mary White Ovington, *Half a Man: The Status of the Negro in New York* (New York: Longmans, Green, 1911).

29   Each of the seven blocks was on the list of Manhattan's worst places to live. In the early 1880s, the Sixth Avenue Line zigzagged at West Third Street between Sixth Avenue and West Broadway, and at Murray Street between West Broadway and Church Street.

30   William D. Howells, *Impressions and Experiences* (London: Ward & Downey, 1889), cited in Hood, *722 Miles*.

31   New-York Historical Society Archives, Prints and Photos Division; "Horse-Drawn Vehicles," in Jackson, *Encyclopedia of New York City*.

32   Martin V. Melosi, *The Sanitary City: Urban Infrastructure in America from Colonial Times to the Present* (Baltimore: Johns Hopkins University Press, 2000).

33   Timothy Gilfoyle, *City of Eros: New York City, Prostitution, and the Commercialization of Sex, 1790–1920* (New York: W. W. Norton, 1992), pp. 214–15.

34   Jacob Riis, *How the Other Half Lives* (New York: Charles Scribner's Sons, 1890).

35   Ibid.

36   New York City Department of Records & Information Services; New York City, New York; *New York City Birth Certificates*; Borough: *Manhattan*; Year: *1883*, Certificate No. 375203.

37   *United States Census for 1830, 1840*, and *1850*, Maryland, Anne Arundel County, Howard District.

38   Groom's address listed on 1880 Marriage Certificate No. 8433, Reel 124, New York City Municipal Archives.

39   Kurt C. Schlichting, *Grand Central's Engineer: William J. Wilgus and the Planning of Modern Manhattan* (Baltimore: Johns Hopkins University, 2012), p. 44. Built in 1871, the massive Grand Central Depot was the terminus for the New York Central & Hudson River Railroad, the New York & New Haven Railroad, and the New York & Harlem Railroad. The structure was replaced in 1913 by today's Grand Central Terminal.

40   Groom's occupation listed on 1880 Marriage Certificate No. 8433; see also *New York City Directories for 1881–82, 1882–83*, New York City Municipal Archives.

41   Bride's address listed on 1880 Marriage Certificate No. 8433; see also *United States Census for 1880*, New York, New York County (Manhattan), ED 20, p. 11. There were numerous African American enclaves dotting Greenwich Village. Today, it is among the wealthiest sections of Manhattan, known as Tribeca, and the trendy Tribeca Hilton Garden Inn has replaced the tenement that once was Margaret Ann's home.

42   *Chicago Tribune*, April 4, 1880.

43   Ellen Corbett arrived on board the *Yorkshire*, a full-rigged transport ship in the Black Ball Line, on August 25, 1851, from Liverpool. *Irish Immigrants: New York Port Arrivals Records*,

1846–1851 (Ellen Corbett); *United States Census for 1880.* The famine caused mass starvation and disease in Ireland, claiming more than a million lives.

44　Madden quoted by Floyd G. Nelson, "The Harlem Limited Broadway Bound," *Pittsburgh Courier,* September 12, 1931. During the mid-1920s, Nelson was the editor of the *Hotel Tattler,* a Black society newspaper (later known as the *Interstate Tattler*).

45　*The Echo: Journal of the Hunter College Archives* (New York: Hunter College of the City University of New York, 1995).

46　Eleventh Commencement of the Normal College of the City of New York, 1880, Hunter College Archives. The institution's eleventh commencement exercise took place on June 17, 1880.

47　Marriage Certificate No. 8433; *United States Census for 1900,* vol. 124, ED 100, sheet 2, line 52.

48　*The Echo,* p. 8. Margaret Madden, New York City Department of Health Death Certificate, May 19, 1924, New York City Municipal Archives, lists years living in New York City.

49　Civil Rights Act of 1875, 18 Stat. 335–337 (1875).

50　"Speech of Hon. James T. Rapier," *New National Era* (Washington, D.C.), June 18, 1874, p.1.

51　Sarah A. Dickey, Clinton, Miss., letter to President Ulysses S. Grant, September 23, 1875, John Y. Simon, *The Papers of Ulysses S. Grant, Volume 26: 1875* (Carbondale: Southern Illinois University Press, 2003), p. 298.

52　*New York Times,* September 8, 1875, p. 5.

53　Campbell Gibson and Kay Jung, *Historical Census Statistics on Population Totals by Race, 1790 to 1990, and by Hispanic Origin, 1790 to 1990, for the United States, Regions, Divisions, and States* (U.S. Census Bureau, Population Division Working Paper No. 56, 2002).

54　*The Crisis* 92, no. 1 (January 1985): 20.

55　Audrey E. Kerr, "Two Black Washingtons: The Role of Complexion in the Oral History of District of Columbia Residents, 1863–1963" (PhD diss., University of Maryland, 1998).

56　Parade description and route, *National Republican,* April 10, 1883, p. 2.

57　"upper crust," Kerr, "Two Black Washingtons."

58　Of the city's 17,244 alley residents, 16,046 were African Americans. Alley population and "stench," James Borchert, "The Rise and Fall of Washington's Inhabited Alleys, 1852–1972," Records of the Columbia Historical Society (Washington, D.C.: By the Society), p. 278.

59　Martha L. Sternberg, *George Miller Sternberg: A Biography* (Chicago: American Medical Association, 1920).

60　"Looking Back on Fifty Years," *Baltimore Afro-American,* September 11, 1954, p. 3.

61　Richard Wright Public Charter School occupies a portion of that block today.

62　*United States Census for 1880.*

63　*Washington Evening Star,* March 27, 1880, p. 9.

64　"Letters to the Editor: Falls Church Negroes," *Washington Post,* October 15, 1948, p. 24.

65　Melvin Lee Steadman, Jr., *Falls Church by Fence and Fireside* (Falls Church, VA: Falls Church Public Library, 1964), p. 215. According to local accounts, Elizabeth Mimetou Foote was a cousin of Chief Logan as well as a brother of Frederick F. Foote, Sr., who was sold as an enslaved person.

66　"Falls Church Negroes," p. 24.

67　*National Park Service: Vicksburg National Military Park.*

68　Ibid. The fact that Black residents cheered as Grant's forces advanced and eventually marched into the city may suggest that there was no need to escape.

69　The house was at 471 School Street SW, Washington, D.C. Eliza was also said to own property on E Street, next to the Fourth Street Police Station.

70   Tours of duty for USS *Tallapoosa*, USS *Worcester*, and USS *Powhatan*: *Disapproved Pension Application File for Seaman William Henderson, Tallapoosa Powhatan (Application Number 44104)*, National Archives and Records Administration, Department of the Interior, Bureau of Pensions, 1849–1930, Series: Case Files of Disapproved Pension Applications of Civil War and Later Navy Veterans, ca. 1861–ca. 1910, Record Group 15: Records of the Department of Veterans Affairs, 1773–2007, NARA Identifier 90727607, originally filed November 3, 1898.

71   Ibid.

72   Kerr, "Two Black Washingtons."

73   *United States Census for 1880.*

74   Leon N. Coursey, "The Life of Edwin Bancroft Henderson and His Professional Contributions to Physical Education" (PhD diss., Ohio State University, 1971), p. 14.

CHAPTER 4: PITTSBURGH PEDIGREE

1   James Parton, "Pittsburg," *Atlantic Monthly* 21, no. 123 (January 1868): 17–36.

2   "No More Smoke!," *Pittsburgh Daily Post*, June 3, 1847, p. 2.

3   *J. M. Kelly's Handbook of Greater Pittsburg, 1895* (Pittsburgh: J. M. Kelly, Publishers, 1895).

4   Joe William Trotter, Jr., *River Jordan: African American Urban Life in the Ohio Valley* (Lexington: University Press of Kentucky, 2014), table 2, African American population in Ohio Valley cities, 1860–1910, p. 28.

5   Ibid., table 2, p. 64.

6   Miles Yancy, "Study to Chronicle Histories of Hill District Ethnic Groups," *New Pittsburgh Courier*, March 10, 1984, p. A4.

7   *Fifth Annual Edition—1890, Directory of Homestead, Munhall, Six Mile Ferry, and Adjacent parts of Mifflin Township, Allegheny County, Pa.* ([Homestead]: M. P. & J. R. Schooley at the Local News Office, [1890]), p. 6.

8   During the late 1800s, Homestead was considered a part of Mifflin Township, Allegheny County, which also included Munhall, Six Mile Ferry, and some adjacent land.

9   The buyout was reportedly for $1.2 million, or about $30 million today. *Harrisburg Daily Independent*, October 17, 1883, p. 1.

10   Allegheny County Department of Real Estate, Lot 138, Plan Book, vol. 4, p. 118. The one-tenth-acre lot sold for $975, or nearly $26,000 today.

11   Hays Family Papers, c1874–c1945, MSS 717, Library and Archives Division, Senator John Heinz History Center, 1887–88. Ledger records show that Captain Hays rented House #3 to C. W. Posey for $10 a month; *Pittsburgh Post-Gazette*, September 12, 1887, p. 6. See also *J. F. Diffenbacher's Directory of Pittsburgh and Allegheny Cities, 1887* (Pittsburgh: Diffenbacher & Thurston, 1887).

12   *1890, Directory of Homestead*, p. 6.

13   They lived at 50 Wilson Street. *Pittsburgh Street Directory, 1888.*

14   Trotter, *River Jordan*. The strikes at Pittsburgh Bolt Company and Black Diamond Steel Works took place in 1875, and at Solar Iron Works from 1887 to 1889.

15   "Largest in the World," *Pittsburgh Daily Post*, January 3, 1887, p. 1.

16   *Champaign Daily Gazette*, May 10, 1887, p. 2.

17   Interview with Henderson, March 1970, cited in Leon N. Coursey, "The Life of Edwin Bancroft Henderson and His Professional Contributions to Physical Education" (PhD diss., Ohio State University, 1971), p. 19.

18   Ishmael Reed, "In Search of August Wilson," *Connoisseur*, March 1987, p. 95.

19   *Pittsburgh Daily Post*, February 11, 1888, p.1.

20   *Pittsburgh Press*, February 5, 1886, p. 1.

21   *Pittsburgh Daily Post*, February 11, 1888, p.2.

22   "gambler," *Muncie Evening Press*, September 10, 1892, p. 7; "thoroughbreds," *Pittsburgh Daily Post*, January 3, 1910, p. 4.

23   Daisy Moore's "disorderly house" was at 32 Bedford Avenue. *Pittsburgh Dispatch*, June 4, 1891, p. 2.

24   *Pittsburgh Press*, January 24, 1888, p. 2.

25   *Pittsburgh Daily Post*, May 18, 1889, p. 1.

26   *J. F. Diffenbacher's Directory*.

27   Sale of 39.9 acres by Peter Elicker to C.W. Posey, both of Mifflin Township, October 24, 1889. Allegheny County Department of Real Estate, Recorder of Deeds, *Deed Book 653*, p. 570–72.

28   *Pittsburgh Dispatch*, August 23, 1890, p. 11.

29   *Pittsburgh Daily Post*, December 6, 1890, p. 3.

30   *Pittsburgh Daily Post*, March 11, 1891, p. 3; April 9, 1891, p. 3; May 8, 1891, p. 8.

31   The *J.S. Neel* had towed more than two million bushels of coal during the prior year. *Pittsburgh Daily Post*, March 18, 1892, p. 7.

32   "About Boats and Boatsmen," *Pittsburgh Daily Post*, May 26, 1892, p. 6.

33   *1896 Homestead Directory* (Homestead, PA: M. P. & J. R. Schooley, 1896). Captain and Anna Posey owned Lots 75, 76, 77, 78, 79, 80, 81, and 82, located on Second Avenue, as specified in the Plan of Lots known as Plumer's Riverside Park Plan No. 2 in the *Allegheny County, Pennsylvania Plan Book, vol. 11*, p. 68. They purchased Lots 75, 76, and 77 for $1,650; Lots 78, 79, and 80 for $1,171; and Lots 81 and 82 for $1,500.

34   Carnegie Bros. & Co. was renamed Carnegie Steel Company in 1892.

35   *Ligonier Echo*, July 20, 1892, p. 1.

36   "River Intelligence," *Cincinnati Enquirer*, December 17, 1894, p. 7.

37   *Pennsylvania Negro Business Directory 1910* (Harrisburg: Jas. H. Howard & Son, 1910), p. 40.

38   Their property included residences with street addresses that included 310, 312, 314, 318, and 320 East Thirteenth Avenue, according to U.S. Census and U.S. City Directory listings.

39   Helen A. Tucker, "The Negroes of Pittsburgh 1907–08," published in *Charities and the Commons*, January 3, 1909, as compiled in *Wage-Earning Pittsburgh* (New York: Survey Associates, 1914).

40   *Pennsylvania Negro Business Directory 1910*, p. 40.

41   Evan Posey Baker, May 17, 2001.

42   Tucker, "The Negroes of Pittsburgh 1907–08."

CHAPTER 5: RITES OF PASSAGE

1   *New York Times*, March 4, 1870, p. 3.

2   Birth Certificate No. 450980.

3   Ibid.

4   Department of Commerce and Labor, Bureau of the Census, *Bulletin 26: Illiteracy in the United States* (Washington, D.C.: Government Printing Office, 1905).

5   Floyd G. Nelson, "The Harlem Limited Broadway Bound," *Pittsburgh Courier*, September 12, 1931.

6   The pushcart location was at 1½ Minetta Lane, right outside where Minetta Tavern is today. Beginning in the 1930s, Minetta Tavern was frequented by several famous writers

and poets including Ernest Hemingway, Ezra Pound, Eugene O'Neill, E. E. Cummings, and Dylan Thomas.

7 "pest spot," Unknown newspaper clipping, May 17, 1914, Minetta Lane Vertical File, Museum of the City of New York.

8 *The New York City Sketches of Stephen Crane, and Related Pieces*, ed. R. W. Stallman and E. R. Hagemann (New York: New York University Press, 1966), pp. 178–79.

9 Jacob Riis, *How the Other Half Lives* (New York: Charles Scribner's Sons, 1890), p. 119.

10 *New York Evening Sun*, November 28, 1903.

11 "playground," "mass of humanity," Minetta Lane Vertical File, Museum of the City of New York.

12 Moses King, *King's Handbook of New York*, 2nd. ed. (Boston: Moses King, 1893), p. 389.

13 John D. Rockefeller, Jr., had the mansion torn down in 1938, following his father's death in 1937. A legendary example of the senior Rockefeller's worth and generosity was when he gave his daughter $1 million on the morning of her wedding in 1889, the equivalent of more than $25 million in today's dollars. *Indianapolis Journal*, October 27, 1889.

14 "How 'the Other Half' in New York Reaches Its Workshops," *New York Times*, June 3, 1906; "Each Has His Body Guard," *New York Times*, January 3, 1892.

15 *New York Evening World*, November 25, 1890.

16 Clifton Hood, *722 Miles: The Building of the Subways and How They Transformed New York* (Baltimore: Johns Hopkins University Press, 1993).

17 Their address was 160 Waverly Place. *New York City Directories for 1890–91, 1903–4, 1905–6*, New York Public Library and New York City Municipal Archives. During the late 1970s, this same location was the legal address of the New York City mobster Carmine Galante, godfather of the Bonanno crime family.

18 In comparison, only 97 such properties were approved for New York City just ten years later. "Decline of Individual Dwellings in New York," *New York Times*, December 30, 1901.

19 Northern Dispensary information, *New York Times*, January 9, 1892, p. 8. The Northern Dispensary was opened in 1831 in what was then the north end of the city. Its original deed restriction states that the building must be used "to serve the worthy poor."

20 Abyssinian Baptist was founded in 1803 in Lower Manhattan, which at the time was home to the city's largest concentration of African Americans. In the early 1860s, as Blacks moved uptown into Greenwich Village, Abyssinian followed, relocating in 1864 to Waverly Place. Its current location is on West 138th Street in Harlem.

21 *United States Census for 1900*, vol. 124, ED 100, sheet 2, line 52.

22 Dudley Allen Sargent, "Are Athletics Making Girls Masculine? A Practical Answer to a Question Every Girl Asks," *Ladies' Home Journal*, March 1912.

23 Ethel Josephine Dorgan, *Luther Halsey Gulick, 1865–1918* (New York: Teachers College, Columbia University, 1934).

24 Joe Willis and Richard Wettan, "Social Stratification in New York City Athletic Clubs, 1865–1915," *Journal of Sport History* 3, no. 1 (Spring 1976): 45–63.

25 "time for sports," Booker T. Washington, *Up From Slavery* (New York: Doubleday, 1901), p.5.

26 Olivia A. Davidson Washington to Mary Elizabeth Stearns, April 11, 1887, in Harlan, *Booker T. Washington Papers*, vol. 2, *1860–-89*, p. 338.

27 "An Account of Addresses by Washington and Mrs. Washington Delivered at Charleston," September 12, 1898, in Harlan, *Booker T. Washington Papers*, vol. 4, *1895–98* (1975), p. 463.

28 The International YMCA Training School was renamed International YMCA College in 1912 and Springfield College in 1954.

29 James Naismith, *Basketball: Its Origin and Development* (New York: Association Press, 1941).

30   Luther Halsey Gulick, MD, *The Efficient Life* (New York: Doubleday, Page, 1907).

31   Naismith, *Basketball*, p. 36.

32   Ibid.

33   Archives of the YMCA, cited in Robert W. Peterson, *Cages to Jump Shots: Pro Basketball's Early Years* (New York: Oxford, 1990).

34   *Kansas City Times*, November 4, 1961, p. 38.

35   *New York Times*, November 18, 1900, p. 7.

36   *New York Times*, October 17, 1897, p. 5. William Strong was the last mayor of New York City while it was still only Manhattan, before expanding in 1898 to include Brooklyn, Queens, Staten Island, and the Bronx.

37   *New York Times*, October 15, 1915, p. 11.

38   Nelson, "Harlem Limited Broadway Bound."

39   The quote is in Patrick Myler, *Gentleman Jim Corbett: The Truth behind a Boxing Legend* (London: Robson Books, 1998).

40   The building housing Grammar School No. 35, at 60 West Thirteenth Street, was converted into a high school and renamed Boys' High School in 1897. It was renamed to DeWitt Clinton High School in 1900, moved to Midtown Manhattan in 1906, and to its present location in the Bronx in 1929.

41   *National Republican*, November 13, 1875, p. 4.

42   *Washington Times*, June 23, 1895, p. 10.

43   "Death Trap For Children," *Washington Evening Times*, April 15, 1896, p. 8.

44   "Looking Back on Fifty Years," *Baltimore Afro-American*, September 11, 1954, p. 3.

45   Edgar S. Martin, *The Playground Movement in the District of Columbia: Report to the Commissioners of the District of Columbia* (62nd Congress, 2nd Session, Senate Document No. 937, 1912).

46   "Looking Back on Fifty Years," p. 3.

47   Ibid.

48   Leon N. Coursey, "The Life of Edwin Bancroft Henderson and His Professional Contributions to Physical Education" (PhD diss., Ohio State University, 1971).

49   "The Small Boy in His Spring Suit," *Buffalo Sunday Morning News*, April 14, 1901.

50   *The Hawaiian Star*, August 10, 1901, p. 8.

51   Typical advertising for Alger novels, "handsomely bound in Illuminated Cloth and finely illustrated," in many American newspapers such as the *Pittsburgh Post-Gazette*, which frequently offered them at a special discounted price of 39 cents.

52   Horatio Alger, Jr., *Fame and Fortune; or, The Progress of Richard Hunter* (New York: A. K. Loring, 1868), p. viii.

53   *The Telegraph Boy* (1879), *The Young Bank Messenger* (1898), *Mark Mason's Victory; or, The Trials and Triumphs of a Telegraph Boy* (1899), and *Adventures of a New York Telegraph Boy* (1900).

54   Gregory J. Downey, *Telegraph Messenger Boys: Labor, Technology, and Geography 1850–1950* (New York: Routledge, 2002).

55   *New York Age*, August 28, 1937; *New York Age*, September 3, 1949.

CHAPTER 6: SATAN'S CIRCUS

1   *New York Times*, January 16, 1900.

2   James Weldon Johnson, *Black Manhattan* (New York: Alfred A. Knopf, 1930), p. 128.

3   *United States Census for 1890, 1900,* and *1910.* Between 1890 and 1900 alone, the Black population of New York City more than doubled to 60,000, and it reached more than 90,000 by 1910. In that same period, the number of African Americans in the District of Columbia grew from 75,000 to 94,000. The Black community in greater Pittsburgh expanded from 13,000 in 1890 to 35,000 in 1910. The population of African Americans in Chicago more than tripled from 14,000 to 45,000 during those years.

4   Johnson, *Black Manhattan.*

5   *United States Census for 1890, 1900,* and *1910.*

6   Gilbert Osofsky, *Harlem: The Making of a Ghetto* (New York: Harper & Row, 1963), pp. 11-12.

7   Jervis Anderson, *This Was Harlem: A Cultural Portrait, 1900-1950* (New York: Farrar Straus Giroux, 1982).

8   "Sports and Amusements of Negro New York," WPA Writer's Project research paper, Schomburg Center for Research in Black Culture, as cited in Anderson, *This Was Harlem.*

9   Johnson, *Black Manhattan.* The Hotel Marshall closed on September 4, 1913.

10 From newspaper advertisements like those in the *New York Age.*

11 *Colored American Magazine,* September 1906, p. 383.

12 Fred R. Moore, *Negro Business Enterprises in New York,* Report of the Fourth Annual Convention of the National Negro Business League, Nashville Tennessee, August 19, 20, and 21, 1903 (Wilberforce, Ohio: Charles Alexander, 1903), p. 69.

13 Jacob Riis, *How the Other Half Lives* (New York: Charles Scribner's Sons, 1890); see also Mary Black, *Old New York in Early Photographs,* 2nd ed. (New York: Dover, 1976).

14 Timothy Gilfoyle, *City of Eros: New York City, Prostitution, and the Commercialization of Sex, 1790-1920* (New York: W. W. Norton, 1992).

15 Ibid.

16 *Harper's Bazaar,* December 22, 1900.

17 Riis, *How the Other Half Lives.*

18 Osofsky, *Harlem,* p. 8.

19 "The Saloon Problem," *New York Times,* February 19, 1906, p. 3.

20 Jimmy Durante, *Night Clubs* (New York: Alfred A. Knopf, 1931).

21 Investigator's Report, March 16, 1910, C14P, box 28, New York Public Library; Investigator's Report, Wilkins Café, undated 1910, C14P, box 28, New York Public Library.

22 Investigator's Report, Welch's Café, undated 1910, C14P, box 28, New York Public Library.

23 Report on Chadwick's Novelty Café, November 21, 1915, box 30, folder 9, COF, as cited by Douglas J. Flowe, *Uncontrollable Blackness: African American Men and Criminality in Jim Crow New York* (Chapel Hill: The University of North Carolina Press, 2020), p. 97.

24 *The Brooklyn Citizen,* September 29, 1905, p. 8.

25 Paul Laurence Dunbar, *The Sport of the Gods* (New York: Dodd, Mead, 1902).

26 Booker T. Washington, *The Future of the American Negro,* (Boston: Small, Maynard & Company, 1902), p. 165.

27 Booker T. Washington to Portia Washington, March 12, 1904, in *The Booker T. Washington Papers,* vol. 7, *1903-4,* ed. Louis R. Harlan and Raymond W. Smock (Champaign: University of Illinois Press, 1977), p. 466. At the time, Portia Washington was a student at Bradford Academy (later Bradford Junior College) in Bradford, Massachusetts, and in 1905 she became the school's first African American graduate.

28 Anderson, *This Was Harlem.*

29 *New York Age,* May 18, 1905.

30 These included the Knights of King Arthur, the Big Brothers, the Boy Scouts, the Men's Guild,

the Brotherhood of St. Andrew, the Men's Bible Class, the St. Agnes Society, the Auxiliary to the Board of Missions, the Auxiliary to the Parish Home for Retired Women, and the Women's Bible Class. *Reaching Out: An Epic of the People of St. Philip's Church, Its First 170 Years* (New York: St. Philip's Church, 1986).

31   Papers on Appeal from Order, St. Christopher Club against St. Christopher Club of New York, Inc., New York State Supreme Court, Appellate Division, First Department, November 10, 1914.

32   "toothbrush," Booker T. Washington, *Up from Slavery* (Garden City, N.Y.: Doubleday, 1901), p. 174.

33   Nina Mjagkij, *Light in the Darkness: African Americans and the YMCA, 1852–1946* (Lexington: University Press of Kentucky, 1994). Of these, forty-one were student-run organizations at Black colleges.

34   Frank Moss, *Story of the Riot* (New York: Citizens' Protective League, 1900), p.1.

35   First quotation, ibid.; second quotation, *New York Times*, August 16, 1900.

36   Arthur J. Harris was subsequently arrested, tried, convicted of murder, and sentenced to life in prison, where he died on December 20, 1908. As cited by Osofsky, *Harlem*, The People vs. Arthur J. Harris, October 29, 1900 (New York City Magistrate's Court), and letter from Harold W. Folletta, Acting Warden, Clinton Prison, to author, August 14, 1961.

37   United States, Selective Service System, World War I Selective Service System Draft Registration Cards, 1917–1918, National Archives and Records Administration, New York State, New York City, Draft Board 153, roll 1786814.

38   *New York Daily Tribune*, August 29, 1900, cited in Osofsky, *Harlem*.

39   Harold X. Connolly, *A Ghetto Grows in Brooklyn* (New York: New York University Press, 1977), pp. 17n10, 21.

40   "Wealthy Negro Citizens," *New York Times*, July 14, 1895.

41   *United States Census for 1910*, including New York City Index; 1905 Brooklyn Census; *Brooklyn City Directories for 1905, 1906, 1907, 1908, 1909*; *New York City Directories for 1905, 1906, 1907, 1908, 1909*; New York City Municipal Archives; Microfilm Reading Room, Genealogy Department, New York Public Library.

42   Gail Lumet Buckley, *The Hornes: An American Family* (New York: Alfred A. Knopf, 1986). The book describes her family and its roots among the borough's privileged African Americans.

43   Clarence Taylor, *The Black Churches of Brooklyn* (New York: Columbia University Press, 1996).

44   St. Augustine's moved to 700 Marcy Avenue in the 1920s and is located today at 4301 Avenue D in Brooklyn.

45   Buckley, *The Hornes*, p. 62.

46   Connolly, *A Ghetto Grows in Brooklyn*.

47   "Negro Business Enterprises in New York," *Colored American Magazine*, July 1904, p. 520. These goods included "pedestals, tabourettes, lamp columns, lamp and vase bodies" in "imitation onyx, agate, fossil wood, and various foreign and American pottery finishes."

48   *New York Age*, February 27, 1908.

49   *New York Age*, July 20, 1905.

50   *Colored American Magazine*, July 1904.

51   *Brooklyn Daily Eagle*, December 7, 1908.

52   Booker T. Washington, *The Negro in Business* (New York: Herte, Jenkins, 1907).

53   Daniel Marsh, *The Challenge of Pittsburgh* (New York: Missionary Education Movement of the United States and Canada, 1917).

54   Oliver Waters, "The Smoky City," *Colored American Magazine*, October 1901.

55 *Colored American Magazine*, October 1901.

56 James Parton, "Pittsburg," *Atlantic Monthly*, January 1868, pp. 17–36.

CHAPTER 7: 1901

1   "Billion Trust Complete," *New York Evening World*, March 2, 1901. The actual transfer of ownership was completed in April 1901.

2   "Mrs. Carnegie's Home," *New-York Tribune*, May 31, 1901.

3   Death Certificate Records, New York City Municipal Archives.

4   Nelson, "The Harlem Limited Broadway Bound," *Pittsburgh Courier*, September 12, 1931.

5   In 1901, the New York City Police Department had 107 horses in service in Manhattan, and of these, 45 were used for mounted duty and 62 for patrol wagons and buggies. "Training Police Horses," *New York Times*, January 27, 1901, p. 6.

6   Maximilian Frances "Max" Schmittberger had a forty-three-year career in the New York Police Department, from 1874 until his death in 1917.

7   "Police Invasion of Little Coney Island," *New York Times*, March 18, 1901, p. 2. Louis and Eddie Waldron were born with the last name Schwartz, their father's name. They changed their surnames to Waldron after 1880. According to Eddie's great-granddaughter, Ruth Foerster, the family may have changed their last name in order to become "Americanized" faster. Later in life, Eddie married a Catholic woman, against the wishes of both sets of parents, and later converted to Catholicism. Waldron family background via personal interview, November 29, 2019.

8   *New-York Evening World*, February 9, 1888, p. 1.

9   Kevin McGruder, *Race and Real Estate: Conflict and Cooperation in Harlem, 1890–1920* (New York: Columbia University Press, 2015).

10 "Waldron Is Discharged," *New-York Tribune*, April 4, 1901, p. 12.

11 Waldron's Dance Hall was located two hundred feet west of Amsterdam Avenue.

12 "Many at Waldron's Dance Unmolested," *New York Herald*, June 3, 1901.

13 Ibid.

14 Committee of Fifteen Records (New York: 1900–1901), Manuscripts and Archives Division, New York Public Library.

15 "Finishing School in Vice for Girls," *New York Herald*, January 17, 1901.

16 *Penal Code of the State of New York* (Albany: Banks, 1881), specifically "§ 277. Theatrical and other performances—The performance of any tragedy, comedy, opera, ballet, farce, negro minstrelsy, negro or other dancing, wrestling, boxing with or without gloves, sparring contest, trial of strength, or any part or parts therein, or any circus, equestrian, or dramatic performance or exercise, or any performance or exercise of jugglers, acrobats, club performances or ropedancers, on the first day of the week, is forbidden; and every person aiding in such exhibition, performance or exercise, by advertisement, posting or otherwise, and every owner or lessee of any garden, building or other room, place or structure, who leases or lets the same for the purpose of any such exhibition or performance or exercise, or who assents to the use of the same for any such purpose, if it be so used, is guilty of a misdemeanor."

17 "Dance Hall Test Case: Argument to Be Heard on the Legality of Opening Such Resorts on Sunday," *New York Times*, January 23, 1901.

18 "Dance Halls Bill Disapproved: Governor Scores Measure Barring Them from Half Mile of Cathedral," *New York Times*, April 9, 1902, p. 5.

19   Goff, John W. to Waldron, Louis and Waldron, Edward, Lots 77, 78, Conveyances, City
      Register's Office, City of New York, Manhattan Business Center.

20   Watson, Steven. *The Harlem Renaissance* (New York: Pantheon Books, 1995).

21   *Wilkes-Barre Times Leader*, 1 June 1903.

22   As seen in advertisements such as *New York Times*, October 14, 1911, p. 22.

23   *Rochester (New York) Democrat and Chronicle*, February 24, 1903.

24   Johnson, James Weldon. *The Autobiography of an Ex-Colored Man* (Boston: Sherman,
      French, 1912).

25   Kevin McGruder, *Race and Real Estate: Conflict and Cooperation in Harlem, 1890–1920*
      (New York: Columbia University Press, 2015), table 2.2, Distribution of African American
      population in Manhattan, 1900, pp. 42–43.

26   New York State Archives, Albany; *State Population Census Schedules, 1905*, AD 23, ED 16,
      New York County (Manhattan).

27   *New York Herald*, cited in McGruder, *Race and Real Estate*, p. 47.

28   McGruder, *Race and Real Estate*.

29   Ibid., table 2.1, Race of residents of the South Side of 135th Street (between Fifth and Lenox
      Avenues), 1900, p. 43.

30   *New York Age*, 25 October 1906, p. 6.

31   DeWitt Clinton High School's second annual commencement exercises were held on June 24,
      1901. *New York Times*, 25 June 1901.

32   *New-York Tribune*, May 30, 1901.

33   Wadleigh High School for Girls was located at 36 East Twelfth Street, between Broadway and
      University Place.

34   Cashboys worked on the sales floors of large stores and collected cash from paying customers
      so that that the salesperson, who called for him by yelling, "Cash!," could continue selling.
      "Sidelights of Cashboy Life," *San Francisco Call*, 22 July 1900, p. 14.

35   *New York Times*, June 9, 1901.

36   *New York Times*, September 14, 1897.

37   *New York Times*, September 5, 1901.

38   *New York Times*, May 14, 1901. The New York Juvenile Asylum incarcerated homeless and
      runaway children in order to house, train, and reform them. The NYJA was located in Wash-
      ington Heights, at 196th Street and Amsterdam Avenue. Those detained were notoriously
      subjected to abuses, and many were sent to the West on "orphan trains," to be placed on farms
      as indentured laborers.

39   "Messenger Service Fails," *New York Times*, 10 May 1901.

40   *New York Times*, April 26, 1901. The last day of trading in the old New York Stock Exchange
      Building was April 26, 1901. The outdated building had been open since December 9, 1865.
      The new building, at 18 Broad Street with an entrance at 11 Wall Street, opened for trading
      on April 22, 1903, and is the current site of the New York Stock Exchange.

41   *New York Times*, 10 May 1901.

42   *Electrical World and Engineer*, May 18, 1901, p. 829.

43   Johnston, W. J. *Telegraphic Tales and Telegraphic History* (New York: W. J. Johnston, 1880).

44   Spargo, John. *The Bitter Cry of the Children John* (New York: Macmillan, 1909). In one favorite
      trick, a messenger boy would be sent for a bottle of whiskey at a nearby hotel, but he would
      know where to purchase it for 50 percent less at another spot, which he would do and then
      pocket the difference.

45   Riis, Jacob. *The Children of the Poor* (New York: Charles Scribner's Sons, 1892).

46   Johnston, *Telegraphic Tales and Telegraphic History.*

47   "Crisis Shown at Opening," *New York Evening World*, May 9, 1901.

48   "Failures before Panic Was Checked," *New York Evening World*, May 9, 1901.

49   *New York Times*, May 9, 1901.

50   "Incidents of the Day," *New York Times*, May 10, 1901.

51   Ibid.

52   "Disaster and Ruin in Falling Market," *New York Times*, May 10, 1901.

53   "Scenes of Disorder in Stock Exchange," *New York Times*, May 10, 1901.

54   "The Northern Pacific 'Corner' Now Broken."

55   "Scenes of Disorder in Stock Exchange."

56   "Market Falls and Panic Soon Reigns," *New York Times*, May 9, 1901.

57   "Northern Pacific Corner Exposed."

58   "Disaster and Ruin in Falling Market."

59   "Wall Street Settlement," *New York Sun*, May 9, 1901.

60   "Disaster and Ruin in Falling Market."

61   "Dies in Vat of Hot Beer," *New York Times*, May 10, 1901.

62   "Scenes of Disorder in Stock Exchange."

63   "The Northern Pacific 'Corner' Now Broken."

64   "Messenger Service Fails."

65   Ibid.

66   "Northern Pacific Corner Exposed."

67   "The Northern Pacific 'Corner' Now Broken."

68   "Crisis Shown at Opening," *New York Evening World*, May 9, 1901.

69   "Incidents of the Day."

70   "Messenger Service Fails."

71   "Negro Boys for Messengers: All the White Boys Discharged in Atlanta and Their Places Filled by Blacks," *New York Times*, June 28, 1903.

72   Floyd G. Nelson, "The Harlem Limited Broadway Bound," *Pittsburgh Courier*, September 12, 1931.

73   *New York County Supreme Court Naturalization Petition Index, 1907–1924*, vol. 442, p. 95, New York City Municipal Archives. There is a conflict between the arrival information listed on Douglas's naturalization documents (departed St. Kitts on May 24, arrived in New York City on June 1, 1901) and the actual ship arrivals listed in multiple independent sources such as the *New York Times*, which state that the *Madiana* in fact reached New York City on June 6.

74   The *Madiana* weighed 3,080 tons, "Cruises from New York," *Washington Evening Star*, March 23, 1901, p. 14.

75   *Buffalo Express*, January 24, 1901, p. 5.

76   "Willett & Gray's Estimates of Cane Sugar Crops at End of 1901," in *The International Year Book: A Compendium of the World's Progress during the Year 1901* (New York: Dodd, Mead, 1902), p. 745.

77   Ibid., p. 444.

78   Within a single two-year span during the mid-1800s, the British colonial islands' share of the world sugar supply dropped from 15 percent to only 2 percent. Sacks, Marcy S., *Before Harlem: The Black Experience in New York City before World War I* (Philadelphia: University of Pennsylvania Press, 2006), p. 20.

79   "Leaving the Caribbean," Howard Dodson and Sylviane Diouf, *In Motion: The African-American*

Migration Experience (New York: New York Public Library, Schomburg Center for Research in Black Culture, 2004).

80   Hubbard, Vincent K. *A History of St. Kitts: The Sweet Trade* (Oxford: Macmillan Caribbean, 2002), p. 125–126.

81   "Table 3: Literacy of Black Immigrants, 1899–1932," in *U.S. Dept. of Labor, Bureau of Immigration, Annual Report of the Commissioner General of Immigration to the Secretary of Labor [1899–1932]* (Washington, D.C.: Government Printing Office [1900–1933]) as cited by Winston James, "Explaining Afro-Caribbean Social Mobility in the United States: Beyond the Sowell Thesis," *Comparative Studies in Society and History* 44, no. 2 (2002): 233. One study found that by 1930, 6 percent of Black Americans listed in the book *Who's Who among Colored Americans* were immigrants, even though less than 1 percent of the country's entire Black population was foreign-born. More than 8 percent of physicians, nearly 5 percent of attorneys, almost 15 percent of businessmen, about 5 percent of clergymen, more than 3 percent of professors, and 4 percent of writers and authors listed were from the West Indies. Watkins-Owens, Irma, *Blood Relations: Caribbean Immigrants and the Harlem Community, 1900–1930* (Bloomington: Indiana University Press, 1996).

82   "Shipping and Foreign Mails," *New York Times*, June 7, 1901, p. 5.

83   *Atlas of the City of New York, Borough of Manhattan, vol. 3 (59th Street to 110th Street); from actual surveys and official plans, 1898*, Lionel Pincus and Princess Firyal Map Division, New York Public Library.

84   United States Bureau of the Census, *Region and Country or Area of Birth of the Foreign-Born Population, with Geographic Detail Shown in Decennial Census Publications of 1930 or Earlier: 1850 to 1930 and 1960 to 1990*. The total was 25,435 if also counting 11,081 residents born in Cuba.

85   Watkins-Owens, *Blood Relations*, p. 4; Gardner Jones, "Pilgrimage to Freedom," Writers' Program series Negroes of New York, p. 25, [Schomburg Library for Research in Black Culture] as cited in Sacks, *Before Harlem*.

86   "Afro-American Notes," *Brooklyn Daily Eagle*, 18 August 1901, p. 6.

87   Carl Nesfield, "All in the Game," *New York Age*, February 6, 1960, p. 15.

88   *New York, Extracted Marriage Index, 1866–1937*, Certificate No. 18205, New York City Municipal Archives.

89   New York State Archives, Albany; State Population Census Schedules, 1905, AD 21, ED 36, New York County (Manhattan), p. 53.

90   *Brooklyn Daily Eagle*, December 31, 1901, p. 9.

91   Frederick M. Binder and David R. Reimers, *All the Nations under Heaven: An Ethnic and Racial History of New York City* (New York: Columbia University Press, 1995).

92   "New York's Latest School," *New York Times*, September 28, 1902.

93   *New York Evening Post*, January 22, 1902.

94   P.S. 188 opened on September 21, 1903. It still stands today and is in full use.

95   *Cortland Evening Standard*, May 6, 1902; see also "New York's Latest School."

96   *Brooklyn Daily Standard Union*, September 22, 1903.

97   "Streetscapes: Charles B. J. Snyder," *New York Times*, November 21, 1999.

98   *New-York Tribune*, September 16, 1906.

99   *Livonia Gazette*, February 22, 1907.

100 *New York Times*, June 5, 1904.

101 Riis, *How The Other Half Lives*, p. 108.

102 *Brooklyn Daily Standard Union*, September 22, 1903, p. 5.

103 Naismith, *Basketball*.

104 Amateur Athletic Union of the United States, Young Men's Christian Association Athletic League of North America and George T. Hepbron, *Official Basket Ball Rules: As Adopted by the Amateur Athletic Union and the Young Men's Christian Association Athletic League of North America, 1908-09* (New York: American Sports, 1908), Group VII, no. 7.

105 Settlement house details, *Handbook of Settlements* (New York: The Russell Sage Foundation, 1911).

106 Gardner Richardson, "The New Gymnasium," *University Settlement Studies* Quarterly 1, no. 4, (1906): 41-45.

107 Eugene C. Gibney, "Basket Ball in Recreation Centers," in *Official Basket Ball Rules, 1913-14* (New York: American Sports, 1913).

CHAPTER 8: PHYSICAL CULTURE

1   Normal School No. 2, later known as the Miner Normal School and the Miner Teachers College, is now the Miner Building on the campus of Howard University.

2   Interview with Henderson, March 1970, cited in Leon N. Coursey, "The Life of Edwin Bancroft Henderson and His Professional Contributions to Physical Education" (PhD diss., Ohio State University, 1971).

3   Ibid.

4   "Demand for Playgrounds," *Washington Evening Times*, June 25, 1901, p. 8.

5   "Extracts Relating To Recreation," The McMillan Report on the "Improvement of Park System, District of Columbia," 1902, as cited in Edgar S. Martin, *The Playground Movement in the District of Columbia: Report to the Commissioners of the District of Columbia* (62nd Congress, 2nd Session, Senate Document No. 937, 1912), p. 4.

6   Ibid, p. 10.

7   Ibid, p. 13.

8   Martin, *Playground Movement*, p. 12-13.

9   *Carlton Avenue YMCA Records*, Kautz Family YMCA Archives, Archives and Special Collections, Elmer L Anderson Library, University of Minnesota.

10 *Brooklyn Life*, January 2, 1904.

11 *New York Times*, February 7, 1904, p. 11.

12 *Brooklyn Daily Eagle*, February 25, 1904.

13 "Rules of Healthful Living," *New York Times*, February 28, 1904.

14 "The Origin and Growth of the Alpha Physical Culture Club," *New York Age*, April 25, 1907.

15 Ibid.

16 1900 U.S. Census.

17 "Alpha Physical Culture Club."

18 Alexander Heffner and Richard D. Heffner, eds., *A Documentary History of the United States*, rev. ed. (New York: Penguin, 2013).

19 Conrad Norman, "The Alpha Physical Culture Club," in *Inter-Scholastic Athletic Association of Middle Atlantic States Handbook for 1910* (New York: American Sports, 1910), p. 27.

20 Herbert Spencer first used the phrase in his 1864 book, *Principles of Biology*, after reading Charles Darwin's *On the Origin of Species by Means of Natural Selection, or the Preservation of Favoured Races in the Struggle for Life* (1859) which is considered the foundation of evolutionary biology. *Principles of Biology* (1864), vol. 1, p. 444. Darwin later wrote, "This preservation, during the battle for life, of varieties which possess any advantage in structure,

constitution, or instinct, I have called Natural Selection; and Mr. Herbert Spencer has well expressed the same idea by the Survival of the Fittest."

21   *New-York Daily Tribune*, January 18, 1904, p. 6.

22   *New York Times*, 20 October 1904; for the cost, see *Hartford Courant*, July 23, 1904.

23   "World's Fair Olympic Games," *Elmira Star-Gazette*, January 16, 1904.

24   *New York Times*, July 20, 1904.

25   *St. Louis Post-Dispatch*, March 26, 1904. Columbia won the intercollegiate title on March 1 by defeating the University of Pennsylvania, 23–12. *Brooklyn Times Union*, March 2, 1904, p. 8.

26   George T. Hepbron, *How to Play Basket Ball*, Spalding's Athletic Library (New York: American Sports, 1904).

27   *Brooklyn Daily Eagle*, January 30, 1904, p. 9.

28   Hepbron, *How to Play Basket Ball*.

29   "Many Changes Among Teachers," *Washington Times*, June 30, 1904, p. 5.

30   Wiggins, David K. "Edwin Bancroft Henderson: Physical Educator, Civil Rights Activist, and Chronicler of African American Athletes," *Research Quarterly for Exercise and Sport* 70, no. 2 (June 1999).

31   Ibid.

32   *Washington Evening Star*, September 7, 1904, p. 2.

33   "Benefits of the Playgrounds: How They Are Directed at the Colored Schools," *Washington Evening Star*, July 25, 1909, p. 24.

34   Harvard University Archives. The other Black student was Eleanor Holmwood, the physical director at Illinois Women's College. Contrary to prior descriptions of Henderson's affiliation with Harvard University, he did not enroll as a full-time regular student there, did not graduate with a regular Harvard University degree, and was not the university's first African American graduate.

35   *Summer School of Arts and Sciences Catalogue of Students in 1904* (Cambridge, Mass.: Harvard University, 1904).

36   Ibid.

37   "Olympic Games Begun," *New York Times*, May 15, 1904. The 1904 Olympic Games officially began on May 14, 1904.

38   "Basket Ball Champions," *Decatur Herald*, July 13, 1904. With their gold medals, the Germans returned home and turned professional, billing themselves as "world's champions." They eventually won 111 straight games from 1908 to 1911 and were subsequently inducted into the Naismith Memorial Basketball Hall of Fame as a team.

39   Wiggins, "Edwin Bancroft Henderson."

40   Gardner Richardson, "The New Gymnasium," *University Settlement Studies* Quarterly 1, no. 4, (1906): 41–45.

41   Poage ran in the 35,000-seat Olympic Stadium. That venue was turned over to Washington University after the Olympics. *New York Times*, July 20, 1904.

42   "Teachers of Physical Training," *Washington Evening Star*, September 15, 1904, p. 16.

43   The school year began on September 19, 1904. "Appointments, Promotions in the Public Schools," *Washington Times*, December 31, 1904, p. 12.

44   Edwin Bancroft Henderson, *The Negro in Sports* (Washington: Associated, 1939), p. 148.

CHAPTER 9: ST. CHRISTOPHER

1   Archives of the Episcopal Church USA.

2   *The Anniversary Book of Saint Philip's Church* (New York: St. Philip's Church, 1943).

3   The United States purchased the Danish West Indies for $50 million in 1917 as a defensive measure against possible German submarine attacks in World War I.

4   St. Augustine's College was a coed Episcopal teachers' institute that was founded in 1867 for freed slaves following the Civil War and initially called the St. Augustine Normal School. At the time Daniel attended, its room, board, and tuition cost $7 a month. *North Carolina and Its Resources* (Winston: M. I. & J. C. Stewart, 1896). The school is known today as St. Augustine's University, a historically Black college.

5   Postulant's Application, October 24, 1899, Archives of the Episcopal Diocese of New York. Founded in 1817, General Theological Seminary is located at 440 West Twenty-First Street in Manhattan. It is the oldest independent seminary in the United States.

6   The Reverend Everard W. Daniel, *The Church on Trial: A Sermon Preached before the Conference of Church Workers among Colored People* (Philadelphia: Church of St. Michael and All Angels', 1916).

7   Daniel's commencement exercises took place on May 14, 1902. "Graduates in Divinity," *New York Times*, May 15, 1902; "Trinity Parish Ordinations," *New York Times*, May 26, 1902.

8   Bragg, George F. *History of the Afro-American Group of the Episcopal Church* (Baltimore: Church Advocate Press, 1922).

9   Everard Washington Daniel to the Right Reverend H. C. Potter, Bishop of New York, October 15,1902, Archives of the Episcopal Diocese of New York.

10   Daniel to Potter, 1902.

11   *United States Census for 1900*, New York, New York County (Manhattan), ED 157, sheet 3B. The building was at 335 West Sixteenth Street, between Eighth and Ninth Avenues.

12   Norman, "The Alpha Physical Culture Club," in *ISAA 1910*.

13   "The Origin and Growth of the Alpha Physical Culture Club," *New York Age*, April 25, 1907.

14   "Candidate's Certificate, Title I, Can. 7, § v. (d) §§ vi, vii," Archives of the Episcopal Diocese of New York, April 30, 1902.

15   Garrie W. Moore, "A Study of a Group of West Indian Negroes in New York City" (Master's thesis, Columbia University, 1913).

16   "New West Side Playground," *Baltimore Sun*, November 5, 1905, p. 5.

17   *New York Times*, May 9, 1906, p. 4.

18   "Negro Parish House," *New-York Tribune*, April 20, 1907, p. 11.

19   The church already had "between three hundred and four hundred members," according to reports. Ibid.

20   *New York Age*, January 21, 1909, p. 3.

21   Nesfield, *New York Age*, February 6, 1960, p. 15.

22   The couple were married on July 25, 1906. *New York, Extracted Marriage Index, 1866–1937*, Certificate No. 18205, New York City Municipal Archives.

23   Local civil registrations and church records identified via correspondence with the St. Kitts National Archives.

24   Death Certificate Records, New York City Municipal Archives.

25   Schuyler B. Stuart, *The Story of the Evergreens Cemetery* (New York: Evergreen Cemetery, n.d.).

26   Floyd G. Nelson, "The Harlem Limited Broadway Bound," *Pittsburgh Courier*, September 12, 1931.

27   Occupations listed in the *New York State Census, 1905*, New York County (Manhattan), AD 5, ED 12, pp. 19, 22.

28   Downey, Gregory J. *Telegraph Messenger Boys: Labor, Communication and Technology, 1850–1950* (New York: Routledge, 2002).

29   *New York City Directory for 1912–13*, New York City Municipal Archives.

30   *New York City Census, 1905*, New York City Municipal Archives; *New York City Directory for 1912–13*, New York City Municipal Archives; views assessed from photographs and descriptions: Vertical Clipping File, "Lower Broadway," Museum of the City of New York; Marcia Reiss, *New York Then and Now* (New York: Dover, 1976); Mary Black, *Old New York in Early Photographs* (New York: Dover, 1973).

31   *New York City Directory for 1905*, New York City Municipal Archives. He was assigned to Room 902.

32   Rockefeller, John D., *Random Reminiscences of Men and Events* (New York: Doubleday, Page, 1916). On the tenth floor was the directors' dining room. Rockefeller particularly enjoyed "the room at the top of the Standard Oil Company's building, where the officers of the company and the heads of departments have had their luncheon served for many years." That changed with the addition of six stories to the structure in 1895.

33   Rockefeller's private office had been moved to Room 1409.

34   *Coeur d'Alene Press*, January 23, 1904.

35   Ibid.

36   Her findings appeared as a nineteen-part series of monthly articles in *McClure's* and were later published in her book, *The History of the Standard Oil Company* (New York: McClure & Phillips, 1904).

37   *St. Louis Republic*, July 14, 1905.

38   *Topeka State Journal*, February 18, 1905.

39   *Los Angeles Herald*, June 11, 1905. John Jr. had joined his father's office in 1897.

40   "Robbers Got $10,000 of Standard Oil Money," *Buffalo Times*, March 21, 1905.

41   *Los Angeles Times*, March 21, 1905.

42   *St. Louis Republic*, July 14, 1905.

43   *Bismarck Daily Tribune*, November 19, 1906.

44   Correspondence between William Anthony Madden and Office of John D. Rockefeller, Jr., February 20, 1940, Standard Oil, folder 1028, box 138, series C, FA312, Business Interests, Office of the Messrs. Rockefeller records, Record Group 2, Rockefeller Family Archives Collection, Rockefeller Archive Center.

45   Horatio Alger, Jr., *Mark Mason's Victory; or, The Trials and Triumphs of a Telegraph Boy* (New York: A. L. Burt, 1899).

46   Lynn Abbott and Doug Seroff, *Ragged but Right: Black Traveling Shows, "Coon Songs," and the Dark Pathway to Blues and Jazz* (Jackson: University Press of Mississippi, 2009).

47   *Brooklyn Daily Eagle*, February 25, 1904.

48   Gail Lumet Buckley, *The Hornes: An American Family* (New York: Alfred A. Knopf, 1986), includes this point and other supporting details relating to the Scottrons, the Smart Set Athletic Club, and Black middle-class life in Brooklyn during that time.

49   For more details about the Scottrons and Hornes, and their friends, see ibid.

50   Ibid.

51   *New York Age*, December 25, 1948.

52   *Baltimore Afro-American*, December 26, 1931.

53 *New York Age*, December 25, 1948. Herbert L. Pratt was married to Florence Gibb on April 28, 1897.

54 *Baltimore Afro-American*, December 26, 1931. Socony-Vacuum eventually became the Socony Mobil Oil Corporation before morphing into Mobil Oil and then ExxonMobil.

55 "New Dances Devised," *Brooklyn Daily Eagle*, December 16, 1894.

56 *Chicago Defender*, April 18, 1931.

57 Samuel Scottron lived at 598 Monroe Street with his wife, Anna, and their children Oscar, Alice, Rowena, and Anna. His two oldest sons, Charles and Cyrus, lived elsewhere. *United States Census for 1900*, Kings County (Brooklyn), Ward 23, p. 15.

58 *Brooklyn Daily Eagle*, July 3, 1902.

59 Local newspapers often ran advertisements for these events, including the *New York Age*. See, for example, *New York Age*, May 11, 1905.

CHAPTER 10: GREAT STRUGGLE FOR VICTORY

1 *Baltimore Afro-American*, January 27, 1906, p. 1.

2 *Baltimore Afro-American*, July 15, 1905, p. 4.

3 "time for sports," Booker T. Washington, *Up From Slavery* (New York: Doubleday, 1901), p.5.

4 Booker T. Washington, Jr., to Booker T. Washington, January 28, 1906, in *The Booker T. Washington Papers*, vol. 8, *1904-6*, ed. Louis R. Harlan and Raymond R. Smock (Champaign: University of Illinois Press, 1979), p. 513.

5 *Washington Evening Star*, January 24, 1903, p. 12.

6 Pinkerton association, *New York Amsterdam News*, January 13, 1926, p. 4.

7 Robert Pinkerton and his family lived in Park Slope at 71 Eighth Avenue.

8 *Inter-Scholastic Athletic Association of Middle Atlantic States Handbook for 1912* (New York: American Sports, 1912).

9 *Baltimore Afro-American*, August 21, 1937.

10 *Baltimore Afro-American*, June 10, 1916.

11 *New York Age*, April 8, 1909.

12 Floyd G. Nelson, "The Harlem Limited Broadway Bound," *Pittsburgh Courier*, September 12, 1931.

13 *Red Raven* reference, *Reaching Out: An Epic of the People of St. Philip's Church, Its First 170 Years* (New York: St. Philip's Church, 1986).

14 "modest means," Robert N. Mattingly, "History of the I.S.A.A.," *ISAA* (1910), p. 15.

15 ISAA history, Ibid, p. 17-23.

16 *University Journal*, May 11, 1906, p. 5.

17 "Mother's Day Nursery Outing Successful," *Brooklyn Standard Union*, July 21, 1906, p. 5.

18 Ibid.

19 *New York Age*, January 14, 1909, p. 3.

20 *New York Age*, July 23, 1908, p. 2.

21 "Irate Divine Wanted Money Back from Charitable Funds," *New York Age*, July 26, 1906, p. 2.

22 Ibid.

23 See "Smart Set Wins," *New York Age*, December 5, 1907, and Lester Walton, "In the Sporting World," *New York Age*, April 8, 1909. About Robert Barnard, see also *ISAA 1910* (New York: American Sports, 1910), p. 68. By 1906, the Clark Settlement House had produced several local basketball stars, including the Jewish stars Sam Melitzer, who played for Columbia University

from 1906 to 1909, and Ira Streusand, who played for City College of New York from 1907 to 1909. See Bernard Postal, Jesse Silver, and Roy Silver, *The Encyclopedia of Jews in Sports* (New York: Bloch, 1965).

24   *ISAA 1910* (New York: American Sports, 1910).

25   *New York Age*, September 23, 1909.

26   Frances Ball, "Browsing Brooklyn," *New York Amsterdam News*, September 5, 1936, p. 10.

27   Gail Lumet Buckley, *The Hornes: An American Family* (New York: Alfred A. Knopf, 1986).

28   Clarence Fleming Lewis lived at 121 West Thirtieth Street. His father was Richard F. Lewis, whose barber shop was at 125 West Thirtieth Street in Midtown.

29   The earthquake struck on January 14, 1907. *New York Age*, January 17, 1907.

30   *New York Age*, August 1, 1907.

31   *Washington Evening Star*, April 3, 1907, p. 9.

32   *New York Age*, October 28, 1909, p. 3.

33   The orchestra had its business office at 321 West Fifty-Ninth Street.

34   *New York Age*, November 21, 1907, p. 6.

35   *Brooklyn Daily Eagle*, January 10 and 29, 1900.

36   *Brooklyn Daily Eagle*, July 9, 1900.

37   "Expected Arrivals," *Brooklyn Daily Eagle*, November 13, 1907.

38   New York City Arrivals, Port of New York, 1907. The Statue of Liberty Ellis Island Foundation.

39   Basketball was normally spelled as two words—"basket ball"—until the late 1910s.

40   "Official Rules—Season 1905–06," *Spalding's Official Basket Ball Guide for 1906–07* (Indianapolis: American Sports, 1905).

41   "Some Rules for Scientific Basket Ball," by J. L. Brewster, *Rochester Evening Times*, in *Spalding's Official Basket Ball Guide for 1906–07* (Indianapolis: American Sports, 1905).

42   Ibid.

43   *New York Age*, November 21, 1907.

44   "His herculean strength": "St. Christopher Wins," *New York Age*, November 21, 1907.

45   Ibid.

46   *Muncie Evening Press*, November 20, 1907, p. 2.

47   *Brooklyn Daily Eagle*, July 9, 1900.

48   *Indianapolis Freeman*, November 30, 1907, p. 6.

CHAPTER 11: A REAL CORKER

1   *New York Age*, December 5, 1907. The game was played on Friday, November 29, 1907.

2   *New York Age*, December 26, 1907.

3   *New York Age*, March 26, 1908.

4   Ibid.

5   The game was played on Monday, January 6, 1908. "Afro-American Notes," *Brooklyn Standard Union*, January 10, 1908, p. 11. The parish house belonged to the Church of the Incarnation and was located at 248 East Thirty-First Street.

6   *New York Times*, June 29, 1908.

7   *New York Times*, August 31, 1915.

8   *Slave Schedule, Eighth Census of the United States, 1860* (Washington, D.C.: National Archives and Records Administration, 1860), M653. The original Hart House still stands and is one of the oldest structures in Eufaula, Alabama, maintained by the Historic Chattahoochee Commission. "[M]ore than $75,000," according to *History of Barbour County, Alabama* (1939) by Mattie

Thomas Thompson. John Cleveland Hart used the funds to build a retail block in Eufaula. In the early 1870s, at a harbor rate of $1.50 each, thousands of bales of cotton were shipped from Eufaula down the Chattahoochee to the Apalachicola River to the Gulf of Mexico, near Panama City, Florida, on their way to New Orleans, Savannah, New York City, and Liverpool.

9 Before sunrise on Election Day, November 3, 1874, one hundred armed White men crowded into the second story rooms overlooking the town's main street and waited in silence until dozens of proud African American residents who had gathered nearby began marching up the street, accompanied by a fife and drum, on their way to vote. When the marchers passed below, the White terrorists opened fire. It was estimated that nearly a hundred Black would-be voters were shot down in the middle of the street, as many as forty of them fatally wounded. Carter, Dan T. *The Politics of Rage: George Wallace, The Origins of the New Conservatism, and the Transformation of American Politics* (Baton Rouge: Louisiana State University Press, 1995).

10 *Official Register of the United States, Containing a List of the Officers and Employees in the Civil, Military, and Naval Service Together with a List of Vessels Belonging to the United States, Vol. 1 (July 1899).* War Department records indicate that Hart was appointed to the USAT *Kilpatrick* in New York City, which means he may have boarded the transport while it was in New York Harbor on July 6, 1899 (*Washington Evening Star*, July 6, 1899). *Captain's boy* was an official job title, a position typically held by a teenager from fourteen to sixteen years old. It involved running errands and helping with chores, in this case as the personal valet for U.S. Army Captain Charles T. Baker, a career naval officer. On July 1, 1899, there were nineteen such transports in the U.S. Army Transport fleet, six of which were in the Pacific. The Kilpatrick was a steamer that carried soldiers, horses, equipment, supplies, and humanitarian aid to Cuba and Puerto Rico in the aftermath of the Spanish-American War, and her cargo capacity was enormous. For example, in 1899, she sailed to Cuba carrying 100,000 feet of lumber, 11,000 sacks of oats, 7,700 bales of hay, 7,000 sacks of flour, 760 kegs of nails, 700 tons of water, 600 tons of coal, 450 boxes of soap, 440 boxes of candles, 375 boxes of bacon, 350 bed springs, 200 bundles of telegraph wire, 200 sacks of coffee, 147 barrels of ham, 100 crates of prunes, 73 boxes of clothes, and 60 tons of ice, not to mention her 150-man crew, according to a captain's report.

11 *Hawaiian Star*, June 8, 1904.

12 *Hawaiian Star*, March 13, 1905.

13 *Honolulu Advertiser*, March 4, 1906, p. 1.

14 *Pacific Commercial Advertiser*, April 8, 1906.

15 *Hawaiian Star*, April 12, 1906, 2nd ed. Hart was a member of the Diamond Head Skating Team.

16 *Pacific Commercial Advertiser*, June 3, 1906, and "major hart leaves today," *Pacific Commercial Advertiser*, August 23, 1906. Hart initially planned to depart in April but rescheduled for a voyage on the same ship in August.

17 Hart sailed aboard the *Logan* to Manila then transferred to the USAT *Kilpatrick* for the remainder of the voyage. *The Hawaiian Star*, August 24, 1906, 2nd ed.

18 *Hawaiian Star*, November 19, 1906, 2nd ed.

19 "The Calamitous typhoon at Hong Kong, 18th September 1906," *Hong Kong Daily Press*, University of Hong Kong Library.

20 "major hart in tangier," *Hawaiian Star*, December 20, 1906, 2nd ed.

21 *Hawaiian Star*, February 14, 1907, 2nd ed.

22 Hart moved into a five-story brownstone mansion at 264 Fifth Avenue on the southwest corner of Fifth and West Twenty-Ninth Street in Manhattan known as the Knickerbocker Flats. The building had upscale retail stores at street level and top floors that had been converted

into lavish apartments used mostly by well-off bachelors. *New York Times*, March 26, 1878. The two French dormers (roofed porthole windows) on the top floor of the current building at that location are the only remaining vestiges of the prior opulent period on that section of Fifth Avenue for several blocks around.

23　*The Anniversary Book of Saint Philip's Church* (New York: St. Philip's Church, 1943).

24　*University Journal*, January 10, 1908, p. 3.

25　Fitzpatrick and Goodwin, *Guide to Black Washington* (New York: Hippocrene Books, 1999). True Reformers' Hall still stands today, across the street from Ben's Chili Bowl, the popular Howard University student hangout with the world's best chili.

26　*University Journal*, January 10, 1908, p. 3.

27　*University Journal*, February 10, 1908, p. 7.

28　Henderson's address there was 1919 11th Street NW, between U and T Streets.

29　*University Journal*, May 10, 1908, p. 1.

30　*Pittsburgh Daily Post*, November 12, 1904, p. 4.

31　"Erecting Unsightly Poles on the Streets," *Pittsburgh Daily Post*, July 26, 1906, p. 3.

32　*Pittsburgh Courier*, December 8, 1934, p. 18.

33　Cum and Chick lived at 320 and 350 East Thirteenth Avenue, respectively. 1910 United States Federal Census.

34　*Homestead Messenger*, cited in Margaret Frances Byington, *Homestead: The Households of a Mill Town* (New York: Charities Publication Committee, 1910), p. 121.

35　Specifically, the Posey's property on Second Avenue was eventually replaced by Carnegie Steel's colossal open hearth and plate mill buildings. After the Homestead Works closed in 1986, the site was reopened as a waterfront shopping complex. The original Second Avenue lots were located approximately where the Eat'n Park restaurant on East Waterfront Drive is today.

36　*Pittsburgh Press*, June 14, 1903, p. 37.

37　Oath of Publication of Notice, State of Pennsylvania, November 5, 1900.

38　Fulton Street, subsequently renamed Fullerton Street, no longer exists. It was covered over to make way for the parking lot of the Civic Arena, more recently known as Mellon Arena, which was built in 1961.

39　*Colored American Magazine*, November 1901.

40　"Colored Club Celebrates," *Pittsburgh Post-Gazette*, November 10, 1907, p. 15.

41　*Colored American Magazine*, November 1901.

42　*Pittsburgh Press*, October 17, 1897, p. 18.

43　*Pittsburgh Press*, March 5, 1899, p. 15.

44　Helen A. Tucker, "The Negroes of Pittsburgh 1907–08," published in *Charities and the Commons*, January 3, 1909, as compiled in *Wage-Earning Pittsburgh* (New York: Survey Associates, 1914), p. 599.

45　*United States Census for 1900*, Pennsylvania, Allegheny County, Homestead Ward 3, ED 0402, p. 2.

46　1900 production was nearly 3 million gross tons, which was about 700,000 tons *more* than the entire output of Great Britain had been in 1885.

47　Bridge, James Howard. *The Inside History of the Carnegie Steel Company: A Romance of Millions* (New York: Aldine Book Company, 1903), p. 295.

48　*Colored American Magazine*, October 1901.

49　*Pittsburgh Daily Post*, November 8, 1908, p. 14.

50　"Pyrotechny," Dick, William Brisbane. *Encyclopedia of Practical Receipts and Processes: Containing Over 6400 Receipts* (New York: Dick & Fitzgerald, 1900), p. 204. "Red fire" contained "20 parts chlorate of pottassa, 24 sulphur, 56 parts nitrate of strontia."

51   *Pittsburgh Daily Post*, November 8, 1908, p. 14.

52   "Basket Ball Tossers Plan Brisk Campaign," *Pittsburgh Daily Post*, October 10, 1908, p. 9.

53   *Liverpool Evening Review*, November 13, 1908, p. 9.

54   *Uniontown Morning Herald*, October 2, 1908, p. 2.

55   Byington, Margaret Frances. *Homestead: The Households of a Mill Town* (New York: Charities Publication Committee, 1910), p. 116.

56   For more on the Homestead High School Class of 1909 Commencement see *Pittsburgh Post-Gazette*, May 16, 1909, p. 11.

57   Moses, Alvin J. "Blazing the Trail," *Interstate Tattler*, April 19, 1929.

58   Personal interview with Evan Posey Baker, Pittsburgh, Pennsylvania, May 17, 2001.

59   Personal interview with Frank E. Bolden, from his home in a telephone call on June 8, 2001. He was a longtime columnist and society observer for the *Pittsburgh Courier*.

60   Clipping, "Wylie Avenue," by John L. Clark, *Pittsburgh Courier*, n.d.

61   Goldman, M. R. "The Hill District as I Knew It," *Western Pennsylvania Historical Magazine* 51 (July 1968).

62   Washington Park was formerly located on the 1200 block of Bedford Avenue, between what used to be Elm Street and Logan Street, overlooked by what used to be Grant Boulevard and nearly in the shadow of Union Station. The park was replaced by the old Civic Arena, renamed Mellon Arena, until that was torn down in 2011. Today, Elm Street and Grant Boulevard have been replaced by I-579. Central High School was formerly located at the corner of Bedford Avenue and Fulton Street.

63   Goldman, M. R. "The Hill District as I Knew It," *Western Pennsylvania Historical Magazine* 51 (July 1968), p. 283.

64   Moses, Alvin J. "Blazing the Trail: Cum Posey an 'All Time' Immortal," *Inter-State Tattler*, April 19, 1929.

65   Pittsburgh Playground Association. "Annual Report of the Pittsburgh Playgrounds and Recreation Parks, 1908."

66   *Pittsburgh Courier*, January 28, 1939.

67   *Pittsburgh Post-Gazette*, November 28, 1908, p. 11.

68   *Wage-earning Pittsburgh* (New York: Survey Associates, 1914).

69   Marsh, Daniel. *The Challenge of Pittsburgh*. New York: Missionary Education Movement of the United States and Canada, 1917.

70   *Pittsburgh Weekly Gazette*, February 15, 1903, p. 11. The new building was purchased in 1903.

71   *Pittsburgh Press*, August 25, 1907, p. 37.

72   *New York Age*, December 3, 1908, p. 5.

73   *Washington Post*, November 27, 1908, p. 1.

74   The beautiful building still stands today, housing the Thurgood Marshall Center for Service and Heritage, the Shaw Heritage Museum and Exhibition Center, and other community organizations. It was recently renovated and is on the National Register of Historic Landmarks.

75   "Artee Fleming Is Dead at 90," *Akron Beacon-Journal*, January 17, 1977, p. 19.

76   *Washington Post*, January 4, 1909, p. 8.

77   "Good Basket Ball Contests Promised," *Washington Evening Star*, March 24, 1909, p. 14.

78   *New York Age*, April 8, 1909.

79   *New York Age*, February 25, 1909.

80   *New York Age*, January 21, 1909, p. 3.

81   *Spalding Athletic Library Official Handbook of the Inter-Scholastic Athletic Association of Middle Atlantic States, 1912* (New York: American Sports, 1912), p. 93.

82 *Spalding Athletic Library Official Handbook of the Inter-Scholastic Athletic Association of Middle Atlantic States, 1910* (New York: American Sports, 1910), p. 61.

83 *New York Age*, January 28, 1909.

84 *New York Age*, July 20, 1905.

85 *Brooklyn Times Union*, February 13, 1909, p. 10.

86 *Amsterdam News*, December 18, 1929.

87 Though some documents list the birth year of Hudson Oliver, Jr., as 1888, his 1905 New Jersey State Census record lists 1890.

88 Her name was Virginia Hewlett.

89 They lived at 188 West Fourth Street. *New York City Directory for 1889.*

90 *New York Age*, March 4, 1909, p. 6.

91 *Brooklyn Daily Eagle*, September 27, 1885, p. 11.

92 *New York Age*, March 4, 1909.

93 *New York Age*, April 8, 1909, p. 6.

94 *Washington Herald*, March 27, 1909, p. 8.

95 *New York Sun*, March 21, 1909, p. 50.

96 Regarding game between Smart Set and Crescent A.C., *Washington Herald*, April 11, 1909, p. 38.

97 This modification was in compliance with the new rules of the local amateur Protective Basket Ball League, to which the Brooklyn Emeralds belonged.

98 *New York Age*, April 8, 1909, p. 2.

99 *New York Age*, April 22, 1909.

100 Ibid., p. 6.

CHAPTER 12: AS OUR WHITE FRIENDS PLAY IT

1 *University Journal*, February 10, 1908, p. 7.

2 *University Journal*, November 19, 1909, V7, No 7.

3 *University Journal*, November 12, 1909, V7, No 6, p. 2.

4 *University Journal*, December 17, 1909.

5 *New York Age*, October 28, 1909, p. 3.

6 The Plaza Rooms were on East Fifty-Ninth Street between Lexington and Third avenues.

7 *New York Age*, December 23, 1909, p. 7.

8 *New York Age*, December 30, 1909, p. 6.

9 *Washington Evening Star*, December 25, 1909, p. 9.

10 *New York Age*, December 30, 1909, p. 6.

11 New York State Supreme Court, Appellate Division, First Department, *Papers on Appeal from Order, St. Christopher Club against St. Christopher Club of New York, Inc.*, November 10, 1914.

12 *New York Age*, January 27, 1910.

13 *New York Age*, September 20, 1906, p. 6.

14 *New York Age*, December 23, 1915. The Manhattan Casino's grand opening was on Friday, June 19, 1903.

15 *New York Age*, August 23, 1906, p. 6.

16 *New York Age*, November 28, 1907, p. 1.

17 *New York Age*, January 20, 1910, p. 7.

18 Ibid.

19 *Washington Evening Star*, February 5, 1910, p. 10.

20   *New York Age*, February 10, 1910, p. 6.

21   *New York Age*, March 3, 1910, p. 6.

22   Young was with the *Pittsburgh Courier* at the time.

23   In 1910, Lent ran from February 9 to March 27.

24   *New York Age*, March 17, 1910, p. 6.

25   *New York Age*, March 31, 1910.

26   *New York Age*, April 7, 1910.

27   Nelson, *Pittsburgh Courier,* September 12, 1931.

28   The game was played on November 7, 1896. A historical marker on the wall of the front plaza of the Mary Roebling State Office Building (exact location, 40° 13.224' N, 74° 45.959' near 20 West State Street, Trenton, NJ 08608) marks the spot where this first pro game was played. The National Basketball Association dedicated it in 1955.

29   This and other fashionable styles were available at H. O'Neill & Co. on Sixth Avenue and Twentieth Street in New York City. "Cheviots" referred to a wool fabric known for its rare elegance and style that was manufactured using wool from Cheviot sheep, a breed found in England, Scotland, and Wales.

30   Hepbron, George T., *How to Play Basketball* (New York: American Sports, 1904).

31   *Spalding Athletic Library Official Handbook of the Inter-Scholastic Athletic Association of Middle Atlantic States, 1910* (New York: American Sports, 1910).

32   Hooks, Ted. "The Sporting World from All Angles," *New York Age*, December 4, 1920.

33   Dougherty, Romeo. "Sport in Greater New York and New Jersey During the Past Twenty Years," *Amsterdam News*, September 18, 1929.

34   The new location was 219 West 134th Street, near Seventh Avenue.

35   St. Philip's Church still stands in that location today as a historical landmark. *New York Age*, May 5, 1910.

36   *Official Handbook of the Inter-Scholastic Athletic Association, 1911* (New York: Spalding Athletic Library, 1911).

37   *Aurora News-Register*, July 22, 1910, p.1.

38   *New York Age*, April 21, 1910, p. 7.

39   *New York Age*, September 29, 1910.

40   Fletcher, Tom. *100 Years of the Negro in Show Business* (New York: Burdge & Company, 1954).

41   *New York Age*, August 22, 1907.

42   *New York Age*, October 17, 1907, p. 1.

43   The first annotated English translation of *The Art of War* was completed and published in early 1910 by Lionel Giles, an assistant curator at the British Museum. At the time it succeeded earlier incorrect translations.

44   *New York Age*, October 13, 1910.

45   *New York Age*, October 20, 1910.

46   *New York Age*, October 12, 1910.

47   "All Stars in Good Trim," *New York Age*, November 3, 1910.

48   *Spalding Athletic Library Official Handbook of the Inter-Scholastic Athletic Association of Middle Atlantic States, 1910* (New York: American Sports, 1910). Even after the Converse Rubber Company began mass-producing canvas sneakers in the 1920s, leather basketball shoes would remain the product of choice among championship-winning African American teams like the New York Renaissance. They outperformed canvas in every category except price, to the point where even Converse produced leather high-tops. Eventually canvas would replace leather as the go-to fabrication of the game. Leather wouldn't come back onto the

court until the emergence of big sneaker brands including PONY, Puma, and Nike in the early 1970s.

49 *New York Age*, October 20, 1910.

CHAPTER 13: WABASH OUTLAWS

1   In the period from 1866 to 1934, there were 353 Black people lynched in Kentucky. Wright, George C. *Racial Violence in Kentucky, 1865–1940: Lynchings, Mob Rule, and "Legal Lynchings"* (Baton Rouge: Louisiana State University Press, 1990).

2   As cited in St. Clair Drake, *Black Metropolis: A Study of Negro Life in a Northern City.*

3   They lived at 715 Belden, just off Lincoln Avenue. The Black population of Ward 23 in 1900 was less than 1 percent.

4   Whatley, Warren C. "African-American Strikebreaking from the Civil War to the New Deal." *Social Science History* 17, no. 4 (1993): 525–58.

5   Drake. *Black Metropolis*. Table 18, "Relationship Between Growth of Total Negro Population and Total Negro Business: 1860–1937."

6   Spear, Allan. *Black Chicago, The Making of a Negro Ghetto, 1890–1920* (Chicago: University of Chicago Press, 1967).

7   Spear, p. 50.

8   Drake. *Black Metropolis*. Figure 6, "Expansion of the Black Belt."

9   Ransom scored two touchdowns and a field goal in the 1902 title game, a 105–0 win over Brooklyn Polytechnic Preparatory School. After graduating from Hyde Park in 1904, he attended Beloit College in Wisconsin, becoming the first African American varsity basketball player in the history of collegiate sports.

10 *Chicago Defender*, October 26, 1912, p. 7.

11 Ida Wells-Barnett, letter to the editor, *Chicago Record-Herald*, January 26, 1912.

12 Odd Fellows Hall was located at 3335 South State Street near East Thirty-Third Street on what was then the northern edge of the city's predominantly Black South Side, across the street from where Illinois Institute of Technology is today. *Daily Times*, January 2, 1911, p. 1.

13 Mjagki, Nina. *Light in the Darkness: African Americans and the YMCA, 1852–1946* (Lexington: University of Kentucky, 2015). There were sixty Black YMCA chapters by 1900. Seventeen were city chapters and forty-three were collegiate branches.

14 Angell, Pauline K. "Julius Rosenwald." *The American Jewish Year Book*, vol. 34, 1932, pp. 141–176.

15 *Chicago Inter Ocean*, January 2, 1911, p. 1.

16 *Davenport (Iowa) Daily Times*, January 2, 1911, p. 1.

17 There were 44,103 Black residents counted in Chicago during the 1910 U.S. Census. "Table 1, Population of Chicago by Ethnic Group: 1900–1944," Drake, St. Clair, *Black Metropolis: A Study of Negro Life in a Northern City*. (Chicago: University of Chicago Press, 1945).

18 William Howard Taft, the twenty-seventh president of the United States, still holds the record as the heaviest president in the history of the United States. He died in 1930 at age seventy-two from heart failure.

19 "News from The Capital City," *New York Age*, May 25, 1911. President Taft made these remarks while addressing an audience of Black students at Howard University.

20 *Chicago Defender*, November 2, 1912, p. 7.

CHAPTER 14: SPORT FOR SPORT'S SAKE

1   *New York Times*, August 9, 1908.

2   Unknown, Author (1923). "Alumni You Outta to Know," *Howard University Studies in History*: Vol. 3: Issue 1, Article 2. Lark's printing business was at 340 Atlantic Avenue. In 1901, Lark would join the United Colored Democracy of Greater New York, which was "cordially received and duly recognized by the great Tammany organization" that controlled New York City politics, graduate from Brooklyn Law School in 1916, and be rewarded with an appointment to Assistant District Attorney of King's County, the first Black person ever to hold a position that high in any criminal justice hierarchy.

3   *New York Amsterdam News*, January 17, 1934, p. 8.

4   *Pittsburgh Courier*, December 11, 1926, p. 13.

5   *Brooklyn Daily Eagle*, August 6, 1908, p. 1. Dougherty lived at 111 Fleet Place, nearly behind where the historic Fleet Street First A.M.E. Zion Church was once located. The woman's name was Elizabeth Jenkins.

6   *Pittsburgh Courier*, December 11, 1926, p. 13.

7   "Sport in Greater New York and New Jersey During the Past Twenty Years" by Romeo Dougherty, *New York Amsterdam News*, December 18, 1929.

8   *New York Amsterdam News*, December 16, 1944.

9   Ibid.

10   Dan, Burley, "Grand Old Man of Press Row Passes On," *New York Amsterdam News*, December 16, 1944.

11   From an oral history interview of Maida Springer Kemp, *Black Women's Oral History Project*, Schlesinger Library, Radcliffe College, p. 2, cited in Irma Watkins-Owens, *Blood Relations: Caribbean Immigrants and the Harlem Community, 1900–1930* (Bloomington: Indiana University Press, 1996), p. 29.

12   McKay, Claude. *Harlem: Negro Metropolis* (New York: E. P. Dutton & Company, 1940), p. 132.

13   See editorial by publisher Fred R. Moore, *New York Age*, July 19, 1924. See also Watkins-Owens, Irma. *Blood Relations: Caribbean Immigrants and the Harlem Community, 1900–1930* (Bloomington: Indiana University Press, 1996).

14   "West Indians in Sport," Romeo L. Dougherty, *New York Amsterdam News*, December 18, 1929, p. 17.

15   Ibid.

16   Ibid.

17   *Chicago Defender*, December 16, 1944, p. 9.

18   *New York Age*, December 8, 1910, p. 6.

19   The Tenth Cavalry "Buffalo Soldiers" Regiment was assigned to Fort Ethan Allen around 1909.

20   *New York Age*, March 30, 1911, p. 6.

21   Leon N. Coursey, "The Life of Edwin Bancroft Henderson and His Professional Contributions to Physical Education" (PhD diss., Ohio State University, 1971).

CHAPTER 15: A JANITOR'S KEY

1   Jones, Alvin J. "Blazing the Trail," *Interstate Tattler*, April 19, 1929.

2   *Reading Times*, January 19, 1910, p. 8.

3   *Pittsburgh Press*, December 18, 1910, p. 20.

4   The Centre Avenue Colored YMCA Branch was and is still located at 1847 Centre Avenue.

5   "Afro-American Notes," *Pittsburgh Press*, January 14, 1912.

6 "Afro-American Notes," *Pittsburgh Press*, November 26, 1911.

7 *Pittsburgh Courier*, November 25, 1911.

8 Ric Roberts, "Dynamic Dorsey Brothers Living Legend in 59-Year-Old Saga of Tan Athletes," *Pittsburgh Courier*, February 24, 1962, p. A22.

9 The site was about where Heinz Field, home of the Pittsburgh Steelers of the National Football League, is located today.

10 Roberts, "Dynamic Dorsey Brothers Living Legend in 59-Year-Old Saga of Tan Athletes."

11 Vann's place, on a twenty-five-by-ninety-three-foot lot near the corner of Collier Street, had cost $3,900.

12 *Pittsburgh Courier*, December 19, 1942. In Posey's 1942 recollections, he mistakenly remembered that the game was played in 1911. The game was indeed played during the 1911–2 season, but the game itself took place on March 8, 1912.

13 *New York Age*, January 26, 1913.

14 *Pittsburgh Courier*, March 23, 1912.

15 *Pittsburgh Courier*, February 12, 1927, p. A5.

16 Moses, Alvin J. "Blazing the Trail: Cum Posey an 'All Time' Immortal," *Inter-State Tattler*, April 19, 1929.

17 As seen in advertisements such as *Cedar Rapids Daily Republican*, January 31, 1913, p. 2.

18 *Lewis's Pittsburgh Street & Trolley Guide* (Pittsburgh: Lewis Publishing Co., 1914).

19 *New York Age*, December 15, 1910, p. 6.

20 *Pittsburgh Courier*, October 31, 1925, p. 13.

21 Timetables and route information, *Book of the Royal Blue, Monthly, Volume 2* (Baltimore: Baltimore & Ohio Rail Road Company, 1898). One can ride the line today on Amtrak's Capitol Limited.

22 Ibid.

23 Ibid.

24 *Lewis's Pittsburgh Street & Trolley Guide*, 1914.

25 *Pittsburgh Post-Gazette*, July 25, 1911, p. 19.

26 *Pittsburgh, Central Business District, Crawford-Roberts, Plate 9*, (Pittsburgh: G. M. Hopkins & Co., 1914).

27 Hotel information, *Pennsylvania Negro Business Directory—1910*, (Harrisburg: James H. W. Howard & Son, 1910); proprietor, *1910 United States Federal Census: Pittsburgh Ward 3, Allegheny, Pennsylvania; Roll: T624_1299; Page: 15B; Enumeration District: 0309.*

28 *Pennsylvania Negro Business Directory—1910.*

29 *The Colored American Magazine*, Vol. IV, November 1901.

30 W. Rollo Wilson, "Eastern Snapshots," *Pittsburgh Courier*, February 28, 1925.

31 W. Rollo Wilson, "Sport Shots," *Pittsburgh Courier*, January 14, 1928, p. A5.

32 *Pittsburgh Courier*, March 2, 1912, p.5.

33 *Pittsburgh Courier*, December 30, 1939, p. 16.

34 *New York Times*, June 30, 1907, p. 26.

35 *Pittsburgh Courier*, December 30, 1939, p. 16.

36 Wilson, *Pittsburgh Courier*, January 14, 1928, p. A5.

37 In 1908, the Collegiate Basketball Rules Committee dropped this rule and the dribbler was once again allowed to shoot for the basket. However, the stubborn AAU kept the rule in place until 1915, when it conceded and the dribble rule at last became uniform for both colleges and amateurs.

38 W. Rollo Wilson, "Sport Shots," *Pittsburgh Courier*, January 20, 1934, p. A4.

39   As described by Black sportswriter Romeo Dougherty, *Pittsburgh Courier*, January 23, 1943, p. 17.

40   Alvin J. Moses, "Blazing the Trail: Cum Posey An 'All Time' Immortal," *The Inter-State Tattler*, April 19, 1929, [n.p].

41   Dougherty, *Pittsburgh Courier*, January 23, 1943, p. 17.

42   *Pittsburgh Press*, March 10, 1912, p. 39.

43   Ibid.

44   *Pittsburgh Courier*, March 16, 1912, p. 1.

45   Ibid.

46   E. S. Crosby, "College Basketball Rules Fair; Should Be Used Universally," *Brooklyn Daily Eagle*, March 7, 1909, p. 60.

47   *Pittsburgh Courier*, March 16, 1912, p. 1.

48   Ibid.

49   Ibid.

50   Wilson, *Pittsburgh Courier*, February 28, 1925.

51   *Pittsburgh Courier*, March 16, 1912, p. 1.

52   *New York Age*, March 14, 1912.

53   *Pittsburgh Courier*, March 16, 1912, p. 1.

54   Ibid.

55   W. Rollo Wilson, "Sports Shots," *Pittsburgh Courier*, January 20, 1934.

56   *Pittsburgh Courier*, March 16, 1912, p. 1.

57   Cum Posey, "Posey's Points," *Pittsburgh Courier*, December 19, 1942.

58   Wilson, *Pittsburgh Courier*, February 28, 1925.

59   *Pittsburgh Courier*, January 23, 1943.

60   Wilson, *Pittsburgh Courier*, February 28, 1925.

61   Dougherty, *Pittsburgh Courier*, January 23, 1943, p. 17.

CHAPTER 16: VIRGIL

1   *Chicago Tribune*, June 2, 1908, p. 12. The park took up the entire block bounded by Elm, Orleans, Hill, and Sedgewick Streets.

2   *Chicago Tribune*, January 14, 1912, p. 23.

3   *Chicago Tribune*, February 11, 1912, p. 22.

4   Cited in John M. Carroll, *Fritz Pollard: Pioneer in Racial Advancement* (Champaign: University of Illinois Press, 1998).

5   *Chicago Tribune*, May 3, 1908, p. 3.

6   *Chicago Defender*, September 14, 1912, p. 7.

7   Pollard was posthumously inducted into the Pro Football Hall of Fame in 2005.

8   *Chicago Defender*, December 7, 1912, p. 8.

9   "Tells How War on Drugs Cuts S. Side's Crime," *Chicago Tribune*, 3 December 1950, p. 13. The Chicago Police Department's Fifth District Police Station was at 4802 South Wabash, at Forty-Eighth and Wabash. Blueitt took charge there on March 1, 1949, as acting captain. He had joined the force in 1929, was promoted to full captain in 1954, then again to district commander in 1960, before retiring in 1963. The old Fifth District is now the Second District or Wentworth Station at Fifty-First and Wentworth, where it moved in 1970; *Kansas City Plain Dealer*, March 11, 1949, p. 1.

10   *Chicago Tribune*, May 3, 1908, p. 3.

11 "Thanksgiving Day Football Game," *Chicago Defender*, December 7, 1912, p. 8.

12 Johnson won the world heavyweight boxing title on December 26, 1908, defeating the reigning world champion, Canadian Tommy Burns, at the Sydney Stadium in Sydney, Australia. The house he bought his mother was at 3344 Wabash Avenue in Chicago.

13 *Chicago Daily Tribune*, July 11, 1912, p. 14.

14 The Café de Champion was located at 41 West Thirty-First Street in Chicago.

15 *Chicago Defender*, November 13, 1948, p. 15.

16 *Chicago Defender*, July 13, 1912, p. 1.

17 *Chicago Daily Tribune*, July 11, 1912, p. 14.

18 Foster lived at 3242 Vernon Avenue.

19 Schorling Park was located at West Thirty-Ninth Street (now West Pershing Road) and South Wentworth Avenue.

20 "Thanksgiving Day Football Game," *Chicago Defender*, December 7, 1912, p. 8.

21 The Wabash Avenue YMCA is included in the National Register of Historic Places.

22 *Chicago Defender*, June 14, 1913, p. 1. They marched down South Wabash to East Thirty-Sixth, over to Dearborn Avenue, then down to East Twenty-Ninth before turning back onto South Wabash and heading up to the YMCA building.

23 *Baltimore Afro-American*, June 21, 1913, p. 3.

24 *Chicago Defender*, June 21, 1913, p. 1.

25 Rosenwald's announcement sparked two dozen campaigns nationwide, but only seven cities would succeed in raising the mandated funds within the specified five-year window. The Twelfth Street YMCA in Washington, D.C., the Senate Avenue YMCA in Indianapolis, the Christian Street Y in Philadelphia, the Paseo YMCA in Kansas City, the Ninth Street YMCA in Cincinnati, the Pine Street Y St. Louis, and the Wabash Avenue YMCA in Chicago would all be opened by 1916. Rosenwald would later extend his five-year deadline for Brooklyn, Baltimore, Columbus, Harlem, Atlanta, and Pittsburgh, each of which subsequently completed successful campaigns and constructed their own Black Y buildings.

26 *Baltimore Afro-American*, June 21, 1913, p. 3.

27 Ibid.

28 *The Negro in Chicago: A Study of Race Relations and a Race Riot by the Chicago Commission on Race Relations* (Chicago: University of Chicago Press, 1922), p. 288.

29 *Chicago Defender*, November 29, 1913, p. 7.

30 "In the Wake of the News" by R. W. Lardner, *Chicago Tribune*, December 3, 1913, p. 18. The archaic adjective "hight" means "named."

31 "lane five gains place in finals," *Chicago Daily Tribune*, January 28, 1914, p. 18.

32 *Chicago Defender*, January 31, 1914, p. 8.

33 *Chicago Defender*, March 11, 1914, p. 16.

34 *Chicago Daily Tribune*, June 14, 1914, p. B4.

35 *Chicago Defender*, June 20, 1914, p. 7.

36 The Colored YMCA in Evanston, Illinois, was located at 1014 Emerson Street. The branch was known as the Emerson Street Colored YMCA.

37 *Chicago Defender*, October 17, 1914, p. 4.

38 *Chicago Tribune*, October 25, 1914, p. 20.

39 *San Francisco Call*, October 30, 1904, p. 23.

40 *Chicago Daily Tribune*, December 1, 1914, p. 16.

41 *Chicago Defender*, October 17, 1914, p. 4.

42 *Chicago Defender*, December 18, 1915, p. 7.

43   *Chicago Defender,* February 6, 1915.

44   *Chicago Defender,* February 6, 1915, p. 4.

45   *Chicago Defender,* April 17, 1915, p. 4.

CHAPTER 17: MADDENING

1   *ISAA 1912* (New York: American Sports, 1912).

2   *Amsterdam News,* January 2, 1929, p. 10.

3   *Baltimore Afro-American,* May 7, 1910, p. 4.

4   *New York Age,* November 21, 1912.

5   Floyd G. Nelson, "The Harlem Limited Broadway Bound," *Pittsburgh Courier,* September 12, 1931.

6   *New York Age,* November 12, 1912, p. 8.

7   Young's Casino information, *New York Age,* July 11, 1912, p. 1.

8   *New York Age,* January 9, 1913, p. 6.

9   *New York Age,* October 31, 1912, p. 6.

10   *New York Age,* November 14, 1912, p. 6.

11   *New York Age,* January 9, 1913, p. 6.

12   Clarence Arthur Perry, *Evening Recreation Centers* (New York City: Department of Child Hygiene of the Russell Sage Foundation, 1910), p. 12.

13   Eugene C. Gibney, "Basket Ball in Recreation Centers," in *Official Basket Ball Rules, 1912–13 (New York: American Sports, 1912).*

14   *New York Times,* April 24, 1916, p. 20.

15   Ibid.

16   ERC 188 won the ERCAL Senior Division basketball championship title in 1912, 1913, and 1914 as well as Junior Division ERCAL titles in 1910, 1911, 1912, 1913, and 1914.

17   Eugene C. Gibney, "Discouraging the Reign of Stars," in *Official Basket Ball Rules, 1914–15 (New York: American Sports, 1914),* p. 68.

18   *New York Age,* January 8, 1914, p. 6.

19   *New York Age,* April 23, 1914.

20   *New York Age,* January 8, 1914.

21   *New York Age,* February 17, 1916.

22   *Hammond Times,* March 13, 1938, p. 37.

23   *Amsterdam News,* August 10, 1935.

24   *New York Age,* October 21, 1915.

25   *New York Times,* October 18, 1914, p. S4.

26   *New York Age,* March 12, 1914.

27   *New York Age,* November 4, 1915.

28   *New York Age,* January 22, 1914, p. 6.

29   *New York Age,* March 19, 1914, p. 6.

30   Ibid.

31   Remarks by Madden, *New York Age,* March 5, 1914, p. 6 and *New York Age,* March 12, 1914, p. 6.

32   *New York Age,* March 5, 1914, p. 6.

33   Ibid.

34   *New York Age,* February 19, 1914, p. 6.

35   Anderson was born in Oxford, Ohio, on April 28, 1866.

36   Remarks about the game, *New York Age*, March 26, 1914, p. 6.
37   Ibid.
38   *New York Age*, April 9, 1914.
39   *New York Age*, April 23, 1914.

CHAPTER 18: SUPREME COURTS

1   New York State Supreme Court, Appellate Division, First Department, *Papers on Appeal from Order, St. Christopher Club against St. Christopher Club of New York, Inc.*, November 10, 1914.
2   *New York Age*, April 13, 1916.
3   New York Department of State, Albany.
4   *New York Age*, August 20, 1914, p. 1.
5   *Amsterdam News* (n.d.) article as cited in New York State Supreme Court, *Papers on Appeal from Order*, November 10, 1914.
6   Ibid.
7   Vestry Minutes, v.6, Subseries I. A. Administrative, St. Philip's Church Records, Schomburg Manuscripts, Archives and Rare Books Division, The New York Public Library.
8   *New York Age*, October 22, 1914, p. 6.
9   *New York Age*, December 3, 1914, p. 6.
10   Ibid.
11   *Omaha Evening Bee*, September 2, 1879, p. 3.
12   *New York Age*, December 10, 1914, p. 6.
13   *New York Age*, December 17, 1914, p. 6.
14   *New York Age*, December 31, 1914, p. 6.
15   Ibid.
16   *New York Age*, January 7, 1915, p. 6.
17   *New York Age*, January 7, 1915, p. 6.
18   *New York Age*, December 17, 1914.

CHAPTER 19: LOENDI

1   "Boost From The Post Office," *Pittsburgh Daily Post*, January 11, 1912, p. 6.
2   *Pittsburgh Courier*, November 22, 1912.
3   *Pittsburgh Press*, February 2, 1913, p. 39.
4   *New York Age*, December 12, 1912.
5   *New York Age*, January 2, 1913.
6   *New York Age*, January 26, 1913.
7   *New York Age*, February 6, 1913.
8   *New York Age*, February 27, 1913.
9   Ibid. Hans "Honus" Wagner was arguably the greatest shortstop ever. Playing for the Pittsburgh Pirates, he won eight straight batting titles, had seventeen straight seasons batting .300 or better, led the league five times in runs batted in, and led seven times in doubles. Wagner became a founding member of the Baseball Hall of Fame in 1936. (He also coached baseball at Carnegie Tech in Pittsburgh for four years, after retiring from the Major Leagues in 1917.)
10   *New York Age*, March 20, 1913.
11   John L. Clark. "Wylie Avenue," in *Pittsburgh Courier*. Ethel had a fifth daughter, but she died as an infant.
12   *Pittsburgh Press*, January 18, 1914, p. 26.

13 From the recollections of Evan Posey Baker, nephew of Cumberland Posey, Jr., gathered in a personal interview in Pittsburgh, May 17, 2001.

14 *Pittsburgh Press*, January 4, 1914, p. 28.

15 *Pittsburgh Press*, February 8, 1914, p. 40.

16 *Pittsburgh Press*, February 15, 1914, p. 39.

17 Remarks about Sell Hall from Bolden interview with author, June 8, 2001.

18 *Pittsburgh Press*, September 27, 1914, p. 39.

19 *Pittsburgh Press*, February 1, 1914, p. 26.

20 In addition, the name "Posey Cumbert" appeared in the *Duquesne Monthly* in a retrospective article some years after *Cumbert* played there.

21 *Duquesne Monthly*, January 1917 vol. 24, no. 4, p. 133.

22 *Pittsburgh Daily Post*, February 10, 1916, p. 11.

23 *Pittburgh Daily Post*, March 12, 1916, p. 40.

24 *Duquesne Monthly*, January 1917 vol. 24, no. 4.

25 According to a survey completed in 1930 ("Social Conditions of the Negro in the Hill District"), the huge influx of African Americans into the Hill District during and following World War I necessitated "a rearrangement of the whole plan of work for Kingsley House," causing the facility to flee the area and move its activities to East Liberty, which resulted in no subsequent contact with the Hill.

26 The hall was at 2616 Fifth Avenue near Robinson Street.

27 *Pittsburgh Daily Post*, February 18, 1917.

28 *Pittsburgh Press*, December 30, 1917.

29 *Pittsburgh Courier*, January 28, 1939.

30 *Pittsburgh Press*, February 3, 1919, p. 48.

CHAPTER 20: OUTLAWS

1 *New York Age*, October 21, 1915, p. 6.

2 *New York Age*, November 4, 1915, p. 6.

3 *New York Age*, November 11, 1915, p. 6

4 *New York Age*, November 4, 1915, p. 6.

5 *New York Age*, December 2, 1915.

6 *New York Age*, November 18, 1915.

7 Ibid.

8 *New York Age*, December 2, 1915.

9 *New York Age*, October 21, 1915.

10 *New York Age*, February 3, 1916, p. 6.

11 *New York Age*, November 4, 1915.

12 *New York Age*, December 9, 1915, p. 6.

13 *New York Age*, November 4, 1915.

14 *New York Age*, December 9, 1915, p. 6.

15 New York Age, December 30, 1915.

16 *New York Age*, December 9, 1915, p. 6.

17 *Baltimore Afro-American*, March 11, 1916.

18 *New York Age*, April 13, 1916.

19 Ibid.

20 *The Crisis* 12, no. 2 (June 1916): 66.

21   *Chicago Defender*, January 15, 1917, p. 9.

22   *Chicago Defender*, February 3, 1917, p. 6.

23   *Chicago Defender*, January 8, 1916, p. 1.

24   *New York Age*, February 1, 1917, p. 6.

25   *Chicago Defender*, March 10, 1917, p. 8.

26   *Baltimore Evening Sun*, October 21, 1921, p. 21.

27   *New York Age*, November 30, 1916, p. 6.

28   *Chicago Defender*, March 10, 1917, p. 8.

29   Ibid.

30   Ibid.

31   *New York Age*, March 22, 1917.

32   Roscoe Lee, "Chicago vs. New York is Sensation of the Basket Ball Season," *Chicago Defender*, March 17, 1917.

33   *New York Age*, March 15, 1917, p. 1.

34   Virgil Blueitt would become a Negro American League umpire during the 1930s and 1940s. He died in 1952 at age fifty-five. A younger brother, "Kinzie" Blueitt, would become a longtime captain in the Chicago Police Department.

35   United States, Selective Service System, *World War I Selective Service System Draft Registration Cards*, 1917–1918 (Washington, D.C.: National Archives and Records Administration), M1509, 4,582 rolls.

36   *New York Age*, March 22, 1917.

37   *Chicago Defender*, April 7, 1917.

38   *Muskogee Times-Democrat*, March 29, 1917.

39   *Chicago Defender*, March 17, 1917.

40   *Chicago Defender*, April 7, 1917.

41   Ibid. Santop was one of the greatest catchers of all time, and Pettus was an all-time great first baseman.

42   Ralph Cooper was the youngest of five children, while Walter was the middle child, fourteen years older than Ralph.

43   *Chicago Defender*, April 7, 1917. The song was composed in 1886 with original lyrics that included instructions for everyone to join in: "When you hear them bells go ding a ling a ling, all join 'round and sweetly you must sing, and when the verse am through in the chorus all join in, there'll be a hot time in the old town tonight!"

44   *New York Age*, November 16, 1916, p. 6.

45   *Chicago Defender*, April 7, 1917.

46   *Chicago Defender*, March 16, 1917.

47   Ibid.

48   *Chicago Defender*, April 7, 1917. Newspaper accounts of African American basketball games during the 1910s were usually limited to a few comments about key plays or player performances. For this game, however, the *Chicago Defender* provided a rare detailed account, and the paper's New York correspondent, Bill White, went to never-before-seen lengths in an effort to describe the action. This was remarkable for the *Defender*, which four years earlier had not even covered basketball in its nearly invisible sports section.

49   Ibid.

50   Ibid.

51   *Oshkosh Northwestern*, March 13, 1935.

52   *Chicago Defender*, April 7, 1917.

53   Ibid.

54   Ibid.

55   *New York Age*, April 26, 1917, p. 6.

56   Ibid. "The play's the thing" appears in the final line of act 2, scene 2 of William Shakespeare's *Hamlet*. The complete line, "The play's the thing / Wherein I'll catch the conscience of the king," was Shakespeare's way of pointing out the greater social role a dramatist played, and Madden's use of that syntax with "the game is the thing" implies he understood the greater social role the athlete played back then, a concept still true today.

57   *Chicago Defender*, December 1917.

58   Historians credit Beau Brummell with introducing the modern men's suit and tie as the established form of fashion for gentlemen.

59   *New York Age*, November 30, 1916.

CHAPTER 21: DEMOCRACY LADS

1   *Coshocton Morning Tribune*, March 31, 1917.

2   Claude McKay, "America" from *Liberator* (December 1921).

3   *Durham Morning Herald*, July 3, 1917.

4   *St. Louis Post-Dispatch*, July 3, 1917.

5   *Minneapolis Morning Tribune*, January 1, 1917, p. 8.

6   *Kansas City Sun*, December 1, 1917, p. 5.

7   "Parade Notice," *New York Age*, July 26, 1917, p. 1.

8   *Chicago Defender*, September 8, 1917, p. 9.

9   *Chicago Defender*, September 22, 1917, p. 10.

10   *Chicago Defender*, November 3, 1917, p. 10.

11   J. E. Patterson, "Thanksgiving Day to Formally Begin Gotham's Basketball Season," *Chicago Defender*, October 13, 1917, p. 5.

12   About the game and who was in attendance, *Chicago Defender*, December 8, 1917, p. 9.

13   *New York Times*, September 24, 1928.

14   *Pittsburgh Press*, March 2, 1919, p. 26.

15   Letter to Romeo Dougherty, *Amsterdam News*, October 2, 1929, p. 13.

16   *Chicago Defender*, December 22, 1917, p. 3.

17   *Chicago Defender*, December 29, 1917, p. 1.

18   Ibid.

19   Ibid.

20   Ibid.

21   *Chicago Defender*, February 23, 1918, p. 7.

22   Ibid.

CHAPTER 22: THE FUTURE OF BASKETBALL

1   *Pittsburgh Press*, February 10, 1918, p. 52.

2   *Pittsburgh Press*, February 3, 1918, p. 48.

3   Cited in Ocania Chalk, *Black College Sport* (New York: Dodd, Mead, 1976).

4   *New York Age*, November 16, 1918.

5   Paul Robeson, *Robeson Speaks*, pp. 293–94.

6   *New York Age*, December 14, 1918.

7   Hallie Elvira Queen, cited by Walker's great-great-granddaughter A'Lelia Bundles, in her book *On Her Ground: The Life and Times of Madam C. J. Walker* (New York: Scribner, 2001). Madam Walker died exactly six months later to the day, on May 25, 1919, at Villa Lewaro in Irving-on-Hudson.

8   World War I officially ended in November 1918.

9   James Reece Europe's brilliant career would end tragically a few months later. In May 1919, at a Tempo Club concert in Boston, a disgruntled band member attacked Europe backstage, superficially wounding him in the neck with a small knife. But doctors discovered that the bandleader's jugular vein had been severed, and they were unable to save him. A few hours later, Europe, aged 38, died. He was given a public funeral by the City of New York (the first black person to receive such a distinction) and buried at Arlington National Cemetery with full military honors.

10   *New York Age*, March 8, 1919, p. 6.

11   *Chicago Defender*, April 5, 1919, p. 11.

12   Ibid.

13   Ibid.

14   Floyd G. Nelson, "The Harlem Limited Broadway Bound," *Pittsburgh Courier*, September 12, 1931.

15   *The Competitor*, v.1 1920, p. 67.

16   Ibid.

17   Murry R. Nelson, *The Effects of Player Contracts in the Battle for Power and Control in Post World War I Professional Basketball*. State College, PA: North American Society for Sport History, 1995.

18   Joe Lapchick, *50 Years of Basketball*, (Englewood Cliffs: Prentice-Hall, 1968).

19   *The Competitor*, v.1 1920, p. 67.

20   *Competitor* 1, no. 3 (March 1920): 70.

21   *Competitor* 1, no. 3 (March 1920): 70.

22   Ibid.

23   Ibid., p. 71.

24   Huiswoud was the brother of Otto Eduard Gerardus Majella Huiswoud, the famous Harlem-based race activist who was committed to black liberation and socialism. Considered a revolutionary in his time, Otto Huiswoud was the only founding member of the American Communist Party of African descent.

25   *Competitor Magazine* (March 1920).

26   *New York Age*. February 7, 1920.

27   The recording, on Okeh Records, sold over 1,000,000 copies that same year and went on to sell over 2,000,000 copies total. With the success of the production, it dawned on record companies that African Americans bought records. Other record labels followed suit, signing up and marketing their own black artists who performed all genres of music on what they called "race records," thus opening up the entire recording industry to African Americans for the first time. Interestingly, Smith began her entertainment career as a teenager dancing in the famous Smart Set Company vaudeville show.

28   *New York Age*, November 13, 1920, p. 6.

29   *Pittsburgh Courier*, January 10, 1924.

30   *New York Times*, September 24, 25, and 26, 1915.

31   Supreme Court of New York, People v. Bambrick, 1915; Supreme Court of New York, Appellate Division, First Department, People v. Frank Reilly, February 15, 1918.

32   Waldron to Committee of Fourteen, September 19, 1918, Correspondence, Committee of Fourteen Records, box 28, Manuscripts and Archives Division, New York Public Library.

33   Mallon to Sisson, January 3, 1919, Correspondence, Committee of Fourteen Records, box 28, Manuscripts and Archives Division, New York Public Library.

34   *New York Age.* "Passing of Manhattan Casino As A Pleasure Resort," February 7, 1920.

35   *New York Age,* January 22, 1921, p. 6.

36   *New York Age,* January 29, 1921, p. 6.

37   The Dunbar Cigar Company shopkeepers were listed as L. Casenava and P. Perez.

38   Irma Watkins-Owens, *Blood Relations: Caribbean Immigrants and the Harlem Community, 1900–1930* (Bloomington: Indiana University Press, 1996), p. 69.

39   According to Irma Watkins-Owens in *Blood Relations,* Roach's claim was true, but only for a while. By 1926 the theater met with hard times due to heavy indebtedness, whereupon new financial backers took over the property and leased it back to the Renaissance Theatre Corporation. By 1933, there were no more Black owners or investors involved in the business.

40   *New York Age,* January 22, 1921, p. 6.

41   *The Competitor,* v.1 1920, p. 67.

42   *New York Age,* April 16, 1921, p. 6.

43   *New York Age,* April 8, 1922.

44   *Competitor Magazine* 3, no. 2 (April 1921): 39–40.

45   *Pittsburgh Courier,* January 23, 1943, referenced in Rob Ruck, *Sandlot Seasons.*

46   Ocania Chalk, in his extensive book *Pioneers of Black Sport* (New York: Dodd, Mead, & Company; 1975), incorrectly identifies Leon Monde as a member of the Spartan Braves at the time the Metropolitan Basketball Association barred him. In fact, Monde had switched to the Borough Athletic Club over the summer.

47   *New York Times,* June 30, 1907, p. 26.

48   New York Age, December 17, 1921.

49   *New York Age,* January 16, 1943, p. 11.

CHAPTER 23: OUT-AND-OUTERS

1   Robert W. Peterson, *Cages to Jump Shots: Pro Basketball's Early Years* (New York: Oxford, 1990), p. 55.

2   *New York Age,* January 20, 1923.

3   Edward "Sol" Butler was one of about ten African Americans who played on White college varsity basketball teams before World War I.

4   Romeo Dougherty. "The Sportive Spotlight." *New York Amsterdam News,* January 3, 1923.

5   *New York Amsterdam News,* January 31, 1923.

6   *New York Age,* March 10, 1923.

7   *New York Amsterdam News,* February 14, 1923, p. 4

8   *New York Amsterdam New*s, February 21, 1923, p. 4.

9   *New York Age,* March 24, 1923.

CHAPTER 24: THE NEW NEGRO

1   New York Amsterdam News. October 3, 1923.

2   William E. Clark, "Professional Basketball Is Magnet for Many New Aggregations in Harlem," "Sport Comment," *New York Age,* November 17, 1923.

3   *New York Amsterdam News*, October 24, 1923.

4   Romeo Dougherty, "The Sportive Spotlight," *New York Amsterdam News*, January 10, 1923.

5   Romeo Dougherty, "The Sportive Spotlight," *New York Amsterdam News*, January 31, 1923.

6   Contrary to popular belief, the Commonwealth Five and not the Harlem Renaissance were the first openly professional all-Black basketball team. The distinction is that the Harlem Rens were the first such team that was Black-owned. The first Black-owned *unofficially* semi-professional Black fives were the New York All Stars, the Monticellos, and the New York Incorporators, followed by the Loendi Big Five, in that order.

7   *New York Amsterdam News*, October 3, 1923.

8   *New York Amsterdam News*, October 24, 1923.

9   *New York Amsterdam News*, October 17, 1923.

10   Robert W. Peterson, *Cages to Jump Shots: Pro Basketball's Early Years* (New York: Oxford, 1990), p. 70–72.

11   New York *Amsterdam News.* October 31, 1923.

12   Chicago *Defender.* December 22, 1923.

13   *New York Age*, April 18, 1925.

14   *Chicago Defender.* February 2, 1924.

15   Romeo Dougherty, "The Sportive Spotlight," *New York Amsterdam News*, February 14, 1923.

16   Few details are available. However, that the Eighth Regiment won this game is surmised from news accounts of the following season, in which the regiment team was introduced and referred to as being the "champions."

17   *Pittsburgh Courier*, October 4, 1924.

18   *Pittsburgh* Courier, October 4, 1924.

19   William E. Clark, "Making Basketball Pay at the Renaissance Casino," "Sport Comment," *New York Age*, November 7, 1925.

20   *Pittsburgh Courier*, September 22, 1924.

21   Ibid.

CHAPTER 25: CHICAGO CRUSADERS

1   "White Boys Act Unmanly at Basket Ball Game," *Chicago Defender*, February 14, 1920, p. 11.

2   "Perrine Is Removed," *Chicago Defender*, December 11, 1920, p.2.

3   "New Life in Athletics at Phillips," *Chicago Defender*, December 10, 1921, p. 10.

4   "Sol Butler Joins Forty Club," *Chicago Defender*, November 20, 1920, p. 9.

5   *Baltimore Afro American*, March 4, 1921, p. 7.

6   *Chicago Defender*, March 5, 1921, p. 6.

7   *Chicago Defender*, May 7, 1921, p. 11.

8   *Chicago Defender*, March 12, 1921, p. 6.

9   *Chicago Defender*, January 7, 1922, p. 10.

10   "Neglect of Boys Shown in Social Service Report," *Chicago Defender*, May 7, 1921, p. 5.

11   *Chicago Defender*, January 1, 1923, p. 10.

12   *Chicago Defender*, March 10, 1923, p.5.

13   *Chicago Defender*, March 1, 1924, p.12.

14   *Chicago Defender*, February 9, 1924, p.11.

15   *Chicago Defender*, March 15, 1924, p.1.

16   *Chicago Defender*, April 5, 1924, p.1.

17   *Chicago Defender*, April 19, 1924, p.10.

18   *Chicago Defender*, May 3, 1924, p.12.

19   *Chicago Defender*, January 17, 1925, p.5.

20   *Norfolk New Journal and Guide*, January 26, 1924, p. 4.

21   "Athletics To Count Toward Degree," *Baltimore Afro American*, February 29, 1924, p. 15.

22   "Legion Post To Give Ball," *Chicago Defender*, November 29, 1919, p. 19.

23   *Chicago Defender*, May 8, 1920, p. 5.

24   *Chicago Defender*, January 14, 1922, p. 10.

25   *Marshalltown Evening Times-Republican*, June 13, 1910, p. 1.

26   *Marshalltown Evening Times-Republican*, July 2, 1910, p. 7.

27   *Marshalltown Evening Times-Republican*, May 24, 1916, p. 3.

28   *Des Moines Bystander*, September 29, 1919, p.4.

29   *Marshalltown Evening Times-Republican*, March 18, 1920, p. 14.

30   The American Professional Football Association had changed its name to the National Football League on June 24, 1922.

31   *Minneapolis Star Tribune*, November 2, 1923, p. 21.

32   *Minneapolis Star*, January 17, 1924, p. 2.

33   *Minneapolis Star*, October 25, 1924, p. 12.

34   *Variety*, February 11, 1925, p. 35.

35   *Variety*, March 17, 1926, p. 1.

36   Ibid.

37   *Chicago Tribune*, June 21, 1926, p. 38.

38   "Globetrotter Idea Gets Start in Coal Office," *Cleveland Call and Post*, June 27, 1953, p. 2D.

39   *Variety*, January 19, 1927, p. 45.

40   *Mason City Globe Gazette*, April 5, 1961.

41   *Sheboygan Press*, December 18, 1926, p. 10.

42   *Marshfield Daily News*, February 16, 1927, p. 3.

43   *La Crosse Tribune*, January 25, 1927, p. 8.

44   *Chicago Defender*, February 19, 1927, p. 9.

45   *Wisconsin Rapids Daily Tribune*, February 19, 1927, p. 8.

46   *Wisconsin Rapids Daily Tribune*, February 21, 1927, p. 5.

47   *Capital Times*, February 4, 1927, p. 13.

48   *Chippewa Herald-Telegram*, February 17, 1927, p. 7.

49   *Appleton Post-Crescent*, December 27, 1926, p. 11.

50   *Pittsburgh Courier*, August 7, 1943, p. 18.

51   Susan J. Rayl, "The New York Renaissance Professional Black Basketball Team," 1923–1950 (PhD diss., Department of Exercise and Sport Sciences, Pennsylvania State University, 1996).

52   *New York Amsterdam News*, November 16, 1927, p. 13.

53   "Savoy Ballroom Opens," *Pittsburgh Courier*, December 3, 1927, p. 6; *Chicago Defender*, December 3, 1927, p. 8.

54   The Philadelphia Warriors would in turn move to California to become the Golden State Warriors.

55   *Sheboygan Press*, December 6, 1927, p. 14.

56   *Sheboygan Press*, December 7, 1927, p. 12.

57   *Naugatuck News*, February 11, 1947, p. 6. In 1947, Wilfred Hetzel claimed to have world's records for making "50 70-foot shots" and "more than 600 40-foot shots," among others.

58   "Negro Collegians to Play Evanston Five Wednesday," *Chicago Daily Tribune*, December 24, 1927, p. 14.

59   "Society," *Chicago Defender*, December 31, 1927, p. 5.

60   *Pittsburgh Courier*, February 11, 1928, p. A5.

61   *Chicago Defender*, February 18, 1928, p. 9.

62   *Chicago Tribune*, January 15, 1926, p. 21.

63   *Sheboygan Press*, January 14, 1927, p. 6.

64   *Streator Times*, March 1, 1928, p. 4.

65   *Sheboygan Press*, January 18, 1928, p. 10.

66   *La Crosse Tribune*, February 14, 1928, p. 16.

67   *Chippewa Herald-Telegram*, February 21, 1928, p. 7.

68   *La Crosse Tribune*, February 16, 1928, p. 11.

69   *Chippewa Herald-Telegram*, February 21, 1928, p. 7.

70   As explained by historian Ben Green in *Spinning the Globe, The Rise, Fall, and Return to Greatness of the Harlem Globetrotters* (New York: HarperCollins, 2005).

71   *New York Amsterdam News*, March 27, 1948, p. 26.

72   *Pittsburgh Courier*, January 7, 1928, p. 15.

73   Rayl.

74   Susan J. Rayl, "The New York Renaissance Professional Black Basketball Team," 1923–1950 (PhD diss., Department of Exercise and Sport Sciences, Pennsylvania State University, 1996).

75   *Chicago Defender*, December 12, 1936, p. 14.

CHAPTER 26: TRUE WORLD CHAMPIONS

1   *The River Press*, February 19, 1936, p.1, 3; *Fallon County Times*, p. 2; *Grass Range Review*, March 19, 1936, p. 4; *Choteau Acantha*, March 19, 1936, p. 1.

2   Personal correspondence with Melanie Cowart, August 3, 2021; Missouri, U.S. Death Certificates, Benson R. Hall.

3   Video of John Isaacs oral history interview, 1986, donated to the Black Fives Foundation Archives in 2020.

4   *New York Age*, February 22, 1936, p. 8.

5   *New York Age*, March 26 and October 28, 1936.

6   *Hammond Times* (Indiana), October 5, 1939.

7   Rayl.

8   *New York Age*, April 10, 1937.

CHAPTER 27: WORLD SERIES OF BASKETBALL

1   *Fitchburg Sentinel*, March 20, 1942.

2   *Pittsburgh Courier*, March 21, 1942.

3   *Enshrinement Program* (Philadelphia: Philadelphia Basketball Hall of Fame, 1989).

CHAPTER 28: THE MISSING NBA TEAM

1   *Chicago Stadium Review, Tenth Annual World's Championship Basketball Tournament, Official Program*, April 8–11, 1948.

2   Susan J. Rayl, "The New York Renaissance Professional Black Basketball Team, 1923–1950" (PhD diss., Department of Exercise and Sport Sciences, Pennsylvania State University, 1996).

3   See, for example, *Daily Capital Journal* (Salem, Oregon), April 10, 1948.

4   "Real Estate, for Rent," *New York Age*, December 4, 1948.

5   *People's Voice*, February 15, 1947, p. 28., cited in Rayl, "The New York Renaissance Professional Black Basketball Team."

6   The ABL had three black players: Bobby Wright with the New York Gothams, Larry Doby signed with the Paterson Crescents, and Preston Wilcox with the Hartford Hurricanes. See ibid.

7   *Muncie Evening Press* (Indiana), December 26, 1947.

8   *Woodstock Daily Sentinel*, January 3, 1947.

9   *New York Age*, November 2, 1946.

10   *Chicago Tribune*, March 23, 1942.

11   George Kroker, "Fan's Fare," *Decatur Herald*, February 23, 1942.

12   *Cincinnati Enquirer*, August 15, 1948.

13   *Pittsburgh Courier*, February 8, 1947.

14   "Rates Clifton Best Young Star," *Pittsburgh Courier*, February 14, 1948.

15   *Richmond Palladium-Item* (Indiana), December 16, 1947, or *Salem News* (Ohio), January 31, 1948.

16   *Minneapolis Star-Tribune*, February 19, 1948.

17   Author's in-person interview with George Crowe, April 24, 2009.

18   *Chicago Defender*, April 17, 1948.

19   *Application for Marriage License*, Indiana Marriage Licenses, 1948, Volume 139, p. 130.

20   *Minneapolis Star Tribune*, July 31, 1948.

21   Ron Thomas. *They Cleared the Lane: The NBA's Black Pioneers* (Lincoln: University of Nebraska Press, 2002), p. 22. According to Thomas, an authority on the topic, Carl Bennett, then general manager of the Fort Wayne Pistons, confirmed the existence of an unwritten rule barring African Americans from the White pro leagues and eventually the NBA.

22   Eventually, league owners would sour of their arrangement with Saperstein, because he would push them into changing their schedules to suit his Globetrotters enterprise and threaten to quit their arrangement if they did not agree. See *Rochester Democrat and Chronicle*, November 29, 1949: "Originally scheduled to play the Royals, the Trotters were matched with the Celts when Abe Saperstein, manager of the Negro cagers, requires a schedule change. In a three-way telephone conversation last night with Maurice Podoloff, president of the NBA, and owner Les Harrison of the Royals, Saperstein declared he wanted a release from the contract, for his Globetrotters are no longer eager to play league teams. Podoloff and Harrison finally yielded after a heated discussion with Saperstein, Royal officials announced."

23   Ron Thomas, *They Cleared the Lane: The NBA's Black Pioneers*.

24   *Syracuse Post-Standard* (New York), December 18, 1948.

25   *Muncie Star Press* (Indiana), July 1, 1949.

26   Ibid.

27   Ibid.

28   Ibid.

29   *Sheboygan Press*, August 1, 1949.

30   *Hartford Courant*, July 2, 1949. Note that the Butler Fieldhouse was renamed as the "Hinkle Fieldhouse" in 1965, after Paul D. "Tony" Hinkle, who had been the school's basketball coach since the Fieldhouse opened in 1928. He also coached football and baseball teams during his Butler career.

31   Ironically, two Indianapolis Olympians players, Alex Groza and Ralph Beard, were suspended from the NBA for life following the 1950–51 season, after they confessed to point shaving during their college careers at Kentucky. The team folded in 1953.

32   *Canandaigua Daily Messenger*, July 28, 1949.

33   *St. Louis Post-Dispatch*, August 4, 1949. "In the big shuffle four teams, Providence and Indianapolis of the BAA and Hammond and Dayton of the NBL were dropped from the ranks," said one wire services release. "The NBL eliminated Hammond, Ind. and Dayton, O.," it continued. When a new committee was organized within the NBA to handle player disputes, the description of its additional purpose struck a similar revealing tone. "This committee also will decide what's to be done with the players on the four teams wiped out," it said.

34   "Oshkosh Out By Gosh," *Wilmington Journal News*, September 10, 1949.

35   *Lafayette Journal and Courier*, December 14, 1949.

CHAPTER 29: VINDICATION

1   Author's email correspondence with George Berger, February 2–6, 2007.

2   Hughes died on May 22, 1967. Langston Hughes Papers, Beinecke Rare Book and Manuscript Library, Yale University.

3   *Baltimore Afro-American*, September 7, 1963, p. A2.

4   Howie Evans, Interview with the Bronx African American History Project. BAAHP Digital Archive at Fordham University, October 1, 2015.

5   Ibid.

6   Howie Evans, Personal Interview via telephone, Claude Johnson, Miami, January 21, 2016.

7   Howie Evans, Interview with the Bronx African American History Project.

8   *New York Age*, November 5, 1955, p. 8.; *Oneonta Star*, February 7, 1956, p. 10.; *Lubbock Avalanche-Journal*, February 12, 1956.

9   Howie Evans, Interview with the Bronx African American History Project.

10   Howie Evans, Personal Interview via telephone, Claude Johnson.

11   Ibid.

12   Howie Evans, "The Unnecessary Abuse of Wilt," *Amsterdam News*, January 23, 1965.

13   Howie Evans, Interview Transcript, Dr. Mark Naison, The Bronx African American Archival Survey at Fordham University.

14   Howie Evans, "Sort of Sporty," *Amsterdam News*, March 27, 1965.

15   Howie Evans, Personal Interview, Claude Johnson, New York City, October 2, 2006.

16   Howie Evans, "Harlem Pro League Hoop Activity Begins," *Amsterdam News*, June 12, 1971; Howie Evans, "Sort of Sporty," *Amsterdam News* (June 12, 1965); Monroe's nickname was "Magic" in the mid-1960s until he later became known as Earl "The Pearl" Monroe.

17   Dave Anderson, "The Doctor Who Makes House Calls," *New York Times*, August 12, 1972.

18   "Howie Evans Joins Riverside Radio Team," *Amsterdam News*, April 24, 1971; "Colonials Settlers," *New York Times*, 30 December 30, 1972; Howie Evans, Interview Transcript, Dr. Mark Naison, The Bronx African American Archival Survey at Fordham University.

19   Howie Evans, *Personal Interview*, Claude Johnson, New York City, October 2, 2006.

20   *Amsterdam News*, February 17, 1973, p. D8.

21   Ibid.

22   File No. 2510, Records Department, Surrogate's Court of the County of New York, Schedule D.

23   File No. 2510, Records Department, Surrogate's Court of the County of New York, Schedule A.

24   The song "You're Nobody 'Til Somebody Loves You" was composed by Russ Morgan, Larry Stock, and James Cavanaugh. Russ Morgan and his Orchestra recorded the tune on Decca Records in 1945.